MW01128103

Tragedy of the Faithful

A History of the III. (germanisches) SS-Panzer-Korps

Wilhelm Tieke

Translated by
Fred Steinhardt

Tragedy of the Faithful

A History of the III. (germanisches) SS-Panzer-Korps

Wilhelm Tieke

Translated by
Fred Steinhardt

Published by
J.J. Fedorowicz Publishing, Inc.
104 Browning Boulevard
Winnipeg, Manitoba
Canada R3K 0L7
Web: www.jjfpub.mb.ca
E-Mail: jjfpub@jjfpub.mb.ca
Telephone: (204) 837-6080
Fax: (204) 889-1960

Printed in Canada
ISBN 0 - 921991 - 61 - 4

Printed by
Friesens Printers
Altona, Manitoba, Canada

Publishers' Acknowledgements

We wish to thank you, the reader, for purchasing this book and all of you who have written us with kind words of praise and encouragement. It gives us the impetus to continue translating the best available German-language books and producing original titles. Our catalog of books is listed on the following pages and can be viewed on our web site at www.jjfpub.mb.ca. We have also listed titles which are near production and can be expected in the near future. Many of these are due to your helpful proposals.

For this book, we wish to thank Max Cuypers for the permission to publish images of relatives of his who fought with various units of the *III. (germanisches) SS-Panzer-Korps*. We also wish to thank Matt Lukes for another great signing box and Shawn Biettner for his research and fact checking.

John Fedorowicz, Mike Olive and Bob Edwards

Editors' Notes

Modern American Army terminology is generally used wherever an equivalent term is applicable. In cases where there may be nuances where we think the reader might enjoy learning the German term, we have included it with an explanation

In cases where the German term is commonly understood or there is no good, direct English equivalent, we have tended to retain the original German term, e.g., *Schwerpunkt* (point of main effort), *Auftragstaktik* (mission-type orders) etc.

In an attempt to highlight the specific German terminology, we have italicized German-language terms and expressions. Since most of the terms are repeated several times, we have not included a glossary. There is a rank-comparison table at the back of the book listing German Army, *Waffen-SS* and US Army equivalents (page 483).

Unit designations follow standard German practise, i.e., an Arabic numeral before the slash (e.g., *1./SS-Aufklärungs-Abteilung 1*) indicates a company or battery formation. A Roman numeral indicates the battalion within the regiment.

Other Titles by
J.J. Fedorowicz Publishing

The Leibstandarte (1. SS-Panzer-Division): Volumes I, II,
    III, IV/1 and IV/2
European Volunteers (5. SS-Panzer-Division)
Das Reich (2. SS-Panzer-Division): Volumes I and II
The History of Panzerkorps "Großdeutschland": Volumes 1,
2 and 3
Panzer Soldiers for "God, Honor, Fatherland":
    The History of Panzerregiment "Großdeutschland"
Otto Weidinger
Otto Kumm
Manhay, The Ardennes: Christmas 1944
Armor Battles of the Waffen-SS, 1943-1945
Tiger: The History of a Legendary Weapon, 1942-1945
Hitler Moves East
Tigers in the Mud
Panzer Aces
Footsteps of the Hunter
History of the 12. SS-Panzer-Division "Hitlerjugend"
Grenadiers, the Autobiography of Kurt Meyer
Field Uniforms of German Army Panzer Forces
    in World War 2
Tigers in Combat, Volumes I and II
Infanterie Aces
Freineaux and Lamormenil—The Ardennes
The Caucasus and the Oil
East Front Drama — 1944
The History of the Fallschirm-Panzer-Korps
    "Hermann Göring"
Michael Wittmann and the Tiger Commanders
    of the Leibstandarte
The Western Front 1944: Memoirs of a
    Panzer Lehr Officer
Luftwaffe Aces
Quiet Flows the Rhine
Decision in the Ukraine: Summer 1943

Combat History of the schwere Panzer-
    Jäger-Abteilung 653
The Brandenburgers—Global Mission
Field Uniforms of Germany's Panzer Elite
Soldiers of the Waffen-SS: Many Nations, One Motto
In the Firestorm of the Last Years of the War
The Meuse First and Then Antwerp
Jochen Peiper: Commander, Panzerregiment
    "Leibstandarte"
Sturmgeschütze vor! Assault Guns to the Front!
Karl Baur: A Pilot's Pilot
Kharkov
Panzer Aces 2
Panzertaktik! Armor Tactics of the German Armed Forces
The Combat History of schwere Panzer-Abteilung 503
The Combat History of Sturmgeschutz-Brigade 276,
    Assault Gun Fighting on the Eastern Front
Normandy 1944
Funklenkpanzer, A History of German Remote- and
    Radio-Controlled Armor Units
Grenadiers, The Autobiography of Kurt Meyer (2nd, revised edition)
The Combat History of schwere Panzer-Abteilung 508,
    In Action in Italy with the Tiger I

In Preparation (Working Titles)

Ju88, A History of the A- and H-Series Aircraft
Brummbär, A History of the German Sturmpanzer
Drama Between Budapest and Vienna
Kursk 1943, A Photo Album
Of Good Conscience, The History of the 4. SS-Polizei-
    Division
The Combat History of schwere Panzerjäger-Abteilung 654

J.J. Fedorowicz Publishing

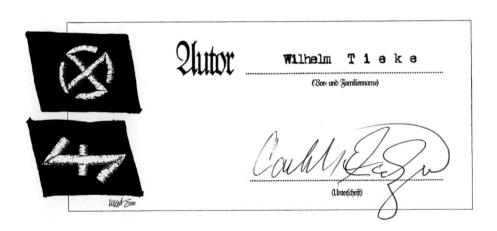

Autor   Wilhelm Tieke

(Vor- und Familienname)

(Unterschrift)

Table of Contents

The Formation of the III. (germanisches) SS-Panzer-Korps

By order of the supreme commander of the *Wehrmacht*, the *III. (germanisches) SS-Panzer-Korps* was activated on 30 March 1943. The German army's great wartime manpower losses forced utilization of all European sources in order to continue the war on the greatly expanded fronts. The first contingent, stemming in part from the replacement battalion of *SS-Panzer-Grenadier-Regiment 9 "Germania"*, which was stationed in the Netherlands, arrived at the training area at Debica in Poland.

Effective 19 April 1943, the headquarters of the *Waffen-SS* ordered the formation of the *III.(germanisches) SS-Panzer-Korps* at the Grafenwöhr training area. The first contingent that had been assembled at Debica/Heidelager was moved to Grafenwöhr. In the first organization lists and strength reports, *SS-Panzer-Grenadier-Division "Wiking"* appears along with *SS-Panzer-Grenadier-Freiwilligen-Division "Nordland"*. Both divisions were to form the corps.

Thanks to the intervention of prominent Dutchmen, *SS-Freiwilligen-Legion "Nederland"*, which was originally intended to join the existing *SS-Panzer-Grenadier-Freiwilligen-Division "Nordland"*, was organized in Thuringia (Germany) as a separate brigade. At the same time, *SS-Panzer-Grenadier-Division "Wiking"* and *SS-Panzer-Division "Totenkopf"* were combined to form a corps. As a result, *SS-Freiwilligen-Brigade "Nederland"* replaced *SS-Panzer-Grenadier-Division "Wiking"* in the *III. (germanisches) SS-Panzer-Korps*.

In February 1943 preparations began for formation of an additional so-called Germanic *SS* division, to be formed from the *SS-Freiwilligen-Brigade "Nederland"*, the *SS-Freikorps "Danmark"* and the *SS-Freiwilligen-Legion "Norwegen"*. The original proposal that it be named *"Waräger"* was dropped. In the end it was designated *"Nordland"*. At that point, *SS-Freiwilligen-Legion "Nederland"* was still on the Eastern Front. It was moved to Thuringia for personnel and political reasons and reorganized as a brigade.

In the Sonneberg area, *SS-Freiwilligen-Panzer-Grenadier-Regiment 46 "de Ruyter" (49 effective 12 November 1943)* was organized with two battalions. The regimental commander was *SS-Sturmbannführer* Collani. The cadre personnel and Collani came from the inactivated *Finnisches Freiwilligen-Bataillon*. *SS-Freiwilligen-Panzer-Grenadier-Regiment 45 "General Seyffard" (48* effective 12 November 194*3)* was also formed with two battalions. Its regimental commander was *SS-Obersturmbannführer* Vitzthum. The first brigade elements were organized at the same time as those regiments.

SS-Brigadeführer und Generalmajor der Waffen-SS Jürgen Wagner was the commander of the *4. SS-Freiwilligen-Panzer-Grenadier-Brigade*. Wagner had commanded *SS-Panzer-Grenadier-Regiment "Germania"* in *SS-Panzer-Grenadier-Division "Wiking"*. *SS-Panzer-Grenadier-Freiwilligen-Division "Nordland"* was directed to the Grafenwöhr training area as its organization site.

SS-Sturmbannführer Vollmer set up the division headquarters at Grafenwöhr. On 1 May 1943 *SS-Brigadeführer und Generalmajor der Waffen-SS* Fritz von Scholz took command of the division. *SS-Sturmbannführer* von Bockelberg was the operations officer.

In addition to the regimental staff, *SS-Panzer-Grenadier-Regiment "Norge"* was formed from the former *SS-Panzer-Grenadier-Regiment "Nordland"*. The remnants of that proven regiment, which had fought for two years as part of *SS-Panzer-Grenadier-Division "Wiking"* in southern Russia, arrived at Camp Auerbach on 10 May 1943. On 12 May *General der Waffen-SS* Felix Steiner and *Generalmajor der Waffen-SS* Fritz von Scholz held the final regimental inspection for *SS-Panzer-Grenadier-Regiment "Nordland"*. Steiner praised the military accomplishments of the regiment and, at the same time, took command of the *III. (germanisches) SS-Panzer-Korps*. After the inspection the men of the regiment left for three weeks of leave.

The *I./SS-Panzer-Grenadier-Regiment "Norge"* was formed from *SS-Freiwilligen-Legion "Norwegen"*. That unit had been formed in the summer of 1941 and had proven itself on the Eastern Front. The Norwegians had been attached to first the *2. SS-Infanterie-Brigade (mot.)* and then the *Lettische SS-Freiwilligen-Brigade*. After heavy fighting, the Norwegians were withdrawn from the Leningrad Front in March of 1943. In May 1943 they were moved to the Grafenwöhr training area where the formation was officially disbanded. With 600 volunteers, the disbanded *SS-Freiwilligen-Legion "Norwegen"* formed the *I./SS-Panzer-Grenadier-Regiment "Norge"*.

The *II./SS-Panzer-Grenadier-Regiment "Norge"* was formed from the cadre of the *II./SS-Panzer-Grenadier-Regiment "Nordland"*. The former *I./SS-Panzer-Grenadier-Regiment "Nordland"* became the *III./SS-Panzer-Grenadier-Regiment "Norge"*. It was planned as an *SPW* battalion.

At the same time, the *13. (Infanterie-Geschütz-)*, *14. (Flak-)* and *16.(Pionier)/SS-Panzer-Grenadier-Regiment "Norge"* were formed. A *15.(Kradschützen)/SS-Panzer-Grenadier-Regiment "Norge"* was also planned but never got past the initial stages and was later dropped.

The organization of *SS-Grenadier-Regiment "Danmark"* went less smoothly. In order to understand what happened it is necessary to look at prior events.

After German forces occupied Denmark on 9 April 1940 and Denmark had joined the Anti-Comintern Pact, German authorities demanded that Denmark take part in the conflict when hostilities broke out with the Soviet Union. With permission from the responsible Danish officials, the *SS-Freikorps "Danmark"* was organized and recruiting begun in all parts of Denmark. The Danish war ministry announced in a circular dated 8 July 1941 that officers and noncommissioned officers, active and reserve, could transfer to *SS-Freikorps "Danmark"* and, at the end of their service there, return to the Danish Army or Navy. Additional regulations governed the logistical demands of the Danish soldiers who volunteered for the *SS-Freikorps "Danmark"*. At the same time, the German mission in Copenhagen guaranteed that *SS-Freikorps "Danmark"* would be committed as an integral unit on the Eastern Front.

On 19 July 1941, 480 volunteers set out from Copenhagen to Hamburg under command of the Danish Lieutenant Colonel Kryssing. Organization and training of *SS-Freikorps "Danmark"* took place in Hamburg and Posen-Treskau under Danish officers.

SS-Freikorps "Danmark" entered service at the front in the so-called *Festung Demjansk*. SS-Obersturmbannführer Frederik von Schalburg commanded it. Within the framework of the *SS-Division "Totenkopf"*, the Danish volunteers fought superbly along the Biakowo —Watschelewchina main supply route, losing two commanders in succession: *SS-Obersturmbannführer* von Schalburg and *SS-Obersturmbannführer* von Lettow-Vorbeck.

After refitting in the rear area in December 1942, the *SS-Freikorps "Danmark"* was thrown back into the bloody fighting in the Welikie — Luki area under *SS-Sturmbannführer* Martinson. On 20 May 1943, the surviving remnants of *SS-Freikorps "Danmark"* were disbanded at Grafenwöhr and *SS-Grenadier-Regiment "Danmark"* was formed from them. Contrary to the promises that *SS-Freikorps "Danmark"* would exist as an integral national unit, non-Danish personnel were incorporated during the course of its enlargement to a regiment. In addition, a non-Dane assumed command of the regiment, *SS-Obersturmbannführer Graf* von Westphalen. The Danes protested and several demanded discharge in their homeland.

General Steiner involved himself in the controversy and pointed out that a small infantry unit that was subordinated to one division after another would be rapidly depleted, since none of the division commanders would have an interest in sparing a unit that was only subordinated to him for a limited time. Therefore, it would be better for the unit to fight within the framework of a single division. The more perceptive officers of the unit acknowledged Steiner's arguments.

The *SS* main office also became aware of the problem and turned to the German foreign ministry, which made contact with the Danish government and initiated joint proceedings. The Danish ambassador in Berlin was included.

On 28 July 1943 the Danish ambassador, Mohr, was in Grafenwöhr. Battalions presented arms and there was a parade in his honor. Mohr then tried to calm the situation and asked the Danish officers and soldiers in the name of the Danish and German government to stay, since the battle against bolshevism was also a part of the Danish mission within the framework of the Anti-Comintern Pact. After the parade, Mohr was the guest of *General der Waffen-SS* Felix Steiner at lunch in the Plassenburg Castle at Kulmbach, where Steiner had his headquarters.

In spite of the involvement of the Danish ambassador, several of the Danes demanded their discharge, among them the last commander of *SS-Freikorps "Danmark"*, *SS-Obersturmbannführer* Martinsen. After those personnel problems had been dealt with, the organization of *SS-Grenadier-Regiment "Danmark"* went smoothly. As with *SS-Panzer-Grenadier-Regiment "Norge"*, the regimental units were formed along with the battalions.

SS-Artillerie-Regiment 11, *SS-Panzer-Abteilung 11* (originally planned as a regiment) and a *Kradschützen-Regiment* (later reorganized as *SS-Panzer-Aufklärungs-Abteilung 11* in August 1943), the *SS-Pionier-Bataillon 11* and the supply and service units of *SS-Panzer-Grenadier-Freiwilligen-Division "Nordland"* were organized in the Grafenwöhr area. *SS-Nachrichten-Abteilung 11 "Nordland"* was formed in Nuremberg. All of the units received their personnel from the existing replacement units. Thus *SS-Pionier-Bataillon 11* received a steady flow of officers, noncommissioned officers and enlisted personnel from the *SS-Pionier-Ersatz- und Ausbildungs-Bataillon Dresden* and from the Engineer School at Hradischko.

SS-Pionier-Bataillon 11 conducted infantry training to establish unit cohesion. Combat engineer training was, of necessity, restricted to assault troop training, mine laying and clearing, instruction in demolitions and a great deal of other instruction since the combat engineering equipment and vehicles were lacking. Similar difficulties existed for all the division units.

SS-Instandsetzungs-Abteilung 11 was formed from the First Platoon of *SS-Instandsetzungs-Abteilung "Wiking"* at Schwabach, near Nuremberg.

SS-Flak-Abteilung 11 was formed at the Arys training area in East Prussia and joined the division at a later date.

SS-Feldersatz-Bataillon "Nordland" formed from drafts from the replacement contingents at Sennheim under command of *SS-Sturmbannführer* Franz Lang.

The battalions and regiments gradually filled out. Difficulties in recruiting from the intended countries resulted in volunteers for the *III. (germanis-*

ches) SS-Panzer-Korps and *SS-Panzer-Grenadier-Freiwilligen-Division "Nordland"* coming from all countries of Europe. Some from the southeast were drafted. Despite understandable initial problems arising from human interaction and compatibility, the formations would prove themselves in the fighting that followed.

In the fourth year of the war, the Germans were forced to mobilize the last remaining manpower reserves as a result of soldier casualties. As a result of an agreement between the Rumanian and German governments, Rumanian citizens of German ethnicity — the ethnic Germans from the Siebenbürgen and Banat regions of Rumania — were conscripted into formations of the *Waffen-SS*. Those conscriptions occured voluntarily in some cases and involuntarily in others. This also occured within the formations of the *III. (germanisches) SS-Panzer-Korps*.

Personnel continually arrived and were assigned to the companies. *SS-Grenadier-Regiment "Danmark"* eventually consisted of 40% Danes, 25% Germans and 35% ethnic Germans from Rumania. It rapidly attained a strength of about 3,200 men. The situation was similar in *SS-Panzer-Grenadier-Regiment "Norge"*. The divisional units were primarily formed from Germans who had received their specialist training in the existing replacement units. Eventually, however, soldiers of other ethnic origins soon entered the pipeline and changed the picture.

Difficulties became universally evident in the issuance of weapons and equipment. Again and again the activation plans were changed. Resourcefulness and inventiveness of the unit commanders nevertheless kept the training moving along.

SS-Sturmbannführer Kausch organized *SS-Panzer-Abteilung 11. SS-Obersturmbannführer* Mühlenkamp had overall responsibility for its formation. At the time, Mühlenkamp was also at Grafenwöhr with units of his *SS-Panzer-Regiment "Wiking"*. A veteran cadre of enlisted personnel, noncommissioned officers and officers gathered around the commander, *SS-Sturmbannführer* Kausch, who had experience at the front with *SS-Panzer-Grenadier-Division "Wiking"*.

In the meantime, *SS-Untersturmführer* Willi had gone to the *Panzer-Lehr-Abteilung* at Erlangen with men who had previous technical training in order to produce the graphic materials for training the tank crews. They worked intensely for eight days, developing the training materials for the *Panzer V (Panther)*. The theoretical training of the tank commanders and crews began. A great many trips were required to obtain all of the materials that a unit requires for its daily routine.

Recruits arrived, including many ethnic Germans from Rumania. All of them were healthy, strong young men with a naturalness and openness that made it a joy to be in a unit with them. The infantry training was soon completed. Then the majority of them proceeded to specialty training with the

Panzer-Lehr-Abteilung at Erlangen, the tank factory at Nuremberg, the Armor School at Wünsdorf and the tank gunnery school at Putlos.

Under *SS-Obersturmbannführer* Mühlenkamp's leadership, the tank training began in a number of old *Panzer III's* and *Panzer IV's*. In addition to that, there were map exercises and radio training.

All of the units had to overcome difficulties during training. However, *SS-Panzer-Grenadier-Freiwilligen-Division "Nordland"* had essentially completed its organization by the beginning of August 1943. At its head was its division commander, *SS-Brigadeführer und Generalmajor der Waffen-SS* Fritz von Scholz, who had formed and led *SS-Panzer-Grenadier-Regiment "Nordland"* with equal skill for the previous three years.

SS-Pionier-Bataillon "Nordland", still in the process of organization, was consolidated with the *16./SS-Panzer-Grenadier-Regiment "Norge"* and the *16./SS-Grenadier-Regiment "Danmark"* at the West Camp at Auerbach. In mid-August 1943, it was transferred along with the combat-engineer units of the *III. (germanisches) SS-Panzer-Korps* and *SS-Freiwilligen-Brigade "Nederland"* to the Beneschau training area in Bohemia for specialty training. There the units were housed in villages outside of the training area, close to the *SS* combat-engineer school at Hradischko. Since they were located right by the Moldau River, training could begin in water-related operations. Additional weapons, vehicles and combat engineering equipment continually arrived.

The training of the regiments of *SS-Freiwilligen-Brigade "Nederland"* was pushed forward in similar fashion in Thuringia, but the brigade still lacked artillery and the brigade units.

In the meantime the organization of the corps units was completed at Grafenwöhr. The chief of the general staff, *SS-Standartenführer* Joachim Ziegler, assembled the corps headquarters and supervised the activation of the corps troops.

After three months of existence, the *OKH* ordered the transfer of the *III.(germanisches) SS-Panzer-Korps* to an area near the front. *General* Steiner asked not to go to the Atlantic coast, citing the requirement that his volunteers had to be employed some place other than the western front. In the end, a move to Croatia was acceptable. The units only had small arms. Tanks, assault guns, vehicles and artillery were still missing.

Transfer To Croatia

At the end of August 1943 the order arrived transferring the *III. (germanisches) SS-Panzer-Korps* to Croatia. On 28 August the corps staff set out from the Bayreuth railroad station. *General* Steiner followed in a road march with a small staff on 29 August and, on 1 September, joined his corps staff in the eastern portion of Agram.

At about the end of the month all the units of *SS-Panzer-Grenadier-Freiwilligen-Division "Nordland"* moved to Croatia. *SS-Freiwilligen-Brigade "Nederland"* followed somewhat later.

On 8 September 1943 at 2020 hours the corps received news of the Italian capitulation. At 2130 hours the units were placed on alert status. The *III. (germanisches) SS-Panzer-Korps* was allocated to *Armeegruppe von Weichs* and attached to the *2.-Panzer-Armee-Oberkommando* under command of *General Dr.* Rendulic. The units of *SS-Panzer-Regiment 5* that had just arrived in Agram, along with *SS-Panzer-Abteilung 11,* proceeded from Agram through Samobar to Karlovac, disarmed the Italian *"Lombardi"* Armored Division, in the process taking Generals Chipione and Pitau captive. The Karlovac area was secured with the focus to the south. In the middle of September *Oberst* Griese's *Polizei-Regiment 14* was attached to *SS-Obersturmbannführer* Mühlenkamp's *Panzergruppe. Polizei-Regiment 14* then advanced southward along the Karlovac—Triest road to secure the area that had been left unsecured by the departure of the Italians. *Bataillon Hack,* a derivative battalion of *SS-Panzer-Grenadier-Regiment 9 "Germania",* was directed to provide support to *Regiment Griese.*

While disarming the Italians, units of the corps in Karlovac and Samobor had to protect Italian officers from their own personnel. *SS-Panzer-Abteilung 11,* still without tanks, received so-called "Badoglio tanks" from the disarmed Italians.

SS-Panzer-Grenadier-Freiwilligen-Division "Nordland" was billeted in the Sisak — Glina — Bosnisch-Nowi area, with the division command post in Sisak. Almost all of the division units were also in Sisak, including *SS-Panzer-Aufklärungs-Abteilung 11. SS-Nachrichten-Abteilung 11* was south of Agram and was attached to the corps. *SS-Panzer-Abteilung 11* was located in Samobar. It had received additional armored vehicles — *Sturmgeschütze* and *Panzer IV's* in addition to the "Badoglio tanks" — and continued its specialized training. The Italian tanks had no radios, only signal disks and small flags for communications. The *3./SS-Panzer-Abteilung 11* was issued the *Sturmgeschütze.* The officers and noncommissioned officers who were still lacking arrived.

Skirmishing began in the partisan areas. The partisans conducted war from ambushes. In those regions there were three parties: the German soldiers, the German-friendly police troops (*Ustascha*) of the ruling regime and the Communist partisans who contended for the land and populace. Major political mistakes often forced the local inhabitants into the partisan camp.

In the Bosnisch-Novi area *SS-Panzer-Grenadier-Regiment "Norge"* — redesignated *SS-Panzer-Grenadier-Regiment 23 "Norge"* on 22 October 1943 — conducted several raids which, however, did not lead to any decisive success. At the end of September *Polizei-Regiment 14* got into a critical situation in Ogulin. For days it had been surrounded by a strong partisan group. An 80-watt radio section of the *2./SS-Nachrichten-Abteilung 11* maintained contact with the *III. (germanisches) SS-Panzer-Korps. General* Steiner flew into the beleaguered city in a *Fieseler Storch* and prepared the relief operation.

During the relief, the *III./SS-Panzer-Grenadier-Regiment 23 "Norge"* was committed into the crisis area by railroad. It debarked at Dugaresa, marching on to Generals-Kistol, which served as the jump-off point. *Polizei-Regiment Griese* was relieved and the area secured toward the south. From a base at Generals-Kistol, *SS-Sturmbannführer* Lohmann's *III./SS-Panzer-Grenadier-Regiment 23 "Norge"* conducted additional operations against the partisans. At the end of October, an assault troop of the battalion advanced to Keitsch and occupied a bridgehead across a stream for several days. Fritz Sivers, a squad leader of the *11./SS-Panzer-Grenadier-Regiment 23 "Norge"*, was killed in that operation. On 21 November the *9.* and *11. Kompanien* of the regiment got into an intense firefight with partisans during which the Norwegian, *SS-Untersturmführer* Lund, was killed. *SS-Panzer-Abteilung 11* conducted an operation with "Badoglio tanks" and assault guns from Samobar against the partisan-held Okitsch Mountain.

SS-Panzer-Grenadier-Regiment 24 "Danmark", which completed its training in its billeting area of Petrinja-Glina, also had to be alert. Individual companies were posted at endangered positions, alternately relieving each other. For all their efforts, the German units controlled no more than the occupied villages. Elsewhere, the partisans were everywhere and nowhere at the same time.

The *I./SS-Panzer-Grenadier-Regiment 24 "Danmark"* was in the most precarious position in Glina. Glina was a village with 2,300 inhabitants. Its only communications were with Petrinja. The village was surrounded by a horseshoe of mountains on which the partisans were located. Repeated fire forced the battalion to an increased level of alertness. On 26 September there was an exchange of prisoners in Glina. Several partisan attacks against Glina, some of them heavy, ensued, but the battalion prevailed.

On 20 November the partisans attacked Glina with about 5,000 men. The battalion had 300 men in position and 150 men in reserve, primarily

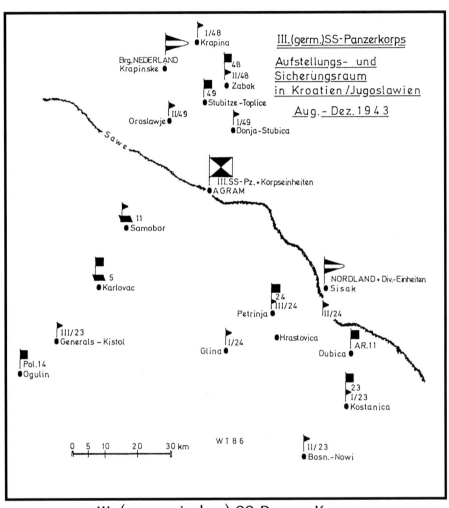

III.(germ.)SS-Panzerkorps

Aufstellungs- und
Sicherüngsraum
in Kroatien/Jugoslawien

Aug.-Dez. 1943

1/48
● Krapina

Brg.NEDERLAND
Krapinske ●

48

II/48
● Zabok

49
● Stubitze-Toplice

II/49
Oroslawje ●

1/49
● Donja-Stubica

III.SS-Pz.+Korpseinheiten
● AGRAM

11
● Samobor

NORDLAND + Div.-Einheiten
● Sisak

5
● Karlovac

24
III/24

Petrinja ●

II/24

III/23
● Generals-Kistol

1/24
Glina ●

● Hrastovica

AR.11
Dubica ●

Pol.14
● Ogulin

23
1/23
● Kostanica

Sawe

0 5 10   20   30 km

WT 86

II/23
● Bosn.-Nowi

III. (germanisches) SS-Panzer-Korps
Formation Area and Security Zone in Croatia
August - December 1943

Danes. They repulsed all the daytime attacks and one nighttime assault with heavy losses to the enemy. Heavy fighting also raged on 21 November. The fighting let up somewhat on 22 November. An attempt was made to reestablish the line of communications with Petrinja. The First Platoon of the *1./SS-Panzer-Grenadier-Regiment 24 "Danmark"* ran into an ambush and was wiped out. *SS-Untersturmführer* Larsen and a few men made it back.

A relief party was sent in support, but that also was without success and suffered three dead and eight missing. On 23 November at 1600 hours the partisans renewed their attack on Glina, supported by three tanks. An anti-tank gun of the *4./SS-Panzer-Grenadier-Regiment 24 "Danmark"* knocked out two of the tanks. The third pulled back and escaped. Heavy fighting continued on 24 and 25 November. Calm was not restored until *Stukas* bombed the partisan mountain positions. The battalion had successfully defended Glina. *SS-Obersturmführer* Norreen, who had acted as temporary commander of the *1./SS-Panzer-Grenadier-Regiment 24 "Danmark"*, was transferred as *Ordonnanzoffizier* to the *III./SS-Panzer-Grenadier-Regiment 24 "Danmark"*.

After the regimental commander, *SS-Obersturmbannführer Graf* von Westphalen had received the reports from the *I./SS-Panzer-Grenadier-Regiment 24 "Danmark"* in Glina, he moved out with the *II.* and *III./SS-Panzer-Grenadier-Regiment 24 "Danmark"* — minus the *5.* and *10. Kompanien* which were committed to security operations at Hrastovica and Petrinja — in order to combat the partisans that had been reported at Gora.

He left the commander of the *III./SS-Panzer-Grenadier-Regiment 24 "Danmark"* in command of the rear area at Petrinja. Soon afterward, the partisans attacked the village of Hrastovica. The fate of the encircled unit in Hrastovica — the *5./SS-Panzer-Grenadier-Regiment 24 "Danmark"* — was sealed before the regimental commander had a clear idea of what had happened. *SS-Sturmbannführer* Jakobsen responded to the call for help from the commander of the encircled company by immediately sending out two available Cossack companies toward Hrastovica, but they were soon involved in heavy fighting and stopped. *SS-Hauptsturmführer* Hämel's *7./SS-Panzer-Grenadier-Regiment 24 "Danmark"*, which had been relieved in Hrastovica two days earlier by the then encircled company, launched an assault from the regimental main body but attacked into thin air. The partisans had disappeared into the mountains. The men of the *7./SS-Panzer-Grenadier-Regiment 24 "Danmark"* found their comrades of the *5. Kompanie* as mutilated corpses. Only a few had escaped the massacre.

SS-Panzer-Aufklärungs-Abteilung 11 had elements of the battalion and its staff billeted in Sisak. On 15 September the *2.* and *3./SS-Panzer-Aufklärungs-Abteilung 11* moved 25 kilometers towards the base of the mountains. The *2./SS-Panzer-Aufklärungs-Abteilung 11* was billeted on a state-owned farm where training, construction of positions, escorting movement columns and details to courses of instruction ensued. On 11 October the *2./SS-Panzer-Aufklärungs-Abteilung 11* moved to Topolavatsch and the *3./SS-Panzer-*

Aufklärungs-Abteilung 11 to a neighboring village. More guard duty, building positions and training. On 15 October, the companies were alerted! Four kilometers away a railroad building went up in the air. The companies headed out to secure two villages. Another alert on 24 October. Units of *SS-Panzer-Aufklärungs-Abteilung 11* moved out on all available vehicles, headed 40 kilometers downstream along the Sava and attacked a partisan camp. They reached the objective but, except for two partisans, the camp was empty. At the beginning of November the battalion received combat vehicles. The *1./SS-Panzer-Aufklärungs-Abteilung 11* received 8-wheel armored cars, the other companies half-tracks.

SS-Panzer-Abteilung 11 in Samobar continued its training. The battalion was still waiting for its tanks. The units of *SS-Panzer-Regiment 5* that were staged at Karlovac were relieved at the end of October by a German infantry division (*Generalleutnant* Niehoff), outfitted with tanks at Erlangen and sent to *SS-Panzer-Grenadier-Division "Wiking"* in Russia.

The same picture held true for *SS-Freiwilligen-Brigade "Nederland"*, which was staged north of Agram. The brigade staff was billeted in Krapinske, *SS-Freiwilligen-Panzer-Grenadier-Regiment 48 "General Seyffard"* in the Zabok area (staff and *II./SS-Freiwilligen-Panzer-Grenadier-Regiment 48 "General Seyffard"* in Zabok and *I./SS-Freiwilligen-Panzer-Grenadier-Regiment 48 "General Seyffard"* in Krapina). The staff of *SS-Freiwilligen-Panzer-Grenadier-Regiment 49 "de Ruyter"* was in Stubitze-Toplice, the *I.SS-Freiwilligen-Panzer-Grenadier-Regiment 49 "de Ruyter"* in Donja-Stubica and the *II./SS-Freiwilligen-Panzer-Grenadier-Regiment 49 "de Ruyter"* in Oroslawje.

At the end of November 1943 *SS-Panzer-Grenadier-Freiwilligen-Division "Nordland"* received orders transferring it to the Leningrad front. The companies were relieved one after another by Cossacks. Partisan activity flared up yet again. The armored units of the division were employed in escorting convoys of vehicles. Some units had to fight their way to the railhead. The *III./SS-Panzer-Grenadier-Regiment "Norge"* embarked on 25 November in Karlovac. *SS-Panzer-Grenadier-Regiment 24 "Danmark"* loaded in Petrinja, where the last transports left on 7 December. The *2./SS-Panzer-Aufklärungs-Abteilung 11*, which had been employed guarding transports, entrained at Agram as one of the last units — other than *SS-Panzer-Abteilung 11*. All of the units were issued warm winter clothing before heading for the Eastern Front.

SS-Freiwilligen-Brigade "Nederland", which had been staged in the area north of Agram, remained in the partisan area for a while and completed its training.

SS-Pionier-Bataillon 11 and the *16./SS-Panzer-Grenadier-Regiment 23 "Norge"* and the *16./SS-Panzer-Grenadier-Regiment 24 "Danmark"* never were sent to Croatia. They were set in march from the troop training area at

Beneschau and arrived at the area of operations at the Oranienbaum pocket ahead of the rest of the division.

The divisional tank battalion was the last unit of *SS-Panzer-Grenadier-Freiwilligen-Division "Nordland"* to leave Croatia, moving out from its billeting area on 22 December 1943 and entraining in Agram. Even during the last night there, the partisans advanced as far as the first houses in Samobor. The *Flak* platoon of *SS-Panzer-Abteilung 11* and the combat outposts took up the firefight and pushed the attackers back. The men of the battalion spent Christmas of 1943 in railroad cars on their way to the front. The planned issue of the *Panzer V Panther* would remain for the future.

At the end of December 1943, *SS-Freiwilligen-Brigade "Nederland"* prepared for departure and followed the *III. (germanisches) SS-Panzer-Korps* into the Oranienbaum pocket. At that time, the brigade was still missing all of its heavy weapons. An artillery battalion intended for the brigade was to be formed at Beneschau; it was still in the initial stages of its formation.

SS-Flak-Abteilung 11 was also not in Croatia. The order transferring it to the northern front reached it at the troop training area at Arys.

SS-Infanterie-Regiment "Nordland" in 1940, after a live-fire exercise. The author, 17-years-old at that time, is fourth from the right.

SS-Infanterie-Regiment "Nordland" in 1940. *SS-Standartenführer* Fritz von Scholz inspects the *I./SS-Infanterie-Regiment "Nordland"* at Klagenfurt.

Leave after the first combat employment at Demjansk. *SS-Sturmbannführer* Martinsen reports the men of *SS-Freikorps "Danmark"*.

Grafenwöhr, July 1943. Inspection of *SS-Grenadier-Regiment "Danmark"*. From the left: the base commander and his adjutant; the regimental commander, *SS-Obersturmbannführer Graf* von Westphalen; *General der Waffen-SS* Steiner; *SS-Obersturmbannführer* Martinsen, commander of the *I./SS-Grenadier-Regiment "Danmark"*.

Above: *General der Waffen-SS* Felix Steiner conversing with Danish volunteers. On the right, in civilian clothing, the Danish minister and ambassador Mohr.

Above left: *Graf* von Westphalen and Mohr at Grafenwöhr, 1943.

Above right: Grafenwöhr. *General* Felix Steiner and the commander of the *III./SS-Grenadier-Regiment "Danmark"*, *SS-Sturmbannführer* Jacobsen.

Security operations in Croatia. Destroyed bridge at Toplica-Lesce.

April 1943 at Staraja-Blismezy (Donez). Officers of *SS-Panzergrenadier-Regiment "Nordland"* who would find employment as commanding officers after the regiment was expanded to a division in the *III. (germanisches) SS-Panzer-Korps*. From the left: *SS-Hauptsturmführer* Bergfeld (half covered); *SS-Obersturmführer* Schlager; *SS-Sturmbannführer* Lohmann (sitting); *SS-Obersturmbannführer* Jörchel; *SS-Sturmbannführer* Collani; *SS-Hauptsturmführer* Meyer; *SS-Obersturmbannführer* Krügel; *SS-Hauptsturmführer* Haupt; *SS-Obersturmführer* Trost (half covered).

View of Narwa — February 1944

View of Iwangorod — February 1944

Left: Rear view of an *Sd.Kfz 250/9* of *SS-Panzer-Aufklärungs-Abteilung 11*. Note the tactical symbol of the *11. SS-Freiwilligen-Panzer-Grenadier-Division "Nordland"*.

Above: Corduroy road in the northern sector.

Below: The command post of *SS-Pionier-Bataillon 11* at a timber-yard in Narwa.

At the command post of the *4. SS-Panzer-Grenadier-Brigade "Nederland"* in the Narwa bridgehead. From the left: *SS-Brigadeführer* Wagner (commander, *4. SS-Panzer-Grenadier-Brigade "Nederland"*); *SS-Sturmbannführer* Ziemssen (brigade operations officer); and, *General der Waffen-SS* Kleinheisterkamp (acting commanding general of the corps for *General der Waffen-SS* Steiner).

Command post of the *11. SS-Freiwilligen-Panzer-Grenadier-Division "Nordland"* at Narwa. Far left: *SS-Sturmbannführer* von Bockelberg (operations officer). Center: Fritz von Scholz, the divisional commander.

Bridgehead Narwa: Cemetery south of the Narwa — Jamburg road.

German military cemetery in destroyed Narwa.

THE 18. ARMEE

In the summer of 1941 the German troops had failed to take Leningrad. The German command focused its attention on the Soviet capital, Moscow. Leningrad's outer suburbs were reached, but then the front stiffened. Long supply routes and the onset of winter saved the city from capture. West of Leningrad, the so-called Oranienbaum pocket remained occupied by Soviet troops who had fallen back into it. At first, the German command granted no great significance to it.

For more than two years the fighting continued around Leningrad. The city was cut off from supply, save what could flow in across the ice of Lake Ladoga. See-saw fighting continued on the Newa, around Schlüsselburg and in the Wolchow area. In the north, the Finns stood guard along their southern border.

During those years, the special nature of the fighting, the wooded marshland and the Russian winter stamped a new kind of frontline soldier: the Wolchow fighter. He was representative of all the soldiers of the northern sector. The German troops had to deal with inadequate supply routes and mud. In the spring and autumn the roads and paths became bottomless. Man and beast sank into the morass. Corduroy roads were constructed as well as strong wooden bunkers and fighting positions that rose above the marshes.

The northern front remained the bastard stepchild of the German army command. The central and southern sectors of the Eastern Front devoured the newly organized German formations. Nothing was left over for the northern sector. Only as the indicators increased toward the end of 1943 that the Russians would relieve Leningrad was the newly formed *III. (germanisches) SS-Panzer-Korps* sent to the *18. Armee*. As 1943 changed to 1944, *Generaloberst* Lindemann's *18. Armee* extended in a broadly stretched arc from the Gulf of Finland to Lake Ilmen, where it joined the *16. Armee*.

The *III. (germanisches) SS-Panzer-Korps* surrounded the Oranienbaum pocket from the mouth of the Luga to Peterhof. The *L. Armee-Korps* was south of Leningrad with the *126., 170.* and *215. Infanterie-Divisionen*. The *LIV. Armee-Korps* extended along the Newa to south of Schlüsselburg with the *11., 24.* and *225. Infanterie-Divisionen*. At the corner post stood the *XXVI. Armee-Korps* with the *61., 227., 254.* and *212. Infanterie-Divisionen* and the Spanish Legion. *Oberst* Wengler held the exposed "Wengler Nose" with one regiment of the *227. Infanterie-Division*. The *XXVIII. Armee-Korps* held the positions on the central Wolchow with the *121. Infanterie-Division*, the *12. Luftwaffen-Feld-Division*, the *21. Infanterie-Division* and the *13.*

Luftwaffen-Feld-Division (at Tschudowo). The *XXXVIII. Armee-Korps* covered to the south to Lake Ilmen with the *2. Lettische Brigade,* the *28. Jäger-Division* and the *1. Luftwaffen-Feld-Division*. On 9 January 1944, *Generaloberst* Model (*Feldmarschall* as of 30 March 1944) took over *Heeresgruppe Nord,* to which the *16.* and *18. Armeen* belonged, relieving the former army-group commander, *Feldmarschall* Küchler.

People of Ugrian stock had settled the area outside of Leningrad and Oranienbaum. The villages were clean; the houses solidly built. The landscape was flat and marshy with alternating meadows and low, marshy woods. Along with the villages of close-set dwellings were numerous separate dwellings and cattle sheds scattered in the landscape. The advance on Leningrad in 1941 swept over the terrain. Almost all of the villages were from 25 to 75% destroyed in the fighting. Corduroy roads led to the command posts and the main supply routes.

The Oranienbaum front was considered a quiet front. It consisted of a strip of coast west of Leningrad with the cities of Oranienbaum and Peterhof. The Russians had held a bridgehead there from the start of the war that was supported from the fortress of Kronstadt.

As 1942 became 1943, the *III. Luftwaffen-Feld-Korps* was formed with the *9.* and *10. Luftwaffen-Feld-Divisionen* and committed at the Oranienbaum pocket, where it relieved army divisions. The commanding general of the *III. Luftwaffen-Feld-Korps* was *Generalleutnant* Odebrecht. However, in November 1943, the corps headquarters was converted into the corps headquarters of the *II. Flak-Korps* and took on other tasks. On 1 December 1942 Odebrecht was named *General der Flak-Artillerie.* The *9.* and *10. Luftwaffen-Feld-Divisionen* remained in their positions.

Since all signs pointed to a Soviet offensive to relieve Leningrad, the German command was forced to strengthen the Oranienbaum front and transferred the newly formed *III. (germanisches) SS-Panzer-Korps* to that sector. That substantially reinforced the sector that had been held by the *Luftwaffen-Feld-Divisionen,* which had little combat experience.

The transfer of the *III.(germanisches) SS-Panzer-Korps* to the Oranienbaum front went under the codename of *Unternehmen Lützow.* On 4 December 1943 the staff of the corps arrived by rail at the Wolossowo railroad station and waited out the pitch-black night. As noon drew near on 5 December the staff detrained and moved into a forest camp at Klopitzy.

SS-Pionier-Bataillon 11 and the combat-engineer companies of *SS-Panzer-Grenadier-Regiment 23 "Norge"* and *SS-Panzer-Grenadier-Regiment 24 "Danmark"* were set in march from the Beneschau troop training area and arrived at the area of operations at the Oranienbaum pocket in advance of the other units of the division. On 6 December the combat-engineer units detrained at Wolossowo and, partly on foot, reached the Klopitzy area. The combat-engineer companies of the regiments were attached to *SS-Pionier-*

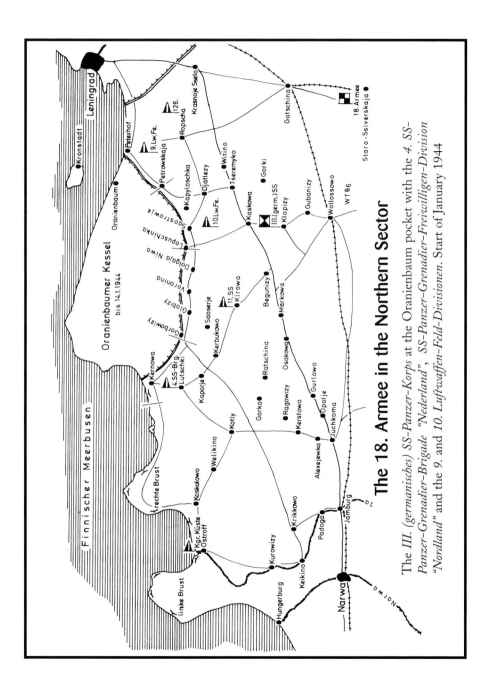

The 18. Armee in the Northern Sector

The III. (germanisches) SS-Panzer-Korps at the Oranienbaum pocket with the 4. SS-Panzer-Grenadier-Brigade "Nederland", SS-Panzer-Grenadier-Freiwilligen-Division "Nordland" and the 9. and 10. Luftwaffen-Feld-Divisionen. Start of January 1944

Bataillon 11. Weapons and equipment of the regimental combat engineers, who had not yet been fully equipped with vehicles, were brought forward in lifts by vehicles of *SS-Pionier-Bataillon 11.* Two days later the combat-engineer units moved to the front and assumed responsibility for minefields and positions for their regiments from the *10. Luftwaffen-Feld-Division.*

In the meantime, the regiments of SS-Panzer-Grenadier-Freiwilligen-Division "Nordland" arrived and detrained at various railroad stations. SS-Panzer-Grenadier-Regiment 24 "Danmark" unloaded in Kotly. SS-Panzer-Grenadier-Regiment 23 "Norge" assembled in the Ragowiczy area and moved in motor-march to the Woronino — Dolgaja-Niwa area.

The commanding general of the *III. (germanisches) SS-Panzer-Korps* had moved in advance of the corps by vehicle. He had gone to the *Führerhauptquartier* (Hitler's headquarters in the field) and the command post of *Heeresgruppe Nord* (*Generalfeldmarschall* von Küchler) and had received a detailed briefing. *General* Steiner then reported to *Generaloberst* Lindemann, the commander of the *18. Armee,* whose command post was southeast of Staro-Ssiverkaja, south of Gatschina. The issue: Should the *III. (germanisches) SS-Panzer-Korps* be committed in the eastern or the western portion of the Oranienbaum front? A Soviet breakthrough to the west to Narwa and the resultant blockade of the retreat route for the entire *18. Armee* was the greatest concern. As a result, *General* Steiner decided to commit his *SS* formations in the western sector.

The battalions of *SS-Panzer-Grenadier-Freiwilligen-Division "Nordland"* took over their positions on 10 December. Company commanders and platoon leaders were sent ahead to familiarize themselves with the terrain and to lead their units into the positions on the following night. On 12 December the relief was considered complete. On 13 December 1943 at 0000 hours the *III. (germanisches) SS-Panzer-Korps* took responsibility for its sector on the Oranienbaum front.

In view of the expected enemy offensive, the corps ordered renewed efforts in the construction of positions. Not only the main line of resistance but also the rear-area positions were improved. Every village was turned into a strongpoint. The main line of resistance — previously consisting only of a series of strongpoints — was tied together by a system of continuous trenches which, as a result of the marshy ground, were often so shallow that men had to bend over when moving in them. Palisades were erected along swampy stretches to block enemy observation.

The enemy remained quiet. However, aside from patrol activity by both sides and the unpleasant activity of enemy snipers, there were no combat operations.

Kampfgruppe Wenning and *Kampfgruppe SS-Polizei-Division* held the coast from the mouth of the Narwa at Hungerburg and along a portion of the land from the center of Koporskii Bay to Gorbowizy. In addition, there were coastal artillery units, Estonian police battalions and veterinary and convalescent companies. The staff was in Ostroff at the mouth of the Luga. With a strength of about 6,400 men, the *Kampfgruppen* held a front about 15 kilometers long.

SS-Panzer-Grenadier-Freiwilligen-Division "Nordland" was committed from Gorbowizy by Nowaja-Burja, with *SS-Panzer-Grenadier-Regiment 24 "Danmark"* to the west and *SS-Panzer-Grenadier-Regiment 23 "Norge"* to the east. The division command post was in Kirowa. The length of the front was about 24 kilometers.

The *10. Luftwaffen-Feld-Division* held the front from Nowaja-Burja to Petrowskaja, with a sector about 22 kilometers long; the *9. Luftwaffen-Feld-Division* held from Petrowskaja to the Gulf of Finland at Peterhof with a front of about 16 kilometers.

General Steiner intended to employ the *4. SS-Panzer-Grenadier-Brigade "Nederland"*, which was still in Croatia, in the sector of *Kampfgruppe SS-Polizei-Division*, which was slated for reorganization. On 14 December 1943 Steiner ordered the reorganization of the coastal sector under a separate command, which he shortly entrusted to Danish *SS-Obersturmbannführer der Waffen-SS* Kryssing. Kryssing, born in 1891, had been an artillery lieutenant colonel in the Danish army. He was the first commander of *Freikorps "Danmark"* and later served on the staffs of *SS-Panzer-Division "Totenkopf"* and *SS-Panzer-Grenadier-Division "Wiking"*. It had been intended to make him the corps artillery commander.

Kryssing's operations officer was *SS-Sturmbannführer* Engelhardt, under whose capable leadership the organizational work of the staff of the *"Kampfgruppe Küste* (coast)" moved forward rapidly. Engelhardt immediately inspected the coastal sector and formed a precise picture of the possibilities for defense. On 18 December Engelhardt reported the results of his reconnaissance to the chief of staff of the *III. (germanisches) SS-Panzer-Korps* and requested the necessary officers, noncommissioned officers and men. The corps helped. When *SS-Obersturmbannführer* Kryssing arrived at the staff billets in Ostroff the most important work had already been done.

The main backstops of *Kampfgruppe "Küste"* were the eleven coastal batteries commanded by *Major* Blum, which were dug in at various points along the coast. From west to east, the lines were occupied as follows (see map): Meeküla (an Estonian police battalion); Hungerburg (two convalescent companies); northeast of Hungerburg (two veterinary companies); around Kirjamo, 10 kilometers west of Ostroff (two convalescent companies); on both sides of the "Left Breast" (a chemical decontamination company); on both sides of the mouth of the Luga (*Marine-Regiment von Beckerath* with the staff in Ust-Luga); west of Welikino (a combat-engineer battalion and a mobile artillery battalion); on the west side of the "Right Breast" (three divisional replacement battalions and a school for noncommissioned officers); on the north and east side of the "Right Breast" (*Marine-Bataillone Hohnschild* and *Schneider*); from there, contact with *Kampfgruppe SS-Polizei-Division*.

The weapons of *Kampfgruppe "Küste"* stemmed from the arsenals of all of Europe. The 7.5 to 15 cm batteries were of French, Polish and Czech origins, as were the small arms. As a result, the approximately 9,000-strong *Kampfgruppe "Küste"* was a rather mixed bag. Reserves consisted of one more veterinary company that was staged at Welikino.

Kampfgruppe SS-Polizei-Division prepared to be relieved. The division was to be reorganized. On 28 December 1943, the advance party of the *4. SS-Panzer-Grenadier-Brigade "Nederland"* arrived from Croatia. One day later, the *II./SS-Freiwilligen-Panzer-Grenadier-Regiment 49 "de Ruyter"* relieved elements of *Kampfgruppe SS-Polizei-Division*. By the start of the new year, the *4. SS-Panzer-Grenadier-Brigade "Nederland"* had taken over the entire *Kampfgruppe SS-Polizei-Division* sector. Only the artillery battalion of *Kampfgruppe SS-Polizei-Division* remained at the front, since the Dutch brigade had no artillery.

The command post of the *4. SS-Panzer-Grenadier-Brigade "Nederland"* was established at Lutschki. *SS-Freiwilligen-Panzer-Grenadier-Regiment 49 "de Ruyter"* was in the eastern sector; *SS-Freiwilligen-Panzer-Grenadier-Regiment 48 "General Seyffard"* was in the western sector. The brigade was still lacking some of its weaponry. Heavy weapons had to be brought forward later. *SS-Panzer-Jäger-Abteilung 54*, which was staged in the area south of Kotly, received *Sturmgeschütze* and *Pak* there. That battalion was committed against partisans in the Kotly area along with forces of *Kampfgruppe "Küste"*. The commander of the brigade's antitank battalion was *SS-Sturmbannführer* Schock. At that point, the brigade had a strength of about 6,000 men. The *SS-Freiwilligen-Panzer-Grenadier-Division "Nordland"* (new designation effective 12 November 1943) held the central sector of the Oranienbaum front.

The division staff was headquartered in a country manor at Kirowa. In addition to staffs of divisional units, the *1./SS-Instandsetzungs-Abteilung 11*, under *SS-Hauptsturmführer* Christiansen, was also located in Kirowa to repair disabled vehicles. Not until Soviet night fighters had repeatedly attacked the area did the staffs build bunkers, which were gradually occupied by the various staff sections.

SS-Panzer-Grenadier-Regiment 24 "Danmark" was committed in the western part of the division sector. The regimental command post was in a bunker complex 4 kilometers north of the village of Saoserje. The complex of approximately 20 bunkers was situated on a small rise that rose above the marsh and was linked to the Kaporje-Popscha main supply route by a corduroy road. The command post of *SS-Artillerie-Regiment 11 "Nordland"* was slightly to its south.

The *III./SS-Panzer-Grenadier-Regiment 24 "Danmark"* was positioned in the western sector, with the *4. SS-Panzer-Grenadier-Brigade "Nederland"* as its outside flank neighbor. The battalion sector extended for three kilometers and included the villages of Petrovizy and Gorbowizy in the main line of resistance. The battalion command post was 1.5 kilometers behind the lines at Kastivskoje. The *I./SS-Panzer-Grenadier-Regiment 24 "Danmark"* linked up with the *III. Bataillon.* Its sector extended east with its right boundary directly west of Woronino. The *II./SS-Panzer-Grenadier-Regiment 24 "Danmark"* was positioned in the area directly south of the assigned front as regimental reserve.

The *II./SS-Artillerie-Artillery Regiment 11* was in support of *SS-Panzer-Grenadier-Regiment 24 "Danmark".* The *1./SS-Pionier-Bataillon 11* was attached to the regiment for construction and improvement of positions. The regimental units were positioned in strongpoints across the sector.

SS-Panzer-Grenadier-Regiment 23 "Norge" was positioned in the Woronino — Nowaja-Burje sector with the *II./SS-Panzer-Grenadier-Regiment 23 "Norge"* to the west, the *III./SS-Panzer-Grenadier-Regiment 23 "Norge"* to the east and the *I./SS-Panzer-Grenadier-Regiment 23 "Norge"* as reserve in the Lopuschinka area. The regimental command post was in a bunker complex at Dolgaja-Niwa. The *I./SS-Artillerie-Regiment 11* was in support of the regiment with the *2./SS-Pionier-Bataillon 11* attached for engineer support.

After the arrival of *4. SS-Panzer-Grenadier-Brigade "Nederland"* in the corps sector, the former regimental commander of *SS-Panzer-Grenadier-Regiment "Norge"*, *SS-Obersturmbannführer* Jörchel, took over *SS-Freiwilligen-Panzer-Grenadier-Regiment 48 "General Seyffard".* The Norwegian regiment was then commanded by *SS-Sturmbannführer* Stoffers.

The *2./SS-Panzer-Aufklärungs-Abteilung 11* entrained in Agram on 8 December 1943 as the last company of the battalion and joined it on 16 December 1943. The battalion moved to the Begunizy — Greblowo area on 29 December 1943 and continued its training. *SS-Hauptsturmführer* Saalbach prepared his battalion for the impending operations with map exercises and command conferences. The battalion surgeon was Dr. Artner.

SS-Obersturmführer Lorenz commanded the *1./SS-Panzer-Aufklärungs-Abteilung 11*, which was equipped with 8-wheel armored cars armed with 20 millimeter cannon and machine guns. *SS-Obersturmführer* Heckmüller commanded the *2./ SS-Panzer-Aufklärungs-Abteilung 11.* It was outfitted with half-tracked vehicles. They were also equipped with 2 cm rapid-fire cannon whose flexible mounts allowed them to also be used against aircraft. The *3.* and *4./SS-Panzer-Aufklärungs-Abteilung 11* were *Panzergrenadier* companies on *SPW* (half-tracked armored personnel carriers). *SS-Obersturmführer* Kaiser commanded the *3./SS-Panzer-Aufklärungs-Abteilung 11*; *SS-Obersturmführer* Viehmann commanded the *4./SS-Panzer-Aufklärungs-Abteilung 11.*

The *5./SS-Panzer-Aufklärungs-Abteilung 11*, the heavy company, was led by *SS-Obersturmführer* Schmidt. It was composed of the company headquarters section, an antitank platoon, an infantry gun platoon, a combat-engineer platoon and a cannon platoon.

The cannon half-tracks were the *Sd.Kfz. 251/9*. On the initiative of the leader of the platoon, *SS-Untersturmführer* Langendorf, the firepower of the company was considerably increased with captured weapons. The platoon had a strength of 1 officer, 7 noncommissioned officers and 30 enlisted personnel. It had 8 armored half-tracks that were equipped with short-barreled 7.5 cm cannon. Each vehicle carried an ammunition basic load of 72 rounds. In winter an additional 72 rounds were carried on sleds designed by Langendorf. Each vehicle mounted a *"Stuka zu Fuß"* (*Stuka* on foot) rocket launcher rack on each side, with either 32 cm high-explosive or 28 cm napalm rounds that could be fired by the driver by means of the vehicle battery. The cannon could also be used for indirect fire.

SS-Panzer-Jäger-Abteilung 11 was staged in the Jamburg area. *SS-Hauptsturmführer* Roensch commanded the battalion; *SS-Obersturmführer* Krohmer the Headquarters Battery. *SS-Hauptsturmführer* Renner commanded the *1./SS-Panzer-Jäger-Abteilung 11*, *SS-Hauptsturmführer* Knobelspieß the *2./SS-Panzer-Jäger-Abteilung 11* and *SS-Hauptsturmführer* Ellesieck the *3./SS-Panzer-Jäger-Abteilung 11*. *Hauptmann* Schulz-Streek (of the army) was assigned to the inexperienced battalion as an advisor. After the battalion had arrived in the rear area of the combat zone, *Sturmgeschütze* were issued to it from the army ordnance supply depot. Gaps in the weapons training were closed.

At the end of 1943, *SS-Panzer-Abteilung 11* arrived at Hungerburg and was given a billeting area there. It was then moved to Jamburg. Individual tank crews were issued *Panthers* that originated in a faulty early-production run and actually did not belong at the front. However, the marked shortage of weapons was already forcing such measures. The *Panthers* served as strongpoints at critical areas of the front, where they were dug in. The tankers of *SS-Panzer-Abteilung 11,* who had waited in vain for their authorized issue of armored vehicles, went to work and, with the help of *SS-Instandsetzungs-Abteilung 11*, made individual vehicles operational.

SS-Freiwilligen-Panzer-Grenadier-Division "Nordland" had a strength of 11,393 men on 31 December 1943.

The *10. Luftwaffen-Feld-Division* held the sector from Nowaja-Burja to Petrowskaja. That sector encompassed about 22 kilometers. *Generalmajor* von Wedel led the *10. Luftwaffen-Feld-Division*. It included: *Jäger-Regimenter (Luftwaffe) 19* and *20*, each with 3 battalions and a 13th and 14th company; *Artillerie-Regiment 10 (Luftwaffe)* with three battalions, *Radfahr-Aufklärungs-Kompanie 10 (Luftwaffe), Panzer-Jäger-Abteilung 10 (Luftwaffe)* and *divisional troops (all numbered 10)*. Its strength was about 10,000 men.

The *9. Luftwaffen-Feld-Division* held the sector from Peterhof (inclusive) to the Gulf of Finland. It was commanded by *Oberst* Michael (effective 1 January 1944: *Generalmajor*) and had a front of about 16 kilometers. It included: *Jäger-Regimenter (Luftwaffe) 17* and *18,* each with three battalions and a 13th and 14th company; *Artillerie-Regiment 9 (Luftwaffe)* with three battalions; a *Füsilier-Bataillon* and *Panzer-Jäger-Abteilung 9 (Luftwaffe)* and the divisional troops. Its strength was about 10,000 men.

At first the front remained quiet. Combat activity diminished on both sides, and there was only limited harassing fire and propaganda activity. Indicative of the activity was the headline one morning in the company newsletter of the *16./SS-Panzer-Grenadier-Regiment 24 "Danmark"*: "The Russians hung aerial propaganda leaflets on the trees during the night!"

The December weather was moderately cold and, as Christmas 1943 approached, a thaw was widespread and the main supply routes in the rear were covered in black ice.

At the end of the year enemy aerial reconnaissance increased. There was a general feeling of approaching danger. Nevertheless, the numbers in the ammunition expenditure reports did not go up. For example, on 29 December 1943, the *III./SS-Panzer-Grenadier-Regiment 24 "Danmark"* reported an expenditure of 110 rifle rounds, 3,670 rounds of machine-gun ammunition, 19 light artillery rounds, 4 heavy artillery rounds and 34 mortar shells. The ammunition expenditure reports from the other battalions were similar. The morning-report strength of the *III.SS-Panzer-Grenadier-Regiment 24 "Danmark"* on 29 December 1943 was 12 officers, 57 noncommissioned officers and 435 enlisted personnel.

On 9 January 1944 the regimental commander of *SS-Panzer-Grenadier-Regiment 24 "Danmark"*, *Graf* von Westphalen, ordered employment of a combat patrol with the mission of bringing back prisoners and blowing up a bunker. *Graf* von Westphalen briefed *SS-Oberscharführer* Hvenekilde, who led the assault troop. The operation miscarried. The combat patrol was spotted prematurely and fell into Soviet hands. All signs pointed toward an imminent Soviet offensive.

On 10 January 1944 the *2./SS-Pionier-Bataillon 11* was withdrawn from *SS-Freiwilligen-Panzer-Grenadier-Division "Nordland"* and attached to the *9. Luftwaffen-Feld-Division* with the mission of constructing positions at the front and serving as boundary protection and operational reserve at the sector boundary between the *9.* and *10. Luftwaffen-Feld-Divisionen.*

SS-Obersturmführer Knepel led his *2./SS-Pionier Bataillon 11* over paths drifted with snow in a motorized night march to the new operational area, which the company reached at about 0500 hours. The company bivouacked in the vicinity of the artillery positions. After a short and intensive scouting of the front with the platoon leaders, the company was directed to construct wood abatis immediately behind the main line of resistance. The increase in enemy aerial activity was striking, as was the registration firing of guns of all calibers on prominent points such as road intersections and the like. Nighttime bombing attacks by the Russian "sewing machine" aircraft on the cities and villages to the rear also increased. The enemy situation reports arriving at the *III. (germanisches) SS-Panzer-Korps* said the Russians were pouring strong forces into the Oranienbaum pocket through Kronstadt Bay. It would soon prove that the failure to eliminate the Oranienbaum pocket was a neglected opportunity that could not be made good.

The Storm Breaks Loose

At the end of 1943 the Soviets achieved significant success in the sector of the *16. Armee* and broke into the German front at several places. The Soviet command saw then that the time had come to launch an assault against the *18. Armee* and free Leningrad.

The high command of the "Leningrad Front" readied for the offensive, positioning the 2nd Shock Army in the Oranienbaum bridgehead, the 42nd Army southwest of Leningrad and the 67th Army north of Mga.

The "Wolchow Front" prepared to have the 59th Army attack Nowgorod, with Pleskau as the operational objective, and to have the 8th and 54th Armies attack from the mid-Wolchow sector.

The 2nd "Baltic Front" was to build on its success at Newel and reach the mid-Düna sector.

The Soviet offensive began at the Oranienbaum bridgehead. On the morning of 14 January 1944 the heavy batteries of the Kronstadt naval fortress, along with the heavy naval guns of the battleship *"Oktjabraska Revoluzija"*, the half-completed cruiser *Lützow*, and the guns of the battleship *"Marat"*, which was lying on the level bottom of the anchorage, along with the batteries of the 2nd Soviet Shock Army, opened a long-lasting heavy barrage on the positions of the *9.* and *10. Luftwaffen-Feld-Divisionen*.

Lieutenant General Fedjuninskij's divisions of the 2nd Shock Army attacked behind the wall of fire. The Soviet XXXXIII Rifle Corps attacked with the 48th, 90th and 98th Rifle Divisions and the 43rd Armor Brigade. In the east — against the positions of the *9. Luftwaffen-Feld-Division* — the CXXII. Rifle Corps attacked with the 131st and 11th Rifle Divisions and the 122nd Tank Brigade . Close behind it followed the 43rd, 168th and 186th

Rifle Divisions and the 152nd Tank Brigade. The 50th Coastal Brigade remained at Peterhof. The main effort hit the boundaries of the two *Luftwaffe* divisions. The first wave achieved a penetration of 5 kilometers.

The next blow hit the German *L. Armee-Korps* a day later on the positions of the *126., 170.* and *215. Infanterie-Divisionen*. The divisions of the 42nd Soviet Army attacked there from the Leningrad area.

The *9. Luftwaffen-Feld-Division* and the *126.* and *170. Infanterie-Divisionen* were partially encircled. Other elements were able to break through to the west. The northern wing of the *18. Armee* collapsed. On 19 January the Soviet 2nd Shock Army and Soviet 42nd Army joined hands at Ropscha. They then assaulted farther to the west against Jamburg. The first objective of the Soviet offensive had been attained; the northern wing of the *18. Armee* was faltering. The Soviet offensive also opened on the southern wing. *Feldmarschall* von Küchler recognized the threatening encirclement and wanted to pull his army group back to the Luga position. Hitler refused and replaced *Feldmarschall* von Küchler with *Generaloberst* Model. Model likewise saw no alternative but to order a withdrawal.

On the morning of 14 January 1944 at 0500 hours, *SS-Untersturmführer* Pauritsch's *2./SS-Pionier-Bataillon 11* set out to continue building wood abatis on the boundary between the *9.* and *10. Luftwaffen-Feld-Divisionen*. The company commander, *SS-Obersturmführer* Knepel, who had been ordered to reconnoiter the *"Finnish Position"* — a blocking position — gave up that plan when, at 0600 hours, a murderous, long-lasting heavy barrage from guns of all calibers began and was supplemented by low-level aerial attacks. On the way to his company, *SS-Obersturmführer* Knepel encountered completely distraught men who were directed to a rally point.

The front-line positions and the wood line presented a gruesome picture. Bunkers had been shot to pieces by the naval guns and the earth plowed up. The woods had been cut down to a height of two meters. Dead and wounded were everywhere. For many soldiers, the first great baptism of fire was too much for their nerves. *SS-Obersturmführer* Knepel hurried with his headquarters section leader from one man to the next. They energized the totally apathetic-appearing men. Severely wounded men were placed on *Akjas* (boat-shaped light sleds) and pulled or carried to the rally point.

By the time those who were left had been briefed, the first Russians, in white winter clothing, had already reached the edge of the woods and infiltrated into the wooded area. One after another, the last weapons of the *Luftwaffe* soldiers fell silent. As the last ones out, Knepel and his headquarters section leader had to clear their retreat route with machine pistol and hand grenades. The remnants of the *2./SS-Pionier-Bataillon 11* were assembled farther to the rear and issued replacement weapons which the *Spieß* (company first sergeant), *SS-Oberscharführer* Willmann, had brought forward.

In the meantime, the *3./SS-Pionier-Bataillon 11* under *SS-Hauptsturm-*

führer Voß had also arrived in the penetration area. That company and the remnants of the *2./SS-Pionier-Bataillon 11* prepared for an immediate counterattack. After a short pause, the combat engineers launched a counterattack into the heavily snowbound, 5 kilometer deep wooded area. Two kilometers into the attack, the two companies ran into the advancing Soviet infantry. The right flank of the *2./SS-Pionier-Bataillon 11* became involved in hard, hand-to-hand combat. For the most part, the surviving *Luftwaffe* soldiers — unaccustomed to combat — had taken flight. Those who had not been killed, wounded or captured had retreated and panicked or were leaderless. As a result, the two *SS* combat engineer companies were entirely on their own and without neighbors on their flanks.

When the danger of being outflanked and encircled became evident, *SS-Hauptsturmführer* Voß ordered a withdrawal. The *2./SS-Pionier-Bataillon 11*, fully involved in hand-to-hand combat, gave covering fire to the *3./SS-Pionier-Bataillon 11* and broke through the encirclement. The two companies occupied new positions on high ground southeast of the woods. The commander of the*2./SS-Pionier-Bataillon 11*, *SS-Obersturmführer* Knepel, was wounded during the breakthrough. The first day of the Soviet offensive had cost the *2./SS-Pionier-Bataillon 11* about 100 men dead or wounded.

In the meantime, the commander of *SS-Pionier-Bataillon11*, *SS-Sturmbannführer* Bunse, had joined his men who were fending off the Soviet masses. Fritz Bunse led his combat engineers back to a shell-torn farmstead that lay like a bastion in the attacker's path. The combat engineers quickly moved into the snow-covered positions and made them defendable again. The careful planning that had surrounded every village with positions then bore fruit. By 1600 hours the light began to fade. The Soviets attacked and ran up against the positions of the engineers. They did not waver. A Soviet battalion was bled white in front of the German positions.

On the following day, artillery and Stalin-organ salvos rained down on the bastion of the combat engineers. Swarms of Soviet airplanes spewed death and destruction on the defenders. The artillery fire mounted to a barrage and thinned the ranks of the combat engineers. The fire then ebbed and the Soviets stormed forward, three T-34 tanks in the lead.

Bunse's companies — totally isolated and without artillery support — did not waver. Two T 34's reached their positions. Two brave combat engineers leapt from their holes in the snow, slapped magnetic hollow charges onto the steel monsters and, at the same moment, the Russian tanks were torn to shreds by the explosions. The third T 34 was knocked out by a *Pak*. The attack by the Russian infantry wavered. Taking advantage of their indecision, a *Sturmmann* sprang up and mowed a grim harvest among the rows of the attackers with his machine gun. That was the signal. The weapons barked from the holes in the snow and the enemy fell back in flight.

In the meantime, all available German formations were thrown into the

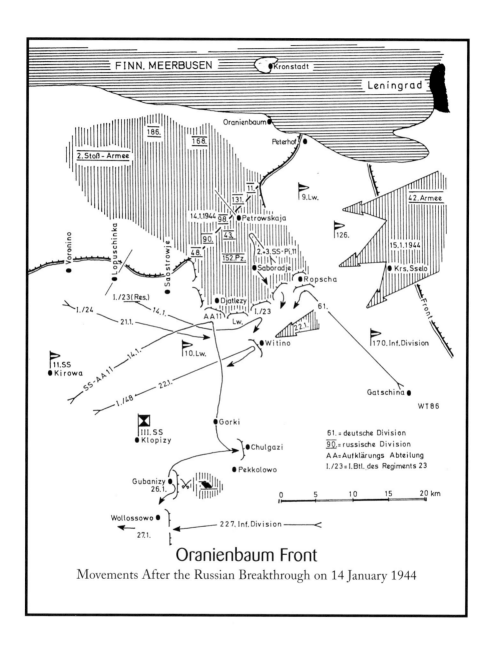

FINN. MEERBUSEN

Kronstadt

Leningrad

Oranienbaum

Peterhof

2. Stoß - Armee

186.

168.

11.

9.Lw.

42. Armee

131.

14.1.1944 98.

Petrowskaja

126.

15.1.1944

Voronino

Lopuschinka

90.

43.

48.

152.Pz.

2.+3.SS-Pi.11

Saboradje

Ropscha

Krs. Sselo

Saostrowje

1./23(Res.)

Djatlezy

1./23

61.

170. Inf. Division

1./24

14.1.

AA 11

Lw.

22.1.

21.1.

Witino

11.SS
Kirowa

SS-AA 11

14.1.

10.Lw.

1./48

22.1.

Gatschina

WT86

III.SS
Klopizy

Gorki

61. = deutsche Division
90. = russische Division
AA = Aufklärungs Abteilung
1./23 = I.Btl. des Regiments 23

Chulgazi

Pekkolowo

Gubanizy
26.1.

0   5   10   15   20 km

Wollossowo

227. Inf. Division

27.1.

Oranienbaum Front
Movements After the Russian Breakthrough on 14 January 1944

33

area of the penetration. The *18. Armee* recaptured the "Wengler Nose" and committed the *61.* and *227. Infanterie-Divisionen* into the area of the penetration. The objective of the 2nd Soviet Shock Army became ever clearer: Ropscha and Gatschina, the key nodal point of the main supply route and railroad network. The *61. Infanterie-Division* stood fast in Ropscha against the enemy assault. The *III. (germanisches) SS-Panzer-Korps* freed up all available forces and committed them in the western penetration area. On 17 and 18 January *Kampfgruppe "Küste"* sent its three infantry replacement battalions and its motorized artillery battalion into the combat zone. The three infantry replacement battalions went to their divisions and right into the midst of the fighting. The artillery battalion was committed at different sectors of the front.

After the location of the Soviet major effort became clear in the morning of 14 January, *SS-Panzer-Aufklärungs-Abteilung 11* was committed in the Djatlezy area by way of Kljassina — Bor. By noon it was employed together with combat-ready units of the *10. Luftwaffen-Feld-Division*. The *2./SS-Panzer-Aufklärungs-Abteilung 11* went to the Kapyloschka — Djatlezy sector. The front held by the *Luftwaffe* ground soldiers had been shattered there as well. The *2./SS-Panzer-Aufklärungs-Abteilung 11* recaptured Djatlezy, where a battalion command post had been located. The Soviets opened up with furious mortar fire. *SS-Obersturmführer* Heckmüller, the commander of the company, called his platoon leaders together. As they left the house, all three platoon leaders were felled by the mortar rounds. *SS-Oberscharführer* Gramlich died shortly thereafter.

SS-Obersturmführer Heckmüller committed his armored cars a bit to the southwest, since it had not been possible to completely clear the village. From a position in the wood line, the crews of the vehicles repulsed all of the enemy assaults with cannon and machine gun fire. The company's operations were complicated by the lack of radios. The headquarters section leader, *SS-Unterscharführer* Pollar, dashed from vehicle to vehicle with his messengers, carrying the orders.

When the Soviets found that they could make no further progress on the road to Alt-Bor, they shifted their effort to the road to Woronino. Heckmüller immediately committed the half of the company available to him. Led by the company headquarters section leader, Pollar, those elements were able to repulse all the attacks on Kapyloschka.

From 17-21 January the command post of the *2./SS-Panzer-Aufklärungs-Abteilung 11* was in Alt-Bor. Heckmüller's company fought shoulder to shoulder with units of a construction battalion — all of whose men were more than 50 — and fended off all the Soviet attempts at a breakthrough at Kosherizy and Bor.

On the morning of 14 January, the *I./SS-Panzer-Grenadier-Regiment 23 "Norge"* was staged as a corps reserve in Lopuschinka, about ten kilometers behind the front. An immobile *Panther* had been dug in on the road to the north and was manned by men of *SS-Panzer-Abteilung 11*. In similar fashion, other immobile *Panthers* had been dug in at Woronino and along the entire front.

Towards noon, the operations order arrived for the *I./SS-Panzer-Grenadier-Regiment 23 "Norge"*. The battalion moved out in motor march to the area west of Ropscha. During the night, *SS-Hauptsturmführer* Vogt led his battalion forward against the location of the penetration. Vogt was a circumspect commander who had already been awarded the *Ritterkreuz* when he was a platoon leader in the western campaign. He called together his officers — Rendemann, von Bargen, Stüwe, Kiefer and Dose — for a situation conference. There was not much that he could tell them. Each of them would have to adjust to the confused situation and take appropriate action.

SS-Panzer-Jäger-Abteilung 11 also helped where it could. Parceled out by company and platoon, the *Sturmgeschütze* were the backbone of the grenadiers.

On the morning of 15 January, six T 34's were suddenly in front of the positions of the *I./SS-Panzer-Grenadier-Regiment 23 "Norge"*. Vogt's battalion received enemy fire from all sides. *SS-Obersturmführer* Rendemann was killed. *SS-Hauptsturmführer* von Bargen's *3./SS-Panzer-Grenadier-Regiment 23 "Norge"* had not been attacked by the six T 34's. *SS-Hauptsturmführer* Ellersiek and the four *Sturmgeschütze* of his *3./SS-Panzer-Jäger-Abteilung 11* arrived in the battalion sector by noon of 15 January. The *3./SS-Panzer-Grenadier-Regiment 23 "Norge"* attacked, supported by the four assault guns. The T 34's, which were waiting in a favorable ambush position, repulsed the German immediate counterattack. The command *Sturmgeschütz* was knocked out. *SS-Hauptsturmführer* Ellersiek was the only one of his crew who could be rescued, and he had severe burns. The *3./SS-Panzer-Grenadier-Regiment 23 "Norge"* fell back a bit, dug itself in and was able to hold. The T 34's did not advance but were able to shell the positions of the company all day long. *SS-Hauptsturmführer* von Bargen and his Norwegian platoon leader (an *SS-Untersturmführer*) were both wounded. *SS-Hauptscharführer* Twesman assumed temporary command of the company.

The *5./SS-Artillerie-Regiment 11* was brought forward to support the *I./SS-Panzer-Grenadier-Regiment 23 "Norge"* and went into position northeast of Djatlezy. *SS-Obersturmführer* Binnerup's battery worked over identified enemy positions with heavy fire the entire day. On the Soviet side, it was primarily Stalin organs that were employed. They caused heavy losses to the battalion.

During the evening, the *I./SS-Panzer-Grenadier-Regiment 23 "Norge"* pulled back about a kilometer to the southwest. The battalion held that line on 18 January and repulsed all Soviet attacks. Again, the losses from Stalin organs and artillery were high.

On 17 January the battalion again had to fall back, occupying a new blocking position north of the main supply route in the Witino — Djatlezy sector. As a result, at that point, the front had swung around to the west. During that withdrawal, *SS-Hauptscharführer* Twesmann received a severe lung wound from a shell fragment and was dragged to the rear in an *Akja*. The battalion adjutant, *SS-Obersturmführer* Fechner, took over the *3./SS-Panzer-Grenadier-Regiment 23 "Norge"*. *Bataillon Vogt* held that position until 21 January. An army assault gun in the battalion's sector knocked out four T 34's, thus playing an important role in the successful defense.

On 17 January *Batterie Lärum*, which was in position south of Woronino, was ordered by *Generalmajor* von Wedel (commander of the *10. Luftwaffen-Feld-Division*) to engage a Soviet armor concentration at Saostrowje. The cannoneers swung their heavy howitzers around 100 degrees. The fire direction center of the battery calculated the data from the map and — after twenty minutes and without observed fire — fired its salvos on the enemy concentration of armor and dispersed it.

After the Russian breakthrough on 14 January, the *1./SS-Pionier-Bataillon 11*, which had been performing combat engineering duties in the sector of *SS-Panzer-Grenadier-Regiment 24 "Danmark"*, was set in march on 15 January to the site of the breakthrough. The main supply route was badly jammed with traffic. The company made only slow progress. It went into action in the sector of *SS-Panzer-Aufklärungs-Abteilung 11* and had its first firefight with the attacking Soviets in broken terrain. The company held, but suffered its first losses.

The sector commander, *SS-Hauptsturmführer* Saalbach, formed a new main line of resistance a bit more to the south on 17 January. His forces consisted of: *SS-Panzer-Aufklärungs-Abteilung 11* and the *1./SS-Pionier-Bataillon 11*, mixed with combat-capable units of the *10. Luftwaffen-Feld-Division*. Soviet antitank guns and snipers forced further improvement of the positions. Cold, wet storms forced construction of bunkers. The position was held for days on end. The German losses were limited, in spite of heavy enemy fire from mortars and infantry guns.

The main thrust of the Soviet 2nd Shock Army was aimed at the capture of Ropscha and toward the south to the major supply route and railroad nodal point, Gatschina.

Gruppe Bunse and the remnants of the *2.* and *3./SS-Pionier-Bataillon 11* defended the ruins of the farmstead until the evening of 17 January, when the *61. Infanterie-Division* could attack. On 17 January the spearheads of the Soviet attack had been in the rear of the combat engineers and threatened the artillery that had been brought up, which was firing from all barrels. Fritz Bunse recognized the danger, threw together a group of radiomen and drivers and launched an immediate counterattack against the Soviets. The artillery was able to pull out to the main supply route. The combat engineers were the last to leave their hotly contested position.

While elements of the *III. (germanisches) SS-Panzer-Korps* sealed off the western portion of the penetration — initially running west-east and later swinging completely to the south — Bunse's combat engineers and the *61. Infanterie-Division* fought their way back to the main supply route. They formed a blocking position there and passed battered remnants of the *L. Armee-Korps* through their position. *SS-Panzer-Aufklärungs-Abteilung 11* was freed up to support the *61. Infanterie-Division*.

On 21/22 January the *II./SS-Panzer-Grenadier-Regiment 24 "Danmark"* (held in reserve up to that point) relieved the *I./SS-Panzer-Grenadier-Regiment 24 "Danmark"* in its positions. After it had been relieved, the *I./SS-Panzer-Grenadier-Regiment 24 "Danmark"* then relieved *the SS-Panzer-Aufklärungs-Abteilung 11* at Djatlezy. The *I./SS-Panzer-Grenadier-Regiment 24 "Danmark"* was reinforced with the regiment's *10. Kompanie* and one of its antitank guns. Additional shifts were made from the still quiet western part of the Oranienbaum front into the endangered eastern section. In the course of those movements, the *8./SS-Panzer-Grenadier-Regiment 24 "Danmark"* was committed at Dolgaja-Niwa in order to free up individual batteries of *SS-Artillerie-Regiment 11* which had supported the hard-fighting *Kampfgruppen* in the area of the penetration.

SS-Panzer-Aufklärungs-Abteilung 11 moved parallel to the enemy forces advancing south. As one of the best and most mobile units of the division, it served as the "fire brigade" and finally had to assist the *61. Division* in that capacity.

The twenty-second of January saw a massed enemy assault on the blocking position east of Witinino on the main supply route. The *2./SS-Panzer-Aufklärungs-Abteilung 11* let the last army formations pass through its positions and then opened fire on the pursuing Soviets.

Until 1900 hours the armored cars of the *2./SS-Panzer-Aufklärungs-Abteilung 11* fended off all infantry attacks, which were supported by heavy mortar fire and the employment of a new kind of phosphorus round. Then the *I./SS-Freiwilligen-Panzer-Grenadier-Regiment 48 "General Seyffard"* (under *SS-Hauptsturmführer* Rühle von Lilienstern) occupied a new blocking position on both sides of Witino. Two companies of *SS-Pionier-Bataillon 54* of *4. SS-Panzer-Grenadier-Brigade "Nederland"* were attached to the battalion.

That *Kampfgruppe* fought off repeated bitter Soviet attacks during the night of 22/23 January. Von Lilienstern and his messengers personally led the thrown-together men in 17 immediate counterattacks to clean up the site of the penetration. He was wounded, but still remained with his battalion, which he later led back along the main supply route toward Jamburg. *SS-Hauptsturmführer* von Lilienstern was awarded the *Ritterkreuz* for that operation.

On 23 January 1944 the front ran as follows: In the Kapyloschka — Djatlezy area was the *I./SS-Panzer-Grenadier-Regiment 24 "Danmark"*. At Djatlezy the front bent back to the south. A *Kampfgruppe* of the *10. Luftwaffen-Feld-Division* (*Rittmeister* Helling), together with the *1./SS-Pionier- Bataillon 11*, started its position at Djatlezy. Farther to the south were the remnants of the *I./SS-Panzer-Grenadier-Regiment 23 "Norge"* and, at Witino, Kampfgruppe von Lilienstern (*I./SS-Freiwilligen-Panzer-Grenadier-Regiment 48 "General Seyffard"*). Mobile *Kampfgruppen* of *SS-Panzer-Aufklärungs-Abteilung 11*, which assisted the *61. Infanterie-Division* in setting up additional blocking positions, were south of the main supply route. The broken German divisions around Leningrad flowed through that blocking position to the west.

The heavy fighting continued on 23/24 January. The Soviet attacks were particularly heavy against the positions of the *I./SS-Panzer-Grenadier-Regiment 24 "Danmark"* with the objective of breaking through the blocking positions on the roads to Woronino, Bor and Tscheremykino. The Soviet attacks were carried out with the employment of armor, artillery and mortars. The *I./SS-Panzer-Grenadier-Regiment 24 "Danmark"* held. The losses were high. Nevertheless, all enemy attacks on Witino were thwarted.

The Russians sought softer spots. At Chulgusi, south of the main supply route, new Soviet assembly positions were spotted. The porous southern front was in danger. *SS-Panzer-Aufklärungs-Abteilung 11*, positioned in the Bol-Chabino — Wolgowo area, received new operations orders: "Eliminate an enemy assembly position in the Chulgusi area!"

SS-Hauptsturmführer Saalbach organized his battalion into two attack groups. The north group included the *1., 4.* and *5./SS-Panzer-Aufklärungs-Abteilung 11* and was commanded by *SS-Hauptsturmführer* Saalbach. Its assembly area was at Wolgowo. The south group consisted of the *2.* and *3./SS-Panzer-Aufklärungs-Abteilung 11.* It was commanded by *SS-Obersturmführer* Heckmüller and assembled at Torrossowo.

After brief preparations, the two attack groups pushed forward to Chuldusi. *Gruppe Heckmüller* bogged down in heavy fighting. The attack did not gain ground until *Gruppe Saalbach* gained an advantage. The *2./SS-Panzer-Aufklärungs-Abteilung 11* lost an armored car to an antitank gun. The commander of the *5./SS-Panzer-Aufklärungs-Abteilung 11*, *SS-Obersturmführer* Schmidt, was wounded. The enemy withdrew in a panicked fashion into the woods to the east. The operation that had been started on 24 January ended successfully, but it was not able to stop the progress of the Soviet operation.

SS-Freiwilligen-Panzer-Grenadier-Division "Nordland" took the precaution of sending its trains to the rear. Trains vehicles were freed up to make the troops more mobile, since the complement of vehicles had never been brought up to the authorized level. The *1./SS-Instandsetzungs-Bataillon 11*, which had

18. Armee (Lindemann)

Positions from the End of 1943 to the beginning of 1944

⬅ Withdrawal after 14 January 1944

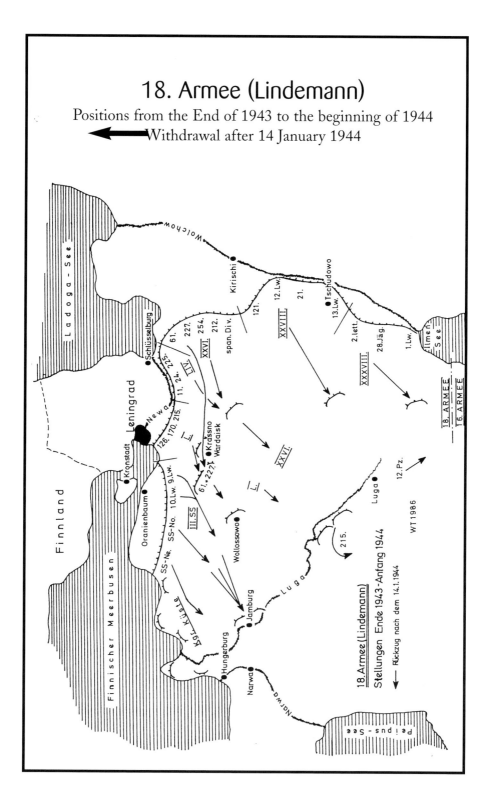

been forward, was moved to Jamburg on 17 January. The staff of *SS-Nachrichtungs-Abteilung 11* followed it, moving first to Alexejewka and later to Jamburg.

On 25 January the companies of the *I./SS-Panzer-Grenadier-Regiment 24 "Danmark"* could no longer hold off the massed enemy attacks. The battalion melted away. The commander, *SS-Hauptsturmführer* Wichmann, and two of his company commanders, *SS-Hauptsturmführer* Hennicke and *SS-Obersturmführer* Hein, were killed. The front ripped open. The Soviets assaulted from three sides. *SS-Hauptsturmführer* Sörensen took over the battalion and gave the order: "Break through to the west, toward Witino!"

Sörensen led the point, *SS-Obersturmführer* Sidon the hard-pressed rear guard. After hard and bloody fighting, the remnants of the *I./SS-Panzer-Grenadier-Regiment 24 "Danmark"* passed through the lines of *Kampfgruppe von Lilienstern* at Witino and were immediately committed south of the village. That blocking position was held until 27 January. The code word *Tauwetter* (thaw) triggered the withdrawal. *SS-Obersturmführer* Sidon and the remnants of the *1.* and *3./SS-Panzer-Grenadier-Regiment 24 "Danmark"* covered the retreat as rear guard.

On 25 January *Kampfgruppe Helling* was also encircled. *Rittmeister* Helling waited for orders. The enemy launched heavy attacks in the afternoon of the following day. Helling conferred with his company officers. *SS-Untersturmführer* Arera proposed an immediate breakout. Dusk began to fall. Off they went! The *1./SS-Pionier-Bataillon 11* was the spearhead. *SS-Untersturmführer* Arera led his combat engineers and the battalion of the *10. Luftwaffen-Feld-Division* that followed in a close-order file of riflemen toward the southwest through a wooded area. *Kampfgruppe* Helling was fired on. Covering squads returned the fire. There were losses. Keep on going! The deep snow interfered with mobility. As night fell the greatest danger had passed. Wounded were cared for, two dead buried. Then the march continued. Hours later, *Kampfgruppe Helling* encountered another blocking group that was withdrawing in similar fashion. After a short pause for a break, they continued westward through the snow-covered woods.

On 25 January *SS-Panzer-Aufklärungs-Abteilung 11* was alerted and, during the afternoon, occupied a semicircular position east of Gubanizy. During the night there were loud tank noises to the east. There was no doubt about it — a strong attack by Soviet armor was imminent. The battalion waited for reinforcements with *Sturmgeschütze*. When loud tank-noises were heard behind them, the units of the battalion in Gubanizy believed the expected armor support was approaching.

However, in the dim light of morning it was not German tanks but a Soviet tank with mounted infantry that rattled along the village street at high speed. It rammed a few half-tracks and disappeared again in the pale dawn light. Not a shot was fired. Damage: several tracks torn off.

In the gray dawn of 26 January *SS-Panzer-Aufklärungs-Abteilung 11* was ready for action outside of Gubanizy. *SS-Hauptsturmführer* Saalbach awaited the clearly impending armor attack with concern. The promised reinforcements had not arrived. Let us now hear from an eyewitness:

In the pale light of the morning, Russian armor broke through the morning gray on a broad front and rattled toward Gubanizy over the open terrain. At first there were seven. Then, behind them, a whole mass of them. In addition to the T 34's, there were all possible types, even old models. The gunners of the *5./SS-Panzer-Aufklärungs-Abteilung 11* brought the enemy tanks into their telescopic sights. Six out of the seven Soviet tanks in the first wave were knocked out. Then it was the second wave's turn. It turned into a tank engagement, the likes of which I had never seen. The bark of the cannon filled the air. Round after round was fired from the barrels of the heavy antitank guns. The crews worked feverishly behind the gun shields. I had counted 61 tanks, many of which were right in front of us at that point. And the battle raged on. *SS-Rottenführer* Spork headed for the Soviets at top speed in his *Kanonenwagen* and knocked out one tank after another over open sights at short range. I could not even hope to guess how long the fighting had gone on, having lost all sense of time. The surviving Russian tanks turned away. The breakthrough attempt was a failure.

On that morning of 26 January, 48 Soviet tanks were knocked out at Gubanizy. Eleven of them fell to the Dutch *SS-Rottenführer*, Casper Spork. The lion's share was credited to *SS-Untersturmführer* Langendorf's *5./SS-Panzer-Aufklärungs-Abteilung 11*. Consider this: One heavy *Pak* platoon with its three 7.5 cm guns and eight *Kanonenwagen*, each with a short-barreled 7.5cm gun, against 61 Soviet tanks. Heavily armored tanks against the lightly armored vehicles of *SS-Panzer-Aufklärungs-Abteilung 11*.

Farther south at Wolossowo a *Kampfgruppe* of the *227.Infanterie-Division* under *Oberst* Wengler had held the important railroad nodal point for days. Wengler's men always referred to Wolossowo as "Wenglerowo", demonstrating their boundless trust in their colonel.

SS-Panzer-Aufklärungs-Abteilung 11 remained north of Wolossowo and awaited new enemy attacks. Men returning from leave who got off the train at Wolossowo were attached to the battalion.

Schwere Panzer-Abteilung 502, which was committed in the same area, was forced to repeatedly clear the retreat routes and suffered significant losses, for instance, almost all of the *1./schwere Panzer-Abteilung 502*. *Major* Jähde, the commander of the heavy tank battalion, had all of his remaining *Tigers* assembled at Wolossowo.

On the morning of 27 January, the armor-supported enemy attack against the Gubanizy — Wolossowo front blazed anew. The front held.

In the meantime, the *III. (germanisches) SS-Panzer-Korps* was in the process of withdrawing. "Wenglerowo" was abandoned. The rear guards held until darkness fell. Vehicles of the *5./SS-Panzer-Aufklärungs-Abteilung 11* covered the withdrawal of *Kampfgruppe Wengler* and the *Tigers*. The combat vehicles of *SS-Panzer-Aufklärungs-Abteilung 11* then provided security for loading the *Tigers* at the Wolossowo railroad station. After the transport train with the special railroad cars loaded with *Tigers* had pulled out of the station heading toward Narwa, the rear guard withdrew to the west.

Withdrawal of the III. (germanisches) SS-Panzer-Korps

The *III. (germanisches) SS-Panzer-Korps* was able to hold off the enemy until 26 January in continuous fighting in a succession of new intermediate positions while the broken divisions of the northern wing of the *18. Armee* retreated to the west. The divisions around Leningrad had lost much equipment and personnel. Among others, *Generalmajor* Michael, the commander of the *9. Luftwaffen-Feld-Division*, was killed on 22 January.

On 26 January the retreat of the *III. (germanisches) SS-Panzer-Korps* began in stages. All formation commanders had been briefed in advance on the previously prepared plans, which would be activated by a code word. The corresponding orders went out that day to the *4. SS-Panzer-Grenadier-Brigade "Nederland"* and to *Kampfgruppe "Küste"*. The corps command post transferred from the forest camp at Klopizy to Opolje. The heavy weapons were withdrawn across the entire corps sector and sent on the march to the rear. The batteries of *SS-Artillerie-Regiment* 11 gradually massed in the area east of Ratschino — Osakowa.

On 27 January the front swung to the south like a closing door. The withdrawal movements were in progress. Heavy weapons and grenadier companies fell back to the northern main supply route along corduroy roads. The *16./SS-Panzer-Grenadier-Regiment 23 "Norge"* blew up important objects and mined the roads in the regimental sector. Only a few of the *Panthers* that had been dug in could be made roadworthy. Most of them were blown up. Bunkers were burning everywhere. The Russians immediately pursued. Strong enemy forces had already infiltrated into the woods south of the old static positions.

They caused problems several times for the retreating units of *SS-Freiwilligen-Panzer-Grenadier-Division "Nordland. SS-Panzer-Grenadier-Regiment 23 "Norge"* swung to the southwest. The trains had been set in march ahead of time. First sergeants and trains officers often had to find their own routes without orders. The trains of the *16./SS-Panzer-Grenadier-Regiment 23 "Norge"*, led by *SS-Hauptscharführer* Waibel, were able to take horse-drawn trains from an army unit under their wing. Their leader had been forgotten and not received any orders.

Fritz von Scholz was almost too late in moving his command post. Advancing enemy forces had already encircled it. Half of the *7./SS-Panzer-Grenadier-Regiment 23 "Norge"* was cut off. The company commander of the *7./SS-Panzer-Grenadier-Regiment 23 "Norge"* launched an immediate counterattack with the remaining men and cleared the way to the division command post in Kirowa, which then moved west. The half of the *7./SS-Panzer-Grenadier-Regiment 23 "Norge"* that had been cut off remained missing.

The *III./SS-Panzer-Grenadier-Regiment 24 "Danmark"* cleared out of its positions without a fight and marched 40 kilometers to Kerstowo on foot. The *II./SS-Panzer-Grenadier-Regiment 24 "Danmark"* temporarily held the Gorbowizy — Kirowa — Begunizy line with *SS-Panzer-Grenadier-Regiment 23 "Norge"*. Farther to the south that day, *SS-Panzer-Aufklärungs-Abteilung 11, Kampfgruppe* Wengler and *Major* Jähde's heavy tanks were at Wolissowo. The enemy repeatedly attempted an encircling pursuit, advancing through the porous front. Again and again the German formations had to fight to clear the route of their retreat. The way was one of combat, torturous exertion and marches through snowbound woods and marshland with wounded and equipment loaded onto *Akjas*. Serving as rearguard, the *16./SS-Panzer-Grenadier-Regiment 24 "Danmark"* carried out demolitions on the Globizy — Krebukowo-North road, blew up the regimental command post at Saoserje and, finally, the bridges at Lamocha.

SS-Panzer-Abteilung 11, with the new honorific of *"Hermann von Salza"*, helped where it could with its few tanks. It lost its first men at Kaporje. *SS-Hauptsturmführer* Holtkamp (commander of the *1./SS-Panzer-Abteilung 11 "Hermann von Salza"*), *SS-Untersturmführer* Schmidichen and a *SS-Unterscharführer* were killed by a direct hit during a reconnaissance.

4. SS-Panzer-Grenadier-Brigade "Nederland" and *Kampfgruppe "Küste"* began their withdrawal on the morning of 28 January 1944. *Kampfgruppe "Küste"* was able to take along part of its weapons and equipment. Most of the static coastal batteries had to be blown up. The conflict between corps and *Führerhauptquartier* was evident in the orders and counter-orders received by Kryssing's staff. *Kampfgruppe "Küste"* received seven orders and counter-orders before it dismantled its telephone switchboard and heard no more from the *Führerhauptquartier*. The staff, which had previously been moved from Ostroff to Welikino, set out in retreat, led by a staff officer, the hereditary Grand Duke of Mecklenburg. As a precaution, *Kampfgruppe "Küste"* had already sent three convalescent companies and five 2-cm *Flak* to protect the 5-ton bridge at Keikino on 26 January. That was the only bridge between the Gulf of Finland and Jamburg. Because of its importance, it had been substantially reinforced under the direction of the former Norwegian combat-engineer officer, *SS-Haupsturmführer* Hoel.

On 28 January the formations of the *III. (germanisches) SS-Panzer-Korps* fought their way back farther to the west. In leapfrog fashion, new blocking positions were repeatedly formed, held for a limited time and then abandoned. While the main body of the divisional artillery of *SS-Freiwilligen-Panzer-Grenadier-Division "Nordland* assembled in the Ratschino area, the infantry units were in the Gomontowo — Begunizy area. The *5./SS-Artillerie-Regiment 11*, under *SS-Obersturmführer* Binnerop, fired off all of its ammunition from its position at Osakowa — 600 rounds by the afternoon. The *III./SS-Artillerie-Regiment 11*, which had taken firing positions east of Ratschino, fired to the north and east.

The remainder of the *I./SS-Panzer-Grenadier-Regiment 23 "Norge"* moved back to the north, parallel to the main supply route. The division commander was with that battalion repeatedly, leading it back through woods and swamps.

The remnants of the *10. Luftwaffen-Feld-Division*, including, among others, *Bataillon Helling* with the attached *1./SS-Pionier-Bataillon 11* and occasionally reinforced by the attachment of *SS-Obersturmführer* von Matt's battery, went into action south of the main supply route. *Batterie von Matt*, firing from a blocking position, stopped strong Soviet attacks. The battery was able to withdraw without losing a gun at the last moment, thanks to covering action by the *1./SS-Pionier- Bataillon 11*.

A Soviet attack wedge assaulted Ragowiczy from the northeast and ran into the *III./SS-Panzer-Grenadier-Regiment 24 "Danmark"*, which was at Kerstowo. Battalion commander Jakobsen committed his *9./SS-Panzer-Grenadier-Regiment 24 "Danmark"* toward Ssergowizy (2 kilometers east of Kerstowo), but it had to withdraw to the south. *SS-Sturmbannführer* Jakobsen, who was still waiting for reports from Ssergowizy, dispatched his *Ordonnanz* (special-duty staff officer), *SS-Untersturmführer* Herlöv-Nielsen. Nielsen did not make it to the company and was captured by the Soviets.

The *III./SS-Artillerie-Regiment 11*, which was still at Ratschino, received orders to pull back to the main supply route. The commander of *SS-Artillerie-Regiment 11*, *SS-Obersturmbannführer* Karl, had previously coordinated the withdrawal with the commander of the *III./SS-Artillerie-Regiment 11*. Karl, who had been ordered to report to the division command post, moved in his vehicle, accompanied by a motorcycle messenger, to the main supply route by the most direct route. Karl was ordered to withdraw his artillery. After he was unable to establish contact by radio, Karl sent the fully briefed motorcycle messenger back to the battalion. He arrived safely. The *III./SS-Artillerie-*

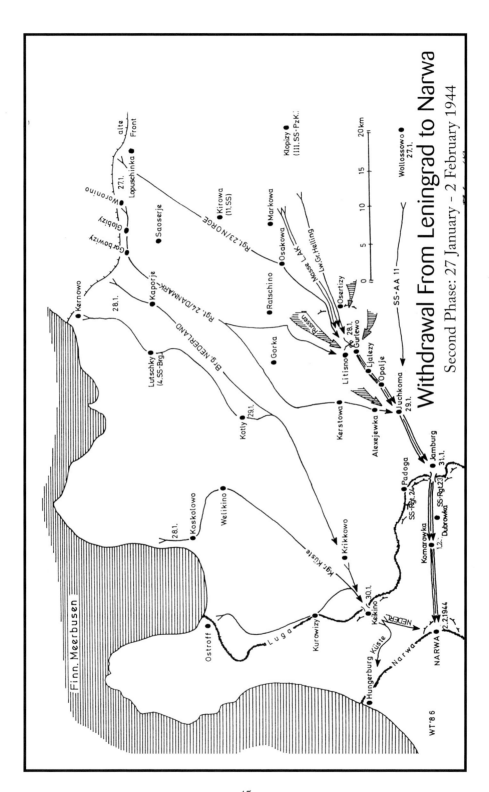

Withdrawal From Leningrad to Narwa

Second Phase: 27 January - 2 February 1944

45

Regiment 11 limbered up and moved out.

Batterie Lärum took the lead. Halfway to the main supply route the lead element was suddenly fired on. Soviets who had broken through attacked from woods on both sides of the trail. Lärum's battery tried to turn around, but was unable to do so on the narrow path. The heavy prime movers and howitzers ended up in the roadside ditches. The surprise was complete and resulted in chaos. The batteries that were following at a distance were able to turn around and reached the main supply route at Gurlowo by another route. Four heavy field howitzers were lost. The cannoneers were able to fight their way through to German troops.

As evening approached, the German defense was concentrated at Kerstowo-Opolje and southward. The *16./SS-Panzer-Grenadier-Regiment 23 "Norge"* arrived during the day at Ljalizy and was attached to an army unit. Ljalizy was attacked by strong Soviet forces, which went around the blocking positions on both sides of the main supply route. Ljalizy, which had been partially lost, was regained in an immediate counterattack. Gurlowo, three kilometers to the east, remained in Soviet hands and, as additional Soviet forces were sent there, it became a serious threat to the German forces still positioned east of it.

SS-Hauptsturmführer Hämel's *7./SS-Panzer-Grenadier-Regiment 24 "Danmark"* at Litisno received orders from Division Commander von Scholz to attack enemy-held Gurlowo. Darkness was already falling. Von Scholz and Hämel watched the enemy movements in Gurlowo from the southeast outskirts of Litisno and firmed up plans for the attack. Hämel assembled his company at Ljalizy — Litisno. The objective of the attack: Gurlowo and clearing the main supply route.

SS-Hauptsturmführer Hämel, who was the second noncommissioned officer in the *SS-Panzer-Grenadier-Division "Wiking"* to have been awarded the German Cross in Gold, was recognized as one of the most reliable officers in the division. For the night attack, *SS-Untersturmführer* Berramsen's motorcycle platoon from *SS-Panzer-Grenadier-Regiment 24 "Danmark"* and two assault guns of *SS-Panzer-Jäger-Abteilung 11* were attached to his company. Hämel's reinforced *7./SS-Panzer-Grenadier-Regiment 24 "Danmark"* attacked toward the east on both sides of the main supply route. Hämel's men stormed forward in a gutsy assault against enemy-occupied Gurlowo. The *Sturmgeschütze* rattled forward along the road, stopping from time to time to be briefed on targets by Hämel. Again and again, *Sturmgeschütz* rounds burst in burning Gurlowo, wiping out one nest of opposition after another, thus assisting *Kampfgruppe Hämel* to a complete success. The fighting on the main supply route and in the village lasted two hours, after which contact was reestablished with the cut-off forces.

That afternoon the remnants of *SS-Panzer-Grenadier-Regiment 23 "Norge"* and of *SS-Artillerie-Regiment 11* were still farther to the east. Beside them were additional withdrawing army formations. Units of *SS-Panzer-Aufklärungs-Abteilung 11* that were coming from the southeast ran into the blocked main supply route. Ten kilometers south of the main supply route was *Luftwaffen-Feld-Bataillon Helling* with the attached *1./SS-Pionier-Bataillon 11*. From various positions the battalion repulsed the attacking enemy.

At the same time as *Kampfgruppe Hämel's* attack, units of *SS-Panzer-Aufklärungs-Abteilung* 11 attacked from the east and broke the Soviet hold at Gurlowo. The remnants of *SS-Pionier-Bataillon 11* were withdrawn after the difficult operations at the Ropscha penetration point and set to combat engineering work. During the morning of 29 January the attachment of the *1./SS-Pionier-Bataillon 11* came to an end. *SS-Untersturmführer* Arera reported back to the commander of *SS-Pionier-Bataillon 11*. The company had been severely decimated by the transport to the rear of its sick and wounded. In the end, there were only eight men left with Arera. The men who were still fit for service were held back by the battalion for pressing combat-engineer work. The *1./SS-Pionier Bataillon 11* had lost nine killed and many wounded.

On 29 January the units flowed back to Jamburg. As noon approached, strong enemy forces had already advanced past Opolje on both sides. Opolje had been under heavy artillery fire since morning. At the last minute the aid station in the church was successfully cleared out and the wounded sent to Narwa. *SS-Panzer-Grenadier-Regiment 23 "Norge"* then evacuated Opolje. *SS-Sturmbannführer* Lohmann's *III./SS-Panzer-Grenadier-Regiment 23 "Norge"*, which was serving as rearguard, passed yet another army formation through its lines and fell back to Jamburg.

The commander of *SS-Panzer-Jäger-Abteilung 11, SS-Hauptsturmführer* Roensch, was killed in that fighting while outside his assault gun. *Hauptmann* Schulz-Streek took over the battalion.

The batteries of *SS-Artillerie-Regiment 11* occupied new firing positions in and on both sides of Jamburg.

East of Jamburg, *SS-Panzer-Grenadier-Regiment 23 "Norge"* held a bridgehead over the Luga. The regimental command post was in the west part of the city. South of the city and west of the Luga were the *16./SS-Panzer-Grenadier-Regiment 23 "Norge"*, remnants of the *I./SS-Panzer-Grenadier-Regiment 23 "Norge"* and army formations.

The command post of *SS-Panzer-Grenadier-Regiment 24 "Danmark"* was temporarily located in Padoga. The *III./SS-Panzer-Grenadier-Regiment 24 "Danmark"* was successfully committed north of Jamburg and the *II./SS-Panzer-Grenadier-Regiment 24 "Danmark"* even farther north. While the main line of resistance was occupied, rearguards still held the area in the vicinity of the Kotly — Juchkoma railroad line. A report on that action follows:

The *16./SS-Panzer-Grenadier-Regiment 24 "Danmark"* was rearguard on the railroad line at Alexejewka. The railroad bridge was blown up, roads were mined and enemy advances repulsed. There was no longer contact with the regiment. After completing its mission, the company fell back. The company approached the main supply route.

In the dreary gray of the winter day, a disorganized mass of infantry rolled toward the west. 300 meters, then 250 meters. The company commander and the headquarters section leader watched spellbound; Bregulla, the leader of the company headquarters section, jabbed *SS-Untersturmführer* Arionius in the side.

"*Untersturmführer*, those are Russians!"

"I know!" replied the company commander dryly.

Without another word being spoken, the company drew closer to the *Rollbahn*. 200 meters, then 150 meters. The Russians became suspicious. That was the time: "Open fire!"

With all its weapons firing and a loud "Hurrah!" the company won the main supply route while the Russians fled headlong. Under fire from Soviet infantry and mortars in the woods south of the road, the company dashed across a 1,000-meter stretch and, with a loss of four wounded, regained contact with friendly forces. Three dead had to be left behind.

Kampfgruppe "Küste" and the *4. SS-Panzer-Grenadier-Brigade "Nederland"* had been withdrawing since 28 January. The *4. SS-Panzer-Grenadier-Brigade "Nederland"* had to make its way back through knee-deep snow and pathless woods. The men dragged weapons and equipment on *Akjas*. Soviet artillery had registered on various lanes through the forest and shelled them frequently. As a result, ways had to be found through the woods themselves, which complicated orientation. The brigade command post in Lutschki went up in flames. Combat engineers blocked the roads against the pursuing Soviets with mines. *SS-Sturmbannführer* Shock's *SS-Panzer-Jäger-Abteilung 54* reinforced the rearguard and then had to withdraw its *Sturmgeschütze* to the south over the bridge over the Luga in Jamburg since the bridge at Keikino was too weak for assault guns. *SS-Obersturmführer* Kuhne's motorcycle company dashed along on snow-covered ways. It provided security, covered open flanks and established contact.

In the Kotly area, the Soviets advanced into the withdrawal *of SS-Freiwilligen-Panzer-Grenadier-Regiment 48 "General Seyffard"* and *SS-Freiwilligen-Panzer-Grenadier-Regiment 49 "de Ruyter"*. The leading elements did not notice. *SS-Hauptsturmführer* Ertel was fired on as he tried to take the movement order to the last battalion of *SS-Freiwilligen-Panzer-Grenadier-Regiment 49 "de Ruyter"*. He made it to the rearguard battalion cross-country. A *Flak* of *the 14./SS-Freiwilligen-Panzer-Grenadier-Regiment 49 "de Ruyter"* engaged the Soviets. The way was cleared. Off to the west, follow *the 4. SS-Panzer-Grenadier-Brigade "Nederland"*!

The *4. SS-Panzer-Grenadier-Brigade "Nederland"* held the pursuing Soviet 47th Army at a distance. As the last units of *Kampfgruppe "Küste"* crossed the Luga bridge at Keikino, the *4. SS-Panzer-Grenadier-Brigade*

"Nederland" occupied new blocking positions in a half circle around Keikino. *SS-Hauptsturmführer* Wanhöfer raced southward from Krikkowo with a combat-engineer squad and blew up the bridge north of Padoga, thus blocking the Krikkowo — Jamburg connection for heavy vehicles.

During the overall withdrawal and the formation of the Luga line, the *4. SS-Panzer-Grenadier-Brigade "Nederland"* crossed back over the Luga to the west, thus giving up its bridgehead at Keikino. On 30 January *SS-Obersturmbannführer* Jörchels' *SS-Freiwilligen-Panzer-Grenadier-Regiment 48 "General Seyffard"* was the last unit to cross the Luga. *SS-Sturmbannführer* Engelhardt, operations officer of *Kampfgruppe "Küste"*, turned over a company of noncommissioned officer candidates to the regiment. *SS-Obersturmbannführer* Jörchel committed that company north of Keikino. The combat engineers of the *4. SS-Panzer-Grenadier-Brigade "Nederland"* blew up the bridge at Keikino during the evening of 30 January.

The commander of *Heeresgruppe Nord, Generaloberst* Model, intended to form a new front behind the Luga. His attention was focussed on the Leningrad — Jamburg railroad and main supply route. Model gave the *III. (germanisches) SS-Panzer-Korps* the mission of holding the Luga and a bridgehead east of Jamburg. *General* Steiner argued to the contrary, stating the Luga line could no longer be held since the Soviets had already crossed the river farther south with their 8th Army and were about to push on to Lake Peipus. In any event, the Luga Line was punctured before it was even occupied. The frozen Luga offered no hindrance to infantry and light formations. Nevertheless, Steiner had to at least make an attempt to hold the Luga Line.

By 31 January 1944 the Soviets had already infiltrated between Kurowizy and the coast at Hungerburg. The noncommissioned officer training company that had been attached to Jörchel's *Regiment* was given the impossible task of guarding a roughly 20 kilometer sector and covering the northern flank. Marshland and primeval forest, with neither roads nor trails, formed the combat zone for the noncommissioned officer candidates. Who would imagine that the Russians would advance through that kind of country? But there, too, they infiltrated like ants, in small groups that later joined together and were soon on the banks of the Narwa River. The weapons of the noncommissioned officer candidates continued to fire, but strongpoint after strongpoint fell silent on the widely-scattered northern flank. Two officers were killed; half of the company was lost. Days passed before the news reached those higher up the chain-of-command.

Farther south, the Soviets attacked the Jamburg bridgehead on 31 January. *SS-Panzer-Grenadier-Regiment 23 "Norge"* held fast.

The pressure shifted to *SS-Panzer-Grenadier-Regiment 24 "Danmark"*. Heavy fighting developed at Padoga, the bridgehead without a bridge. The *II. and the 16./SS-Panzer-Grenadier-Regiment 24 "Danmark"* held their own. Two hours later, a dangerous penetration threatened to tear open the front of the regiment. *SS-Obersturmführer* Seebach and his *5./SS-Panzer-Grenadier-Regiment 24 "Danmark"* hurled the Soviets back in an immediate counterattack. Even though he received his seventh wound in that fighting, Seebach did not leave his company. Seebach was awarded the *Ritterkreuz* for that decisive action.

One day later, on 1 February, the Soviets massed new forces. In the sector of the *III./SS-Panzer-Grenadier-Regiment 24 "Danmark"* increased enemy pressure fell on the *9./SS-Panzer-Grenadier-Regiment 24 "Danmark"* of *SS-Untersturmführer* Darm as well as on the remnants of the *10./SS-Panzer-Grenadier-Regiment 24 "Danmark"*. The latter company had been employed there after having come back from Djatlezy where it had been committed with the *I./SS-Panzer-Grenadier-Regiment 24 "Danmark"*.

The battalion commander hurried forward, was fired upon by the Russians and wounded. In spite of his wounds, *SS-Sturmbannführer* Jakobsen assembled his reserve company. The Soviet penetration in the sector of the *9./SS-Panzer-Grenadier-Regiment 24 "Danmark"* had broadened. The company commander of the *11./SS-Panzer-Grenadier-Regiment 24 "Danmark"*, *SS-Obersturmführer* Worsöe-Larsen, a Dane, fell in the attack. He had been leading his company from the front. *SS-Sturmbannführer* Jakobsen was wounded a second time that day and had to be dragged back by his messengers. The Soviet submachine gun battalion was able to hold its own and maintain a dangerous bridgehead on the west bank of the Luga.

On 31 January, the *16./SS-Panzer-Grenadier-Regiment 23 "Norge"* was south of Jamburg on the bend of the Luga River. On that day *SS-Panzer-Grenadier-Regiment 23 "Norge"* repulsed all enemy attacks on the Jamburg bridgehead. The Soviets looked for success elsewhere.

The *16./SS-Panzer-Grenadier-Regiment 23 "Norge"* had occupied its positions during the course of the day. The remnants of the *I./SS-Panzer-Grenadier-Regiment 23 "Norge"* closed up to the south. A 2 cm multi-barreled *Flak* from the *14./SS-Panzer-Grenadier-Regiment 23 "Norge"* took position in the company's sector in the small group of buildings at a farmstead on some high ground. The *Flak* was positioned as if it were on a silver platter, but it had an extremely good field of fire. *SS-Untersturmführer* Brünestedt was the leader of the *Flak* section.

As darkness fell, everything was still quiet. At about 2000 hours the company commander of the *16./SS-Panzer-Grenadier-Regiment 23 "Norge"*, *SS-Untersturmführer* Schirmer, made another round, checking his positions. He stayed longer with his Third Platoon, which was farthest to the south. The terrain was shielded from observation by *Balkas* (ravines) and patches of woods. Schirmer returned to his command post at 2100 hours. A little later men of the *I./SS-Panzer-Grenadier-Regiment 23 "Norge"* passed by. Schirmer learned from an officer of that battalion that the pre-arranged flare signals had been fired and that the battalion had to pull back to the railroad line.

SS-Untersturmführer Schirmer was determined to remain there with his company since he had not received any orders to withdraw. Schirmer went back to Hokkerup's platoon. *SS-Unterscharführer* Hokkerup reported that there was no longer contact to the south with the *I./SS-Panzer-Grenadier-Regiment 23 "Norge"* and the Soviets had probably pressed forward. *SS-Untersturmführer* Schirmer mounted an immediate counterattack with his Third Platoon and made it to the positions that had been abandoned. After a short, intense fight the platoon fell back again and occupied a blocking position. The night was uncanny!

At the same time, Soviet groups had gone around the south flank of the *16./SS-Panzer-Grenadier-Regiment 23 "Norge"* and reached the company command post. The command post changed hands several times. *SS-Untersturmführer* Dall arrived from the *13./SS-Panzer-Grenadier-Regiment 23 "Norge"* at the same time as *SS-Untersturmführer* Schirmer to look into the cause of the night-time shooting. At that moment the Russians again attacked and were soon right at the command post bunker. Schirmer directed his platoons into position. The occupants of the bunker heard the Russians above them. *SS-Untersturmführer* Dall did not waste time. Over the intact telephone line he called the firing position of the *13./SS-Panzer-Grenadier-Regiment 23 "Norge"*: "Fire on the strongpoint!"

The men in the firing position delayed, thinking there must be an error. Dall repeated the order, with emphasis: "Fire on our own strongpoint! Fire *now*! The Russians are on the bunker on top of us!"

Seconds later the heavy 15 centimeter shells howled down and burst around the company command post. The bunker shook and quaked, but it kept its occupants safe. In a short time the Soviets were driven off. Then *SS-Untersturmführer* Schirmer and his platoons pulled back and took position with their front facing south.

As the day dawned on 1 February, the Soviets had already brought heavy weapons forward into a wooded area that jutted towards the lines of the *16./SS-Panzer-Grenadier-Regiment 23 "Norge"*. Additional columns could be seen in a valley moving west. The heavy infantry guns of the *13./SS-Panzer-Grenadier-Regiment 23 "Norge"* shelled the columns until noon. Brünestedt's *Flak* and the small arms of the combat engineers engaged the infantry forces.

Jamburg was abandoned on 1 February. The Luga bridge went up in the air. In order to counter the dangerous penetration south of Jamburg, the *II./SS-Panzer-Grenadier-Regiment 24 "Danmark"* was shifted behind *SS-Panzer-Grenadier-Regiment 23 "Norge"* and committed south of the main supply route with its front facing southeast. The *16./SS-Panzer-Grenadier-Regiment 24 "Danmark"* was also committed there, where it was able to hold off the enemy forces at Komerowka until evening.

SS-Panzer-Grenadier-Regiment 24 "Danmark" and *SS-Panzer-Grenadier-Regiment 23 "Norge"* fought their way back in a leapfrog fashion to the Narwa line. The *III./SS-Panzer-Grenadier-Regiment 23 "Norge"* was the rearguard and repeatedly repulsed heavy attacks by the pursuing Soviets. Three times elements of the *III./SS-Panzer-Grenadier-Regiment 23 "Norge"* prevented chaos by launching immediate counterattacks led by the battalion commander, Lohmann. *SS-Sturmbannführer* Lohmann was able to repulse a furious Soviet attack right outside the regimental command post with hastily assembled radio operators and drivers. Lohmann was wounded in the fighting.

On both sides of Jamburg and north of Keikino the Luga defenses were torn open. The artillery had already been pulled back behind the Narwa. *Generaloberst* Model was indignant. He ordered *SS-Obersturmbannführer* Karl to move his *SS-Artillerie-Regiment 11* forward again. However, the Luga line could no longer be held. As the operations officer of *Kampfgruppe Küste* visited the corps headquarters in the eastern outskirts of Narwa, the commanding general, Felix Steiner, gave the following instructions to *SS-Sturmbannführer* Engelhardt:

> Assemble the remnants of *Kampfgruppe Küste* and all of the other units you can find in and around Hungerburg and organize a defense along the Narwa from the mouth of the river as far south as you can. *4. SS-Panzer-Grenadier-Brigade "Nederland"* and *SS-Panzer-Grenadier-Regiment "Nordland"* are still holding the Luga line, but I do not know how long they will continue to do so.

One day later, on 31 January, the official order went out to *Kampfgruppe Küste*: "The Russians have broken through the Luga position. The Narwa River main line of resistance is to be occupied immediately."

SS-Freiwilligen-Panzer-Grenadier-Division "Nordland" moved quickly to Narwa. *4. SS-Panzer-Grenadier-Brigade "Nederland"* arrived from Keikino. The formations were assembled as quickly as possible and put into the river front and the Narwa bridgehead. Stragglers, alarm units, navy troops and the remnants of the divisions from Leningrad held the front along the river. The Narwa-East bridgehead was held by *4. SS-Panzer-Grenadier-Brigade "Nederland"* and *SS-Freiwilligen-Panzer-Grenadier-Division "Nordland"*.

During the final hours of the influx into the bridgehead, *SS-Rottenführer* Spork of the *5./SS-Panzer-Aufklärungs-Abteilung 11* was on his own one more time. His *Kanonenwagen* dashed to the east yet again and knocked out several Soviet self-propelled guns and numerous trucks in front of the German lines. Once again, he brought the enemy to a halt.

Tired and depressed, the German formations occupied the new position. They soon discovered that the *Panther* line only existed on paper. Other than a few positions that had barely been begun and a short stretch of antitank ditch, the men found nothing. Despite their exhaustion, hunger and filth, they immediately had to set to work building new positions and bunkers. The Soviets had closed up along the entire line and were preparing a new assault.

While the combat troops arrived at the Narwa, a mighty stream of refugees abandoned the city and headed west.

The Fighting For Estonia

The city of Narwa lies on a flat ridge of the Baltic highlands that stretch through Estonia to the gates of Leningrad. Surrounded by impenetrable forests and marshland, it had controlled the isthmus between the Gulf of Finland and Lake Peipus for centuries. Narwa was founded in the thirteenth century by Danes and turned into a strong fortress against Russia by the German military religious orders. The fortress was greatly strengthened under *Ordensmeister* Hermann von Brüggenau-Hasenkamp. Its emblem was a lofty tower, called the *"langer Hermann"* ("tall Hermann").

Opposite the *langer Hermann* was the Russian fortress of Iwangorod, built by order of Grand Duke Ivan III. The triumphant battle of the 17-year-old Swedish king, Karl XII, flared up around Narwa, where he defeated the numerically vastly superior Russian forces. Narwa received its defeat at the hands of Peter the Great, who placed the country under the throne of the czars. Not until 1919 did Estonia achieve temporary independence.

Soldiers from all the countries of Europe prepared to defend Narwa. At their sides stood the men of the *20. Waffen-Grenadier-Division der SS (estnisch)*, which consisted entirely of Estonians.

Narwa was the next Soviet objective. Three armies — the 47th, the 2nd Shock and the 8th — prepared to break open the defensive front at Narwa. The newly-formed main line of resistance extended along the river from Hungerburg. North of Narwa it leaped to the east bank of the river at Ssivertsi to form a bridgehead extending as far as the village of Dolgaja-Niwa (inclusive), then springing to the west bank at Kreenholm and continuing along the west bank. The Narwa River front was meant to run along the west bank. A lot of marshy terrain interfered with the construction of the front. The Soviets were quicker and formed a bridgehead at Krivasso.

The German defensive front was constructed at all possible speed. The formations were a thrown together hodgepodge. Men of the army, the *Luftwaffe*, Estonian volunteers and the men of *SS-Freiwilligen-Panzer-Grenadier-Division "Nordland"* and *4. SS-Panzer-Grenadier-Brigade "Nederland"* responded to the orders of determined officers. Both efforts and sacrifices were great. The Soviets attacks bogged down in front of the German positions due to the determination of the defenders.

Kampfgruppe "Küste" was staged on the Gulf of Finland with its staff at Auga. In its sector: An Estonian police battalion at Mereküla with a coastal battery to its west; one coastal battery south of Mereküla; *Marine-Bataillon Hohnschild* as far as Hungerburg; *Marine-Bataillon Schneider* in Hungerburg and 1.5 kilometers upstream. At first, the stretch extending to Sivertsi was held by a motley group that were replaced in the early days of February by *Kampfgruppen Kausch*, *Gehrmann* and *Wengler*. The sector from the match factory at Ssivertsi through the northern outskirts of Narwa was held by *SS-Pionier-Bataillon 54*.

In the bridgehead, from north to south: *4. SS-Panzer-Grenadier-Brigade "Nederland"*, with *SS-Freiwilligen-Panzer-Grenadier-Regiment 48 "General Seyffard"* at and south of Popovka. *SS-Freiwilligen-Panzer-Grenadier-Regiment 49 "de Ruyter"* extended from outside of Lilienbach as far as the main road to Jamburg. *SS-Panzer-Grenadier-Regiment 24 "Danmark"* was in the southern portion of the bridgehead.

In the wooded terrain along the Narwa, from east to west: Remnants of *SS-Panzer-Grenadier-Regiment 23 "Norge"*, police units and *Kampfgruppen* of the *61.,225.* and *170. Infanterie-Divisionen*. The Soviets were already attacking the Narwa bridgehead in the first days of February.

Tigers of *schwere-Panzer-Abteilung 502* that arrived at Narwa via rapid-transport by rail from Wolossowo provided a substantial strengthening to the fortifications of the bridgehead. In that regard, here is some information provided by *Leutnant* Otto Carius of *schwere-Panzer-Abteilung 502*. These remarks also sketch a portrait of *SS-SS-Brigadeführer und Generalmajor der Waffen-SS* Fritz von Scholz. *Leutnant* Carius did not know *Generalmajor* von Scholz.

We were ordered to report to the division commander of *SS-Freiwilligen-Panzer-Grenadier-Division "Nordland"* and support the division in repulsing Soviet attacks on the bridgehead. We struggled through to Narwa and moved over the bridge. I finally found the division command post in a bus. I reported to the operations officer, who was housed in a second bus with his staff. I was then summoned to the division commander.

I climbed up into the other bus and was surprised to meet a man who was the very personification of goodness and modesty. During my entire time at the front I never encountered a division commander who could compare with Fritz von Scholz. He was one with his troops and the men idolized him. His soldiers called him "Old Fritz". During the time we worked together, he treated me like a son.

We then turned to a discussion of the situation. It turned out that my skepticism regarding the "*Panther* Position" was justified.

"Look," "Old Fritz" explained to me. "In reality, the position only exists on paper. I have laid out a proper bridgehead line and your mission is to help my men construct and fortify that line."

Two days later, Narwa was already under heavy Soviet artillery fire and a bridge had already been eliminated. I proposed repositioning my *Tigers* on the west bank near the main bridge. In that fashion we could assist at any time yet, at the same time, avoid the danger of being cut off by the loss of the bridge. Fritz von Scholz agreed.

Just as my *Tigers* got oriented in the western part of Narwa, *Feldmarschall* Model appeared. After I had reported to him, he thundered at me and ordered me and my *Tigers* to move back over. He said: "You are personally responsible to me to ensure that no Russian tanks break through. None of your *Tigers* will be knocked out due to enemy fire. We need every gun tube."

Our guest performance with *SS-Freiwilligen-Panzer-Grenadier-Division "Nordland"* soon came to an end. We covered the sector until the front had stabilized itself. We were then employed between Narwa and Hungerburg.

Between Hungerburg and Narwa

By the start of February, the Soviet 47th Army had already attempted to form a bridgehead between Hungerburg and Narwa. At Kudruküla it finally succeeded in tearing open the defensive front along the river. *Kampfgruppe "Küste"* reserves, led personally by *SS-Brigadeführer und Generalmajor der Waffen-SS* Kryssing, and supported by three tanks , threw themselves against the Soviets and forced them back over the river. After that, the front at Hungerburg was divided into two commands. The coastal sector was then the responsibility of *Kampfgruppe "Küste"*; the Hungerburg — Narwa sector belonged to *Kampfgruppe Berlin*. *Generalleutnant* Berlin was the commander of the *227. Infanterie-Division*, which was still fighting piecemeal. *Kampfgruppe Berlin's* staff was at Mereküla.

One night, after the destruction of the Soviet bridgehead at Kudruküla, the remnants of the *7./SS-Panzer-Grenadier-Regiment 23 "Norge"*, led by *SS-Oberscharführer* Schacher, reached the river there. For 14 days they had marched through enemy territory, living on a single sack of flour which they had found somewhere. They lost their Norwegian *SS-Untersturmführer* to German fire in crossing the river. Barely 30 men from the company that had been scattered at Kirowa were saved. However, that was not the only group that was able to fight its way through.

On 29 January, elements of *SS-Panzer-Abteilung 11 "Hermann von Salza"* — without any tanks — broke out of Jamburg. After a wearisome march with the equipment on sleds and men of the headquarters Company dragging the *Flak* by hand, they arrived in Voka on the coast. They were promptly employed as infantry in the river sector Kudruküla — Riigi. Kausch's command post was set up in the woods on the river bank southwest of Kudruküla. The trains were staged in positions at Jaaksoni. The battalion surgeon, *Dr.*

Lotze, set up a dressing station with the trains of the Headquarters Company.

During the night of 3 February, the Russians penetrated along the boundary between *Kampfgruppe Kausch* and *Kampfgruppe Wengler* (*227. Infanterie-Division*). The scout platoon of *SS-Panzer-Abteilung 11 "Hermann von Salza"*, the battalion reserve, launched an immediate counterattack and threw the Soviets back across the ice. The positions were improved. On the following night another enemy raiding party was repulsed. Four dead Soviets were left lying on the ice.

During the night of 6 February, one man crossed over the ice. As he got to the final third of the river, he stood up and called out: "Don't shoot, comrades!" Too late. A burst of machine-gun fire cut down the supplicant. During the day the scout platoon of *SS-Panzer-Abteilung 11 "Hermann von Salza"*, which had been committed, was fired on by sharpshooters. There were losses.

On 8 February a Soviet assault troop again attacked the boundary between *Kampfgruppe*n *Kausch* and *Wengler* at Riigi. The Soviets gained a firm hold at the location of *Kampfgruppe Wengler* since the river bank there could not be observed. A flank assault by the scout platoon of *SS-Panzer-Abteilung 11 "Hermann von Salza"* threw the Soviets back again.

By 11 February the Soviets had already brought up strong forces. That day they tried again to gain a bridgehead at Riigi. *SS-Unterscharführer* Stöckle, platoon leader of the scout platoon of *SS-Panzer-Abteilung 11 "Hermann von Salza,"* wrote the following:

0715 to 0745 hours: Artillery and mortar fire-for-effect on the Riigi sector. Enemy attack position spotted behind the Kegelberg (14,7). 0750 hours: Soviet attack (about 50 men) on the sector boundary. 0820 hours: The attack came to a halt in concentrated German defensive fire. 39 enemy dead counted. Renewed heavy enemy fire on our positions. 1410 hours: An enemy assault troop directly in front of our neighboring company (*Grenadier-Regiment 366/Wengler*). We worked around their flank. The enemy pulled back. Our own losses: 2 men wounded and *SS-Unterscharführer* Moser killed by a hit from an antitank gun. Our young soldiers made it through their baptism of fire.

During the night of 12 February: Three men crawled over the ice. Our machine guns barked. In the middle of the ice they stood up and one shouted, "Don't shoot! *SS-Oberscharführer* Schenke here!" They reached our position, unwounded. They were stragglers from the retreat. The last three of 38. They had eaten tree bark and plants. They had hidden themselves by day and marched by night. The dead man on the ice from 6 February was also identified as a man from that platoon.

On 12 February the Soviets advanced again between Riigi and Ssivertsi and were able to penetrate at several places across the ice into the weakly held German river positions. While Wengler's grenadiers were able to hold on at Riigi and Wanhöfer's combat engineers at the northern outskirts of the city of Narwa, the front fell apart in between.

The combat engineers of the *4. SS-Panzer-Grenadier-Brigade "Nederland"* held the cemetery south of Ssiverti. The Soviets stormed against the bulwark repeatedly. The commander of *SS-Pionier-Bataillon 54*, *SS-Hauptsturmführer* Wanhöfer, hurried to the front and personally led the operation. He pulled out enough men from his battalion line to put together a strong assault troop and set it to recapture a section of trenches that had been lost. Soon they were back in German hands. However, the forces did not suffice to do anything else.

In the meantime, the *III. (germanisches) SS-Panzer-Korps* committed all its available forces into the area of the penetration and sealed it off to the west. The Soviet spearhead was only 300 meters from Pähklemäe and, as a result, was almost on the main supply route.

At about midnight, a small *Kampfgruppe* led by *SS-Sturmbannführer* Krügel set out against the Soviets. A motorcycle platoon from *SS-Panzer-Grenadier-Regiment 23 "Norge"*, led by *SS-Oberscharführer* Wienke, was at the Pähklemäe dairy farm. Additional companies followed, one at a time. The penetration was sealed off. At the same time, assault guns from *SS-Freiwilligen-Panzer-Grenadier-Division "Nordland"* and *4. SS-Panzer-Grenadier-Brigade "Nederland"* moved to the outskirts of Narwa and secured it toward the north.

The bridgehead at Ssivertsi was extremely significant to both the Germans and the Soviets. If it were further enlarged, it would lead to the fall of the city of Narwa and thus to the encirclement of the troops in the bridgehead. That would clear the route to Estonia for the Soviets.

The *16./SS-Panzer-Grenadier-Regiment 23 "Norge"*, which had spent the night laying mines in the Narwa bridgehead, was committed at Pähklemäe, as were the *16./SS-Panzer-Grenadier-Regiment 24 "Danmark"* and the *11./SS-Panzer-Grenadier-Regiment 23 "Norge"*. The *16./SS-Panzer-Grenadier-Regiment 23 "Norge"* reinforced *Alarmkompanie Landmesser* in Ssivertsi. *Alarmkompanie Landmesser* had been seriously reduced on 12 February to a small fraction of its former self by heavy artillery fire. *SS-Obersturmführer Landmesser*, twice wounded, remained at the front.

Soviet batteries pounded the German positions still holding out during the morning of 13 February. *Kompanie Landmesser*, *Kompanie Schirmer* and *SS-Pionier-Bataillon 54* at the northern edge of the Ssivertsi cemetery were especially hard hit. From positions on the higher east bank of the river, the Soviets engaged every visible target with their antitank guns.

After heavy fire preparation, the Soviets moved out from Ssivertsi and across the ice against the cemetery. *SS-Hauptsturmführer* Wanhöfer hurried over the uprooted gravestones to the riverbank, where his combat engineers held their positions. Many attackers who had been shot were scattered on the ice. During a period of relative calm, the combat engineers rooted out Soviets who had already penetrated into a section of trenches. The Soviets responded with a murderous fire on the west bank from their heavy weapons.

It got lively again on the far bank. In tightly packed groups, the Soviets stormed across the ice. A German forward-observer who was in a position on the riverbank directed the defensive fire. Rounds striking the ice left dark holes into which Soviet soldiers sank. The others fled back. Then the German artillery fire shifted to the vegetated areas on the east bank and smashed the assembly positions. The final attack of the day had been crushed. The time had come for the German counterattack on the Ssivertsi bridgehead.

It was *SS-Sturmbannführer* Schock's *Sturmgeschütze* that pressed forward to Ssivertsi from the outskirts of Narwa. Heavy antitank gun fire engaged them from the east bank. *SS-Sturmbannführer* Schock was killed. The assault guns had to fall back.

Landmesser's and Schirmer's companies were able to batter their way forward and throw the Soviets out of various positions. By evening, the force was exhausted. The Soviets had been forced back in concentric attacks. However, the Soviets still controlled German movements from their positions on the east bank and could bring them to a standstill during the day. Rations and ammunition had to be brought forward by *Tigers*, which took the wounded back with them on their return trips.

The division order to Schirmer's *16. SS-Panzer-Grenadier-Regiment 23 "Norge"* read: "Attack Ssivertsi: Objective is the Swedish Memorial in the northern ruins." *SS-Untersturmführer* Schirmer refused to execute the order, based on the condition of his battered company. Fritz von Scholz went forward, satisfied himself as to the conditions he saw there, and rescinded the order. Schirmer's and Landmesser's companies remained in their positions. Significant losses continued. The remnants were relieved by *Hauptmann* Lempke's company.

Meter by meter, *SS-Sturmbannführer* Krügel's *Kampfgruppe* wrested Ssevertsi from the enemy. Krügel was wounded. *SS-Hauptsturmführer* Thöny assumed command. Finally the *Kampfgruppe* succeeded in capturing the ruins of Ssevertsi. The enemy then stiffened his resistance at Vepsküla. The *11./SS-Panzer-Grenadier-Regiment 23 "Norge"* committed an assault troop with no success. The leader of the assault troop, *SS-Oberscharführer* Hollinger, was wounded.

The *13./SS-Panzer-Grenadier-Regiment 23 "Norge"* and *SS-Artillerie-Regiment 54* battered the enemy at Vepsküla with heavy fire. The Soviets held on doggedly in good positions and foxholes on the steep riverbank, strengthening the area they held night after night. *SS-Unterscharführer* Nielsen, section leader of the mortar section of the *11./SS-Panzer-Grenadier-Regiment 23 "Norge"*, counted 72 heavy and super-heavy Russian mortars in the Vepsküla area from his position in the attic of a house. Soon afterward, he was wounded and blinded by a round from those much-feared weapons. A *Hauptmann* had assumed temporary command of the *11./SS-Panzer-Grenadier-Regiment*

23 "Norge" by the time it was relieved by the Estonians. The company's strength was 31 men. A *SS-Rottenführer* led the remnants of the *16./SS-Panzer-Grenadier-Regiment 24 "Danmark"* — all of 20 men — which had been in action in the same area.

At the site of the northern penetration at Riigi, grenadiers of *Grenadier-Regiment 366* (*Oberst* Wengler), slowly pushed the enemy back. *Leutnant* Carius' *Tiger* platoon, which had been brought forward, played an essential role in *Oberst* Wengler's success. Bit by bit, the enemy held trenches were rolled up in good teamwork between the grenadiers and the *Tigers*.

When the advance guard of the *20. Waffen-Grenadier-Division der SS (estnisch)* arrived on 20 February, the Soviet bridgehead had been reduced to a limited area at Vepsküla. One by one the battalions arrived and assumed the Hungerburg — Narwa sector while the German divisions were being reorganized. *SS-Freiwilligen-Panzer-Grenadier-Regiment 46* (*SS-Standartenführer* Tuuling) was committed south of Hungerburg with its *I. Bataillon* (*SS-Hauptsturmführer* Silvert) south of Kudruküla and its *II. Bataillon* (*SS-Obersturmführer* Weber) at Riigi. *SS-Freiwilligen-Grenadier-Regiment 45* (*SS-Sturmbannführer* Riipalu) occupied the positions with its *I. Bataillon* (*SS-Hauptsturmführer* Triik) between Vasa and Vepsküla and its *II. Bataillon* (*SS-Hauptsturmführer* Maidla) extending from Ssivertsi to the northern outskirts of the city of Narwa, where it linked up with *SS-Pionier-Bataillon 4.*

Hardly had the positions been occupied when the Soviets' struggle for the little bridgehead flared up anew. On 29 February the 22-year-old *SS-Unterscharführer* Nugiseks closed the breach. He and his assault troop stormed forward twice. Twice the Estonian attackers were forced to the ground 50 meters in front of the Russian trenches. Nugiseks' men leaped to their feet one more time and, in bitter hand-to-hand fighting, forced their way into the Soviet trenches. The subsequent attack by stronger forces of the *20. Waffen-Grenadier-Division der SS (estnisch)* ended with the destruction of the Soviet bridgehead. The road along the riverbank was clear of the enemy; the main supply route was no longer in acute danger.

After the close of the fighting between Hungerburg and Narwa, *SS-Sturmbannführer* Krügel and the Estonian *SS-Unterscharführer* Nugiseks were awarded the Knight's Cross.

Two days after the formation of the Soviet bridgehead at Ssivertsi, the Soviets carried out an amphibious landing at Mereküla.

Soviet attack on the northern flank of the *18. Armee*. On 19 January 1944, the *schwere Panzer-Abteilung 502* is alerted.

Oberleutnant Otto Carius: Knight's Cross recipient and the company commander of the *2./schwere Panzer-Abteilung 502*. Fellow soldiers: Knight's Cross recipient Albert Kerscher and *Unteroffizier* Engesser.

A T 34 knocked out by *schwere Panzer–Abteilung 502*.

Major Jähde, the commander of *schwere Panzer–Abteilung 502*.

The Soviet Landing Operation at Mereküla

In order to reap the benefits of their successful breakthrough between Ssivertsi and Riigi to the fullest, the Soviet command prepared a landing operation. Its intent was to link up with the forces at Ssivertsi in order to unhinge the Narwa defenses from the rear.

After several unit movements, the Baltic coast was held as follows: An Estonian police battalion held from east of Mummassaare to Mereküla. A naval coastal artillery battery with four 10 cm captured guns was in the dunes. The battery was fixed. Six 2 cm *Flak* were employed for antiaircraft defense. The terrain approaching the coast was secured with barbed-wire entanglements. The staff of the *227. Infanterie-Division* (*Kampfgruppe Generalleutnant Berlin*) was at Mereküla. Mereküla was a tiny fishing village with 30 houses and two churches. Berlin's command post was surrounded with barbed wire entanglements. *Marine-Bataillon Hohnschild* held the Mereküla sector as far as directly west of Hungerburg. *Marine-Bataillon Schneider* was in Hungerburg. Between Mereküla and Kiwisaare was a naval battery with 15 cm guns. The staff of *Kampfgruppe "Küste"* was in the little fishing village of Auga.

The entire coastal sector was under the command and control of *Kampfgruppe "Küste"*. The commander was the Danish *Generalmajor* Kryssing. The operations officer was *SS-Sturmbannführer* Engelhardt. *Generalmajor* Kryssing's son, serving as an *SS-Untersturmführer* in *SS-Aufklärungs-Abteilung 11*, was wounded and sent in a vehicle from Wolossowo to Jamburg where he fell into enemy hands. *SS-Untersturmführer* Kryssing has been missing ever since.

During the night of 13/14 February, twelve small steamers and trawlers plowed the waves of the Gulf of Finland toward the west. They were escorted by several Soviet destroyers. Soon they were off the city of Hungerburg. They then changed course and headed for the coast. The engines of the little armada gave off a subdued humming. Above and below deck were Soviet soldiers in special outfits. There was whispering, final handshakes. The chemical-protective outfits were secured everywhere. The pants had suspenders and the boots were of one-piece construction. Weapons and equipment were secured on their shoulders. The landing battalion consisting of specially selected soldiers tensely awaited action.

The coast could be made out as a dark streak in the distance. The engines were throttled down. Small boats were lowered. The landing battalion disembarked and was rowed to the shore by marines. The boat trip ended a good fifty meters from dry land. The Soviets jumped into the cold water and waded ashore. Hardly a word was spoken. The water softly lapped at the rubber coveralls. Only the subdued crunch of the gravel on the bottom could be heard. Would the surprise succeed?

Two squads of the *3./Bataillon Hohnschild* were overpowered, but the firefight alerted the front. Soon Berlin's command post was surrounded. The all-around defense held. The *3./Bataillon Hohnschild* sealed off the coast to the north. The naval battery to the southwest took up the firefight. The guns alternately shelled the beachhead and the landing flotilla. They could clearly be seen in the light of illumination rounds. Three landing ships ran aground after being fired on, the others reached the open sea. The Soviets who had landed repeatedly charged the steep slope to eliminate the battery. Hundreds of them were killed on the steep, heavily vegetated slope with its multiple barbed-wire entanglements.

How did things look from the viewpoint of the staff of *Kampfgruppe "Küste"*? At about 0330 hours heavy infantry and artillery fire could be heard. *SS-Sturmbannführer* Engelhardt rushed to the coast with 50 to 70 men of the headquarters guard in Auga. There he found a squad of *Bataillon Hohnschild* already firing. Nobody knew what was really going on at first.

In the meantime, *Generalmajor* Kryssing began to form a picture through telephone reports. The staff of *Kampfgruppe Berlin* was surrounded in Mereküla and requested help. Two squads of the *3./Bataillon Hohnschild* had vanished. The company command post was defending itself against an attack on Mereküla from the west. Kryssing alerted the reserves of Hohnschild's and Schneider's battalions. *SS-Sturmbannführer* Engelhardt, who had returned to the command post, established contact with *SS-Aufklärungs-Abteilung 11*, which was in Puhkowa. Then the defense measures went into effect.

SS-Sturmbannführer Engelhardt, who was the man most familiar with the terrain, led the 50-man-strong reserve companies of Hohnschild's and Schneider's battalions and a 2 cm *Flak-* platoon from Auga against Mereküla. It was still dark — about 0530 hours — when those forces reached Mereküla and were able to establish contact with the staff of *Kampfgruppe Berlin*. The Soviet landing force was between the fixed battery, Berlin's command post and the naval reserves. When it got light, *Korvetten-Kapitän* Hohnschild took command of the German forces at Mereküla.

At 0900 hours additional German forces attacked the Soviets who had landed. *SS-Sturmbannführer* Engelhardt came from the northeast with three tanks and 30 infantrymen. Elements of *SS-Panzer-Aufklärungs-Abteilung 11* — including *Kanonenwagen* of the *5./SS-Panzer-Aufklärungs-Abteilung 11* — attacked from the southeast. Twelve *Stukas* showed up at the same time. Someone had reported that Mereküla was already in Soviet hands. Two *Stukas*

peeled off in bombing runs. There were friendly casualties. White flares clar-
ified the situation and the other ten *Stukas* turned away.

At 1000 hours the landing operation was finally crushed. 300 dead lit-
tered the battlefield. 200 Soviets were captured. The German naval battalion
west of Mereküla had born the greatest share of the defense. Seventy-five
Soviets escaped into the woods, where they were hunted down and captured.
A stroke of luck: The intact German telephone lines had made it possible to
coordinate the countermeasures. The Soviets had failed to discover the telephone cable that had been run in the trees.

As the men inspected the battlefield they discovered another 50 dead in
the waves of the Baltic sea. What had happened to them? They had stumbled
or been wounded. While the heavy equipment on their upper bodies forced
them under, the air trapped in their rubber pants shot upward and they
drowned. There were a hundred pair of rubber-clad legs jutting from the
waters of the Baltic Sea.

The Southern Front at Narwa

While German divisions still flowed into the Narwa bridgehead, the
Soviet 8th Army had already established a bridgehead at Krivasso. After the
battered German divisions had been assembled, they arrived too late to occupy the southern front at Narwa in time. The Soviet 8th Army under Major
General Suchomlin (effective 1 March: Major General Stanikow), strengthened the Krivasso bridgehead and thus formed a jump-off point for an
advance to the north that would cut off the *III. (germanisches) SS-Panzer-
Korps* in the Narwa bridgehead. The remnants of the *170. Infanterie-Division*
and elements of the *227. Infanterie-Division* that were defending were forced
back. *Panzer-Grenadier-Division "Feldherrnhalle"*, remnants of the *61.
Infanterie-Division* and additional *Kampfgruppen* were brought in as reinforcements.

On 24 February 1944 the Soviets reached the railroad line between the
Waiwara railroad station and the church. That advance was designated the
"West Sack" by the Germans. On both sides of the road, which ran due north
to the *Kinderheimhöhe* (children's home hill), were two battalions of the *61.
Infanterie-Division*. They held the so-called "boot". A second Soviet advance
along the Lipsus road reached the railroad at the Auwere station. That

advance was called the "East Sack". As a result, the Wesenburg — Narwa railroad line was cut in two places.

The situation was extremely dangerous. Anyone with any common sense could figure out that the Soviets would reinforce their forward forces and, in a further advance, reach the Wesenburg — Narwa main supply route. That would seal the fate of the defenders of Narwa and open the way to Estonia. All units located in that combat zone were alerted!

The *Tigers* of the *2./schwere-Panzer-Abteilung 502* were first on the scene as they moved to the threatened position at the front to strengthen the thin security screen. Four *Tigers* went to the "West Sack" and two to Lembitu at the "East Sack".

The *11. SS-Freiwilligen-Panzer-Grenadier-Division "Nordland"* freed up all available forces and sent them to the endangered "West Sack". For the most part, it was the bled-white companies of *SS-Panzer-Grenadier-Regiment 23 "Norge"* that came directly from employment at Ssivertsi, along with *Kampfgruppen* formed from trains elements and staffs. For example, a squad from the staff of *SS-Panzer-Abteilung 11*, led by *SS-Unterscharführer* Kipp, went into action at the Waiwara church.

In the morning hours of 25 February regimental commander Stoffers led a *Kampfgruppe* from *SS-Panzer-Grenadier-Regiment 23 "Norge"* in an attack southeast of the Waiwara railroad station to choke off the "West Sack" from the west. Storming forward behind *SS-Untersturmführer* Stock, the Norwegian grenadiers broke into the enemy main line of resistance. *SS-Untersturmführer* Stock and many men were wounded or killed during the assault. The attack bogged down. Stoffers met a soldier's death in the attack. Although that counterattack did not itself lead to success, it brought with it the result that the Soviets ceased their attack out of the "West Sack".

The first attempt to squeeze out the "West Sack" failed. An army mortar battalion, along with the *13./SS-Panzer-Grenadier-Regiment 23 "Norge"* and the *Kanonenwagen* of *SS-Panzer-Aufklärungs-Abteilung 11*, supported the attack. In order to get increased elevation for their guns, the *Kanonenwagen* had to position themselves with their rear in the ditch. Their heavy weapons were not able to fully replace the missing artillery. The front was a stalemate.

In order to prevent further penetration to the main supply route, four *Tigers* of the *2./schwere-Panzer-Abteilung 502* remained at the "West Sack" and two at the "East Sack" at Lembitu on 25 February. They supported the small number of infantry and earned unheard of respect from the Soviets. Forces of the *61. Infanterie-Division* were in the "boot" and on both sides of it. Directly east of Auwere, *Panzergrenadier-Division "Feldherrnhalle"* linked up with those forces.

During the night of 25 February the Russians had positioned a well-concealed antitank gun at the railroad embankment at Auwere. Only the muzzle brake could be made out with difficulty. *Leutnant* Carius and *Feldwebel* Kerscher moved forward with their *Tigers*. Before the antitank gun could get a round off it had been eliminated by the 8.8cm *Tiger* rounds. That was only the beginning.

In order to clean up the dangerous penetration, *Oberst Graf* Strachwitz was detailed to *Heeresgruppe Nord* as a senior armor commander. *Generaloberst* Lindemann wanted to clean up the penetration north of Krivasso first. That marshy area on the southern Narwa front was truly not armor terrain. Nevertheless, *Oberst Graf* Strachwitz set out to carry out his assigned mission. After intensive terrain reconnaissance, the first task was to reduce the "West Sack" in an operation similar to Stoffer's. The preparations were made. The operation was rehearsed behind the front.

At that time the *Tigers* of *schwere-Panzer-Abteilung 502* formed the nucleus of the defenses along the railroad line. On 27 February the Russians started to also attack at night, using their "coal shovels" (night-flying aircraft). All signs pointed to the Soviet bridgehead being pumped full through its Krivasso umbilical cord.

At 0900 hours on 17 March a heavy artillery barrage pounded the entire *61. Infanterie-Division* sector and also the western positions of *Panzergrenadier-Division "Feldherrnhalle"*. The Russians were determined to gain the main supply route advancing from the "East Sack". The weak units of the *61. Infanterie-Division* were smashed, the remnants falling back to the main supply route. At about 1000 hours, six T 34's circled around the *Kinderheimhöhe* and headed for the main supply route. A Soviet battalion had crossed the railroad embankment at Lembitu and followed the tanks. Success seemed near!

At that moment on the razor's edge, *Leutnant* Carius was 1000 meters west of Chundinurk with two *Tigers*. He was exactly in the right spot. He could observe the front from Lembitu to Auwere disintegrating.

The headphones of *Feldwebel* Kerscher crackled in the second *Tiger*. *Leutnant* Carius developed the plan of attack. Motors howled; the *Tigers* charged the Soviets. Within a scant ten minutes, six T 34's were aflame. Then the Soviet battalion was shot to pieces in the open area. In high gear, the *Tigers* dashed to the railroad embankment, knocked out five antitank guns and remained at the main line of resistance. They waited in vain for the infantry that they had requested by radio. Fortunately, a third *Tiger* was sent forward to join them.

The enemy made another attempt at 1340 hours. That time he had five T 34's, a KV I and a battalion of infantry. They, too, were shot to pieces. Three *Tigers* were holding the main line of resistance.

At 1515 hours a Soviet regiment staged south of Lembitu. There was no longer an artillery forward observer available. *Leutnant* Carius directed the

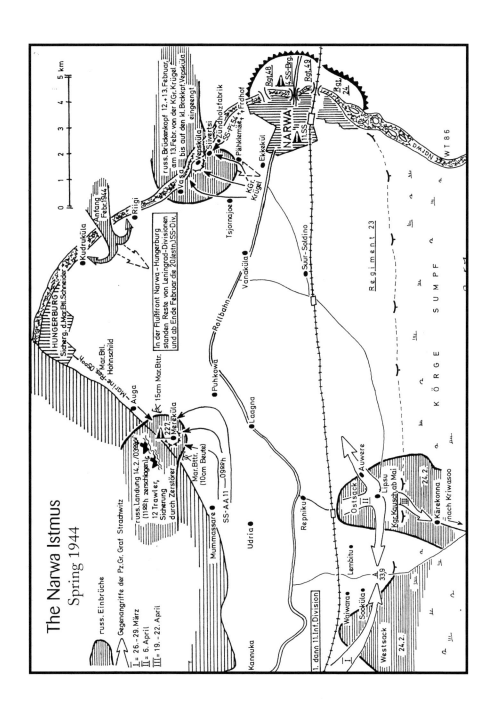

The Narwa Istmus
Spring 1944

russ. Einbrüche

Gegenangriffe der Pz.Gr. Graf Strachwitz

I = 26.–29. März
II = 1.– 6. April
III = 19. – 22. April

In der Flußfront Narwa – Hungerburg standen Reste von Leningrad-Divisionen und ab Ende Februar die 20.(estn.)SS-Div.

russ. Brückenkopf 12.+13.Februar, am 13.Febr. von der KGr. Krügel bis auf den kl. Brückopf. Vepsküla eingeengt

russ. Landung 14.2./0500ʰ (11ᵘʰ zerschlagen), 12 Trawler, Sicherung durch Zerstörer

15cm Mar.Bttr.

Mar.Bttr. (10cm Beute)

SS-AA 11 ___ 0500ʰ

Marine-Res.(Rgt.)900

Sicherg. d.Mar.Btl.Schneider

Mar.Btl. Hohnschild

HUNGERBURG

Anfang Febr.1944

Kudruküla

Riigi

Vepsküla
Siivertsi
Zündholzfabrik
SS-Pi.54
Pähklemäe
Ekeküll
Vasa
KGr. V
Krügel V

NARWA
1.SS

Rgt. 48
4.SS-Brg.
Rgt. 49

Rgt. 24

SS
Frdhof

WT 86
DMJDN

Tsjornojoe

Suur-Soldino

Vanaküla

Rollbahn

Regiment 23

KÖRGE   SUMPF

Puhkowa

Laagna

227.

Merekūla

Mummassare

Udria

Repniku

Kannuka

Waiwara
Lembitu
Sooküla

Westsack   24.2.

△ 33,9

Ostsack
Lipsu
Auwere

KGr.Kausch ab Mai

Käärekonna
nach Kriwasoo

24.2.

1. dann 11.Inf.Division

I
II
III

Auga

0   1   2   3   4   5 km

German artillery barrage himself. The attack position was decimated!

At 1615 hours came the last attack in battalion strength. It was supported by T 34 tanks. That, too, collapsed under the *Tigers'* fire. At that point, three *Tigers* had destroyed 14 T 34's, one KV I and five antitank guns without a single friendly loss. *Major* Haase got together some men from his *Grenadier-Regiment 162* and sent them forward as security for the *Tigers*, which had, in the meantime, pulled back a bit for security reasons.

On 18 March, the unshakable *Leutnant* Carius continued his operations against the old main line of resistance and, in particular, against the strongpoint in the ruins east of Lembitu. With a handful of infantry he captured one strongpoint after another in the ruins. During the night the Soviets had strengthened them and positioned heavy weapons there. That evening the kills totaled four T 34's, one T 60, seven antitank guns and one 4.7cm antiaircraft gun.

After the breakthrough at that point failed, the Russians tried to get through at point 33.9 on the north-south road that led directly to the *Kinderheimhöhe. Leutnant* Carius' terse combat report read:

19 March. 1200 hours: After a preparation by artillery and mortars, [Russian] attack on the north-south road at point 33.9. Destroyed six T 34's, one KV I, one T 60, one 7.62 cm antitank gun. At 1600 hours launched an immediate counterattack to the south. 1700 hours: 1 T 34, knocked out. 1800 hours: Another T 34 knocked out. Reached old main line of resistance again at 1900 hours.

20 March. 0515 hours. Russian attack in company strength at Lembitu. Repulsed at 0630 hours. One T 34 destroyed. 1145 hours: Attack in company strength at Lembitu. Repulsed at 1230 hours. One T 34, one antitank gun knocked out.

21 March. 0300 hours: Central ruins captured by Russians. 0445 hours: Counterattack with ten infantry. 0600 hours, ruins back in our hands. Two 7.62 cm antitank guns destroyed.

0830 hours: Ruins again evacuated. Four men dead, six men bolted.

1200 hours: Radio sets brought to farmstead with a *Tiger*, radio at the ruins inoperative. Impossible to reach on foot. Two T 34's destroyed at point 33.9.

1600 hours: Counterattack against central ruins. Situation restored at 1700 hours. One vehicle got stuck. One *Tiger* damaged by a direct mortar hit and one man wounded. Destroyed two T 34's and two antitank guns.

22 March. 1000 hours: Attack at point 33.9. Two T 34's knocked out. Attack was repulsed.

With that, the Soviet attack toward the main supply route foundered at that location as well. Between 17-22 March 1944, *Oberleutnant* von Schiller's *2./schwere-Panze-Abteilung 502* destroyed 38 Soviet tanks of various types, four assault guns and 17 antitank and antiaircraft guns. *Leutnant* Carius played a decisive part in holding the front south of the *Blauberge* (Blue Hills).

At the same time as the attacks on Lembitu and Point 33.9, a Soviet assault wave decimated the Estonians at Sirgala. The Soviets advanced through Riwimaa on a very narrow front. They moved with tanks along narrow paths in the woods. *SS-Panzer-Grenadier-Regiment 23 "Norge"* had to take action. With support from the heavy infantry weapons of the *8., 12.* and *13./SS-Panzer-Grenadier-Regiment 23 "Norge"*, the grenadiers mounted an immediate counterattack. They forced the enemy back in dense wooded, marshy terrain. Infantry guns — particularly the heavy infantry guns of the *13./SS-Panzer-Grenadier-Regiment 23 "Norge"* — had a particular share in that success, as prisoners later confirmed. Companies of the *II.* and *III./SS-Panzer-Grenadier-Regiment 23 "Norge"*, led by *SS-Sturmbannführer* Krügel, led the assault. Elements of *SS-Panzer-Aufklärungs-Abteilung 11* also participated. *SS-Obersturmführer* Kaiser, the commander of the *3./SS-Panzer-Grenadier-Regiment 23 "Norge"*, was killed.

While *SS-Hauptsturmführer* Bergfeld remained in the firing position of the *13./SS-Panzer-Grenadier-Regiment 23 "Norge"*, *SS-Untersturmführer* Dall took part in the assault toward Sirgala as a forward observer. Suddenly, he and his two radio operators were completely alone. A T 34 stood at a fork in the road. Dall had already gone too far to turn back. He happened to have a *Panzerfaust*. For him, there was only one way out: "It's you or me!"

The radio operators, who were somewhat farther back, got support from a machine gun. The Germans soon realized that the tank was damaged and the crew was busy trying to fix it. Dall was in the T 34's blind spot, but when he took aim with the *Panzerfaust*, he came under small-arms fire. The German machine gunner covered the prone Dall. Whenever the Soviets tried to get out of the tank, the German machine gun ripped off a burst and forced the crew back inside again. The cat and mouse game continued for half an hour until the tank crew was outwitted and *SS-Untersturmführer* Dall was able to get off the fatal round. The T 34 burned and the Russians lost another tank.

The massive rounds of the heavy infantry guns again tore into the woods and suppressed the last opposition. The Norwegian grenadiers captured Sirgala and reoccupied the old main line of resistance. The Estonians lay in the bunkers and woods positions, shot up and defeated. In the captured Soviet mortar positions there were also the bodies of women who had crewed the mortars. During the following night, the Norwegian *Kampfgruppe* was relieved by a *Jäger-Regiment* and found quiet at Surr-Soldino.

Strachwitz' Operation "West Sack" got going on 26 March. An artillery barrage began at 0555 hours. The upper portion of the "West Sack" was cut off and rolled up by three tanks moving one behind another. In that difficult maneuver, only three tanks could move along a narrow embankment through marshy terrain. Ammunition was sent along by personnel carrier. Soldiers of *Infanterie-Regiment 23* and *Infanterie-Regiment* 24 of the *11.Infanterie-Division* assaulted on both sides of the tanks. The fighting was over after three days. On the evening of 29 March, the west edge of the "boot" was reached and the "West Sack" no longer existed.

On the morning of 6 April 1944 a large number of *Flak* weapons of all calibers opened up with a barrage on the "East Sack" from all sides. Artillery formations from positions in the rear joined in the performance, including 28 cm howitzers and a *Nebelwerfer* unit that fired napalm. Four *Tigers* from the *2./schwere-Panzer-Abteilung 502* — commanded by Kerscher, Carius, Zwetti and Gruber — moved forward at top speed under the protection of that barrage from their assembly position at the *Kinderheimhöhe*. They approached the railroad embankment, crossed it, knocked out the antitank guns and advanced deep into the "East Sack" toward Auwere. More tanks and *SPW* from *Gruppe Strachwitz* followed them. Mine and antitank gun belts posed no problem.

After reaching the assigned objective, assault troops of battalions from *Panzergrenadier-Division "Feldherrnhalle"* broke off to the east and west at the base of the "sack" and established contact with the German forces at the bottom of the "sack". It was a terrible night. There were still Russians from an entire Soviet division in the area. Strachwitz' tanks had reached the objective so quickly and with such surprise that the Soviet division commander could only escape captivity with great difficulty. His operations officer was captured. According to his statements, the Russians had expected an operation at the base of the "sack" like Operation "West Sack".

Extensive obstacles had been carefully constructed — trees were fitted with trip wires that would set off concealed mines. They then sealed the fate of the Soviets. The Russians had not expected a frontal German attack, the more so since overlapping belts of antitank obstacles had been established. Surprise was complete. Soviet tanks were scattered everywhere on the wooded lanes, abandoned or immobilized. The "East Sack" had been punctured at its extremity and rolled up from the bottom. Strachwitz was pleased; the grenadiers of the *61. Infanterie-Division* in the "boot" were happy. The nerve-wracking "boot" that had depleted their strength no longer existed. The "East Sack" and "West Sack" had been eliminated. Only the Krivasso bridgehead and the vital Lipsus road remained.

On 19 April the third Strachwitz operation began, with the destruction of the remaining bridgehead at Krivasso as its objective. In the meantime, a thaw had set in. At that point, the tanks could not move even one meter from the road without sinking into the marshy terrain.

The third "Strachwitz Operation" was initiated with *Tigers* in the lead. It advanced from the east along the Suur-Soldino — Auwere road. A *Panzergruppe* with *Panzer IV's* advanced from the north to the south over the former "boot sole" and Point 33.9 and sank into the mud.

The *Tiger* in the lead of the main effort encountered a mine. Because of the marshy ground, the *Tigers* that followed were unable to pass. Precious hours were lost. The Russians were alerted, mined the approach route and committed assault guns. The attack bogged down. The *2.* and *3./Grenadier-Regiment 401 (170. Infanterie-Division)* as well as units of *Grenadier-Regiment 151 (61. Infanterie-Division)* were able to break into the first enemy positions. The fighting was bitter. The *I./Grenadier-Regiment 399* tried to help the forward companies. The Russians were stronger. The German forces had to fall back. Another fearsome night followed. The assault was to continue the following day.

On 20 April the *Stukas* of *Schlachtgeschwader 3* under *Oberstleutnant* Kuhlmey took off from Reval with Krivasso and two Soviet underwater bridges as their targets. They dove on the bridge sites and artillery positions. Two *Stukas* were shot down. The others were unable to find the underwater bridges since they were built barely below the surface of the water and could not be identified. Whenever vehicles moved over them, the water covered their wheels. A number of Russian observation balloons flew above Krivasso. Observers directed the fire of the heavy artillery from them. When danger loomed, the balloons were hauled down and disappeared in the thick brush along the riverbank.

On 20 April the attack was renewed. *Kampfgruppe "Feldherrnhalle"* finally got to a dry spot. After gaining 800 meters of ground, the Soviet defense became too strong. Two *Tigers* were knocked out. Out of there! A new main line of resistance was formed at the northern edge of the Körge Marshes. The Soviet bridgehead continued to threaten the German defense at Narwa. *Oberst Graf* Strachwitz was awarded the Diamonds to his Knight's Cross and was sent to another part of the front. The *Tigers* of the *2./schwere-Panzer-Abteilung 502* were transferred to the Pleskau area. *Leutnant* Famula, *Oberst Graf* Strachwitz' aide, was killed on 22 April. He had been responsible in large part for the success of "Operation East Sack". He was posthumously awarded the Knight's Cross on 15 May. The third Strachwitz Operation remained stuck in the marshes. The newly arrived *SS-Vielfachwerfer-Batterie 521* — a multiple-tube rocket launcher battery — had gone into firing position at Auwere and supported the Strachwitz operations. *SS-Hauptsturmführer* Flecke commanded it.

After reorganization of the formations of the *III. (germanisches) SS-Panzer-Korps*, the *II.* and *III./SS-Panzer-Grenadier-Regiment 23 "Norge"* were committed between the Narwa bridgehead and *Panzergrenadier-Division "Feldherrnhalle"* was employed in the Narwa riverbank position along the woods. The remnants of *I./SS-Panzer-Grenadier-Regiment 23 "Norge"* were consolidated with the *III./SS-Panzer-Grenadier-Regiment 23 "Norge"*. *SS-Hauptsturmführer* Vogt and a cadre were sent to Germany to reform the *I./SS-Panzer-Grenadier-Regiment 23 "Norge"*. A similar procedure was carried out with the *I./SS-Panzer-Grenadier-Regiment 24 "Danmark"*. As a result, both regiments were reduced to having only two battalions.

In the meantime, a number of personnel changes also took place. *SS-Obersturmbannführer* Knöchlein took over command of *SS-Panzer-Grenadier-*

Regiment 23 "Norge" after the death of *SS-Sturmbannführer* Stoffers. *SS-Sturmbannführer* Krügel had commanded *SS-Panzer-Grenadier-Regiment 24 "Danmark"* in the Narwa bridgehead ever since Easter.

SS-Panzer-Grenadier-Regiment 23 "Norge" was again committed as an integral whole south of Narwa. During the operations in February and March it had been split up frequently and committed as separate companies. The combat engineers of the *16./SS-Panzer-Grenadier-Regiment 23 "Norge"* constructed the regimental command post in Jaola. The command post of *SS-Hauptsturmführer* Gürz' *III./SS-Panzer-Grenadier-Regiment 23 "Norge"* was located a little to the south in the brickyard.

The sector of the *III./SS-Panzer-Grenadier-Regiment 23 "Norge"* included, from east to west: Two islands in a river and a projecting section of the Narwa river bank that lay across from the rear defenses on the "Rectangle", "Triangle" and "Brush" woods. One part of the main line of resistance followed the Mulgu Creek, then bent sharply south west of the "Rectangle" woods. The workers' houses and peat-diggings were partially in German hands. The battalion boundaries ran opposite the notorious "Snake" woods into the Körge Marshes. *SS-Sturmbannführer* Scheibe's *II./SS-Panzer-Grenadier-Regiment 23 "Norge"* linked up with the battalion along the wooded marshes to the west.

As soon as they reached the southern front, the men of *SS-Panzer-Grenadier-Regiment 23 "Norge"* set about constructing positions. They built bunkers and palisades. Schirmer's combat engineers laid minefields and built "Target" bridge over the Mulgu Creek. Kilometers of corduroy road were laid.

Combat activity was limited to small operations. Assault troop activity flared up in efforts to dispose of the overturned industrial rail cars that obstructed the field of fire at the peat diggings. Snipers nested in the trees all along the edge of the woods. As long as the treacherous moor was frozen, patrols and assault troops crossed it. They were always local operations. The focal point of all the troubles was the "Snake" woods in the Körge Marshes.

The thaw set in at the beginning of April and rain added to the mess. The marshes were impassable, the roads bottomless. Frozen and often soaked to the skin, the men of *SS-Panzer-Grenadier-Regiment 23 "Norge"* stayed in positions along lanes and clearings in the woods and in gasoline drums and barrels that could only be reached over corduroy roads. The squad base camps were in bunkers and wooden sheds. The enemy was in the same situation. The bottomless moor prevented any large combat operations.

It was during that period that the third Strachwitz operation got bogged down in the morass. Even though the *III. (germanisches) SS-Panzer-Korps* joined in with heavy weapons, it did not help. The marshes were stronger. The divisional artillery of the *11. SS-Freiwilligen-Panzer-Grenadier-Division "Nordland"* turned its cannon around and, as needed, fired in two directions. The Krivasso bridgehead was past the stage where it could be eliminated, but the lines of communications to Narwa remained open.

The reorganization of *Armee-Abteilung Narwa* was completed by the end of April. The *III. (germanisches) SS-Panzer-Korps* was positioned at Narwa, the *XXXXIII. Armee-Korps* (*11., 58.* and *122. Infanterie-Divisionen*) in the center and the *XXVI. Armee-Korps* (*225., 170.* and *227. Infanterie-Divisionen*) along the western Narwa. *Armee-Abteilung Narwa* formed *Division zur besonderen Verwendung 300* (Special-Purpose Division 300) from the staff of the destroyed *13. Luftwaffen-Feld-Division*. Its line units consisted of Estonian border regiments 1-4. That purely Estonian formation with German leadership went into action on the north shore of Lake Peipus and was directly subordinate to *Armee-Abteilung Narwa*. Soon, however, *Armee-Abteilung Narwa* had to give up the *XXXXIII. Armee-Korps* and, in July, also the *XXVI. Armee-Korps* to other hard-pressed positions along the front. From that time on, the Narwa front was defended entirely by the *III.(germanisches) SS-Panzer-Korps*.

What was the situation in the corps sector at the end of April? The *Panzergrenadier-Division "Feldherrnhalle"* and the *61. Infanterie-Division* had been withdrawn. The *11. Infanterie-Division* took over the sector extending from south of *Kinderheimhöhe* to southwest of Sirgala. *Kampfgruppe Kausch* was inserted between the positions of *SS-Panzer-Grenadier-Regiment 23 "Norge"* described above and the *11. Infanterie-Division*. It consisted of two companies of *SS-Panzer-Abteilung 11 "Hermann von Salza"* that were committed as infantry, two Estonian companies and the *1.* and *3./SS-Pionier-Bataillon 11. SS-Obersturmbannführer* Kausch's *Kampfgruppe* was entrusted with the defense of the Lipsus road to Krivasso, one of the most dangerous sectors of the front. The main line of resistance crossed the road south of Lipsus and Wanamoisa.

The *11. Infantry-Division* had the sector of front formerly containing the "West Sack" and the "East Sack". It faced south. The battle-tested East-Prussian *11. Infanterie-Division* was commanded by *Generalleutnant* Reymann. To the rear of the division were the commanding heights of the "Blue" Hills. The staffs were dug in there. New tunnels were continually dug into the hill. Rear-area units were brought up to improve the blocking positions.

The Narwa Bridgehead

On 1 and 2 February, the formations of the *III. (germanisches) SS-Panzer-Korps* poured into the Narwa bridgehead. Tired and burnt out, the battered companies occupied the designated positions and clawed themselves firmly into the ground. The formations were a colorful mix of units.

The divisional commanders, von Scholz and Wagner, set up the defense as soon as possible. Soon, however, the sharply pursuing Soviet armies — the 47th, 2nd Shock and 8th Armies — pressed against the new defensive sector.

As one of many, *SS-Hauptsturmführer* Per Sörensen and the remnants of the *I./SS-Panzer-Grenadier-Regiment 24 "Danmark"* held positions along the Narwa — Jamburg road. To their north stood the volunteers of *4. SS-Panzer-Grenadier-Brigade "Nederland"*, to their south, units of *SS-Panzer-Grenadier-Regiment 23 "Norge"* and *SS-Panzer-Grenadier-Regiment 24 "Danmark"*. Primary support came from the *Tigers* of the *2./schwere-Panzer-Abteilung 502* and the *1./SS-Panzer-Abteilung 11 "Hermann von Salza"*, along with assault guns from the division and the brigade.

The powerful attack against the bridgehead failed. Artillery barrages from *SS-Artillerie-Regiment 11* and *SS-Artillerie-Regiment 54* protected it. *Tigers* and *Panthers* moved forward and knocked out antitank and infantry guns. Soon General Goworow had to recognize that there was no getting through along the main road. A short respite set in. The Germans reorganized their formations.

Both the *9.* and *10. Luftwaffen-Feld-Divisionen* had been so decimated that reconstitution was out of the question. Both divisions had lost their commanders. *Oberst* Michael (*9. Luftwaffen-Feld-Division*) was killed on 22 January 1944. *Generalmajor* von Wedel (*10. Luftwaffen-Feld-Division*) died on 5 February 1944. *Luftwaffe* ground soldiers and officers took their places in the ranks of the *III.(germanisches) SS-Panzer-Korps*, where they were soon completely assimilated. The members of the army formations that had joined up with the *11. SS-Freiwilligen-Panzer-Grenadier-Division "Nordland"* and *4. SS-Panzer-Grenadier-Brigade "Nederland"* were considered to have been attached to those formations and later returned to their own units.

In the meantime, the bridgehead position grew stronger from day to day. The reorganization of the companies was continued, entailing the unavoidable consequence that new sector assignments were a daily event. There was hard fighting around Lilienbach. *SS-Hauptsturmführer* Thöny's *Kampfgruppe "Norge"*, along with additional immediate reserves, had to assist *4. SS-Panzer-Grenadier-Brigade "Nederland"* at critical times.

Narwa was strengthened into a fortress. Night after night the combat engineers of *SS-Pionier-Bataillon 11* and *SS-Pionier-Bataillon 54,* as well as the regimental combat engineers, moved into the bridgehead and built palisades and barbed-wire entanglements, field positions and machine-gun positions and dug kilometers of communications trenches. They kept the bridgehead intact, in spite of constant attacks by Soviet aircraft and artillery. Smoke pots were positioned to protect the main bridge. Within a few seconds, the bridge and fortress could be covered in smoke.

SS-Artillerie-Regiment 11 and an artillery battalion of *SS-Artillerie-Regiment 4* of the *4. SS-Polizei-Panzergrenadier-Division* — attached to *4. SS-Panzer-Grenadier-Brigade "Nederland"* — played a large role in the defensive success of the first days in the bridgehead. The supporting artillery battalion was eventually incorporated into the Dutch brigade. *SS-Artillerie-Regiment 11* was in a firing position south of the main supply route. The commander of *SS-Artillerie-Regiment 11, SS-Obersturmbannführer* Karl, had his command post in the Hermannsburg.

Following its activation at the Arys Training Area in East Prussia, *SS-Flak-Abteilung 11* was supposed to be moved forward to the division at the Oranienbaum Pocket. During its railroad transport through the Baltic area, the battalion was involved in a major railroad accident (probably sabotage). Almost all of the officers were injured. The battalion had to be sent back to Arys. At the beginning of March, the battalion finally arrived in Narwa from Arys. Three batteries of 88's and one 3.7cm battery were a welcome addition to the divisional firepower. The *Flak* battalion provided point protection for the bridge and artillery positions and also performed artillery tasks occasionally.

After the Russian failures to break out at Ssivertsi, on the Meréküla beachhead and from the Krivasso bridgehead, General Goworow, the commander of the 3rd Baltic Front, tried other means.

During the night of 6/7 March 1944, Russian bomber wings droned over the city, dropping death and destruction. One bomb struck the demolition charge on the railroad bridge, which went up in the air in a mighty detonation. Bombs burst everywhere in the inner city and buildings collapsed like houses of cards. *SS-Pionier-Bataillon 11* suffered a large number killed at Petri Square.

The next night, Kreenholm and the southern portion of the bridgehead were the focus of the bombing. As the last wave turned away after twelve hours of bombing, the Soviet artillery opened up a murderous intense barrage on the city and bridgehead. An observation balloon far to the east directed the fire of the Soviet heavy artillery. Vehicles and wooden houses burned everywhere. Narwa was destroyed in two nights of bombing.

SS-Panzer-Grenadier-Regiment 24 "Danmark" lost 34 vehicles in those attacks. The *13. (IG)/SS-Panzer-Grenadier-Regiment 24 "Danmark"* lost a third of its guns while the *14.(Flak)* lost two thirds. Similar losses were suffered by all of the other units staged in Narwa.

The main weight of the Soviet attack then fell upon *SS-Freiwilligen-Panzer-Grenadier-Regiment 48 "General Seyffard"*, which defended the northern portion of the bridgehead at Popovka. The regiment's commander, *SS-Obersturmbannführer* Jörchel, committed his last reserves. Tröger's and Breimann's battalions held. The Soviet attack collapsed in the face of a strong defense and immediate counterattacks. The efforts of those regiments were mentioned in the Armed Forces Report for 15 March 1944: "During the last few days of fighting in the northern sector of the Eastern front, the Dutch *SS-Freiwilligen-Panzer-Grenadier-Regiment 48 "General Seyffard"* excelled under the leadership of *SS-Obersturmbannführer* Jörchel."

Soon after, the Soviets started again at Lilienbach, where *SS-Freiwilligen-Panzer-Grenadier-Regiment 49 "de Ruyter"* was positioned. Soviet infantry and armor succeeded in penetrating the positions at Lilienbach. The *9./SS-Panzer-Grenadier-Regiment 24 "Danmark"* and remnants of *Kampfgruppe Thöny* from the *11. SS-Freiwilligen-Panzer-Grenadier-Division "Nordland"* were assembled under *SS-Obersturmführer* Sidon and committed in the endangered sector. In several immediate counterattacks the enemy was hurled back and the main line of resistance reestablished. *SS-Obersturmführer* Sidon was severely wounded and his *9./SS-Panzer-Grenadier-Regiment 24 "Danmark" 24* almost totally wiped out. The efforts of Sidon's company, including the remnants of *Kampfgruppe Thöny*, were recognized by the award of the *Ehrenblattspange* to *SS-Obersturmführer* Sidon.

The struggle for Lilienbach went on without a break. Tanks that had broken through frequently had to be engaged by close-combat means. The commander of the *14./SS-Freiwilligen-Panzer-Grenadier-Regiment 49 "de Ruyter"*, *SS-Hauptsturmführer* Dievel, was killed at the dairy. The seesawing, bloody fighting continued.

The Russians next attempted to break through to the bridge just north of the main supply route. The hour had come for the *1./SS-Panzer-Abteilung 11 "Hermann von Salza"*. It had been positioned at the command post of the *4. SS-Panzer-Grenadier-Brigade "Nederland"*. In repeated, spirited assaults, *SS-Obersturmführer* Rott's *Panthers* stopped the enemy armored attack. *SS-Oberscharführer* Wild was especially conspicuous in that action. His *Panther* platoon thwarted a deep Russian thrust toward the main bridge. The enemy tanks remained knocked out near the cemetery.

During those critical hours, Wagner, the commander of the Dutch brigade, kept on top of the situation. Constantly on his feet, without sleep, he directed the defense of his brigade. Unceasingly the field telephones rang and the radio broke static; it was important to direct reserves, ammunition and rations to the proper place.

The struggle for Lilienbach went on for two days. *SS-Freiwilligen-*

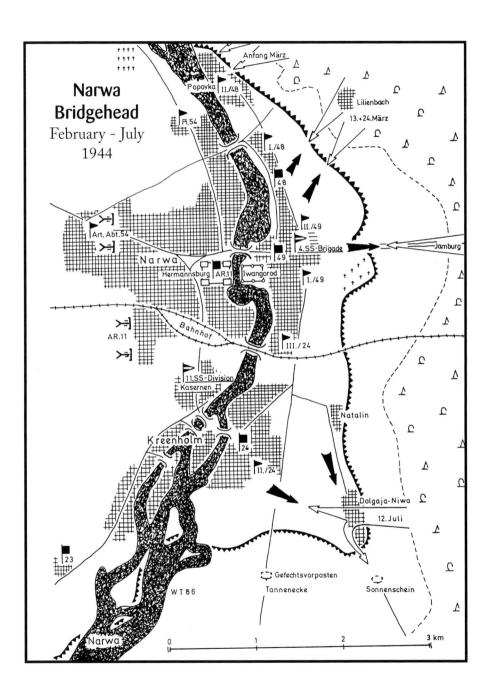

Narwa Bridgehead
February - July
1944

Anfang März

Popovka II./48

Lilienbach

Pi.54

13.+24.März

I./48

48

II./49

Art.Abt.54

4.SS-Brigade

Jamburg

Narwa

49

Hermannsburg AR.11 Iwangorod

I./49

AR.11

Bahnhof

III./24

11.SS-Division

Kasernen

Natalin

Kreenholm

24

II./24

Dolgaja-Niwa

12.Juli

23

Gefechtsvorposten

WT86

Tannenecke

Sonnenschein

Narwa

0   1   2   3 km

Panzer-Grenadier-Regiment 49 "de Ruyter" suffered tremendously. Enemy penetrations, defense and immediate counterattacks followed one another in quick succession. The regimental commander Collani bore a heavy responsibility. Would his regiment hold?

In the end, the front at Lilienbach was so entangled that is was frequently impossible to determine what was happening. Again and again the barrages of Soviet artillery pounded down on the bridgehead. German artillery, directed by indomitable forward observers in the foremost positions, supported the hard-fighting grenadiers and halted the advancing enemy tanks. Lilienbach was finally lost. The German positions were pulled back to the "Devil's Meadow" and established as quickly as possible.

After days of local fighting, a renewed, heavy artillery barrage hailed down on the "Devil's Meadow" — "Park Forest" sector during the night of 13/14 March. Under protection of darkness, taking advantage of the moment of surprise, the enemy succeeded in penetrating the new, hurriedly constructed makeshift positions. The battalion commander of the *II./SS-Freiwilligen-Panzer-Grenadier-Regiment 49 "de Ruyter"*, *SS-Hauptsturmführer* Diener, was killed. A company commander was wounded in the immediate counterattack. The acting commander of the neighboring company, *SS-Untersturmführer* Scholz, recognized from the sound of the fighting that the Russians had begun to roll up the position. Scholz immediately launched a counterattack with a small, hastily assembled group of courageous men and threw the enemy back out. *SS-Untersturmführer* Scholz then assumed command of the entire sector and repulsed the ensuing enemy attacks. On the following day, the regiment's adjutant, *SS-Hauptsturmführer* Ertel, assumed temporary command of the battalion, which he then turned over to *SS-Hauptsturmführer* Frühauf a short while later.

After further local assaults, a renewed, extraordinarily heavy barrage began to pound the Lilienbach Hill — "Devil's meadow" — "Park Forest" sector during the midday hours of 22 March. It struck the *5./SS-Freiwilligen-Panzer-Grenadier-Regiment 49 "de Ruyter"* with its full weight, pulverizing and smashing it. The Soviets succeeded penetrating with 150 men on an extremely narrow front. The battalion commander, *SS-Hauptsturmführer* Frühauf, scraped together grenadiers, messengers and communications men and launched an immediate counterattack against the enemy who had penetrated the lines. The counterattack threatened to fall apart several times in the defensive fire of the numerically far-superior enemy, but, again and again, Frühauf's example carried the men forward. After half an hour of combat, the enemy was thrown out and the old main line of resistance reoccupied. Scholz and Frühauf played a decisive role in holding the bridgehead during those critical March days.

During the nights that followed, friend and foe fortified and improved their positions. A war of nerves set in with all its bitterness. Snipers lurked everywhere, causing unexpected casualties and death to those who were not careful.

The southern portion of the bridgehead remained relatively calm during that series of fighting. The positions of *SS-Panzer-Grenadier-Regiment 24 "Danmark"* began south of the road at the cemetery. They then crossed the railroad line, jumped like a finger to the village of Dolgaja-Niwa and then ran west to the river, including two small river islands. *SS-Panzer-Grenadier-Regiment 23 "Norge"* linked up with the regiment in the southern part of Kreenholm on the west bank of the river. Artillery and trains elements of the *11. SS-Freiwilligen-Panzer-Grenadier-Division "Nordland"* were mostly in Kreenholm. The division command post was in the former Estonian barracks south of the railroad station property.

The positions of *SS-Panzer-Grenadier-Regiment 24 "Danmark"* were slightly elevated. The enemy positions ran parallel, about 800 meters to the east in a densely vegetated zone. With the help of the *1./SS-Pionier-Bataillon 11*, Dolgaja-Niwa had been turned into a strong bastion. Prolonging the Dolgaja-Niwa finger, a German combat outpost (Code name *Sonnenschein* = sunshine) had been established 400 meters out. South of Usküla, *SS-Panzer-Grenadier-Regiment 24 "Danmark"* held another combat outpost (Code name *Tannenhecke* = spruce hedgerow).

All sorts of tasks fell to the combat engineers. Crossings required constant attention and maintenance. The railroad bridge was made passable again. The northern bridge, which was under constant infantry fire, was made usable for messenger traffic. The Kreenholm suspension bridge was reinforced. Farther north, a cable car was put in service to carry ammunition and supplies and, if necessary, sometimes even a man over the river. Assault boats were at the ready south of Kreenholm. A 60-ton ferry was on standby so that tanks could be put across the river even if the bridges were destroyed. With the onset of the thaw, the combat engineers repeatedly had to blow up ice jams at the bridges. *SS-Pionier-Bataillon 11* had only two officers available, other than its surgeon, *SS-Hauptsturmführer* Kurz. Convalescent officers started returning as spring progressed.

SS-Artillerie-Regiment 11 and the artillery battalion of *4. SS-Panzer-Grenadier-Brigade "Nederland"* played a major role in the defense against the Soviet attacks. *SS-Sturmbannführer* Schlüter's battalion was north of the main supply route and operated in the sector of the *4. SS-Panzer-Grenadier-Brigade "Nederland"*. *SS-Obersturmbannführer* Karl's *SS-Artillerie-Regiment 11* was in the southern part of the city of Narwa and screened the southern portion of the bridgehead, along with the sector along the wooded river banks. On occasion it became involved in the fighting at Auwere and turned its howitzers toward that target. Later on, the defense of the Narwa — Narwa Riverbank positions was in the hands of the *8., 12.* and *13./SS-Panzer-Grenadier-Regiment 23 "Norge"* and with the *"Stuka zu Fuß"* that had been positioned in the wooded riverbank area. That support was later augmented by *SS-Vielfach-Werfer-Batterie 521* (Flecke) at Auwere.

The divisional dressing station was in the cellar of the fabric mill on Kreenholm Island. Surgeons and medics carried out their duties there with self-sacrificing devotion.

On 9 April 1944 (Easter Monday), the commander of *SS-Panzer-Grenadier-Regiment 24 "Danmark"*, *SS-Obersturmbannführer Graf* von Westphalen, was wounded by shrapnel on the Kreenholm bridge. On Whit Sunday, 28 May 1944, he died in the hospital at Reval as a result of his thigh injury. *SS-Sturmbannführer* Albrecht Krügel assumed command of *SS-Panzer-Grenadier-Regiment 24 "Danmark"* on the following day.

In the meantime, *SS-Hauptsturmführer* Hämel took over the *II./SS-Panzer-Grenadier-Regiment 24 "Danmark"* from *SS-Sturmbannführer* Walter, who had stayed with his battalion during the retreat in spite of wounds and had become seriously ill in the bridgehead.

In the quiet sector, an assault troop of the *II./SS-Panzer-Grenadier-Regiment 24 "Danmark"* blew up the "Walter Bridge", three kilometers south of Usküla. Another operation, which went under the codename *"Stinkfisch"* (foul fish), failed and took casualties. It had been given the objective of blowing up a Soviet base camp in a farmstead.

On 7 June the Soviets made their first attempt to eliminate combat outpost *"Sonnenschein"*. The attack was repulsed. *SS-Untersturmführer* Berthelsen, who was the acting commander of the *7./SS-Panzer-Grenadier-Regiment 24 "Danmark"*, was killed in the fighting. *SS-Untersturmführer* Madsen assumed command of the company.

An unusually heavy harassing fire opened up on the bridge positions and hinterland at about noon on 12 June. It finally shifted and included the positions of *SS-Panzer-Grenadier-Regiment 24 "Danmark"*. A further enemy barrage, which included massive amounts of smoke rounds, covered the positions at Dolgaja-Niwa as far as the command post of the *II./SS-Panzer-Grenadier-Regiment 24 "Danmark"* with thick smoke. *SS-Untersturmführer* Madsen fired the flare signal that Krügel had directed to be fired if an extreme situation existed. Madsen realized the positions of his *7./SS-Panzer-Grenadier-Regiment 24 "Danmark"* would be the enemy's point of main effort.

Under cover of the tall underbrush that had resisted all attempts at burning it out, and under the protection of the rolling barrage, the enemy suddenly appeared in front of the positions of the *7./SS-Panzer-Grenadier-Regiment 24 "Danmark"* which had just finished issuing rations. Serious fighting ensued. Two platoon leaders were killed in the hand-to-hand fighting. Only the squad of Danish *SS-Unterscharführer* Christoffersen, which was on the northern wing, was able to hold its position, doggedly defending itself. *SS-Hauptsturmführer* Hämel had reached his forward command post in the meantime and intercepted the retreating elements of the company.

On receipt of Madsen's flare signal, all of *SS-Artillerie-Regiment 11* laid down a final-protective fire directly east of Dolgaja-Niwa. A Soviet regiment stormed forward from the 800-meter distant wood line to reinforce the approximately 200-man strong assault force in Dolgaja-Niwa. They ran right into the artillery barrage. Few reached the German lines.

At the same time, about 120 men of the penetration force turned westward. The remainder attacked combat outpost "Sonnenschein".

Under the fire direction of SS-Hauptsturmführer Lärum, the combined fire of the 8., 12. and 13./SS-Panzer-Grenadier-Regiment 24 "Danmark" greeted the wedge advancing to the west. Eight and twelve centimeter mortars, as well as the light and heavy infantry guns, poured rounds down on the enemy who had found cover in a railway trench. Lärum, who had his observation post in the attic of the fabric mill, "nailed" the Soviets to the spot.

The German countermeasures were also coming into play. SS-Hauptsturmführer Meier advanced on Dolgaja-Niwa from the north with elements of his 9./SS-Panzer-Grenadier-Regiment 24 "Danmark" The regimental tank hunter-killer platoon and the regimental combat engineers moved out to the east from the command post of the 8./SS-Panzer-Grenadier-Regiment 24 "Danmark". They were supported by two assault guns and reached the railway trench. About 40 Russians surrendered. The rest had been killed by the regiment's heavy weapons.

At the same time, SS-Unterscharführer Christoffersen and his squad, who were in the positions of the 7./SS-Panzer-Grenadier-Regiment 24 "Danmark", launched an immediate counterattack and rolled up the enemy-occupied German trenches from north to south. SS-Unterscharführer Christoffersen, truly a model of a simple soldier who copes with the situation and combines courage and resolve, motivated his men to take decisive action. By the time that the German immediate counterattack had fully developed, Christoffersen's squad had already done half the job. SS-Hauptsturmführer Hämel awarded Christoffersen the Iron Cross, First Class and recommended him for the Knight's Cross.

The sobering after-action report of the II./SS-Panzer-Grenadier-Regiment 24 "Danmark" read:

After heavy artillery preparation with extremely heavy use of smoke rounds as far back as the battalion command post, the enemy worked his way right up to the battalion positions and, when the fire stopped, captured the positions of the 7./SS-Panzer-Grenadier-Regiment 24 "Danmark". After the enemy had advanced into Dolgaja- Niwa, he attacked forward combat outpost "Sonnenschein" in an enveloping attack with his main effort at Dolgaja-Niwa. The strongpoint was only able to hold out for a limited time against the superior enemy. Most of the 25 personnel were killed. Ten men were missing. Two men were able to fight their way out. Several charred bodies lay in a bunker. The battalion surgeon was sent to forward combat outpost "Sonnenschein" to identify the bodies. It must be assumed that several of the men reported missing had been killed in the bunker. According to the reports of the surviving two men, three to four men had been captured. The combat situation permitted no clear picture. *SS-Hauptsturmführer* Hämel had proceeded to the forward-most lines, where *SS-Unterscharführer* Christoffersen and his squad had remedied the situation with an immediate counterattack.

At the same time as the attack on Dolgaja-Niwa, the enemy mounted attacks against Natalin and Usküla with a strength of about 40-60 men in each attack force. Those attacks were repulsed. Those attacks were apparently diversionary maneuvers.

After heavy German artillery preparation, the remaining elements of the *7./SS-Panzer-Grenadier-Regiment 24 "Danmark"*, the regimental combat engineers, the regimental anti-tank platoon, two assault guns and elements of the *9./SS-Panzer-Grenadier-Regiment 24 "Danmark"* regained possession of Dolgaja-Niwa and *"Sonnenschein"*.

Losses: 90 killed and wounded. 3 light machine guns.

Captured: 1 antitank gun, 2 heavy machine guns, 4 light machine guns.

The commander of the forward combat outpost, *SS-Untersturmführer* Koopman, was killed in the action.

On 5 July 1944 the *II./SS-Artillerie-Regiment 4* arrived in the Narwa sector. It had been raised at Beneschau near Prague. The guns were unloaded at Suur-Soldino and moved to their firing positions. That finally gave the *4. SS-Panzer-Grenadier-Brigade "Nederland"* an artillery regiment.

SS-Obersturmbannführer Jörchel went to a training course. *SS-Obersturmbannführer* Benner, coming from the Finland front, assumed command of *SS-Freiwilligen-Panzer-Grenadier-Regiment 48 "General Seyffard"*. Standing in for *General* Steiner, *General der Waffen-SS* Kleinheisterkamp temporarily assumed command of the *III.(germanisches) SS-Panzer-Korps*. *SS-Brigadeführer und Generalmajor der Waffen-SS* Augsberger commanded the *20. Waffen-Grenadier-Division der SS (estnisch)*. There was also a change at *Kampfgruppe "Küste"*. *Generalmajor* Kryssing was ordered to a training course. His successor was *Oberstleutnant* von Bülow.

During June and July, Narwa lay under oppressive heat. New fires started throughout the ruins. Combat engineers had to blow up entire blocks of houses to prevent the spread of the flames. The heavy air attacks had left Narwa a dead city.

Danger was in the air. The defenders of Narwa could sense it. The heavy guns at Jamburg registered their rounds on the railroad facilities and roads in the hinterland. Russian long-range artillery accomplished the unbelievable in hitting the *"langer Hermann"*, leaving a gaping hole in its wall. The enemy also conspicuously reinforced himself on the southern Narwa front and in front of the bridgehead.

A large-scale blow against the Narwa bridgehead was impending. Substantial Soviet forces had been freed up by the capitulation of Finland, some of which were thrown in against the Narwa front. The German command planned to evacuate Narwa so as to parry the Soviet thrust in a significantly shortened front at the *"Tannenberg-Stellung"*, 20 kilometers to the west.

The bridgehead was to be cleared on 16 and 17 July. The evacuation order had to be rescinded, since the Russians had learned of it, according to the interrogation of two prisoners. In that tense situation, the Russians launched a surprise attack on the afternoon of 17 July, ejected the occupants of command post *"Sonnenschein"* and occupied it.

Again, it was the cool action of a single soldier that saved the situation. All alone, unnoticed by the Soviets, the forward observer of the *13./SS-Panzer-Grenadier-Regiment 24 "Danmark"* remained in a bunker with his radio. He radioed a short situation report on what was happening outside. He then called down fire from the heavy weapons on his own surroundings and reported where the rounds impacted. An immediate counterattack launched a short time later by the *II./SS-Panzer-Grenadier-Regiment 24 "Danmark"* — led by the Danish *SS-Untersturmführer* Spleth — hurled the Soviets back. They left several prisoners and dead behind. *SS-Untersturmführer* Spleth was killed in the counterattack.

Nerves remained strained on both sides. On 24 July *SS-Artillerie-Regiment 11* and *SS-Artillerie-Regiment 54* fired continuous barrages on known assembly positions. By doing so, they introduced the final act of the battle for the Narwa bridgehead.

The Evacuation of Narwa

On 22 June 1944, on a 400-kilometer front, a major offensive broke loose against the central sector of the Eastern Front. After several days, the German divisions were smashed and wiped out. On 10 July, contact between *Heeresgruppe Mitte* and *Heeresgruppe Nord* finally tore apart. Twenty-nine Soviet rifle divisions and one tank brigade moved through the 25-kilometer gap and advanced along the Düna River toward Lithuania and Latvia. That placed *Heeresgruppe Nord* in grave danger. The *16. Armee*, fighting at Newel and without contact to the south, had to bend and extend itself to the west.

As if that were not enough, the 2nd Baltic Army opened its major offensive on 11 July against the southern wing of the *18. Armee* south of Pleskau. The *18. Armee* had to give up the *"Panther"* Position and fall back on the

"Marienburg" Position along the Pleskau — Jakobstadt railroad line.

On 24 July the 3rd Baltic Army launched its blow against *Armee-Abteilung Narwa* with 20 divisions. With that, the entire northern front was ablaze.

In view of the situation, *Armee-Abteilung Narwa* prepared to evacuate the city and Hungerburg and to fall back to the significantly shorter *"Tannenberg"* Position about 20 kilometers west of Narwa and go over to the defense.

At the regimental command posts and in the command post of the *11. SS-Freiwilligen-Panzer-Grenadier-Division "Nordland"*, some of whose battalions had moved to the Repiknu forest camp, the quiet staff work began.

The work of the staff signals officer should be mentioned here. It was he who was responsible for the complicated signals network. Radio and telephone links needed to be thought out and established, for they were the nerve fibers of the division. Without them, plans and execution, brain and hand could not be coordinated. A glance at the signal officer's map revealed a bewildering array of strokes, codenames and zigzag lightning flashes that marked the locations of the radio positions. Only the specialist could make sense of that. But that apparent chaos of strokes, lines, codenames and lightning strokes testified to the careful thinking of the signals officer and represented the practical functioning of an indispensable instrument of command for the commander and staffs of the fighting elements.

The enemy continually tested the positions in the bridgehead, but always ran into determined opposition. All non-essential trains elements started being sent back to the Kothla — Järwe area on 19 July.

On 23 July the pullback orders for the units in the bridgehead arrived. They established how the withdrawal would work. Those orders would be set in motion at H-Hour.

However, the Soviet attack had already begun in the sector of the East-Prussian *11. Infanterie-Division* on 24 July. It employed strong infantry units that fought to clear lanes for the later advance of armor. At the same time, the Soviets were able to gain a foothold on the west bank of the Narwa in the Riigi — Hungerburg area after expending a great deal of men and equipment. The intention was obviously to envelop the forces of the *III. (germanisches) SS-Panzer-Korps* that were in the Narwa defenses and destroy them in a pincers movement. While the *11. Infanterie-Division* warded off all attacks, the *20. Waffen-Grenadier-Division der SS (estnisch)* was unable to reduce the bridgehead on the lower course of the Narwa.

In the meantime, work was going on at full speed on the *"Tannenberg"* Position. Combat engineers, *SS-Bewährungskompanie 103* (penal company) and naval units helped finish the work.

In the midst of its reorganization, *SS-Panzergrenadier-Bataillon*

"Langemarck" was assembled and set in march from Beneschau to Narwa. On 24 July that battalion arrived in Toila, disembarked and occupied the *Kinderheimhöhe*. The battalion was commanded by *SS-Hauptsturmführer* Rehmann and formed from the remnants of *SS-Sturmbrigade "Langemarck"*.

On 24 July at 2330 hours, H-Hour was executed. First, the Narwa bridgehead was evacuated. *SS-Panzer-Grenadier-Regiment 24 "Danmark"*, minus the *7./SS-Panzer-Grenadier-Regiment 24 "Danmark"*, and the *I./SS-Freiwilligen-Panzer-Grenadier-Regiment 49 "de Ruyter"* crossed the bridges and headed back to the west. *SS-Freiwilligen-Panzer-Grenadier-Regiment 48 "General Seyffard"* and the *7./SS-Panzer-Grenadier-Regiment 24 "Danmark"* also crossed the bridges, but remained on the west bank in the city of Narwa another 24 hours as rear guard.

The withdrawal plan established four intermediate positions before reaching the new main line of resistance. The four positions would be occupied in leapfrog fashion and then evacuated. The first intermediate position (A) was at Vanaküla and in the Riverbank Woods at the workers' houses across from the notorious "Snake Woods". Those blocking positions were about six kilometers west of Narwa. Blocking position B was at Puhkova, Suur-Soldino (echeloned forward somewhat to the east) and at Samokras. The C positions were at Walge, east of the Repikno settlement, along the railroad embankment south of Repikno and directly east of Auwere. Intermediate position D was at Udria, Auwere railroad station and 2 kilometers west of Lipsu. The plan was very precise. Would it be possible to follow it?

The war diary of *Heeresgruppe Nord* has the following entry under 26 July 1944: "2230 hours: Narwa and the Narwa bend evacuated. *"Tannenberg"* Position occupied: the *11. SS-Freiwilligen-Panzer-Grenadier-Division 'Nordland'* on the right, *4. SS-Panzer-Grenadier-Brigade 'Nederland'* on the left."

The Soviet official general staff work reported under 26 July 1944: "Marshal Goworow occupied Narwa."

And, in a general situation report for 26 July 1944, it merely stated that the enemy sharply pursued the withdrawal movement of *Armee-Abteilung Narwa*.

What, however, was hidden behind those brief sentences? How did it look to the combat elements?

The bridgehead was given up at midnight on 25 July 1944. The companies reached the west bank of the river by way of the Kreenholm, railroad and main bridges. The withdrawal took place unnoticed by the enemy. At 0200 hours, the suspension, Kreenholm, railroad and main bridges went up in the air. At that point the enemy woke up and followed in pursuit. For a long time, timbers, chunks of iron and clods of earth rained down in the water and on the adjoining riverbank area. One bridge, however, remained standing. Both fuses had failed!

SS-Hauptsturmführer Wanhöfer, commander of *SS-Pionier-Bataillon 54*, stood at that bridge. "Damn! The bridge is not covered. Fast-moving enemy advance-guard units can take it with no problem!"

It would have taken too long to search for the damaged places in the fuses. Wanhöfer shouted to his driver: "Drive to Petri Square immediately! Load up with explosives, as much as you can, and come back by the quickest route!"

While the *VW-Kübelwagen* dashed off, a squad of combat engineers established security. Anxious minutes crept by. The mortar fire that had been covering the bridge suddenly stopped. Were the Soviets there?

A flare hissed up into the air. A German machine gun ripped off a burst. Finally the vehicle returned.

Combat engineers dragged mines and crates of explosives onto the bridge. They paid no attention to the fire directed at them. Other soldiers provided covering fire. In a few moments the hasty charge was ready.

A quick dash behind a protecting wall. Then the bridge went up in the air. The enemy was faced with a river without a bridge. On the east side, in the old German positions, the Russians found undestroyed bunkers and trenches — and large quantities of propaganda material (psychological warfare material) — that had been skillfully prepared by *SS-Standarte "Kurt Egger"*.

On 25 July, a hail of fire of all calibers renewed on an extremely narrow area of the Estonian positions facing the Soviet bridgehead. It pulverized them completely. Once again, counterattacks were able to hold the enemy within bounds, but for how long?

SS-Freiwilligen-Panzer-Grenadier-Regiment 48 "General Seyffard", the *II./SS-Freiwilligen-Panzer-Grenadier-Regiment 49 "de Ruyter"* and the *7./SS-Panzer-Grenadier-Regiment 24 "Danmark"* were still in Narwa. The artillery forward observers were also at the front. New firing positions had been established farther to the west.

By the morning of 25 July an unbroken stream of heavy bombers flew over the city from the east. The last ruins crumbled under the Soviet bombs. Soviet artillery batteries then took over the final work of destruction.

The diary of the forward observer of the *4./SS-Artillerie-Regiment 54* noted for 25 July:

0600 hours: Heavy barrage on Narwa and the main supply route. Aerial attacks came in waves. Observation position in the tower of the cotton mill in the southern part of Narwa. I directed the battery in shelling mortars that were going into position. Over there (on the east side of the Narwa River) it teemed with Russians. Visibility was very limited due to the large number of burning houses. The cotton mill was also burning. At 1700 hours the order arrived: Everyone must be past grid line 61 by 1800 hours. The Russians have formed a bridgehead north of us and would cut the main supply route by then.

What do the brief sentences in the war diary reveal?

Once again General Goworow had massed a major portion of his forces at Hungerburg and Riigi — this time achieving success! The dam was broken. The courageous Estonians fell back under the immense pressure. The Soviets poured into Estonia. Small Soviet infiltration squads were already firing on the main supply route.

Early that afternoon, *SS-Hauptsturmführer* Wanhöfer and his remaining combat engineers raced westward on the main supply route in three vehicles. After three kilometers they encountered the first outposts, lying in the roadside ditch and facing north. The solders barely raised their heads. One of them yelled: "Keep moving, fast! The first Russians are 500 meters in front of us!"

Little fountains of dust leaped up in front of the vehicles. While everyone else ducked their heads as low as they could, the drivers hunched down behind their steering wheels like cats.

With an immense expenditure of artillery and unending waves of aerial attacks, the Soviets attempted to tear open the blocking positions in the south on that same 25 July. The two Estonian companies of *Kampfgruppe Kausch* were pushed back on the Lipsus Road. By noon, Kausch's command post was encircled. Kausch kept his nerve and ordered countermeasures over the functioning radio. At the same time, the command post and the *1.* and *2./SS-Pionier-Bataillon 11*, acting as infantry in *Kampfgruppe Kausch*, mounted an immediate counterattack toward the south. After heavy fighting, the old main line of resistance was regained and held until *Kampfgruppe Kausch* completed its withdrawal. An hour later, *SS-Obersturmführer* Gärdtner, who was the acting commander of the *2./SS-Pionier-Bataillon 11*, was killed by a fragment from an antitank gun round.

During that same period of time, the division staff in the Repiknu forest camp (codename: *Wartburg*) was in the process of evacuating. Low flying aircraft attacked repeatedly. The fighting positions were quickly reoccupied. The move finally got going at about 1100 hours. The staff moved through Auwere to Saksamas (1 kilometer west of the Waiwara railroad station) where the new command post for the *11. SS-Freiwilligen-Panzer-Grenadier-Division "Nordland"* was established.

The Russians were also attacking with strong forces in the southern sector and pushed hard against the units that were pulling out. *SS-Panzer-Grenadier-Regiment 24 "Danmark"* reached the *"Tannenberg"* Position along the railroad line. The *7./SS-Panzer-Grenadier-Regiment 24 "Danmark"*, serving as rear guard, followed the regiment during the evening hours of 25 July without having any enemy contact. *SS-Hauptsturmführer* Trautwein's *11./SS-Panzer-Grenadier-Regiment 24 "Danmark"*, which was the strongest company of the regiment at the time, was staged at the division command post in the Repiknu forest camp as the divisional reserve. As a precaution, it occupied a portion of the positions of *SS-Panzer-Grenadier-Regiment 23 "Norge"*, since that regiment was having difficulties in its withdrawal due to a premature bridge demolition.

As did *SS-Panzer-Grenadier-Regiment 24 "Danmark"*, *SS-Panzer-Grenadier-Regiment 23 "Norge"* was withdrawing along the railroad line. Combat engineers performed demolitions at suitable sites along the stretch. The *5./SS-Panzer-Grenadier-Regiment 23 "Norge"* covered the work of the engineers in leapfrog fashion, reaching "Line D" at Auwere, where *Kampfgruppe Kausch* also arrived.

What was happening with the rear guard at Narwa?

On 25 July, at about 1700 hours, the order arrived: "By 1800 hours, all units must have crossed grid line 61 (Hungerburg — Soldino) toward the west." *SS-Untersturmführer* Madsen's *7./SS-Panzer-Grenadier-Regiment 24 "Danmark"* made it back to the railroad line without enemy contact. For the *II./SS-Freiwilligen-Panzer-Grenadier-Regiment 49 "de Ruyter"* and *SS-Freiwilligen-Panzer-Grenadier-Regiment 48 "General Seyffard"*, however, the retreat route — the main supply route — was already barred. The blocking positions at Vanaküla (A) were already in Russian hands.

SS-Freiwilligen-Panzer-Grenadier-Regiment 48 "General Seyffard" fought its last fight during this withdrawal operation. There is a report of the events by the *4. SS-Panzer-Grenadier-Brigade "Nederland"* in the German Federal Archives in Freiburg from which one can reconstruct the individual phases that follow.

In addition to the regimental formations, the following units were attached to the regiment: the *7./SS-Panzer-Grenadier-Regiment 24 "Danmark"*, the *II./SS-Freiwilligen-Panzer-Grenadier-Regiment 49 "de Ruyter"*, *Bataillon Rebane* of the *20. Waffen-Grenadier-Division der SS (estnisch)*, the penal platoon of the *4. SS-Panzer-Grenadier-Brigade "Nederland"* and *SS-Panzer-Jäger-Abteilung 54* (minus one battery).

The withdrawal had been planned in phases, in each of which a new intermediate position would be occupied and held according to a time schedule. The left-hand neighbor of the regiment proper was *Bataillon Rebane*, the right-hand neighbor, the *II./SS-Panzer-Grenadier-Regiment 23 "Norge"*. The latter battalion was covering to the south at the workers' housing.

In addition to the precarious position of having to conduct a time-phased withdrawal under enemy pressure, *SS-Obersturmbannführer* Benner, the regi-

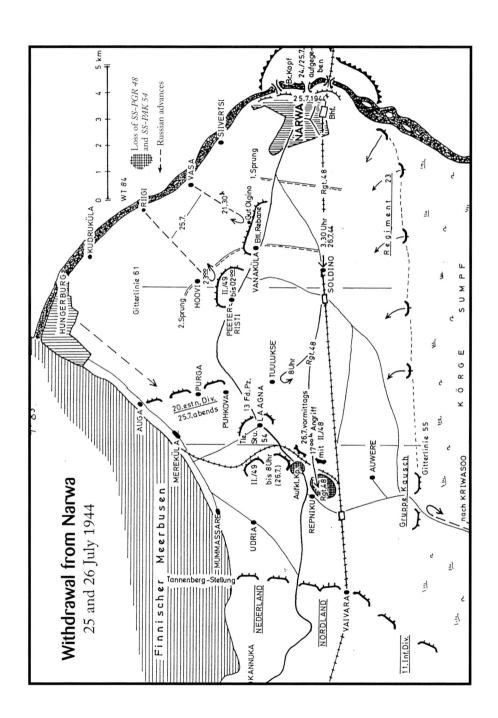

Withdrawal from Narwa
25 and 26 July 1944

mental commander, had only taken over command of *SS-Freiwilligen-Panzer-Grenadier-Regiment 48 "General Seyffard"* from *SS-Obersturmbannführer* Joerchel two days previously. Benner had come from the *11. SS-Freiwilligen-Panzer-Grenadier-Division "Nordland"* and was, therefore, not fully familiar with the situation. The same unpromising situation held true in regard to coordination with subordinate and superior commands.

SS-Freiwilligen-Panzer-Grenadier-Regiment 48 "General Seyffard" was directed to coordinate with *SS-Artillerie- Regiment 54 (SS-Sturmbannführer* Schlüter). *SS-Nachrichten-Kompanie 54* maintained wire and radio communications. However, wire contact was totally lost after 1700 hours due to constant incoming artillery fire.

Benner's greatest concern was getting out the artillery and heavy infantry weapons that were still in firing positions in the Narwa area. He had been given the choice of using the Narwa — Reval main supply route or the railroad route or both.

As evening approached on 25 July, Benner received orders by radio from the *4. SS-Panzer-Grenadier-Brigade "Nederland"* for the withdrawal to the "Tannenberg Position". The time for H-Hour (exact start of withdrawal movement) could not yet be determined since *SS-Artillerie-Regiment 54* had just started changing positions, and it could not yet be determined when that movement would be completed.

The commander of *SS-Artillerie- Regiment 54 "Nederland"*, *SS-Sturmbannführer* Schlüter, received a separate order, however. It stated that by 1800 hours all guns had to be withdrawn to the west past gridline 61. The change of position for the *9./SS-Artillerie-Regiment 54* was delayed until about 2100 hours because of the lack of prime movers. Batteries that had already occupied the intermediate position and were directed by three forward observers supported *SS-Freiwilligen-Panzer-Grenadier-Regiment 48 "General Seyffard"* to the end.

At 2000 hours, *SS-Obersturmbannführer* Benner called the commanders of the *I.* and *II./SS-Freiwilligen-Panzer-Grenadier-Regiment 48 "General Seyffard"* (*SS-Sturmbannführer* Betzweiser and Breymann), the *II./SS-Freiwilligen-Panzer-Grenadier-Regiment 49 "de Ruyter"* (*SS-Hauptsturmführer* Frühauf) and *SS-Artillerie-Regiment 54* (*SS-Sturmbannführer* Schlüter) as well as *SS-Utersturmführer* Römmelt, platoon leader of the *1./SS-Panzer-Jäger-Abteilung 54*, to his command post in Narwa.

They discussed the withdrawal to the "Tannenberg Position". At 2110 hours the senior special-staff officer of the brigade, *SS-Untersturmführer* Steinfeld, brought the written withdrawal order. At 2130 hours the adjutant of a regiment of the *20. Waffen-Grenadier-Division der SS (estnisch)* came and reported that the Russians had reached the main supply route at the estate at Olgino. At that point, *SS-Haupsturmführer* Frühauf was ordered to secure or clear the highway with support from Römmelt's two assault guns. *Bataillon*

Rebane, which was at Olgino, was to take part in that operation.

SS-Hauptsturmführer Frühauf and his *II./SS-Freiwilligen-Panzer-Grenadier-Regiment 49 "de Ruyter"* moved west on the road in combat order. His battalion made contact with elements of the Estonian *Bataillon Rebane* at Vanaküla. At 2130 hours, in a nighttime counterattack, the Soviets were thrown back to the north at the Olgino estate. They were just shy of the main supply route. Römmelt's two *Sturmgeschütze* had supported the counterattack. *Bataillon Rebane* secured the area while Frühauf and his battalion moved on.

Around 2300 hours, Soviet forces had reached the main supply route at Peeterristi. They were forced back by *Bataillon Frühauf* and the main supply route was secured in that area.

At 2150 hours *SS-Obersturmbannführer* Benner received a radio message from the brigade (transmitted at 2105 hours) that H-hour had been set at 2200 hours. In the meantime, a radio message had already arrived advancing the time to 2315 hours for the second movement back and 2400 hours for the third bound. The reason for advancing the times was the rapid advance of the Soviets against the *20. Waffen-Grenadier-Division der SS (estnisch)*.

The question of whether the bounds to the rear could be kept according to the schedule was overcome by events. *SS-Obersturmbannführer* Benner replied to the messages that he could not pull out his infantry and antitank guns at the directed H-Hour. It is not possible to determine exactly what orders Benner issued from the report in the Federal Archives in Freiburg.

A withdrawal order to *Bataillon Rebane* through a liaison officer of *SS-Freiwilligen-Panzer-Grenadier-Regiment 48 "General Seyffard"* makes evident that the time for the withdrawal and the individual bounds was postponed again. The order was later paraphrased by Rabane and his adjutant:

The withdrawal is to begin with the *II./SS-Panzergrenadier-Regiment 47* (Rebane) on the left and the *II./SS-Freiwilligen-Panzer-Grenadier-Regiment 48 "General Seyffard"* (Breymann) on the right. Southern boundary: Hill Taravälja (1 kilometer north of Soldino). H-hour: 2300 hours, at 2330 hours everything moves. Second bound at 0030 hours at the line Hoovi — Vanaküla — Soldino. Third bound 0130 hours individually to Kannakula. Detailed instructions from *SS-Hauptsturmführer* Frühauf.

At 2300 hours Rebane learned from the adjutant of *SS-Freiwilligen-Panzer-Grenadier-Regiment 48 "General Seyffard"* and *SS-Hauptsturmführer* Frühauf that H-hour had been postponed to 2330 hours which is probably what happened.

For *SS-Obersturmbannführer* Benner and his two battalion commanders the question remained open whether the main supply route was still usable at the Olgino estate and Peeterristi or whether the Russians had blocked it. They decided to only use the railway line. There was no way that they could have known that, in fact, the main supply route was open between 2200 and

0200 hours. During that time period individual vehicles had moved across that stretch of road, though under heavy fire. Whether Benner knew that remains unknown.

SS-Hauptsturmführer Frühauf, who had secured the main supply route with his *II./SS-Freiwilligen-Panzer-Grenadier-Regiment 49 "de Ruyter"* at Peeterristi, received orders from *SS-Freiwilligen-Panzer-Grenadier-Regiment 48 "General Seyffard"* to fall back to the west at 0100 hours. He waited to execute the order until the last Estonian unit passed through at 0200 hours. There was no radio traffic at the time. Frühauf and Rebane must have correctly presumed that *SS-Freiwilligen-Panzer-Grenadier-Regiment 48 "General Seyffard"* had chosen to withdraw along the railroad line.

Anyone who has taken part in a retreat knows that, after the start of the withdrawal movement, each battalion, indeed, each company, is more or less on its own. It has to adhere to the orders that were given and radio contact breaks down. The companies, for the most part, did not even have small radio sets, let alone the large, long-range sets. The *4. SS-Panzer-Grenadier-Brigade "Nederland"* had given *SS-Freiwilligen-Panzer-Grenadier-Regiment 48 "General Seyffard"* the choice of using the railroad line or the main Narwa — Reval supply route or both. The most obvious choice would have been to use the main supply route with its considerably better condition. Benner chose the railroad line because he believed the main route was blocked. That was the great tragedy.

Accordingly, all of *SS-Freiwilligen-Panzer-Grenadier-Regiment 48 "General Seyffard"* assembled at the Narwa/Kreenholm railroad station after H-Hour had been announced and moved out along the railroad line as far as Soldino, where the first elements arrived at about 0330 hours on 26 July. By the time the last elements of the regiment arrived it was 0500 hours.

According to statements made later by soldiers of the regiment who made their way back to German lines, *SS-Obersturmbannführer* Benner learned at the Soldino rest area that Russian forces were already on the railroad and had blocked the main supply route at Peeterristi with strong forces. Benner resolved to attack at Peeterristi because he suspected that German forces were still in that area. In addition, it seemed to him that it would be too risky to initiate fighting in the matted, marshy woodlands along the railroad. However, he changed his decision after a route had been scouted from Soldino to Laagna. In fact, elements of *SS-Panzerjäger-Abteilung 54* with assault guns and *Bataillon Frühauf* were still in that area at 0800 hours waiting for the regiment, although the pressure from the enemy was steadily increasing.

At 0530 hours the regiment moved out from Soldino toward Laagna. The trail in the woods eventually led into a marshy area where the heavy vehicles soon bogged down. It was no longer possible to turn back. Trees were felled and a corduroy road constructed. That took precious time.

At that time the security positions of *SS-Panzer-Grenadier-Regiment 23* *"Norge"* at the Körge Marsh and of *Kampfgruppe Kausch* at Auwere were already being evacuated, as planned. There, too, the Soviets followed close on the heels of the withdrawing forces.

SS-Freiwilligen-Panzer-Grenadier-Regiment 48 "General Seyffard" was seriously restricted in its movements. It was under continuous attack by Soviet ground-attack aircraft, as well as constant artillery fire that was directed from an observation balloon in the Körge Marsh.

As was later determined, the Russians soon had a bridge back in service at Narwa and pushed forward along the main supply route and in the sector toward the coast with strong forces supported by numerous tanks. The *III. (germanisches) SS-Panzer-Korps* was thus placed in a dangerous situation while it was in the process of moving. There was a real possibility that the Soviets would occupy the Tannenberg Position as their own before the Germans got there. At the same time that the schedule fell apart on 26 July due to the considerably delayed movement of *SS-Freiwilligen-Panzer-Grenadier-Regiment 48 "General Seyffard"* and the blocking positions that had been set up to receive it, only the first few positions were occupied in the Tannenberg Position. The Tannenberg Position was only about eight kilometers wide and was bounded on the north by the Gulf of Finland and on the south by the marshy woods. In the center were the commanding heights of the Blue Hills.

On 26 July, at about 0800 hours, the lead battalion of the regiment, the *I./SS-Freiwilligen-Panzer-Grenadier-Regiment 48 "General Seyffard"*, finally reached the area south of Tuulukse. At that same time, *Bataillon Frühauf* was forced to fall back from the area west of Laagna under strong enemy pressure. When the *I./SS-Freiwilligen-Panzer-Grenadier-Regiment 48 "General Seyffard"* emerged from the woods and tried to attack Tuulukse, it was met with heavy fire from about 300 Red Army soldiers. Thirteen Soviet tanks, which also opened fire, were confirmed at Laagna. The heavy infantry and antitank guns of the regiment went into position at the edge of the woods and engaged the enemy forces at Laagna until the guns had expended all their ammunition. In the course of that action, four Soviet tanks were knocked out.

An advance by assault guns of the *4. SS-Panzer-Grenadier-Brigade "Nederland"* to enable a passage of lines by *SS-Freiwilligen-Panzer-Grenadier-Regiment 48 "General Seyffard"* at Laagna was thwarted by Russian armor. During that engagement, *SS-Rottenführer* Bruins knocked out eight Soviet tanks with his assault gun. Two *Sturmgeschütze* and acting battery commanders von den Kuyl and Pempelt were lost. Around 0800 hours the *II./SS-Freiwilligen-Panzer-Grenadier-Regiment 49 "de Ruyter"* also had to evacuate its blocking position between Laagna and Repniku — along the railroad at the Auwere railroad station — Mereküla under intense enemy pressure. *SS-Obersturmführer* Kuhne's *SS-Panzer-Aufklärungs-Kompanie 54*, which was meant to remain until 0900 hours as rearguard, was encircled in a farmstead at Repniku and wiped out.

There at Repniku, within a few kilometers of the lifesaving German passage position, the fate of *SS-Freiwilligen-Panzer-Grenadier-Regiment 48 "General Seyffard"* was sealed. After all of the ammunition for the heavy weapons had been expended at about 0900 hours, *SS-Obersturmbannführer* Benner ordered that the heavy weapons and vehicles be blown up. At 0907 hours the regiment made its final radio transmission to *the 4. SS-Panzer-Grenadier-Brigade "Nederland"*: "We are fighting our way through the forest south of Laagna to the west."

Presumably because of the unfavorable terrain conditions, radio communications was intermittent. At 1003 hours the brigade queried the regiment yet again by radio: "Where are you? There are still German forces in Repniku, but also Russian forces. Do not go off the air without letting us know."

The regiment received that radio transmission and then blew up its two remaining radio vehicles. Based on that transmission, *SS-Obersturmbannführer* Benner decided to push through to Repniku. Before the regiment had regrouped and changed its direction of march, the situation on the main supply route had changed again. The Soviet spearhead was already at the *Kinderheimhöhe*. The German lines east of the hill hadn't even been occupied by that point. The Soviets had already brought up artillery that had opened heavy fire on the German forces that were falling back on the Blue Hills. Russian ground-assault aircraft provided support.

The *11./SS-Panzer-Grenadier-Regiment 24 "Danmark"* was relieved by the *III./SS-Panzer-Grenadier-Regiment 23 "Norge"* during the midday hours in the position south of the railroad line and was moved forward west of the hill massif onto the main supply route and toward the east. *SS-Hauptsturmführer* Trautwein and his *11./SS-Panzer-Grenadier-Regiment 24 "Danmark"* threw back the Soviets who had penetrated and occupied the main line of resistance east of the *Kinderheimhöhe*. Trautwein's company, along with elements of the *20. Waffen-Grenadier-Division der SS (estnisch)* and remnants of the naval battalion, were thus at the most exposed position of the front and held it for the time being. To the north, there was contact with the *II./SS-Freiwilligen-Panzer-Grenadier-Regiment 49 "de Ruyter"*, which had already occupied the main line of resistance. To the south, there was still no contact with the *10./SS-Panzer-Grenadier-Regiment 24 "Danmark"*.

Soviet artillery fire increased against the hill massif on the afternoon of 26 July. *Kampfgruppe Rehmann* (from *SS-Freiwilligen-Sturmbrigade "Langemarck"*) had already been hard hit. *SS-Hauptsturmführer* Rehmann, *SS-Untersturmführer* Swinnen, and the battalion adjutant were wounded. A little later, the company commanders of the *1.* and *2./Kampfgruppe Rehmann*, *SS-Untersturmführer* van Bockel and *SS-Untersturmführer* van Moll, were killed. The battalion adjutant, *SS-Untersturmführer* van Leemputten, died of his wounds on 17 August. As a result, *Kampfgruppe Rehmann* was nearly bereft of leaders at the beginning of the fighting. *SS-Untersturmführer* D'Haese assumed command of the *Kampfgruppe*, which had been severely decimated by artillery and aerial attack.

At that time *SS-Freiwilligen-Panzer-Grenadier-Regiment 48 "General Seyffard"* was five kilometers to the east. It had changed its direction of march from Tuulukes and turned to the south, then again west toward Repniku. After an arduous, slow march through marshy woods, it had reached the wood line at gridline 55. Reconnaissance revealed enemy positions at the north-south railroad embankment that was one kilometer farther west.

SS-Obersturmbannführer Benner discussed the plan of attack with Betzwieser and Breymann. The *II./SS-Freiwilligen-Panzer-Grenadier-Regiment 48 "General Seyffard"* was to be in the lead. Its mission was to break through the Soviet positions and then secure to the sides to enable the remainder of the regiment to pass through. It was a reasonable decision, but hours had gone by since the last radio message from the brigade and there were no longer any German forces at Repniku.

The attack began at 1730 hours. Within a few minutes, *SS-Obersturmbannführer* Benner was killed at the head of his troops. Confusion set in. Nevertheless, large parts of the regiment made it through under heavy enemy fire from the railroad embankment. Smaller elements fell back into the jump-off positions at the edge of the woods. Those who broke through suffered substantial losses due to fire from three sides. Cohesion was lost. The isolated groups were scattered or wiped out. The fight to the death of the regiment was over by 1800 hours. Individual groups sought to reach the German lines on their own. Those who were not captured hid in the brush- and marshland between the railroad and the road between the Auwere railroad station and Repniku until it was dark.

Only a few individuals were able to make it to the German lines, among them the Dutch *SS-Untersturmführer* Nieuwendijk-Hoek, who confirmed that Benner had been killed. The statements of the soldiers who made their way back to German lines, though sometimes contradictory, made possible the dramatic reconstruction of the end of *SS-Freiwilligen-Panzergrenadier-Regiment 48 "General Seyffard"* with its two battalions and regimental units. Particularly dramatic was the fact that the units manning passage positions and the regiment missed each other by no more that a few hours and a few kilometers.

In its closing summary, the report on the loss of *SS-Freiwilligen-Panzergrenadier-Regiment 48 "General Seyffard"* on 26 July 1944, stated:

> The fight by *SS-Freiwilligen-Panzer-Grenadier-Regiment 48 "General Seyffard"* made possible the withdrawal of all of the brigade artillery and elements of the artillery of the division adjoining on the right (*11. SS-Freiwilligen-Panzer-Grenadier-Division "Nordland"*). The artillery had been substantially endangered by the situation of the division adjoining on the left (*20. Waffen-Grenadier-Division der SS (estnisch)*).

In addition, strong enemy forces were pinned by the regiment and the enemy suffered considerable losses. That the "Tannenberg Position" could be held in the ensuing heavy fighting was the result of the heroic battle of *SS-Freiwilligen-Panzer-Grenadier-Regiment 48 "General Seyffard"*.

Little is known of the individual fates of the officers, noncommissioned officers and enlisted personnel.

According to reports by German radio surveillance units, a Soviet artillery unit took twelve Germans captive on 26 July at 0820 hours at the Auwere railroad station. Another unit reported the capture of four men of *SS-Freiwilligen-Panzer-Grenadier-Regiment 48 "General Seyffard"* after a fight that same day. It was evident from the radio traffic of the Soviet 2nd Guards Engineer Brigade at noon on 28 July that fighting was still in progress behind its positions and that support was required at one place.

On 30 July 1944 another unit captured four members of *SS-Panzer-Aufklärungs-Kompanie 54* and *SS-Pionier-Bataillon 54* who had wandered around in the woods since 27 July. Bad news is seldom revealed in its totality by any military command in war. Thus the cloak of silence was spread over the fate of *SS-Freiwilligen-Panzer-Grenadier-Regiment 48 "General Seyffard"* in the following **secret** message of 25 August 1944:

The *Reichsführer* has ordered that in the publicity regarding the heroic fight of *SS-Freiwilligen-Panzergrenadier-Regiment 48 "General Seyffard"*, considering the fact that elements of the regiment still exist, it will only be stated that a *Kampfgruppe* of the regiment sacrificed itself in heroic battle to the end.

Right: *SS-Hauptsturmführer* Frühauf, the commander of the *II./SS-Freiwilligen-Panzer-Grenadier-Regiment 49 "de Ruyter".*

Above: The bridgehead at Narwa with a view of Iwangorod. In the foreground on the right was the command post of the *4. SS-Panzer-Grenadier-Brigade "Nederland"*.

Right: *SS-Sturmbannführer* Kausch and *General der Waffen-SS* Kleinheisterkamp.

Below right: *SS-Obersturmführer* Meißner, the headquarters commander of the *11. SS-Freiwilligen-Panzer-Grenadier-Division "Nordland"*. He was killed in action at Wuwere in March 1944.

Top: *SS-Untersturmführer* Schneider, a Norwegian, and *SS-Oberscharführer* Abel outside of Iwangorod.

Above: The bivouac area in the woods at Mummassare in the spring of 1944. The Knight's Cross has been awarded to *SS-Sturmbannführer* Krügel, the commander of *SS-Panzer-Grenadier-Regiment 24 "Danmark"*, *SS-Sturmbannführer* Saalback, the commander of *SS-Panzer-Aufklärungs-Abteilung 11* and *SS-Untersturmführer* Langendorf, the commander of the *4./SS-Panzer-Aufklärungs-Abteilung 11.*

Above: The headquarters company of *SS-Panzer-Aufklärungs-Abteilung 11* at Mummassare in Estonia.

Middle right: April 1944. A social get-together in the rest and relaxation facility of *SS-Panzer-Grenadier-Regiment 24 "Danmark".* It was 400 meters behind the front lines in Narwa. The regimental physician, *SS-Sturmbannführer Dr.* Schlegel, and *SS-Hauptsturmführer* Broberg can be seen.

Right: Men of the divisional switchboard for the *11. SS-Freiwilligen-Panzer-Grenadier-Division "Nordland"* at Narwa in the spring of 1944.

Winter 1943/1944: Unit trains at Kothla-Järwe.

Narwa in the spring of 1944. Officers of the *4. SS-Panzer-Grenadier-Brigade "Nederland"*, from left to right: *SS-Hauptsturmführer* Hofer, the commander of the *II./SS-Artillerie-Regiment 54*; *SS-Hauptsturmführer* Frühauf, the commander of the *II./SS-Freiwilligen-Panzer-Grenadier-Regiment 49 "de Ruyter"*; *SS-Sturmbannführer* Wiemssen, the operations officer of the brigade; *SS-Brigadeführer und General der Waffen-SS* Jürgen Wagner, the brigade commander; *SS-Hauptstrumführer* Steenholt-Schütt, the brigade adjutant; *SS-Hauptsturmführer* Meyer, the commander of the *I./SS-Freiwilligen-Panzer-Grenadier-Regiment 49 "de Ruyter"*; *SS-Obersturmbannführer* Collani, the commander of *SS-Freiwilligen-Panzer-Grenadier-Regiment 49 "de Ruyter"*; *SS-Hauptsturmführer* Schlüter, the commander of the *I./SS-Artillerie-Regiment 54*; and, *SS-Hauptstrumführer* Wanhöfer, the commander of *SS-Pionier-Bataillon 54*.

Above: The spring of 1944. Assault guns formed the immediate ready-reserve in Narwa.

Left: Fighting at Narwa — a break in the action.

Right: 8.8 cm *Flak* of *SS-Flak-Abteilung 11* at Narwa.

SS-Brigadeführer Fritz von Scholz at the award ceremony for the award of the Knight's Cross to *SS-Hauptsturmführer* Hämel.

SS-Panzer-Aufklärungs-Abteilung 11 in January 1944. From the left: *SS-Untersturmführer* Eriksen (Adjutant), *SS-Hauptsturmführer* Saalbach (Battalion Commander), *SS-Obersturmführer* Lorenz (commander of the *1./SS-Panzer-Aufklärungs-Abteilung 11)* and *SS-Obersturmführer* Persson (commander of the *3./SS-Panzer-Aufklärungs-Abteilung 11*).

A knocked-out *Panther* at the Narwa bridgehead.

The main dressing station at Narwa.

The Narwa City Hall after the Soviet aerial bombardment.

A position along the Narwa between Hungerburg and Riigi.

Kreenholm

The Narwa Position. Dead Soviet soldiers on the ice in front of the position.

Dead soldier of a Soviet patrol on the ice of the Narwa at Riigi. In the foreground is a dead German soldier from the *11. SS-Freiwilligen-Panzer-Grenadier-Division "Nordland"*.

The Tannenberg Position. *Sturmgeschütze* with mounted infantry on the march.

A *Panther* of the *SS-Panzer–Abteilung 11 "Hermann von Salza"*.

Combatants at Narwa.

Positions in the Narwa bridgehead in 1944.

Officers of *SS-Artillerie-Regiment 11* in Narwa. From left to right: Karl, Knötzinger, Grabenhorst, Kuhnke, von Matt and Töper.

Top right: April 1944 in Narwa. From left to right: *SS-Sturmbannführer* Otto Vollmer, quartermaster of the *11. SS-Freiwilligen-Panzer-Grenadier-Division "Nordland"*; *SS-Sturmbannführer Dr.* Schlegel, the regimental surgeon of *SS-Panzer-Grenadier-Regiment 24 "Danmark"*; *SS-Sturmmann* Sandström; *SS-Sturmbannführer* Alfred Fischer (in front), the commander of the *II./SS-Artillerie-Regiment 11*; *SS-Sturmbannführer Dr.* Hans Siebert, the regimental surgeon of *SS-Artillerie-Regiment 11*.

Middle right: From the left: *SS-Sturmbannführer* Riipalu of the *20. Waffen-Grenadier-Division der SS (estnisch)*; *SS-Brigadeführer* Ziegler, the commander of the *11. SS-Freiwilligen-Panzer-Grena-dier-Division "Nordland"* (killed in action on 2 May 1945); and *SS-Oberstrum-bannführer* Kausch, the commander of *SS-Panzer-Abteil-ung 11 "Hermann von Salza"*.

Below: Platoon leader and Knight's Cross recipient *SS-Oberscharführer* Will with the company commander of the *1./SS-Panzer-Abteilung 11 "Hermann von Salza"*, *SS-Oberstrumführer* Rott.

Panther of *SS-Panzer-Abteilung 11 "Hermann von Salza"*.

The maintenance section of *SS-Panzer-Abteilung 11 "Hermann von Salza"* works on the running gear of a *Panther*.

The "Tannenberg" Position

The "Tannenberg" Position started in the north at the Gulf of Finland, ran for about three kilometers through flat terrain and cut the Narwa — Reval road. At that point, the Blue Hills formed the nucleus of the defense. The Blue Hills consisted of three large hills that commanded the surrounding landscape far and wide: The *Kinderheimhöhe*, Grenadier Hill and Hill 69.9, along whose slopes the road ran. From there the "Tannenberg" Position proceeded farther south, cutting between the railroad stations at Auwere and Waiwere on the Narwa — Reval railroad line. It then bent to the southwest.

The northern section of the "Tannenberg" Position was on flat land. The hills commanded the coastal strip. In the troubled history of Estonia, it had held great significance as the gateway to the country since ancient times. Peter the Great once had his command post in the collapsed positions of Hill 69.9. In more recent times, the *61.* and *11. Infanterie-Divisionen*, as well as *Graf Strachwitz*, had located their command bunkers in the hill. On the west slope of Hill 69.9, *SS-Panzer-Grenadier-Regiment 24 "Danmark"* and *SS-Freiwilligen-Panzer-Grenadier-Regiment 49 "de Ruyter"* now had their command posts there. *SS-Panzer-Grenadier-Regiment 23 "Norge"* held the southern front. An endless lowland with impenetrable primeval forest stretched in front of the positions. The forest could only be traversed at a few places. In those locations Russian supply lanes were named for birds and places, lanes that would play a roll in later fighting. That was the area of operations for the "Tannenberg" Position.

The *4. SS-Panzer-Grenadier-Brigade "Nederland"* was in the northern section of the "Tannenberg" Position. From north to south: Elements of the *20. Waffen-Grenadier-Division der SS (estnisch)*; *SS-Pionier-Bataillon 54*; and, the *I.* and *II./SS-Freiwilligen-Panzer-Grenadier-Regiment 49 "de Ruyter"*, the latter in contact with the *11. SS-Freiwilligen-Panzer-Grenadier-Division "Nordland"* at the road. From the road to the south: The *III.* and *II./SS-Panzer-Grenadier-Regiment 24 "Danmark"* and the *III./SS-Panzer-Grenadier-Regiment 24 "Danmark"*, with the Danish battalion in contact with the *11. Infanterie-Division*. The *II./SS-Panzer-Grenadier-Regiment 23 "Norge"* was the division reserve. The *Kinderheimhöhe* was held by *Kampfgruppe "Langemarck"*, whose antitank elements were in position at the foot of the hill. Grenadier Hill and Hill 69.9 were held by the remaining Estonians and two companies of *SS-Pionier-Bataillon 11*.

The forward-most positions, on both sides of the road, were held by the *II./SS-Freiwilligen-Panzer-Grenadier-Regiment 49 "de Ruyter"* (*SS-Hauptsturmführer* Frühauf) on the northern side and the *III./SS-Panzer-*

111

Grenadier-Regiment 24 "Danmark" (*SS-Sturmbannführer* Kappus) on the southern side.

Late in the afternoon of 26 July, heavy Soviet artillery fire already covered the sector that had been occupied, with particularly heavy concentrations on the *Kinderheimhöhe* and the main supply route. The *6. SS-Freiwilligen-Sturmbrigade "Langemarck"* was practically without officers and suffered heavy losses from the artillery. *SS-Hauptsturmführer* Meggl, commanding the *13./SS-Freiwilligen-Panzer-Grenadier-Regiment 49 "de Ruyter"*, was killed on the *Kinderheimhöhe* while searching for an observation position. The enemy's intention was obvious: Break through to the west on the main supply route.

As darkness fell, five Soviet tanks with accompanying infantry advanced through the main line of resistance directly south of the road, throwing back a weak naval company. The five tanks took position in front of the *Kinderheimhöhe* while the accompanying infantry dug into the hill's eastern slope, thus securing a good jump-off position. The next day, 27 July, would be decisive.

The five enemy tanks remained quiet, but the *11./SS-Panzer-Grenadier-Regiment 24 "Danmark"* and the regimental motorcyclists spotted them and sent back a report. *SS-Unterscharführer* Mellenthin led his regimental tank hunter/killer team forward at about midnight. After a short discussion of a course of action, the plan for destroying the tanks proceeded and, one after another, all of the enemy tanks were destroyed with close-combat means. The major share of that success was credited to the 20-year-old *SS-Unterscharführer* Mellenthin. He raised his score of knocked-out tanks to seven in the next few days using the *Ofenrohr* (German bazooka equivalent) and the *Panzerfaust.*

During the next half-hour, the Soviets poured mortar fire down on the German positions. The hunter/killer team remained in the main line of resistance, which ran only 200 meters east of the *Kinderheimhöhe* in some places.

On 27 July 1944, at 0600 hours, the Soviet artillery fire escalated to barrage intensity. Shells of all calibers rained down for hours on the positions between the railroad and the road and concentrated on the three hills, blanketing them in thick clouds of smoke. The few remaining assault guns and tanks of the of the divisional antitank and armor battalions were sent forward to *SS-Panzer-Grenadier-Regiment 24 "Danmark"*, which would be at the focal point of the enemy's main effort. Under *SS-Obersturmbannführer* Kausch's command, the armor staged behind a ridge of Hill 69.9 that extended to the south.

SS-Hauptsturmführer Fleck's *SS-Vielfach-Werfer-Batterie 521* went into firing position in the rear area of *SS-Panzer-Grenadier-Regiment 24 "Danmark"*. The forward observer, *SS-Unterscharführer* Lerner, established his observation point at the command post of the *III./SS-Panzer-Grenadier-Regiment 24 "Danmark"*. Fleck's battery consisted of armored multiple-rocket launchers similar to the Russian Stalin Organs. With six launchers, each capable of discharging 48 rounds in two to three seconds, the battery had tremendous firepower.

The Soviets attacked at about 0900 hours with strong infantry and armored forces, achieving dangerous penetrations in the main supply route — Tirtsu area through the *10.* and *11./SS-Panzer-Grenadier-Regiment 24 "Danmark"*. *SS-Hauptsturmführer* Trautwein, commanding the *11./SS-Panzer-Grenadier-Regiment 24 "Danmark"*, was severely wounded in the stomach. The Soviets advanced to within 50 meters of the positions of the *11./SS-Panzer-Grenadier-Regiment 24 "Danmark"*, the regimental motorcyclists and the hunter/killer team and, from that range, shot up the trenches. North of the main supply route, an antitank gun belonging to the *4. SS-Panzer-Grenadier-Brigade "Nederland"* opened fire. After the first shock was overcome, 12 Russian tanks were knocked out with *Panzerfäuste*. The *9./SS-Panzer-Grenadier-Regiment 24 "Danmark"* rolled its northern flank back to Chundinurk. All contact with the *10.* and *11./SS-Panzer-Grenadier-Regiment 24 "Danmark"* was lost. The Soviets pushed forward through the gaps.

A short time later, heavy attacks hit Chundinurk and the sectors of the *II./SS-Panzer-Grenadier-Regiment 24 "Danmark"* and the *III./SS-Panzer-Grenadier-Regiment 23 "Norge"*. The attacks originated from Auwere, Lembitu and Sooküla. Although the aforementioned battalions held, contact was lost with the *9./SS-Panzer-Grenadier-Regiment 24 "Danmark"* at Chundinurk. The Soviets stormed forward against *SS-Hauptsturmführer* Herbert Meier's company from three sides. German artillery and the regiment's heavy weapons laid down final protective fire and ceaselessly shelled the enemy assembly positions east of Tirtsu, Repiknu, Auwere, Lembitu and Sooküla. Thanks to timely spotting by forward observers, enemy attacks were effectively combated at the onset and advancing packs of tanks were intensely shelled, immobilizing many of them.

After overrunning the main line of resistance east of the *Kinderheimhöhe*, the main thrust of the attack turned against the hill itself, leaving the *9., 10.* and *11./SS-Panzer-Grenadier-Regiment 24 "Danmark"* continuing to defend isolated strongpoints.

The attack hit the remnants of the *6. SS-Freiwilligen-Sturmbrigade "Langemarck"* like an avalanche. The *Kampfgruppe* fought on bitterly under *SS-Untersturmführer* D'Haese. However, they were ejected from their positions and fell back to Grenadier Hill in small groups. The Flemish volunteer, Remi Schrijnen, was positioned at the foot of the *Kinderheimhöhe* with a 7.5 cm *Pak*. He waited in vain for the order to fire. His antitank gun, which was employed in an ambush position, could only fire when so ordered. It had already been outflanked by the Soviet infantry and armored forces that streamed past the northern side of the hill to the west. Schrijnen was certain that no firing order would arrive. His *Pak* barked at the Russian tanks on its flank. In a short time, four T 34's were ablaze and the tracks had been shot off two more. The gun crew then withdrew to the west.

While the Flemish were thrown back, the *II./SS-Freiwilligen-Panzer-Grenadier-Regiment 49 "de Ruyter"* held its positions north of the *Kinderheimhöhe*. *SS-Hauptsturmführer* Frühauf was wounded. *SS-Obersturmführer* Scholz took over command of the battalion. Battalion tank hunter/killer teams knocked out several Russian tanks.

It was then time for the German armor to launch its immediate counterattack. North of the hill massif, *SS-Obersturmbannführer* Kausch committed 12 assault guns under *SS-Obersturmführer* Stübben into the fight. Using flexible combat tactics, they were finally able to scuttle that day's enemy armored thrust.

The crisis intensified around Chundinurk. There continued to be no contact with the *II./SS-Panzer-Grenadier-Regiment 24 "Danmark"*. Enemy groups that flowed past both sides of Chundinurk — defended by *SS-Hauptsturmführer* Meier and his *9./SS-Panzer-Grenadier-Regiment 24 "Danmark"* — isolated and threatened the command post of the *III./SS-Panzer-Grenadier-Regiment 24 "Danmark"*. The command post was located in a group of houses between Grenadier Hill and the railroad line. *SS-Sturmbannführer* Kappus called for help. The weak *7./SS-Panzer-Grenadier-Regiment 23 "Norge"* was attached to Kappus and went into position in a small patch of woods north of the group of houses.

The *II./SS-Panzer-Grenadier-Regiment 24 "Danmark"* (*SS-Hauptsturmführer* Hämel) had its *5.* and *6. Kompanien* in the main line of resistance. The *7./SS-Panzer-Grenadier-Regiment 24 "Danmark"*, which had been the last company of the regiment out of Narwa, was not in action. It was recuperating west of Hill 69.9. The *8./SS-Panzer-Grenadier-Regiment 24 "Danmark"* was in a firing position at the Waiwara church. The mortars were emplaced in a quarry about 600 meters west-southwest of the western outskirts of Chundinurk.

The flank of Hämel's battalion was also threatened. Weak forces of the Estonian *I./Panzergrenadier-Regiment 47* were sent to him at about noon on 27 July. Hämel's *II./SS-Panzer-Grenadier-Regiment 24 "Danmark"*, along with the attached Estonian battalion, launched an immediate counterattack to reestablish contact with the *9./SS-Panzer-Grenadier-Regiment 24 "Danmark"*. *SS-Hauptsturmführer* Hämel was wounded in the engagement. The counterattack threw back the Soviets who had already nearly reached the mortar positions of the *8./SS-Panzer-Grenadier-Regiment 24 "Danmark"*. It was possible to reestablish tenuous contact.

The linchpin of the defense remained the *Kinderheimhöhe*, which had been lost, and the endangered Grenadier Hill, which was held by the Estonian and Flemish soldiers. Several attempts by engineer units failed to close the great gaps in the main line of resistance east of the *Kinderheimhöhe* and Tirtsu and to help the elements of the *III./SS-Panzer-Grenadier-*

Regiment 24 "Danmark" which was holding on to the east.

About noon on 27 July there was a meeting at the command post of *SS-Panzer-Grenadier-Regiment 24 "Danmark"*. The command post had been moved from the north slope to the southwest slope of Hill 69.9. The division commander, von Scholz, the regimental commander, Krügel, the acting commander of the *1./SS-Pionier-Bataillon 11* and several other officers were present. The first decision: The *1./SS-Pionier-Bataillon 11*, which had been attached to *SS-Panzer-Grenadier-Regiment 24 "Danmark"*, was to send another combat patrol forward into the main line of resistance. The acting commander requested permission to lead the assault troop. Fritz von Scholz denied his request.

SS-Untersturmführer Arera assembled the combat patrol. In spite of the desperate situation, he was still able to find volunteers. *SS-Rottenführer* Glaser led the patrol.

The meeting in the bunker continued. All options were carefully considered. Fritz von Scholz always proved to have a particular gift for dealing with such situations. As always, when the situation was at its worst, he was up front with his men.

Von Scholz left the command post. He wanted to get to *SS-Hauptsturmführer* Lärum, whose *13./SS-Panzer-Grenadier-Regiment 24 "Danmark"* was in a firing position nearby. He then wanted to get an overview of the combat situation with *SS-Sturmbannführer* Kappus.

At that moment, the Russian artillery again laid down heavy fire. The regimental adjutant, *SS-Hauptsturmführer* Ternedde, decided to send a messenger with von Scholz as a guide. At almost the same moment, he and *Haupsturmführer* Lärum rushed out into the open. Fritz von Scholz was hit in the head by shrapnel. They quickly got the wounded man to the command post of *SS-Panzer-Grenadier-Regiment 24 "Danmark"* and placed him on a cot. He was unconscious.

The first men of the combat patrol returned in about two hours, their uniforms filthy and torn, their faces like stone. The operation had miscarried. The leader of the patrol, *SS-Rottenführer* Glaser, had been killed.

The Germans then wanted to dislodge the Russians with a night attack. Again it was the combat engineers of the *11. SS-Freiwilligen-Panzer-Grenadier-Division "Nordland"*, along with Estonian battalions.

At about 1800 hours, the company commanders of the *1. and 3./SS-Pionier-Bataillon 11* were briefed by *SS-Obersturmbannführer* Krügel and *SS-Obersturmbannführer* Bunse. The plan:

2200 hours: Artillery barrage on the *Kinderheimhöhe*. Estonians to attack on both sides of the hill massif with support from *Sturmgeschütze* with the objective of closing the gaps in the main line of resistance east of the *Kinderheimhöhe*. After the gap in the main line of resistance has been plugged, there will be a flare signal of four successive white flares. Then the *1./SS-Pionier-Bataillon 11* is to attack from the north and the *3./SS-Pionier-Bataillon 11* from the south against the eastern slope of the *Kinderheimhöhe* with the objective of cutting off the Soviet forces on the hill.

The jump-off positions were reached by 2130 hours. Exactly at 2220 hours a barrage by artillery and *Nebelwerfer* pounded the *Kinderheimhöhe*. *Sturmgeschütze* from *Gruppe Kausch* rolled eastward with the grenadiers from the *20. Waffen-Grenadier-Division der SS (estnisch)* past both sides of the hill massif. Sounds of heavy fighting could be heard in the main line of resistance.

Instead of four successive white flares, yellow, red and green flares were fired. Enemy attacking! But the combat engineers were to attack even if the gap in the main line of resistance had not been filled.

SS-Untersturmführer Arera had organized his combat engineer company into two assault groups: *SS-Unterscharführer* Frömmelt led one, *SS-Unterscharführer* Simanski the other. At about 2250 hours, Arera started with the *1./SS-Pionier-Bataillon 11* from the north and *SS-Untersturmführer* Schimpf from the south with the *3./SS-Pionier-Bataillon 11*.

They made it to the hill. The Soviets defended. The Germans stormed the last part of the hill with a "Hurrah!" and the Soviets fell back. The eastern slope was held at bay with hand grenades and machine-gun fire. At that point contact had to be established between the *1.* and *3./SS-Pionier-Bataillon 11*. *SS-Unterscharführer* Wolf, a headquarters section leader, prepared to assault the eastern slope. Arera tried to establish contact with the *3./SS-Pionier-Bataillon 11* with two messengers. A flare signal was fired, the signal for an Estonian battalion to occupy the high ground.

When *SS-Untersturmführer* Arera reached the southern slope, he believed he had men from the *3./SS-Pionier-Bataillon 11* approaching him. Arera called to them, receiving rifle fire in return. The combat engineers reacted by hurling hand grenades. While throwing, *SS-Untersturmführer* Arera was severely wounded by a round to the stomach. The messengers dragged him back. The company's medic, *SS-Unterscharführer* Genat, cared for the wounded man. He was then evacuated to the command post of *SS-Freiwilligen-Panzer-Grenadier-Regiment 49 "de Ruyter"*. The severely wounded *SS-Untersturmführer* gave his report. A *VW- Schwimmwagen* then took him to battalion surgeon, *SS-Hauptsturmführer Dr.* Kurz. An ambulance next carried him on through heavy artillery fire to the main dressing station. *Oberarzt Dr.* Nagel, a surgeon who had saved the lives of many wounded men, operated.

The assault troop that was advancing from the south also ran into a strong defense. *SS-Untersturmführer* Schimpf was killed south of the nursery. Weak Estonian battalions of the *20. Waffen-Grenadier-Division der SS (estnisch)* were able to occupy the *Kinderheimhöhe* during the night, but the nursery on the south slope was bitterly defended and remained in Soviet hands.

General Goworow believed that he could sweep the Germans away with his first assault. But General Goworow had found a worthy opponent in *General der Waffen-SS* Felix Steiner, an opponent who drew on the entire range of his ability. Steiner knew that his force was greatly inferior in men and equipment. That did not faze that gifted man. His approach was to make best use of the available means. The bled-white battalions and regiments could only stand up so long to those mass assaults. Armor was practically unavailable, so only artillery was left!

Under the direction of the corps artillery commander, *Oberst* Kresin, and his operations officer, *Hauptmann* Ossenkop, *SS-Artillerie-Regiment 11* and *SS-Artillerie-Regiment 54*, the entire corps- and *Flakartillerie*, the naval coastal artillery, *Werfer-Batterie Flecke* and all the regimental heavy weapons were consolidated. New fire plans were created. Final protective fire areas for the entire front were numbered in a single unified system and given coordinates on the map. In that way, the fire of all the heavy weapons could be directed rapidly on a single critical point. In the course of that reorganization, the *8., 12.* and *13./SS-Panzer-Grenadier-Regiment 24 "Danmark"* consolidated under the fire direction of *SS-Hauptsturmführer* Lärums in the area southwest of Hill 69.9 — Kirikükla. The same thing happened to the *8., 12.* and *13./SS-Panzer-Grenadier-Regiment 23 "Norge"*.

What was happening on the other side?

As a result of the determined employment of several construction brigades, the Soviets had a bridge ready at Narwa in a very short time. Men and equipment flowed in unceasing streams over the crossings. General Goworow wanted to force the decision. Before long he had amassed eleven rifle divisions and six tank brigades in front of the *Tannenberg* Position. Eleven divisions against four that did not even have the numerical strength of two. When the ball dropped, the ratio was 1 to 4.

SS-Hauptsturmührer Bergfeld took over command of the *II./SS-Panzer-Grenadier-Regiment 24 "Danmark"* during the night of 28 July. *SS-Untersturmführer* Dall then led his former *13./SS-Panzer-Grenadier-Regiment 23 "Norge"*. The wounded *SS-Hauptsturmführer* Hämel went from the dressing station to the *11. SS-Freiwilligen-Panzer-Grenadier-Division "Nordland"* field hospital at Kothla-Järwe.

General der Waffen-SS Fritz von Scholz followed the same route. Chief surgeon *Dr.* Riedweg cared for the severely wounded general and, on 28 July 1944, sent him on to the special surgical facility at Wesenberg. A locomotive departed with a single boxcar. *SS-Hauptsturmführer* Hämel lay beside von Scholz on the straw in the boxcar. The bloody head bandage on the division commander was surrounded by flies. Hämel tore his mosquito net off and the attending medic spread it over the head of the division commander. Fritz von Scholz spoke no more. His breath became short. When the wounded were unloaded at Wesenberg, Fritz von Scholz was dead.

SS-Brigadeführer Ziegler, the chief of staff of the *III. (germanisches) SS-Panzer-Korps*, assumed command of the *11. SS-Freiwilligen-Panzer-Grenadier-Division "Nordland"*. He, in turn, was replaced by the divisional operations officer, *SS-Obersturmbannführer* von Bockelberg. *SS-Sturmbannführer* Weitzdörfer became the division's new operations officer.

In the early morning hours of 28 July the fighting renewed. The *Kinderheimhöhe*, split between Estonians and Russians, remained the hot spot. After quickly moving into attack positions and a brief artillery preparation, *SS-Sturmbannführer* Scheibe led the 5. and 6./*SS-Panzer-Grenadier-Regiment 23 "Norge"* and the remnants of a naval battalion in a counterattack against the north and east slopes of the *Kinderheimhöhe*.

Soviet artillery, however, laid down an intense barrage as soon as the units left the attack position. Low-flying aircraft later joined in. The trenches that led over the entire hill massif were, at that point, quite literally plowed up. The Estonians on the west side of the hill were smashed. The counterattack drowned in its own blood. The remnants fell apart but were able to regroup on Grenadier Hill. The Estonians also had to fall back to that position. Flemish, German and Estonian soldiers were now elbow to elbow.

But that was not enough! The Soviets promptly launched an attack against Grenadier Hill. Individual groups of the enemy succeeded in reaching the eastern slope. The situation was totally confused.

What was going on in the Grenadier Hill — railroad line sector? *SS-Unterscharführer* Lerner, the *Werfer-Batterie 521* forward observer, noted in his diary:

0830 hours: The enemy pounded the entire sector. Extremely heavy fire of all calibers on our position and the rear area. The telephone line is out. Repair party searching for the break.

0855 hours: Dust and powder smoke prevent any observation. Situation report: Infantry attack expected but not yet identified.

Continuous salvoes from *Batterie Flecke*, as planned. Unable to observe effect.

1000 hours: The enemy is attacking with armor and infantry and achieves a penetration.

That attack struck the 9./*SS-Panzer-Grenadier-Regiment 24 "Danmark"* at Chundinurk. The final protective artillery fires were called to devastating effect. Individual Russian tanks that had broken through were knocked out by *Panzerschrecks* and *Panzerfäuste* or forced to turn back. Two *Sturmgeschütze* were positioned near the command post of the *III./SS-Panzer-Grenadier-Regiment 24 "Danmark"* to counter the repeated Soviet attempts at an armored breakthrough on the Chundinurk — Kiruküla road. They successfully took part in all the fighting in that sector and were able to knock out several Soviet tanks in the course of the next few days.

After the collapse of the main line of resistance east of Chundinurk and on both sides of Tirtsu, the entire area north of the Chundinurk — Kiruküla road as far as the hill massif became a no-mans-land, seriously endangering the remnants of the *III./SS-Panzer-Grenadier-Regiment 24 "Danmark"*. To guard against the elimination of the command post or of having the position rolled up from the rear, units of the *7./SS-Panzer-Grenadier-Regiment 23 "Norge"* were moved into the wooded area north of the command post. Under the leadership of an unshakeable young Norwegian *SS-Unterscharführer*, all attacks launched from south of and from the hill massif proper were repulsed. The elements of the *7./SS-Panzer-Grenadier-Regiment 23 "Norge"* knocked out several Russian tanks. On 28 July the battalion adjutant, *SS-Untersturmführer* Efsen, was killed at the regimental command post by a Russian sniper's bullet.

After the failure of the enemy attacks, an attempt was made in the afternoon to establish contact with the remnants of the *10.* and *11./SS-Panzer-Grenadier-Regiment 24 "Danmark"* that were presumed to still be in the main line of resistance. A platoon-sized element of the *III./SS-Panzer-Grenadier-Regiment 24 "Danmark"*, along with a *Panther* from *SS-Panzer-Abteilung 11*, made the effort. The rifle platoon made good progress past the road fork east of Chundinurk toward Tirtsu. The *Panther* supported the advancing grenadiers with its fire. A Soviet antitank gun made a vain attempt from the railroad embankment to knock out the *Panther*. When the German attack neared Tirtsu, the Soviets leaped out of the trenches and ran back. The platoon occupied the main line of resistance to the extent that its weak forces allowed. There was no contact to the north. There were not enough men to adequately occupy the regained portion of the main line of resistance. The next day, the platoon had to fall back to Chundinurk under heavy enemy pressure.

At about 1700 hours, seven enemy tanks with mounted infantry attacked from the direction of Lembitu. There, too, the German artillery fired with good effect. The situation report of *SS-Werfer-Batterie Flecke's*: "Battery's salvos right on target. Position in our hands."

The struggle for Grenadier Hill continued throughout the day. The fighting was conducted by groups out of contact with one another. Both Grenadier Hill and the *Kinderheimhöhe* were repeatedly under heavy artillery fire. Late in the afternoon the Soviets "weaseled" their way back to the *Kinderheimhöhe*.

At sunset the *7./SS-Panzer-Grenadier-Regiment 24 "Danmark"* launched another assault on the *Kinderheimhöhe* with 50 men, including 20 Flemish soldiers. After quickly assembling for the attack on the northern slope of Grenadier Hill, they attacked from the northwest against the *Kinderheimhöhe*. The Soviets repulsed the attack. The acting company commander, *SS-Untersturmführer* Madsen, was wounded. That was the last attempt to recapture the *Kinderheimhöhe*. Like a dark shroud, the night covered everything. General Goworow wanted to finally force a decision on the third day of fighting at the "Tannenberg" Position. He brought up everything he could get hold of. The 29th of July 1944 was to be the decisive day.

In the morning, an extremely heavy artillery barrage covered the entire eastern sector of the "Tannenberg" Position. The main concentration was from Grenadier Hill to Chundinurk. Successive waves of Soviet aircraft bombed Grenadier Hill and the artillery positions. Low-flying aircraft were on the hunt over the battlefield for targets on the ground. Grenadier Hill was shrouded in a giant mushroom cloud of smoke from the bursting shells.

The inevitable enemy attack with strong armored support followed at the foot of the hill. In the sector from the main supply route to Tirtsu more than 100 tanks of all types approached the German positions. The combined German artillery formations fired. Salvo after salvo crashed into the packs of tanks and the following infantry, but the Soviets rolled forward in spite of significant losses.

The small German hedgehog positions east of the *Kinderheimhöhe* were bypassed. Dealing with them would only have slowed down the attack. Onward, Onward! That was the Soviet motto. And the isolated German strongpoints were powerless to prevent the Soviets from flooding past. They had had to count every cartridge, every hand grenade for a long time. Every round must score a hit! And they only fired when they were directly threatened. If they had only had enough ammunition! They held out under such conditions and hoped they would be relieved and the main line of resistance regained.

So it was that the remnants of the *10.* and *11./SS-Panzer-Grenadier-Regiment 24 "Danmark"*, Mellenthin's tank-destroyers and Hektor's motorcyclists, were caught up in a hopeless situation. *SS-Oberscharführer* Hektor was wounded and dragged back. *SS-Untersturmführer* Bertramsen, successor to *SS-Hauptsturmführer* Trautwein as commander of the *11./SS-Panzer-Grenadier-Regiment 24 "Danmark"*, was killed. And so it was that they shed their blood east of the *Kinderheimhöhe* as the fighting raged far behind them.

SS-Unterscharführer Lerner, forward observer for *SS-Werfer-Batterie Flecke*, reported from his observation point near Kappus' command post:

0830 hours: Enemy artillery pounds the entire sector and rear area, particularly the firing positions of the heavy weapons.

0900 hours: Observation no longer possible. Sounds of advancing infantry. Attack not yet identifiable.

0955 hours: About 40 tanks in front of our position, including Stalins. Request support from 8.8 cm *Flak*.

1000 hours: Enemy is attacking in regimental strength along both sides of the railroad line.

1020 hours: Enemy stopped by the fire of our heavy weapons. Situation report:

Negligible penetrations. Heavy infantry losses. Request faster fire-mission times.

On Grenadier Hill, *SS-Hauptsturmführer* Bachmeier had been handed the reins, but what could he do? For the moment, very little!

The remnants of his II./SS-Panzer-Grenadier-Regiment 23 "Norge", the few surviving Flemish soldiers of the 6. SS-Freiwilligen-Sturmbrigade "Langemarck", the Estonians of the 20. Waffen-Grenadier-Division der SS (estnisch) and a few survivors of the naval battalion fought in small groups. German, Flemish, Estonian and Norwegian men — men who had not even known each other up to that point — lay in shot-up fighting positions, bunkers and bomb craters, fighting on without contact with each other, no longer receiving orders nor, for that matter, waiting for them. The inferno of bursting shells and bombs raged on and on around them. And the Soviets worked their way forward from the west slope of the Kinderheimhöhe.

But it was not just from the *Kinderheimhöhe* that the infantry and armor assaulted. The *II./SS-Freiwilligen-Panzer-Grenadier-Regiment 49 "de Ruyter"*, which had been led by *SS-Obersturmführer* Helmut Scholz since *SS-Hauptsturmführer* Frühauf had been wounded, held its ground. The Russians stormed past the battalion's southern flank. Tanks were knocked out with *Panzerfäuste* and the Soviet infantry paid a high toll in blood, but the battle moved on to the west, past the dead and the knocked-out tanks.

Schrijnen's 7.5 cm *Pak* was positioned on the northern slope of the hill massif. He was located in an ambush position again and was supposed to wait for the order to fire. His crew had been lost to death and wounds, leaving Schrijnen all alone. One man, one loaded gun and 30 approaching tanks!

The gun barked at the tanks. The gun shield had long since been destroyed. The extractor had also been damaged. Schrijnen fired, then leaped in front of the barrel to shove the jammed expended cartridge case out with the cleaning rod. Three Stalin tanks blazed. Four more T 34's shared the same fate. Schrijnen's *Pak* bellowed like a gut-wounded hound until a Stalin tank finally smashed it in his hands at short range. Schrijnen was tossed aside, wounded for the eighth time.

The battle raged on past Schrijnen. Onward to the west!

The Soviets were already at the road that ran parallel to the front. One armored wedge turned to the south once it was west of Grenadier Hill. As a result, the hill appeared lost. They stormed onward, on the connecting road on the northern slope of Hill 69.9. The tanks clattered forward, mercilessly shooting the bunkers on the northern slope to pieces. The command post of *SS-Freiwilligen-Panzer-Grenadier-Regiment 49 "de Ruyter"* was also hit. *SS-Obersturmbannführer* Collani was severely wounded. When the Soviets stood outside his shot-up command post, he committed suicide.

Just when the breakthrough succeeded and Grenadier Hill appeared lost, *SS-Obersturmbannführer* Kausch committed his tanks and assault guns into the fray. Only they could bring the chaos to an end!

Like enraged wasps, they moved out of their "nest" behind the southern outcropping of Hill 69.9 and threw themselves upon the enemy armor that had advanced so far to the west. In a war of movement, they broke off the enemy spearhead and swept behind the fleeing Red Army soldiers and tanks. They trapped them and blew them to bits.

What was happening on Grenadier Hill? Bachmeier had fortified the west slope with a few men. He had long since lost any concept of the "big picture". Bombs, impacting rounds and tanks down below! Shelled, plowed-up positions! Infantry fire from German and Russian weapons! Who could make sense out of that? Bachmeier had to wait helplessly because there was nothing further that he could do.

On the east slope of Grenadier Hill was a dying radioman from the naval coast artillery observation post. His radio set was still intact. Below him he saw Russian armor and called down fire from his battery. The rounds landed among the enemy tanks. Several were rendered immobile. A little later he saw more of them in the west turning toward the south. In his head, he was thinking: "Grenadier Hill is surrounded". Red Army soldiers were also working their way over from the *Kinderheimhöhe* to Grenadier Hill. With the last of his ebbing strength, he called down fire on his own position on Grenadier Hill. Not far from him was *SS-Sturmmann* Keilert of the *5./SS-Panzer-Grenadier-Regiment 23 "Norge"*. He saw the Russians coming and opened fire. Then another murderous artillery barrage came down and, as far as he could tell, it was coming from the west.

In search of protection, Keilert leaped into a shattered dugout. The fire let up. Suddenly three German helmets were in front of him — worn by Russians. "Get up and come with us!" they shouted at Keilert. But before Keilert could get his senses together, the three Russians had all been torn apart by a direct hit from a round. Keilert was also wounded. He received 15 fragments, including one in his eye and one embedded in a lung.

Keilert dragged himself farther. He found a bunker that had survived the shelling. He found comrades there: An *SS-Unterscharführer* from Breslau who had been wounded by a bullet that had passed through his lower leg; a Norwegian who had bled to death; and, a very young grenadier, who was unwounded but in a severe state of shock. Keilert, who was greatly weakened by that time, joined up with them.

Below him, the main guns of the tanks were bellowing. *Sturmgeschütze* and the few tanks from *SS-Panzer-Abteilung 11 "Hermann von Salza"* were mopping up. It was not mass and equipment that were decisive but courage and death-defying determination. *SS-Obersturmbannführer* Kausch's *Panzergruppen* had decided the outcome!

They hunted down the retreating T 34's. They came upon *SS-Sturmmann*

Schrijnen's smashed gun and almost a dozen damaged or destroyed enemy tanks in front of it. They loaded the wounded Schrijnen on board and brought him back.

Up above, on the hill, everything was in a state of confusion! While the noise of battle below ebbed away toward the east, additional groups of Russians were coming over from the *Kinderheimhöhe* onto Grenadier Hill. But all that they found were dead and wounded enemy and plowed-up earth.

Soon the Soviets up on the hill saw that the pullback was in progress down below. They also prepared to pull out, but before they left they searched through the tortured, plowed-up eastern slope of Grenadier Hill for German, Estonian, Flemish and Norwegian soldiers. It was only dead and wounded that they found. Whoever was unable to walk was shot out of hand. Keilert was still able to respond to the demand to come out of the bunker. He saw no other way out. Then, as they left, a Russian submachine gun chattered, extinguishing all life in the bunker.

Keilert was a prisoner, along with 19 other wounded men. They were brought over from Grenadier Hill to the *Kinderheimhöhe* by 15 Russians.

On the western slope of Grenadier Hill, *SS-Hauptsturmführer* Bachmeier organized the survivors. One step at a time, the hill was taken back. More men emerged from shell-smashed bunkers, men who had survived the inferno on Grenadier Hill. By the evening of 29 July, Grenadier Hill was entirely in German hands once more.

And in the railroad-line sector? After the morning's unsuccessful attack, *SS-Unterscharführer* Lerner's diary noted the following for the afternoon:

Strong harassing fire. Barrages and carpet bombing. Radio and field telephone are out. Messenger underway to *Batterie Flecke* requesting pre-planned fires. Infantry assembling east of this position. Battery fire with observed good effect. Minor enemy penetrations.

A bitter defensive battle was waged that cost both sides immense casualties. During the first three days, 113 Soviet tanks were knocked out. Many wrecked tanks were in the field of craters. One German *Sturmgeschütz* stood on its nose in a bomb crater, but most of the knocked-out armored vehicles were recovered during the night and put back in service by the untiring maintenance troops. The Russians did the same. Recovery parties and demolition squads often ran into each other during the night and engaged in firefights.

The German artillery played a large role in the successful defense. It had continually and effectively engaged enemy concentrations. A German/ Estonian *Stuka* wing flew missions from Reval against Narwa and the Soviet battery positions. One or two aircraft were lost in every *Stuka* attack.

The last two days of July saw renewed heavy fighting; the *Schwerpunkt* was once again the hill massif. Giant, gray-black smoke clouds enshrouded

Grenadier Hill and darkened the cloudless blue sky. Grenadier Hill held!

Attacks launched from the Tirtsu and Auwere area also failed. Spotted early, they were smashed by the German artillery. One attack carried out by twelve Stalin tanks foundered on the stubborn defense of the *II./SS-Freiwilligen-Panzer-Grenadier-Regiment 49 "de Ruyter"*. Again it was *SS-Obersturmführer* Scholz who was an example to his men. When the Russian tanks appeared right outside the ruined cellar in which his command post was located, he knocked out two with *Panzerfäuste*. Not one of the twelve Stalin tanks got through. Not one of them made it back to their own lines. In one of the tanks a map was found with the march route to Reval marked on it.

After the death of *SS-Obersturmbannführer* Collani, the regimental adjutant, *SS-Hauptsturmführer* Ertel, commanded *SS-Freiwilligen-Panzer-Grenadier-Regiment 49 "de Ruyter"*. It was thanks to his cool-headed leadership that the regiment and, with it, the sector to the Baltic Sea successfully withstood all the Soviet attacks.

The high point of the battle was 29 July. Even though heavy fighting continued on 30 and 31 July, the relentless advance of the Soviet assault abated. The Russian strength slowly ebbed.

Here is the story of *SS-Unterscharführer* Scholles, operations clerk for *SS-Panzer-Grenadier-Regiment 24 "Danmark"*, who was regularly called on to serve as "a jack of all trades". After repelling two enemy attacks, the soldiers on Grenadier Hill were nearly out of ammunition by midday. Scholles was given the task of bringing ammunition forward to Grenadier Hill with a group of Estonians. As he described it:

At the north slope of Hill 69.9, we dashed to the west slope of Grenadier Hill and paused for a bit. I looked for a suitable way to Grenadier Hill. The communications trenches had been plowed up. Dead were everywhere. A gruesome picture and a fearful stench under the burning heat of the noonday sun. At the northeast slope of Hill 69.9 there were dead Russians and Germans on the communications road across the position. All of the bunkers on the north slope of Hill 69.9 had been shot to pieces and burnt out, in spite of their unique position on the slope. The stink of decomposing corpses flowed from the collapsed bunkers. An artillery barrage forced us to take full cover.

After the enemy fire let up, we made it at a dead run across the 250 meters of open, flat terrain to the west slope of Grenadier Hill. We made our way up the slope with difficulty. I headed for Bachmeier's command post, which was in a crater-shaped defile. We found *SS-Hauptsturmführer* Bachmeier in a tunnel. He maintained a positive view of the situation.

Suddenly Soviet artillery opened fire. After twenty minutes it shifted to infantry fire. A breathless messenger ran up and reported an enemy penetration to Bachmeier. Without delay, Bachmeier set out at the front of a strong reserve squad in an immediate counterattack and cleaned up the penetration.

The morning of 1 August remained surprisingly peaceful. Heavy ship

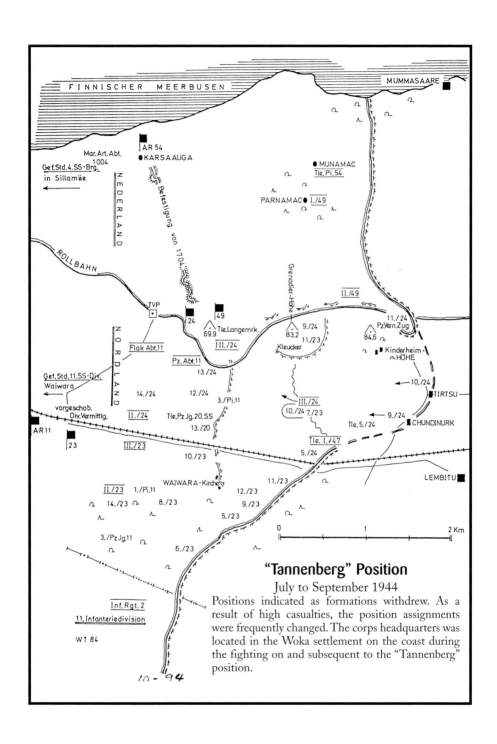

FINNISCHER MEERBUSEN

MUMMASAARE

AR 54
● KARSA AUGA

Mar.Art.Abt.
1004
Gef.Std.4.SS·Brg.
in Sillamäe

● MUNAMAC
Tle.Pi.54

NEDERLAND

Befestigung von 170.+

● MUNAMAC
Tle.Pi.54

PARNAMAC● I./49

ROLLBAHN

Grenadier-Höhe

II./49

11./24
Pz.Vern.Zug

TVP
49
24

9./24
83.2
11./23
Kleucker

84.6

Kinderheim-
HÖHE

Tle.Langemrk.
69.9

III./24

10./24
TIRTSU

Flak Abt.11

Pz.Abt.11
13./24

NORDLAND

Gef.Std.11.SS-Div.
Waiwara

14./24   12./24
3./Pi.11

III./24
10./24 7./23

9./24
Tle.5./24
CHUNDINURK

vorgeschob.
Div.Vermittlg.

II./24   Tle.Pz Jg.20.SS
13./20

Tle. I./47

AR 11

23

III./23

10./23

5./24

LEMBITU

WAIWARA-Kirche

11./23

II./23   1./Pi.11
14./23   8./23

12./23
9./23

5./23

3./Pz Jg.11

6./23

0   1   2 Km

"Tannenberg" Position
July to September 1944

Positions indicated as formations withdrew. As a
result of high casualties, the position assignments
were frequently changed. The corps headquarters was
located in the Woka settlement on the coast during
the fighting on and subsequent to the "Tannenberg"
position.

Inf.Rgt.2
11.Infanteriedivision

WT 84

10-94

traffic was observed at sea. The German command figured that, after the failure of the Soviet attack on Grenadier Hill, there would be an attempt at landing from the sea. As a precaution, the countermeasures that had been prepared under the codename *"Seelöwe"* (sea lion) were set in motion. However, the first of August remained relatively quiet. The *Wehrmachtbericht* reported that day:

On the isthmus of Narwa, the enemy did not continue his offensive due to heavy losses. The following formations played an outstanding and significant role in the successful defense against the recent Soviet offensive: The *III. (germanisches) SS-Panzer-Korps*, commanded by *General der Waffen-SS* Steiner, with the *11. SS-Freiwilligen-Panzer-Grenadier-Division "Nordland"* and the *4. SS-Panzer-Grenadier-Brigade "Nederland"*, the *20. Waffen-Grenadier-Division der SS (estnisch)*, the East Prussian *11. Infanterie-Division*, as well as the units of the *Kriegsmarine* that had been committed on land and army-level artillery and rocket-launcher units.

On 2 August, the battle for Grenadier Hill flared up again in full force. Bachmeier's men held. Penetrations were eliminated with immediate counterattacks. Enemy attacks supported by armor on Chundinurk and along the railroad embankment were shattered by German artillery. A small penetration southwest of Chundinurk was cleaned up in an immediate counterattack by the Estonians attached to the *II./SS-Panzer-Grenadier-Regiment 24 "Danmark"*. The enemy forces who had penetrated were Mongols.

Another attempt failed to regain contact with the surviving elements of the *10.* and *11./SS-Panzer-Grenadier-Regiment 24 "Danmark"* and the regimental platoons that were still in the former main line of resistance. The relief party that had been put together from *SS-Panzer-Grenadier-Regiment 23 "Norge"* was dispersed.

The 3rd of August brought more hard fighting at Grenadier Hill, with isolated penetrations that could be cleaned up. During the night, the *Kinderheimhöhe* was the target of heavy German artillery barrages which were significantly reinforced by employment of *SS-Werfer-Batterie 521*. The fire effectively destroyed the attack position of a Soviet division so that it was unable to move out for the attack on Grenadier Hill it had planned for 4 August. As a result, 4 August remained relatively calm.

The Russians attacked Grenadier Hill three times on 5 August. They only had weak artillery support. The single penetration could be isolated. After bringing up reserves, the last penetration was cleaned up by about 2300 hours. The forward observer of *Werfer-Batterie Flecke* reported those activities on the same date: Sound of fighting at 12 — 413. 2300 hours: Sound of infantry weapons coming from Grenadier Hill and the south slope. Sector active."

SS-Hauptsturmführer Bachmeier, commander of the forces on Grenadier Hill, was wounded. The acting commander of *SS-Bewährungskompanie 103*, *SS-Obersturmführer* Kleucker, took his place. The Russian offensive against the "Tannenberg" Position had failed.

Extensive regrouping followed on the German side. Chundinurk was abandoned. The group of houses around the command post of the *III./SS-Panzer-Grenadier-Regiment 24 "Danmark"* was built into a strong bastion between Grenadier Hill and the railroad line. The command post, itself, was moved to the west slope of Hill 69.9. The remnants of the *9./SS-Panzer-Grenadier-Regiment 24 "Danmark"* and the Estonians held the strongpoint. To the north of it were the remaining elements of the *7./SS-Panzer-Grenadier-Regiment 23 "Norge"*.

Gradually a few survivors of the *10.* and *11./SS-Panzer-Grenadier-Regiment 24 "Danmark"* and the regimental platoons fought their way back to the new German defensive front. The *10./SS-Panzer-Grenadier-Regiment 24 "Danmark"* was reorganized under the acting command of *SS-Untersturmführer* Jessen; the *11./SS-Panzer-Grenadier-Regiment 24 "Danmark"* was reorganized under *SS-Obersturmführer* Thorkildsen. The remnants of *SS-Bewährungskompanie 103* were given back their insignia, ranks and decorations and consolidated with *SS-Panzer-Grenadier-Regiment 24 "Danmark"* as rehabilitated soldiers.

The dead were buried and positions rebuilt. Everyone attempted to improve his positions. *SS-Obersturmbannführer* Bunse assumed command of *SS-Freiwilligen-Panzer-Grenadier-Regiment 49 "de Ruyter"*. *SS-Pionier-Bataillon 11* went to *SS-Hauptsturmführer* Voß.

The days that followed saw small-scale attacks that were, in part, supported by armor. Not until 12 August did the Russians test the front in the Narwa isthmus with stronger combat reconnaissance. Sixty Russians assaulted Grenadier Hill and were thrown back. About 200 Soviets attacked from the direction of Lembitu and Sooküla. They were repulsed far from the main line of resistance by concentrated fire from the heavy weapons. The fighting continued in the form of intense artillery duels throughout the day.

The *Armee-Abteilung Narwa* newspaper, printed in Reval, caught the mood:

The new day rises, beaming, from the nighttime shadows over the isthmus of Narwa. Fog lies like a milky veil over the Gulf of Finland. Men of the *11. SS-Freiwilligen-Panzer-Grenadier-Division "Nordland"* and the *4. SS-Panzer-Grenadier-Brigade "Nederland"* hold the trenches; Estonians are on guard in their foxholes.

The artillery forward observer sits at an advanced post in the main line of resistance. The scissors-telescope peers over the stony rim of the parapets, turning from point to point. The road to Narwa shines like a bright ribbon through the valley. To its right and left rise small hills in the otherwise level landscape.

Observation post X (Grenadier Hill): It is approaching 0700 hours. Nine enemy tanks are approaching. The scissors-scope can distinguish enemy infantry, some mounted on the tanks and others pushing forward behind them. Soviet mortars open up with a hail of fire. Their antitank guns support them. The artillery forward observer calmly reports his observations to the command post, which then gives firing data to the batteries. Everything is prepared for immediate action.

Suddenly the earth quakes directly in front of the observation post. Stalin organs! The nine Soviet tanks also open fire and roll forward toward Hill X. Two more tanks emerge from the left and five more roll forward along the Narwa road. Heavy fire lashes out at them from the guns of the artillery and the *Flak*. Then the steel giants form a hedgehog position beyond the reach of the weapons of the defending infantry. They position themselves on both sides of the main supply route and fire to all sides to enable their infantry to break through. The observer determines the exact location of the armored hedgehog and calls down fire on it. A dull roar drowns out the clear song of the light weapons for a few seconds. The shells burst directly beside the tanks. The hedgehog position dissolves immediately, and the Soviet tanks head back north, except for one that was torn to bits by German rounds.

1555 Hours: Eight more enemy tanks roll forward. Another joins them. Our batteries again open fire. Armor plates burst asunder and dirty smoke swirls high. Direct hit! Panic stricken the other tanks immediately turn to the north and make it to the protection of the woods. It takes exactly five minutes to force the enemy to abandon his plans for a penetration.

The day draws to an end without terminating the struggle for the gateway to the Baltic region. Signal flares burn in the darkness, the muzzle flashes of the guns flare everywhere. The marching of companies can be heard in the darkness. It is all just a transition to the new day.

The tally from *SS-Artillerie-Regiment 54* supplements that account: Thirty Russian tanks were destroyed through open sights or the timely fire direction provided by the forward observers. Numerous enemy concentrations and attacks were thwarted. One *Kampfgruppe* was assembled from the trains positions and committed as infantry in the main line of resistance. The regiment's two quad-*Flak* platoons shot down six low-flying aircraft.

On 19 August, *SS-Obersturmführer* Scholz turned over command of the *II./SS-Freiwilligen-Panzer-Grenadier-Regiment 49 "de Ruyter"* to the regimental adjutant, *SS-Hauptsturmführer* Ertel, so that he could attend to the healing of an injury. The battalion held the so-called "finger", a stretch of trenches northeast of the *Kinderheimhöhe* that had remained in German hands.

At the end of August, the enemy attacked the "finger" with a penal battalion after a heavy fire preparation and was able to break into the trenches. Contact was lost with the platoons there. German artillery and heavy infantry weapons opened a sudden, heavy fire. They laid down a dome of fire over the penetration and provided a screen for the immediate counterattack.

SS-Oberscharführer Walther, who had come to the *II./SS-Freiwilligen-Panzer-Grenadier-Regiment 49 "de Ruyter"* in Narwa from a *Luftwaffen-Feld-Division*, led an assault troop that hurled back the Soviets who had broken in. He reestablished contact with the companies that had been cut off. Prisoners were taken.

On 29 August, *SS-Hauptsturmführer* Ertel turned the battalion over to

SS-Hauptsturmführer Petersen.

Both sides expended immense quantities of men and equipment in the bitter struggle for the "Tannenberg" Position. After the fighting, the battlefield was a dreary, cratered landscape saturated with water-filled shell holes stretching from the Baltic Sea in the north and ending in the forested marshland to the south. The *Kinderheimhöhe* and Grenadier Hill had been plowed up by bombs and shells. Bizarre, isolated, splintered tree stumps stretched toward heaven and completed the portrait of the tortured earth. There was not a tree left on Hill 69.9, either. The slender birches lay as if mowed down. Woods and thickets had become a field of stubble.

When, in the course of this book, there is talk of companies and batteries, it must be remembered that the strengths of the units in men and equipment steadily shrank — often dramatically in a short period of time — and they received practically no replacements. At the same time, the defensive sectors remained the same. That resulted in a double burden on the units. The *III. (germanisches) SS-Panzer-Korps*, whose divisions in the Narwa bridgehead had long-since lacked their authorized strengths, shrank yet more with significant losses during the defensive fighting at the *"Tannenberg"* Position. Companies that had comprised 100 men at Narwa had melted away to the point where the strongest of them had no more than 50 men and many were down to squad strength. Replenishment from army units and the *Luftwaffen-Feld-Divisionen* did not significantly alter the picture. *SS-Feld-Ersatz-Bataillon "Nordland"* in Toila did its best to fill the existing gaps, but it remained "a drop of water in the bucket".

The military performance of the officers and men was beyond measure. Day and night the staffs performed their behind-the-scenes work, trying to keep track of the course of the fighting. Improvisation and tactical insight repeatedly mastered critical situations. The commanders barely managed to sleep during the course of the fighting. Again and again it was a matter of conducting defensive and offensive operations and personally intervening when the situation demanded it.

In the staffs and command posts, radio and field-telephone operators struggled to maintain communications and, in so doing, provided the prerequisites for the successful coordination of all arms on the battlefield. Whenever cables and radio sets went out, unshakable messengers made their way through the broken landscape and reestablished contact.

The major burdens of the fighting, however, lay on the shoulders of the grenadiers and combat engineers who were welded together with their officers and noncommissioned officers into a brotherhood borne of combat.

Credit must also be given to the tanks and assault guns that rolled forward repeatedly and slugged it out with the packs of Soviet armor.

The artillery regiments, the *Flak* batteries, the *gepanzerte SS-Vielfach-*

Werferbatterie 521 and the heavy companies of the grenadier regiments played an essential role in the successful defense as well.

Supply, repair and support units also accomplished immense tasks. The maintenance sections worked ceaselessly in returning damaged tanks and vehicles to service. In Ontika, on the Soviet flight-path to Reval, *SS-Instandsetzungs-Abteilung 11* had an assortment of watch duties to perform in addition to its own work.

High praise goes to the surgeons and medics who fought with all their skill for the lives of the torn and wounded comrades that the battle took by thousands. The long rows of graves at the military cemetery on the beach at Reval bore silent witness to the murderous fighting.

Fairness also demands recognition of the endeavors of the enemy, who fought and died with equal effort and under equal privations.

Two personal accounts illustrate how individual humans stand on the razor's edge between life and death in the middle of the fight. The first account will follow the story of the young German soldier, Keilert, who had been wounded and then captured by the Soviets and taken from Grenadier Hill to the *Kinderheimhöhe*:

We were escorted over from Grenadier Hill to the *Kinderheimhöhe* by at least 15 Russians. On the way over, we repeatedly had to abandon cover since the trenches were either destroyed or blocked by the dead. Whenever we emerged, we were fired on by machine guns and carbines so that another three Russians fell along the way. From that we concluded that it was our comrades who were doing the firing. Even though I had the best intentions in the world, I no longer had the strength to attempt to escape. It would have been impossible in any case. The experiences of the last 48 hours were so crushing and the stench of the rotting corpses was so penetrating — it was very hot that day — that I only wanted to get out of there. It didn't matter where.

At the *Kinderheimhöhe*, Russians stood with their rifles ready, preparing for our execution. A Mongol officer intervened energetically. It was thanks to his efforts that we were spared. I shall never know why. We were conducted back to the Russian artillery positions and locked up in a barn. One after another we were interrogated. On the next day we were loaded on a truck and taken to Jamburg via Narwa. We were deloused, bathed and again interrogated. We were taken to the university clinic at Leningrad on a hospital train (boxcars with wooden bunks and white-covered sacks of straw). There, a Jewish female doctor removed the shell fragment from my eye and took the one from my lung. Three more came out on their own after the area became infected. Then followed six years of Soviet captivity.

SS-Unterscharführer Illum, the platoon sergeant of the tank hunter/killer team of *SS-Panzer-Grenadier-Regiment 24 "Danmark"*, wrote the following concerning the struggle and the end of his platoon as well as that of the regimental motorcyclists and the *11./SS-Panzer-Grenadier-Regiment 24 "Danmark"*. They met their end on the main supply route to Narwa, east of the *Kinderheimhöhe*. The final days of the *10./SS-Panzer-Grenadier-Regiment 24 "Danmark"*, which was employed a bit farther to the south, was similar. The narrative starts with the Soviet armored breakthrough directly south of the main supply route during the morning of 26 July 1944.

We were sent forward at about midnight to the positions east of the *Kinderheimhöhe*. The positions right at the road were occupied by naval infantry. They breathed a sigh of relief at our arrival, since we were considered to be "tank-busters".

We stopped between the *11./SS-Panzer-Grenadier-Regiment 24 "Danmark"* and the regiment's motorcycle platoon. *SS-Oberscharführer* Hektor and *SS-Untersturmführer* Bertramsen showed us the Soviet tanks that had broken through. They could be seen several hundred meters behind our position. The *Kinderheimhöhe* had already been partly occupied by Soviet infantry which had followed the tanks.

We talked over our plan. We had to eliminate all the tanks, if possible, with a single blow. Since several of the tanks were in bad positions for us, *SS-Unterscharführer* Mellenthin and another volunteer would go around the tanks through a depression and give the signal to fire...

Mellenthin set out with his comrade. They got behind the tanks through the depression that led toward the *Kinderheimhöhe* while the other "tank busters" waited in extreme tension.

Mellenthin finally gave the signal. The projectiles hissed from the barrels of our *Ofenrohre*. Mellenthin fired at the same instant. In a fraction of a second, three jets of flame shot out of the tanks, but the *Ofenrohre* had been reloaded by then and additional projectiles were on the way. There were more dull detonations and jets of flame leaping high. Four tanks were knocked out. The fifth tank started its engine and tried to get away, but it was already too late. Within a few seconds, he was also ablaze.

Mellenthin and his comrades came back with beaming faces. Before long the Russians pounded our positions with an hour of barrage fire from their mortars. We had to crouch way down in the trenches, and we suffered losses.

When things calmed down again we thought we would be relieved, but, since more tank attacks were expected, we had to remain and take position between the *11./SS-Panzer-Grenadier-Regiment 24 "Danmark"* and the motorcycle platoon.

The next morning our positions were pounded for two hours with an intense barrage. The trenches were plowed up. It was a cloudless, hot summer day. We lost lots of men. Since we had Russians both in front of and behind us, our morale sank to zero.

When the barrage suddenly shifted to our rear, we knew they would come. And come they did — we were struck speechless.

Engines roared. Thirty Soviet Josef Stalin and T 34 tanks rolled toward our positions along and south of the main supply route. We had only one thought: How were we going to survive this?

North of the main supply route a 7.5 cm *Pak* from the *4. SS-Panzer-Grenadier-Brigade "Nederland"* opened fire, but it was not long before the gun fell silent. The tanks rolled closer and closer.

Sixty to eighty meters in front of our positions they came to a halt. The muzzles of their cannon lowered and they opened fire on our positions at extremely short range. We leaped and crawled for our lives.

After the moment of terror was past, a head popped up here and there, aimed and fired a *Panzerfaust*. First one tank burned, then another, and, all at once, the old fighting spirit was back again. Columns of smoke rose everywhere from burning Russian tanks. When fourteen tanks were burning, the others gave up and moved back.

Our own losses were very high. The commander of the *11./SS-Panzer-Grenadier-Regiment 24 "Danmark"* , *SS-Hauptsturmführer* Trautwein, was severely wounded, as were *SS-Untersturmführer* Bertramsen and *SS-Oberscharführer* Hektor. Dead and wounded lay everywhere in the shot-up trenches. The worst of it was that contact with the *10./SS-Panzer-Grenadier-Regiment 24 "Danmark"* had been lost. The section of trench between them and us was occupied by Russians, and they continued to pour troops through it.

After darkness fell we received rations and ammunition. The wounded were taken to the rear, but the dead had to lie where they were since there were not enough stretchers.

During the night, the Soviets attempted to recover their knocked-out tanks. Our artillery fired harassing fire. The Russians were able to drag away two or three damaged tanks. An *SS-Oberscharführer* from the *11./SS-Panzer-Grenadier-Regiment 24 "Danmark"* took over command and we had to spread out farther. At the same time, the *11. /SS-Panzer-Grenadier-Regiment 24 "Danmark"* set up defenses facing south.

The next morning the heavy barrage broke out again. After about an hour, the Soviets came again with tanks and used the same method they had the day before. This time our positions had been so shot up that they were no more than shallow trenches. The enemy tanks were more careful. They kept back farther, so we were only able to destroy three tanks.

That time infantry followed, but when the tanks had to cease fire so as not to endanger their own infantry, we grabbed our weapons and let loose with all that we had. The Soviet infantry attack fell apart. The tanks fell back. We were totally exhausted.

The main supply route was then under Russian control, which cut our contact with the *4. SS-Panzer-Grenadier-Brigade "Nederland"*. Soviet sharpshooters fired on every movement in our trenches. We had already lost several men to head wounds. We waited, longing for darkness to fall.

During that night, *SS-Unterscharführer* Mellenthin and I were the only surviving noncommissioned officers and our platoon had a total of nine men left from the erstwhile 28. The motorcycle platoon and the *11./SS-Panzer-Grenadier-Regiment 24 "Danmark"* still had a strength of about 30 men. There was no more naval infantry.

We placed the dead on the slope behind us. The wounded had to remain until they could be taken away. During the night the Russians moved forward with nine tanks, and we looked forward with misgivings to the next day. We only had one machine gun with a little ammunition and a few *Panzerfäuste* in our platoon. All of the *Ofenrohre* had been destroyed by direct hits. We had no contact with the regiment. We sent a volunteer off to the regiment's command post. Would he make it through?

We stayed out of contact. A new, dreadfully hot day dawned. The wounded moaned softly and constantly asked for water. The only thing we could give them was a few drops of cold tea and some brandy. When would things start up again?

However, that morning we heard a familiar drone of engines from the west. It grew louder and louder. Then we saw 40 *Stukas*. Flight after flight flew over our position. The Russian anti-aircraft opened fire. Shell burst after shell burst, side by side — I didn't think a single plane would make it through.

But plane after plane tipped its wings and peeled off in its dive. Bomb after bomb fell on the Russian assembly positions. Steel, fire and dirt flew high and it seemed as if the entire earth were shaking and tilting. Aircraft after aircraft approached right above our heads. They flew low over our heads and we cheered as they flew away.

Barely two hours later our *Stukas* were back again, and our enthusiasm knew no bounds.

That afternoon they came yet a third time. Again we enthusiastically watched the planes depart. Suddenly, I noticed a *Stuka* was missing one of its landing gear and the machine was constantly losing altitude. The airplane touched the earth right in front of our machine-gun position. It spun around several times and then remained stationary. The Plexiglas canopy was shoved open and a *Feldwebel* and an *Unteroffizier* jumped out, positioning themselves with a machine pistol at the ready. They were happy when we waved to them.

We soon had them in safety, since the Russian sharpshooters were still a danger. There was no saving their aircraft. After we took belts with 900 rounds of machine-gun ammunition from the wings, we blew up the machine.

Naturally, the aircrew wanted to go back. *SS-Unterscharführer* Mellenthin wanted to go back with them and take a report to the regimental command post. Mellenthin came back late in the night. He had made it through with the fliers. We were to remain where we were because there was to be another attempt to take back the *Kinderheimhöhe*. However, the attack did not succeed. As a result, we remained east of the *Kinderheimhöhe* in a hopeless outpost.

During the night, the wounded were supposed to be carried back, but no more stretcher parties could make it through, so we placed all the wounded in the last intact bunker.

More extremely heavy artillery fire pounded our positions next morning. Again there were dead and wounded. As the Russian infantry started its attack, we still had one machine gun, two machine pistols, a few hand grenades and a little bit of ammunition. We were twelve in all.

We desperately tried to defend ourselves, but the Russians soon infiltrated past on our right (south) and an unequal struggle began for the stretch of trench south of the main supply route.

The Soviets then very skillfully rolled up our trenches with hand grenades. We fell back toward the main supply route, alternating fire and movement. But our way was blocked there by a Soviet tank that had the road under fire. Two men fell in the first attempt to cross the road. The Soviets called on us twice to surrender, but we had experienced too much to have any faith in being treated properly.

In the end, we were forced together close to the main supply route. On the far side we could see the positions of the *4. SS-Panzer-Grenadier-Brigade "Nederland"*. Salvation was so close we could almost touch it, but the main supply route still lay between us.

I tried to orient myself while *SS-Unterscharführer* Mellenthin and *SS-Rottenführer* Jörgensen held the Russians down with the machine gun. In spite of my warning, a man jumped up beside me. He tried to make it across the road but was shot down in the middle of it. A mortar round burst behind us and, as I turned around, Mellenthin came toward me. He had been hit by shrapnel and his head was bleeding profusely. I applied an emergency bandage. After I had finished that, *SS-Rottenführer* Jörgensen collapsed, shot in the stomach. His younger brother, who was still one of the living, did not want to leave him in the lurch, though it was more than doubtful whether he would survive. A little later a shot rang out, followed by a loud cry. *SS-Rottenführer* Jörgensen had shot himself in his brother's arms. The younger brother then leaped out of the trench and ran in the opposite direction before we could do anything to stop him.

I wanted to blind the Soviet tank by stirring up dust with the last hand grenades. We crawled close to the main supply route. I threw first one, then another hand grenade and the men leaped up and dashed across the road. The dust that had been stirred up covered them. As Mellenthin and I leaped from the trench as the last men to leave, the Soviet infantry had already made it to the final bend in the trench system.

Only one of the last seven men was hit while crossing the main supply route. He was shot in the leg but made it with us to the Dutch trenches. We were saved!

The second half of August and the first half of September were marked by regrouping and refitting. *SS-Hauptsturmführer* Ternedde assumed command of the *III./SS-Panzer-Grenadier-Regiment 24 "Danmark"*. *Hauptmann* Lührs, who had been transferred from the army to the *Waffen-SS*, became regimental adjutant. The *Sturmgewehr 44* (assault rifle) was introduced. Minefields were laid and an integrated system of trenches extended across the landscape. After *SS-Hauptsturmführer* Bachmeier was wounded, *SS-Obersturmführer* Kleucker took command of hotly-contested Grenadier Hill.

The east slope of Grenadier Hill was mined in such a fashion that, in the event of an attack, explosives could be set off and the enemy forced back by avalanches of stones. In the course of laying minefields in the Grenadier Hill area, *SS-Obersturmführer* Arionus had both legs torn off by a mine accident during the night of 13 September. Arionus, who had taken over the *3./SS-Pionier-Bataillon 11* after returning from convalescence, was taken to the aid station where, fully conscious, he dictated a letter to his wife and then his parents. Finally, he dictated one to his battalion commander and then died.

The *20. Waffen-Grenadier-Division der SS (estnisch)* held a sector between the *Division zur besonderen Verwendung 300* and the East Prussian *11. Infanterie-Division*. At the southern extreme, extending to the shore of Lake Peipus, was the *Division z.b.V. 300*, which had been formed from German divisional units and Estonian rifle regiments.

The East Prussians of the *11. Infanterie-Division* were outstanding fighters. During the period from 24-27 July, they had repulsed six enemy attacks whose objective had been to clear paths for armored formations that would follow. The courageous East Prussians held, protecting the backs of the forces fighting along the isthmus.

However, the Soviets were already advancing towards East Prussia, Riga and the Dorpat Isthmus, thus undermining the "Tannenberg" Position, which was left projecting far to the east. Construction on a blocking position at Konju was stopped. In the west the invasion raged and the capitulation of Finland caused great difficulties. In recognition of that situation, a withdrawal from the "Tannenberg" Position was inevitable. The undefeated volunteers from all the lands of Europe were forced to give up the positions for which they had fought so intensely.

1944: *SS-Standartenführer* von Bockelberg, the chief of staff of the *III. (germanisches) SS-Panzer-Korps* (left), and *SS-Brigadeführer* Ziegler who became the commander of the *11. SS-Freiwilligen-Panzer-Grenadier-Division "Nordland"* after the death of Fritz von Scholz.

1944: The commander of *SS-Panzer-Grenadier-Regiment 24 "Danmark"*, *SS-Sturmbannführer* Krügel, presents awards to deserving men. Right: The regimental adjutant, *SS-Hauptsturmführer* Ternedde.

Pilots with the Fieseler *"Storch"* assigned to the *III.(germanisches) SS-Panzer-Korps.*

Summer 1944: The brigade command post of the *4. SS-Panzer-Grenadier-Brigade "Nederland"* at Sillamäe. Left: *SS-Sturmbannführer* von Bock, the operations officer.

The command post of the *III. (germanisches) SS-Panzer-Korps* at Sillamäe. From left to right: *SS-Brigadeführer* Augsberger, the commander of the *20. Waffen-Grenadier-Division der SS (estnisch)*; *SS-Sturmbannführer* Riipalu, the commander of *SS-Grenadier-Regiment 45*; *SS-Sturmbannführer* Kausch, the commander of *SS-Panzer-Abteilung 11 "Hermann von Salza"*; *SS-Brigadeführer Ziegler*, the commander of the *11. SS-Freiwilligen-Panzer-Grenadier-Division "Nordland"*; *SS-Obergruppenführer* Steiner, the commanding general of the *III. (germanisches) SS-Panzer-Korps*; *SS-Sturmbannführer* Schlüter, the commander of *SS-Artillerie-Regiment 54*; and *Oberst* Kressin, the corps artillery commander.

A *Panther* advances.

Summer 1944: The *Kinderheimhöhe*.

Summer 1944: The Tannenberg
Position. Here: Hill 69.9.

Nature calls!

Top: A recovery vehicle of the maintenance company of *SS-Panzer-Abteilung 11* *"Hermann von Salza"*.

Above: *SS-Nachrichten-Abteilung 503* (the corps signals battalion). Here: Laying cable on the coastal road in Estonia.

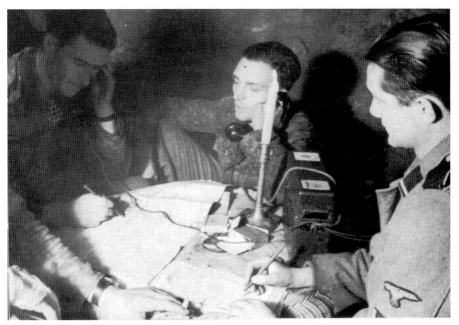

Summer 1944: "Stalactite Cavern". The command post of *SS-Panzer-Grenadier-Regiment 49 "De Ruyter"*.

A *Sd.Kfz. 222* of the *2./SS-Panzer-Aufklüarungs-Abteilung 11*.

This page and top of facing page: Several views of multiple-rocket-launcher vehicles of *SS-Vielfachwerferbatterie 521* which supported the *III. (germanisches) SS-Panzer-Korps* extensively in the Tannenberg Position. The battery was commanded by *SS-Hauptsturmführer* Flecke

Opposite page, bottom: A *Kanonenwagen* of the *5./SS-Panzer-Aufklärungs-Abteilung 11.*

A forward observer conducts his business.

Position on the *Kinderheimhöhe*.

Fire Brigade in
the Northern Sector

On 22 June 1944 the central sector of the Eastern Front collapsed under the weight of the large-scale Soviet offensive. Soviet divisions stormed through the resulting gap between the northern front and those units of the central front that were still holding. One Soviet assault group rapidly gained ground south of the Düna. The specter of encirclement loomed over *Heeresgruppe Nord*. No help could be expected from *Heeresgruppe Mitte* in closing the threatening gap. *Heeresgruppe Nord* was forced to move all available forces into the area of the penetration. *SS-Panzer-Aufklärungs-Abteilung 11* was one of that small number of formations.

SS-Panzer-Aufklärungs-Abteilung 11 was rushed by rail to the Düna. The rail transport rolled through Dünaburg and was then sent on toward Jakobstadt because the Russians had already pushed past Dünaburg to the west. *Abteilung Saalbach* was in the Jakobstadt area on 10 July. The trains had to be unloaded on an open stretch of track in some instances. *SS-Panzer-Aufklärungs-Abteilung 11* went right into combat.

On 14 July, Hitler assembled the various commanders-in-chief, including the commanders of *Heeresgruppen Mitte* and *Nord*, at the *Führerhauptquartier*. *Generaloberst* Frießner, at that time commander-in-chief of *Heeresgruppe Nord*, was ordered to advance southwest with an immediately assembled assault group to reestablish contact with *Heeresgruppe Mitte*.

The *Kampfgruppe* was formed by the evening of that same day. It was led by *General der Kavallerie* Kleffel. The *Kampfgruppe* consisted of the *61.* and *225. Infanterie-Divisionen* as well as *SS-Panzer-Aufklärungs-Abteilung 11*. The *Kampfgruppe* moved out and individual formations made contact with *Heeresgruppe Mitte*, but the area was too great. Contact broke again.

SS-Panzer-Aufklärungs-Abteilung 11 — frequently referred to at that time as *Panzergruppe Saalbach* — was an extremely hard-hitting and rapidly mobile unit that was given a multiplicity of tasks in such a threatening situation. It had two armored car companies, two *SPW* companies and one heavy company. It was often split up into separate companies. It parried with the Soviet corps along the way to the Baltic; it repeatedly attacked the enemy formations. Reconnaissance, immediate counterattacks, blocking missions and the closing of gaps alternated in unbroken succession. Moves of up to a hundred kilometers in a single night were not uncommon. Soon *SS-Sturmbannführer* Saalbach's group was being spoken of by friend and foe alike. German units breathed a sigh of relief when they knew *Kampfgruppe Saalbach* was near, and the Soviets warned their formations in the clear: "Warning! *Panzergruppe Saalbach* approaching!"

Panzergruppe Saalbach thus played a substantial role in preventing the Soviets from attaining their objective of Riga. Oriented southwest, *SS-Panzer-Aufklärungs-Abteilung 11* screened the Latvian capital from the Soviet advance to the Baltic coast at Tuccum.

During that same time period, the southern pillar of *Heeresgruppe Nord* was under assault. Bit by bit, the front crumbled at Polozk. *Schwere-Panzer-Abteilung 502* tried to stem the Soviet tide east of Dünaburg. Even though its *Tigers* knocked out numerous enemy tanks, the Soviet thrust was only delayed. On 24 July, Dünaburg fell to the Soviets. On that same day, *Oberleutnant* Carius, commander of the *2./schwere panzer-Abteilung 502* was wounded and fell into Soviet hands. He was rescued in an assault by elements of his company at the last moment, after a Soviet commissar thought he had executed him with a pistol shot in the back of his neck and had fled with Carius' map board. That day the Soviets proclaimed the death of the famed *Tiger* officer but, by a miracle, Carius was alive.

Along with those ground formations mentioned above, praise must be given to *Major* Rudel's *III./Schlacht-Geschwader 2*, which attacked the enemy armor with successive waves of *Ju 87* dive-bombers, destroying numerous Russian tanks.

While *SS-Panzer-Aufklärungs-Abteilung 11* and other formations covered the southern flank of *Heeresgruppe Nord*, the Soviets reached the Baltic Sea on 1 August at Tuccum. They had advanced on a narrow front between Autz and Mitau.

Heeresgruppe Nord was effectively cut off when the Russians reached the Baltic Sea at Tuccum. The Soviets were already bringing forward new forces to capture the Latvian capital from the west and south. Nevertheless, *Generaloberst* Schörner, who had been entrusted with the command of *Heeresgruppe Nord* on 25 July 1944, was confident. The *OKH* promised assistance. For the advance to Riga from the west, the legendary "*Panzergraf*", *Generalmajor Graf* Strachwitz, was chosen. But the armored formations that were intended for the attack did not arrive — for the simple reason that no more were available. Hyacinth *Graf* Strachwitz, a master of improvisation with the old cavalry spirit, finally set forth with ten tanks and 15 *SPW* instead of the promised three armored divisions to break through to Riga.

After the Soviets captured Tuccum on 1 August, the *SS-Panzer-Ausbildungs- und Ersatz-Regiment* and the *SS-Panzer-Aufklärungs-Ausbildungs-Abteilungen 1* and *2*, which were at the "*Seelager*" training area near Dondangen in Latvia, were combined to form a *Panzerkampfgruppe* under *SS-Obersturmbannführer* Groß. The harbor cranes clattered in Windau harbor as they loaded all that was superfluous from the above-named replacement units for the return to Germany.

Panzer-Brigade Groß then advanced on Tuccum. On 8 August, with support from a makeshift armored train, it attempted to recapture Tuccum on its own. The attempt failed. *Brigade Groß* pushed on past Tuccum to reestablish contact to the east with *General der Kavallerie* Kleffel's *Kampfgruppe*.

After *Graf* Strachwitz had made his preparations, *Panzergruppe Groß* was attached to him. On 20 August, Strachwitz attacked Tuccum with the improvised formation. The armored force captured the city in a *coup de main*. The 48 Russian tanks that were assembled in the city's market place were destroyed by the 20 cm shells of the naval guns of the heavy cruiser *"Prinz Eugen"*. In a rapid thrust, Strachwitz assaulted toward Riga and reached the Latvian capital.

Panzer-Brigade Groß reached the Doblen — Autz road with its infantry forces on 26 August. Elements of *SS-Infanterie-Bataillon Runge* fought with the Russians at the village of Janiarauniki and Hill 50. Runge's battalion was then pulled out of *Brigade Groß* and attached to *Infanterie-Regiment 174* of the *81. Infanterie-Division*.

However, before Strachwitz could fend off the threat to Riga, a new threat loomed against the northern wing of *Heeresgruppe Nord* in the Dorpat Isthmus, a threat that particularly endangered the *III. (germanisches) SS-Panzer-Korps*, which was still located far to the east in the *"Tannenberg"* Position.

On 12 August 1944, the Soviets broke through the *"Modohn"* Position 45 kilometers southwest of Pleskau. The divisions on the southern wing of the *18. Armee* were swept away. Slowly the German divisions fell back to the line extending from the southern point of Lake Wirz to Walk. *Heeresgruppe Nord* tasked *Armee-Abteilung Narwa* with blocking Estonia between Lake Wirz and Lake Peipus. By calling on its last reserves, the Soviet advance was blocked until 16 August. Again, the *III./Schlacht-Geschwader 2* of *Major* Rudel played a decisive role. Thirty divisions of the 3rd Baltic Front were held back. But soon the Soviets sent part of their forces north against Dorpat. Four Soviet rifle divisions and one tank division, as well as two motorized brigades, pressed against the German defensive front between Lake Wirz and Lake Peipus. The *207. Sicherungs-Division* — a security division composed of older men and only lightly armed — was thrown back in a punishing struggle of attrition. The way to Dorpat appeared to be open!

From all points of the compass, units — most of them small — were thrown into the endangered sector. The *III. (germanisches) SS-Panzer-Korps*, which had just finished the heavy fighting in the *"Tannenberg"* Position, sent *Generalmajor der Waffen-SS* Jürgen Wagner to the Dorpat area. With his *staff from the 4. SS-Panzer-Grenadier-Brigade "Nederland"*, he took command of the forces that the *III. (germanisches) SS-Panzer-Korps* had freed up. His own brigade remained in the *"Tannenberg"* Position under *Oberst* Friedrich.

During the night of 15/16 August, the units of the newly formed *Kampfgruppe Wagner* were pulled out of their positions in the *"Tannenberg"* Position and from the rear area of the *III. (germanisches) SS-Panzer-Korps*. Included were the last tanks and assault guns from the *11. SS-Freiwilligen-Panzer-Grenadier-Division "Nordland"* and the *4. SS-Panzer-Grenadier-Brigade "Nederland"*. A battalion of the *5. SS-Freiwilligen-Sturmbrigade "Wallonien"* that was only starting its initial organization in the coastal sector west of the *"Tannenberg"* Position was added to the force mix. The motorized units moved south.

On 16 August, at about 2100 hours, the *II./SS-Artillerie-Regiment 54* (*SS-Hauptsturmführer* de Veer) was withdrawn from the *"Tannenberg"* Position. It entrained at the Jöhwi railroad station and was sent to Dorpat.

On that day the Soviets landed with the 25th Inland-Naval Brigade at Mehikoorma on the west shore of Lake Peipus.

Kampfgruppe Wagner passed Dorpat and formed a line of defense south of the city. Estonian paramilitary forces with armbands were incorporated, along with remnants of broken German units. *Grenadier-Regiment 23 (11. Infanterie-Division)*, the Flemish *SS* battalion, the *III./Werfer-Regiment 3* and the *II./Artillerie-Regiment 58* held off further advances on Dorpat for the time being.

Panzer-Verband Graf Strachwitz, which was still fighting at Riga, was sent on through by high-speed transport to Estonia, reaching Elva on 23 August. Strachwitz was meant to intercept the Soviet advance against the southern end of Lake Wirz with his formation, which included, among others, *Brigade Groß* and *SS-Panzer-Aufklärungs-Abteilung 11*. *Graf* Strachwitz was eliminated as commander while the preparations were still in progress by an automobile accident.

As early as 19 August the battalion of the *5. SS-Freiwilligen-Sturmbrigade "Wallonien"* was already engaged in heavy fighting with a Soviet assault force at Patska. With four tanks, the battalion captured Windmill Hill at Patska and the village itself and checked the Soviet advance. The thin front was penetrated at other points.

The *II./SS-Artillerie-Regiment 54* then occupied firing positions on both sides of Dorpat but was moved forward about 20 kilometers east-southeast of Dorpat on 20 August, where it then supported the Estonians and *Füsilier-Bataillon 11 (11. Infanterie-Division)* which were engaged in heavy defensive fighting.

The men of *Füsilier-Bataillon 11* and the forward observer of the *4./SS-Artillerie-Regiment 54* would never forget that 20 August. The Russians stormed forward against the thinly held positions. The Estonians were thrown back. *Rittmeister* Hansen's fusiliers were all that was left. The *1./Füsilier-Bataillon 11* of *Leutnant* Buchholz on the left wing was the most

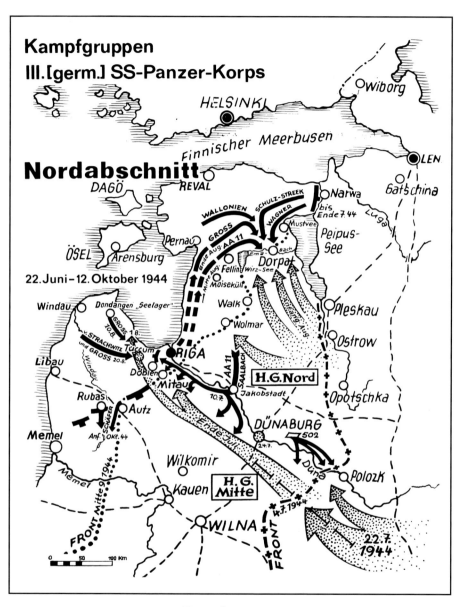

Kampfgruppen
III. (germanisches) SS-Panzer-Korps
22 June - 12 October 1944

149

hard pressed. The battery commander of the *4./SS-Artillerie-Regiment 54*, *SS-Untersturmführer* Horstmann, ran to the aid of *Leutnant* Buchholz and his men. The radio link was reestablished. The Russians came on in hordes. The *1. Schwadron* — the honorific applied in a fusilier battalion — counted no more than 20 combatants.

SS-Untersturmführer Horstmann understood his craft. "Fire with delayed fuses." Within 40 minutes the battery had fired 350 rounds. That stopped the Soviets, costing them more than 200 infantrymen and 15 antitank guns, as well as 13 heavy machine guns.

The Soviets reacted with heavy fire from antitank guns and a new attack with fresh forces. *Rittmeister* Hansen's fusiliers were forced to fall back. The *II./SS-Artillerie-Regiment 54* took up new firing positions at Meliste.

On 21 August, *Generalmajor* Wagner had some control of the situation at the front in the Dorpat area. Along Lake Peipus and along the Werro — Dorpat road there were signs that the Soviet assault was headed north. The Soviets reached the village of Kambi on the Werro — Dorpat road.

SS-Sturmbannführer Degrelle and his Flemish battalion were committed in the Kambi area with the mission of fixing the Soviets. Three *Pak* blocked the road to the north. Friendly artillery was in support. The Soviets gave up Kambi, but repeatedly renewed their attack. Degrelle's battalion had a second mission: Blowing up the railroad line to Dorpat.

On 21 and 22 August there was no breakthrough. On 23 August all hell broke loose.

On that day Noo fell. Degrelle's battalion held its position. A small *Kampfgruppe* under *SS-Untersturmführer* Gillis held a position on the road to Dorpat with three *Pak*. Again and again the Soviets attacked. Gillis lost his three guns. They were recaptured from the Soviets in an immediate counterattack and then three Soviet tanks were knocked out.

Generalmajor der Waffen-SS Wagner implored Degrelle to hold the vital hill position at Kambi. *Major* Rudel's *Stukas* attacked, unceasingly working over the attacking Soviets with bombs and on-board weapons, but it was not enough. The Walloons had to fall back before the overwhelming Soviet pressure. They fought their way through to the north and occupied new positions west of Dorpat and south of the Em Creek.

Panzer-Brigade 101 and *Panzer-Brigade Groß* moved out on 24 August against Elwa and Noo. They had arrived in the meantime from Latvia. *SS-Panzer-Aufklärungs-Abteilung 11*, which also belonged to *Kampfgruppe Graf Strachwitz*, captured the village of Tamsa farther north. But the Soviets proved to be stronger. In the evening of 24 August they reached the southern point of Lake Wirz, thus separating *Armee-Abteilung Narwa* and the *18. Armee*. The Soviet objective was Pernau on the Gulf of Riga. *SS-Panzer-Aufklärungs-Abteilung 11* joined *Kampfgruppe Wagner*. The other formations of *Kampfgruppe Graf Strachwitz* fell back to the southwest.

From that time on, *SS-Panzer-Aufklärungs-Abteilung 11* was a pillar of strength for *Kampfgruppe Wagner*. Often split up into small elements, it attacked east, only to then turn back to the west, soon to attack again in another location. *Kampfgruppe Saalbach* attacked wherever danger threatened.

On 25 August 1944 the struggle for Dorpat began. Elements of the *11. Infanterie-Division* (the *I./Grenadier-Regiment 33*), the *I./Sturmgeschütz-Brigade 393* and the Estonians were thrown back after bitter fighting. At 1800 hours the Red flag waved over Dorpat. *SS-Unterscharführer* Behnke of the *5./SS-Panzer-Aufklärungs-Abteilung 11* defended the Dorpat airfield with his 7.5 cm *Pak*. The Soviets attacked with superior forces, but Behnke and his gun crew did not waver. They repeatedly swung their gun around in all directions and knocked out the attackers.

Dorpat, the old university city south of Em Creek, had been lost. On 25 August the Soviets were able to advance east and west of the city from small bridgeheads over Em Creek and move on farther to the north. West of Dorpat, at the village of Noela, the volunteers of *SS-Bataillon "Wallonien"* offered a stubborn defense. East of the city were Estonian units of limited value in combat. The *II./SS-Artillerie-Regiment 54* provided support, but had to repeatedly displace to new positions to the rear.

The Soviet objective was to effect the junction of their two bridgeheads north of the city of Dorpat and thus reach the road and railroad line linking Dorpat and Reval. On 25 August the way seemed clear. Estonian self-defense units, civil personnel, German trains elements — all streamed in wild confusion to the north. Only a few troops stood against the Soviet assault. *Generalmajor* Wagner no longer knew the meaning of the word sleep, but he did finally manage to gain control of the confused situation with his small number of war-hardened formations.

Along with the defense of Noele, *SS-Sturmbannführer* Degrelle was given the mission of forming a blocking position on the plateau north of Dorpat along the line Parna —Lombi — Keerdu. Degrelle sought out all that were left: Wounded, drivers and payroll clerks. There wasn't much left. On the previous evening, the last of the battalion's *Pak* had been destroyed in an unequal struggle with Soviet tanks. *SS-Untersturmführer* Gillis, the soul of the defense, had been wounded. But on 25 August the defense held fast on the hills north of Dorpat.

Unceasingly the vehicles of *SS-Panzer-Aufklärungs-Abteilung 11* raced from hotspot to hotspot. On 26 August two *Flak* and two 10.5 cm howitzers belonging to a blocking position were surrounded in Haage, near Dorpat. *SS-Standarten-Oberjunker* (officer candidate) Schwarck of the *5./SS-Panzer-Aufklärungs-Abteilung 11* led his cannon platoon in a relief attack on Haage and was able to free the beleaguered army comrades from their unfortunate situation.

The remnants of the tank and assault-gun battalions of the *11. SS-Freiwilligen-Panzer-Grenadier-Division "Nordland"* sacrificed themselves during that fighting. In the Dorpat area they repeatedly stood fast against advancing Soviet armor. Initially, it was seven assault guns of the *SS-Panzer-Abteilung 11 "Hermann von Salza"* and six *Sturmgeschütze* of the *SS-Sturmgeschütz-Abteilung 11* that carried on the fight under *SS-Hauptsturmführer* Schulz-Streek. Soon, however, there were none left. *SS-Untersturmführer* Becker was the only officer to survive. Among others, *SS-Untersturmführer* Stamm and *SS-Untersturmführer* Stübben were killed.

The men of *SS-Bataillon "Wallonien"* formed the decisive blocking position during the final days of August on the high ground along the line Parna — Lombi— Keerdu. All the Soviet attacks broke against their stubborn defense. The Walloons were praised three times in the orders of the day of the *III. (germanisches) SS-Panzer-Korps.* After the fighting concluded, *General* Steiner awarded the Iron Cross to more than 200 of the Walloons. *SS-Untersturmführer* Gillis was decorated with the Knight's Cross and *SS-Sturmbannführer* Degrelle received the Oakleaves to the Knight's Cross. The Walloons were sent back to Germany by ship for re-fitting.

While every kilometer of ground was being hotly contested along the Dorpat front, the *II. Armee-Korps* approached to take over the defense of the Dorpat Isthmus. *Generalmajor* Wagner had brilliantly performed his mission.

East of Dorpat, Estonian battalions took their place in the front. On 31 August they attacked to reduce the Soviet bridgehead over Em Creek. On 1 September the Soviet bridgehead no longer existed. As a result, Em Creek was the front once again. The *II./SS-Artillerie-Regiment 54*, which had occupied firing positions in the Alewi area and later moved its observation positions forward into the Saia — Lamba area, supported the operation. During the first days of September, that sector was reinforced by *Heeres-Artillerie-Abteilung 153.* The Soviets had built corduroy roads south of Em Creek and brought in a fresh division. On 4 September offensive operations were conducted against Dorpat, Kavastu and Mäkse to improve the German positions.

On 13 September the *II./SS-Artillerie-Regiment 54* was relieved by the *II./SS-Artillerie-Regiment 11.* The *II./SS-Artillerie-Regiment 54* reached Voldi by road march. From there it proceeded by rail to Toila and then reoccupied its old firing positions in the *"Tannenberg"* Position.

During the first days of September, the Soviets started regrouping for their great fall offensive.

— Objective No.1: Riga! Cut off the German Northern Front and regain the Baltic region.

— Objective No.2: Pernau! Advance directly south of Lake Wirz to the Baltic Sea.

— Objective No.3: Reval! Advance from the Dorpat area.

The Soviet plans were extremely dangerous for the *18. Armee*, especially for *Armee-Abteilung Narwa* and the *III. (germanisches) SS-Panzer-Korps* which was positioned farthest to the east.

On 16 September, the 3rd Baltic Front started combat reconnaissance patrols in the Dorpat Isthmus. They attained favorable jump-off positions between Dorpat and Lake Peipus. Two days later the Soviets were at Mustvee, the northwest corner of Lake Peipus. *SS-Panzer-Aufklärungs-Abteilung 11* had to intervene again, this time to cover the withdrawal of the *III. (germanisches) SS-Panzer-Korps* from the *"Tannenberg"* Position.

Staff officers of the *III. (germanisches) SS-Panzer-Korps*. From left to right: Krieger, Hahn (*11. SS-Freiwilligen-Panzer-Grenadier-Division "Nordland"*) and Steinfeldt (*4. SS-Panzer-Grenadier-Brigade "Nederland"*)

The field hospital of the *11. SS-Freiwilligen-Panzer-Grenadier-Division "Nordland"* in Reval. Seen here are medics and Estonian nurses. Right: *SS-Sturmbannführer Dr. Dittmar* (commander of the field hospital).

SS-Brigadeführer Wagner, the commander of the *4. SS-Panzer-Grenadier-Brigade "Nederland"*, and his adjutant, *SS-Sturmbannführer* von Bock, while conducting reconnaissance in the Dorpat area, where elements of the brigade had to be committed.

Above: *SS-Brigadeführer* Wagner, Degrelle and Degrelle's adjutant Schäfer during the fighting at Dorpat and along Lake Peipus in September 1944.

Right: 1 June 1944: The burial of *SS-Obersturmbann-führer Graf* von Westphalen, the commander of *SS-Panzer-Grenadier-Regiment 24 "Danmark"*, at the military cemetery on the beach at Reval.

Left: The grave of von Westphalen.

Below: Those in attendance, from left to right: *SS-Standartenführer Dr.* Schlosser, the divisional surgeon of the *11. SS-Freiwillig-en-Panzer-Grenadier-Division "Nordland"*; *SS-Obersturmbann-führer Dr.* Riedweg, a staff officer; *SS-Sturmbannführer* Krügel, the commander of *SS-Panzer-Grenadier-Regiment 24 "Danmark"*; and, *SS-Sturm-bannführer Dr.* Schlegel, the regimental surgeon of *SS-Panzer-Grenadier-Regiment 24 "Danmark"*.

Withdrawal From Estonia

Felix Steiner, commanding general of the *III. (germanisches) SS-Panzer-Korps*, was ordered to report to the *Führerhauptquartier* at Rastenburg on 10 September 1944. At that meeting, Hitler revealed to him a plan that would entail the destruction of the *III. (germanisches) SS-Panzer-Korps* and its volunteers from all the parts of Europe. In that conversation, Hitler let the cat out of the bag:

> I have decided to pull out of Estonia. However, I cannot lose control of the eastern Baltic Sea, since that would stop the ore traffic from Sweden. Therefore it is necessary to hold a bridgehead at Reval.

Steiner knew how Hitler would proceed. Doubtless he intended to have the volunteers fall back on Reval and leave it to them to hold the bridgehead. Steiner was entirely against it. Hitler knew that. Without a farewell, he turned away from Steiner and departed. His final words were: "*Heeresgruppe Nord* will receive appropriate instructions!" But the final decision and concrete instructions did not follow.

Without delay, *General* Steiner flew back to Estonia and immediately arranged for the partial motorization of the East Prussian *11. Infanterie-Division* and the *20. Waffen-Grenadier-Division der SS (estnisch)*. Any and all vehicles were collected and divided among the two divisions. All administrative, work service, police and other official agencies were informed and given the recommendation that their personnel should be immediately transported back to Germany.

General Steiner found an ally in *Generaloberst* Schörner (commander-in-chief of *Heeresgruppe Nord*). Schörner likewise saw no operative significance in a bridgehead at Reval and exerted pressure convinced the *OKH* not to do it.

Despite the possible military ramifications, Steiner informed the Estonians about the impending withdrawal. At his headquarters, Steiner revealed the withdrawal decision to the Inspector of Estonian Volunteers, Major General Sodla, and the Inspector of the Estonian Self-Defense Forces, Colonel Sinka.

"Do you know, *General*, what you have just told us? You have pronounced the death sentence on the Estonian people!" exclaimed Colonel Sinka, breaking the icy silence.

"Move right back to Reval without delay! Put all who wish to flee on the railroad and on the ships in the harbor and send them west! I can do no more!" Steiner answered. And, in all truth, there was no more that he could do. The evacuation measures were begun without permission from the *OKH*.

The Soviet offensive between Lake Peipus and Schaulen started on 14 September. The German front broke in several places. Again and again, Hitler balked at the idea of pulling out of Estonia. *Generaloberst* Schörner flew to the *Führerhauptquartier* to personally obtain permission for withdrawing from Estonia. He outlined the situation. Contrary to expectations, Hitler approved the withdrawal after a short discussion. *"Unternehmen Aster"* began.

Without informing the *OKH*, *Generaloberst* Schörner had already given the order to start preparations for withdrawal from the Narwa position. In the evening of 15 September, *Armee-Abteilung Narwa* and the *III. (germanisches) SS-Panzer-Korps* ordered that the trains elements should be evacuated. All officers up to the rank of *Major* were limited to one rucksack as luggage. Commander calls and coordination meetings followed one after another.

On 18 September 1944 the order for *"Unternehmen Aster"* was issued. It briefly and clearly specified how Estonia would be evacuated:

1.   The *III. (germanisches) SS-Panzer-Korps* falls back when darkness falls to the west and, in a single move, goes all the way back to Pernau. Last units leave Wesenberg on the evening of 19 September.

2.   The *II. Armee-Korps* holds the current line and withdraws on 19 September as rapidly as possible.

3.   *Gruppe Gerok* (*Generalmajor* Gerok) foils the enemy advance on Reval with combat elements. It defends Reval and the Baltic port until the conclusion of embarkation on ships.

4.   The Eastern Baltic Naval Command carries out the evacuation no later than 22 September, concluding with the transport of *Gruppe Gerok* to the Baltic islands.

At 1800 hours on 18 September, *SS-Panzer-Grenadier-Regiment 24 "Danmark"* issued its regimental order to its companies. That order can serve as an example of similar orders that went out to all the units of the *III. (germanisches) SS-Panzer-Korps:*

1.   Enemy advances from the Dorpat area to the northeast and from the Walk area to the west and southwest. In front of our own sector the enemy formations that were confirmed in August are still present.

2.   Finland's capitulation eliminates the need for continuing to hold Estonia.

3.   The regiment withdraws from its positions with all units at 2000 hours.

4.   The heavy weapons of the regiment (the *13.* and *14./SS-Panzer-Grenadier-Regiment 24 "Danmark"*) will cover the withdrawal of the rifle com-

panies.

5. Communication after 1900 hours will be by radio.

6. Rearguard: *6./SS-Panzer-Grenadier-Regiment 24 "Danmark"* and the regiment's machine-pistol- and combat-engineer platoons. They will remain until 2300 hours on Grenadier Hill and Hill 69.9. The regiment will attach a 30-watt radio section to the *6./SS-Panzer-Grenadier-Regiment 24 "Danmark"*.

7. The regiment's assembly area will be Kothla-Järwe.

> *II./SS-Panzer-Grenadier-Regiment 24 "Danmark"*: Konju
> *III./SS-Panzer-Grenadier-Regiment 24 "Danmark"*: West of
> Konju in the former trains area.

8. Order of march from Kothla-Järwe:

> Regimental command & control section
> *II./SS-Panzer-Grenadier-Regiment 24 "Danmark"*
> *III./SS-Panzer-Grenadier-Regiment 24 "Danmark"*
> *13./SS-Panzer-Grenadier-Regiment 24 "Danmark"*
> *14./SS-Panzer-Grenadier-Regiment 24 "Danmark"*
> Supply companies and trains elements.

9. The regimental command post will remain at Hill 69.9 until 2000 hours. After 2000 hours it will be on the move. Communications will be by radio.

10. Medical aid station will be west of Hill 69.9 until 2000 hours.

The formations of the *4. SS-Freiwilligen- Panzergrenadier- Brigade "Nederland"* and the *11. SS-Freiwilligen-Panzer-Grenadier-Division "Nordland"* withdrew from the positions according to plan. The artillery assembled on the road to Konju and moved west.

The *II./SS-Freiwilligen-Panzer-Grenadier-Regiment 49 "de Ruyter"*, which had been taken over by *SS-Sturmbannführer* Petersen, had already been withdrawn from the *"Tannenberg"* Position and had been attached to the *II. Armee-Korps* as a rear-guard formation.

SS-Panzer-Grenadier-Regiment 23 "Norge" pulled out of its positions at Waiwara, marched on foot to Sillamäe and climbed onto the vehicles that were waiting there.

There was a delay for *SS-Panzer-Grenadier-Regiment 24 "Danmark"*. The heavy weapons could not be pulled out of position as planned. The vehicles and prime movers were held up at the Konju bridge and were not able to proceed against the stream of withdrawing vehicles.

In the meantime, the rifle companies of *SS-Panzer-Grenadier-Regiment 24 "Danmark"* had already withdrawn from their positions. The *6./SS-Panzer-Grenadier-Regiment 24 "Danmark"* remained on Hill 69.9 as rear guard.

Grenadier Hill was held by the regiment's machine-pistol and combat-engineer platoons. They had recently been reformed at the Toila forest camp. Those platoons were the last units in contact with the enemy and had to simulate full occupation of the main line of resistance.

At 2030 hours the heavy weapons of *SS-Panzer-Grenadier-Regiment 24 "Danmark"* delivered one more barrage. Excess ammunition was fired off. At 2100 hours the heavy weapons limbered up. The companies moved to the west. Only the rear guard remained in the positions.

The account that follows details the experience of the rear guard, which was, at that point, the eastern-most element on the entire Eastern Front:

The platoon leaders, *SS-Hauptscharführer* Christensen (regimental combat-engineer platoon) and *SS-Hauptscharführer* Schwabenberg (regimental machine-pistol platoon) ceaselessly made the rounds of the positions, which were thinly held throughout. From Grenadier Hill they strained their ears and peered down at the road below. Nothing could be seen or heard. They knew that their platoons were now alone on Grenadier Hill and covering the withdrawal of their comrades.

The *6./SS-Panzer-Grenadier-Regiment 24 "Danmark"* withdrew from Hill 69.9 at 2200 hours. The rear-guard platoons were to follow at 2300 hours.

The German withdrawal did not remain concealed from the Russians. Vehicle noises and the artillery barrage that was not followed by any assault troop operations strengthened Russian suspicions of a German withdrawal. Soviet combat patrols hesitantly probed forward and found the German positions empty.

The rear-guard platoons withdrew from Grenadier Hill at 2300 hours. It was high time. As the Germans descended the west slope of Grenadier Hill, the Russians were already on the road probing westward. While the Russians searched the abandoned bunkers, the German platoons marched silently alongside the road toward the west.

The rear-guard platoons from *SS-Panzer-Grenadier-Regiment 24 "Danmark"* marched on foot to a small bridge south of Sillamäe where a rearguard from the *I./SS-Freiwilligen-Panzer-Grenadier-Regiment 49 "de Ruyter"* was waiting for them to pass through its lines. Then the bridge went up in the air.

The stream of vehicles flowed to the west in two parallel rows. Here and there, explosions thundered through the night and fires lit up the darkness. The *11. SS-Freiwilligen-Panzer-Grenadier-Division "Nordland"* and the *4. SS-Panzer-Grenadier-Brigade "Nederland"* reached Kothla-Järwe in the morning of 19 September.

The last units reached Wesenberg at about noon on 19 September 1944. There was a "clearance sale" at the army rations dump. The men hauled wine, *Schnaps*, cigarettes and foodstuffs to their vehicles.

Several kilometers outside of Weißenstein the army fuel dump was being cleared. All vehicles filled their tanks and any spare fuel containers. On the other side of Weißenstein military police directed them toward Pernau. The units billeted themselves in small villages and woodland clearings and waited for new orders.

The East Prussian *11. Infanterie-Division*, which had defended the Narwa Isthmus to the last as part of the *III. (germanisches) SS-Panzer-Korps* (south of the *11. SS-Freiwilligen-Panzer-Grenadier-Division "Nordland"*), got hold of every vehicle it could lay its hands on to be able to execute its withdrawal as rapidly as possible. Its horse-drawn division artillery trotted more than 150 kilometers without a break and brought the precious weapons to safety. The horses accomplished unimaginable feats. The grenadier companies, packed like sardines on requisitioned vehicles, proceeded southwest just as fast as the motorized units of the corps.

The *20. Waffen-Grenadier-Division der SS (estnisch)*, which had defended south of the *11. Infanterie-Division*, proceeded in similar fashion to Riga and, from there, by ship to German territory, where it was reformed at the Neuhammer Training Area. Several units were lost during the withdrawal.

The *Division z.b.V. 300*, which had been formed from Estonian border-guard formations and had been positioned north of Lake Peipus on the Narwa River front, was unable to make contact in repeated attempts. The drama of that division should be told briefly.

*

In May 1944 the *Division z.b.V. 300* was formed from the staff of the shattered *13. Luftwaffen-Feld-Division* and Estonian border-guard formations. It was directly subordinated to *Armee-Abteilung Narwa*. The division was comprised of German divisional units, four regiments of border guards, six batteries of light and heavy field howitzers and a *Jäger-Bataillon* (light infantry).

The division had a sector to defend that was slightly larger than the combined sectors of the 11. SS-Freiwilligen-Panzer-Grenadier-Division "Nordland", the 4. SS-Panzer-Grenadier-Brigade "Nederland", the 11. Infanterie-Division and the 20. Waffen-Grenadier-Division der SS (estnisch). Because of the extraordinary length of front, and for better command and control, the division was divided into two brigades. The terrain in the combat sector consisted of extensive marshland with few trails. To supply the division, two stretches of narrow-gauge railroad, about 30 kilometers in length, were built. They connected with Jewe. In addition, the division's combat-engineer battalion built a 30-kilometer corduroy road to Jisaku. At its endpoint, the corduroy road divided and linked the brigades to the north and south with the division staff. Other than that, there was only a small hard-surface road along the north shore of Lake Peipus leading westward from the little village of Vihtse.

On 18 September, the Soviet 2nd Shock Army, which had assumed command in the Dorpat area, attacked the blocking positions on the Dorpat

Isthmus. It was unable to break through between the *87. Infanterie-Division* and the *207. Sicherungs-Division* of the *II. Armee-Korps*. However, it did break through the Estonian self-defense formations positioned to the north. *General* Hasse channeled his *II. Armee-Korps* back to Oberpahlen and Fellin. The forces of the 2nd Shock Army (Lieutenant General Fedjuninskij) that had broken through stormed northward along Lake Peipus. That was the day that the withdrawal order went out to the *III. (germanisches) SS-Panzer-Korps*. The *11. SS-Freiwilligen-Panzer-Grenadier-Division "Nordland"*, the *4. SS-Panzer-Grenadier-Brigade "Nederland"*, the *11. Infanterie-Division* and the *20. Waffen-Grenadier-Division der SS (estnisch)* were able to carry out their planned withdrawal. For *Division z.b.V. 300*, however, the withdrawal movement was far more difficult due to the inadequate roads, which finally sealed its fate.

To the details…On 18 September, at 0830 hours, the division commander, *Generalmajor* Höfer, received news from his operations officer, *Major Freiherr* von Hammerstein, that "strong Soviet forces have broken through east of Dorpat through the Em Creek position and are advancing north!" That news was shortly followed by the withdrawal order from *Armee-Abteilung Narwa*. Plans for the withdrawal were made in all possible haste.

The northern brigade of *Division z.b.V. 300*, which was led by *SS-Obersturmbannführer* Engelhardt, had to fall back to the west over the corduroy road. *Regiment 6* from the southern brigade also had the same withdrawal route. The other regiment of the southern brigade was to use the road along the shore of Lake Peipus.

The *Division z.b.V. 300* started its withdrawal at 1800 hours. Three infantry regiments, several batteries of artillery, a *Jäger-Bataillon* and the attendant trains elements were all to use a single, narrow corduroy road that stretched for 25 kilometers. Each regiment had 384 one-horse and 16 four-horse wagons. One of the officers made the following report:

> I had to leave my command post at 2100 hours in order to perform traffic control duties with my staff. Chaos ruled where the corduroy roads of the northern and southern brigades came together. No one had told us that half of the southern brigade was to march back with us on the same corduroy road. There was no rest for us from 2200 to 0200 hours during the night of 19 September. All of the units had to be funneled in on a single road. The Estonians did not understand any German. Everything had to be accomplished by pushing and poking. The small Baltic horses got stuck in the mud holes again and again.

On 18 September, because of the developments along the western shore of Lake Peipus, *SS-Panzer-Aufklärungs-Abteilung 11* was sent south. *SS-Hauptsturmführer* Flecke's *SS-Vielfach-Werfer-Batterie 521* was attached. *Kampfgruppe Saalbach* hurled itself against the spearheads of the Russian attack, but the area was bare of troops. *Kampfgruppe Saalbach* felt as though it were a drop in the bucket. In the meantime, the bulk of *Division z.b.V. 300* was lost.

The units of *Division z.b.V. 300* had to make a turn south from Jisaku to get to the only bridge over the broad and deep Pungerja River. The total strength of the division at that point amounted to about 1700 men. In order to ward off the threatening catastrophe, the division quickly organized three *Kampfgruppen* that were led by German colonels and equipped in makeshift fashion with motor vehicles to gain mobility. But they also got lost in the vast area of operations. *SS-Obersturmbannführer* Engelhardt led one *Kampfgruppe*. Each had a strength of about 600 men.

SS-Panzer-Aufklärungs-Abteilung 11, which had won a legendary reputation between Riga and Dorpat as *Panzergruppe Saalbach*, repeatedly halted Russian spearheads in a war of movement. At Mustvee and Torma it temporarily stopped the Soviets and then moved to Wesenberg. More was not possible.

The fate of most of the *Division z.b.V. 300* was sealed in the wooded region on both sides of the marshy Pungerja. The Estonian 8th Rifle Corps, one of the units formed by the Soviets under Lieutenant General Pern, and formations of the Soviet 2nd Shock Army reached that region. There, Estonians in Russian uniforms shot Estonians in German uniforms. Most of the soldiers of the division vanished in the wooded swamps.

*

The *III. (germanisches) SS-Panzer-Korps* fell back from Estonia in leapfrog fashion. It wanted to form a blocking position at Pernau, Walk and Wolmar against the pursuing Soviets. The Soviets were attempting to thrust through to the sea and cut off the retreating German forces. The two sides were engaged in a race.

In the evening of 19 September, the *5./SS-Panzer-Aufklärungs-Abteilung 11* was positioned west of Wesenberg as rearguard. After the pursuing enemy had been stopped by an immediate counterattack, an order went out to the company by radio at 0200 hours:"*5.SS-Panzer-Aufklärungs-Abteilung 11* withdraw and return to the battalion!"

The company moved the entire night. Shortage of fuel forced it to tow vehicles. *SS-Untersturmführer* Schirmer reported in to the battalion at 0900 hours on 20 September. The vehicles were immediately refueled. A Soviet armored advance forced the renewed immediate commitment of the company, but soon the battalion headed west as ordered. In the meantime, the *II. Armee-Korps* swung to the south.

The *5./SS-Panzer-Aufklärungs-Abteilung 11,* which included a combat-engineer platoon, received the mission of holding a bridge on the retreat route open until ten *Sturmgeschütze* involved in rearguard fighting had made it past the bridge. The demolition order that *SS-Untersturmführer* Schirmer received read: "When the tenth assault gun has crossed the bridge, blow it!"

The perfectly straight road cut a streamed at right angles. To the west on

163

both sides of the road were small groups of bushes in which Schirmer set up his security. On both sides of the road, echeloned to the rear, were two farmsteads in which *Kanonenwagen* and *SPW* were positioned. Behind the right-hand farmstead was a road leading east. It was secured by one *Kanonenwagen* and a 7.5 cm *Pak*. On the far side of the stream the terrain was covered in light vegetation. There was a village about 400 meters away. Schirmer and his messenger were in a ditch on the near side of the bridge.

The *5./SS-Panzer-Aufklärungs-Abteilung 11* waited for almost two hours, but no *Sturmgeschütze* came. Sounds of armor could be heard from the village on the far side of the stream. Russian infantry gradually worked its way through the vegetation and up to the stream. There was intermittent infantry fire. Schirmer had a message sent to the battalion by radio. The answer: "Follow the demolition order!"

Schirmer dashed forward to the bridge and shortened the fuse. Infantry fire. The situation became critical. And still no *Sturmgeschütze* to be seen. Once again, the answer to a radio request: "Follow the demolition order!"

Schirmer dashed forward again to attach a satchel charge. Then the first *Sturmgeschütz* arrived, followed by two more that were moving in reverse and firing at the same time. Four Soviet tanks followed. The infantry fire intensified. The first *Sturmgeschütz* rolled over the bridge and sheared off to the side to give covering fire to the others. Finally, the remaining two crossed the bridge. A *Leutnant* shouted from one of them: "Blow the bridge! We are the last ones. The other seven assault guns broke out to the north. Confirmed by radio!"

Green light for Schirmer. A T 34 had already got to within 80 meters of the bridge. High time! Would everything work?

Schirmer ran for the bridge. Soviet infantry fired madly. The fire was returned from the German side. The first and second fuses were lit. Schirmer ran back and tossed himself down 40 meters from the bridge as it went up into the air. Pieces spiraled through the air. A chunk struck Schirmer's pistol holster, breaking both pistol grips. Alternating fire and movement, the company worked its way back. It then mounted up and raced back to the battalion.

The withdrawal from Estonia did not proceed without problems. At times the columns were split far apart. Two vehicles of *SS-Panzer-Grenadier-Regiment 24 "Danmark"* had to be blown up at Wesenberg as the enemy neared. In the end, *SS-Unterscharführer* Diedrich of the *10./SS-Panzer-Grenadier-Regiment 23 "Norge"* rolled south on a single tire with part of his platoon. He only rejoined his company just outside of Riga. The supply sergeants and the maintenance personnel had their hands full.

All installations of military importance were demolished by the combat engineers: Railroad lines, bridges and the oil refineries in Kothla-Järwe — the only ones in Estonia—that processed the rich oil-shale deposits.

In the meantime, *Generalmajor* Gerok's *Kampfgruppe* formed a bridgehead at Reval. It included naval formations, Estonian home-guard formations, a *Heeres-Artillerie-Abteilung*, a *Kampfgruppe* of the corps *Panzerjäger-Abteilung* and elements of the *11. Infanterie-Division* and the *20. Waffen-Grenadier-Division der SS (estnisch)*. By 19 September the positions had been occupied.

The Soviets attacked the bridgehead position at Reval on 21 September. In the meantime, the embarkation of German formations in Reval harbor had been proceeding in high gear. On 22 September the companies of *Kampfgruppe Gerok* fell back to the harbor. In the afternoon, the last German torpedo boats — "*T-23*" and "*T-28*" — cast off and fired at the pursuing Soviets. On 22 September the Red flag waved over Estonia's capital city. By 22 September the ships of the Eastern Baltic command under *Admiral* Burchardi had transported approximately 80,000 German soldiers, civil personnel, Estonians and wounded.

Pernau fell on 23 September. Hapsal, across from the island of Dagö, fell on 24 September.

Kampfgruppe Bunse (the *I./SS-Freiwilligen-Panzer-Grenadier-Regiment 49 "de Ruyter"* and additional elements of the *4. SS-Freiwilligen-Panzergrenadier- Brigade "Nederland"*) continued to hold a small bridgehead at Pernau for three more days to secure the embarkation of German formations in the small harbor. The new line of defense was the Pernau River south of the city. After the bridge over the river had already been blown up, a small German reconnaissance formation showed up. The combat engineers of the *4. SS-Panzer-Grenadier-Brigade "Nederland"* quickly constructed a makeshift crossing of poplar trunks laid close together. That enabled the rearguard unit which had been forced off course to continue its withdrawal.

The reinforced motorcycle platoon of *SS-Freiwilligen-Panzer-Grenadier-Regiment 49 "de Ruyter"* held a road intersection south of the city for a longer period of time.

The rear guards of the *4. SS-Panzer-Grenadier-Brigade "Nederland"* moved rapidly to the southwest. Large tracts of woods, villages and individual farmsteads in forest clearings followed each other in varied succession. The woods gleamed picturesquely in the rusty autumn colors.

Again there was a traffic jam. *SS-Pionier-Bataillon 11*, which was in the rearguard, put out close security. The commander of the combat engineers, *SS-Haupsturmführer* Wanhöfer, hurried back to find out what was the cause of the jam. Vehicles coming from two directions were halted at a fork in the road. On some high ground was an *Oberst*. Wanhöfer turned to him:

"*Herr Oberst*, the rearguard has closed up. The vehicles have to get going!"

"The road is impassable and must be fixed first!" answered the *Oberst*. After receiving further condescending answers, Wanhöfer left — with his doubts.

A little later he reached the first vehicle. A completely intact stretch of road stretched ahead of him. When he questioned the driver, he got the answer: "We were stopped by an *Oberst!*"

Wanhöfer instructed the driver: "Move out now!"

The long line of vehicles got moving. When Wanhöfer got back to the fork in the road, the *Oberst* was no longer there.

SS-Panzer-Aufklärungs-Abteilung 11 and *Kampfgruppe Bunse* (the *4. SS-Freiwilligen-Panzergrenadier-Brigade "Nederland"*) were diverted south. The reconnaissance battalion blocked the road to Pernau Bay east of Moiseküll. *Kampfgruppe Bunse* held blocking positions at Wolmar.

The divisions of the *II. Armee-Korps* were moving behind the *XXVIII. Armee-Korps* (*30.* and *61. Infanterie-Divisionen*). Further to the south, the *L. Armee-Korps* was defending against superior enemy forces.

On 24 September *Kampfgruppe Petersen*(the *II./SS-Freiwilligen-Panzer-Grenadier-Regiment 49 "de Ruyter"*) was positioned at the Lemmer River south of Pernau and blocked the coastal road to the south. Here is the after-action report of *Kampfgruppe Petersen*:

During the morning hours of 24 September 1944, *Kampfgruppe Petersen* held its position on the Lemmer. The reconnaissance that had been conducted during the day resulted in no contact with the enemy.

At 1930 hours the combat outposts reported the approach of three tanks and 20 trucks with mounted infantry. Two enemy tanks succeeded in reaching the road south of the Lemmer by way of the beach and continuing to advance along it. The third enemy tank was destroyed in close combat. The enemy infantry attempted to break through the friendly positions but were bloodily repulsed.

The enemy then launched a massed armor attack along the coast and on the road with about 20 tanks. He was able to break through our main line of resistance. Five more tanks were destroyed at close quarters in the main defensive area. Several enemy tanks advanced as far as the staging area of our own combat vehicles and were combated there by the reserve and the drivers. They were able to destroy four more tanks. (*SS-Rottenführer* Strapatin particularly excelled in that action. Through his coolness, the combat vehicles were saved from certain destruction.)

Deeply affected by his losses, the enemy turned back and returned to his jump-off position. Two of the withdrawing tanks were destroyed by our reserves, which had been brought forward in the meantime.

During the ensuing break in the fighting, the battalion withdrew under heavy pressure from the enemy. The enemy attempted to make contact with the moving column from behind and engage it in combat. *SS-Unterscharführer* Spork alternately brought two light infantry guns into position. He destroyed one tank, that way covering the withdrawal.

The two tanks that had broken through in the first attack were knocked out by the *4./SS-Artillerie-Regiment 54* and by the leader of the radio section of the divisional communications center.

During a change of position of the light infantry guns, two enemy tanks advanced by surprise. The first rammed the vehicle from behind, but was knocked out by a *Panzerfaust*. The second rolled along the column. The men of the rammed vehicle ran after the enemy tank and destroyed it from behind with a *Panzerfaust*. In order to protect the main body of the battalion from further attacks by enemy tanks, the commander ordered demolition of the bridge north of Haynach, even though his adjutant and a number of men were still on the northern side of the small coastal river as rearguard.

The following soldiers destroyed Russian tanks in close combat:

Staff, *II./SS-Freiwilligen-Panzer-Grenadier-Regiment 49 "de Ruyter"*

SS-Rottenführer Straptin: 2 tanks
SS-Unterscharführer Seifholz: 1 tank

5./SS-Freiwilligen-Panzer-Grenadier-Regiment 49 "de Ruyter"

SS-Unterscharführer Schuur: 3 tanks
SS-Rottenführer Kist: 1 tank

6./SS-Freiwilligen-Panzer-Grenadier-Regiment 49 "de Ruyter"

No names available

7./SS-Freiwilligen-Panzer-Grenadier-Regiment 49 "de Ruyter"

SS-Untersturmführer Teunissen: 1 tank

8./SS-Freiwilligen-Panzer-Grenadier-Regiment 49 "de Ruyter"

SS-Sturmmann Rieger: 1 tank
Light infantry guns: 2 tanks

4./SS-Artillerie-Regiment 54

SS-Untersturmführer Horstmann: 1 tank
Light field howitzer: 1 tank.

The soldiers of *Kampfgruppe Petersen* would not forget the night of 24/25 September 1944. On the morning of 25 September they were on the coastal road on the border of Estonia and Latvia.

While the *III. (germanisches) SS-Panzer-Korps* fell back to the south, the *XXVIII.* and *L. Armee-Korps* defended in the Walk — Wolmar line. Both corps melted away. Contact was lost. The *L. Korps* was hardest hit. The commanding general, *General der Infanterie* Wegener, was killed in the front lines. The *21. Infanterie-Division* was smashed and reduced to no more than one small *Kampfgruppe*.

SS-Flak-Abteilung 11 was attached to the *Kampfgruppe* of the *21.*

Infanterie-Division. In ceaseless, self-sacrificing service with the few infantry-men of the *21. Infanterie-Division,* the battalion maintained exemplary comradeship and fell back from position to position to the southwest. After the conclusion of the fighting, the divisional commander of the *21. Infanterie-Division* awarded the German Cross in Gold to the battalion commander, *SS-Obersturmbannführer* Plöw, and the battery commander of the *4./SS-Flak-Abteilung 11, SS-Obersturmführer* Holzboog.

It was no better with the other corps of the *18. Armee.* The *18. Armee* was facing collapse. Indicative of the situation is its after-action report:

> In the defensive fighting that has lasted since 14 September, the *18. Armee* has faced almost 70 Russian rifle divisions, two armored corps and numerous separate armored formations…Due to heavy losses, ten of the 18 divisions of the *18. Armee* can only be considered Kampfgruppen.

While the German corps between Walk and Wolmar were involved in heavy fighting, the Soviet III Guards Corps also attacked between the Misa and Kekava Rivers. Its objective was Riga. Alarm units of the *I. Armee-Korps* barely held a bridgehead at Kekava. The bridgehead was broadened in counterattacks. The *11. SS-Freiwilligen- Panzergrenadier- Division "Nordland"* was committed in that endangered sector. The *III. (germanisches) SS-Panzer-Korps* eventually took command of the sector.

The new march objective for the *11. SS-Freiwilligen-Panzer-Grenadier-Division "Nordland"* for 22 September was 30 kilometers north of Riga! In the afternoon of 21 September, the division crossed the Estonian-Latvian border on the coastal road.

On the morning of 22 September, the division received the attack order for the next day. The soldiers of the division mounted up. After exactly one hour, they were moving through Riga. Then to the southeast. Russian aircraft bombed the Latvian capital unceasingly.

The Baldone, Doblen and Autz Areas of Operation

As the evening of 22 September 1944 approached, the regiments of the *11. SS-Freiwilligen- Panzergrenadier- Division "Nordland"* bivouacked in the extensive pine forests south of Kekava. The corps headquarters was in Tigurgas; the command post of the division in Gulbji. For days five German divisions had held off the Soviet assault on Riga. The Soviet command kept throwing new formations into the battle for Riga. On the German side, the *11. SS-Freiwilligen- Panzergrenadier- Division "Nordland"*, the *225. Infanterie-Division*, elements of the *11. Infanterie-Division* and elements of the *14. Panzer-Division* entered the fray.

During the evening of 22 September, *SS-Panzer-Grenadier-Regiment 24 "Danmark"* was attached to the *14. Panzer-Division* and the following order issued to the battalions:

1.   The enemy continues to attack Riga with strong infantry and armored forces and has gained deep penetrations in some places.

2   On 23 September, *SS-Panzer-Grenadier-Regiment 24 "Danmark"* is to attack from the area north of Lidakas and Vaci against the streambed of Kekava Stream. The villages of Lidakas and Vaci and the woods north of the stream are to be cleared of the enemy; the enemy is to be thrown back across the stream.

3.   Assembly area: *III./SS-Panzer-Grenadier-Regiment 24 "Danmark"* on the left in the woods northeast of Lidakas; *II./SS-Panzer-Grenadier-Regiment 24 "Danmark"* on the right in the woods northeast of Vaci.

4.   Attack sector for the *III./SS-Panzer-Grenadier-Regiment 24 "Danmark"*: From the left regimental boundary to Lidakas (inclusive). Adjoining to the right, the *II./SS-Panzer-Grenadier-Regiment 24 "Danmark"* to Vaci (inclusive).

5.   Attack start: 23 September, 0700 hours.

6.   The *13.* and *14./SS-Panzer-Grenadier-Regiment 24 "Danmark"* are to occupy the reconnoitered positions by daybreak and cover the regiment's attack. The *14./SS-Panzer-Grenadier-Regiment 24 "Danmark"* is to occupy positions allowing simultaneous ground and aerial engagement.

7.   The attack will be supported by tanks and assault guns of the *14. Panzer-Division*.

8.   Communications links by radio and wire are to be established immediately upon occupying the assembly positions.

9.   The regimental command post will be in Celmini as of 22 September, 2300

hours.

SS-Panzer-Grenadier-Regiment 23 "Norge" went into its assembly position in extensive woods in the line Dekmeri — Katlapji. The few tanks and assault guns of the *11. SS-Freiwilligen- Panzergrenadier- Division "Nordland"* assembled in the Senbegi area. The *I./SS-Artillerie-Regiment 11* went into position to the north at Tici. The *11.* and *225. Infanterie-Divisionen* established security to the east in the extensive woods. The plan intended the forces to conduct a flank attack into the Soviet tank brigade that had advanced from Baldone on the road to Cempulli. It was located at Blunavas.

The units reached their assigned areas. The night was calm. Only a few "lame ducks" occasionally disturbed the silence of the night. Fires burned everywhere.

The new day, 23 September, dawned. The glowing sun rose in the east. Air and artillery liaison officers arrived at the regimental command post. Shortly before the start of the attack, the news arrived that the arrival of the tanks from the *14. Panzer-Division* would be delayed. The start of the attack was postponed, but before the new order could reach the battalions, the *II. SS-Panzer-Grenadier-Regiment 24 "Danmark"* (Bergfeld) had already moved out for the attack. That meant that the *III./SS-Panzer-Grenadier-Regiment 24 "Danmark"* (Ternedde) also had to start.

The companies energetically launched their attacks. The enemy fell back. German artillery fired salvoes on the stream bed while German ground-attack planes struck the enemy artillery positions. After a bitter defense, Lidakas was in the hands of the *III./SS-Panzer-Grenadier-Regiment 24 "Danmark"* at 1030 hours. The *6.* and *11./SS-Panzer-Grenadier-Regiment 24 "Danmark"* were only a few hundred meters from the stream bed, which was strongly held and studded with machine guns and antitank guns. Even though the tanks and assault guns of the *14. Panzer-Division* had arrived by then, the enemy resistance increasingly stiffened.

The critical point had been reached! The Russians launched a counterattack with armored forces and infantry. Enemy infantry fell on the companies from the rear from woods that had not been cleared. The situation was extremely tense. The *II./SS- Artillerie-Regiment 11* and the heavy weapons of *SS-Panzer-Grenadier-Regiment 24 "Danmark"* fired unceasingly into the stream bed and shelled the attackers. Russian artillery and Stalin organs poured down barrages on the Germans. Aircraft from both sides joined the ground fighting in that spectacle from hell.

The *6.* and *11./SS-Panzer-Grenadier-Regiment 24 "Danmark"* fell back a little and were received by the reserves. By 1300 hours the enemy counterattack was broken.

The regiment advanced again and was supported by some tanks of the *14. Panzer-Division*. Again, the *6.* and *11./SS-Panzer-Grenadier-Regiment 24*

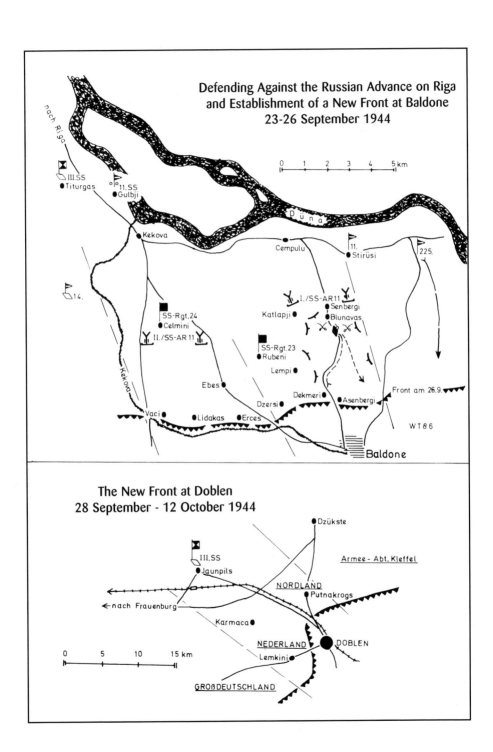

Defending Against the Russian Advance on Riga
and Establishment of a New Front at Baldone
23-26 September 1944

0 1 2 3 4 5 km

nach Riga

III.SS
Titurgas
11.SS
Gulbji
Kekova
Düna
Cempulu
11.
Stirüsi
225.
14.
I./SS-AR 11
Senbergi
Katlapji
Blunavas
SS-Rgt.24
Celmini
II./SS-AR 11
SS-Rgt.23
Rubeni
Lempi
Kekova
Ebes
Dekmeri
Asenbergi
Front am 26.9.
Dzersi
Vaci
Lidakas
Erces
WT 86
Baldone

The New Front at Doblen
28 September - 12 October 1944

Dzükste

III.SS
Jaunpils

Armee - Abt. Kleffel

NORDLAND
Putnakrogs

nach Frauenburg

Karmaca

NEDERLAND
Lemkini
DOBLEN

0 5 10 15 km

GROßDEUTSCHLAND

171

"Danmark" were in the stream bed. However, the attack ground to a halt in the Soviet defensive fire. The Soviets launched another counterattack.

On both sides, the heavy weapons fired with everything they had. Low-flying aircraft swept over the battlefield. Two German and four Soviet tanks were burning. Finally there was a break in the fighting at about 1700 hours. Both sides were exhausted and had suffered numerous casualties. *SS-Panzer-Grenadier-Regiment 24 "Danmark"* had lost nearly 300 men. As a result, it no longer had any strength to attack.

During the night, the main line of resistance was pulled back at various places. The last reserves were sent forward. The regiment's machine-pistol platoon, the communications platoon and an alarm company formed from trains elements held Lidakas. Regimental commander Krügel anxiously awaited the new day. Would the regiment's thin line withstand a new attack? *SS-Panzer-Grenadier-Regiment 24 "Danmark"* had been forced over from the attack to the defense.

The 24th of September opened with a heavy artillery barrage in the regimental sector. Contrary to expectations, the enemy only made weak probes and fell back at the first signs of defense. As the afternoon approached the enemy artillery fire also let up.

On 25 September there were sizeable troop movements in the enemy rear area. It remained relatively quiet in the regimental sector.

*

On 23 September at 1400 hours, *SS-Panzer-Grenadier-Regiment 23 "Norge"* attacked to the east from the line Dekmeri — Katlapji. At the same time, armored units from the *11. SS- Freiwilligen- Panzergrenadier- Division "Nordland"* launched an attack from the north. Both were advancing against the Soviet tank brigade's armored spearhead that had advanced as far as Blunavas. In the dense woods, there was only one course open to the Russians — withdraw to the south. The *I./SS-Artillerie-Regiment 11* fired from the north. To the east, nothing could be seen in the woods where the security forces of the *11.* and *225. Infanterie-Divisionen* were positioned. From the west came the attack by the Norwegians. The Soviets were faced with a dangerous development!

The attack of *SS-Panzer-Grenadier-Regiment 23 "Norge"* rapidly gained ground in the open woodland. Soon, however, the Soviet strength became apparent. Enemy armor and infantry teemed in the woodland lanes and clearings. For the first time the Norwegian grenadiers saw Sherman tanks that had come from Allied Lend-Lease shipments. After the attack had got off to a promising start, heavy enemy fire set in. Sherman and Stalin tanks blocked the path of the regimental grenadiers . A bitter struggle began that cost both sides numerous losses. Russian tanks were destroyed by *Pak* and in close combat. On the very first day of the attack, the *11./SS-Panzer-Grenadier-*

Regiment 23 "Norge" lost its commander, Norwegian *SS-Obersturmführer* Sondborg.

The attack continued on 24 September. The attack again gained ground. *SS-Unterscharführer* Petrat of the *10./SS-Panzer-Grenadier-Regiment 23 "Norge"* knocked out a Stalin tank with a *Panzerfaust* in a daredevil move. Shortly after that he was cut down by a burst of submachine gun fire, but the attack was moving again. The Soviets lost several tanks that day in similar fashion.

The commander of the *10./SS-Panzer-Grenadier-Regiment 23 "Norge"*, *SS-Obersturmführer* Dirks, was wounded. One of his platoon leaders, *SS-Hauptscharführer* Stolz, died a soldier's death. After initial success, the resistance stiffened. The attack went no farther. Without a moment's break, salvos from the heavy weapons burst in the treetops and sent innumerable fragments scything to the earth. The regiment dug in and held the line it had won.

On 25 September *SS-Panzer-Grenadier-Regiment 23 "Norge"* regrouped. Again there was extremely heavy enemy artillery and mortar fire. And, again, the regiment attacked. By evening it was close to Baldone in the line Dekmeri — Asenbergi. It lacked the strength to attack the city.

On 26 September the front stabilized along the line Vaci — Erkes (*SS-Panzer-Grenadier-Regiment 24 "Danmark"*) and Dekmeri — Asenbergi (*SS-Panzer-Grenadier-Regiment 23 "Norge"*). To the east there was contact with the *225. Infanterie-Division* and elements of the *11. Infanterie-Division* that had advanced the same distances.

During the morning, the Soviets succeeded in breaking into the sector of the *III./SS-Panzer-Grenadier-Regiment 23 "Norge"*. *SS-Hauptsturmführer* Gürz was killed while leading the reserves in cleaning up the penetration. The immediate counterattack received significant assistance through good fire support form the *12./SS-Panzer-Grenadier-Regiment 23 "Norge"*, which was led by *SS-Obersturmführer* Ahlf. *SS-Unterscharführer* Blahs, headquarters-section leader of the *11./SS-Panzer-Grenadier-Regiment 23 "Norge"* was wounded.

The regiment made preparations to be relieved. The commander of the *III./SS-Panzer-Grenadier-Regiment 23 "Norge"*, *SS-Hauptsturmführer* Martin Gürz, was decorated with the Knight's Cross for his battalion's outstanding performance.

*

During the night of 26 September, *SS-Panzer-Grenadier-Regiment 24 "Danmark"* was relieved by an army unit. *SS-Panzer-Grenadier-Regiment 23 "Norge"* left its positions a day later. Under the pressure of the German counterattack, the Soviets were forced to halt their attacks on Riga. Soviet forces shifted to the west. The withdrawal route of *Heeresgruppe Nord* through Riga — Tuccum appeared secure. However, the Soviet command soon assembled new forces to try again north of Doblen.

The units of the *11. SS-Freiwilligen-Panzer-Grenadier-Division "Nordland"* made it back through Riga and along the Riga beach on the only available, clear route out of the area. They moved southwest of Riga. Elements of *SS-Panzer-Grenadier-Regiment 24 "Danmark"* were temporarily put up in the barracks north of Mitau, where *"Freikorps Danmark"* had been stationed once in 1942.

The *11. SS-Freiwilligen-Panzer-Grenadier-Division "Nordland"* assembled a few kilometers outside of Tuccum. Again, it headed south. Fertile fields, marshland, woods, stately isolated farms and tidy villages succeeded each other. Labor companies and civilians were building positions and tank obstacles everywhere. The first hazy, cloud-draped day of a beautiful autumn came to an end. A wild night's journey began. Again and again the columns lost contact with one another. At every halt, the drivers fell asleep from exhaustion. The division reached the area north of Doblen at midnight. That was where the main effort of the next Soviet attack was expected.

New orders were expected on 28 September for commitment north of Doblen. The intelligence map showed strong concentrations of Soviet troops in the Doblen area. In the afternoon, the divisions of the *III. (germanisches) SS-Panzer-Korps* relieved army formations. The *11. SS-Freiwilligen-Panzergrenadier- Division Nordland"* occupied positions north of Doblen. The *4. SS-Freiwilligen- Panzergrenadier- Brigade "Nederland"* had returned to the corps in the meantime. It took up positions west of Doblen. The positions were well constructed. They lay in open woodland and were studded with numerous heavy weapons. After a peaceful 29 September, heavy enemy artillery fire began on 30 September. The companies reported strong enemy movements. It became increasingly clear that the Russians had discarded their plan to attack there in order to try elsewhere. A race began. German and Soviet forces side-slipped in parallel to the west, since there was not yet any German front south of Libau.

German troop movements followed those of the enemy. *Panzergrenadier-Division "Großdeutschland"* was withdrawn and shifted to the Autz area. The *11. SS-Freiwilligen-Panzer-Grenadier-Division "Nordland"* and the *4. SS-Panzer-Grenadier-Brigade "Nederland"* followed. During the night of 5/6 October, the remaining formations of the corps were relieved in the Doblen area and shifted to the area around Autz. But it was relatively quiet there as well. The German command had countered the enemy troop concentrations with concentrations of strong forces in the area of the expected attack.

*

The area north of Moscheiken appeared to be the new focus of the Soviet concentration. *Sperrgruppe Schäfer* (blocking group) was formed to counteract the threat. It consisted of the combat-engineer battalions of the *11. SS-Freiwilligen-Panzer-Grenadier-Division "Nordland"* and the *4. SS-Panzer-*

Grenadier-Brigade "Nederland" as well as *SS-Panzer-Aufklärungs-Abteilung 11*, the corps security company and the *1./SS-Artillerie-Regiment 54.*

Initially, *Sperrgruppe Schäfer* was committed in the Autz area. After the regiments of the *III. (germanisches) SS-Panzer-Korps* had taken over the positions, *Sperrgruppe Schäfer* was shifted farther west.

In the Moscheiken area the Soviets exerted heavy pressure against the *32.* and *201. Infanterie-Divisionen. Sperrgruppe Schäfer* was inserted between those divisions. *SS-Obersturmbannführer* Schäfer, the commander of the corps engineers, reported to the command post of the *201. Infanterie-Division* in Rubas and received his orders. *Sperrgruppe Schäfer* was to occupy a sector south of Rubas along the Vadakalis River. However, before the main line of resistance could be occupied, the Russians had already occupied it in areas. *Sperrgruppe Schäfer* was finally able to occupy its positions, albeit using an extremely unfavorable approach march. All the lines of communication ran perpendicular to the designated main line of resistance. Further, there was marshland to the rear.

On 8 October enemy forces had already broken through the neighboring unit on the left, the *201. Infanterie-Division.* The withdrawal route for *Sperrgruppe Schäfer* was in danger. *SS-Obersturmbannführer* Schäfer ordered a withdrawal. In leapfrog action, *Sperrgruppe Schäfer* boxed its way back, supported by fire from the *I./SS-Artillerie-Regiment 54* and the armored cars of *SS-Panzer-Aufklärungs-Abteilung 11,* which covered the complete withdrawal.

A new main line of resistance was established in the Aswinsi — Bugisi area. Firing from the new position, the artillery of *Sperrgruppe Schäfer* disrupted an enemy assembly position in battalion strength. At 1700 hours, the enemy penetrated into the right-neighbor's sector, the *32. Infanterie-Division. Sperrgruppe Schäfer* had to fall back again to the area south of Micini. The batteries fired on the pursuing enemy.

In the afternoon of 9 October a friendly armored force launched a counterattack. The main line of resistance was moved forward again.

On 10 October heavy enemy vehicular movement was heard in the "Mushroom Woods" in front of *SS-Pionier-Bataillon 11.* At 1500 hours about 600 Russians attacked the battalion. The attack fell apart under concentrated artillery fire. On the following day, when vehicle noises were heard again — this time in the "Fire Station" — and intentions for an attack were apparent, the artillery shelled the assembly positions for a fire for effect.

On 12 October the German artillery laid down barrages on enemy concentrations in the "Birch Patch" and on the tank trail.

The *I./SS-Artillerie-Regiment 54* was placed under the operational control of the *32. Infanterie-Division.* In the days that followed the Soviet attacks abated. The German positions were improved. Bunkers and trenches were constructed. Minefields secured the area in front of the positions. When army units relieved *Sperrgruppe Schäfer* some days later, the *III. (germanisches) SS-Panzer-Korps* was already engaged in heavy defensive fighting in the Skuodas — Preekuln area. It got its own combat-engineer battalion back as the requisite reserve. In that area of operations, elements of *SS-Panzer-Aufklärungs-Abteilung 11* had taken over the sector from the *14. Panzer-Division*.

SS-Vielfach-Werfer-Batterie 521 (Flecke) was disbanded due to a shortage of ammunition. The men were transferred to *SS-Panzer-Grenadier-Regiment 23 "Norge"*.

In the meantime, *Heeresgruppe Nord* prepared for Operation "Thunder", which had as its objective the final withdrawal of German troops to Kurland. On 6 October the withdrawal movement began. In a few days' time, the divisions of the *18. Armee* had to follow behind the rear of the *16. Armee* into Kurland. The passage was through a narrow corridor 45 kilometers long and 6 kilometers wide between Riga and Schlock. In the process, the corridor crossed two rivers, the Düna and the Aa. In the morning of 13 October 1944 the Düna bridge at Riga went up in the air. Riga had been evacuated. Operation "Thunder" was completed.

*

On the southern wing of the Kurland front, the Soviets continued their attacks in full strength. With 29 rifle divisions and 8 armored brigades, they reached the Schaulen — Moscheiken area and, in mid-October, the Baltic Sea north of Memel. With that, Kurland was encircled. The commander-in-chief of the *Heeresgruppe, Generaloberst* Schörner, had made plans for the evacuation and tried in vain to persuade Hitler to pull the army group back to East Prussia. The *III. (germanisches) SS-Panzer-Korps*, the *14. Infanterie-Division* and *General* Busse's *I. Armee-Korps* with its *11., 126.* and *87. Infanterie-Divisionen* were to have formed the spearhead of the breakthrough that, in all probability, would have succeeded. Instead, a time of great sacrifice began in the history of the German Army in Kurland. A time of sacrifice which would continue through the capitulation.

At the same time as the Soviet advance to the Baltic Sea, units of the Soviet 6th Guards and 51st Armies — with five tank brigades and 31 divisions — attacked between Skuodas and Preekuln toward Libau and threatened the German formations that were fighting there.

Preekuln – Skuodas

In the course of 12 October 1944, the *11. SS-Freiwilligen-Panzergrenadier-Division "Nordland"* was committed to the endangered southern sector. It was becoming clear that the enemy objective was the capture of Libau harbor, thus eliminating the supply source for the German forces fighting in Kurland. The *11. SS-Freiwilligen-Panzergrenadier-Division "Nordland"* moved across Kurland to reach its new operational area. It passed through Frauenburg. Night fell. Everywhere, burning villages marked the course of the front. The *SS-Panzer-Abteilung 11 "Hermann von Salza"* had been reduced to no more than a few tanks. They were committed into action under *SS-Obersturmführer* Rott.

At the same time, the *4. SS-Freiwilligen-Panzergrenadier-Brigade "Nederland"* was also rolling south. Before it arrived at its intended area of operations, however, the Russians broke through in the sector of the *11. Infanterie-Division* north of the Tirs-Purvs Marshes and assembled substantial forces in the "Mushroom Woods" for the subsequent breakthrough to Libau. It was necessary for the *4. SS-Freiwilligen-Panzergrenadier-Brigade "Nederland"* to take action to screen the establishment of the southern front. The I./*SS-Freiwilligen-Panzer-Grenadier-Regiment 49 "de Ruyter"* set out for the northeast of the Tirs-Purvs Marshes, then east toward the stem of the "mushroom". The II./*SS-Freiwilligen-Panzer-Grenadier-Regiment 49 "de Ruyter"* started from the east and was soon able to establish contact with the other battalion. Command and control of the battalions in the pathless woods turned out to be difficult.

Artillery coordination was effected through carefully worked out target-reference points. Orientation from one reference point to the next was by means of airbursts that could be spotted from the battalion's position. The Soviets were surrounded in the Mushroom Woods. Platoon-size elements broke out. Soviet tanks and heavy weapons fell into German hands. With the help of elements of the *11.* and *87. Infanterie-Divisionen*, the enemy forces were wiped out in two days of fighting. *SS-Hauptsturmführer* Petersen, the commander of the II./*SS-Freiwilligen-Panzer-Grenadier-Regiment 49 "de Ruyter"*, distinguished himself and received the Knight's Cross later. After the two infantry divisions had closed the gap in the front, *SS-Freiwilligen-Panzer-Grenadier-Regiment 49 "de Ruyter"* returned to its own sector of the front.

After having had its formations parceled out for various operations, the *III. (germanisches) SS-Panzer-Korps* was again employed as an organic whole. On 15 October the regiments took over the positions of various *Sperrgruppen* and elements of the *14. Panzer-Division*.

On the evening of 15 October, the lines of the *III. (germanisches) SS-Panzer- Korps* ran from north to south as follows:

II./SS-Panzer-Grenadier-Regiment 23 "Norge": North of the Preekuln — Vainode railroad line to Hill 39.1.

III./SS-Panzer-Grenadier-Regiment 23 "Norge": South of the railroad line with main strong point at "Horsehead Hill". Boundary with the *II./SS-Panzer-Grenadier-Regiment 24 "Danmark"* east of Klein- Trekni.

II./SS-Panzer-Grenadier-Regiment 24 "Danmark": Klein-Trekni — Trusi — Trekni.

III./SS-Panzer-Grenadier-Regiment 24 "Danmark": Grudulis — Birkstal — marshes south of Purmsati.

II./SS-Freiwilligen-Panzer-Grenadier-Regiment 49 "de Ruyter": East of Annenhof along the railroad line.

I./SS-Freiwilligen-Panzer-Grenadier-Regiment 49 "de Ruyter": Railroad line Preekuln — Skuodas to Hill 17.1 at Ozoli.

Kampfgruppe Aigner (Remaining elements of the *4. SS-Panzer-Grenadier-Brigade "Nederland"* and others): Ozoli to Flossen. The small Apda River was the border between Latvia and Lithuania and also the boundary with the *11. Infanterie-Division*.

The command post of the *III. (germanisches) SS- Panzer-Korps* was located at Goldnieki, 2 kilometers north of Susten.

The command post of the *11. SS-Freiwilligen-Panzer-Grenadier-Division "Nordland"* was at Maki, directly west of the Wartaga River on the Preekuln — Libau main road.

The command post of the *4. SS-Freiwilligen- Panzergrenadier- Brigade "Nederland"* was in a group of houses southeast of Susten.

The main dressing station was in the village of Paplaken, close to the Paplaken forest camp.

The field trains elements were in the Susten area, west of the Wartaga River.

After the Soviet breakthrough attempts at Doblen, Autz and Moscheiken had failed, the fighting shifted to the southern front in Kurland. The front wandered from east to west and gradually became stronger. Enemy troop movements made it clear that the Skuodas — Preekuln — Vainode area of operations would be the scene of heavy fighting.

On 16 October 1944 a barrage pounded the entire sector of *SS-Panzer-Grenadier-Regiment 23 "Norge"* and the *30. Infanterie-Division*. The barrage

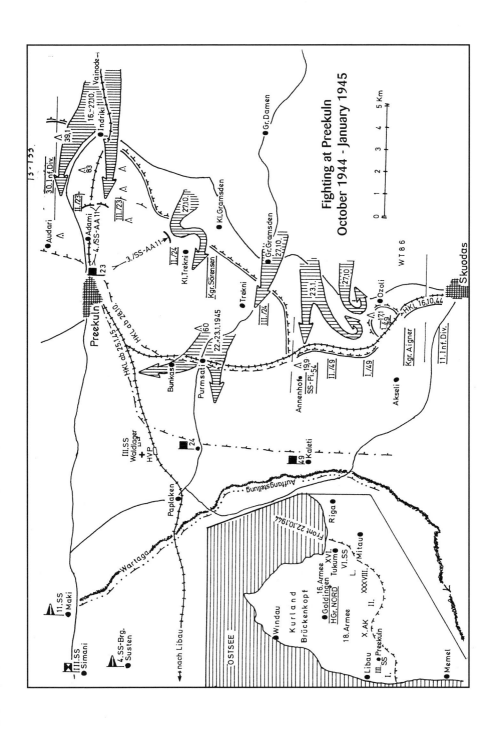

Fighting at Preekuln
October 1944 - January 1945

5 Km
0   1   2   3   4   5

N

was substantially intensified by a hail of bombs dropped by dive-bombers and Martin bombers. The *11. SS-Freiwilligen-Panzer-Grenadier-Division "Nordland"* and the *30. Infanterie-Division* were only able to hold their own with difficulty. The *4. Panzer-Division* was inserted in the gap that existed between the two divisions. It was able to intercept an attack formation at Audari. The enemy lost 164 tanks and 80 aircraft in that sector by 22 October.

How did it look on 16 October in the sector of *SS-Panzer-Grenadier-Regiment 23 "Norge"*? Some of its companies had only begun to occupy their sectors during the night. As a result, the Soviet attack in unfamiliar terrain hit all the harder in the morning of 16 October. The companies, which had received replacements and whose strength again averaged 100 men, melted away in the first hour of the barrage.

SS-Hauptsturmführer Spörle and his *II./SS-Panzer-Grenadier-Regiment 23 "Norge"* were north of the railroad line. The focal point of their defense was Hill 39.1. They clung to their positions and fought back desperately against superior armor and infantry forces. Contact with higher headquarters was lost on both sides. Spörles' battalion held firm. His *7./SS-Panzer-Grenadier-Regiment 23 "Norge"* was defending on three sides in the north.

On the southern wing of the battalion, the *5./SS-Panzer-Grenadier-Regiment 23 "Norge"* fought with equal desperation. The company commander and the platoon leaders had fallen. The enemy attained a penetration. *SS-Hauptscharführer* Lüngen, the leader of the *Pak* platoon of the *8./SS-Panzer-Grenadier-Regiment 23 "Norge"*, assumed command of the orphaned company. With eight men and two *Sturmgeschütze*, *SS-Hauptscharführer* Lüngen mounted an immediate counterattack and closed the gap in the lines.

In spite of all the courage of the Norwegian grenadiers, the enemy attained a wider penetration. When the enemy approached the command post of the *II./SS-Panzer-Grenadier-Regiment 23 "Norge"*, *SS-Hauptsturmführer* Spörle attacked with two assault troops and two *Sturmgeschütze* and hurled him back. In the evening of the first day of the attack, Spörle's battalion held its positions, even though severely decimated.

The weight of the Soviet offensive also hit the *III./SS-Panzer-Grenadier-Regiment 23 "Norge"* on 16 October. *SS-Hauptsturmführer* Hoffmann's battalion held its own in seesaw fighting in the sector south of the Preekuln — Vainode railroad line. The main effort struck the *10./SS-Panzer-Grenadier-Regiment 23 "Norge"*, positioned on Horsehead Hill. Because the company was not familiar with the positions — it had just occupied them during the night — the company suffered heavy losses. The heavy platoon was hardest hit. It was practically in the open while serving as the reserve.

In the hard fighting that ensued, it was the veteran soldiers who held the positions with steely resolve. The numerous young replacements experienced an extremely difficult baptism of fire. Most of the young soldiers stayed close to the experienced soldiers and rose to the occasion. Only a few fled from the positions.

The northern part of Horsehead Hill was assaulted by the Soviets. All the officers of the *10./SS-Panzer-Grenadier-Regiment 23 "Norge"* were killed or wounded. In the confusion of the fighting, *SS-Unterscharführer* Diedrichs collected several men of the company around him and recaptured Horsehead Hill in an immediate counterattack. The counterattack was supported by a 2 cm *Flak*. The former main line of resistance was completely reoccupied during the night by the collected remnants of the battalion.

During the fighting on 16 October contact was lost between the *II.* and *III./SS-Panzer-Grenadier-Regiment 23 "Norge"*. On 17 October the Soviets spotted the gap. There was heavy fighting that day west of Indriki. The machine-pistol platoon of *SS-Panzer-Grenadier-Regiment 23 "Norge"* was given the mission of sealing the gap. The platoon leader was killed and his platoon melted away. An assault troop from the *5./SS-Panzer-Grenadier-Regiment 23 "Norge"* raced in from the north. An assault troop from the *10./SS-Panzer-Grenadier-Regiment 23 "Norge"* attacked from the south. The gap was closed by evening. The regimental machine-pistol platoon warded off all further enemy attacks.

The Soviets repeatedly attacked in the regimental sector until 22 October, but the companies held their positions. The few *Sturmgeschütze* and the artillery of the *11. SS-Freiwilligen-Panzer-Grenadier-Division "Nordland"* played a major role in the successful defense.

Soviet secondary attacks on both sides of Preekuln involved *SS-Panzer-Grenadier-Regiment 24 "Danmark"* in the fighting. The focus of the fighting was at the enemy-held village of Trekni on the Groß-Gramsden — Purmsati road. The regiment's sector had been stretched to the limit and was only thinly held. After strong artillery and mortar fire, the *11./SS-Panzer-Grenadier-Regiment 24 "Danmark"* was forced back west of the poplar-lined lane at Trekni. A dangerous gap formed.

The regiment's machine-pistol platoon was alerted and moved forward to launch an immediate counterattack. However, before the platoon had reached its attack position, it was spotted and fired on by Soviet artillery. Even before the platoon could move out for the attack, it had suffered four dead and fourteen wounded. The machine-pistol platoon (Schwabenberg) finally reached the line that the *11./SS-Panzer-Grenadier-Regiment 24 "Danmark"* was holding. The fighting shifted to the *10./SS-Panzer-Grenadier-Regiment 24 "Danmark"*, positioned farther to the west. The *11./SS-Panzer-Grenadier-Regiment 24 "Danmark"* shifted slightly to the west and joined the other company in successfully repulsing the enemy attack. Schwabenberg's men — totaling three noncommissioned officers and 25 enlisted personnel — then had to hold a sector stretching about 1,000 meters. The Soviets finally achieved a penetration in the sector of the *10./SS-Panzer-Grenadier-Regiment 24 "Danmark"*. Albrecht's *11./SS-Panzer-Grenadier-Regiment 24 "Danmark"* and Schwabenberg's machine-pistol platoon were then cut off from contact in both directions.

A new attack began at 1600 hours. The machine guns hammered away. Soon ammunition ran low. Slightly wounded rebelted ammunition. Albrecht raced from one machine-gun position to another, intervening in person at dangerous spots. Schwabenberg's and Albrecht's men held the positions. As evening approached, however, the situation became critical. The Russians had worked their way forward along numerous drainage ditches. Albrecht fired three red flares. The *II./SS-Artillerie-Regiment 11* laid down final protective fire. Even though there was no forward observer, the fire was effective. The Soviets halted their attack.

During the night, *SS-Hauptsturmführer* Ternedde reorganized his battalion's positions. Ammunition and rations were sent forward. The wounded and dead were taken back. The *13./SS-Panzer-Grenadier-Regiment 24 "Danmark"* sent up *SS-Oberscharführer* Noach as a forward observer. A young Norwegian *SS-Untersturmführer* took over fire direction for the artillery.

On 17 October the Soviets attacked again in the morning, but the attack collapsed under the concentrated fire of the heavy weapons. There was a pause in the fighting.

At 0900 hours the entire sector was pounded with murderous artillery and mortar fire. After 20 minutes, the fire suddenly shifted to the rear. With an "Urrah!" the Soviets stormed toward the German positions. German machine guns and assault rifles barked, punctuated by the bursting rounds from the heavy weapons. That attack was also repulsed.

On 18 and 19 October additional, weaker attacks struck the sector of the *III./SS-Panzer-Grenadier-Regiment 24 "Danmark"* and were repulsed. The *II./SS-Panzer-Grenadier-Regiment 24 "Danmark"* also repulsed weak enemy attacks. As before, there was a gap between the two battalions at the Gramsden — Purmsati road. Elements of the *3./SS-Panzer-Aufklärungs-Abteilung 11* under *SS-Obersturmführer* Pehrsson were inserted as a stop-gap measure.

SS-Panzer-Grenadier-Regiment 24 "Danmark" was forced to exhaust all its reserves to strengthen the extremely tenuous front in its sector. *SS-Hauptsturmführer* Sörensen, formerly a company commander in *"Freikorps Danmark"*, was given the mission of organizing a *Kampfgruppe* that would be inserted between the *II.* and *III./SS-Panzer-Grenadier-Regiment 24 "Danmark"*. The *5./SS-Panzer-Grenadier-Regiment 24 "Danmark"*, *Alarmkompanie Roßman* (formed from trains units) and Schwabenberg's machine-pistol platoon were attached to it. *Kampfgruppe Sörensen* based its defense of the sector around the village of Kelputi, which was directly across from Trekni.

After fruitless attempts, contact was finally established between the battalions during the night of 23/24 October. On 23 October a reconnaissance patrol ran into a strong Soviet combat patrol. One noncommissioned officer was killed. He and four wounded were recovered under cover of darkness.

During the following days, the enemy was relatively inactive. Heavy weapons activity was normal. The companies reported much track noise from Trekni and substantial enemy movements during the day, suggesting preparations for an attack. There were similar reports from the sector of *SS-Panzer-Grenadier-Regiment 23 "Norge"*. On the German side, it also appeared that people were not satisfied with the situation as it stood. Armor officers reconnoitered assembly positions and terrain suitability. Work went on at a feverish pace to improve the German positions. The usual observations and enemy activity continued on 24 and 25 October.

During the forenoon hours of 26 October, an intense artillery barrage battered the sector of the *6./SS-Panzer-Grenadier-Regiment 24 "Danmark"*. A Soviet assault formation broke through the company's positions. *SS-Hauptsturmführer* Bergfeld committed his battalion's last reserves. The penetration was cleaned up during the afternoon.

The enemy was quiet during the night that followed. Everyone expected a Soviet offensive soon, however. The advance in the sector of the *6./SS-Panzer-Grenadier-Regiment 24 "Danmark"* was considered an attempt to feel out the front.

On 27 October 1944, the Soviets launched an offensive with 45 rifle divisions and a tank corps, to which an additional two tank corps would soon be added. The main effort: The center of the Kurland front. The objective: Divide the German forces in Kurland. The German front quaked under the fire of 2,000 Russian guns. The south flank of the offensive struck the *III. (germanisches) SS-Panzer-Korps* with its full fury.

At 0600 hours heavy artillery fire covered the positions of the *11. SS-Freiwilligen-Panzergrenadier-Division "Nordland"*. By 0900 hours it intensified into a truly murderous barrage, which finally included the entire sector of the *III. (germanisches) SS-Panzer-Korps*.

SS-Panzer-Grenadier-Regiment 23 "Norge" was engaged in a hopeless struggle. The Soviets attacked with superior infantry and armored forces. Under the crushing intensity of the artillery fire, the companies had shrunk to platoon size. The front could no longer be held. The *III./SS-Panzer-Grenadier-Regiment 23 "Norge"* had to give way and was forced back to the northwest. Spörles' *II./SS-Panzer-Grenadier-Regiment 23 "Norge"* fought its way back to the west. There was a broad gap between the two battalions on both sides of the Preekuln — Vainode railroad line. Contact with the *30. Infanterie-Division* to the north was also lost.

As noon approached, *SS-Panzer-Aufklärungs-Abteilung 11* was moved up. It had been held in reserve until given the alarm. *SS-Obersturmführer*

Schirmer reported to the command post of *SS-Panzer-Grenadier-Regiment 23 "Norge"* with his *4./SS-Panzer-Aufklärungs-Abteilung 11*. The command post was directly southeast of Preekuln and was preparing to defend itself. An 8.8 cm *Flak* was the mainstay of the command post defense.

Schirmer's company was briefed. It moved into the assembly area at the ridge directly south of Adami on foot. Schirmer was to establish contact with the *III./SS-Panzer-Grenadier-Regiment 23 "Norge"* to the southwest. His company consisted of 60% replacements. The *4./SS-Panzer-Aufklärungs-Abteilung 11* threw the enemy back in a dashing attack and formed a new main line of resistance. The Soviets mounted an immediate counterattack with armored support, including flamethrower tanks. Signs of panic were evident among the replacements but, once again, it was the few "old salts" that the inexperienced soldiers looked to and whose leadership they followed. On the company's right wing, an *SS-Unterscharführer* knocked out a flamethrower tank with a *Panzerfaust*. The other Russian tanks did not dare move ahead. The situation was saved. The *4./SS-Panzer-Aufklärungs-Abteilung 11* held the blocking position.

A dangerous gap continued to yawn toward the *II./SS-Panzer-Grenadier-Regiment 23 "Norge"*. The *3./SS-Panzer-Aufklärungs-Abteilung 11* was inserted there during the night on both sides of the Preekuln — Vainode railroad line. An army *Sturmgeschütz* battery moved into an attack position along the ridge east of Preekuln.

In the morning of 28 October the Soviets renewed their attack. Schirmer's and Persson's companies initially repulsed all attacks. The Soviets employed increased artillery and mortar fire. At 1100 hours the enemy attacked with armor support. The *Sturmgeschütze* fell back to a more favorable position. The struggle raged back and forth, with both sides suffering substantial losses. As noon approached, *SS-Obersturmführer* Schirmer was severely wounded. The headquarters-section leader, *SS-Unterscharführer* Stuhn, assumed command of the company. He had previously become known for a courageous single-handed operation with the *SS-Freiwilligen-Panzer-Grenadier-Division "Nordland"*. Stuhn had spent three days and nights in civilian clothes behind Russian lines and then returned with exact reports on enemy armor concentrations. During this critical fighting, he and the men of the *4./SS-Panzer-Aufklärungs-Abteilung 11* made the Soviets pay for every meter of ground.

SS-Unterscharführer Stuhn was killed in the heavy fighting that continued on 29 October. The two companies of *SS-Panzer-Aufklärungs-Abteilung 11* and both battalions of *SS-Panzer-Grenadier-Regiment 23 "Norge"* were pulled back to a line directly south and southeast of Preekuln. The *10./SS-Panzer-Grenadier-Regiment 23 "Norge"* left its positions with three noncommissioned officers and 16 enlisted personnel. The fighting strengths of the other companies of *SS-Panzer-Grenadier-Regiment 23 "Norge"* were comparable.

On 30 October the Soviets were pressing against the new positions. *SS-Unterscharführer* Diderichs, the acting company commander of the *10./SS-Panzer-Grenadier-Regiment 23 "Norge"*, was severely wounded that evening while defending against an enemy assault. *SS-Unterscharführer* Schellenberger, who had been transferred from the army, assumed command of the remnants of the company.

The uncertainty about Soviet intentions had ended on 27 October. The positions of *SS-Panzer-Grenadier-Regiment 24 "Danmark"* also rocked under the Soviet hurricane of fire. *SS-Obersturmbannführer* Krügel watched the developments with concern, for he well knew the weakness of his front. At 0930 hours a radio message was passed on to him: "The *5./SS-Panzer-Grenadier-Regiment 24 "Danmark"* has repulsed the enemy attack. The German lines are still intact!" Krügel was pleased.

Up front, the fighting continued in the positions. Again and again the dirt-brown-clad Soviet soldiers charged against the thin lines of *SS-Panzer-Grenadier-Regiment 24 "Danmark"*. The grenadiers were in makeshift positions fifty to sixty meters apart. Initially, the main effort was directed against the village of Kelputi. Before long, however, the enemy also assaulted the village of Trusi, which was held by the *6./SS-Panzer-Grenadier-Regiment 24 "Danmark"*. At 1030 hours, battalion commander Bergfeld had a radio message sent to the regiment: "Deep penetration in the sector of the *6./SS-Panzer-Grenadier-Regiment 24 "Danmark"*. The *7./SS-Panzer-Grenadier-Regiment 24 "Danmark"* is still holding firm."

The *5./SS-Panzer-Grenadier-Regiment 24 "Danmark"* confirmed the report at 1100 hours: "The enemy has broken through in the sector of the *6./SS-Panzer-Grenadier-Regiment 24 "Danmark"* and is behind us."

By then, Krügel had already been in a forward command post for some time (Hill 28.3). He replied: "Hold the positions!"

At 1110 hours, *Alarm-Kompanie Roßman* reported from the Kelputi sector: "Strong enemy infantry and armored attack on the entire company sector." At the same time, an enemy assault threw the *10./SS-Panzer-Grenadier-Regiment 24 "Danmark"* and elements of the *11./SS-Panzer-Grenadier-Regiment 24 "Danmark"* southwest of the Gramsden — Purmsati road back to the edge of the woods southwest of Grudulis. On both sides of the road, not far from the poplar-lined lane at Trekni, units of the *11./SS-Panzer-Grenadier-Regiment 24 "Danmark"* and Schwabenberg's machine-pistol platoon held their positions. Strong enemy forces flowed past them on both sides.

At 1120 hours the companies were told by radio: "Hold on, no matter what!"

The *II./SS-Artillerie-Regiment 11* of *SS-Sturmbannführer* Fischer and the *III./SS-Artillerie-Regiment 11* of *SS-Sturmbannführer* Potschka fired for all they were worth but, before long, the combatants were so intermingled that no forward observer could sort out the confusion. At 1140 hours, a forward observer of the *II./SS-Artillerie-Regiment 11* reported: "Enemy in the sector of the *5./SS-Panzer-Grenadier-Regiment 24 "Danmark"*; positions of the *Alarmkompanie* penetrated." At 1145 hours the forward observer's radio operator transmitted a new report: "*5. Kompanie* and *Alarmkompanie* have been overwhelmed by the enemy. Situation of Schwabenberg's machine-pistol platoon is unclear."

SS-Unterscharführer Illum from the machine-pistol platoon was with a small bunch of men north of the road not far from the poplar-lined lane at Trekni. The Russians had pushed far past them on both sides. They then started to attack the little group; they were supported by two tanks. Illum fired the last *Panzerfaust*. It missed, but the tanks moved back. Illum's men repulsed the Russian infantry, but the situation remained desperate. The men finally made it to the west side of the road through a concrete culvert. The positions there were all plowed up.

At last they made it to the remnants of the *11./SS-Panzer-Grenadier-Regiment 24 "Danmark"*, which had taken a stand in a stretch of trench to await the fall of darkness. From the *11./SS-Panzer-Grenadier-Regiment 24 "Danmark"* there were two noncommissioned officers and seven enlisted personnel; there were two noncommissioned officers and six enlisted personnel from the machine-pistol platoon. In addition, there was the Norwegian *SS-Untersturmführer*, who was the forward observer for the *II./SS-Artillerie-Regiment 11*, and another wounded *SS-Unterscharführer*. They waited for darkness, since the flat terrain made a daylight withdrawal impossible.

At 1300 hours the Soviets were in front of Hill 28.3. The *5./SS-Panzer-Grenadier-Regiment 24 "Danmark"* had taken position northwest of Hill 28.3 in a wooded defile. The *8./SS-Panzer-Grenadier-Regiment 24 "Danmark"*, with its infantry guns and mortars, was to the north. The *6.* and *7./SS-Panzer-Grenadier-Regiment 24 "Danmark"* stayed in their positions to the east at the edge of the woods between Trusi and Egli. The pressure was greatest at Hill 28.3, where *Kampfgruppe Sörensen* defended. At 1310 hours the last radio message from the regiment to the companies: "Hill 28.3 is to be held under all circumstances!"

The batteries of the *II./SS-Artillerie-Regiment 11* were in position behind the hill. Krügel occupied the hill with his messengers and two *Sturmgeschütze*. Additional men who had become separated from their units made their way to him during the afternoon. By 1600 hours the acute danger was past. Roßmann assembled the remnants of his *Alarm-Kompanie* and incorporated it into the defenses of Hill 28.3.

As darkness fell, the remnants of the *11./SS-Panzer-Grenadier-Regiment 24 "Danmark"* and Schwabenberg's platoon laid the wounded *SS-Unterscharführer* in a shelter-half and made it to the southern wood-line at

Grudulis with him. On their way, they came across a captured antitank gun that was manned by men of the *12./SS-Panzer-Grenadier-Regiment 24 "Danmark"*. They sent the horse-drawn limber with the driver, the wounded man and a situation report back to the battalion. They then set up for defense along a path through the woods and waited for orders and the new day. They had no contact with other companies.

On 28 October the main effort was again directed against Hill 28.3. The Soviets launched an early morning attack and captured the hill. Two *Sturmgeschütze* supported the immediate counterattack, which recaptured Hill 28.3. The Russians who had infiltrated to the north between the *5.* and *6./SS-Panzer-Grenadier-Regiment 24 "Danmark"* made their presence felt with flanking fire.

Early in the afternoon the German forces were forced to give up Hill 28.3 after it had been bypassed to the north. The *14./SS-Panzer-Grenadier-Regiment 24 "Danmark"* and the *II./SS-Artillerie-Regiment 11* evacuated their positions behind the hill under enemy infantry and mortar fire. The two *Sturmgeschütze* and Krügel and his messengers covered the withdrawal of the heavy weapons. At about 1600 hours the rearguard established itself along the poplar-lined lane northeast of Purmsati. Two *Sturmgeschütze* and two 2 cm *Flak* of the *14./SS-Panzer-Grenadier-Regiment 24 "Danmark"* remained there and laid down well-aimed fire on the pursuing enemy. Nevertheless, the Russians were able to occupy the Purmsati railroad station. The rapidly established new main line of resistance of *SS-Panzer-Grenadier-Regiment 24 "Danmark"* ran along the Preekuln — Skuodas railroad line. As the day went on, all the companies of the regiment fell back to that line.

As evening approached, a *VW-Schwimmwagen* raced up the poplar-alley at Purmsati toward Gramsden. It proceeded through the German lines without its occupants realizing that they had crossed them. Thirty minutes later, one of the occupants made it back. He reported: "*Schwimmwagen* with division adjutant *SS-Sturmbannführer* Witten ran into the enemy! Witten and a messenger are dead! I was able to get away!"

Krügel immediately sent a combat patrol forward, which was able to recover the bodies, which had been completely plundered.

During the night, Krügel requested reinforcements for the Purmsati sector from division commander Ziegler. In the course of that planning, operations clerk *SS-Unterscharführer* Scholles was given the task of establishing contact with *SS-Pionier-Bataillon 54,* which had just been released from *Sperrgruppe Schäfer* and was staging in the Sprogy area. During the reinforcement of the front, *Feld-Ersatz-Bataillon 11* was attached to *SS-Panzer-Grenadier-Regiment 24 "Danmark"*. In that capacity it was redesignated *Bataillon zur besonderen Verwendung "Nordland"*. The replacement battalion had just come from the Autz area of operations.

At about midnight, *Kampfgruppe Sörensen*, consisting of about 40 men, was relieved at Purmsati by *Bataillon z.b.V. "Nordland"*. It then remained with that battalion as its reserve. *Kampfgruppe Sörensen* consisted of one squad each from the *5./SS-Panzer-Grenadier-Regiment 24 "Danmark", SS-Artillerie Regiment 11*, the *Alarm-Kompanie* and the divisional supply battalion.

After a restless 29 October, during which the enemy repeatedly attempted to break through the German positions at Purmsati, he intensified his efforts as night fell and with more success. Advancing along the poplar alley, the Russians were able to knock out one rifle position after another with mortars and to ambush the reserves of *Kampfgruppe Sörensen* that were coming forward. That group was only able to escape capture with difficulty. It waded through a pond. The enemy worked his way forward along numerous drainage ditches. It was an uncomfortable night. The command post of the *3./Bataillon z.b.V. "Nordland"* set up an all-around defense at the schoolhouse at Purmsati. Sörensen and Roßmann also set up there. Lang's command post (*Battailon z.b.V. "Nordland")* was in Gulby.

Under decisive leadership, the Purmsati defensive front firmed up steadily. Two *Sturmgeschütze* were sent as reinforcements from the *11. SS-Freiwilligen-Panzergrenadier- Division "Nordland"*. With their help, the German position was improved in a night attack. At the railroad station, at the stock pond and throughout the terrain, high-explosive shells exploded and had a lasting effect. The Soviets were driven out of the drainage ditches. The new main line of resistance strengthened, with Purmsati as its major support. Before daybreak, the defense of Purmsati was further strengthened with two *Panthers* from *SS-Panzer-Abteilung 11 "Hermann von Salza"*.

With daybreak, heavy artillery fire rained down and concentrated on the school. Enemy attacks were repulsed along the poplar alley and at the stock pond. There was a penetration at the railroad embankment. An immediate counterattack with support from a *Sturmgeschütz* restored the lines. The Russian artillery fired without a pause, and the German artillery, which set the Purmsati railroad station on fire with a new kind of incendiary round, did not hesitate in its reply.

During the midday hours, the enemy increased his effort. He launched an attack with infantry and tanks along the poplar alley and moved straight at the school. The *Panthers* sneaked up and opened fire. Several rounds followed in quick succession. The first Russian tank was on fire, the second went up in the air, the third burned and the last was disabled. The enemy responded with furious fire from super-heavy mortars, but even that failed to force the defenders out of their positions.

That evening the situation again became critical. The main line of resistance north of Purmsati was considerably weakened by losses. The enemy succeeded in penetrating there. A little later the Russians also penetrated at the stock pond. Friendly tanks again rolled forward. One of the German tanks was so seriously damaged while cleaning up that penetration that it had to be towed away under cover of darkness. The school at Purmsati again stood as a bastion and served as the bedrock of the defense the entire sector. Again the German tanks denied the Russians their gains.

The 31st of October brought a perceptible reduction in the intensity of the fighting at Purmsati. Around 1600 hours there was another 20-minute period of intense artillery fire on the school at Purmsati. The enemy attack that followed bogged down. Persistent enemy attacks at the poplar alley, at the stock pond and at the railroad line were repulsed. During the night, a 75-man group from the corps hospital was sent forward to the *3./SS-Bataillon z.b.V. "Nordland"*. *Kampfgruppe Sörensen* was withdrawn and disbanded at the command post of *SS-Panzer-Grenadier-Regiment 24 "Danmark"*.

After the conclusion of the fighting, the commander of *SS-Artillerie-Regiment 11, SS-Obersturmbannführer* Karl, and the commander of the *III./SS-Artillerie-Regiment 11, SS-Sturmbannführer* Potschka, were awarded the Knight's Cross on 26 December 1944. The following were awarded the *Ehrenblattspange* (Honor Roll Clasp): *SS-Obersturmbannführer* Lang, the commander of *SS-Bataillon z.b.V. "Nordland"*; *SS-Hauptsturmführer* Per Sörensen, the commander of a *Kampfgruppe*; *SS-Hauptsturmführer* Ternedde, the commander of the *III./SS-Panzer-Grenadier-Regiment 24 "Danmark"*; *SS-Unterscharführer* Jonstrup, of the headquarters company of *SS-Panzer-Grenadier-Regiment 24 "Danmark"*; and, *SS-Sturmbannführer* Fischer, commander of the *II./SS-Artillerie-Regiment 11*. *SS-Unterscharführer* Jonstrup, an old timer at the front, had been severely wounded by a shell fragment that tore away half of his jaw. Before he even looked for the dressing station, he dragged himself to the forward regimental command post and set down in writing the situation of *Alarm-Kompanie Roßmann*. At that time, during the midday hours of 27 October, his report was extremely important.

What was happening on 27 October 1944 in the sector of the *4. SS-Panzer-Grenadier-Brigade "Nederland"*? After *SS-Freiwilligen-Panzer-Grenadier-Regiment 49 "de Ruyter"* had cleaned up the Soviet penetration north of the Tirs-Purvs Marshes, the brigade staff assumed the Kaleti sector. Up to mid-October, it had commanded a colorful assemblage of formations in the Autz sector — *Bataillon z.b.V. "Nordland"* and army battalions. Once there, the *III. (germanisches) SS-Panzer-Korps* was again being employed as a single, coherent unit.

Due to the lack of adequate forces, the sector of the *4. SS-Freiwilligen-Panzergrenadier- Brigade "Nederland"* was only weakly held. The defense centered on strongpoints on several commanding hills. The northern boundary was with the *SS-Freiwilligen-Panzer-Grenadier-Division "Nordland"*. The boundary between the *III./SS-Panzer-Grenadier-Regiment 24 "Danmark"* and the *II./SS-Freiwilligen-Panzer-Grenadier-Regiment 49 "de Ruyter"* was the little river Birkstal, about four kilometers south of Purmsati.

The major offensive that began on 27 October 1944 also included on its fringes the sector of the *4. SS-Freiwilligen- Brigade "Nederland"*. A Soviet attack formation set out from Gramsden toward Kaleti but was limited in its width by the marches on both sides of the avenue of approach. Repeated artillery barrages pounded the defenders on both sides of the road. Petersen's battalion held, but for how long?

The Soviet attack bogged down at Purmsati. In an effort to get it moving again, the Russians attempted to push in the south flank at Purmsati. Ternedde's *III./SS-Panzer-Grenadier-Regiment 24 "Danmark"* held. The Soviets pounded the positions of the *II./SS-Freiwilligen-Panzer-Grenadier-Regiment 49 "de Ruyter"* with a great expenditure of artillery and mortar fire, achieving an eventual penetration. *SS-Untersturmführer* Rieth, battery commander in *SS-Artillerie- Regiment 54 "Nederland"*, had been directing the fire of his entire battalion in that sector for days. Rieth attacked the Soviets with his fire-direction personnel and some stragglers and forced them back.

A German "bridgehead" over the railroad embankment was reduced and the personnel from the *II./SS-Freiwilligen-Panzer-Grenadier-Regiment 49 "de Ruyter"* had to fall back. The equipment of a wire signals intelligence section was lost.

At the same time, the Soviets also attacked the positions of the *I./SS-Freiwilligen-Panzer-Grenadier-Regiment 49 "de Ruyter"* from Rudbarzi. The main effort of the assault turned against the key terrain of Hill 17.1 at Ozoli on the southern wing of the battalion. Hill 17.1 was defended by *SS-Standarten-Oberjunker* Schluifelder's *1./SS-Freiwilligen-Panzer-Grenadier-Regiment 49 "de Ruyter"*. Schluifelder, who had been transferred to the *4. SS-Panzer-Grenadier-Brigade "Nederland"* from the *Luftwaffe* in Narwa, was the soul of the defensive fighting. Nevertheless, the enemy was able to gain a footing on the hill. In seesaw, bitter fighting, however, Schluifelder and his men were able to restore the former situation until the fighting ebbed at the beginning of November. Schluifelder, the defender of Hill 17.1, was promoted for bravery and awarded the Knight's Cross.

In the first days of November, *SS-Sturmbannführer* Lohmann, who had returned from convalescent leave, replaced *SS-Obersturmbannführer* Bunse as commander of *SS-Freiwilligen-Panzer-Grenadier-Regiment 49 "de Ruyter"*. The command post of the regiment was at Keleti.

The heavy fighting in the sector of the *III. (germanisches) SS-Panzer-Korps* drew to a close. The units could then carry on with the improvement of the positions and the pressing need for refitting. The average fighting strength of the companies was brought up to 40-50 men. In the first days of November, the fall rains set in and transformed the terrain into a "mudscape". Filth clung to the men, who worked without a break, stood watch, and then went back to work again on the positions. The main line of resistance consisted of a chain of squad positions that were formed around elevated sectors of terrain. The water table was within 50 cm of the surface in the low-lying places. Combat engineers laid wire obstacles and minefields in front of the positions.

SS-Obersturmbannführer Krügel was awarded the Oakleaves to the Knight's Cross on the 16th of November. Soon afterward he went on leave. While he was gone, *SS-Obersturmbannführer* von Boch und Pollach, the operations officer of the *11. SS-Freiwilligen-Panzergrenadier-Division "Nordland"*, filled in for him as acting commander of *SS-Panzer-Grenadier-Regiment 24 "Danmark"*.

During the first days of November, the *"Nationalkomitee Freies Deutschland"* — an organization consisting of turncoat Germans — began an intensive loud-speaker propaganda campaign, which had no apparent effect on the members of the *III. (germanisches) SS-Panzer-Korps*. An attack on *Bataillon Lang* by 30 members of the "National Committee" was repulsed. The attackers wore German uniforms and were only identified by a red armband. In the area of operations north of Preekuln, however, they did achieve success in a *coup de main* that was later made known as a warning example to all the companies. Here's what happened: Late in the evening, an officer and 30 men appeared as relief at the command post of a grenadier company. The next morning the entire company had disappeared, and there was a yawning gap in the battalion sector. Fortunately, it was promptly spotted and closed.

On 12 November, operations subsidiary to the second Battle for Kurland extended to include Purmsati/Bunkas (suburb of Purmsati, 600 meters to its north). At 1700 hours heavy artillery fire opened up on that sector. An attack by 300 Soviets, launched behind a screen of artificial smoke, collapsed in the fire of the German heavy weapons, far in front of the main line of resistance.

On 24 November 1944 another Soviet attack followed on the *III./SS-Panzer-Grenadier-Regiment 24 "Danmark"* south of Purmsati. We can read about that attack in the notes of *SS-Unterscharführer* Lerner, who was assigned as a forward observer to the *4./SS-Artillerie-Regiment 11* after *SS-Werferbatterie 521* (Flecke) had been disbanded due to lack of ammunition. His experience was an example of all of the forward observers who often stood, fought and died in unfavorable conditions with the grenadiers in the front line:

I was on my way to report in the early morning hours of 24 November 1944 to *SS-Hauptscharführer* Albrecht at the company command post of the *11./SS-Panzer-Grenadier-Regiment 24 "Danmark"*. I couldn't report in to the commander, however, as there was an enemy attack in progress on the main line of resistance against the company's thinly held lines. A 20-minute Russian barrage forced Albrecht's company to the ground. His key heavy machine gun was eliminated by a direct hit. Albrecht worked like a man possessed to keep his men in the position, for the chance was one in four that an enemy penetration was likely.

In that situation and time of need, with scant contact with the battery, which had not yet even registered its guns, I received the following impossible fire mission: "Entire battery — Base line company command post — Add 200 meters —

Everything you've got — Report when ready!" The commander of the 4./SS-Artillerie-Regiment 11, a Dane or Norwegian, quickly reported the battery was up.

Under the cover of fire from their heavy weapons, the Russians worked their way to within 200 meters of the battered position of the *11./SS-Panzer-Grenadier-Regiment 24 "Danmark"*. They would storm our positions after a sudden cessation of fire.

"Fire!"

And then there was nothing to do but to wait for a few anxious seconds. Would the fire fall too short? Would it be over?

Several rounds fell worrisomely short, but on line. The *4./SS-Artillerie-Regiment 11* pounded the attacking Russian battalion to bits right in front of our main line of resistance. Albrecht and his company did the rest. Finally, in the evening, I was able to report to Albrecht. In his face was concern and sadness over the loss of his magnificent soldiers and concern regarding the even more tenuous manning of his lines, but there was also unmistakable joy at the day's success.

The award recommendation for the Iron Cross, First Class for *SS-Unterscharführer* Lerner read:

…He promptly spotted the enemy in his attack position and immediately called down fire from the battery. Without regard to enemy machine gun and machine-pistol fire, Lerner remained at his observation post at the front and directed the fire against the attacking enemy with great calmness and precision so that the attack was brought to a halt. When the enemy made additional attempts to attack, Lerner directed the fire with such skill that the enemy was halted 80 meters in front of the German lines and shot to pieces. As a forward observer, he played a major role in holding the main line of resistance in this sector…

That same day the Soviets also attacked in the sector of the *4. SS-Freiwilligen-Panzergrenadier-Brigade "Nederland"*. *SS-Rottenführer* Kutzner was positioned with his company, the corps security company, in the sector of the *I./SS-Freiwilligen-Panzer-Grenadier-Regiment 49 "de Ruyter"*. The corps security company consisted of the remnants of *Bataillon Runge* of *Panzer-Brigade Groß*, which had formerly been attached to the *81. Infanterie-Division* in the Tuccum — Mitau — Doblen area. *SS-Rottenführer* Kutzner gives us the following report based on his diary notes:

We still had 25 men in the company. There were two light machine guns, two machine pistols and 16 carbines. We had an 800-meter sector. All Hell broke loose on 24 November.

The sun had scarcely risen when I heard the "whump" of Russian mortars as they opened fire on the platoon next to us. I checked out the situation with my binoculars and spotted a poorly camouflaged 7.62 cm antitank gun in the sector in front of us. Along with it were four heavy machine guns and ten light machine guns. It was an attack position.

A messenger went to the company command post. Then things started happening around us, too. The salvos came over without a break. In addition, three antitank guns opened fire into the railroad embankment. It kept up that way until nightfall. We were pressed into the dirt the entire day. Our artillery joined in. We held the position.

A heavy infantry gun from the *4. SS-Panzer-Grenadier-Brigade "Nederland"* took out the most dangerous antitank gun with two rounds. An ensuing pause in the fire indicated something was up. How right I was! Right beside us, where there was another company from the brigade, we could hear bursts of machine-pistol fire, exploding hand grenades and shouting. The Russians had penetrated. There were two possibilities: Immediate counterattack or seal it off until the "fire brigade" arrived.

Strength was lacking for the immediate counterattack. Despite that, two men tried it and drew the short straw in a hand-grenade duel. If the Russians attacked frontally along the creek, it would be all over.

Red flares went up. Final protective fire! The Soviets came no farther. I took my MG 34 and crawled along with my ammunition carrier into a foxhole. In the next foxhole I heard commands in Russian. As long as I fired at them, they kept their heads down. When I moved back, zipped right over the foxhole. Four Russians leaped forward from the left. Ratatata! They fell. Wrach — Wrach! Six hand grenades in front of us. As long as our supply lasted, we threw right back. I swung the machine gun around — tata— Damn! Misfire!

My comrade took the carbine, fired, and collapsed. A round to the head. I cleared the stuck round, raised the machine gun high and fired. Then something hit me in the back so that I jumped up high and fell back. The same burst of machine-pistol fire had caught my ammunition carrier. Stomach wound! He cried out loudly in pain. Why didn't the Russians come? I pulled myself together again and crawled across the open field. Two Dutch soldiers gave me covering fire. I fell in a drainage ditch up to my stomach and dragged myself to the platoon leader's hole. I was bandaged with a field dressing and dragged myself on to the company command post where I had to wait for darkness. In the meantime they also dragged back my two wounded comrades. As we were taken to the rear during the night, the Sturmgeschütz company that had been held in reserve rolled forward to iron out the penetration.

After the failure of the second attempt to break through at Libau, the third battle started on 21 December. It had the same objective. Twenty Soviet divisions attacked the German positions on a 35-kilometer front in an attempt to get to the Frauenburg — Libau road. The desired breakthrough and the attempt to split *Heeresgruppe Nord* were thwarted by the steadfastness of the German divisions.

Generaloberst Schörner, commander-in-chief of *Heeresgruppe Nord*, understood how to thwart the enemy intentions and support his threatened positions in good time. The third battle of Kurland was over by the end of December. After it ended, the *16. Armee* reported a total of 25,547 casualties and the *18. Armee* 41,141 casualties in the three battles. In addition, *Armee-Abteilung Kleffel* had lost 5,415 casualties in the first battle. A breakthrough to East Prussia that had repeatedly been planned finally had to be called off since the Soviets had penetrated far to the west. The only communication with Germany was maintained by the *Kriegsmarine* through the harbors of

Libau and Windau. The convoys steadily plowed through the Baltic Sea, bringing replacements and equipment to Kurland and taking the wounded back with them.

At the beginning of January 1945, *Generaloberst* Schörner was awarded the Diamonds to the Knight's Cross and left the army group to assume command of the central sector of the Eastern Front. *Generaloberst Dr.* Rendulic came in his place.

Heeresgruppe Nord was renamed *Heeresgruppe Kurland* and specially recognized by the creation of a silver-gray cuffband with the *Hochmeister* coat of arms, the elk head and, in the center, the word "Kurland".

In Germany in the meantime, Anglo-American bomber squadrons reduced one city after another to rubble and ashes. On the Western Front, the Ardennes offensive bogged down. Rumania had long since been occupied by the Soviets, and the Red Army continually pressed forward in Hungary and in the Balkans.

*

During the third battle of Kurland, the sector of the *III. (germanisches) SS- Panzer- Korps* remained relatively quiet. The commanders used the time for rebuilding and refitting their units. Each company was regularly pulled from the lines in order to allow it time to enjoy a few days relaxation at the Paplaken forest camp. At the same time, the unit that was resting was the corps reserve and had to be prepared for action at short notice.

Before the *II./SS-Panzer-Grenadier-Regiment 24 "Danmark"* was relieved in the sector north of Purmsati by *SS-Panzer-Aufklärungs-Abteilung 11* it carried out an unsuccessful combat patrol to bring in prisoners. After six days of brief refitting in the Paplaken forest camp, it relieved *Bataillon Lang* on both sides of Purmsati during the night of 13 December.

Hard frost set in and snow fell in mid December. The Soviets launched heavy air attacks on Libau. German fighter planes shot down numerous enemy aircraft. West of Purmsati, two Soviet airmen jumped from their burning aircraft and were captured. When interrogated, they revealed that the main Soviet airbase was at Baranowitschi. Shortly before Christmas another thaw set in.

After thorough analysis of the situation, a combat patrol was to go out in the sector of the *III./SS-Panzer-Grenadier-Regiment 24 "Danmark"* and bring in a prisoner to determine the enemy situation. Albrecht's *11./SS-Panzer-Grenadier-Regiment 24 "Danmark"* was chosen to carry out the patrol. The plan was for it to capture an enemy listening post at the railroad embankment in front of the company. A special "bravery leave" was promised for the successful completion of the combat patrol. Almost the entire company volunteered, but only a few were selected by the leader of the patrol.

194

The operation was carefully prepared. *SS-Unterscharführer* Lerner's task was to provide covering fire for the operation with the combined fire of the batteries of *SS-Artillerie-Regiment 11*. After completion of the preparations, *SS-Hauptscharführer* Albrecht was able to report that the combat patrol was ready.

The designated night arrived. The men were rested and the operation was rehearsed one more time by the glimmer of the "Hindenburg" lights in the company command post. Present were the battalion commander, Ternedde, and the commanders of *SS-Panzer-Grenadier-Regiment 24 "Danmark"* and *SS-Artillerie-Regiment 11*.

There stood the members of the combat patrol, all of them in plain field-gray with snow smocks. Their pockets had been emptied of any personal possessions. They wore no indications of rank or decorations. The oldest was father of two children, the youngest barely 17 years old. Where the belt buckle was to be found on other soldiers, there was a conspicuous '08 pistol on the youngest one. His pockets were stuffed full with ammunition for the pistols and machine pistols.

At 2200 hours it was time. The company commander and the other commanders said farewell to the men of the combat patrol and shook their hands.

It did not take long for the men to reach the forward-most trenches and disappear into the darkness. The diversionary combat patrol sent out by the elements on the right — *4. SS- Freiwilligen- Panzergrenadier- Brigade "Nederland"* — ran onto mines. The enemy was alerted, but the Russians in the listening post at the railroad embankment were unconcerned and remained quiet. The patrol took the final 20 meters in a dash. Without a single shot being fired, they collared the occupants of the enemy listening post. In forcing the occupants out of the listening posts, a concealed communications wire to a bunker at the railroad embankment was activated. In an instant, all hell broke loose. The Russian who had already been captured was able to escape.

Everywhere it teemed with Russians. The patrol was only able to get away with difficulty, but then a massive artillery duel began. It was the patrol's bad luck that there must have been an enemy forward observer in one of the bunkers. He was able to call down well-directed fire from heavy weapons, which then considerably complicated the patrol's withdrawal.

The last men of the patrol did not reach their jump-off position until 0400 hours under cover of darkness. Almost all of them had been wounded. The young man with the '08 pistol was the only one who came back without injury. Slightly wounded comrades brought the patrol leader to the company command post of the *11./SS-Panzer-Grenadier-Regiment 24 "Danmark"*. The old man of the patrol did not get to see the younger soldiers again on a "bravery leave". He stayed behind in front of the main line of resistance at the railroad embankment between Purmsati and Ozoli.

On 22 December, winter finally arrived with light frost and heavy snow-fall.

The Christmas of 1944! The corps front was calm. In the bunkers and combat positions were Christmas trees. The walls were decorated with Christmas greens. Here and there, "Hindenburg lights" replaced the missing candles. Sweets, canned goods and tobacco were distributed in abundance.

*

At Purmsati, the main line of resistance ran right through the village. The school and the area around the stock pond were German territory. The railroad station belonged to the Russians. The group of farmsteads known as Purmsati/Bunkas — one kilometer north of Purmsati where a road forks off toward Gulby — was only a field of ruins. The German soldiers lived in what remained of the cellars. The Russian trenches were on the far side of the occasionally very flat railroad embankment. It was there that the Soviets started an assault with infantry and strong armored forces and crushed the ruins even flatter.

SS-Panzer-Aufklärungs-Abteilung 11 was in the Purmsati/Bunkas sector as 1944 turned to 1945. The *II./SS-Panzer-Grenadier-Regiment 24 "Danmark"* was in Purmsati itself and the *III./SS-Panzer-Grenadier-Regiment 24 "Danmark"* was to its south.

The *3./SS-Panzer-Aufklärungs-Abteilung 11* had a remarkable experience on New Year's Eve that is well worth recounting.

On the previous day, the Russians had occupied a slight rise on the far side of the railroad line and constructed a machine-gun position there. That allowed them to work over the German positions in a most unpleasant fashion. The company commander therefore gave the leader of the mortar platoon the task of knocking out the machine-gun position with its mortars.

In the brightly moonlit New Year's Eve, the platoon leader hurried forward so he could be briefed at the foremost German position. On the way there a wild outburst of gunfire began. A few more leaps and the mortarman landed in a German machine-gun position.

"What's happening?" he asked, breathlessly.

"Over there they're firing into the air to celebrate New Year's; we had to give a suitable reply!"

Tracers arced back and forth. To the right and left, more weapons joined in the celebration, welcoming the New Year with gunfire. What a spectacle from Hell!

After the wild gunfire had died down, the number one machine gunner turned to the mortar-platoon leader: "They must be dead drunk over there — listen to 'em!"

Fifty meters away was a Soviet outpost that was occupied by four men during the night. After the gunfire had ended completely, they could hear something quite unusual from that direction. Someone was playing a harmonica.

The platoon leader made his calculations for the following day. This night, for once, the usual sounds of vehicles in the Russian rear area were not audible. Then a voice from over there drunkenly asked, "Comrade, why are you so sad?"

The men in the German position held their breath in amazement. Nothing like that had ever happened to them before. A German machine gun ripped off an answer. As the noise of the weapon died away, the voice over there asked: "Why are you shooting, comrade?"

"If you come over and play the harmonica for us, then we won't fire any more!"

An awkward murmuring could he heard from the other side. Then, three shadows raised themselves from the dark background of an overturned railroad car. A few runs sounded from the harmonica. Then a ponderous Russian melody began. The front listened, spellbound.

A second, lively melody — a Cossack dance — set the Russian soldier in the center of the trio to wild movements. Then, as he attempted a deep bow at the end, he fell over. Comrade alcohol showed his effects. Peals of laughter rang through the New Year's Eve from both sides.

The conversation got going again. Now both sides described Christmas gifts in bastardized forms of either language. When the word *Pantoffel* — the German word for "slipper" — came up, a Russian wanted an exact explanation.

In the comprehensive explanation of that useful object, the word *Pantoffel* was transformed into the nicer sounding diminutive of *Tuffli*. With that, the curiosity grew even greater.

There was silence on the other side — a lot of guessing going on. Then the conversation was off and running again. For a long time it revolved around the *Tufflis*. If the old lady had known what debates her well-intentioned Christmas package to an unknown soldier would release, she would certainly have sent a second pair so that the Russian could also have had the pleasure of a warm pair of slippers. But one could only try to imagine it: Slippers at the front, in the bunker!

Finally, after the *Tuffli* theme had been thoroughly worked over, it appeared that the time had come for a swap of Russian *Machorka* for German tobacco.

On each side, a figure drew up out of the positions. With careful steps, they walked out into no-man's-land and approached each other. But before the exchange could take place, the shot of a German sentry who had not been informed cracked overhead and the two partners in the exchange leaped wildly back to their own lines.

On New Year's morning, the war resumed. In mid-January 1945, the *II./SS-Panzer-Grenadier-Regiment 24 "Danmark"* relieved *SS-Panzer-Aufklärungs-Abteilung 11* in the rotation.

*

The daily reports of enemy movements presented new riddles to the German command. Did they indicate new assembly positions or the withdrawal of enemy forces? To answer that question, additional combat patrols were ordered sent out to bring back prisoners.

In the evening of 2 January 1945, a combat patrol of *SS-Panzer-Aufklärungs-Abteilung 11* ran into a Russian minefield and had to turn back without results. It lost one dead and seven wounded. A new attempt was made at Purmsati. A combat engineer of *SS-Pionier-Bataillon 11* was killed and another severely wounded while clearing a lane through the mines.

During the following night a combat engineer from the regimental combat-engineer platoon was killed in a third attempt. He was shot through the heart. The next night a combat engineer was wounded in a fourth try. By the time a combat patrol from *SS-Panzer-Grenadier-Regiment 24 "Danmark"* was able to set out, the enemy was warned. Several bunkers were destroyed, but the desired prisoner was still lacking.

The offer of three weeks of special leave for bringing in a prisoner clearly indicated the German command's interest in prisoners. The German command at Kurland was driven to those measures by necessity. Due to its own lack of forces, it needed prisoners to find out what the enemy was up to and identify planned enemy offensives in time. That allowed it to pull reserves out of less threatened positions on the front and stage them at the focal points of impending offensives.

SS-Unterscharführer Janke, a squad leader in the newly refitted *SS-Panzer-Aufklärungs-Abteilung 11* was asked whether he would make a single-handed attempt to penetrate the enemy trenches and bring back a prisoner. Janke, who came from the Warthegau, spoke perfect Polish. He pondered the situation and told his superiors about a crazy plan he had in mind.

Janke went to the trains area and asked the *Hiwis* working there about Russian practices in positional warfare. He learned that the soldiers rarely knew the password and were only likely to know it if action was expected from the Germans.

"What if someone is asked for the password? What happens then?" asked Janke.

"Then give a sharp, confident answer and don't show any uncertainty," said the Russian volunteers at the field kitchen.

"Take off your uniform and give it to me!" Janke ordered the Russian.

The uniforms were quickly exchanged. Janke threw a German overcoat over it and strolled back to the position.

Janke planned to carry out his plan in a wooded position north of Purmsati. Stands of old trees with islands of thick undergrowth appeared to favor his intentions. He spotted minefields and wire obstacles in front of the lines. The trenches were close to each other.

Accompanied by a messenger, who had also donned Russian uniform, Janke was able to approach close to the Russian trenches. From a thicket, they observed an isolated sentry in the trench whom they intended to grab.

"You stay here and cover me. I'm going into the trench to the left. If I can't do it alone, come and help me!"

The messenger objected, but Janke said that because he didn't know Russian, it would be better if he provided covering fire with his machine pistol. Janke crawled off without his belt, but he had a pistol and hand grenades in his pants pockets.

Just before Janke reached the trench, the single Russian sentry departed, apparently to relieve himself. He left his rifle leaning against the wall of the trench. Janke was in the trench in a flash. He unloaded the Russian rifle, put it back in its place and waited for the sentry to return.

When the sentry took too long returning, Janke proceeded along the Russian trench. Unexpectedly, he came upon a commissar who was cleaning his machine pistol. Janke could hear other voices nearby.

The commissar asked what he wanted. Janke replied that he was from the adjoining company and had come to visit a friend, whom he named. The commissar, however, did not know the ostensible friend.

"Then there's probably no point in looking!" said Janke and strolled back.

The single sentry was not yet back. When Janke heard excited voices behind him in the trench, he figured he had been discovered. He swung himself up out of the trench and disappeared into the nearby underbrush with the messenger. A Russian patrol hurried past in the trench.

After a few tense, anxious minutes, the two Germans in Russian uniforms made it back to the German positions at another location. When the German sentry pulled the shelter-half off the machine gun to open fire, Janke shouted: "Don't fire — we're German!"

***

With the start of the new year, *SS-Untersturmführer* Birkedahl-Hansen assumed command of the *8./SS-Panzer-Grenadier-Regiment 24 "Danmark"*. It had been under the temporary command of *SS-Untersturmführer* Raßmussen, the battalion adjutant, when *SS-Obersturmführer* Kure became ill.

After the combat reconnaissance failed to bring in prisoners, uncertainty continued regarding enemy intentions. The German positions were strengthened. Numerous *"Stuka zu Fuß"* — heavy rockets fired from simple launch frames — were set up throughout the corps sector. The maintenance companies of *11. SS-Freiwilligen-Panzer-Grenadier-Division "Nordland"* and the *4. SS-Panzer-Grenadier-Brigade "Nederland"* tirelessly welded together new launch frames.

The Eighth of January 1945 saw lively enemy artillery activity, primarily in the Purmsati sector. Considerable enemy activity could be seen in the rear areas. What was happening? Reinforcement or relief?

Vehicle concentrations at Hill 28.3 and at Trekni were observed on 9 January. The heavy companies and *SS-Artillerie-Regiment 11* opened fire on identified targets. The forward observer of the *8./SS-Panzer-Grenadier-Regiment 24 "Danmark"*, *SS-Unterscharführer* Laursen, succeeded in setting the biggest nuisance ablaze — the "Haunted House", directly north of the Purmsati school. He employed well-directed fire from infantry guns and mortars. Soon after that, Laursen's observation position received a direct hit. His radio operator was killed immediately. Laursen died in the field hospital.

The fire abated during the day of 10 January. More guesswork concerning the enemy's intentions. A new patrol was prepared to reconnoiter the enemy situation, but it never took place.

On 12 January a Danish machine gunner at Purmsati brought a Russian back through the minefield to the German lines in an unparalleled act of boldness. The confused Russian was brought to the command post of the *II./SS-Panzer-Grenadier-Regiment 24 "Danmark"*. By chance, the regimental commander, Krügel, and the artillery commanders, Fischer and Karl, were there in addition to the battalion commander, *SS-Sturmbannführer* Bergfeld. The reconnaissance patrol referred to above was made superfluous. The Dane received the Iron Cross, First Class and was able to go on leave shortly thereafter.

Interrogation of the prisoner confirmed considerable regrouping, refitting and the concentration of significant forces in the entire corps sector.

During the same night, the *II./SS-Panzer-Grenadier-Regiment 24 "Danmark"* was relieved by the *Bataillon z.b.V. "Nordland"*. It then spent one night in Paplaken and, the following night, relieved *SS-Panzer-Aufklärungs-Abteilung 11* in the sector north of Purmsati. *SS-Sturmbannführer* Bergfeld turned over the battalion to *SS-Hauptsturmführer* Per Sörensen and became the new divisional adjutant.

Further regrouping took place the next day. *SS-Panzer-Aufklärungs-Abteilung 11* relieved the *III./SS-Panzer-Grenadier-Regiment 24 "Danmark"* south of Purmsati. After a short break, the battalion assumed positions south of Preekuln. To the north at Preekuln, the *III./SS-Panzer-Grenadier-Regiment 23 "Norge"* was in a position that had contact in the north with the *30. Infanterie-Division*. The *II./SS-Panzer-Grenadier-Regiment 23 "Norge"* was in the Paplaken forest camp.

On 20 January the Soviet artillery registered on important targets. It became increasingly clear that the ruined houses of Purmsati/Bunkas and the road leading to Gulbji would be the probable *Schwerpunkt* of the attack.

During the nights there were loud vehicular and track noises. The *11. SS-Freiwilligen-Panzer-Grenadier-Division "Nordland"* ordered an increased level of alert. The commanders continually inspected the positions and made final preparations. Just as before a storm, a certain level of nervousness was evident. As the morning of 23 January approached, reports from the front arrived with increasing frequency. *SS-Hauptsturmführer* Sörensen was also up front with his battalion every night. It had become an article of faith that wherever Sörensen was, was also where the Russians were coming. At 0330 hours a call from the regimental adjutant, *SS-Haupsturmführer* Lührs, to the battalion adjutant, *SS-Untersturmführer* Raßmussen: "Enemy attack at daybreak is certain!"

Raßmussen notified Sörensen. He considered all the options one more time, but there was nothing left to do but wait.

The same held true for the northern neighbor, the *III./SS-Panzer-Grenadier-Regiment 23 "Norge"*. Ternedde also had to wait.

Soviet artillery opened the fourth Battle of Kurland with a heavy barrage on the morning of 23 January 1945. Eleven divisions of the Red Army attacked the German lines on both sides of Preekuln. The objective was Libau. The full weight of the attack struck the *30. Infanterie-Division* and the *III. (germanisches) SS-Panzer-Korps*. As soon as the *Schwerpunkt* of the Soviet offensive was recognized, the *18. Armee* released operational reserves from less threatened portions of the front and sent them to the site of the Soviet main effort. As a result, the *14. Panzer-Division* arrived in the Preekuln — Purmsati— Kaleti area of operations.

An intense barrage hailed down on the positions of the *11. SS-Freiwilligen-Panzer-Grenadier-Division "Nordland"*. The heaviest concentration was north of Purmsati. *SS-Panzer-Grenadier-Regiment 24 "Danmark"* was the hardest hit initially. In addition to smaller guns, the heavy 17.2-centimeter shells and the new "suitcase-size" salvos of the 28-cm Stalin organs pounded the defenders' positions. Giant, dark craters rose from the white snowscape.

After that hail of fire, more than 40 Soviet tanks attacked the German positions from the Pauseri — Waldhof — Klabji area and pulverized anything that stood against them. Infantry followed in tight-packed masses.

Nevertheless, courageous survivors attacked the tanks again and again. Ten Soviet tanks were destroyed in front of the *6./SS-Panzer-Grenadier-Regiment 24 "Danmark"* at Purmsati/Bunkas, six of them by one Danish grenadier with *Panzerfäuste*. Farther to the north, the *7.* and *11./SS-Panzer-Grenadier-Regiment 24 "Danmark"* engaged the Soviet infantry and tanks that were trying to reach the Purmsati — Paplaken road. In spite of all the determination with which the defenders clung bitterly to their positions, it was an unequal fight. The defenders began to thin out.

The radio reports that follow are from the companies of the *II./SS-Panzer-Grenadier-Regiment 24 "Danmark"* after all the field-telephone wires had been cut by fire and the Russian artillery fire had shifted to the rear: "*7./SS-Panzer-Grenadier-Regiment 24 "Danmark"*: Everything still fine in our sector."

There was no report from the *6./SS-Panzer-Grenadier-Regiment 24 "Danmark"*, which was committed to the south at Purmsati/Bunkas. Then, another report from the *7./SS-Panzer-Grenadier-Regiment 24 "Danmark"*: "Strong infantry and armor attack on the sector of the *6./SS-Panzer-Grenadier-Regiment 24 "Danmark!"*

A little later, another report from the *7./SS-Panzer-Grenadier-Regiment 24 "Danmark"*: "Tanks have overrun the *6./SS-Panzer-Grenadier-Regiment 24 "Danmark"*. Enemy assault turning against our front!" That was the last radio report from the Purmsati/Bunkas area of the fighting that day.

Shortly thereafter the Soviet armor overran the *7.* and *11./SS-Panzer-Grenadier-Regiment 24 "Danmark"*. There was likewise intense fighting in those sectors.

The main line of resistance fell apart north of Purmsati. It had been pounded to bits. The batteries of *SS-Artillerie-Regiment 11* fired at their maximum rate, but the Soviets rolled inexorably west. Almost all of the heavy weapons of Birkedahl-Hansen's *8./SS-Panzer-Grenadier-Regiment 24 "Danmark"* were put out of action. Birkedahl-Hansen and *SS-Rottenführer* Wirth ran from firing position to firing position, firing the *"wilde Säue"* (wild sows), as the heavy rockets were known in soldier slang. Both of the heavy machine guns of the company went into position and opened fire on the advancing Soviets. When they got as far as the small patch of woods west of Bumeistari — Gulbji, the Russians came to a halt before the barrels of the *13./SS-Panzer-Grenadier-Regiment 24 "Danmark"*. *SS-Hauptsturmführer* Sörensen and *SS-Hauptsturmführer* Lärum quickly formed a new main line of resistance with the remnants of their battalions.

As noon approached, the Russians attacked the Purmsati sector. *Bataillon Lang* held. Farther to the south, *SS-Panzer-Aufklärungs-Abteilung 11* held fast in its positions along the railroad embankment.

Late in the afternoon, the *II./SS-Panzer-Grenadier-Regiment 23 "Norge"* launched an immediate counterattack in the sector of *SS-Panzer-Grenadier-Regiment 24 "Danmark"*. It succeeded in pushing the German lines forward somewhat, thus improving them.

In the evening, the strength figures showed the following: Three men returned from *SS-Untersturmführer* Spahn's *6./SS-Panzer-Grenadier-Regiment 24 "Danmark"* at Purmsati/Bunkas. The *7./SS-Panzer-Grenadier-Regiment 24 "Danmark"* consisted of only *SS-Untersturmführer* Madsen and 14 men. The *8./SS-Panzer-Grenadier-Regiment 24 "Danmark"* had lost four dead, 30 wounded, one *Pak*, one infantry gun, two *"Maultier"* tracked prime movers and four heavy mortars. Things looked no better for the *III./SS-Panzer-Grenadier-Regiment 24 "Danmark"*.

During the night, the *14. Panzer-Division* moved forward to reinforce the decimated formations.

After the *II./SS-Panzer-Grenadier-Regiment 24 "Danmark"* had been overrun, the main effort turned against the *III./SS-Panzer-Grenadier-Regiment 24 "Danmark"* to the north. The fighting was quite bitter there as well. The battalion fell back under enemy pressure. Almost all the leadership was eliminated. The companies suffered heavy losses. The commander of the *9./SS-Panzer-Grenadier-Regiment 24 "Danmark"*, *SS-Obersturmführer* Maagard Hansen, was killed. The *III./SS-Panzer-Grenadier-Regiment 24 "Danmark"* finally held with its northern wing at Jogli and maintained tenuous contact with the *III./SS-Panzer-Grenadier-Regiment 23 "Norge"* roughly along the line of the Preekuln — Libau railroad.

On 24 January, after hours of combat, the *14. Panzer-Division* temporarily regained possession of the ruins of Purmsati/Bunkas. Both sides made extensive use of heavy weapons.

On the morning of 25 January, the thermometer dropped to thirty degrees below zero Celsius (22 degrees below zero Fahrenheit). While heavy artillery fire continued throughout the day, the main effort of the attack shifted to the Purmsati — Kaleti area. *Bataillon Lang* fought bitterly at Purmsati but could not prevent giving up the place as the day went on. Strong Russian air formations blanketed the German artillery positions with bombs on that cold, but clear day. That day the *"Stuka zu Fuß"* also proved to be an effective weapon in the Purmsati sector.

How did things look on 23 January 1945 in the sector of the *4. SS-Freiwilligen-Panzergrenadier-Brigade "Nederland"*?

There were two *Schwerpunkte*: the Groß Gramsden — Kaleti road with the commanding high ground at Annenhof and, in the south, Hill 17.1 directly east of the Ozoli railroad station. If the Soviets wanted to break through to the coast and Libau, they would first have to take that key terrain.

On the morning of 23 January, extremely heavy artillery fire covered the positions of the *4. SS-Panzer-Grenadier-Brigade "Nederland"*. The thin lines were literally pounded into the ground. *SS-Untersturmführer* Schluifelder and his *1./SS-Freiwilligen-Panzer-Grenadier-Regiment 49 "de Ruyter"* held the Ozoli hill (Hill 17.1). Schluifelder was the soul of the defense. After several immediate counterattacks, Hill 17.1 remained firmly in the hands of what had become a small band of men, even though the enemy had successfully penetrated on both sides.

The *II./SS-Freiwilligen-Panzer-Grenadier-Regiment 49 "de Ruyter"* held out north of the Gramsden — Kaleti road; the *I./SS-Freiwilligen-Panzer-Grenadier-Regiment 49 "de Ruyter"* held onto its positions south of the road. That was the focal point of the fighting. *SS-Sturmbannführer* Schlüter's *SS-Artillerie-Regiment 54 "Nederland"* supported the hard-fighting grenadiers. Thanks to good fire direction, *SS-Obersturmführer* Behler, commander of the *3./SS-Artillerie-Regiment 54*, was able to smash all of the enemy attacks in front of the main lines. On the first day of the fourth Battle of Kurland the *4. SS-Freiwilligen-Panzergrenadier-Brigade "Nederland"* had essentially held its positions.

SS-Brigadeführer Wagner followed the reports from the front with concern. He knew the Russians would not give up and would attack with new reserves.

There were also concerned faces at the command post of *SS-Freiwilligen-Panzer-Grenadier-Regiment 49 "de Ruyter"*. *SS-Sturmbannführer* Lohmann pondered all the options yet again, but the prospects remained dim. His regiment had already suffered substantial casualties on the first day. There was no hope of replacements. Artillery remained the main source of support. There was no rest at the regimental command post that night.

On 24 January 1945 extremely heavy artillery fire covered the positions of the *4. SS-Panzer-Grenadier-Brigade "Nederland"*, which held its positions in the main line with four battered battalions. From north to south: *SS-Panzer-Pionier-Bataillon 54* (*SS-Hautsturmführer* Wanhöfer); the *II./SS-Freiwilligen-Panzer-Grenadier-Regiment 49 "de Ruyter"* (*SS-Sturmbannführer* Petersen); the *I./SS-Freiwilligen-Panzer-Grenadier-Regiment 49 "de Ruyter"* (*SS-Sturmbannführer* Unger); and, the hastily assembled *Kampfgruppe* under *SS-Hauptsturmführer* Aigner.

The southern bastion, the Ozoli Hill, fell into Russian hands after seesaw fighting. Only a few survivors of the *I./SS-Freiwilligen-Panzer-Grenadier-Regiment 49 "de Ruyter"* made it through to the west. *SS-Untersturmführer* Schluifelder, seriously wounded, shot himself before he could be captured. The main line of resistance fell back to the west behind the railroad line.

The main effort of the attack, however, took place on both sides of the Gramsden — Kaleti road. After the Soviet artillery barrage subsided, the infantry assaulted. The hour had come again for *SS-Obersturmführer* Behler, the artillery forward observer. All of the field-telephone wires had been cut. He directed the fire by radio. Nevertheless, the Soviets were able to penetrate the main line of resistance on both sides of the road. The Soviets encircled the hill in the afternoon. With a few men, Behler broke out to the west in hand-to-hand combat.

In the same area of the fighting, *SS-Obersturmführer* Hellmer's company from the *II./SS-Freiwilligen-Panzer-Grenadier-Regiment 49 "de Ruyter"* held its positions that day in bitter defensive fighting even though the main line of resistance broke on both sides of it. A Russian armored advance along the Gramsden — Kaleti road pushed forward far to the west. A single *Flak* of the *4. SS-Panzer-Grenadier-Brigade "Nederland"* fired to the last at the Soviet tanks, though its 2-cm tracer rounds had no more than a psychological effect.

On that day, *Kampfgruppe SS-Pionier-Bataillon 54* got off lightly. The *Kampfgruppe* was located in the northern portion of the brigade sector and consisted of a reinforced combat engineer company, a reconnaissance company and two 2cm *Flak* platoons. *Kampfgruppe Wanhöfer* held its positions. During the night, however, it was forced by a deep enemy penetration to pull back to the west to the new improvised main lines. That night reserves arrived. The *II./Infanterie-Regiment 323* of the *218. Infanterie-Division* occupied a blocking position west of Kaleti. To its north, elements of the *14. Panzer-Division* stood in reserve.

On 25 January, the Soviets continued their attack. Murderous artillery fire again covered the German positions. Lohmann's battalions were burnt to a cinder. Artillery was again the mainstay of the German defenses. The high ground around Annenhof — Meiri — Ozolnieki was lost. And, again, bitter fighting played itself out. The cohesion of the German formations was torn apart. Command and control in large formations was impossible. Every squad, every company fought on its own.

SS-Obersturmführer Hellmer's company and the *I./SS-Artillerie-Regiment 54*, its fire directed by *SS-Obersturmführer* Behler, again stood out for its stubbornness. After a bitter defense, the observation post of the *II./SS-Artillerie-Regiment 54* was also encircled. There, it was a lowly cannoneer who took the initiative. He was the radio operator for the forward observer of the *II./SS-Artillerie-Regiment 54*. When the hill was lost, he led others and recaptured it in an immediate counterattack. *SS-Kanonier* Jenschke, whose camouflage smock concealed his rank, led a small group of determined men forward. Even noncommissioned officers followed his orders.

The *SS-Pionier-Kampfgruppe Wanhöfer* again held its positions that day, but contact was lost with *SS-Bataillon Petersen*. *SS-Untersturmführer* Horstmann wrote in his diary for 25 January 1945:

During the two days of heavy fighting, the companies in the main line of resistance have been almost totally wiped out. Not a single man has returned to the rear. Now only several places in the former lines are still defended as strongpoints. They are surrounded by the enemy. The battalion command posts are now forward strongpoints and the road is the main line of resistance.

Petersen and Unger (both battalion commanders) and seven men defend the entire village of Kaleti...

During the night, the southern wing of *SS-Pionier-Kampfgruppe Wanhöfer* was outflanked by the enemy and attacked from the rear. An inexorable stream of Soviets moved west on the Gramsden — Kaleti road. The combat engineers repulsed several night attacks. At about midnight, two *Sturmgeschütze* belonging to the *4. SS-Panzer-Grenadier-Brigade "Nederland"* pushed through to the *Kampfgruppe* with mounted grenadiers, but it was no longer possible to establish a cohesive front.

At about the same time, the Soviets were outside the command post of *SS-Freiwilligen-Panzer-Grenadier-Regiment 49 "de Ruyter"*, two kilometers northwest of Kaleti (the settlement of Grantini). Inside the command post a command conference was in progress with the commander of the SPW-Bataillon of the *14. Panzer-Division* and the battalion commanders of *SS-Freiwilligen-Panzer-Grenadier-Regiment 49 "de Ruyter"*. The forward outposts were occupied by the signals platoon and the messengers. They brought the Soviet advance to a standstill. In the morning the regimental command post was moved to Klein-Kaleti. The lines were pulled back to Kaleti.

During 26 January 1945, the sector of the *11. SS-Freiwilligen-Panzer-Grenadier-Division "Nordland"* remained relatively quiet thanks to the intervention of the *14. Panzer-Division*. On the other hand, the fighting flared up anew in the sector of the *4. SS-Freiwilligen-Panzergrenadier-Brigade "Nederland"*. Soviet armor was advancing on Kaleti. *Sturmgeschütze* — the remnants of *Sturmgeschütz-Abteilung "Nederland"* — knocked out Soviet tanks, but then had to fall back to the west.

North of Kaleti an immediate counterattack by *Sturmgeschütze* with mounted infantry was repulsed. In the process, the commander of the *7./SS-Freiwilligen-Panzer-Grenadier-Regiment 49 "de Ruyter"*, SS-*Obersturmführer* Grabow, was severely wounded. An immediate counterattack by assault guns of the *14. Panzer-Division* brought only temporary relief.

Kampfgruppe Wanhöfer, which still stood as a breakwater northeast of Kaleti, was attacked at noon by enemy tanks. They barred the withdrawal route of the combat engineers. It then became a matter of life or death. Wanhöfer gave the order: "Break through to the German lines!"

The remnants of the *Pionier-Kampfgruppe* fought their way to the high ground northwest of Kaleti. SS-*Hauptsturmführer* Wanhöfer was severely wounded but was rescued at the last moment ahead of the approaching enemy tanks.

At 1240 hours the Soviets were already between Kaleti and Klein-Kaleti. The units of the *II./Infanterie-Regiment 323* of the *218. Infanterie-Division* that were in the blocking position defended desperately, but would they be able to repulse the attack?

On the high ground north of Grantini, directly south of the small Birkstal River (between Kaleti and Klein-Kaleti) was the instructional platoon of *SS-Untersturmführer* Krämer. His platoon was in a position to attack the enemy's flank and brought him to a halt.

On that day it became clear that the new main line of resistance could not be held with the small number of bled-white forces available.

West of the Wartage River a new blocking position was established by alarm units from Libau. The command post of *SS-Freiwilligen-Panzer-Grenadier-Regiment 49 "de Ruyter"* moved there. *SS-Sturmbannführer* Petersen established himself in Klein-Kaleti with the remnants of the *4. SS-Panzer-Grenadier-Brigade "Nederland"*.

On 27 January an extremely heavy artillery barrage covered Klein-Kaleti. Petersen and his men held the village. An army assault gun battalion, which also had radio contact with a cannon battery, brought temporary relief. Petersen held on for another night until he received permission to withdraw.

The remnants of the *4. SS-Freiwilligen-Panzergrenadier-Brigade "Nederland"* held on in the Krute — Klein - Kaleti—Kodeli sector until relieved by forces of the *14. Panzer-Division* and the *218. Infanterie-Division*. *SS-Freiwilligen-Panzer-Grenadier-Regiment 49 "de Ruyter"* was decimated, having a combat strength of only 80 men. The fourth Battle for Kurland was over.

In conclusion, we will let *SS-Untersturmführer* Horstmann's diary speak. It echoes the impressions of the fighting of those days:

That was the most heroic battle I ever experienced — the defense of the *4. SS-Panzer-Grenadier-Brigade "Nederland"*! Everyone remained in his position until he fell. The attacks were brought to a standstill in front of the barrels of the artillery. The guns *were* the main line of resistance. But even then, we did not fall back until we were relieved.

*

The *30. Infanterie-Division*, which was in and around Preekuln, was also decimated in that fighting. *General* Ranck's *121. Infanterie-Division* was thrown into the Preekuln area and held the city in spite of extremely heavy losses. Preekuln was not evacuated by *Kampfgruppe Ranck* until 22 February.

In Kurland, *SS-Flak-Abteilung 11* was attached to the *19. Grenadier-Division der SS (lettisches Nr. 2)* and the *VI. Waffen-Armeekorps der SS (lettisches)* under *SS-Obergruppenführer und General der Waffen-SS* Walter Krüger. It proved itself in numerous operations north of Frauenburg. A large number of Russian tanks lay scattered in front of the barrels of the Flak battalion. Krüger wanted to keep the battalion in his corps, but when the *III. (germanisches) SS-Panzer-Korps* was moved to Pomerania, the battalion returned to the division. It was transported by sea to Pomerania.

Sea Transport To Pomerania

On both sides of Preekuln the German divisions were forced to fall back to the Wartaga sector, where the terrain favored the establishment of a new defensive front.

The *III. (germanisches) SS-Panzer-Korps* needed to be transported to Germany for necessary reorganization and was thus released from attachment to *Heeresgruppe "Kurland"*. That decision was obviously viewed with bitterness by many of the soldiers who remained in Kurland. They felt themselves in a hopeless situation, as the facts soon proved.

All the rumors and hopes for a large-scale German counterattack increasingly diminished. After the Soviet advance to the Oder, the *III. (germanisches) SS-Panzer-Korps* was chosen as the mainstay of the newly-formed *Heeresgruppe "Weichsel"*. After refitting and reorganization, the corps was to attack Zhukov's deep northern flank. *General der Waffen-SS* Steiner was ordered to organize the *11. Panzer-Armee*. *General* Unrein, formerly commander of the *14. Panzer-Division*, assumed command of the *III. (germanisches) SS-Panzer-Korps*.

The Pomeranian *32.* and the *215. Infanterie-Divisionen* also made the journey to Germany along with the *III. (germanisches) SS-Panzer-Korps*. Later, elements of the *11. Infanterie-Division* and the *14. Panzer-Division* were also evacuated. In addition, the wounded and 125 fathers of large families were also transported to Germany from every division in Kurland.

During the night of 28 January the remaining elements of the *III. (germanisches) SS-Panzer-Korps* were withdrawn from the front and arrived at daybreak in the Sutsas area, where the trains elements were located. *Heeresgruppe "Kurland"* praised the departing *III. (germanisches) SS-Panzer-Korps* in an order of the day.

*

The elements of *SS-Panzer-Abteilung 11 "Hermann von Salza"* without any tanks had already been loaded on ship in the harbor of Libau on 10 and 11 November 1944. They made the journey by sea to Germany on cargo ship *H 27* and disenbarked at Gotenhafen. In the Landeck area, south of Danzig, the units were rebuilt with new personnel, but the men waited in vain for tanks. At the end of January 1945 the battalion moved to Grafenwöhr. It had hardly arrived there when the old and new transports were reloaded and rolled to Pomerania.

In the final days of January, the remaining elements of the *III. (germanis-*

ches) SS-Panzer-Korps reached the Libau area. The cargo ships were loaded in bitterly cold weather. The hooks that were meant to secure the wheels of the vehicles slipped repeatedly. During the loading of *SS-Panzer-Grenadier-Regiment 24 "Danmark"* two vehicles fell into the harbor and were lost.

Every ship captain tried to load his ship as fast as humanly possible. Major difficulties arose from the inadequate loading facilities. The *"Traute Faulbaum" (II./SS-Panzer-Grenadier-Regiment 24 "Danmark"),* the *"Hernid Visor VII" (III./SS-Panzer-Grenadier-Regiment 24 "Danmark"),* the *"Malgache" (SS-Panzer-Grenadier-Regiment 23 "Norge"),* the *"Moira" (*elements of *the 4. SS-Panzer-Grenadier-Brigade "Nederland"),* the ferry ship *"Deutschland" (SS-Nachrichten-Abteilung 11* and *SS-Pionier-Bataillon 11),* the *"Minden" (SS-Freiwilligen-Panzer-Grenadier-Regiment 49 "de Ruyter"),* the *"Sesostris" (SS-Artillerie-Regiment 54),* the *"Comet"* and *"Karin von Bornhofen" (*units of *SS-Panzer-Aufklärungs-Abteilung 11* and staff*)* and other ships were loaded. The report that follows is from the command-post clerk of the *II./SS-Panzer-Grenadier-Regiment 24 "Danmark".*

The waiting was finally over and the uncertainty at an end. In the afternoon of 29 January the loading order for 30 January reached us. We were to move out at 0200 hours. Heavy snow started to fall. It took a long time to get the vehicles on the road and move out. The cold and wet penetrated to our bodies, even through the felt boots and winter clothing. As morning approached, a thaw set in. After short spells of driving and endless waiting, we were finally in Libau at 1500 hours and were shown to the barracks.

Wait — Wait! At 1700 hours the transportation orders for the battalion arrived. The rifle companies consisted of little more than trains elements. I was given the task of finding out where the ship was to be docked. Together with *SS-Untersturmführer* Christensen from the combat-engineer platoon, I looked in the military harbor, the north harbor and at the *U-Boot* wharf. All in vain!

Finally, I was informed at a naval office that our ship, the 1500-ton *"Traute Faulbaum",* was in the northern harbor at that very moment. We quickly drove back and directed the battalion to the embarkation point. In spite of inadequate loading facilities, the embarkation went quickly. On 30 January our "tub" left Libau harbor and, once outside, was escorted by *Schnellboote* (E-boats). Our ship steamed west through heavy seas.

The ferry ship *"Deutschland",* which arrived late, was loaded in an extremely short time. *SS-Sturmbannführer* Schlotter, commander of *SS-Nachrichten-Abteilung 11* and transport officer-in-charge for the *"Deutschland",* consulted with the naval officers and the commander of *SS-Pionier-Bataillon 11.* It was necessary to join the convoy. All available men, grenadiers, combat engineers and signaleers shoveled coal on the ship and made it possible to join the convoy. With the *"Malgache"* and a destroyer, the convoy immediately made full speed. When it was as far as Memel, it was attacked by a Soviet submarine, but the escort destroyer was able to drive the attacker off with depth charges.

Some of the convoys were separated by fog. New convoys formed up in the Danzig roadstead. The journey continued. In the waters of the Baltic Sea the "landlubbers" saw the floating remains of the women from the *"Wilhelm Gustloff"*, which the Soviets had torpedoed the previous day. It had sunk with its passengers, who were primarily refugees from East Prussia. Elements of the *4. SS-Panzer-Grenadier-Brigade "Nederland"* went down with the transport *"Moira"*.

The endeavors of the *Kriegsmarine* call for special praise in this connection. Without a break, the predominately small warships steamed through the waters of the Baltic Sea and escorted the convoys that served Kurland to the very end. Again and again they had to ward off attacking enemy ships and aircraft. German ships were lost in so doing.

The division adjutant of the *11. SS-Freiwilligen-Panzer-Grenadier-Division "Nordland"*, *SS-Sturmbannführer* Bergfeld, along with the corps quartermaster, *SS-Obersturmbannführer* Sporn, made the journey to Germany in mid-January 1945. There they arranged for the personnel reconstitution of the corps with the *OKH*. The new corps was created on paper. Considerable work had to be done.

In the course of the reorganization, the *4. SS-Freiwilligen-Panzergrenadier-Brigade "Nederland"* was redesignated as the *23. SS-Freiwilligen-Panzergrenadier-Division "Nederland"*.

*

Although sources are meager, we will attempt to reconstruct additional aspects of the maritime transport of the corps out of Kurland and to Stettin in Germany to conclude this chapter. The sources quoted are from the *"Lagebuch des Wehrmachts-Führungsstabes"* (Situation Book of the *Wehrmacht* Operations Staff = *LB*) and excerpts from the notes on the *"Teilnahme des Oberbefehlshabers der Kriegsmarine (Großadmiral Dönitz) an der Führerlagen"* ("Participation of the Commander-in-Chief of the Navy (*Großadmiral* Dönitz) in the Command Situation Conferences" = *KM*).

KM: 18 January 1945. Regarding the transport of three divisions of *Heeresgruppe Nord* to Germany (effective 25 January 1945: *Heeresgruppe Kurland*), the Commander-in-Chief of the Navy reported that an adequate amount of shipping capacity is available. The time required for the transport depends on the loading capacity of the harbor of Libau and on the weather conditions, which are presently and for the immediate future unfavorable (storms from the west). It is hoped that the *4. Panzer-Division* can be transported within the space of three days.

To clarify the loading capacity, a presentation to Hitler by the Commander-in-Chief of the Navy 18 March 1945 follows:

a)   Allowing for maintaining current supply shipments, for troop transports from Norway at the current level and for transport of wounded and refugees, the following shipping is available for transports from Kurland: 28

ships with 110,729 gross (register) tonnage.

b)   With that shipping capacity the following can be transported in a single round trip: 23,250 men, 4,520 horses and 3,160 vehicles.

c)   Considering probable enemy action and interference from weather, a round trip between Libau and Swinemünde will average 9 days.

d)   The capacity of the ports of Libau and Swinemünde are adequate for that transport movement if transports of wounded and refugees are conducted at harbors other than Swinemünde.

e)   Prerequisite for the operation is the maintenance of coal supplies for the escort ships, transports and shipyard repair facilities at the current level.

f)   Unusual increase in enemy action (heavy losses of shipping, destruction of harbors) cannot be calculated in advance and therefore is not included in the above figures.

It is clear from this report that Hitler considered bringing the Kurland armies back to Germany but then decided not to. Concern for an adequate supply of coal and oil for the ships is evident in all reports.

LB: 26 January 1945. The *4. SS-Polizei-Panzergrenadier-Division* will come from Hungary to *Heeresgruppe Weichsel*; the *III. (germanisches) SS-Panzer-Korps* (Dutch and Nordic soldiers) will be brought from *Heeresgruppe Kurland*.

LB: 27 January. The transports are not disturbed by the enemy. 14,000 men were brought from Libau. Up till now, 22,000 men have been brought from Libau in spite of the bad weather.

KM: 31 January. With regard to the loss of the passenger liner *"Wilhelm Gustloff"* due to submarine torpedoes on the outer route north of the Stolp Banks, the Commander-in-Chief of the Navy stated that overall losses among the transports in the Baltic Sea have, so far, remained within the limits allowed for. As painful as that specific loss may be, it must be viewed as particularly fortunate that losses to date have not been greater. In spite of that, it must be pointed out that Russian submarines are only able to enter the Baltic Sea with so little trouble because of a lack German airborne antisubmarine forces. Because of the shortage of German security forces, the navy must concentrate on the immediate security of the convoys...

LB: 1 February. Twelve transport ships are en route from Kurland to Swinemünde, including six with the *III. (germanisches) SS-Panzer-Korps*. 800 men from the steamer *"Wilhelm Gustloff"* were rescued.

KM: 1 February. The accelerated transport of *SS-Panzer-Korps Steiner* from Kurland, the *4. SS-Polizei-Panzergrenadier-Division* from the west, the *163. Infanterie-Division* from Norway and the *Marine-Schützen-Brigade* (naval rifle brigade) from *Marine-Oberkommando Nordsee* (naval high-command) depend on the situation in the Stettin — Stargard — Reetz area.

LB: 2 February. The *389.* and then the *281. Infanterie-Divisionen* will be shipped out after the current transport to Stettin of the *III. (germanisches) SS-Panzer-Korps* and the remainder of the *4. Panzer-Division* and the *32. Infanterie-Division* is completed. Fourteen ships are currently en route to Stettin.

KM: 2 February. In conjunction with the aerial attack on the inner city of Berlin today, the Commander-in-Chief of the Navy expressed his concerns regarding aerial attacks on Stettin and Swinemünde, which would have extremely serious consequences due to the high concentration of military vehicles, shipping capacity, refugees and wounded…The jamming of Swinemünde with refugees has continued to increase. At the present time there are about 35,000 refugees already there with another 22,000 on the way to Swinemünde.

LB: 3 February. Nine transport ships had arrived in Stettin by evening with units of the *III. (germanisches) SS-Panzer-Korps.*

LB: 4 February. Six steamers arrived in Stettin. The weather has improved. The flow of shipping is going smoothly.

LB: 5 February. A third of the *III. (germanisches) SS-Panzer-Korps* has now unloaded in Stettin. One third is waiting to disembark.

LB: 6 February. The combat echelons of the *III. (germanisches) SS-Panzer-Korps* have now left Kurland. Half of them have disembarked at Stettin.

LB: 8 February. The enemy has penetrated into Reetz…Nineteen ships carrying the *III. (germanisches) SS-Panzer-Korps* have arrived at Stettin. Fifteen are still waiting in the fog outside of Swinemünde.

LB: 9 February. Twenty-seven ships have unloaded at Stettin; eight in the roads…

KM: 9 February. The *Führer* particularly recognized the performance of the *Kriegsmarine* in the transport of the *III. (germanisches) SS-Panzer-Korps* from Libau to Stettin and said that this sea transport went faster than the transport by land of the divisions in the west to the east.

LB: 10 February. There are now 1,000 men of the *III. (germanisches) SS-Panzer-Korps* that have disembarked at Stettin. The *389. Infanterie-Division* has disembarked at Gotenhafen. (Author's Note: The 1,000 figure is probably a typographical error; the figure was more likely 10,000.)

LB: 11 February. The Lloyd-Steamer *"Steuben"* sank. Of the 2,500 wounded and 1,000 refugees on board, 600 were saved.

LB: 13 February. Thirty-three ships with the *III. (germanisches) SS-Panzer-Korps* have entered the port of Stettin, but not all of them have yet unloaded.

LB: 14 February. …Arnswalde has been encircled…

LB: 17 February. A 9,000 gross (register) ton transport was damaged by a mine outside of Stettin. It was possible to run it aground so that the cargo and the troops on board could be saved.

According to information provided by a former member of *SS-Artillerie-Regiment 11,* the advance parties of the battalions and of the *11. SS-Freiwilligen-Panzer-Grenadier-Division "Nordland"* were transported from Libau to Stettin on the steamer *"Bukarest".*

Additional material has become available in War Diary Number 4 of the *4. SS-Panzer-Grenadier-Brigade "Nederland"*, which has recently come to light. According to it, advance parties of the corps headquarters and of the division and the brigade were transported on the steamers *"Elbe"* (first transport group), *"Ilmenau"* (second transport group) and *"Preußen"* (third transport group). Elements of the brigade staff and the corps' *SS-Pionier-Bataillon 103* were transported with transport group seven on the steamer "R.O.I.". The *I./SS-Freiwilligen-Panzer-Grenadier-Regiment 49 "de Ruyter"*, *SS-Pionier-Bataillon 54* and *SS-Aufklärungs-Kompanie 54* were shipped from Libau to Stettin in transport group eight on the steamer *"Michael Ferdinand"*. No other information could be found.

SS-Sturmbannführer Lohmann and *SS-Hauptsturmführer* Ertel with recently decorated enlisted personnel and noncommissioned officers of *SS-Freiwilligen-Panzer-Grenadier-Regiment 49 "de Ruyter"* after the Second Battle for Kurland.

On the way from Kurland to Pomerania by boat.

Opposite page, top to bottom. Top: September 1944: Movement of the divisional field hospital of the *11. SS-Freiwilligen-Panzer-Grenadier-Division "Nordland"* from Reval to Lithuania. **Middle:** The harbor at Libau. **Bottom:** February 1945: Naval transportation from Kurland to Stettin.

This tanker takes a swig from a large container, much to the amusement of his comrades.

Members of the *2./SS-Panzer-Aufklärungs-Abteilung 11* on their way to Pomerania by sea.

A *U-Boot* provides escort as a troop transport makes its way into Stettin.

The Situation in Pomerania

On 12 January 1945 the Soviets broke through the German Narew-Weichsel (Vistula) position and advanced westward in several assault wedges. Three-million Soviet soldiers overran the 750,000 poorly armed German soldiers who faced them. On 26 January, the German *2. Armee* was forced back behind the lower Weichsel. Königsberg was encircled. Farther south, in the Braunsberg-Heiligenbeil pocket, German formations were engaged in a hopeless battle. Refugee treks flowed over the ice of the Frische Haff to Frische-Nehrung. Danzig was the center of bitter fighting.

In the south, Soviet divisions had reached lower Silesia. In the north, on the lower Weichsel, Field Marshal Rokossowski's 2nd White Russian front was pinned for the time being. Marshal Zhukov's 1st White Russian Front led the main effort of the offensive. It was intended to advance through Posen to Frankfurt/Oder. Posen was encircled but did not fall until 23 February. Bromberg held out for a longer time. Schneidemühl was encircled and defended itself until 14 February. The garrison broke through the encirclement on 13 and 14 February in the direction of Deutsch-Krone.

After a turbulent approach march, Zhukov's 1st and 2nd Guards Tank Armies were already at Küstrin on the Oder at the beginning of February and, as a result, at Berlin's front door. Zhukov's flank forces secured to the north along the Bahn — Pyritz— Arnswalde— Kallies line. Farther to the east was a gap of 100 kilometers.

To ward off the danger of a German flank attack, the 2nd White Russian Front was ordered to advance from the Weichsel toward Pomerania in the direction of Schlochau. The Polish 1st Army — five infantry divisions and nine additional brigades — was inserted between the 1st and 2nd White Russian Fronts. That secured the vast Soviet assault wedge to the north.

After the German positions on the Weichsel had been overrun in mid-January, the cohesiveness of the German formations was lost. The situation was overcome by events.

On 23 January a new army-group staff was formed under Himmler, the Commander-in-chief of the Replacement Army, with the mission of assembling the German formations between the Weichsel and the Oder and forming a new defensive front along the Warthe — Netze line with its front facing south. On 24 January Himmler established his field headquarters at Deutsch-Krone. Gradually, all the replacement units in the Pomeranian area were gathered into *Heeresgruppe Weichsel*. It was an assortment of hastily assembled *Kampfgruppen* formed from replacement units and men who had become separated from their units.

At Konitz and on the Netze River, the *15. Waffen-Grenadier-Division der SS (lettische Nr. 1)* conducted the defense. It was in the process of being totally reorganized. *SS-Freiwilligen-Regiment 33 (lettisches Nr. 4)* under *Oberst* Januns reached the Netze, but the attempt to advance farther to Bromberg and establish contact with the German garrison of the city failed. The *33. Waffen-Grenadier-Division der SS "Charlemagne"*, commanded by *General* Puaud, fought at Konitz. At the beginning of March, the remainder of that division was integrated into the defense of Kolberg. It fought for days on end in the city's defense, shoulder to shoulder with the German defenders.

At the Hammerstein Training Area — the staging area for the replacements for the *III. (germanisches) SS-Panzer-Korps* — *Offizierslehrgruppe Scheibe* (officer-training group) and *Unterführer-Ausbildungs-Bataillon Hämel* (noncommissioned officer training group), along with *SS-Freiwilligen-Panzer-Grenadier-Regiment 48 "General Seyffard"*, which was in the process of reorganization, were combined to form *Kampfgruppe Scheibe*. That *Kampfgruppe* was attached to *Korps Tettau*.

Elements of *SS-Panzerjäger-Abteilung 11*, which was in the process of reorganization, advanced from Neuhammer/Queis to join the units of the *III. (germanisches) SS-Panzer-Korps* which were engaged. At Arnswalde, Bahn and Pyritz, German formations were engaged with the flank forces of the 1st White Russian Front.

After the success of the breakthrough on the Weichsel in mid-January, *General der Waffen-SS* Felix Steiner was tasked with the defense of Eastern Pomerania, which he was to accomplish with the yet-to-be organized *11. Panzer-Armee*. *General* Unrein assumed command of the *III. (germanisches) SS-Panzer-Korps*. At the time it was still in transports at sea.

The German lines gradually firmed up with their front to the south. Between the Oder and Lake Madü stood *Korps Hörnlein*, to which the *4. SS-Polizei-Panzergrenadier-Division* was to be attached. The division was in the process of being transported from the Balkans. However, that division was transferred to the east shortly afterward and joined the *10. SS-Panzer-Division "Frundsberg"* to form the *XXXIX. Panzer-Korps* under *General* Decker at Stargard. In the same area of operations, *Panzer-Jagd-Brigade Munzel* and elements of the *28. SS-Freiwilligen-Panzergrenadier-Division "Wallonien"* had engaged the Russians who were advancing on Stettin.

In the Arnswalde sector, 3,000 men of *Nebelwerfer* replacement units were defending in the encircled city. To the north of that, the *III. (germanisches) SS-Panzer-Korps* was staging. At Neuwedell *Fallschirmjäger-Regiment 25*, commanded by *Major* Schacht, defended the city for days on end. To the east of the city was the *402. Infanterie-Division* under *Generalmajor* von Schleinitz. In mid-February, the *X. Armee-Korps* and *Korps Tettau* were staged yet farther to the east. The danger of a German flank attack forced the Soviet

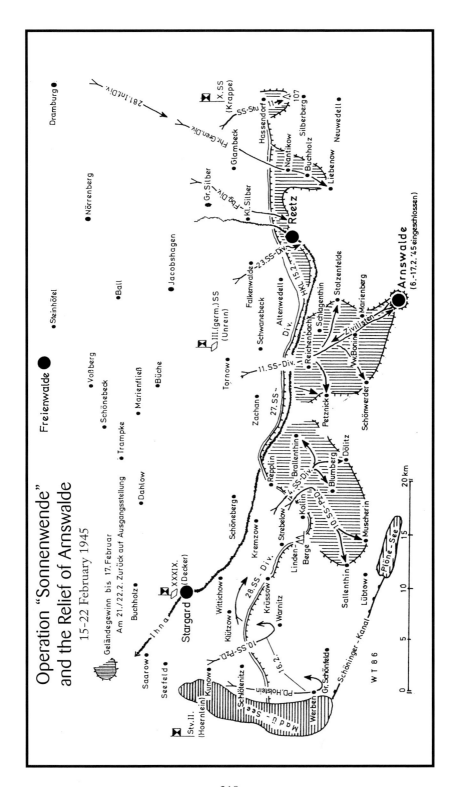

Operation "Sonnenwende" and the Relief of Arnswalde
15–22 February 1945

Geländegewinn bis 17.Februar
Am 21./22.2. Zurück auf Ausgangsstellung

Freienwalde ●

Arnswalde (6.–17.2. '45 eingeschlossen)

Reetz

Stargard (Decker)

XXXIX.

Stv.II. (Hoernlein)

X.SS (Krappe)

III.(germ.)SS (Unrein)

281.Inf.Div.
Fhr.Gren.Div.
Fbg.Div.
Gr.Silber

SS-Stu
107
SS-Stu
Hassendorf
Glambeck
Nantikow
Buchholz
Silberberg
Liebenow
Neuwedell

Dramburg ●
Nörrenberg ●
Steinhöfel ●
Ball ●
Jacobshagen ●
Voßberg ●
Schönebeck ●
Trampke ●
Marienfließ ●
Büche ●
Dahlow ●
Buchholz ●
Saarow ●
Seefeld ●
Kunow ●
Schöltenitz ●
Werben ●
Gr.Schönfeld ●

Kl.Silber
Falkenwalde
Altenwedel
Schwanebeck
Reichenbach
Schlagenthin
Stolzenfelde
Marienberg
Bonin
Zivilisten
Schönwerder
Petznick
Döbitz
Blumberg
Muscherin
Sallenthin
Lübtow
Tornow ●
Zachan ●
Repplin ●
Brallenthin
Kolin
Schönberg ●
Kremzow ●
Strebelow
Linden-Berge
Krüssow
Warnitz
Wittichow ●
Klützow ●

HKL 15.2.
–23.SS-Div.
11.SS-Div.
27.SS–
24.SS-Div.
10.SS-P.D.
28.SS-Div.
10.SS-PZD.
16.2.
PD.Holstein

Madü-See
Plöne-See
Schöninger-Kanal

Ihna

W T 8 6

0   5   10   15   20 km

command to first conquer Pomerania and then march on Berlin. The many German pockets in the Soviet rear area were eliminated. The 2nd White Russian Front and the 1st Polish Army started north from the Schneidemühl — Schlochau area with the objective of reaching the Baltic Sea and splitting up *Heeresgruppe Weichsel*. After initial successes, the attack bogged down on 19 February.

Steiner's *11. Panzer-Armee* had seven full and five incomplete divisions with which it was to hold the front in Lower Pomerania. However, the *OKH* directed the *11. Panzer-Armee* to attack south against the Russian deep northern flank. In a clear appreciation of the situation, *Generaloberst* Guderian pressed for an immediate attack so as to thwart Zhukov's attack on Berlin and gain time. Steiner first wanted to carry out the emergency refitting of his battered formations and start on 22 February. Guderian, the Chief of Staff of the *OKH*, prevailed. As a result, the *11. Panzer-Armee* started its attack to the south on 16 February 1945.

Korps Becker was able to force Zhukov's forces back and reached the southeast point of Lake Madü by evening. In the center, the *III. (germanisches) SS-Panzer-Korps* forced its way through to Arnswalde. The left-wing corps gained ground to the south east of Reetz and screened the eastern flank of the area of the attack.

Marshal Zhukov, who saw the danger approaching his 1st White Russian Front, swung his two tank armies to the north and staged the Soviet 67th Army, which was far superior to the *11. Panzer-Armee*, behind them. That brought the German flank attack to a standstill.

The Russians achieved a penetration south of Frankfurt. *Heeresgruppe Weichsel* had to immediately shift the *10. SS-Panzer-Division "Frundsberg"* there. The *4. SS-Polizei-Panzergrenadier-Division* was thrown into the Dirschau — Rummelsburg area and attached to *General* von Kessel's *VII. Panzer-Korps*, where it had to endure hard fighting with the *7. Panzer-Division. General* Decker's *XXXIX. Panzer-Korps* thus became a corps without troops. The *11. Panzer-Armee* had been forced to send valuable forces to other endangered places at the front and, at the end of February, went over to the defense.

Splitting *Heeresgruppe Weichsel* remained the objective of the Soviet command. Elements of the 1st and 2nd White Russian Fronts, along with the 1st Polish Army, started an advance to the Baltic Sea at the end of February. Neusettin was encircled at the end of February. Rummelsberg was captured on 3 March and Belgard on 4 March. The Soviets reached the Baltic at Kolberg on 5 March. With that, *Heeresgruppe Weichsel* was split in two.

During the fighting in central Lower Pomerania, the 1st White Russian Front opened its offensive against the *III. (germanisches) SS-Panzer-Korps* on 1 March from the Stargard — Reetz area. Superior armored forces achieved a breakthrough in two days. The German forces were forced back to the west.

The Altdamm bridgehead held temporarily. The Soviets reached Gollnow and the eastern shore of the Haff (sound) from the north on 7 March. On 18 March the last defenders of Kolberg left the encircled city by sea.

On 18 March, the attack was resumed against the Altdamm bridgehead. A penetration at Finkenwalde forced the defenders to evacuate the bridgehead on 20 March.

In East Pomerania, the German formations were thrown back to Danzig-Gotenhafen. Many formations were wiped out in the intense fighting. At the very end there was fighting on the Hela peninsula. Only a small number of men could be evacuated by sea.

With that, *Heeresgruppe Weichsel* had been destroyed. Himmler had proven himself incapable of leading large military formations. He laid down his authority as Commander-in-Chief of *Heeresgruppe Weichsel* and took shelter in illness.

The III. (germanisches) SS-Panzer-Korps in Pomerania

Between the Weichsel and the Oder the front moved slowly to the west, drawing more and more German formations into the maelstrom. The units engaged were burnt-out formations, units composed of stragglers or hastily assembled *Kampfgruppen*. They fought delaying actions but could no longer halt the Russian advance.

On 3 February 1945, while the regiments of the *III. (germanisches) SS-Panzer-Korps* were still afloat on the Baltic Sea, the newly formed *SS-Panzer-Jäger-Abteilung 11* of the *11. SS-Freiwilligen-Panzer-Grenadier-Division "Nordland"* entered the delaying actions in Pomerania, fighting alongside German infantry at Hassendorf.

One day later the Soviets reached the Ihna River southwest of Zachan. On the same day, the newly organized *schwere SS-Panzer-Abteilung 503* (Hertzig) arrived in Arnswalde and took its place in *Generalmajor* Voigt's defensive front, which was further strengthened with the addition of the *SS-Begleit-Bataillon Groß* (the escort battalion of the Commander-in-Chief of

Heeresgruppe Weichsel, Himmler).

The Soviets continued to advance on both sides of Arnswalde. Heavy fighting flared up along the outer defensive ring around Arnswalde. *SS-Obersturmbannführer* Kausch arrived in the area of the fighting with his *SS-Panzer-Regiment 11 "Hermann von Salza"*, which was not yet ready for combat.

Kausch's unit, which was in and around Landeck, had been moved to Grafenwöhr by rail at the end of January. It had scarcely been unloaded, when the order arrived moving it to the front in Pomerania. As a result, the same train was reloaded and then rolled toward Stettin. In Stettin the unit was issued 30 assault guns and 30 *Panzer V's*. It then road marched to the area north of Arnswalde.

On 6 February 15 *Sturmgeschütze* of *SS-Panzer-Regiment 11 "Hermann von Salza"*, under *SS-Obersturmbannführer* Kausch, advanced toward Arnswalde from the north and helped *SS-Begleit-Brigade Groß* recapture Schönwerder. In the evening, *Gruppe Kausch* moved on to Reetz. Petznick, Schlagenthin, Pammin and Stolzenfelde were occupied by the Soviets. Schönwerder was lost again. *SS-Begleit-Brigade Groß* went back to the defensive ring around Arnswalde. At Nantikow, units of *Kampfgruppe Schulz-Streek* had been encircled for two days. Other units of *Kampfgruppe Schulz-Streek* were south of the city of Reetz. Farther to the east, *Fallschirmjäger-Regiment Schacht* and elements of the *402. Infanterie-Division* held positions in the Neuwedell area. Two regiments of the *28. SS-Freiwilligen-Panzergrenadier-Division "Wallonien"* that were not yet combat ready arrived in Stargard on the morning of 6 February and occupied the Scheidersfelde — Kremzow — Repplin area.

Adjoining to the east were *Bataillon Oehms* (with staff in Zadelow) and *Bataillon Rehmann* (with staff in Zachan). Both battalions belonged to the *27. SS-Freiwilligen-Grenadier-Division "Langemarck"* which had been in the process of reorganization in the Lüneberger Heath area. The situation also forced the commitment in the Pomeranian area of the two battalions that were barely combat ready.

The German main line of resistance stabilized along the Ihna. The units of *Kampfgruppe Schulz-Streek (Sturmbann 11)* that had been encircled at Nantikow fought their way through to the new lines.

In the meantime, the first units of the *III. (germanisches) SS-Panzer-Korps* arrived in Pomerania. It was intended that the *23. SS-Freiwilligen-Panzergrenadier-Division "Nederland"* be reconstituted in the Gollnow area. The division staff was in Gollnow. The *11. SS-Freiwilligen-Panzergrenadier-Division "Nordland"* was staged in the Massow area with the division staff in Massow.

While inspecting the strongpoints held by *Kampfgruppe Schulz-Streek*, its

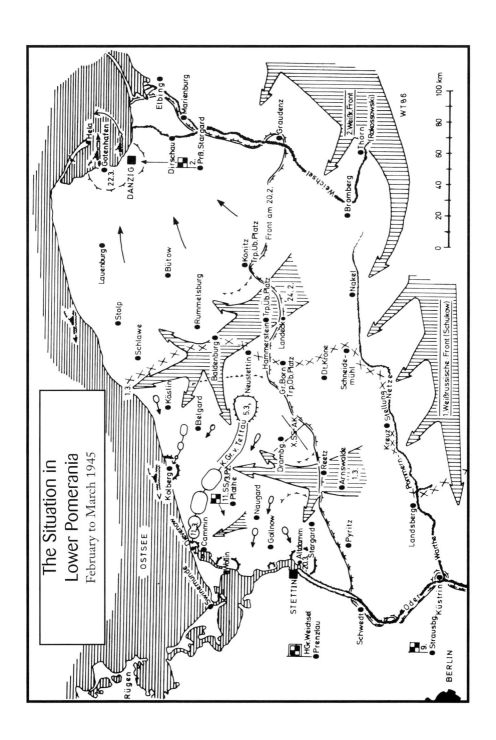

The Situation in
Lower Pomerania
February to March 1945

OSTSEE

Rügen

Swinemünde

Swinemünde

Wollin

Cammin
1.3.

Kolberg

Belgard

Köslin

1.3.

Schlawe

Stolp

Lauenburg

Bütow

Rummelsburg

Baldenburg

Neustettin

Gr.v.Tettau 5.3.
11.SS/3.Pz.K
Plathe

Naugard

Gollnow

Altdamm
20.3.
Stargard

Drambg

X.SS-AK

Reetz

Arnswalde
1.3.

Pyritz

STETTIN

Schwedt

Prenzlau

HGr.Weichsel

Landsberg

Strausbg
9.

Küstrin

Warthe

Oder

BERLIN

Hammerstein Trp.Üb.Platz
Landeck

24.2.

Gr.Born
Trp.Üb.Platz

Dt.Krone

Schneide-
mühl

Nakel

Konitz
Trp.Üb.Platz

Front am 20.2.

Kreuz Stellung
Pommern-
Netze

1.Weißrussische Front (Schukow)

DANZIG

Dirschau

2.
Prß.Stargard

Elbing

Marienburg

Prß.Stargard

Graudenz

Thorn
(Rokossowski)

2.Weißr.Front

WTB6

Bromberg

Weichsel

Hela
Gotenhafen
(22.3.

100 km

80

60

40

20

0

commander determined that the Russians had broken through east of Reetz and were advancing to the north. *SS-Sturmbannführer* Schulz-Streek briefed his *3. Bataillon* on the extremely dangerous situation. *SS-Obersturmführer* Pappert took immediate action. His extra long-barreled 7.5-cm *Pak* took up the firefight. *SS-Sturmbannführer* Schulz-Streek was wounded and made it to the hospital in Stargard, where his arm was put in a cast, the root of a tooth was pulled and his lower jaw was splinted. He remained in the hospital for two days, then left and made it on highway 104 to Kallies, which had been captured by the Russians. He fell back to the north and, finally, crossed the lines between Kallies and Dramburg.

The enemy's intentions were unmistakable: Advance north to Nörrenberg. The security forces of the *III. (germanisches) SS-Panzer-Korps* positioned northwest of Reetz were reinforced by the *Führer-Begleit-Division* (*Generalmajor* Remer), which had detrained on 8 February at Freienwalde and had immediately been employed at the new *Schwerpunkt* northeast of Reetz. At the same time, the *III. (germanisches) SS-Panzer-Korps* committed additional units into the area as fast as they arrived. *SS-Panzer-Flak-Abteilung 11* arrived at Jakobshagen. The *II./SS-Panzer-Grenadier-Regiment 23 "Norge"*, which had just arrived from Kurland, was directed on to Altenwedell. The staff of *SS-Freiwilligen-Panzer-Grenadier-Regiment 49 "de Ruyter"* was moved to Ravenstein with the command group (minus the regiment). A *Kampfgruppe* was assembled under the regimental commander, *SS-Obersturmbannführer* Lohmann, which included the staff of *SS-Freiwilligen-Panzer-Grenadier-Regiment 49 "de Ruyter"*, the *II./SS-Panzer-Grenadier-Regiment 23 "Norge"*, a bicycle company, an army antitank company and a police unit. The *Kampfgruppe* was attached to the *Führer-Begleit-Division*.

***

This section is a first-hand account by a former tanker of *schwere SS-Panzer-Abteilung 503*, Fritz Kauerauf, who provides insight into the desperate fighting in Pomerania.

With the Königstiger at the Front

After forty years, with the help of the Comrade's Association of *Korps Steiner*, I was finally able to locate *SS-Oberscharführer* Philipp Wild of *SS-Panzer-Abteilung 11 "Hermann von Salza"* of the *11. SS-Freiwilligen-Panzer-Grenadier-Division "Nordland"*, which led to a spontaneous and heartfelt reunion on 26/27 April 1985. The two of us were able to put the experiences we shared on 8 and 9 February 1945 in Pomerania in order as if it had been yesterday! Here is my report:

At daybreak on 8 February 1945, I, Fritz Kauerauf (22), at that time an *SS-Untersturmführer* in *schwere SS-Panzerabteilung 503* (the *Königstiger* battalion of the *III. (germanisches) SS-Panzer-Korps)* was ordered to report to the commander of *SS-Panzer-Abteilung 11 "Hermann von Salza"*, *SS-Obersturmbannführer* Paul-Albert

(Peter) Kausch, at the battalion command post. "Take a *Königstiger* and *SS-Oberscharführer* Wild's three *Sturmgeschütze*, move with them over the Ihna bridge to Ziegenhagen and Klein-Silber and cut off the Russian advance that has been reported there!" After giving me that mission, Kausch accompanied me outside and introduced me to *SS-Oberscharführer* Wild. He then sent us off and wished us success in our mission.

I assumed command of *SS-Unterscharführer* Lindl's *Königstiger*. I knew its crew well. Lindl went with us for a bit, but then had to stay behind.

We moved forward from the command post, which was south of Jakobshagen, behind the hills west of the Ihna. We advanced as far as that high ground and then saw the whole shebang in broad daylight! An endless Russian march column was moving from south to north along the ridge east of the Ihna with tanks, artillery, every kind of vehicle and also horse-drawn units. *SS-Oberscharführer* Wild had been attached to me because of his expertise in successful armored attacks. In 1944 *Feldmarschall* Model had awarded him the Knight's Cross in Kurland. He agreed with me that something had to be done immediately. He said, "If their march continues, they will get through to the Baltic. They could cut off our corps still arriving from Kurland." At that point in time, it had not yet completely arrived by sea at Stettin.

Since our four armored vehicles were far too weak to take on the superior enemy forces that we had spotted, I sent Wild back to get reinforcements for our attack. He did, in fact, do exactly that. Within a very short time, two more *Königstiger* under *SS-Oberstumführer* Kaes and about ten more *Sturmgeschütze* from the *1./SS-Panzer-Abteilung 11 "Hermann von Salza"* and a company of *Fallschirmjäger* joined us. We were later joined by the assault guns of *SS-Panzerjäger-Abteilung 11* under *SS-Sturmbannführer* Schulz-Streek. Towards noon we deployed from the line of march toward Ziegenhagen. We had to make our first firing halt before we reached the Ihna, since several antitank gun positions at the edge of Ziegenhagen had to be taken out. The *Fallschirmjäger* advanced on both sides of the road across the small bridge over the Ihna to Ziegenhagen.

We then followed across the bridge and into Ziegenhagen along with the *Fallschirmjäger*. There were two *Sturmgeschütze* in the lead and our *Königstiger* right behind. It started out as house-to-house fighting, but after the road swung to the left, we advanced relatively well as far as a right-hand curve. However, the two *Sturmgeschütze* in front of us were brought to a halt at the right-hand curve by heavy antitank fire. The problem turned out to be a Russian antitank gun beside the church at a range of about 150-200 meters. That was where our road joined the route of the Soviet advance march to Groß-Silber. An intense firefight developed between our *Sturmgeschütze* and the Russian antitank gun. However, because of a rise in the road, neither could get at the other. The rounds always went over for both parties. The attack had bogged down.

In that situation it was up to me, with the greater height of our *Königstiger*, to get the attack moving again. I had one of the assault gun commanders describe the antitank position to me. Then, during a precisely measured break in the firing, we rounded the corner with our *Königstiger* so quickly that we surprised the Russian antitank gun and knocked it out with a high-explosive round. We immediately pressed forward, bringing both of *SS-Oberstumführer* Kaes' *Königstiger* behind us. Wild's *Sturmgeschütze* followed right behind. The success of the undertaking now rested squarely on us, and us alone. However, we were again brought to a halt. This time it was a hasty minefield that had been laid on the street between two houses. The Russian rifle fire increased against our armor. It was particularly noticeable when we wanted to toss out empty shell casings. The *Fallschirmjäger* fought their way up to us, from house-wall to house-wall at the edge of the road and we gave each other mutual cover. The Russians still had control of the village.

My request for combat engineers to remove the mines remained unanswered. Finally, I was told to get out myself and remove the mines. Easier said than done. Help then came from an unknown fellow officer who leaped past our tank into the cover of the house that stood beside the hasty minefield on the right. He had a laundry bag full of demolition materials and was in dress uniform! Perhaps he had just come back from the hospital? It seemed totally unbelievable, but from there, by leaping back and forth and laying demolition cartridges or hand grenades, he blew up one mine after another! Five or ten times! That was an amazing performance that none of those who watched will ever forget. That unknown *SS-Untersturmführer*, whom we covered as best we could with our on-board machine guns, accomplished yet another feat that was decisive for the further progress of our attack. From behind a house he spotted a danger approaching our tank and, wildly gesticulating in the street and pointing to the fork in the road, identified it to us.

I called for a change of ammunition, which meant that Bruno Tuschkewitz, the loader, removed the roughly 1.2-meter-long high-explosive round from the breech and replaced it with an armor-piercing projectile. Thank God! It that very moment a muzzle brake that could only belong to a Josef Stalin tank appeared; it was half as high as a house and the Russian armored giant rolled directly at us at a range of 50 meters. "12 o'clock, armor piercing, Josef Stalin, aim between hull and turret — Fire!" Fritz Lukesch fired. The Russian tank came to an immediate halt. Its hatches were thrown open and our crew immediately began to celebrate.

Since the barrel was still aimed directly at us, I shouted with all my strength down into our tank, "Don't be crazy! Give it another one!" And then, again, "Give it another!" At that point, the Josef Stalin was burning brightly in front of us, its ammunition continuously exploding. But then what did we see? Two more tanks of the same type came up beside and to the left of the knocked-out Russian tank. Their crews must have had quite a shock, since they bailed out and ran away. We did not fire on those tanks since their guns were elevated. Obviously they had not figured on encountering us. They had probably never seen a *Königstiger* so close at hand.

The *Fallschirmjäger* waved joyfully to us and we were congratulated over the radio. But there was more to do! After the fire in the giant tank had died down a bit, we forced our way past it. We were then on the Russian route of advance and chased the Russians off in every direction. The road then belonged to us, the *Fallschirmjäger* and the tanks and assault guns that followed. *SS-Oberscharführer* Wild was still with us. We fought our way forward, always escorted by the *Fallschirmjäger*, well knowing that success had already been achieved.

Two or three ricochets glanced off of us. However, all in all, the Russian route of advance to the north had been cut for the time being. As evening approached we were at the southern outskirts of Klein-Silber, facing in the direction of Reetz. We formed a hedgehog with the three *Königstiger*. There were still about seven *Fallschirmjäger* with us. That was too few to relieve each other in two machine-gun positions. The

Fallschirmjäger had put in an extraordinary effort. They were completely exhausted. Nevertheless, they hung in there.

Kaes and I attempted to get back to the forward command post on foot during the night, but it was impossible. All hell was still loose in the village behind us. We heard that the unknown *SS-Untersturmführer* who had blown up the mines and warned us had been killed by a mortar round. We were all very shaken by that. We intended, however, that he would get the Knight's Cross for his deed. Later during the night a supply vehicle got to us and brought each *Königstiger* a drum of fuel (200 liters). There were no rations. But, then, we had no appetite either. Fueling from the drums was backbreaking work! Through it all, lost Russians and riderless *Panje* horses and their wagons ran through the area. In order to get some sort of rest, we "hung", as one might say, every which way inside the tight space of our tank. At the very top, on the commander's cupola, there was a sentry. We hardly got any sleep since the Russian artillery of the units that were pushing to the rear constantly fired into the village.

As morning drew near, the order arrived to capture the rest of the village to the east. For that we had to move back about 100 meters. In the process, there was a misunderstanding and, in spite of what had been coordinated, we were again at the point. The situation didn't seem right for a successful continuation of the attack. It didn't seem necessary to us to continue the attack in that direction either, since the terrain could be dominated from other locations. That later turned out to be the case. Since we also had no infantry to do what the *Fallschirmjäger* had done the day before, and since security for the tanks is an absolute requirement for close-in combat, I radioed a request for infantry. Instead of an answer, we got increasingly insistent attack orders. I finally called down to the driver: "Menke, are we moving or not?" The answer from the crew came in chorus, U*ntersturmführer*, we are moving." Since the radio was inadvertently on, that conversation was even heard by the *Korps Steiner* staff, as I later discovered (at that time *SS-Armeeoberkommando 11*). *Korps Steiner* was listening in on both us and the Russians. That brought a commendation to our crew. However, they never learned of it.

I then radioed: "Rainbow, this is Eagle 1, move forward to the outskirts of the village, follow me!" To our crew: "Step on it to the outskirts of the village!" Menke moved us forward. It was only about 500-600 meters, and I hoped that the tanks and assault guns would follow along behind us. If they did that, then our operation would probably succeed even without infantry. However, when we got to the outskirts of Klein-Silber we found ourselves entirely alone again!

Suddenly all our attempts to make radio contact failed, and my last request to close up to us — since we would otherwise have to fall back — went unanswered. We could not comprehend why nobody followed us. It was only later in the field hospital that I learned that *SS-Obersturmführer* Kaes' *Königstiger* had been set on fire by the Russians. It was directly behind us and blocked the street for the following *Sturmgeschütze*. Fortunately, Kaes and his crew got away with no more than a good scare. We set a time limit of 15 minutes for ourselves, since we could not hold at that spot any longer. When nobody joined us, we slowly moved back, firing occasionally at the Russians. However, we only made it half way back. In the meantime, the Russians had constructed a roadblock from handcarts and farm machines that blocked our way.

We attempted to move slowly around the barrier, but slid off the road to the left rear in such a way that our main gun pointed at the sky. It was no longer possible to make effective use of the bow or coaxial machine guns. The Russians immediately came and climbed on our tank. They set ladders up against it, and we were helpless in a flash. I ordered our driver, Menke, to move forward on the street again at full throttle and to move to the right through an opening between the buildings and out of the place. At first that seemed to work. But before we were completely out, a mighty detonation shook our tank and there was a spurt of flame. Our tank came to an immediate halt.

"Bail out!" I shouted to those down below. After the second direct hit struck the turret and smashed my left shinbone, I jumped out of the cupola. I felt a third direct hit as I leaped from the tank. I saw one comrade run away. Actually, there were two who got away. They took exactly the right direction and made it to our hedgehog position from the night before. Our third *Königstiger* and a *Sturmgeschütz* were behind the road embankment. The *Königstiger* had been immobilized by electrical problems and could only fire its two machine guns. Our *Fallschirmjäger* from yesterday were also still there. However, I knew nothing of that as I collapsed before our knocked-out tank.

As I fell, I raised my arms high and cried out loudly due to the Russians standing all around. On the ground, however, I pulled my pistol out of my pants pocket. But the Russians did not pay any attention to me at the moment. The sight of the burning *Königstiger* was more important to them. Our comrades died inside it: gunner Fritz Lukesch, a 17-year-old Transylvanian Saxon, and Bruno Tuschkewitz, the loader, who believed to the last that he would recapture his Pomeranian homeland. Their *Königstiger* became their grave!

The radio operator, Beißer, whom I saw run away, and the driver, Menke, escaped with burns. The front slope of our knocked-out *Königstiger* and the main gun could be seen from the *Sturmgeschütz* that our men had reached. They also quickly realized that I was still lying there. As I started to crawl to a stall for small animals that consisted of two huts with a door between, both the Russians in the barnyard and our *Sturmgeschütz* became active. The *Sturmgeschütz* started firing high-explosive rounds into the farmstead and around the shed in front of which I was lying. The rounds kept striking a little farther out so that the fragments wouldn't hit me but would force the Russians to stay under cover.

In the meantime, with the wire from my headphones and a bit of wood, I attempted to put a tourniquet on my left leg. My foot still hung painlessly within the twisted shoe in the shredded leather pants. I then lay on my stomach and waved toward the *Sturmgeschütz*. Suddenly, I felt a pain in my right and left thighs. Behind me stood a Russian who was firing at me from the hip with a machine pistol. He hit me with the first two rounds but was then unable to keep the burst on target as it pulled away to the left. I turned myself and shot him with my pistol. I also fired on another who looked around the corner. The Russian I had shot was dragged by the feet around the corner of the shed. I then lay on my back and kept an eye on the two corners of the shed. No more Russians came out. One hand grenade was thrown and landed by my lower body.

I was able to grab it and toss it away. However, it was hardly out of my hand when it went off and I received a 4-5 centimeter long strip of tin through my lower lip that stuck between my lower front teeth. I was able to pull it out again. I cried out again loudly after the explosion in the hope that the Russians would think that I was finally done for. However, another Russian, appeared in the center of the little stall. He was the second one I was able to properly gun down. They did not concern themselves with him, however. I suddenly saw, and the Russians behind the little double-stall must have also seen, that three men from our *Sturmgeschütz* were working their way forward to us along the outer edge of the farm houses of the village.

They got as far as the next barnyard and were almost within calling distance when they went back and disappeared at the *Sturmgeschütz*. I was deeply depressed. Then, however, I crept as far as the slat door between the two little stalls and saw, right behind it, a Russian machine gun with the ammunition drum on top and two men lying behind it. They did not notice me because the sounds of combat continued to dominate. I had long since inserted the second magazine in my pistol. I then took aim through a crack in the slat door to shoot the Russian duo at their machine gun, who where so close to me. I concentrated on saving one round for myself. However, that was not the way it worked out. I aimed, fired, aimed, fired and aimed again. I could no longer identify anything, and I fired again. The receiver locked to the rear! Empty! Throw the pistol away, far away! No, I'm not done for! Crawl, crawl and crawl some more. Just keep crawling until I am there where my comrades had been! I ordered myself to do that and I did it. I was able to disappear under a heap of potato tops. I was angry at myself that I could not pull my wrecked leg under the pile, and then I passed out.

The next thing I remember is seeing a Russian *Rata* wheeling in a cloudy sky. A *Fallschirmjäger* stood by my feet firing into the air with an assault rifle and two of our men in leather uniforms called to me: "*Untersturmführer*, where can we grab hold of you?" I happily yelled back, "Grab my shoulders and let's get out of here!" In one dash, without a break, they dragged me the 200-300 meters across the field to the *Sturmgeschütz*. Only when we were there did the third man, our *Fallschirmjäger*, run back. The commander of our third *Königstiger* came to the *Sturmgeschütz* and reported his tank totally disabled. I ordered him to blow up the breechblock of the main gun and set the tank on fire, which he then did. I no longer know who rode with me on the *Sturmgeschütz*. In any case, they delivered me to the medical clearing station at about 0930 hours. I was able to identify one of my rescuers later. His name was Leonhard Theunissen and he did not return from the fighting around Berlin. Someone found his *Soldbuch* and mailed it to his parents without commentary or return address. His last letter dealt with the fact that he had to blow up his tank in Klein-Silber and, in so doing, all his things were burned up. "God protect you!" was his last greeting to his parents.

When I was carried from the medical clearing station to the ambulance, several men from *SS-Panzer-Abteilung 11 "Hermann von Salza"* were standing there. One of them whispered in my ear: "*Untersturmführer*, we all saw what happened. Take care!" In the hospital I heard that the grenadiers of the *11. SS-Freiwilligen-Panzer-Grenadier-Division "Nordland"* occupied the area that we had captured and made it possible a week later to relieve the beleaguered Arnswalde. What is more, it was possible to transport a portion of the *Königstiger* of our *schwere SS-Panzer-Abteilung 503* that came out of Arnswalde by rail for the defense of Danzig.

During the breakthrough to Arnswalde, Knight's Cross recipient *SS-Oberscharführer* Philipp Wild was also knocked out and went to hospital with rather severe wounds.

After the war, an *SS-Hauptsturmführer* from the staff of *SS-Armeeoberkommando 11* (Steiner) told me that it had been listening in on the Russian radio during our attack. At the time I heard this toward the end of 1945, I was in the garrison dispensary at Ratzeburg at Below Barracks (an *SS* hospital guarded by the British). He told me the staff took great pleasure when it determined that the Russians were greatly agitated because our lead *Königstiger* had knocked out the three Josef Stalin tanks and our tank column had moved onto the route of the Russian advance.

Felix Steiner wrote the following in his book, *"Die Freiwilligen, Idee und Opfergang"* (The Volunteers: Idea and Sacrifice), published in 1958 by Plesse Verlag K.W. Schütz, Göttingen, (page 317): "The *11. SS-Freiwilligen-Panzer-Grenadier-Division "Nordland"*, which was following, attacked a long Soviet column that had broken through. The attack proceeded from the line of march and destroyed the Soviet column. The front then held. The refugees could then continue to flood across the Oder.

***

On 9 February bitter fighting raged northeast of the city of Reetz. Groß-Silber was recaptured by the *Führer-Begleit-Division* at about 1500 hours. The village was lost to the Soviets again in the evening.

During that time, the main body of the *III. (germanisches) SS-Panzer-Korps* was still at sea. The ships steamed west in hazy weather. Attacks by Soviet aircraft and submarines were expected at any time. The men's nerves were taught. The life jackets they wore for the passage did not give them a sense of security.

On 4 February about 50 ships were in the roads of Swinemünde. The escorts had tripled in size since passing Hela. Thick fog limited visibility to 100 meters. The sirens howled and the ships' bells tolled at short intervals. Shipwrecks were everywhere, which complicated entry into the sea-canal leading to Stettin. In spite of the heavy fog, the transports continued onward to Stettin and berthed at the harbor's wharves. Modern harbor facilities made for rapid unloading. One after another, the last ships with the units of the *III. (germanisches) SS-Panzer-Korps* arrived. On 7 February the motor ship *"Hernid Visor VII"* arrived in Stettin harbor with the *III./SS-Panzer-Grenadier-Regiment 24 "Danmark"*. *SS-Sturmbannführer* Ternedde reported his battalion to *Großadmiral* Dönitz, who greeted the ships as they made port.

The units reached their staging areas by motor march. A few days of rest followed. Replacements arrived. The *III. (germanisches) SS-Panzer-Korps* was replenished with replacement units from Kienschlag (Bohemia). The companies were reorganized with a strength of 1 officer, 9 noncommissioned officers and 60 enlisted personnel. *SS-Panzer-Grenadier-Regiment 24 "Danmark"* formed a new *16. Kompanie*, which was intended as a regimental reserve.

It was intended that the *23. SS-Freiwilligen-Panzergrenadier-Division "Nederland"* would get the newly reorganized *SS-Freiwilligen-Panzer-*

Grenadier-Regiment 48 "General Seyffard". However, under *SS-Obersturmbannführer* Scheibe, that regiment had been badly mauled in the fighting in the Landeck — Flederborn area and in the Polzin Pocket. Only remnants of that regiment were able to break through to the west through Divenow. As a result, the newly re-formed *SS-Freiwilligen-Panzer-Grenadier-Regiment 48 "General Seyffard"* was decimated before it ever got to its parent division. An additional regiment was organized in Kienschlag under *SS-Obersturmbannführer* Klotz. That regiment later made its way to the *23. SS-Freiwilligen-Panzergrenadier-Division "Nederland"*, though still not ready for combat. Because of losses, it was merged with *SS-Freiwilligen-Panzer-Grenadier-Regiment 49 "de Ruyter"*.

In the meantime, the enemy achieved new penetrations in the Arnswalde — Reetz area. The ring around Arnswalde was drawn tighter. Hohenwalde, Schulzendorf and Kähnsfelde were lost. On 12 February, the Russians demanded that *Kampfgruppe Voigt*, which was encircled in Arnswalde, capitulate. Voigt declined. The *Kampfgruppe* was supplied by air. During the days that followed, the Soviets forced their way to the outskirts of the city of Arnswalde and captured the railroad station.

In the evening of 7 February the Soviets penetrated into Reetz. The little country town was the center of important road networks and, thus, the point of departure for further Soviet advances. *Kampfgruppe Lohmann*, a hastily assembled formation, was already there. The newly formed *Kampfgruppe Schäfer*, led by the commander of the corps combat engineers, *SS-Standartenführer* Schäfer, assembled there. *Kampfgruppe Schäfer* included the combat engineer battalions of the *11. SS-Freiwilligen-Panzer-Grenadier-Division "Nordland"* and the *23. SS-Freiwilligen-Panzergrenadier-Division "Nederland"*. The next day the battalions of *SS-Freiwilligen-Panzer-Grenadier-Regiment 49 "de Ruyter"* arrived, reinforcing the forces around Reetz.

The situation at Arnswalde intensified, but its defenders remained confident. The civilian population and 11,000 refugees held out with them, awaiting the promised relief of the city.

The situation south of Stargard developed into a crisis. The *28. SS-Freiwilligen-Panzergrenadier-Division "Wallonien"* was positioned there with two regiments and *Volkssturm* units in a tenuous line of defense. The Soviets sought to reach Stargard. The *28. SS-Freiwilligen-Panzergrenadier-Division "Wallonien"* stood its ground in heavy fighting at Repplin. The next day comprehensive Soviet regroupings were observed. The division launched a limited attack to the south to thwart the movements.

At daybreak on 9 February the battalions of *the 28. SS-Freiwilligen-Panzergrenadier-Division "Wallonien"* opened an attack to the south, commanded by *SS-Obersturmbannführer* Degrelle. The Faule Ihne was crossed on both sides of Streelow. In a dashing attack, the Walloon volunteers captured

Heinrichsthal and Karlsburg and took the commanding Linden Hills. The Russians launched an immediate counterattack with armored support but were not successful. The Walloon volunteers held the tactically important high ground. A German counterattack launched at the same time by units of the *XXXIX. Panzer-Korps* farther to the west did not make it past the Warnitz/Damnitz railroad station. The villages of Warnitz and Damnitz remained in Soviet hands. During the night, *the 28. SS-Freiwilligen-Panzergrenadier-Division "Wallonien"* was pulled back into its jump-off positions. One company was sent to Krüssow, but found that it had already been occupied by the Soviets. A counterattack on Krüssow the following day was unsuccessful. The Soviets held the village.

After a few days of familiarization and training, the *11. SS-Freiwilligen-Panzergrenadier-Division "Nordland"* was alerted on 14 February and told to be prepared to relieve Arnswalde. Operation *"Sonnenwende"* (solstice) got under way. Its objective was to relieve Arnswalde, advance to Landsberg/Warthe and strike the divisions of Marshal Zhukov in their deep northern flanks. The battalions got to their assembly positions in rainy weather.

The attack forces of the *11. Panzer-Armee* staged along a line south of Stargard — Reetz — Kallies. On 16 February, the German attack to the south began. The west wing, the *XXXIX. Panzer-Korps* with the *10. SS-Panzer-Division "Frundsberg"* and the *4. SS-Polizei-Grenadier-Division,* rapidly gained ground to the south. In the center, the *11. SS-Freiwilligen-Panzergrenadier-Division "Nordland"* on the west and the *23. SS-Freiwilligen-Panzergrenadier-Division "Nederland"* on the east attacked Arnswalde. They were followed by two battalions of the *27. SS-Freiwilligen-Grenadier-Division "Langemarck"* and the *281. Infanterie-Division* (Ortner). The *Führer-Begleit-Division* (*Generalmajor* Remer) and the *Führer-Grenadier-Division* (*Generalmajor* Mäder) advanced in the Reetz — Hassendorf avenue of approach. The *402. Infanterie-Division* (*General* von Schleinitz) and the *5. Jäger-Division* (*Generalmajor* Sixt) were to mount a fixing attack on Kallies.

Before the attack began on 16 February, the *11. SS-Freiwilligen-Panzer-Grenadier-Division "Nordland"* had to fight for a favorable jump-off position. The *II./SS-Panzer-Grenadier-Regiment 24 "Danmark"* made it to the Ihna through Zachan. In thin morning fog the companies passed through the security line of the *27. SS-Freiwilligen-Grenadier-Division "Langemarck"*, crossed the Ihna at Fährzoll and formed a bridgehead. The combat engineers worked at a feverish pace as they reinforced the light wooden bridge at Fährzoll. The first vehicles rolled over the bridge at noon. The *II./SS-Panzer-Grenadier-Regiment 24 "Danmark"* closed up. Tanks and the *SPW-Bataillon* of the *Führer-Begleit-Division* followed. Elements of *SS-Panzer-Abteilung 11 "Hermann von Salza"* and the divisional *SPW-Bataillon* as well as the *3./SS-Panzer-Jäger-Abteilung 11* and Klösel's platoon from the *1./SS-Panzer-Jäger-Abteilung 11* advanced by surprise through Reichenbach to Marienberg and established contact with the encircled units at Arnswalde.

The *II./SS-Panzer-Grenadier-Regiment 24 "Danmark"* and the *III./SS-Panzer-Grenadier-Regiment 23 "Norge"* were committed at Reichenbach. The large, single-street village was soon in German hands. The *II./SS-Panzer-Grenadier-Regiment 23 "Norge"* advanced farther to Schlagenthin but was unable to free the village from the Soviets.

Let us now take a look at the operations of the *II./SS-Panzer-Grenadier-Regiment 24 "Danmark"*. They are indicative of the efforts made by all of the attacking battalions:

In a smoothly flowing road march, the battalion reached the bridgehead that had been formed by the *III./SS-Panzer-Grenadier-Regiment 24 "Danmark"*. The battalion dismounted by a mill south of the Ihna and organized for the attack. The *6./SS-Panzer-Grenadier-Regiment 24 "Danmark"* was on the left, the *7. Kompanie* on the right and the *5. Kompanie* behind it as reserve. The *8. Kompanie* was already in firing position. Friendly armor was out ahead, moving through Reichenbach buttoned up. There were surprised Soviet forces everywhere, but they made no use of their heavy weapons. The companies charged forward, gripped with the fever of the attack. Soon they were on the first hill. The village of Reichenbach lay beyond a shallow depression on the far rise.

A knocked-out antitank gun was on the road. Farther down the road hasty withdrawal actions could be observed. Several houses were on fire in Reichenbach. The *II./SS-Artillerie-Regiment 11* and elements of *SS-Artillerie-Regiment 54* supported the attack. *SS-Sturmbannführer Sörensen* knew that there was no time to lose. Charge into the fleeing Soviets, giving the enemy no time to get organized. Forward!

With long steps, Sörensen strode forward. He was followed by *SS-Untersturmführer* Raßmussen, *SS-Untersturmführer* Stippernitz and *SS-Unterscharführer* Scholles. The companies were having a hard time dragging weapons and equipment and could not keep up. Soon Sörensen's group had reached the eastern outskirts of the village. Dead Russians, dead animals and full baggage carts were everywhere. Saddled horses were in a courtyard. The men proceeded onwards, weapons ready to fire. A window opened and a head peered out shyly. At that point, the battalion's assault platoon also showed up. Two men entered the house. A heart-wrenching sight greeted them. Women cried for joy over their rescue.

Sörensen, his party and the assault platoon waited at the southern outskirts of the village for the arrival of the companies. *SS-Untersturmführer* Madsen's *7./SS-Panzer-Grenadier-Regiment 24 "Danmark"* finally arrived, panting and gasping. It was followed shortly by the *6./SS-Panzer-Grenadier-Regiment 24 "Danmark"*. At last the *5./SS-Panzer-Grenadier-Regiment 24 "Danmark"* arrived. Its commander, *SS-Hauptsturmführer* Fendler, had been wounded and *SS-Hauptsturmführer* Seyb had assumed temporary command. The *6./SS-Panzer-Grenadier-Regiment 24 "Danmark"*, which had been wiped out in Purmsati/Bunkas, had been formed anew and was now commanded by *SS-Obersturmführer* Engelbrecht. *SS-Obersturmbannführer* Krügel then drove up. Under no circumstances could the enemy be allowed to organize. After a short discussion, new attack orders were issued:

7./SS-Panzer-Grenadier-Regiment 24 "Danmark" on the right: Take and hold

Hochberg!

6./SS-Panzer-Grenadier-Regiment 24 "Danmark" in the center: Take and hold Hohenfriedberg!

5./SS-Panzer-Grenadier-Regiment 24 "Danmark" on the left: Take the storage sheds in the *VW* sub-division at Bonin and hold them. If strong enemy resistance develops in the patch of woods north of the *VW* plant, go into position!

The companies moved out again at 1300 hours. The *6./* and *7./SS-Panzer-Grenadier-Regiment 24 "Danmark"* reported at 1345 hours: "Attack objective reached. Weak enemy resistance broken!" Shortly afterward the *5./SS-Panzer-Grenadier-Regiment 24 "Danmark"* also reached its objective. The battalion and regimental command posts were set up in Reichenbach. With few exceptions, the village had been abandoned by the civilian population. Everywhere the livestock was in its stalls, the cows with swollen udders. *SS-Wirtschafts-Bataillon 11* was tasked with transporting the livestock away.

On 16 February, the German advance to the south was intended to be in full swing. *SS-Panzer-Grenadier-Regiment 23 "Norge"* was unable to capture Schlagenthin on that day either, however. That, in turn, tied *SS-Panzer-Grenadier-Regiment 24 "Danmark"* to its former main line of resistance.

The *XXXIX. Panzer-Korps* advanced along Lake Madü to the south with the intention of having units swing to the east from the southern point of Lake Madü and then unite with the forces advancing on Arnswalde, thus forming a pocket between Lake Madü and Arnswalde. The advance to the south was successful. The swing to the east was thwarted by the Soviets. The *28. SS-Freiwilligen-Panzergrenadier-Division "Wallonien"* attacked the commanding Linden Hills one more time and captured them, but neither that day nor the next was it possible to unite with the forces assaulting toward the south. The Soviets brought up reinforcements. The *XXXIX. Panzer-Korps* did not get past the southern point of Lake Madü. A hard fate awaited *SS-Untersturmführer* Capelle's company of Walloon volunteers, who had advanced far ahead onto the Linden Hills.

On 16 February heavy fighting developed in the sector of the *III. (germanisches) SS-Panzer-Korps*. Repeated attempts failed to attain the attack objectives. Companies of the *27. SS-Freiwilligen-Grenadier-Division "Langemarck"* fought in the west around Brallenthin and Petznick. Brallenthin was captured late in the afternoon. The Soviets held their own in Petznick. *SS-Panzer-Grenadier-Regiment 24 "Danmark"* was forced to stay on the high ground south of Reichenbach. *SS-Panzer-Grenadier-Regiment 23 "Norge"* fought at Schlagenthin and was only able to capture portions of it in the evening. The attack at Stolzenfelde bogged down.

SS-Freiwilligen-Panzer-Grenadier-Regiment 49 "de Ruyter" fought without success around Reetz in the sector of the *23. SS-Freiwilligen-Panzergrenadier-Division "Nederland"*. The *1./SS-Freiwilligen-Panzer-Grenadier-Regiment 49 "de Ruyter"* (command post at Neuglück) attacked along both sides of the Ravenstein — Reetz road, supported by *SS-Panzer-*

Jäger-Abteilung 54 (Aigner). The attack bogged down in concentrated Soviet fire at the cemetery in the northern part of the city. During the attack an isolated *Sturmgeschütz* that was trying to enter the city from the west through the Arnswalde gate was knocked out by gunfire and blocked the entrance to the city. The *II./SS-Freiwilligen-Panzer-Grenadier-Regiment 49 "de Ruyter"* was thereupon withdrawn from its position north of Reetz and brought around to the south to the *I./SS-Freiwilligen-Panzer-Grenadier-Regiment 49 "de Ruyter"* in an attempt to capture the city from the south from the Altenwedell area and break open the Soviet defense around the rifle club clubhouse. While crossing the Ihna, the Russians were already attacking with armor. As a result, the attack of the *II./SS-Freiwilligen-Panzer-Grenadier-Regiment 49 "de Ruyter"* also ground to a halt.

Elements of the *Panzer-Regiment* and *Oberstleutnant* Wolf's *Panzergrenadier-Regiment* of the *Führer-Begleit-Division* moved out from Klein-Silber to capture Reetz from the northeast. That attack, too, was brought to a halt in front of a strong antitank gun position. It only got to the Konraden railroad station. The rest of the *Führer-Begleit-Grenadier-Division* further to the right captured Steinberg and Kreuz, but was brought to a standstill outside of Nantikow.

The *281. Infanterie-Division* drove its attack forward by way of Glambeck, Hill 116 and Hassendorf. By evening, the division had gone as far as *Reichsstraße* 104. *Kampfgruppe Schulz-Streek*, which was advancing in that sector, reached Hill 107 south of Hassendorf. Late in the afternoon the enemy launched an immediate counterattack with armor to regain possession of the hill. The enemy attack was stopped by fire from the *Sturmgeschütze*. *Kampfgruppe Schulz-Streek* knocked out 24 T 34's.

On 17 February the *XXXIX. Panzer-Korps* again failed to get any farther at Lake Madü. Zhukov had thrown significant armored forces against it. *SS-Untersturmführer* Capelle's company, hanging onto its positions on the Linden Hills in desperate fighting, was shelled from all sides by T 34 and *Stalin* tanks. Neither reinforcements nor ammunition and food could get through to the encircled company, which melted away by the hour.

The *11. SS-Freiwilligen-Panzergrenadier-Division "Nordland"* tried to broaden its area to Arnswalde on 17 February. *SS-Panzer-Grenadier-Regiment 23 "Norge"* captured all of Schlagenthin and pushed its line of combat outposts to Stolzenfelde.

SS-Panzer-Grenadier-Regiment 24 "Danmark" received the following attack order:

1. *VW* Plant at Bonin, Schönwerder and Gut Marienfelde are held by strong enemy forces.

2. *SS-Panzer-Grenadier-Regiment 24 "Danmark"* is to attack from its positions on 17 February.

3. The *III./SS-Panzer-Grenadier-Regiment 24 "Danmark"* is to attack the *VW* plant at Bonin at H-hour, supported by elements of the *SPW-Bataillon* of the *Führer-Begleit-Division* and also three *Sturmgeschütze* from the *11. SS-Freiwilligen-Panzer-Grenadier-Division "Nordland"*. It is to capture the plant and form a new main line of resistance facing south.

4. After completion of the attack on the *VW* plant at Bonin, the *SPW* and *Sturmgeschütze* are to turn around and, swinging from the *VW* plant at Bonin toward Schönwerder, support the attack of the *II./SS-Panzer-Grenadier-Regiment 24 "Danmark"*.

5. The *I./SS-Grenadier-Regiment 66 "Langemarck"* is to launch its attack at the same time as the *III./SS-Panzer-Grenadier-Regiment 24 "Danmark"* and capture Gut Marienfelde. A combat-outpost line facing Petznick is to be established.

6. After completion of these two attacks, the *II./SS-Panzer-Grenadier-Regiment 24 "Danmark"* — *16./SS-Panzer-Grenadier-Regiment 24 "Danmark"* as reserve — is to attack Schönwerder with the mission of capturing and holding it.

7. The forward command post will be at Hochberg at 1200 hours.

The companies staged without significant interference from the enemy. The assault companies were in the lead, followed by the battalion staffs with commanders, adjutants and messengers, *Nebelwerfer* liaison, field-telephone wire units and, in addition, the 30-watt radio station of the communications battalion. The messengers were nearby.

SS-Sturmbannführer Ternedde's *III./SS-Panzer-Grenadier-Regiment 24 "Danmark"* attacked the *VW* plant at Bonin. He was supported by *SPW's* and *Sturmgeschütze*. They were met by a stiff defense. The companies worked their way forward by bounds and broke the enemy resistance. The *VW* plant at Bonin was soon in the possession of the *III./SS-Panzer-Grenadier-Regiment 24 "Danmark"*.

The Flemish soldiers' attack on Gut Marienfelde did not go as smoothly. The Soviets defended fiercely. The company commander of Oehm's battalion which was attacking Gut Marienfelde was killed at the very beginning. The fighting at the sheep farm continued for a long time. The company was reduced to two weak platoons.

Gut Marienfelde was a threat to the flank of *SS-Panzer-Grenadier-Regiment 24 "Danmark"*. Nevertheless, late in the afternoon, *SS-Obersturmbannführer* Krügel ordered the attack to be launched against Schönwerder. While *SS-Sturmbannführer* Sörensen's *II./SS-Panzer-Grenadier-Regiment 24 "Danmark"* moved out, the previously coordinated flare signal rose above Marienfelde. That indicated the farm was in the hands of the Flemish soldiers.

The *II./SS-Panzer-Grenadier-Regiment 24 "Danmark"* advanced on both sides of the Reichenbach — Schönwerder road. A broad plain stretched in front of the first known enemy positions. The companies worked their way forward to the enemy by bounds. The *Sturmgeschütze* fired on the wood line. The first Russians took flight after 15 minutes. The *6.* and *7./SS-Panzer-Grenadier-Regiment 24 "Danmark"* could no longer be held back. They broke into the Soviet positions. Russian machineguns, antitank rifles and rifles were scattered about. Bed linens, blankets and warm furs were left in the field positions. Two of the *Sturmgeschütze* that were moving along the road were disabled by mines. The third met the same fate shortly before it got to Schönwerder. The *SPW's* swung out to the east. Enemy resistance stiffened in front of the village. Antitank guns barked and *SPW's* were knocked out by direct hits. Heavy defensive fire pounded the attackers just as they got to Schönwerder. A barrage of mortar fire forced Sörensen's companies to the ground. *SS-Obersturmbannführer* Krügel went up front.

New orders went out to the companies. *SS-Untersturmführer* Madsen fired up his *7./SS-Panzer-Grenadier-Regiment 24 "Danmark"*. It broke into Schönwerder in a gutsy assault. The other companies followed. Darkness was already falling, which prevented the *II./SS-Panzer-Grenadier-Regiment 24 "Danmark"* from pushing its combat-outpost line to the Stargard — Arnswalde railroad line. Contact was established to the east with the *III./SS-Panzer-Grenadier-Regiment 24 "Danmark"*, some of whose units had reached the railroad line. Contact was also established with the units in Marienberg. The *16./SS-Panzer-Grenadier-Regiment 24 "Danmark"* was inserted in the long western flank facing the brush-covered and wooded terrain. It would also establish contact with the *I./SS-Grenadier-Regiment 66 "Langemarck"*. There was also heavy fighting that day around Petznick. At that point, *SS-Panzer-Grenadier-Regiment 24 "Danmark"* had its east flank directly west of the city of Arnswalde. Seven tanks of the *11. SS-Freiwilligen-Panzer-Grenadier-Division "Nordland"* arrived in Arnswalde at about 1600 hours.

What was the situation on 17 February in the sector of the *23. SS-Freiwilligen-Panzergrenadier-Division "Nederland"*?

The *I./SS-Freiwilligen-Panzer-Grenadier-Regiment 49 "de Ruyter"* repeated its attack from the cemetery against Reetz, again to no avail. The city was strongly held and could not be taken in a frontal attack. Numerous enemy weapons, particularly artillery, dominated the town in the valley from the hills southeast of it. Therefore *SS-Obersturmbannführer* Lohmann decided against any additional frontal attacks. He requested the enemy weapons first be eliminated by capturing the commanding hills in a pincers attack. The *II./ SS-Freiwilligen-Panzer-Grenadier-Regiment 49 "de Ruyter"* was again sent north and occupied positions north of Reetz along the Walkmühle — Konraden railroad station line.

The day was also filled with fighting for the *Führer-Begleit-Division*, the *Führer-Grenadier-Division* and elements of the *281. Infanterie-Division*. An attack by the mixed *Kampfgruppe Wünsch* of the *Führer-Begleit-Division* from Nantikow against Buchholz miscarried. The *Kampfgruppe* had to be withdrawn from the fighting due to heavy losses.

With support from the *5./Artillerie-Regiment 281* and the *I./Grenadier-Regiment 368 (281. Infanterie-Division)*, the *Führer-Begleit-Division* was able to capture Buchholz in an enveloping attack and also advance halfway to Liebenow. From that line, the division repulsed Russian armored assaults.

Additional crises arose during the night for the division. From the east came a night attack on Nantikow, where the division command post was located. The division's *Sturmgeschütz-Abteilung*, under *Hauptmann* Tornau, repulsed all the enemy armored attacks.

The Eighteenth of February started under a bad sign in the sector of the *XXXIX. Panzer-Korps*. Zhukov committed his guards tank units, forcing the *XXXIX. Panzer-Korps* back out of several villages in the direction of Stargard. The German offensive was thus transformed into a defensive action.

The death struggle of Capelle's company of the *28. SS-Freiwilligen-Panzergrenadier-Division "Wallonien"* began on the Linden Hills. T 34 and Stalin tanks rolled against the lines from all sides. Soon the remaining *Panzerfäuste* had been expended. *SS-Untersturmführer* Capelle was still in touch with the division by radio. Relief was impossible. The Walloon volunteers were killed and ground up in their foxholes by tank tracks. Severely wounded men fought on to their last breath. In the end, only the command post was left. Capelle fired his pistol to the last. Severely wounded, he fired the final round into his own head. The fighting had lasted the entire day. Only two wounded Walloon volunteers made it to the German lines during the night.

During the night a new main line of resistance was established along the line Lake Madü — Schlötenitz — Streesen — Schiedersfeld — Kremzow. *General* Decker's armored formations were withdrawn.

The Eighteenth of February remained quiet in the sector of the *11. SS-Freiwilligen-Panzergrenadier-Division "Nordland"*, but reconnaissance revealed that the enemy had been conspicuously reinforced along the Stargard — Arnswalde railroad line. During the night, a Soviet patrol was able to make its way to the Reichenbach road at Marienfelde and fire on supply vehicles. As a result, another company of the *27. SS-Freiwilligen-Grenadier-Division "Langemarck"* was inserted between Marienfelde and the *II./SS-Panzer-Grenadier-Regiment 24 "Danmark"*.

Heavy fighting raged in Arnswalde around the military base and in the vicinity of the railroad station. Wounded flowed out through the two-kilometer lane that *the 11. SS-Freiwilligen-Panzer-Grenadier-Division "Nordland"* had opened the day before. That evening, the commanding general of the *III. (germanisches) SS-Panzer-Korps, General* Unrein, appeared in Arnswalde and discussed further measures with the Arnswalde area commander, *Generalmajor* Voigt. *Sturmgeschütze* from the *1./SS-Panzer-Jäger-Abteilung 11* were sent forward to the defenders of Arnswalde.

In the sector of the *23. SS-Freiwilligen-Panzergrenadier-Division "Nederland"* the situation remained essentially unchanged.

During the morning of 18 February, the enemy launched a strong flank attack against Nantikow. It was supported by ground-attack aircraft. The *Führer-Begleit-Division* and the *Führer-Grenadier-Division* held their own. A little later an enemy armored attack struck Hill 107 south of Hassendorf. *Kampfgruppe Schulz-Streek*, which was positioned there, repulsed the attack and caused the enemy heavy losses. The *Kampfgruppe* destroyed 17 enemy tanks, several antitank guns and other guns and captured three T 34 tanks.

During that time, the *Führer-Begleit-Division* (Remer) readied itself to continue the attack to the south. The jump-off position was Buchholz. The intermediate objectives of the attack were Neuhof, Bethanien and Liebenow. The high ground along that line was barred by a strong Soviet antitank gun and tank barrier that could not be broken. The situation became critical in the afternoon. The German attack forces were pulled back to Buchholz. A German main line of resistance was established at the road. It held in spite of the onset of enemy attacks. The division was withdrawn during the night and the sector was taken over by the *Führer-Grenadier-Division*. The *Führer-Begleit-Division* and, later, the *Führer-Grenadier-Division* were needed by the army group in other places. That marked the termination of the offensive toward the south. The German forces proved to be too weak in relation to the steadily strengthening forces of Marshal Zhukov.

On 19 February, the *Führer-Grenadier-Division* (Mäder) prepared for yet another attack on Liebenow. That evening *Heeresgruppe Weichsel* ordered the termination of the attack. That was the end of the German offensive.

On 20 February, the *Führer-Grenadier-Division* was also withdrawn. The *281. Infanterie-Division* took over the Reetz — Buchholz — Nantikow — Hassendorf sector. It, in turn, was relieved between 21 and 23 February by the *5. Jäger-Division*. The main line of resistance there was gradually forced back toward the north.

As a result of that development, the evacuation of the city of Arnswalde became pressing, the more so since strong enemy attacks with the objective of encircling the city were expected.

On 19 February there was a meeting in the city between the local area commander, *Generalmajor* Voigt, and the commander of the *11. SS-Freiwilligen-Panzergrenadier-Division "Nordland"*, *SS-Brigadeführer und Generalmajor der Waffen-SS* Ziegler, which determined the plan for the evacuation of the city. An enemy armored assault was repulsed at Friedrichsruh, three kilometers northeast of Arnswalde. The Third Platoon of the *1./SS-Panzer-Jäger-Abteilung 11* knocked out two Soviet KV 1's, one T 34 and one Stalin tank.

On 19 and 20 February, the enemy pressure increased against *SS-Panzer-*

Grenadier-Regiment 23 "Norge" and SS-Panzer-Grenadier-Regiment 24 "Danmark". Heavy barrages from Stalin organs, mortars and guns of all calibers covered their positions. Enemy attacks from both the Schönwerder estate and the railroad station at Schönwerder were broken up by the fire of the heavy weapons of SS-Panzer-Grenadier-Regiment 24 "Danmark" in front of its lines.

The Soviet barrages reached their high point on 21 February. Schönwerder burned. During the night, the cattle were driven off toward Reichenbach by the supply battalion of the 11. SS-Freiwilligen-Panzer-Grenadier-Division "Nordland".

Late in the afternoon of 21 February the battalion adjutants gave the following situation report to the company headquarters-section leaders for them to pass on to their company commanders. The situation report for SS-Panzer-Grenadier-Regiment 24 "Danmark", which is similar in content to what SS-Panzer-Grenadier-Regiment 23 "Norge" was given, reads:

Enemy strength has significantly increased in front of the entire sector of 11. SS-Freiwilligen-Panzer-Grenadier-Division "Nordland". The division has advanced far forward and has long flanks, which cannot be maintained. The offensive that began with good initial success has bogged down with the attainment of the intermediate objective of freeing Arnswalde. It has now run into strong enemy reserves. Although the 27. Freiwilligen-Grenadier-Division "Langemarck" was unable to capture the village of Petznick, the 11. SS-Freiwilligen-Panzer-Grenadier-Division "Nordland" was able to capture the large villages of Reichenbach, Schlagenthin and Schönwerder, thus opening a corridor to Arnswalde. In view of an impending enemy attack, the decision has been made to pull the front back to the Ihna. The time for the evacuation of Schönwalde will be determined after the beginning of the evacuation of Arnswalde. A verbal order will be given for dismantling the field-telephone system. The signals sections of the companies will switch to "listening silence". The withdrawal movement will begin with the code word "Adelheid". Until then, the companies are to maintain all their accustomed activity (flares, infantry harassing fire, etc) and, on receipt of the withdrawal order, quietly and inconspicuously withdraw to the VW plant at Bonin. Each company is to leave one squad as rear guard, which will, under the command of a yet-to-be appointed officer, continue to occupy the position and simulate a fully occupied position through infantry harassment fire. A signals section will be assigned to each battalion to maintain communications. Times and detailed orders will follow separately.

The company commanders had hardly been given that information when the withdrawal order from the regiment arrived:

1. Commencing 2300 hours on 21 February 1945, the II. and III./SS-Panzer-Grenadier-Regiment 24 "Danmark" will withdraw from their positions to the VW plant at Bonin. The rear guard is to remain in the old positions until 22 February, 0100 hours.

2. The III./SS-Panzer-Grenadier-Regiment 24 "Danmark" is to remain at the VW plan at Bonin and receives the rear guard. It is to remain there until 22 February as the regimental rear guard.

3. The *II./SS-Panzer-Grenadier-Regiment 24 "Danmark"* is to move back in a single bound through Reichenbach to Fährmühle where it is to occupy the ridge line lying north of Reichenbach, focusing on Petznick.

4. After passage of lines by the rearguard of the *11. SS-Freiwilligen-Panzer-Grenadier-Division "Nordland"* (*III./SS-Panzer-Grenadier-Regiment 23 "Norge"* and *III./SS-Panzer-Grenadier-Regiment 24 "Danmark"*) the *II./SS-Panzer-Grenadier-Regiment 24 "Danmark"* is to withdraw over the Ihna to Zachan.

5. The commander of the *II./SS-Panzer-Grenadier-Regiment 24 "Danmark"* is responsible for the demolition of the Ihna bridge.

6. *SS-Panzer-Grenadier-Regiment 24 "Danmark"* is to assemble east of Stargard.

The withdrawal movement of the combat units began in Arnswalde. Civilians and wounded soldiers had already left the city the previous night.

Kampfgruppe Voigt left the city of Arnswalde in three march groups at 1700, 1800 and 1900 hours. It passed through Marienberg, Reichenbach and Fährzoll. The rearguard, commanded by *SS-Obersturmbannführer* Groß, withdrew at 2000 hours. The rearguard consisted of one assault-gun battery, one light *Flak* battery and two rifle companies. Müller's platoon, which was providing cover at Friedrichsruh, was picked up and taken away by the *Sturmgeschütze*. With that, the city of Arnswalde was evacuated. *Generalmajor* Voigt reported the withdrawal of his *Kampfgruppe* to the commanding general of the *III. (germanisches) Panzer-Korps*, *General* Unrein, in Tornow at midnight.

What was the situation for *SS-Panzer-Grenadier-Regiment 24 "Danmark"*, which was securing the southern flank? The men of the regiment heard the non-stop movement of the stream flowing north. They had to remain and cover their comrades' withdrawal!

At 2300 hours the *II.* and *III./SS-Panzer-Grenadier-Regiment 24 "Danmark"* withdrew from the positions at Schönwerder. One squad from each company remained in the positions for another two hours. As ordered, the *III./SS-Panzer-Grenadier-Regiment 24 "Danmark"* occupied a rearguard position south of the *VW* plant at Bonin. The *II./SS-Panzer-Grenadier-Regiment 24 "Danmark"* pulled back to Fährmühle.

The rearguards left in the old positions felt like they were sitting on hot coals. Such operations were nerve-wracking. Flares rose in the sky. Here and there a machine gun rattled. *SS-Untersturmführer* Gordon, who commanded the rearguard of the *II./SS-Panzer-Grenadier-Regiment 24 "Danmark"*, went quietly from squad to squad. At last, the hour-hand of his watch pointed to the numeral "one". It was time!

At 0300 hours a heavy barrage fell on the old positions and on Schönwerder. The men of the rearguard grinned in a satisfied manner. The Russians had not yet noticed the positions had been abandoned.

At 0500 hours on 22 February, the *II./SS-Panzer-Grenadier-Regiment 24 "Danmark"* occupied the designated bridgehead position at Fährmühle. The stream flowing out of Arnswalde flowed ceaselessly; at daybreak it would cease abruptly.

The *III./SS-Panzer-Grenadier-Regiment 24 "Danmark"* held its position at the *VW* plant at Bonin. The Soviets were not certain until the morning hours of 22 February that the German positions were empty. They felt their way forward hesitantly and occupied Schönwerder. As noon approached, Russian cavalry attacked the *VW* plant at Bonin. The *III./SS-Panzer-Grenadier-Regiment 24 "Danmark"*, which was positioned there as rearguard, repulsed the advance. After that, it remained quiet.

As dusk fell, the divisional aid station of the *11. SS-Freiwilligen-Panzer-Grenadier-Division "Nordland"* pulled out of Reichenbach and moved to the rear. Around 2000 hours the *II./SS-Panzer-Grenadier-Regiment 24 "Danmark"* was placed in a heightened state of alert, with its attention focused on Petznick. The first rearguard elements of the division arrived and crossed over the Ihna bridge that *SS-Sturmbannführer* Sörensen's *II./SS-Panzer-Grenadier-Regiment 24 "Danmark"* had to keep open until the end. At about 2200 hours, *SS-Sturmbannführer* Ternedde's *III./SS-Panzer-Grenadier-Regiment 24 "Danmark"* conducted the passage of lines. Forty-five minutes later the *III./SS-Panzer-Grenadier-Regiment 23 "Norge"*, coming from Schlagenthin, also passed over the bridge. After the passage was complete, the *II./SS-Panzer-Grenadier-Regiment 24 "Danmark"* evacuated the Fährmühle bridgehead.

SS-Sturmbannführer Sörensen gave the order to blow up the Ihna Bridge. The demolition party made its final preparations. Then the *10./SS-Panzer-Grenadier-Regiment 23 "Norge"* came through. After the company had crossed, the bridge flew up into the air.

The new front ran south of Stargard as far as the Ihna; it then followed the course of the small river north of Reetz. After that, it followed (approximately) *Reichsstraße 104* — Konraden and Hassendorf — as far as Wildforth.

The Soviet armies armed themselves for the final assault that would split *Heeresgruppe Weichsel* in two. A second thrust targeted Stettin, with the objective of destroying the formations that were in the western part of Lower Pomerania, including the formations of the *III. (germanisches) SS-Panzer-Korps*.

The German formations were regrouped. In the course of 24 February, *SS-Panzer-Grenadier-Regiment 24 "Danmark"* moved through Stargard to the area south of the city and relieved an army unit. It had been billeted in the Dahlow —Barskewitz area. Within the regiment's sector, the *III./SS-Panzer-Grenadier-Regiment 24 "Danmark"* was to the west, holding from Lange-Berge to Streesen; the *II./SS-Panzer-Grenadier-Regiment 24 "Danmark"* was to the east, holding from Streesen to the Faule Ihna. The latter battalion maintained contact with *28. SS-Freiwilligen-Panzergrenadier-Division "Wallonien"*. The regimental command post was at Gut Klützow.

28. SS-Freiwilligen-Panzergrenadier-Division "Wallonien" was positioned farther to the east in the area on both sides of Kremzow. Two battalions of the *27. SS-Freiwilligen-Grenadier-Division "Langemarck"* were south of Zadelow — Zachan. *Begleit-Bataillon Groß* was at Fährzoll. *SS-Panzer-Grenadier-Regiment 23 "Norge"* held as far as Altenwedell. *SS-Freiwilligen-Panzer-Grenadier-Regiment 49 "de Ruyter"* was positioned from west of Reetz to the Konraden railroad station. The *5. Jäger-Division* was at Steinberg and *Kampfgruppe Schulz-Streek* was at Hassendorf, where it maintained contact to the *X. SS-Panzer-Korps* under *General* Krappe.

The Soviet offensive began on 28 February against the central portion of the army-group front. Things also got active on the western Pomeranian front.

In the Ihna sector, the enemy increased pressure on the *23. SS-Freiwilligen-Panzer-Grenadier-Division "Nederland"*, which was able to hold on at the Reetz cemetery and at *Reichsstraße 104*.

The Russians also tested the German front south of Stargard. A heavy artillery barrage came down on the positions of the *III./SS-Panzer-Grenadier-Regiment 24 "Danmark"*. It was holding a blocking position on the Lange Hills facing toward Stargard. Its position was on the important Highway 158, the only one between Lake Madü and the Faule Ihna. The *11./SS-Artillerie-Regiment 11* returned the fire and shelled the villages of Warnitz and Krüssow. It remained quiet in the Streesen sector, but the forward observers of the *8.* and *12./SS-Panzer-Grenadier-Regiment 24 "Danmark"*, along with those of the *II./SS-Artillerie-Regiment 11,* flooded the command channels with reports of enemy activity. Enemy formations moved from east to west with infantry, artillery, vehicles and tanks. New *Schwerpunkte* developed south of Stargard and between Lake Madü and Pyritz. On 28 February the reports of enemy activity gave rise to nervousness everywhere on the German side.

SS-Artillerie-Regiment 54 "Nederland", which had been constantly employed in the hot spots of the fighting with two light battalions ever since Narwa, started organizing a new heavy battalion in Pomerania. The light batteries gave up personnel. The commander of the new battalion was *SS-Sturmbannführer* Hofer. Guns and prime movers were lacking. The *9./SS-Artillerie-Regiment 54* was supposed to receive 8.8 cm *Flak*. The new Soviet offensive, however, broke into the middle of the training and organizational program.

The Soviet offensive against Stettin began at almost the same time as the advance to the Baltic Sea from the Neustettin area. The Soviet command wanted to conquer Lower Pomerania first and then initiate the decisive blow against Berlin.

On 1 March 1945 the positions of the *III. (germanisches) SS-Panzer-Korps* were shaken under the blows of the Soviet artillery and armor formations. Massed infantry attacked the entire corps front. The front broke at many places under the weight of the Soviet blows. In the corps sector on 1 March two *Schwerpunkte* crystallized. The first was along the Faule Ihna at Petznick, Brallenthin and Repplin . The second was at Reetz.

The companies of the *27. SS -Freiwilligen-Grenadier-Division "Langemarck"* — they never even constituted a regiment in strength — had been bled white. They held positions at Brallenthin and Repplin along the Faule Ihna. They were thrown back. Russian infantry and armor captured Brallenthin and Repplin, then crossed the Ihna from there and moved north. Soon Suckow was also in their hands. As noon approached on 1 March, Russian armor was positioned on *Reichsstraße 104* outside of Schönberg. The men of the *28. SS-Freiwilligen-Panzergrenadier-Division "Wallonien"* in Collin and Strebelow held their positions and had to watch the stream of Soviets flow past their flanks without being able to do anything about it. The shortage of ammunition for the heavy weapons was already becoming evident. The division received orders to evacuate Collin and Strebelow and form a blocking position at the village of Kremzow, thus blocking an important highway to Stargard. Kremzow held!

The second *Schwerpunkt* was Reetz. The defense also collapsed there under the weight of the Soviet artillery and the armored steamroller. *SS-Obersturmbannführer* Lohmann's *SS-Freiwilligen-Panzer-Grenadier-Regiment 49 "de Ruyter"* was forced to give way. With armor and infantry formations following close behind, the Soviets captured the important *Reichsstraße 104*. The main body of the regiment fell back to the north and organized for defense in Falkenwalde. The regimental command post, and the command post of the *II./SS-Artillerie-Regiment 54*, were also located there. Elements of the *II./SS-Freiwilligen-Panzer-Grenadier-Regiment 49 "de Ruyter"*, pulling security at Konraden (northeast of Reetz), missed the link-up and fell back to the north.

In the corps command post the reports piled in, one after another. Soviet armor was everywhere! *General* Unrein and the chief of staff, *SS-Obersturmbannführer* von Bockelberg, saw only one option: Swing the east wing at Reetz back toward the west to Freienwalde with the hinge point at Stargard, which was still holding. *Reichsstraße 158* (Stargard — Freienwalde) would serve as the blocking line.

The few German tanks were sent from one sector to the other in dribs and drabs. Once again, tanks and assault guns were the backbone of the severely battered battalions, but they could not hold their own against the massive Soviet superiority in armor. As if that were not enough, there was a constant and universal shortage of ammunition and fuel, since the supply units could no longer find "their" tanks. One example: On the afternoon of 1 March, the trains units of *SS-Panzer-Grenadier-Regiment 24 "Danmark"* in Barskewitz suddenly found themselves face to face with a Soviet armor formation and, at the last minute, fled to Dahlow. In Ravenstein in the morning hours, the elements of the *III./ SS-Artillerie-Regiment 54* that did not have any guns — the battalion was still in the process of being organized — had to fall back to Falkenwalde before Soviet tanks. A trains unit of *27. SS - Freiwilligen-Grenadier-Division "Langemarck"* was surprised at Saatzig by a Soviet armored spearhead. On both sides of *Reichsstraße 104* the situation was totally confused.

Units of *Kampfgruppe "Langemarck"* assembled in Pansin and Wulkow. *SS-Obersturmbannführer* Lohmann formed a blocking position at Falkenwalde with his *SS-Freiwilligen-Panzer-Grenadier-Regiment 49 "de Ruyter"*. During the reorganization of his regiment, units of *SS-Panzer-Jäger-Abteilung 11*, which had been securing northeast of Reetz, pushed through and made their way into the regimental position. Falkenwalde held!

The assembly area of the *23. SS-Freiwilligen-Panzergrenadier-Division "Nederland"* on 2 March was in the village of Kasshagen, two kilometers north of Jakobshagen. At 0500 hours *SS-Freiwilligen-Panzer-Grenadier-Regiment 49 "de Ruyter"* pulled out of Falkenwalde. The *3./SS-Pionier-Bataillon 11* was nearby. Lohmann established a new position in Jakobshagen. Twenty Soviet tanks advanced into the midst of the organization of the new position. Ten were knocked out. *SS-Obersturmbannführer* Lohmann ordered: "Fall back to Ball!" He was wounded soon afterward. Elements of the *II./SS-Freiwilligen-Panzer-Grenadier-Regiment 49 "de Ruyter"* that had become separated from their units in Konraden forced their way from Konstantinopel to the regiment. Elements of *SS-Flak-Abteilung 11*, which had been in Jakobshagen, closed up. The main body of the *23. SS-Freiwilligen-Panzergrenadier-Division "Nederland"* reached the city of Freienwalde by evening, passing through Ball — Langenhagen. Other units were in Rehwinkel at 1400 hours. Stalin tanks attacked, shelling the farmer tracks to Charlottenfelde, where units of *SS-Artillerie-Regiment 54* were moving to the rear. Traffic jams were inevitable. Trucks got stuck. Stalin tanks kept up their fire. The *1./SS-Artillerie-Regiment 54* lost its guns.

On 1 March the corps command post moved to Daarz. The staff continued studying ways to get the units back under control.

What was the situation on 2 March at Stargard?

During the night of 2 March *SS-Panzer-Grenadier-Regiment 24 "Danmark"* was relieved by a *Füsilier-Bataillon*. It assembled in Klützow and rolled through Stargard to Dahlow. A few kilometers outside of Stargard the *II./SS-Panzer-Grenadier-Regiment 24 "Danmark"* was stopped by military police. *SS-Sturmbannführer* Sörensen received a new operation order in a sealed envelope:

Proceed without stopping to Freienwalde. Report to the *23. SS-Freiwilligen-Panzergrenadier-Division "Nederland"* there as the corps reserve. A liaison officer is to be detailed to the corps command post in Daarz."

The battalion was quartered in a large commercial structure. The night was quiet. While the *28. SS-Freiwilligen-Panzergrenadier-Division "Wallonien"* remained in its positions at Streesen and Kremzow on 2 March and *SS-Sturmbannführer* Methieu's battalion provided an outstanding example of steadfastness in Kremzow, the Flemish soldiers of *Kampfgruppe "Langemarck"* were forced back to Wulkow and Zartrig. They defended in a desperate manner, but they were overwhelmed by the superior Soviet forces.

As early as 2 March, Soviet armor had already pushed forward on the Barskewitz — Büche — Rehwinkel line with spearheads as far as *Reichsstraße 158* (Stargard — Freienwalde). All available tanks and assault guns of *the 11. SS-Freiwilligen-Panzer-Grenadier-Division "Nordland"*, as well as *SS-Sturmbannführer* Herzig's remaining *Tigers* of *schwere SS-Panzer-Abteilung 503*, launched an immediate counterattack to the southeast from the Trampke — Schönebeck — Voßberg line. The Soviets fell back before the German armored advance.

During the evening and night, the *III./SS-Panzer-Grenadier-Regiment 24 "Danmark"* took positions on both sides of Büche. The three tanks that were pulling security there moved to the rear. Büche was occupied by the *9./SS-Panzer-Grenadier-Regiment 24 "Danmark"*. Company commander *SS-Untersturmführer* Birkedahl-Hansen's report offers one impression of that operation:

The *9./SS-Panzer-Grenadier-Regiment 24 "Danmark"* was to occupy the southern outskirts of Büche and employ patrols to maintain contact with the *10./SS-Panzer-Grenadier-Regiment 24 "Danmark"*, which was in position two kilometers to the north. The Russians had been driven out of Büche. Everywhere there were the bodies of women and children who had been run down by Soviet tanks as they were attempting to flee. Two German tanks provided security in the southern part of the village. There were five charred and blackened Soviet T 34's in front of them. After briefing us on the situation, our tanks moved to the rear. I positioned one of my two platoons in the southern part of the village at the bridge that formed the entrance to the village between the two lakes. The second platoon went into position in the northern part of the village. At 2300 hours on 2 March, six Russian tanks with mounted infantry came and destroyed the first platoon south of the bridge. Nevertheless, the second platoon and two *Pak* north of the bridge were able to form a new defense and block entry. During the night, several infantry attacks on the bridge were repulsed. Calls for help requesting support by German tanks and artillery went unanswered. There was nothing available! The end was in sight.

The Russians attacked at 0600 hours on 3 March. Both *Pak* were spotted and destroyed by T 34's before they could get off a single round. The platoon leader of the second platoon knocked out one Russian tank with a *Panzerfaust*. The others then reached the northern portion of the village.

The order came to withdraw along the lake to Marienfließ. Half way there, a Russian tank cut off our withdrawal route. One *Panzerfaust* was fired, but without getting a hit. The enemy tank used smoke. Under cover of the smoke, the rest of the company made it to Marienfließ. Marienfließ was immediately attacked from the east by Soviet infantry. The retreat continued to Trampke!

In Trampke the *9./SS-Panzer-Grenadier-Regiment 24 "Danmark"* still had 20 men. The *10./SS-Panzer-Grenadier-Regiment 24 "Danmark"* arrived. It had also suffered heavy losses. West of Trampke, together with *SS-Untersturmführer* Thorkildsen (company commander, *11./SS-Panzer-Grenadier-Regiment 24 "Danmark"*), I succeeded in bringing the remaining men of the battalion into position. But soon the packs of Russian tanks were also there and forced us out of the position with gunfire. We fired two *Panzerfäuste*. The enemy tanks fell back somewhat. We made it to Dahlow. The *III./SS-Panzer-Grenadier-Regiment 24 "Danmark"* occupied a blocking position.

In the gray dawn of 3 March, *SS-Panzer-Aufklärungs-Abteilung 11* was positioned in and around Voßberg. The report by the commander of the mortar platoon of the *3./SS-Panzer-Aufklärungs-Abteilung 11* follows:

The population had evacuated Voßberg in good time. After my mortar platoon was in position, *SS-Unterscharführer* Kunze and I looked for a place where we could get a bit of sleep. We found two bed frames. The mattresses and featherbeds were missing.

A hellish crash had us wide awake in a hurry. We got up in terror and ran to the kitchen. Brramm! Our eardrums hurt. We threw a hasty glance back and saw dust and walls collapse on the bed where Kunze had just been sleeping. "Lucky one more time!" Kunze shouted as he ran away.

Crouching low, we dashed to our vehicles. Lindenau ran up to me and yelled: "We're trapped! T 34's are advancing against the west entrance to the village."

Then tank cannon barked. The men of our battalion came back from the eastern part of the village and reported: "Heavy enemy attack on the village!"

The second platoon hurried to reinforce the outskirts of the village. The Soviet forces were overwhelmingly superior.

A *Königstiger* rolled through the village and filled the entire village street. Its commander, an *SS-Unterscharführer*, ran ahead and directed the giant tank to the western outskirts.

Ten Russian T 34's waited on a winding road for the *Tiger*, which then stopped. Main guns bellowed. After four minutes, four T 34's were ablaze. The others took flight.

"Out of the village!" was the next order. Our precipitous flight led past the knocked-out enemy tanks. One vehicle got stuck at a viaduct. 150 meters beyond it I spotted three Russian antitank guns. Smoke grenades made us invisible. We got the stuck vehicle moving again and continued to the southwest.

A few kilometers farther, we raced around a curve. In front of us was a small village. At the entrance the Russians were busy unhitching an antitank gun from a Panje cart. The command vehicle raced wildly past the Panje cart. My vehicle couldn't swing around it. The Panje cart shattered against my armor.

The Russians had broken through everywhere. We were directed into a blocking position, but shells plowed into the crews as they dismounted. The Russians had gotten there ahead of us! "Keep going back!"

Another glimpse of the fighting at Freienwalde: The *II./SS-Panzer-Grenadier-Regiment 24 "Danmark"* occupied positions at the northeast corner of the city. The *6./SS-Panzer-Grenadier-Regiment 24 "Danmark"* was to the south and the *7./SS-Panzer-Grenadier-Regiment 24 "Danmark"* to the north of the road leading toward Steinhöfel — Nöblin. Before the companies could dig in, however, Russian tanks rolled up. *SS-Sturmbannführer* Sörensen ordered a pullback to the outskirts of the city, where the companies threw the enemy back from prepared positions. Only the first platoon of the *6./SS-Panzer-Grenadier-Regiment 24 "Danmark"* was unable to pull out in time. With Lake Groß Starlitz at its back, *SS-Oberscharführer* Pösch and his platoon fought an unequal fight. The Soviets attacked from three sides. Pösch's men fought desperately. The Russians brought up six tanks that fired on one foxhole after another from a range of 300 meters. Pösch's platoon melted away with no way to get at the tanks. In a last, desperate struggle, the remaining men of the platoon fought their way along the south shore of the lake with machine pistols and hand grenades. Only *SS-Oberscharführer* Pösch and four men made it to the southern part of Freienwalde. Five of his men were captured, the others were killed.

In the positions at the outskirts of the city of Freienwalde, the German units repulsed all of the Russian attacks for the remainder of 3 March. Concentrated fire from the German heavy weapons hit the enemy concentrations. Enemy movements toward the west were observed north and south of the city. The city lay under constant enemy artillery fire. The *II./SS-Panzer-Grenadier-Regiment 24 "Danmark"* maintained contact with the regiment through the command post of *SS-Pionier-Bataillon 54*. The *5./SS-Panzer-Grenadier-Regiment 24 "Danmark"* was employed to cover the flank on the northern outskirts of Freienwalde.

While there was already heavy fighting on the eastern outskirts of Stargard, the rest of the *28. SS-Freiwilligen-Panzergrenadier-Division "Wallonien"* held positions south of the city in the villages of Klützow and Wittichow. It hurled back all the Soviet attacks from the south and southeast. During the night, the units of the division, swinging far to the west around Stargard, made it back and took positions defending the northern outskirts of the city.

On 3 March the cities of Stargard and Freienwalde continued to hold out, but the defenses between the two cities collapsed. The German command made efforts to establish a new defensive line in the line Stargard — Masow. That meant an additional shifting to the west of the northern wing of the corps front. With that, the movement of the *III. (germanisches) SS-Panzer-Korps* front from an east-west to a north-south direction was completed.

At about 1700 hours the adjutant of *SS-Obersturmführer* Schoofs' *SS-Pionier-Bataillon 54*, which was committed in the same sector, briefed the commander of the *II./SS-Panzer-Grenadier-Regiment 24 "Danmark"* regarding the situation: "The enemy is north of the city. The situation there is not clear. Voßberg, south of Freienwalde, is in Soviet hands. Strong enemy forces have crossed the Freienwalde — Stargard road and continue to advance to the west!"

Under cover of darkness, strong Russian forces worked their way close to the positions at the outskirts of the city so as to rush them by surprise in the gray light of dawn. It was a form of attack that had been employed a lot recently.

SS-Obersturmführer Schoofs informed *SS-Sturmbannführer* Sörensen of the following at 2200 hours: "If the situation gets worse, we plan to evacuate Freienwalde. The road to Kannenberg is still open. It is the only link to the west. Friendly *Flak* blocking positions and units of *SS-Panzer-Abteilung 11 "Hermann von Salza"* are committed in the Sassenberg area."

At 0155 hours the withdrawal order arrived for the *II./SS-Panzer-Grenadier-Regiment 24 "Danmark"*:

The *II./SS-Panzer-Grenadier-Regiment 24 "Danmark"* is to pull out of its positions commencing at 0230 hours on 4 March. It is to occupy the railroad station and railroad line as regimental rearguard until 0600 ours. At 0600 hours the battalion is to continue to withdraw to Karkow. Karkow is to be held until 0900 hours. At 0900 hours it is to withdraw again to Kannenberg as rearguard. Briefing will be given there by a liaison officer of the *23. SS-Freiwilligen-Panzergrenadier-Division "Nederland"*.

The *23. SS-Freiwilligen-Panzergrenadier-Division "Nederland"* inconspicuously evacuated its positions. The *II./SS-Panzer-Grenadier-Regiment 24 "Danmark"* occupied the railroad station and railroad line as ordered. The last formations had passed through them by 0600 hours, including three 8.8 cm guns belonging to a *Luftwaffe Flak* battalion. The Russians pushed forward hesitantly from the southeast. The *II./SS-Panzer-Grenadier-Regiment 24 "Danmark"* fell back again and, at 0900 hours, occupied a new rearguard position at Karkow. It then fell back again to Kannenberg.

Kannenberg was successfully defended for the entire day by the *II./SS-Panzer-Grenadier-Regiment 24 "Danmark"*, *SS-Pionier-Bataillon 54* and units of *Fallschirmjäger-Regiment Schacht*. To its south, at Sassenburg and Rossow, *Sperrgruppe Kausch* held firm (elements of *SS-Panzer-Regiment 11* and *SS-Flak-Abteilung 11*). Elements of *SS-Panzer-Aufklärungs-Abteilung 11* were positioned at Alt-Damerow. In the Kietzig — Buchholz area were elements of *SS-Panzer-Grenadier-Regiment 23 "Norge"* and *SS-Panzer-Grenadier-Regiment 24 "Danmark"*. Stargard was lost in the morning hours. The Soviets pushed farther to the west against the entire line in an unequal battle with the burnt-out and decimated German formations.

Again and again the Russians advanced rapidly, allowing the Germans no time to form a new main line of resistance. As a result, the German defenses were again torn apart on 4 March 1945.

At 1830 hours the order went out by radio to the forces in Kannenberg:

"Friendly forces withdraw to Massow, commencing 2100 hours!"

The *II./SS-Panzer-Grenadier-Regiment 24 "Danmark"* made it to the small Pomeranian town of Massow by forest trails through the isolated village of Wittenfelde. The closely-following enemy forced the German command to rush the establishment of a new main line of resistance east of Massow in the defensive sector of the *23. SS-Freiwilligen-Panzergrenadier-Division "Nederland"*. The dire situation forced *Generalmajor der Waffen-SS* Wagner to act quickly. The troops were hastily thrown into positions without regard to order, but the main line of resistance was in place east of Massow on the morning of 5 March.

SS-Pionier-Bataillon 54 secured the flank in the north toward Freiheide. *Aufklärungs-Abteilung 115* was committed east of the road to Freiheide with its northern wing swung back. *Fallschirmjäger-Regiment Schacht* covered the road to Falkenberg. Farther to the southeast of Daarz, the remnants of *23. SS-Freiwilligen-Panzergrenadier-Division "Nederland"* organized themselves for defense.

The Fifth of March was a day filled with fighting. The enemy mounted an attack on the road to Falkenwalde, which the *Fallschirmjäger-Regiment* repulsed. *23. SS-Freiwilligen-Panzergrenadier-Division "Nederland"*, farther to the south, was under heavy enemy pressure and was hard pressed to ward off all the attacks. Enemy artillery, which had been brought forward, maintained steady fire on Massow and Daarz. An enemy reconnaissance-in-force was repulsed at Hill 85. As a result of that, strong enemy forces bypassed it to the north. Since noon, the *10. SS-Panzer-Division "Frundsberg"* had been engaged in heavy fighting in Neuendorf, northwest of Massow. The Russians shifted farther to the north and occupied the small town of Speck on the road to Gollnow. Gaps yawned everywhere in the German defensive front. *SS-Pionier-Bataillon 54* was withdrawn to reinforce another place on the front. *Aufklärungs-Abteilung 115* stretched its northern wing to the west. The *5./SS-Panzer-Grenadier-Regiment 24 "Danmark"* was similarly employed for screening to the north and occupied the forester's house at Massow with a combat outpost. It had orders to fall back when the enemy approached.

Elements of *SS-Panzer-Grenadier-Regiment 23 "Norge"* and *SS-Panzer-Aufklärungs-Abteilung 11* fended off enemy attacks at Parlin and Lenz. East of Mulkenthin, the *III./SS-Panzer-Grenadier-Regiment 24 "Danmark"* organized for defense. The remnants of *28. SS-Freiwilligen-Panzergrenadier-Division "Wallonien"* were in Lübow, Saarow and Seefeld. The southern wing of the corps front bent back to the northern point of Lake Madü.

On 5 March the *III./SS-Panzer-Grenadier-Regiment 24 "Danmark"* was engaged in heavy fighting east of Mulkenthin. The Soviets attacked in the morning with infantry and tanks. The German companies, with strengths of about 30 men and defending sectors averaging 600-800 meters long, were faced with an impossible task. *Panzerfäuste* weren't enough against the packs

250

of Russian tanks. There were no other armor-defeating weapons. The *9./SS-Panzer-Grenadier-Regiment 24 "Danmark"* was defending to the north of the isolated farmstead of Seehof; the *14./SS-Panzer-Grenadier-Regiment 24 "Danmark"* was at the brickyard. However, the units of *SS-Panzer-Grenadier-Regiment 24 "Danmark"* were forced to fall back. The Russians then had to bring up heavy weapons and refuel their tanks. The enemy tanks had barely moved to the rear when the *III./SS-Panzer-Grenadier-Regiment 24 "Danmark"* attacked again with the *13.* and *14./SS-Panzer-Grenadier-Regiment 24 "Danmark"* and regained its old positions.

The day did not go so well in the sector of the *28. SS-Freiwilligen-Panzergrenadier-Division "Wallonien".* Reduced to a single weak regiment, the Walloon volunteers held positions at Lübow and Saarow in the gray morning of 5 March. The two villages were on opposite sides of the Ihna. The left bank of the river was elevated and covered with trees. The right bank was open and broken only by a railroad embankment that ran west of the houses of Lübow. Fifteen heavy Soviet tanks attacked Lübow from the east. Without antitank defenses, the Walloon volunteers were powerless. They were dispersed in desperate individual actions. Some succeeded in making it over the Ihna to Saarow.

The Russian attack rolled on. Soon 21 Soviet tanks with accompanying infantry were at the southern outskirts of Saarow. The houses collapsed under the impacts of the rounds from the main guns. The tanks rolled through the village to the north. One Walloon volunteer sought shelter behind the open door of the church and knocked out the lead tank with a *Panzerfaust*. The attack came to a halt and the Walloon volunteers withdrew to the west.

Other elements of the *28. SS-Freiwilligen-Panzergrenadier-Division "Wallonien"* were in Seefeld at that time. Forty-one enemy tanks attacked there. *SS-Obersturmbannführer* Degrelle employed nearby artillery in the fight against the tanks. Firing over open sights, the artillerists took on the tanks. The Russian armor fell back.

On 6 March the *10. SS-Panzer-Division "Frundsberg"* successfully defended Neuendorf. Units of the *23. SS-Freiwilligen-Panzergrenadier-Division "Nederland"* warded off the enemy in the Daarz area. At about 1000 hours the Russians took the forester's house at Massow without a fight. Farther to the north, there was fighting at the road to Gollnow. Enemy forces infiltrated between Neuendorf and Massow and threatened the artillery positions at Resehl. The artillerists of *SS-Artillerie-Regiment 54* organized for close-in defense.

On 6 March there was heavy fighting along the *Autobahn*. *SS-Panzer-Grenadier-Regiment 23 "Norge"* fought a delaying action as it fell back on Wachlin. The Soviets were poised that evening with massed armored forces directly east of Groß- and Klein-Wachlin. *SS-Panzer-Aufklärungs-Abteilung 11* held on there as rearguard.

The mortar platoon of the *3./SS-Panzer-Aufklärungs-Abteilung 11* went into position at a farmstead that took up almost the entire hill and registered on target reference points. Enemy artillery shelled the place. The German forces withdrew; the Russians followed up with tanks and infantry. The time had arrived for the mortars of the *3./SS-Panzer-Aufklärungs-Abteilung 11*.

"Add twenty on Erich!" the observer directed. The men worked feverishly. Round after round left the barrels of the 8 cm mortars.

"Great! Drop thirty on Manfred. Five rounds!" The crews worked rapidly, changed targets, aimed anew, corrected and again changed targets. The other platoons repulsed the last Soviet assault.

Russian artillery covered Wachlin with shellfire. Attics were smashed; flames broke out and lit up the night.

The link to the observer broke. Nevertheless, the mortars continued to fire on individual target reference points. The buildings burned all around. Stifling smoke settled into the lungs. Russian machine guns chattered in threatening proximity. Russian tanks were only 200 meters distant.

"Dismantle! Fall back!" came the eagerly anticipated withdrawal order from the acting company commander. Motors howled and the vehicles raced out of the farmstead and over the fields to the west.

Massow still held on but was under attack from three sides. Encirclement threatened!

SS-Sturmbannführer Sörensen, *Major* Wolf (commander of *Aufklärungs-Abteilung 115*) and *Major* Schacht (commander of the *Fallschirmjäger*), proposed a plan to *Generalmajor der Waffen-SS* Wagner for pulling back the front. Wagner asked the corps and the corps radioed back, "The present main line of resistance must be held!"

The officers proposed that, in the event that Massow were encircled, the companies would be split into partisan groups, a measure born out of necessity. Security was strengthened at the combat positions. Radio operators, drivers and soldiers from the trains units took up their weapons.

On 7 March at 0300 hours the withdrawal order arrived. The companies immediately fell back and put together a new defense along the Resehl line, with the *II./SS-Panzer-Grenadier-Regiment 24 "Danmark"* serving as its *Schwerpunkt*. The 5. and *7./SS-Panzer-Grenadier-Regiment 24 "Danmark"* were positioned at the southeast edge of Resehl along the road to Massow. By 0900 hours the *7./SS-Panzer-Grenadier-Regiment 24 "Danmark"* had already established enemy contact. About 60 Russians worked their way under cover to within 50 meters of the line of defense. An immediate counterattack by the company threw the Russians back.

At the same time heavy fighting raged around Daarz. *The 23. SS-Freiwilligen-Panzergrenadier-Division "Nederland"* was no longer able to hold the place and fell back. Rosenow was lost soon after. With that, the situation also became critical southwest of Resehl. Strong enemy concentrations at Daarz made clear that additional attacks would follow. An immediate counterattack on Rosenow bogged down.

At 1630 hours a heavy barrage landed on the eastern portion of Resehl followed by an enemy attack on Daarz. The men of the *II./SS-Panzer-Grenadier-Regiment 24 "Danmark"* and *Aufklärungs-Abteilung 115* fought back but were forced to fall back on account of the gap to the south. They formed a hedgehog defense on three sides in Resehl. The following order reached the German forces in Resehl that evening:

The enemy has captured Gollnow. The *10. SS-Panzer-Division "Frundsberg"* is already pulling out of the Neuendorf area towards Lüttgenhagen. Friendly forces in Resehl are to fall back through Großenhagen at 2330 hours and report to the command post of the *23. SS-Freiwilligen-Panzergrenadier-Division "Nederland"* in Lüttgenhagen. Move at all possible speed since the main line of resistance has already been evacuated on either flank. Surprise attacks must be expected from both north and south.

How did things look to the south on 7 March?

SS-Panzer-Grenadier-Regiment 23 "Norge" was engaged in heavy fighting on both sides of the *Autobahn*. The remnants of *SS-Flak-Abteilung 11* assembled in Hinzendorf and occupied positions on the eastern outskirts. The Soviets were already attacking Hinzendorf with infantry and tanks in the morning hours. The *Flak* gunners knocked out several Russian tanks. The rest fell back.

Farther to the south, the *III./SS-Panzer-Grenadier-Regiment 24 "Danmark"* defended southwest of Bruchhausen. Armor also attacked along with infantry. The battalion fell back to the edge of the woods. Two German tanks rolled up and joined the battalion in an immediate counterattack that forced the Russians back.

The enemy pressure on Hinzendorf increased. In the evening hours came a new, significantly stronger, attack by armor with infantry support. That attack, too, was brought to a halt. Russian artillery fired without a pause. Hinzendorf was ablaze from one end to the other. The staff of the *11. SS-Freiwilligen-Panzergrenadier-Division "Nordland"* moved under heavy fire from Hinzendorf to Karlsbach and, during the night, farther back to Augustwalde.

As evening approached, *SS-Sturmbannführer* Kurz and the remnants of his *Flak* battalion fell back to a patch of woods south of Hinzendorf. In the meantime, Hinzendorf had been occupied by the Soviets and was now under fire from the *Flak*. As midnight drew near, the remnants of the divisional *Flak* battalion headed back toward Augustwalde.

That day another attack ensued against the *III./SS-Panzer-Grenadier-*

Regiment 24 "Danmark", which had gone into position at the edge of the woods east of Karolinenhorst. Soviet cavalry attacked the southern wing of the battalion position, which was held by the regimental assault- and combat-engineer platoon. The riders came to within 150 meters, at which point all Hell broke loose. In addition to the infantry weapons, two 2cm *Flak* of the *14./SS-Panzer-Grenadier-Regiment 24 "Danmark"* fired on the charging riders, mowing them down. The *III./SS-Panzer-Grenadier-Regiment 24 "Danmark"* and the divisional *Flak* battalion pulled back to Augustwalde and Hohenkrug almost simultaneously.

On 8 March, at about 0200 hours, *SS-Sturmbannführer* Sörensen reported the arrival of his *II./SS-Panzer-Grenadier-Regiment 24 "Danmark"* to the command post of the *23. SS-Freiwilligen-Panzer-Grenadier-Division "Nederland"* in Lüttgenhagen. The battalion was immediately directed on and reached Christinenberg at 0700 hours. The *11. SS-Freiwilligen-Panzer-Grenadier-Division "Nordland"* left rearguard forces in Lüttgenhagen until dawn.

Day after day, the numerically weak German formations were forced back to the west. Gaps yawned everywhere in the hastily formed lines, and before the German main line of resistance could even take proper shape, the Russians had broken through it again. It was a hopeless battle that the Germans fought under increasing compulsion to save the civilian population of Pomerania and make it possible for them to flee. Many refugee columns made their way to the west. Russian aircraft mercilessly strafed them. One column was attacked with bombs and on-board weapons on the Stargard — Freienwalde road. In Reichenbach, Schlagenthin and all the villages between that the German soldiers regained from the Russians, the civilian population that had not fled had suffered a hard fate. Often the German soldiers looked into women's eyes that were wide with terror. That always renewed the soldiers' strength to carry on in hopeless situations until the last civilians had escaped from their homes.

Every day patrols were sent out from the *1.* and *2./SS-Panzer-Aufklärungs-Abteilung 11* in order to provide information on the enemy's intentions to the senior leadership. *SS-Untersturmführer* Andresen and *SS-Unterscharführer* Ihle were the most successful patrol leaders.

In conclusion it must be said that it was a tactical masterpiece to hold the corps together under extremely heavy enemy pressure and under total enemy air superiority and pull the corps back successfully from an east-west direction to a north-south one in a difficult turning maneuver. During the movements, the corps command post constantly relocated and communications links repeatedly failed.

In addition to the commanding general, *General* Unrein, the soul of that tactical command and control was the corps chief of staff, *SS-Oberstumbannführer* von Bockelberg. He worked out the difficult operation with clear understanding and almost mathematical precision. Without that brilliant leadership, all the bravery of the soldiers would have accomplished nothing.

The notes of a liaison officer that are reproduced below allow us to perceive somewhat the immense tension of those days:

As Ordonnanz-Offizier I, I had no rest during that time. Because the communications often broke down, or because the reports from the divisions did not give a clear picture of the situation, I had to go to the divisions two or three times a day. You can imagine what it meant to undertake that journey during the day with complete enemy control of the air and during the night with the uncertainties about where the front was. Sometimes I had to wait at some bridge during the night with an armored radio vehicle to observe the withdrawal of our units and the ultimate demolition of the bridge and report those activities to the corps. Once, I wanted to go back to the corps command post but, when I got there, I found it had already been evacuated and was occupied by Russians. You had to have a sixth sense and a lot of situational awareness to avoid running into the enemy. (*SS-Hauptsturmführer* Ertel)

The Altdamm Bridgehead

On 5 March the Soviet and Polish divisions reached the Baltic Sea at Kolberg. Encircled Kolberg maintained its defense until 18 March. The last defenders got away by sea.

Two advances ensued from the Kolberg — Polzin area toward the west. One was aimed at Divenow, the other to the southwest through Gollnow toward Stettin.

At the beginning of March, *Kampfgruppe Scheibe* and the headquarters and supply company of *SS-Panzer-Jäger-Abteilung 11* fought its way back to the Divenow bridgehead through Polzin and Kolberg. The latter company, under *SS-Hauptsturmführer* Kuhl, had been caught up in the pocket of Kolberg but, nevertheless, was able to fight its way out. With minimal losses, it rejoined the German lines at Divenow. On 12 March those forces of the *III. (germanisches) SS-Panzer-Korps* crossed the Oder.

On 7 and 8 March 1945, the exhausted formations of the *III. (germanisches) SS-Panzer-Korps* occupied the Altdamm bridgehead. At the time, it still had contact with the Greifenhagen bridgehead.

On the morning of 8 March, the *II./SS-Panzer-Grenadier-Regiment 24 "Danmark"* reached Christinenberg, northeast of Lake Dammsch. One by one, additional German forces arrived in that area.

The northern part of the bridgehead — from Lübzin to Hornskrug — was held as follows: One naval company; remnants of the *II./SS-Panzergrenadier-Regiment 21 "Frundsberg"*; the *II./SS-Panzer-Grenadier-Regiment 24 "Danmark"*; the remnants of *Aufklärungs-Abteilung 112*; Schacht's *Fallschirmjäger*; the remnants of *23. SS-Freiwilligen-Panzergrenadier-Division "Nederland"*; and, *SS-Artillerie-Regiment 54* in the Birkhorst area. The *23. SS-Freiwilligen-Panzergrenadier-Division "Nederland"* had overall command of the sector.

The central sector — Hornskrug and the Autobahn — was defended by *SS-Panzer-Aufklärungs-Abteilung 11* and the remnants of *SS-Panzer-Grenadier-Regiment 23 "Norge"*.

Adjoining to the south were the III./SS-Panzer-Grenadier-Regiment 24 "Danmark", elements of SS-Pionier-Bataillon 11 and SS-Flak-Abteilung 11 (Rosengarten).

Remnants of the *27. SS-Freiwilligen-Grenadier-Division "Langemarck"* and the *28. SS-Freiwilligen-Panzergrenadier-Division "Wallonien"* were at Höckendorf and Finkenwalde.

Strong enemy forces were already exerting pressure on all the combat outposts of the *II./SS-Panzer-Grenadier-Regiment 24 "Danmark"* by noon on 8 March. The outposts fell back. A Russian follow-up attack forced units of the *II./SS-Panzer-Grenadier-Regiment 24 "Danmark"* and *Aufklärungs-Abteilung 115* out of Sophinthal and Rörchen. Since there was danger of being cut off, *SS-Sturmbannführer* Sörensen ordered a withdrawal to Friedrichsdorf. Widely separated, the men made it to the village. Antitank-gun and machine-gun fire dispersed the withdrawing units. *Major* Schacht, in command of that sector, ordered an immediate counterattack. The groups turned around, reinforced by the *5./SS-Panzergrenadier-Regiment 21 "Frundsberg"*.

In the meantime, *SS-Untersturmführer* Stippernitz and the liaison officer of *Aufklärungs-Abteilung 115* — ignorant of the other developments — had mounted an immediate counterattack with five men against Sophinthal and forced the Russians back as far as the church. The former main line of resistance was reoccupied, but it became increasingly difficult to hold. The Russians brought more and more heavy weapons into position at the edge of the woods east of Sophinthal and Rörchen and they could observe every movement in the village. The main line of resistance remained open as far as Fuchsberg. There was fire from antitank guns and mortars of various intensity during the afternoon. In the evening, the mess truck of the *6./SS-Panzer-Grenadier-Regiment 24 "Danmark"* was destroyed by a direct hit from an antitank gun. The *Spieß*, the maintenance sergeant and the cook were killed. The company fighting in the northern part of Sophinthal did not receive any

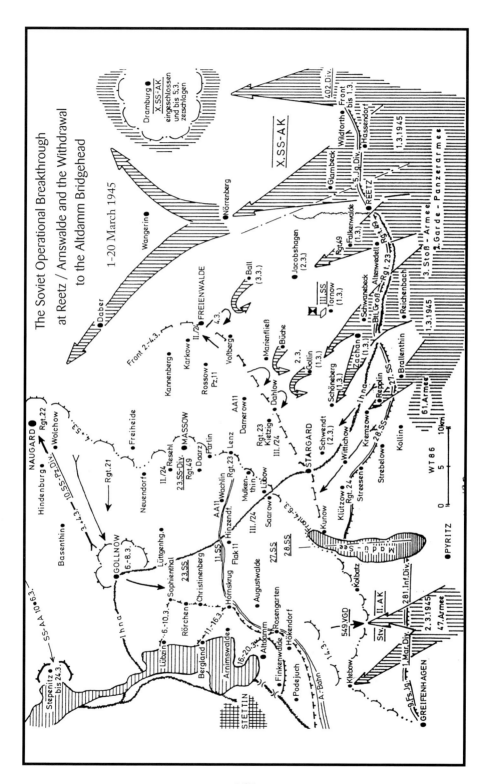

The Soviet Operational Breakthrough
at Reetz / Arnswalde and the Withdrawal
to the Altdamm Bridgehead

1–20 March 1945

257

rations.

At about 2100 hours the enemy attacked the northern part of the village from the church. *SS-Obersturmführer* Engelbrecht's men defended themselves with hand grenades and machine pistols. The force of the attack was broken in the middle of the village. Engelbrecht reorganized his squads. At about 0400 hours on 9 March he heard tanks and voices in front of him.

The main line of resistance was pulled back a bit to give a better field of fire. At 0700 hours Sophinthal — Rörchen were under heavy mortar fire, which was followed by an infantry attack with armored support. A struggle ensued for every house. A Stalin tank was rendered immobile by a *Panzerschreck*. Ammunition and hand grenades were running out. In the southern part of the village, the defenders — soldiers from *SS-Panzer-Grenadier-Regiment 24 "Danmark"*, the *10. SS-Panzer-Division "Frundsberg"*, *Aufklärungs-Abteilung 115* and the *Fallschirmjäger* — were squeezed together, but they held. Three German tanks rolled forward in support but only made it as far as Christinenberg. There was no way to cross the open stretch leading to Rörchen. Soviet antitank guns fired incessantly, even firing on the wounded who dragged themselves back over the meadow to Friedrichsdorf.

At about 1300 hours the Soviets renewed their assault with fresh forces, supported by one tank and several assault guns. Another attack came from the east against the units of *Aufklärungs-Abteilung 115* and the *Fallschirmjäger* who were holding their positions. It threw them back. The men of the *6.* and *7./SS-Panzer-Grenadier-Regiment 24 "Danmark"* who were still in the southern part of the village were at their wits end.

At 1400 hours the order came to fall back on Friedrichsdorf. Widely dispersed, the men ran across the open terrain. Antitank guns and mortars fired all the while. The men made it to Friedrichsdorf almost without losses. The commanders of the *6.* and *7./SS-Panzer-Grenadier-Regiment 24 "Danmark"* assembled their men. The battalion assault platoon arrived. The road to Christinenberg as well the northern outskirts of Friedrichsdorf were secured by two German tanks. New positions were taken as fast as possible at the edge of the village. Between the two companies and the assault platoon there were 2 officers, 5 noncommissioned officers and 30 men. The same picture held true for the elements of the *10. SS-Panzer-Division "Frundsberg"*, *Aufklärungs-Abteilung 115* and the *Fallschirmjäger*. *SS-Hauptsturmführer* Seyb and his *5./SS-Panzer-Grenadier-Regiment 24 "Danmark"* were employed with the regiment. The strength of that company was 31 men. That was all that was left of the *II./SS-Panzer-Grenadier-Regiment 24 "Danmark"*. In the afternoon of 10 March the remnants of *SS-Freiwilligen-Panzer-Grenadier-Regiment 49 "de Ruyter"* were forced to evacuate Christinenberg. Extremely heavy artillery and mortar fire covered the Christinenberg sector throughout the entire day.

During the night of 11 March the batteries of *SS-Artillerie-Regiment 54* evacuated their firing positions at Birkhorst and occupied new firing positions in the area south of Arnimswalde. Those elements of the *10. SS-Panzer-Division "Frundsberg"* that were still to the north at Lübzin and Ibenhorst followed the batteries. A new main line of resistance was established in the line Bergland — Friedrichsdorf. The makeup of the units that held the new main line of resistance and the command structure were remarkable. The entire sector was under *Generalmajor der Waffen-SS* Wagner. *Major* Schacht of the *Fallschirmjäger* commanded the northern sector as a regimental commander. Elements of the *II./SS-Panzer-Grenadier-Regiment 24 "Danmark"*, the *10. SS-Panzer-Division "Frundsberg"*, a naval company, *Fallschirmjäger-Regiment 25* and the men of *Aufklärungs-Abteilung 115* belonged to his command. The sector as far as Hornskrug was held by the remnants of *SS-Freiwilligen-Panzer-Grenadier-Regiment 49 "de Ruyter"* and was commanded by *SS-Obersturmbannführer* Klotz, who had just arrived with replacements from Kienschlag.

The new positions had hardly been occupied when the units reported that the Soviets had already worked their way up to the new main line of resistance under cover of darkness and dug in.

That Russian tactic, which had been much used of late, had proven quite successful. Under cover of darkness the Soviets "weaseled" their way forward, dug themselves in and then, at daybreak, attacked with all their strength. The Germans were almost incapable of effectively combating the enemy concentrations that built up due to lack of ammunition for the heavy weapons.

In the gray light of dawn, enemy infantry and armored concentrations were reported on the Christinenberg — Friedrichsdorf road.

On 11 March, at about 0700 hours, the Soviets broke out of the positions that they had occupied during the night and penetrated both north and south of Friedrichsdorf. However, *SS-Sturmbannführer* Sörensen and his hastily assembled *Kampfgruppe* held the village for the time being. It was only when the enemy reached the Friedrichsdorf — Oberhof road that it became dangerous for Sörensen's *Kampfgruppe*. At 1300 hours the German forces fell back under enemy pressure along Lake Dammsch to Arnimswalde. With that, the position at Friedrichsdorf became untenable. Sörensen's *Kampfgruppe* fought its way through to Oberhof and took a firm stand there. That day, the fighting was marked by intense activity of Russian heavy weapons.

On that day as well, the commanders of both the *6.* and *7./SS-Panzer-Grenadier-Regiment 24 "Danmark"* were wounded and put out of action. The *8./SS-Panzer-Grenadier-Regiment 24 "Danmark"*, the heavy company, was also without a commander. Its commander, the veteran *SS-Obersturmführer* Kure, had to go to aid station seriously ill. On 11 March the *II./SS-Panzer-Grenadier-Regiment 24 "Danmark"* shrank to 20 men, who were led by *SS-Untersturmführer* Stippernitz. The battalion adjutant, *SS-Untersturmführer* Raßmussen, assumed command of the *8./SS-Panzer-Grenadier-Regiment 24*

"Danmark". *Major* Schacht wanted to employ the heavy company as infantry. He finally relented after Raßmussen convinced him that the company could still make effective use of its weapons. *SS-Untersturmführer* Raßmussen scraped up ammunition from all sources. During the night that followed, the *8./SS-Panzer-Grenadier-Regiment 24 "Danmark"* had all its weapons in action from its new positions at Arnimswalde.

Hornskrug, the breakwater of the northern front, continued to be successfully defended by *SS-Panzer-Aufklärungs-Abteilung 11*. Elements of the *10. SS-Panzer-Division "Frundsberg"* later reinforced the reconnaissance battalion there.

In the southern part the sector of the *III.(germanisches) Panzer-Korps* was the *11. SS-Freiwilligen-Panzergrenadier-Division "Nordland"*, commanded by *Generalmajor der Waffen-SS* Ziegler. As was the case with the *23. SS-Freiwilligen-Panzergrenadier-Division "Nederland"*, the units attached to it came from a variety of sources. The remnants of *SS-Panzer-Grenadier-Regiment 23 "Norge"* held positions south of Hornskrug. *SS-Panzer-Grenadier-Regiment 24 "Danmark"* was in charge of the sector around Augustwalde. Belonging to it were the *III./SS-Panzer-Grenadier-Regiment 24 "Danmark"*, *SS-Pionier-Bataillon 11* and *SS-Flak-Abteilung 11*. The corps boundary with the *XXXII. Armee-Korps* was at Höckendorf. The remnants of the *27. SS-Freiwilligen-Grenadier-Division "Langemarck"* and the *28. SS-Freiwilligen-Panzergrenadier-Division "Wallonien"* were attached to it.

SS-Obersturmführer Hund and the remnants of the *6.* and *7./SS-Panzer-Grenadier-Regiment 23 "Norge"* had been holding positions at the *Autobahn* south of Hornskrug for quite some time.

The *III./SS-Panzer-Grenadier-Regiment 24 "Danmark"* and elements of *SS-Flak-Abteilung 11* blocked *Reichstraße 104* to Altdamm at Hohenkrug. Soon, however, the main line of resistance had to be pulled back to the west after heavy attacks by Soviet infantry and armor. While *SS-Flak-Abteilung 11* positioned itself firmly east of Rosengarten, thus controlling *Reichstraße 104* and the *Autobahn* (to the north) with its weapons, the *11./SS-Panzer-Grenadier-Regiment 24 "Danmark"* and the regimental platoons established themselves securely at Hammermühle and Plänebach. Adjoining to the north were the *10.* and *9./SS-Panzer-Grenadier-Regiment 24 "Danmark"*. The regimental command post was in Stutthof.

Those positions were also soon under extremely heavy Soviet artillery fire. T 34 and Stalin tanks supported the infantry attacks. The *10.* and *11./SS-Panzer-Grenadier-Regiment 24 "Danmark"* were forced from their positions. The former positions were regained in immediate counterattacks. Enemy penetrations at Rosengarten forced *SS-Flak-Abteilung 11* to fall back to Altdamm. During the night of 15 March the *III./SS-Panzer-Grenadier-Regiment 24 "Danmark"* also evacuated its positions and fell back to the outskirts of the city of Altdamm.

The situation remained unchanged in the Bergland — Oberhof — Hornskrug sector from 12 to 15 March. The units became smaller and smaller. *SS-Oberscharführer* Vandborg changed positions going from Arnimswalde to Oberhof several times with his mortars of the *8./SS-Panzer-Grenadier-Regiment 24 "Danmark"*, thus providing well-directed fire support for the companies holding the positions.

On 15 March, the *III./SS-Panzer-Grenadier-Regiment 24 "Danmark"* defended on both sides of the Altdamm railroad station. The *11./PHR24* and the regiment's machine-pistol platoon were positioned east of the railroad station on the eastern side of an antitank ditch. A surprise enemy attack forced them out of their positions. The leader of the headquarters section of the *11./SS-Panzer-Grenadier-Regiment 24 "Danmark"*, *SS-Unterscharführer* Kruse, left the company command post at the very last moment. He flung two cans of gasoline at the pursuing Soviets and set the canisters on fire with a burst from his machine pistol. Kruse got away behind the resultant raging Hell of fire and smoke. The deep antitank trench was the next obstacle he had to surmount. With great effort and under covering fire from the *10./SS-Panzer-Grenadier-Regiment 24 "Danmark"*, he made it.

In the afternoon, the Russians attacked along the Stargard — Altdamm railroad line and captured the railroad station. At about 1500 hours an immediate counterattack against the Altdamm railroad station was unsuccessful.

On 16 March, another immediate counterattack by the *11./SS-Panzer-Grenadier-Regiment 24 "Danmark"* (10 men) and the regimental machine-pistol platoon (9 men) was led by *SS-Obersturmbannführer* Krügel. The Soviets successfully defended the railroad station and repulsed the counterattack. The commander of *SS-Panzer-Grenadier-Regiment 24 "Danmark"*, *SS-Obersturmbannführer* Krügel, was killed in that action. A new main line of resistance was then established at a road directly west of the Altdamm railroad station.

It was not until 28 March 1945 that the *Wehrmachtsbericht* reported:

SS-Obersturmbannführer Krügel, recipient of the Oakleaves to the Knight's cross and commander of *SS-Panzer-Grenadier-Regiment 24 "Danmark"*, demonstrated extraordinary bravery during a counterattack. He died on the field of battle during that fighting.

The Sixteenth of March brought a climax to the fighting at Altdamm. An extremely heavy Soviet artillery barrage covered the entire sector as far as Hornskrug, which was evacuated that day. The remnants of *Regiment 23 "Norge"* were also forced back to the Altdamm — Gollnow railroad line from their positions at the *Autobahn*. *SS-Obersturmbannführer* Paetsch, commander of *SS-Panzer-Regiment "Frundsberg"*, died on the field of battle that day. He had provided support everywhere with his few remaining tanks. It became senseless to hold the northern portion of the bridgehead in the face of such overwhelmingly superior enemy forces. The remaining formations of the *III.*

(germanisches) SS-Panzer-Korps were forced into a continually shrinking perimeter. It is remarkable that, with the end in sight, the soldiers continued to hold out, making an orderly withdrawal possible.

During the evening hours of 16 March, the batteries of the *I.* and *II./SS-Artillerie-Regiment 54* displaced to Altdamm. The *III./SS-Artillerie-Regiment 54* was being reorganized west of the Oder.

At about 2000 hours the northern part of the bridgehead was evacuated. On 11 March *Gruppe Stippernitz* still had 21 warriors (the remainder of the 6. and *7./SS-Panzer-Grenadier-Regiment 24 "Danmark").* All that were left when the bridgehead was evacuated were *SS-Untersturmführer* Stippernitz and two men. They wearily pulled out of the positions alongside the equally severely decimated *8./SS-Panzer-Grenadier-Regiment 24 "Danmark"* and, in the morning of 17 March, reached Stettin/Scheune by an exhausting foot march through Altdamm-Zollhaus. The fighting continued in the reduced Altdamm bridgehead. On 17 March a strong enemy attack from the railroad station property struck the *III./SS-Panzer-Grenadier-Regiment 24 "Danmark".* *SS-Obersturmführer* Thorkildsen, the commander of the *11./SS-Panzer-Grenadier-Regiment 24 "Danmark",* was killed. The remnants of *SS-Panzer-Grenadier-Regiment 24 "Danmark"* fell back to the cemetery. *SS-Haupsturmführer* Ternedde, as acting regimental commander, was able to hold off all Soviet attacks until 19 March with the remnants of the regiment — about 50 men including radio operators and drivers.

SS-Flak-Abteilung 11 was directly to the south, fighting primarily as infantry. To the north were the remnants of the *23. SS-Freiwilligen-Panzergrenadier-Division "Nederland", SS-Panzer-Grenadier-Regiment 23 "Norge"* and *SS-Panzer-Aufklärungs-Abteilung 11.* The *Flak* battalion was moved to the Hornskrug — Altdamm road when the enemy attacks intensified there.

Without a let-up, the Russians hammered away at the constricted bridgehead with rounds of all calibers. The ground heaved as if in an earthquake. Wherever one looked, one saw exhausted, bearded *Landser* coated with chalk dust. Few rations made it to the front, but the hunger was easier to deal with than the exhaustion. Eyes burned like fire but stayed open. The unceasing attack waves granted the defenders no moment of rest. The men fought for every house in the ruins of Altdamm. The few remaining German heavy weapons were positioned in the courtyards and supported the warriors in the foxholes in front with their fire. At the northeast outskirts of the city were elements of *SS-Panzer-Aufklärungs-Abteilung 11.* By some miracle, the mortar platoon of the *3./SS-Panzer-Aufklärungs-Abteilung 11* still had all six mortars in position. A platoon leader of the *3./SS-Panzer-Aufklärungs-Abteilung 11, SS-Oberscharführer* Hoppe, was blinded by an explosive projectile and had to be taken to the rear.

To gain some understanding of the severity of the fighting, another report follows:

In the evening the new commander ordered me to relieve our forward observer. He had suffered a nervous breakdown. That told me a lot, for he was no weakling.

It was not that far that I had to go, but it seemed like an eternity before I could get to him. Shells were bursting everywhere. I ran through the darkness and through the bright light of scorching fires, beneath flares that lit up the night for long seconds. Finally I slid down the remains of a set of cellar stairs.

A stale reek of blood, oil and body odors greeted me. Illumination came from a burning wick in an oil-filled tin can. A staff *SS-Untersturmführer* sat on a stool and fumbled with a receiver in hopes of getting some sort of news about the overall situation. Two severely wounded men were on the cement floor and being attended to by a medic. The forward observer whom I was to replace sat on the edge of a field-cot with his head buried in hands that ran nervously through his hair. In grotesque contrast, another *SS-Untersturmführer* from the staff sat on a vegetable crate picking lice. Now and again he threw a glance over his shoulder. At last, with wavering voice, he said: "Horrible! Everything is going to Hell for us!"

The commander came into the cellar, heard the reports and noticed the groaning men on the floor. Like a father, he kneeled down and spoke softly to them, but their answers were only a gurgling groan. When asked a question about something, the medic only helplessly shook his head. Before leaving, the commander stood thinking for a moment, then saluted the two dying men and left the cellar with the forward observer.

On 18 March the Soviets went for the final decision. On the hills of Buchheide Forest they had massed numerous heavy weapons that covered any German movement with a hail of rounds. *Korps Hörnlein* pulled back across the *Autobahn* bridge. Units were forced to the north. *Autobahn* bridges and railroad bridges north of Podejuch were blown up. *Sturmbataillon "Wallonien"*, which had been formed from the remnants of *28. SS-Freiwilligen-Panzergrenadier-Division "Wallonien"* and commanded by *SS-Sturmbannführer* Dierickx, was committed at Finkenwalde. The Walloon volunteers held the area around the Altdamm — Podejuch railroad line. In the end, they were pulverized by an intense artillery barrage. On 19 March, *Bataillon Dierickx* was forced to abandon Finkenwalde, but was then able to reform in a position at the Altdamm —Stettin railroad embankment. Supported by two German tanks, the battalion held the route to Stettin open for the withdrawal of the *III. (germanisches) SS-Panzer-Korps*. After the Soviets penetrated and advanced as far as the Altdamm — Zollhaus road, the Russians were forced back by an immediate counterattack. Once again, the withdrawal route of the *III. (germanisches) SS-Panzer-Korps* had been preserved from danger.

As early as the night of 18/19 March, the heavy weapons and vehicles rolled through Zollhaus to Stettin. Combat engineers blew up all the installations and buildings in the city of Altdamm that would be useful to the enemy. Even the tower-bunker in which the command post of the *11. SS-Freiwilligen-Panzergrenadier-Division "Nordland"* had been located was blown up. At about 1900 hours the remnants of *SS-Panzer-Grenadier-Regiment 24 "Danmark"* withdrew from the positions at the cemetery. While assembling to move out, an artillery salvo rained down and killed an additional six men. A severely wounded *SS-Unterscharführer* of the *12./SS-Panzer-Grenadier-Regiment 24 "Danmark"* was loaded onto a baby buggy and taken to Stettin in that, since all the vehicles had already left.

In the meantime the Soviets had adjusted fire from several antitank guns on the withdrawal route to Zollhaus. Their observers spotted the flames coming from exhaust pipes and called down fire. Fortunately, almost all of the vehicles of the corps had already been sent back. For those that had not, it became a life-or-death movement.

During the night of 19/20 March 1945, at about midnight, the regimental machine pistol platoon performed rearguard duty at the Zollhaus — Stettin highway bridge, which had been prepared for demolition. The bridge went up in the air.

Fifteen hundred meters south of the bridge, the rearguard of *Bataillon Dierickx* and two German tanks crossed back over the Oder on the railroad bridge north of Finkenwalde. Then that bridge also went up in the air.

That was the end of the fighting in Lower Pomerania. It also ended with practically the destruction of the *III. (germanisches) SS-Panzer-Korps*. It had fought to the point of self-sacrifice to aid the flight of the Pomeranian populace. At the end, only decimated regiments and battalions remained. Entire companies had been wiped out. Pomerania was lost. The German troops that were still fighting in Danzig/Hela and Königsberg — Pillau could no more affect the outcome than those still fighting in the Kurland bridgehead. In the west, the Allies were already far into Germany. Mainz, Siegen, Frankfurt and Würzburg were already in their hands. All that remained was a dim and muddled hope for a political chess move. Rumors abounded, including the one that the Allies would make a common front with the Germans against communism.

*

The staff of the *11. Panzer-Armee* was withdrawn for other duties before the retreat to the Oder. It was replaced by the *3. Panzer-Armee* under *Generaloberst* Raus, later *General* von Manteuffel.

The commander of *Fallschirmjäger-Regiment 25*, *Major* Schacht, after fighting in the Reetz-Kallies area.

Hetzer of the *Waffen-SS* and *Fallschirmjäger* of *Fallschirmjäger-regiment 25* conduct an immediate counterattack in the area of Kallies.

Fallschirmjäger of *Fallschirmjäger-Regiment 25* during a break in the fighting.

Reorganization West of the Oder

The shattered battalions and separate formations of the *III. (germanisches) SS-Panzer-Korps* assembled for reorganization in the Wussow — Sommersdorf — Wattin area southwest of Stettin.

Replacements arrived. For the most part, they were older men from the *Kriegsmarine*, the *Luftwaffe* and staffs that had been disbanded. Their morale was understandably poor in light of the overall situation and the fighting that could be expected. The official routine continued. The emphasis was on training for combat. The remaining officers, noncommissioned officers and men of the field units looked to the coming days with some concern. Without a doubt, their combat power had shrunk significantly.

On 27 March 1945 the units moved to the Altküstrienchen — Schwedt — Gartz area to push forward the reorganization. But the movement there had another special reason behind it, as an army order made clear:

The enemy has concentrated his 61st Army on the eastern bank of the Oder in front of Schwedt — Gartz. The *III. (germanisches) SS-Panzer-Korps* will be attached to the *3. Panzer-Armee* (*General* von Manteuffel) during its further reorganization.

After many difficulties, the fuel necessary for the movement was provided. The allotment was so tightly measured that vehicles had to tow one another to the day's destination. Several companies had to be moved by shuttling vehicles back and forth, since many vehicles had been lost during the operations in Pomerania.

The reorganization was completed in a tense atmosphere. In spite of gnawing doubts and dark suspicions, the units pushed on with the combat training. The defense of Germany had become bitterly serious and quite literal. *General* von Manteuffel issued the following: "The Oder is the front — not a single step to the rear!"

After the evacuation of the Altdamm bridgehead, the less battered batteries of *SS-Artillerie-Regiment 11* and *SS-Artillerie-Regiment 54* took up new firing positions west of the Oder. *SS-Artillerie-Regiment 11* was in the area southwest of Schwedt; *SS-Artillerie-Regiment 54* was northwest of Schwedt.

The elements of the *23. SS-Freiwilligen-Panzergrenadier-Division "Nederland"* were billeted in the area northwest of Schwedt, where they continued their training. *SS-Freiwilligen-Panzer-Grenadier-Regiment 48 "General Seyffard"*, commanded by *SS-Obersturmbannführer* Scheibe, who had returned to the division after employment in the Polzin — Divenow area, was reconstituted with two battalions.

SS-Freiwilligen-Panzer-Grenadier-Regiment 49 "de Ruyter" was reconstituted in the Gartz area under *SS-Obersturmbannführer* Lohmann, who had returned from convalescence. The regimental command post was in Gasekow; the regiment was attached to *General* Fronhöfer's *547. Volks-Grenadier-Division*.

The *28. SS-Freiwilligen-Panzergrenadier-Division "Wallonien"* and the *27. SS-Freiwilligen-Grenadier-Division "Langemarck"* were also being reconstituted in the same sector. It would be more accurate to refer to it as an attempted reconstitution, since men and weapons were lacking. The Walloon volunteers received a total of two weak regiments. The *27. SS-Freiwilligen-Grenadier-Division "Langemarck"* fared no better. The latter was almost always referred to as *Kampfgruppe Schellong*.

The *11. SS-Freiwilligen-Panzer-Grenadier-Division "Nordland"* was moved to the area west of Schwedt — Freienwalde to carry on with its reorganization. The divisional command post was in Alt-Künkendorf; the command post of *SS-Panzer-Grenadier-Regiment 24 "Danmark"* in Hohenlandin. *SS-Artillerie-Regiment 11* was in Dobberzin, *SS-Panzer-Grenadier-Regiment 23 "Norge"* in Liepe, *SS-Panzer-Regiment "Hermann von Salza"* had one battalion in Albrechtshöhe; the *II. Abteilung* was in Frauenhagen.

The *547. Volks-Grenadier-Division* was positioned along the Oder front with the *1. Marine-Division* to its south. The staff of the *III. (germanisches) SS-Panzer-Korps* moved at that time from Stettin to Steinhöfel.

Replacements arrived daily and were allocated to the companies. The severely battered *II./SS-Panzer-Grenadier-Regiment 24 "Danmark"* was formed anew with a strength of 80 men per company. After receiving 100 men from *SS-Panzer-Regiment 11 "Hermann von Salza"* — all of them veteran frontline soldiers who could no longer be provided with tanks — there was new energy in the companies.

The reconstituted *I./SS-Panzer-Grenadier-Regiment 24 "Danmark"* was transferred to the *5. SS-Panzerdivision "Wiking"* and never returned to the *11. SS-Freiwilligen-Panzer-Division "Nordland"* again. The same happened to the newly organized *I./SS-Panzer-Grenadier-Regiment 23 "Norge"*.

On 7 April, the *11. SS-Freiwilligen-Panzergrenadier-Division "Nordland"* received orders to occupy blocking positions and positions covering the artillery firing positions west of Schwedt. The companies relieved each other in 72-hour shifts.

The order directed that the units in the covering positions would remain quiet and inconspicuous during the day. During the night, positions would be constructed and patrols would be sent to the units committed at the Oder to maintain contact. A few kilometers south of Berkholz, the Karlshof fortress stood on a commanding hill, with the Oder and the small town of Schwedt in the valley below. On the other bank the ground rose steeply. It was a picturesque landscape. Nothing suggested war. Not a round was fired. The Karlsberg was the pivot point of the position of the *II./SS-Panzer-Grenadier-Regiment 24 "Danmark"*. The position ran along advantageous high ground from north to south. The *7./SS-Panzer-Grenadier-Regiment 24 "Danmark"* was on a small lake; at that time it was led by *SS-Oberscharführer* Pösch. A few hundred meters to the west, at Lake Pagel, *SS-Unterscharführer* Steindor's newly-formed assault platoon constructed the battalion command post. Warm April sun and a small, blue lake surrounded with meadows and woods allowed the men to forget the war.

During that time period, *SS-Obersturmbannführer* Klotz assumed command of *SS-Panzer-Grenadier-Regiment 24 "Danmark"*.

The first days of April proceeded in the same manner for all the other units of the *III. (germanisches) SS-Panzer-Korps* as well. A small squad of British volunteers who had been assigned in Stettin to *SS-Panzer-Aufklärungs-Abteilung 11* returned to the corps staff and were later employed in a medical role. On 16 April 1945, the order went out to the *11. SS-Freiwilligen-Panzer-Grenadier-Division "Nordland"* to fully occupy the blocking positions. The final battle loomed ahead.

What was the situation on the lower Oder?

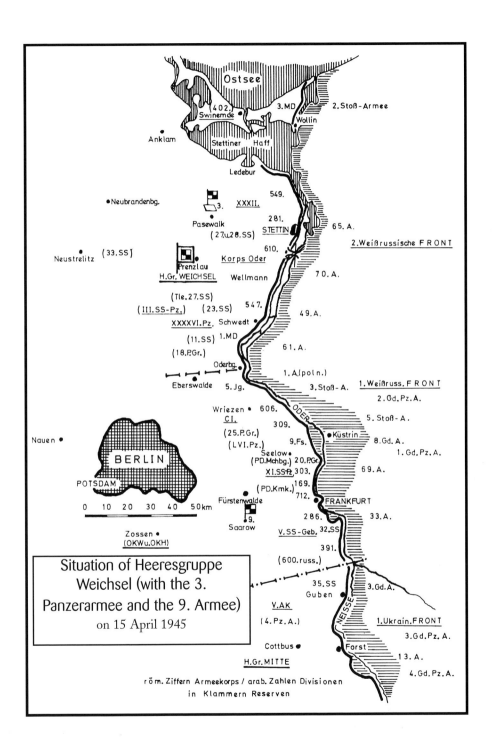

Ostsee

402. Swinemde · 3.MD · Wollin · 2.Stoß-Armee

Anklam

Stettiner Haff

Ledebur

· Neubrandenbg.

3. XXXII.

549.

Pasewalk
(27.u.28.SS)

281.
STETTIN

65. A.

2.Weißrussische FRONT

Neustrelitz (33.SS)

610.
Korps Oder

Prenzlau
H.Gr. WEICHSEL   Wellmann

70. A.

(Tle.27.SS)

(III.SS-Pz.)   (23.SS)

547.

XXXXVI.Pz. Schwedt ·

49.A.

(11.SS) 1.MD

(18.P.Gr.)

61. A.

Oderbg.

Eberswalde   5. Jg.

1.A.(poln.)

3.Stoß-A.

1.Weißruss. FRONT

2.Gd.Pz.A.

Wriezen · 606.
CI.

5. Stoß - A.

Nauen ·

(25.P.Gr.)
(LVI.Pz.)

309.

9.Fs.

· Küstrin

8.Gd. A.

BERLIN

Seelow·
(PD.Mchbg.) 20.P.Gr.

1.Gd.Pz.A.

POTSDAM

XI.SS-Pz.303.

69. A.

0 10 20 30 40 50km

(PD.Kmk.) 169.
712.

Fürstenwalde ·

· FRANKFURT

Zossen ·
(OKWu.OKH)

9.

Saarow ·

286.

33.A.

V.SS-Geb. 32.SS

**Situation of Heeresgruppe
Weichsel (with the 3.
Panzerarmee and the 9. Armee)
on 15 April 1945**

391.
(600.russ.)

35.SS
Guben

3.Gd.A.

V.AK
(4.Pz.A.)

1.Ukrain.FRONT

3.Gd.Pz.A.

Cottbus ·

Forst

13. A.

H.Gr.MITTE

4.Gd.Pz.A.

röm. Ziffern Armeekorps / arab. Zahlen Divisionen
in Klammern Reserven

The positions of *Heeresgruppe Weichsel* ran from the mouth of the Oder to where the Neiße joined the Oder. After Himmler had left, *Heeresgruppe Weichsel* was commanded by *Generaloberst* Heinrici. To the south, at the Neiße, the sector of *Heeresgruppe Mitte* started.

General von Manteuffel's *3. Panzer-Armee*, located in the Stettin area, belonged to *Heeresgruppe Weichsel*, as did *General* Busse's *9. Armee* in the Küstrin — Frankfurt/Oder area.

The *3. Panzer-Armee* had the *XXXII. Armee-Korps* at Stettin and *SS-Korps Oder* to its south. The *XXXXVI. Armee-Korps* was at Schwedt. Stationed as reserves, from north to south, were the *23. SS-Freiwilligen-Panzergrenadier-Division "Nederland"*, the *11. SS-Freiwilligen-Panzer-Grenadier-Division "Nordland"* and the *18. Panzergrenadier-Division*.

The *9. Armee* had in its front, from north to south: the *101. Armee-Korps*, the *XI. SS-Korps* (Frankfurt/Oder), and, to its south, the *V. SS-Korps* as far as the mouth of the Neiße. For reserves it had the *LVI. Panzer-Korps* with the *25. Panzergrenadier-Division*, the *20. Panzer-Division* and *Panzer-Division "Müncheberg"*.

That was the organization that awaited the Soviet attack on Berlin.

Operation Berlin

During the course of 1944, the German Eastern Front fell back as far as the Weichsel. On 12 January 1945, the Red Army began a new offensive from that position. It tore the German Narew — Weichsel position apart in several places. The assault wedges of the Red Army moved to the borders of the Germany.

Marshal Zhukov's 1st Belorussian Front (equivalent to a *Heeresgruppe*) was the main effort. It advanced through Posen and Schneidemühl and reached the Oder in the Frankfurt — Küstrin area at the end of January/beginning of February 1945. A German counterattack into Zhukov's deep north flank (Operation *"Sonnenwende"*) had to be halted after initial success due to inferiority of forces. At that time the German Ardennes offensive on the Western Front had failed and the Western Allies had regained the initiative there. The German front in Lower Pomerania — extending from Schwedt on the Oder through Deutsch-Krone and Schlochau to the southwest border of East Prussia — gradually had to be pulled back to the lower Oder under enemy pressure. The German *2. Armee*, which was cut off in East Prussia, was smashed by Rokossowski's 2nd Belorussian Front.

Heeresgruppe Weichsel, which had been newly formed from the final call-up of the last reserves, could not close the giant gap in the front between Lower Pomerania and Silesia. The remnants of the *9. Armee* that were fighting in that area could not stop the Red Army. The front fell back to the Oder and the Neiße.

During the critical days of February, it was the small units that occupied and held the Oder — Neiße line. They were led by lower-ranking officers who did not wait for orders from "above". The front along the rivers was gradually strengthened and reinforced by bringing forward the "last reserves". The pressure also eased because the Russians needed an operational pause to bring up reserves and supplies.

At that point, the Red Army prepared "Operation Berlin", which was to bring about the final victory over the German eastern armies. They refitted their formations, brought up reserves and heavy artillery and moved their airfields forward.

The 1st Belorussian Front and the 1st Ukrainian Front were the formations that would carry the burden of the offensive, with more than two million soldiers and a corresponding issuance of heavy weapons, armor and aircraft.

The 1st Belorussian Front would carry the major part of the burden in the attack on Berlin. It was in the Schwedt — Frankfurt/Oder sector. Zhukov moved his nine infantry armies, two tank armies and two air armies into their jump-off positions by mid-April. Transport trains with an aggregate length of 1,200 kilometers rolled through Poland. More than seven million rounds of artillery ammunition were brought forward.

In the Oder positions, each side overdid itself in the propaganda battle. Loudspeakers aimed at the enemy broadcast news and observations of the situation. With varying arguments, comparisons were made between the battle before Moscow at the end of 1941 and the impending battle for Berlin. "Berlin remains German, Vienna will be German again and Europe will never be Russian!" blared from the German side. The Russian route of advance was placarded with signs proclaiming: "Forward to Berlin!"

Heeresgruppe Weichsel included the Swinemünde Defense Area (Ansat), the *3. Panzer-Armee* (von Manteuffel) and the *9. Armee* (Busse). The Swinemünde Defense Area was responsible for the defense and security of the islands and coastline of the Stettiner Haff. The *3. Armee* held the Oder Front from Stettin to Oderberg (north of Bad Freienwalde). The *9. Armee* continued to the south as far as the junction where the Neiße flows into the Oder. The *4. Panzerarmee* (Graeser), which belonged to *Heeresgruppe Mitte*

(Schörner), held the front southward along the Neiße from there.

The headquarters of *Heeresgruppe Weichsel* were located in Prenzlau. At first, Himmler, the *Reichsführer-SS* and Commander-in-Chief of the Replacement Army, commanded *Heeresgruppe Weichsel*. Himmler was replaced by *Generaloberst* Heinrici on 22 March 1945.

General Theodore Busse's *9. Armee* was positioned at the probable *Schwerpunkt* of the enemy's attack in the Oderberg — mouth of the Neiße sector at the start of April 1945. It had 11 divisions in the front lines and the *25. Panzergrenadier Division* in reserve. Busse's *9. Armee* had 489 combat-ready tanks and assault guns on 8 April 1945. All of the divisions had been refitted in makeshift fashion, many with hastily assembled replacement units. In addition to meager division artillery, the *9. Armee* had two *Volks-Artillerie-Korps* and two *Panzer-* or *Panzerjäger-Abteilungen* available. The *23. Flak-Division* was directed to support the army. Its batteries were, for the most part, built into stationary positions on the Oder Front and were, therefore, not mobile.

Busse's opponent, Marshal Zhukov, wrote the following on page 599 of "The Memoirs of Marshal Zhukov":

On the whole the work to prepare the Berlin Operation had no parallel in scale of intensity. Concentrated on a fairly narrow sector of the front and within short time limits were 68 infantry divisions, 3,155 tanks and self-propelled guns and about 42,000 artillery and mortar pieces. We were quite sure that with these capacities our forces would smash the enemy within the shortest possible span of time.

In addition, Marshal Zhukov had more than 5,000 combat aircraft at his disposal. By 10 April 1945, Zhukov's formations had built 23 bridges over the Oder between Bad Freienwalde and the mouth of the Neiße.

The Germans could do little to counter that. *General* Busse wrote in his study:

...unbelievable concentrations of enemy forces. Tempting targets for aerial attack — if we had possessed enough aircraft and fuel — or for concentrated artillery fire — if the guns and, above all, ammunition had been available.

Thus, Zhukov could fill up his Oder bridgehead with almost no interference. Hitler still did not believe that the main effort would take place there. He expected that the main thrust would be directed at Forst, with a rapid advance to the middle Elbe. There, they would unite with the Americans. That mistaken expectation led him to take four divisions away from *General* Busse — including the *10. SS-Panzer-Division "Frundsberg"* — and send them to the Neiße.

The German soldiers on the Oder Front saw what was going to come at them. With their limited means and options, they prepared for the defense according to the motto: "If Berlin is to be defended at all, it must be defended at the Oder!" They also clung to the hope that there would still be a rupture between the Russians and the Western Allies. They did not want to believe that the western powers would give central Europe to the Russians.

The Allies laid down guidelines for Germany's unconditional surrender at the Yalta conference in February 1945. Stalin, Roosevelt and Churchill agreed on the essential questions regarding Germany, but differences of opinion already became evident regarding the political structure of the future Europe. It became increasingly clear that the Soviet Union intended to advance the boundaries of its sphere of influence as far as possible into Western Europe. Churchill wanted to prevent that, but it also became evident that he would have to abandon his plans for a Poland and a Czechoslovakia fashioned after his notions. It was also evident that the Soviet Union would not let go of the area of the Balkans that it conquered. In view of the great increase in territory and power, Churchill — with hardly any support from Roosevelt — later stated resignedly: "We've slaughtered the wrong pig!"

By the beginning of March 1945, the Western Allies had reached the Rhine on a broad front. In Hungary the German Lake Balaton Offensive was in progress. It brought no relief to the Oder Front in the form of a regrouping of the Red Army. On the contrary, the Red Army conquered all of Hungary and the eastern portion of Austria, including Vienna. The German army group in Italy negotiated with Allied emissaries in Switzerland in hopes of gaining a separate armistice. At the same time, Allied bombers reduced more and more German cities to cinders and ashes, destroyed all important bridges and stretches of railroad. As a result, the Germans had great difficulties moving units. In April 1945, *Heeresgruppe Model* was smashed in the Ruhr Pocket. Following that, three American, one British and one Canadian army advanced into central and northern Germany. In Czechoslovakia *Heeresgruppe Schörner* held positions at the Altvater Mountains and along a line running from Ölmütz — west of Brünn — west of Vienna.

The Western Allies could easily have advanced to Berlin, but differences in military objectives arose between the political and military commands of Great Britain and the USA. Churchill and Field Marshal Montgomery pleaded for the capture of Berlin, but Roosevelt turned that down based on the Yalta agreements.

Already, during the Arnhem operation — Operation "Market Garden" — the ambitious Montgomery had his eyes firmly set on Berlin as the final objective. As the troops of the Western Allies drew near to the Elbe, those plans were brought forward again. Churchill also wanted to continue to Berlin in order to set the boundary for the Russian sphere of influence at the Oder.

The Soviets saw a serious danger threatening their plans for Berlin in the accelerated advance of the Western Allies to the Elbe. Stalin's mistrust grew with the receipt of Eisenhower's March 28 telegram in which he laid out his plans in detail for the Russian high command (STAVKA), something he had never done before. Stalin believed it was a deception to gain time and answered it with the following telegram on 29 March 1945:

I received your telegram of 29 March. Your plan to split the German forces by uniting the Western Allies with the Soviet armed forces fully corresponds with my own concept...The meeting should take place in the Erfurt — Leipzig — Dresden area. A second meeting could take place in the Vienna — Linz — Regensburg area. The Soviet armed forces will direct their major effort in that direction. Berlin has lost its previous strategic significance. Therefore, the Soviet high command will employ only second-line troops for the attack on Berlin. The time of the Soviet offensive will probably be in the second half of May. (Gosztony, "Der Kampf um Berlin 1945", p. 122).

Stalin thus attempted to divert attention from his true objective and gain time.

On 30 March 1945 Stalin summoned the commanders of the 1st Belorussian and 1st Ukrainian Fronts to Moscow to finalize the details for the attack on Berlin. There was no mention of beginning "in the middle of May" or of "second-line troops" as had been discussed in the letter to Eisenhower on 29 March.

Eisenhower did, in fact, follow the plans he had described to Stalin in his telegram of 28 March. On 31 March he also informed Montgomery of his plans. Regarding the question of Berlin, the American told the Briton:

You will note that in none of this do I mention Berlin. That place has become, for me, nothing but a geographical location, and I have never been interested in these. My purpose is to destroy the enemy's forces and his powers to resist.

General Bradley, the Commander-in-Chief of the US 12th Army Group, and his staff evidenced no interest in Berlin either. The press officer of the army group wrote the following in that regard: "The occupation zones were already marked on our army maps." Bradley amplified, "If the zones of occupation had not already been determined, I would have agreed with the attack (on Berlin) on political grounds. However, I saw no sense in suffering losses in fighting for a city we would then have to turn over to the Russians." (Gosztony, p. 107). Montgomery was resigned to the fact in his memoirs: "It was useless for me to pursue the matter further. We had had so much argument already on great issues; anyhow, it was now almost too late."

In agreement with Montgomery, Churchill wrote the following to President Roosevelt on 1 April:

...The Russian armies will no doubt overrun all Austria and enter Vienna. If they also take Berlin will not their impression that they have been the overwhelming contributor to our common victory be unduly imprinted in their minds, and may this not lead them into a mood which will raise grave and formidable difficulties in the future? I therefore consider that from a political standpoint we should march as far east into Germany as possible, and that should Berlin be in our grasp we should certainly take it. (Churchill, "The Second World War: Triumph and Tragedy", Volume 6, p. 465.)

Churchill and Montgomery continued to attempt to get the Americans to march on Berlin. On 7 April 1945, General Eisenhower explained to the Joint Chiefs of Staff of the Western Allies:

If it should turn out after the capture of Leipzig that we can move ahead towards Berlin without heavy losses, I want to do it...I would be the first to admit that war is waged in pursuance of political aims and if the Combined Chiefs of Staff should decide that the Allied effort to take Berlin outweighs purely military considerations in this theater, I would cheerfully readjust my plans and thinking so as to carry out such an operation.

Many German officers and soldiers built their hopes on such a development of the situation. From that point of view, the defense at the Oder still made sense. Many hoped they would take to the field against the Russians together with the British and Americans. That hope intensified with the death of President Roosevelt on 12 April 1945. However, "Operation Berlin" began four days later. With that, reality won the upper hand.

Leutnant K reveals what he thought of the situation and his mood at the time in the passage that follows. He had fought his way through with a break-out group from the encircled city of Posen to the Reetz area in East Pomerania. There he passed through the lines of the *11. SS-Freiwilligen-Panzergrenadier-Division "Nordland"*. After initial hesitation, he and his friend *O* remained with that division until the end of the war. *Leutnant* K wrote:

The *III. (germanisches) SS-Panzer-Korps*, whose replacements were processed through *Feld-Ausbildungs-Regiment Lang*, to which O and I now belonged, consisted of divisions whose ranks were made up mostly of European volunteers who were fighting against Bolshevism...

"The Oder is the main line of resistance!" That is what was to be read in one order of the day from the commander...We also read the order of the day from the Führer headquarters: "Berlin remains German, Vienna will again be German and Europe will never be Russian!" What language!

In those days, however, a remarkable change took place in us, and the National Socialist officer attached to us supported that change in our outlook with his instruction.

The clear insight that our last bulwark against the Soviet armies was erected here on the Oder reduced our picture of the situation to the essentials: How to stop the Russians from also conquering central Germany. It was so clear to every one among us what would happen to Europe and its way of life if the Soviets crossed the Oder and conquered Germany that we suddenly tried to discover a common interest between the western powers and us. An absolute turnabout of the Allies did not seem, on closer examination, as if it would be the first case of necessary realism in world history...

We knew that the Red Army was on the other side of the Oder, fired up with the prospect of reaching Berlin and the Elbe and that nothing that would stop that was beyond consideration. We waited for the Western Allies to come through. The miracle of the Oder did not take place.

One day in the first week of April, the commanding general of the *III. (germanisches) SS-Panzer-Korps*, *SS-Obergruppenführer* Felix Steiner, spoke to us.

I noted that Steiner was loved by the troops. Silver haired, large, broad-shouldered, with a winning appearance. He had a good face and a calm voice; he was a fine old gentleman.

Steiner spoke. I listened. The man who spoke was a man who was weary, infinitely weary, not in body, but in his soul. He said that the apparatus of the state no longer functioned. We had to see how we could help ourselves. I was terrified. Yes, it had gotten to that. The state was no longer in order. It no longer functioned for us! Nothing could have made our situation clearer to me in that hour of hopelessness than those words of the weary general who stood before us. It did not "function" any more. The conviction of the infallibility of the organization of the German state had been so strong in me that the thought that it was no longer in order pressed down on me with immense weight. What would happen to us now? Was there any way for us young soldiers to personally come through this great collapse? I knew of none...I felt empty and perplexed. In the days that followed I simply tried my best to forget the weary general and his words...

When *Generaloberst* Heinrici replaced Himmler in command of *Heeresgruppe Weichsel* on 22 March 1945, Himmler indicated to him that the time had arrived to negotiate with the western powers and that he had taken the first steps through a Swedish middleman. From that viewpoint, the Oder defense still made sense for Heinrici. He also hoped that the English and Americans would continue their advance through Berlin to the Oder. There were already secret negotiations in progress in Switzerland leading in that direction between representatives of the Western Allies and the Germans regarding a capitulation of the German Army in Italy.

General Steiner was also active in that respect. In his book, *"Die Freiwilligen"*, on page 323, he wrote:

All forces that were available anywhere had to defend the Oder to hold off the impending offensive...Then it would be up to the Western Allies to advance through the thin German front on the Elbe — which could be yet thinned even further — to Berlin and on to the Oder. That was the suggestion I made to Himmler. I also requested simultaneous diplomatic talks to end the war. It had to be clear to anyone with any common sense that the war would end in a few weeks.

Steiner was supported in that thinking by his adjutant, Dr. Riedweg, a relative of the former Minister of War, von Blomberg. Right up to the end, Steiner sent officers of his staff to Bad Wiessee in an effort to persuade von Blomberg, who was in retirement there, to go to his daughter-in-law in western Germany and make contact with Field Marshal Montgomery to start negotiations. A German military regime under von Blomberg was also under discussion, but von Blomberg rejected all of that. Steiner:

...It was necessary to ask all directorates and ministries for their cooperation. But, with few exceptions, none of the ministries was still capable of any initiative and all of them had resigned themselves to inaction. One could only hope for an initiative from Himmler. He had to take action, since the war had become senseless...

Even as the Battle for Berlin began, Steiner was still thinking of arresting Hitler. The commander of the *4. SS-Polizei-Division*, *SS-Standartenführer* Harzer, wrote the following in that regard:

On 23 April 1945 Steiner visited me at my command post and asked if I had a reliable regiment available with an energetic commander. He intended to send it to Berlin and arrest Hitler so that, as a minimum, the completely senseless fighting against the Western Allies could be halted. The Russian advance on Nauen made that plan irrelevant.

Steiner's command post at the time was already at Oranienburg and his corps' original divisions, the *11. SS-Freiwilligen-Panzer-Grenadier-Division "Nordland"* and the *23. SS-Freiwilligen-Panzergrenadier-Division "Nederland"*, had been sent to other hard-pressed army corps. The corps headquarters of the *III. (germanisches) SS-Panzer-Korps* had been redesignated as *Armee-Abteilung Steiner*, a grandiloquent name behind which stood only hastily thrown together units with little combat power. When Steiner said farewell to his old division commanders, he sent them on their way with the advice to avoid letting their formations get drawn into Berlin, but they could not prevent that from happening. As a result, Berlin was also defended by volunteers from many lands of Europe whose motivation was the battle against Bolshevism. A tragedy of the faithful!

Having presented the greater political and military setting, we shall now move to the actual events of the fighting.

The Storm Breaks

The Soviet high command prepared well for "Operation Berlin". It was a pincers operation in the proper German style, employing both Zhukov's 1st Belorussian Front and Konjew's 1st Ukrainian Front, which had concentrated at the Neiße.

Since the end of March 1945, the *III. (germanisches) SS-Panzer-Korps* was positioned west of Schwedt with the *11. SS-Freiwilligen-Panzer-Grenadier-Division "Nordland"* and the *23. SS-Freiwilligen-Panzergrenadier-Division "Nederland"*. The formations which had been badly battered in Lower

Pomerania were refitted. Together with the *18. Panzergrenadier-Division*, they formed the operational reserve of Heeresgruppe Weichsel.

The German staffs at the front saw what was coming at them. When local advances began to feel out the German front on 15 April, they knew that the offensive would follow directly. The corps headquarters of the *LVI. Panzerkorps*, which was arriving from East Prussia with its experienced commanding general, Weidling, was inserted as the command responsible for the Seelow sector. During the night of 15/16 April the first position in the Küstrin — Frankfurt sector was evacuated and the second position, the main position — the "Hardenberg position" — was occupied.

During that same night, Berlin experienced its 378th aerial attack of the Second World War. At the same time, the last Russian assault troops poured into the Oder and Neiße bridgeheads and waited for Stalin's order: "The Red Army is to capture Berlin!"

Marshal Zhukov, the Commander-in-Chief of the 8th Guards Army, General Tschuikow, and other high staff officers of the Red Army waited for the beginning of "Operation Berlin" at the command post of the 8th Guards Army on the Reitweiner-Nase. Zhukov wrote of it in his memoirs:

The hands of the clock seemed to be moving slower than ever before. To kill the remaining 15 minutes, we all decided to have some hot tea, which was made right there in the dug-out by a young girl…We sipped our tea in silence, each of us deeply engrossed in his thoughts.

Exactly three minutes before the start of the artillery barrage we all came out of the dug-out and took up our places at the observation post.

From this point in daylight, the entire Oder terrain could be observed very well. At the time the whole area was enveloped in a pre-dawn fog. I glanced at my watch. It was 0500 hours.

At 0500 hours Moscow time, 0300 hours German time, the Russian artillery thundered. Zhukov continued:

In that same instant, the entire area was brilliantly lit up by the fire of many thousands of guns, mortars and our legendary "Katyushas", followed by the deafening thunder of the explosions of shells, mines and aerial bombs…

It seemed that no living being could have survived in the enemy positions. After 30 minutes of powerful artillery pounding during which the enemy did not return a single round — thus indicating that his defenses had been disrupted and completely neutralized — it was decided to mount the general assault. (Zhukov op. cit. p.603.)

On the German side, the forward positions had been evacuated and the main line of resistance occupied. The Russian artillery preparation fell on empty ground.

When the Russians then launched their infantry attack, 143 antiaircraft searchlights blazed in the Küstrin — Reitwein sector. Zhukov wrote:

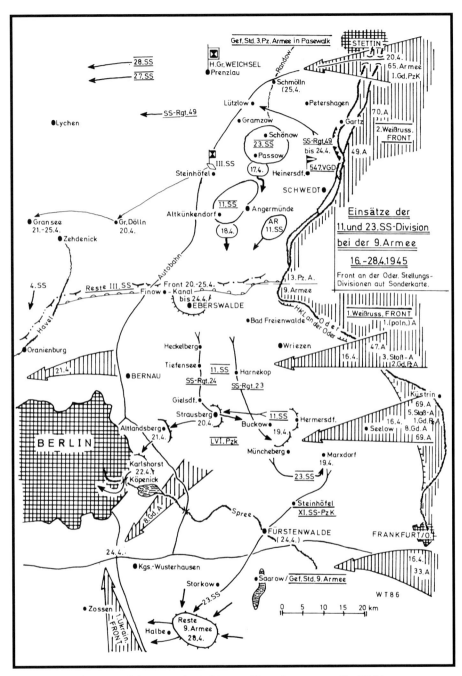

Employment of the 11. and 23. SS-Freiwilligen-Panzergrenadier-Divisionen
"Nordland" and "Nederland" with the 9. Armee
16-28 April 1945

279

Over one hundred billion candlepower illuminated the battlefield, blinding the enemy and picking out of the darkness the attack objectives for our tanks and infantry. It was an immensely fascinating and impressive sight, and never before in my life had I felt anything like what I felt then.

The forward German positions having been evacuated, Zhukov's "secret weapon" proved ineffective, since the beams of the searchlights only penetrated 150 meters into the curtain of powder, smoke and dust.

Since the beginning of April, *schwere SS-Panzerabteilung 502* (Hartrampf) had been staged in the Diedersdorf — Lietzen area and was the operational reserve of the *XI. SS-Panzer-Korps* (Kleinheisterkamp). *SS-Hauptscharführer* Streng, commander of a *Tiger* in the *2./schwere SS-Panzer-Abteilung 502*, reported the following about the beginning of the Russian offensive on Berlin:

It still had to be night, but outside, in the field of vision of the periscope, the eastern horizon was ablaze. From the marshy Oder lowlands to the hills just in front of Lebus and Reitwein all the way to Seelow...the entire terrain seemed to be on fire! In front of us and behind us, everything was under a murderous rain of steel. Heavy artillery fired across the Oder. Twenty, thirty flying shadows swooped over the ruined houses dropping clusters of heavy phosphorus and high-explosive bombs in every patch of woods, on the German artillery and *Flak* positions waiting behind roads and folds of terrain, far to the rear of the front lines.

From the foremost foxhole to the rearmost trenches, the Germans waited behind their machine guns, fighting positions, optics, radio sets and map tables for the decisive hour. Reserves moved into their assembly positions and defensive areas. From the foremost infantry battalion to the German headquarters at Zossen in the rear, radio message followed radio message in unbroken succession.

Then swarms of German fighters and bombers also joined the battle. The air shook with the thunder of motors and propellers. 0700 hours arrived, then 0800 hours.

For half an hour the rising and falling noise of infantry weapons could be heard. Through it, the hammering staccato of the machine guns seemed to be getting closer...

Because the first German positions had been evacuated, the Russian artillery preparation fizzled. As the Soviet assault troops advanced, they ran into stubborn resistance from the main German positions. The attack threatened to bog down. German counterattacks started at critical positions. The *Tigers* of *schwere SS-Panzer-Abteilung 502* knocked out eleven Russian tanks at Dolgelin.

At 1400 hours, Stalin telephoned Marshal Zhukov from Moscow and checked up on the situation for himself. Stalin was displeased with the slow progress of the offensive and ordered the immediate employment of the entire 1st Guards Tank Army (Katukow). The tank army was to pass through the 8th Guards Army and capture the Seelow Heights. At the end of the telephone call Stalin informed the commander in chief of the 1st Belorussian Front that the 1st Ukrainian Front had broken through the German front on the Neiße on its first attempt and was making good progress toward the west and northwest. Stalin's playing one front against the other made Zhukov nervous and drove him to push for progress, since he wanted to go down in history as the conqueror of Berlin.

As a result of the employment of the tank army at that point, a bottleneck developed at the offensive *Schwerpunkt* in front of Seelow. Tanks and infantry got in each other's way. In another telephone conversation in the evening of 16 April, Zhukov promised Stalin that the Seelow Heights would be captured the next day.

A critical situation developed at Seelow, which was held by remnants of the *20. Panzergrenadier Division* and units that had been brought up from *Panzer-Division "Müncheberg"* and the *25.Panzergrenadier-Division.* Additional crises existed at Freienwalde, in the sector of the *5. Jäger-Division* and *Division 606*; with the *9. Fallschirmjäger-Division* northeast of Seelow; at Lebus (*169.* and *712. Infanterie-Divisionen*); and, south of Frankfurt/Oder. Nevertheless, the German front essentially held on the first day of the attack.

The approximately 235,000 men of the *9. Armee* had fought courageously. General Busse, the Commander-in-Chief of the *9. Armee*, wrote in his study:

Considering the imbalance of forces, 16 April was a great defensive success…The condition of the troop units at the *Schwerpunkte* was a cause of concern…The losses in personnel and equipment could no longer be made good…The *Luftwaffe* (about 300 aircraft) had provided effective support for the ground troops, but could not prevent the Russians from controlling the air. The fuel supplies of the *Luftwaffe* were enough for two days, at the most, of such intense operations.

On 17 April the *18. Panzergrenadier-Division* and the *11. SS-Freiwilligen-Panzergrenadier-Division "Nordland"* were brought out of army-group reserve to reinforce the hard-pressed *LVI. Panzer-Korps.* The *18. Panzergrenadier-Division* was committed in the Seelow area and the *11. SS-Freiwilligen-Panzer-Grenadier-Division "Nordland"* was committed in the Ihlow — Hermersdorf area (east of Strausberg).

***

The *23. SS-Freiwilligen-Panzergrenadier-Division "Nederland"* was attached to the *XI. SS-Panzer-Korps* and staged in the area southwest of Seelow. It included: *SS-Freiwilligen-Panzer-Grenadier-Regiment 48 "General Seyffard"*, which had been newly re-formed; the *II.* and *III./SS-Artillerie-Regiment 54*; and, the division units. *SS-Freiwilligen-Panzer-Grenadier-Regiment 49 "de Ruyter"* — still split up and attached to a variety of units — initially remained in the positions at Gatow and Gartz, as did the *I./SS-Artillerie-Regiment 54.*

The *11. SS-Freiwilligen-Panzergrenadier-Division "Nordland"* was also needed in the area of the Seelow penetration. In the afternoon of 16 April, the regimental adjutant, *SS-Hauptsturmführer* Lührs, called the battalions: "Prepare to move! Additional orders to follow!"

The staff of *SS-Panzer-Grenadier-Regiment 24 "Danmark"* was in Hohenlandin. There were also elements of the *II./SS-Panzer-Grenadier-Regiment 24 "Danmark"* there. Other units of that battalion were in Niederlandin. The *III. SS-Panzer-Grenadier-Regiment 24 "Danmark"* was in and around Flemsdorf.

After being re-formed, the companies consisted of two assault platoons, each with three squads and a platoon headquarters and, a covering platoon with four squads. The squads each had two machine guns. Each company also had about 50 assault rifles, four rifles with telescopic sights and eight rifle-grenade launchers, giving an unprecedented firepower. The heavy companies (*8./* and *12./SS-Panzer-Grenadier-Regiment 24 "Danmark"*) had three 7.5 cm *Pak*, three 7.5 cm infantry guns, two mortar platoons, each with four 8 cm mortars, and two heavy-machine gun platoons, each with four heavy-machine guns.

With the onset of darkness, the companies sent everything that was not essential to the rear. During the night of 16/17 April, the order arrived to pull out of the positions and assemble in Hohenlandin. The field telephone lines were quickly recovered. A heavy artillery barrage could be heard to the south. The heavens were lit up red. The sound of fighting could be heard to the north. Soviet heavy artillery fired in regular intervals on Berkholz. The companies reached Hohenlandin at the beginning of daylight.

Regimental commander Klotz briefed battalion commanders Sörensen and Ternedde. The regiment was no longer fully motorized. Many of the vehicles remained in Pomerania. The regimental order:

1. The enemy is attacking with superior forces in the Küstrin — Frankfurt/Oder sector. After a level of fire preparation never before experienced on the Eastern Front — barrages reaching far into the depth of the battlefield as far as the division command post — his armor and infantry formations have achieved threatening initial successes.

2. The *III. (germanisches) SS-Panzer-Korps* is to transfer to the Strausberg — Eberswalde area on 17 April.

3. *SS-Panzer-Grenadier-Regiment 24 "Danmark"* is to move out on 17 April at 1000 hours.

4. *SS-Panzer-Grenadier-Regiment 24 "Danmark"* is to assemble in the forest east of Strausberg and organize immediately for defense with front facing east and north-east.

5. The first units to move via road march:

Regimental Headquarters and Headquarters Company

13. and *14./SS-Panzer-Grenadier-Regiment 24 "Danmark"*
Staff of *II./SS-Panzer-Grenadier-Regiment 24 "Danmark"* and the *8./SS-Panzer-Grenadier-Regiment 24 "Danmark"*
All of the *III./SS-Panzer-Grenadier-Regiment 24 "Danmark"*

The rifle companies of the *II./SS-Panzer-Grenadier-Regiment 24 "Danmark"* are to be brought forward immediately after the arrival of the regiment in the area of operations by the personnel carriers of the *III./SS-Panzer-Grenadier-Regiment 24 "Danmark"*.

The *15./SS-Panzer-Grenadier-Regiment 24 "Danmark"* and the regimental field-replacement company are to follow the regiment on foot.

6. The road march will be conducted with appropriate spacing for air defense.

The *15./SS-Panzer-Grenadier-Regiment 24 "Danmark"* was a newly formed horse-drawn element. The field-replacement company was to assemble reserve manpower and follow the regiment.

At 1000 hours the column moved out. The regiment reached the area specified in the orders by way of Angermünde — Eberswalde — Tiefensee. While the staff of the *II./SS-Panzer-Grenadier-Regiment 24 "Danmark"* and the *8./SS-Panzer-Grenadier-Regiment 24 "Danmark"* remained in Gielsdorf, the *III./SS-Panzer-Grenadier-Regiment 24 "Danmark"* reached the Hermersdorf — Münchhofe area.

***

SS-Panzer-Aufklärungs-Abteilung 11 was already in action on 17 April, supporting the badly battered companies of the *9. Fallschirmjäger-Division* as they were slowly forced back to the west.

SS-Panzer-Aufklärungs-Abteilung 11 occupied new blocking positions northwest of Seelow. Units of the *3./SS-Panzer-Aufklärungs-Abteilung 11*, together with army personnel, repulsed an enemy infantry attack. Soon afterward the rattle and rumble of Soviet armor could be heard in a patch of woods not far to the front of the position. The leader of the blocking unit ordered it to fall back to a wooded area to the west. The mortars of the *3./SS-Panzer-Aufklärungs-Abteilung 11* also changed position. Everyone watched the developing situation closely from the sparse, high-standing woods. Three infantrymen had remained in the old position — three volunteers with *Panzerfäuste*.

The engine noise grew stronger. An armored giant pushed aside the last tree trunks providing a hindrance in the patch of woods and moved into the open. Two more followed beside the first one, and another two in its tracks. The Russian tanks moved out into the field and fired on the last of the withdrawing infantry. They must have felt nothing could stop them.

Everyone tensely followed the movements of the Russian tanks as they rolled forward, close together and with no infantry escort. The three men in the former position seemed devoid of nerves. The earth already shook. The

Russian tanks fired on the edge of the woods and paid no attention to the former positions.

When the Soviet tanks were within 30 meters, three heads emerged from cover. Fire spurted from the *Panzerfäuste* — and three tanks were hit. The third one turned in a circle due to a broken track.

Again the three steel helmets emerged. *Panzerfäuste* hissed. Two more tanks burned. The third — gutshot — received the mercy shot. Five Soviet tanks burned. They had been destroyed by three unknown German soldiers who then ran back.

Two companies of *SS-Panzer-Aufklärungs-Abteilung 11* went into position on both sides of the Seelow —Müncheberg road. There was a 7.5 cm *Pak* on the road and the *3.* and *4./SS-Panzer-Aufklärungs-Abteilung 11* were employed as infantry to either side of it. The vehicles were staged farther to the west. The *3./SS-Panzer-Aufklärungs-Abteilung 11* dug in along a small patch of woods.

In the midst of the digging, someone shouted "Russians!" and pointed toward the opposite edge of the woods. The spades flew to the side.

Men were running across the field, directly toward the positions of the *3./SS-Panzer-Aufklärungs-Abteilung 11*. The characteristic helmets of German *Fallschirmjäger* were clearly recognizable. They had run out of ammunition as they defended against an enemy attack and had been forced to give up their blocking position.

Seventy *Fallschirmjäger* of the *9. Fallschirmjäger-Division* received ammunition from the men of the *3./SS-Panzer-Aufklärungs-Abteilung 11*, mounted an immediate counterattack and hurled the Soviets back. While that was happening, Soviet tanks rolled forward on the highway. The only *Pak* received a direct hit. The Soviet escorting infantry charged. The blocking position collapsed and the German companies fell back to the west.

***

As the situation became increasingly fluid, the *Königstiger* of *schwere SS-Panzer-Abteilung 503* (Herzig) formed the first battering rams. One of them, commanded by *SS-Hauptscharführer* Körner, started out by knocking out seven Russian tanks near Grunow, bringing the Russian infantry attack to a halt.

In the forenoon hours of 19 April, *SS-Obersturmführer* Müller's *Tiger* knocked out 23 Russian tanks between Grunow and Bollersdorf. When he moved back to get more ammunition, Russian tanks followed. At that point, they became engaged with other *Tigers* of the battalion, which were in position and ready to engage. Numerous additional Russian T-34 and KV I tanks were destroyed.

At about 1300 hours Körner's section of *Tigers* supported the counterattack of *SS-Panzer-Grenadier-Regiment 23 "Norge"* on Bollersdorf. On departure from the assembly area, Körner discovered two Russian T-34 tanks that were covering the refueling and resupply of ammunition of a large armored formation that had moved up along the road from Bollersdorf to Strausberg and was at Bollersdorf itself. Surprise and chaos prevailed among the Russians when the *Tiger* main guns opened fire. Armor and supply vehicles were so close together that they got in each other's way when the fight started.

At about 1700 hours yet another armored engagement took place on the heights west of Bollersdorf. During that engagement, Körner's and *Untersturmführer* Schäfer's *Tigers* again knocked out numerous enemy tanks. All in all, the Russians lost 70 tanks in the area east of Strausberg.

Körner knocked out another 17 tanks on the outskirts of Berlin. That brought his total to 101 tanks and 26 antitank guns destroyed. Körner, Schäfer and the battalion commander, *SS-Sturmbannführer* Herzig, were awarded the Knight's Cross in Berlin on 29 April.

In spite of those defensive successes, the final dams broke on 18 April. The Russian assault wedge advancing through Wriezen and south of the Oder-Spree Canal tributary — the northern arm of the Russian pincers — rapidly gained ground to the west. Only south of Eberswalde was a bridge-head still held by the *25. Panzergrenadier-* and the *5. Jäger-Division*. The southern arm of the Russian pincers around Berlin, on the other hand — which was moving forward from Frankfurt/Oder — was still impeded in its advance by the formations of the *V. SS-Gebirgs-Korps* (Jeckeln), by the *32. SS-Division* and the *286. Infanterie-Division*.

Marshal Zhukov wrote in his memoirs that, on 20 April, his long-range artillery opened fire on Berlin: "With that, the historical assault on the German capital had begun."

***

While *SS-Sturmbannführer* Sörensen waited for his *II./SS-Panzer-Grenadier-Regiment 24 "Danmark"* in Gielsdorf, *SS-Sturmbannführer* Ternedde's *III./SS-Panzer-Grenadier-Regiment 24 "Danmark"* went into position at the edge of the woods west of Hermersdorf. It maintained contact to the south with *SS-Panzer-Grenadier-Regiment 23 "Norge"* (west of Münchhofe — Dahmsdorf). There was a unit of about 500 youths of the "Hitler-Jugend" to the north. They ranged in age from 15 to 17 years. In front of them on 18 April were still *Kampfgruppen* of the *9. Fallschirmjäger-Division* in Hermersdorf and Obersdorf. The *Fallschirmjäger* were already warding off enemy attacks in Obersdorf.

In Hermersdorf the situation became increasingly critical. There the Russians attacked with armor. Alongside the *Fallschirmjäger* were the remnants of an 8.8 cm *Flak* battalion. *SS-Sturmbannführer* Ternedde also sent elements of his *III./SS-Panzer-Grenadier-Regiment 24 "Danmark"* to that blocking group. The village was held until evening. After the *Flak* had expended all its ammunition, those forces fell back to the wood line designated in the orders.

The Nineteenth of April began with gloomy prospects. Superior Soviet armored formations with escorting infantry were already beating against the *"Hitler-Jugend"* positions and those of the *III./SS-Panzer-Grenadier-Regiment 24 "Danmark"* and *SS-Panzer-Grenadier-Regiment 23 "Norge"* in the morning hours. First came an artillery barrage. The units melted away. The wood was ablaze from end to end. Soviet fighter-bombers attacked constantly. In spite of all that, the defenders did not waver.

That day it was the individual warrior who put his life on the line and knocked out the Soviet tanks. Damaged enemy tanks were everywhere. The teenage boys of the *"Hitler-Jugend"* unit fought like old soldiers in the midst of the Soviet assaults, but the unit melted away to a tiny group and could do nothing to prevent the penetration from succeeding. As a result, Ternedde's battalion holding to the north was threatened. The picture looked no better for *SS-Panzer-Grenadier-Regiment 23 "Norge"* either. *SS-Hauptsturmführer* Spörle, commander of the *II./SS-Panzer-Grenadier-Regiment 23 "Norge"*, was killed on the field of battle.

The regimental command post was initially in Buckower Palace. The regiment was distributed along the wood line, with the individual formations frequently out of contact with one another. It had to fall back. Whenever it reorganized for the defense, the sound of Soviet tank guns could already be heard to the rear or on the flanks. Soon nobody had even a rough idea of where the front ran. The woody terrain prevented any overall view. It was in that situation that *SS-Panzer-Grenadier-Regiment 23 "Norge"* fought its way back to Strausberg.

During the night of 19/20 April, the *III./SS-Panzer-Grenadier-Regiment 24 "Danmark"* and the regimental units pulled out of the burning woods south of Buckow and fell back through Garzau to Hohenstein. The *16./SS-Panzer-Grenadier-Regiment 24 "Danmark"* and the regiment's assault platoon were the last ones to leave. After *SS-Untersturmführer* Fahrenbacher was wounded, *SS-Oberscharführer* Illum led those elements. After a difficult march they wanted a few hours of rest in Garzau, but Soviet tanks and infantry were soon advancing into the village. The formations of *SS-Panzer-Grenadier-Regiment 24 "Danmark"* withdrew to Hohenstein where, in the meantime, other units of the regiment had already arrived and formed a new main line of resistance south and east of the village.

On 19 April the fighting flared up around Hohenstein. The elements of *SS-Panzer-Grenadier-Regiment 24 "Danmark"* held on for some time but, when 20 Soviet tanks pushed their way into town, the German elements had to leave. Southwest of Hohenstein, *SS-Panzer-Grenadier-Regiment 23 "Norge"* was also fighting and falling back. The Soviets did not push the pursuit. In the evening, *SS-Panzer-Grenadier-Regiment 23 "Norge"* and *SS-Panzer-Grenadier-Regiment 24 "Danmark"* held positions in a wide semi-circle east of Strausberg.

On 20 April, Soviet artillery pounded the entire sector from Gielsdorf to Strausberg. The Soviets themselves advanced behind the rolling wall of fire. *SS-Pionier-Bataillon 11,* which had been positioned east of Gielsdorf, fell back to the eastern outskirts of the town. *SS-Sturmbannführer* Sörensen, a battalion commander without a battalion, talked with the commander of the combat engineers. Neither of them believed that the *II./SS-Panzer-Grenadier-Regiment 24 "Danmark",* which was to have been brought back by the vehicles of the *III./SS-Panzer-Grenadier-Regiment 24 "Danmark",* would still be able to get to Gielsdorf. Sörensen attached his *8./SS-Panzer-Grenadier-Regiment 24 "Danmark"* to the combat engineers and moved to the north with his staff to look for his battalion. But they didn't get far. In the next village the antitank barriers had been closed and the church bells were ringing to announce that the Russians were coming. They had already outflanked the *11. SS-Freiwilligen-Panzergrenadier-Division "Nordland"* to the north. Sörensen ordered: "Back to Gielsdorf!"

On 20 April heavy fighting raged east of Strausberg. Soviet infantry and armor were able to achieve penetrations and work their way forward through parks and garden plots. The command post of the *11. SS-Freiwilligen-Panzer-Grenadier-Division "Nordland"* was in the cellar of a large airport building. A few hundred meters to the east, at the eastern edge of the Strausberg airport, was the command post of *SS-Panzer-Grenadier-Regiment 24 "Danmark".* It was in a former *Flak* position. A bit farther to the south was the command post of *Regiment 23 "Norge".* The division was holding its position, but the Soviets kept throwing new forces into their assault. The hail of shells of all calibers poured down on the German positions with ever increasing fury, tearing larger and larger gaps in the lines.

The main thrust of the armor-supported attacks was aimed at the command post of *SS-Panzer-Grenadier-Regiment 24 "Danmark".* The regimental commander, *SS-Obersturmbannführer* Klotz, and the commander of the *III./SS-Panzer-Grenadier-Regiment 24 "Danmark", SS-Sturmbannführer* Ternedde, decided to join their men, who were a few hundred meters to the east. They tried to go forward with their vehicle and the radio section through a little depression. As the vehicle emerged from the depression, it received a direct hit from an armor-piercing round. *SS-Obersturmbannführer* Klotz showed only faint signs of life. Ternedde, with a head wound, was unconscious. The senior liaison officer, *SS-Untersturmführer* Gräf, lost his left leg at the thigh. Three men of the radio section who were crouching behind them in the vehicle were killed. Only the driver escaped without injury.

Ignoring the artillery and armor-piercing rounds striking around the vehicle, the driver dragged his regiment's commander, *SS-Sturmbannführer* Ternedde and the liaison officer into the vehicle, whose motor was still running. With one hand he plugged the hole in the leaking fuel tank. With the other, he steered the vehicle and raced back to the division command post. There he unloaded *SS-Obersturmbannführer* Klotz, who had died on the way. Ternedde and Gräf were brought to the hospital at Alt-Landsberg. Ternedde refused a transfer to a hospital in his country and was taken to the trains units at Mahlsdorf.

Gielsdorf had already been evacuated. Supported by two assault guns of the *11. SS-Freiwilligen-Panzer-Grenadier-Division "Nordland"*, the combat engineers fought for every patch of woods. Sörensen ran into Voß, who was standing beside a *Sturmgeschütz*, pointing out targets. Soviet antitank guns were also firing. The *Sturmgeschütze* held their positions and fired into Gielsdorf, but it was easy to see it could not last much longer. A radio message from the division was passed to *SS-Sturmbannführer* Sörensen: "*SS-Obersturmbannführer* Klotz has been killed; *SS-Sturmbannführer* Ternedde wounded. *SS-Sturmbannführer* Sörensen is to immediately assume command of *SS-Panzer-Grenadier-Regiment 24 "Danmark"* and report to division headquarters for a briefing."

SS-Sturmbannführer Sörensen attached his heavy company to *SS-Pionier-Bataillon 11* and started back. On the way, the battalion staff came upon the trains units, which were moving back to Seeberg. One portion of the signals section joined up. At the division headquarters, *SS-Sturmbannführer* Bergfeld briefed Sörensen. *SS-Untersturmführer* Raßmussen was given the task of moving north to search for the *II./SS-Panzer-Grenadier-Regiment 24 "Danmark"*.

SS-Sturmbanführer Sörensen passed through Alt-Landsberg on his way to Strausberg. The roads were jammed with columns trying to get through to the west.

At about 1000 hours, Sörensen's vehicle arrived at the command post of the *11. SS-Freiwilligen-Panzergrenadier-Division "Nordland"* in the cellar at the edge of the Strausberg airport. The remains of *SS-Obersturmbannführer* Klotz were in the process of being loaded onto a *Volkswagen*. One last time, the new commander saluted his dead predecessor. Klotz was laid out in a small chapel. The rush of events that day prevented his men from burying him.

Generalmajor der Waffen-SS Ziegler briefed the new commander of *SS-Panzer-Grenadier-Regiment 24 "Danmark"*. Soon afterward, Sörensen was at his command post, which was also the command post of the *III./SS-Panzer-Grenadier-Regiment 24 "Danmark"*. *SS-Untersturmführer* Dirksen, who had received a battlefield commission, commanded the *III./SS-Panzer-Grenadier-Regiment 24 "Danmark"*.

The intensity of infantry action had cooled down somewhat in the sector of *SS-Panzer-Grenadier-Regiment 24 "Danmark"*, but heavy artillery fire continued to pound the positions, the airfield and the military facilities. The enemy achieved a penetration at the airport in the afternoon. Three Soviet tanks were knocked out by an 8.8 cm *Flak*. The *16./SS-Panzer-Grenadier-Regiment 24 "Danmark"* and regimental assault platoon ironed out the penetration. The main line of resistance held. Undamaged aircraft parked on the airfield were blown up. There were additional penetrations during the course of the day north and south of the division.

By the evening of 20 April, there was no avoiding the necessity for the withdrawal of the division. The regiments were to evacuate their positions upon receiving a code word and fall back to Alt-Landsberg. *SS-Panzer-Grenadier-Regiment 24 "Danmark"* was to take up new positions in the village of Buchholz. But events did not work out as planned.

At about 1900 hours the Russians attacked. *Luftwaffe* ground forces positioned north of *SS-Panzer-Grenadier-Regiment 24 "Danmark"* fell back. The north flank was open. Soon afterward, the enemy was on the improved-surface road to Strausberg. The *11. SS-Freiwilligen-Panzergrenadier-Division "Nordland"* had to fall back. In all due haste the companies withdrew from their positions. Vehicles moved across the airfield and made it to the available exit to the main road to Strausberg.

SS-Panzer-Grenadier-Regiment 23 "Norge" reached Alt-Landsberg during the night, but *SS-Panzer-Grenadier-Regiment 24 "Danmark"* did not. The roads west were hopelessly jammed with traffic. At times panic threatened, but squad and platoon leaders kept control of their new and combat-inexperienced men. A barrage of fire from *Stalin* organs and mortars covered the southeast outskirts of the city, but had not yet reached the highway. Traffic piled up yet again in Strausberg. Bombs fell. There was only one thing to do: Step on the gas and get through!

SS-Panzer-Grenadier-Regiment 24 "Danmark" assembled west of the city on the southern shore of Lake Strausberg. After waiting for hours, it moved a few kilometers farther. There was no contact with the division. However, the assigned mission was still: "*SS-Panzer-Grenadier-Regiment 24 "Danmark"* is to occupy Buchholz!"

SS-Sturmbannführer Sörensen doubted whether Buchholz was still really free of the enemy, so he sent in a patrol . In the meantime, his companies set up security with several tanks and assault guns.

While *SS-Panzer-Grenadier-Regiment 24 "Danmark"* still waited at Strausberg for the reconnaissance results from Buchholz, *SS-Panzer-Grenadier-Regiment 23 "Norge"* had already reached Alt-Landsberg and organized for the defense. Sörensen and his formation went farther to the southwest on trails in the woods and waited.

On the preceding day, however, some Soviet armored spearheads had already reached the outskirts of Berlin. *Generalmajor* Bärenfänger's blocking group at Mahlsdorf smashed one of them.

The trains units of *SS-Panzer-Grenadier-Regiment 24 "Danmark"* which were staged at the time in Mahlsdorf, were threatened during the night by four Soviet tanks that moved around in the village. The wounded *SS-Sturmbannführer* Ternedde, who was convalescing with the trains units, committed the drivers and repair section. Two Soviet tanks were destroyed by *Panzerfäuste* and the others moved off. Ternedde led the trains units of *SS-Panzer-Grenadier-Regiment 24 "Danmark"* to the palace on the lake at Lake Müggel. Since Soviet armored spearheads were also advancing there, Ternedde and his trains units fell back into the Grune Woods.

During the night of 20/21 April at the command post of *SS-Panzer-Grenadier-Regiment 23 "Norge"* in Alt-Landsberg, not one of the officers knew how far the Soviets had advanced. The adjutant sent out old, veteran soldiers in a patrol.

A motorized patrol moved toward Eggersdorf. All around them, fires lit up the night. *SS-Oberscharführer* Zühlke sat on the edge of one side of the *Volkswagen* with his machine pistol ready to fire. The windshield was folded down. They moved slowly past houses. Here and there a weak glimmer of light shone through the blacked-out windows. From time to time they stopped, then moved onward again, only to stop again. Movements in the shadows ahead. After tense moments they spotted women with baby buggies.

Zühlke asked: "Where are you going?" The answer revealed perplexity. "We don't know either! People say the Russians have broken through, so we are taking off to Berlin…Is it true that the Russians rape all the women?" The *SS-Oberscharführer* tried to come up with some fitting reply, since the truth would not do. He had seen too much during the counterattack at Schlagenthin in Pomerania. "Go to Berlin," he said, "and disappear in the big city. Then it will not be so bad!"

Two kilometers farther they spotted movements among the shadows of the houses by the light of the dying fires. The stopped the Volkswagen and worked their way forward, where they then took to the ground. A motor roared. Tank tracks ground and screeched. Flashlights shone. The wind carried bits and pieces of words: *"Idi, idi, pistra!"* The men had found out what they needed to know. They ran to the vehicle and sped back.

During that night, *SS-Sturmbannführer* Sörensen and the remnants of *SS-Panzer-Grenadier-Regiment 24 "Danmark"* reached the *Autobahn* ring west of Fredersdorf by way of Herzfelde. The regiment had been forced well to the south by the enemy advance at Gielsdorf and Strausberg. On 21 April the command post of *SS-Panzer-Grenadier-Regiment 24 "Danmark"* was in Friedrichshagen. For the time being, the *11. SS-Freiwilligen-Panzergrenadier-Division "Nordland"* was able to hold its positions on both sides of *Reichsstraße 1* at the *Autobahn* ring.

In the afternoon, the Soviets achieved a penetration east of Neuenhagen. The *16./SS-Panzer-Grenadier-Regiment 24 "Danmark"* and the regiment's assault platoon were loaded on trucks and committed into the area of the penetration. They occupied positions on the Dahlwitz-Hoppergarten branch line facing north, supported by two *Sturmgeschütze* from the division. The Soviets attacked again, this time supported by four T 34's. One *Sturmgeschütz* knocked out two of them. The situation became untenable as darkness fell. The Soviets had already moved farther, outflanking them to the north. The remnants of both divisional regiments occupied new positions on both sides of Mahlsdorf.

***

What was the overall situation in the Battle for Berlin?

After Zhukov's divisions had torn apart the cohesion of *General* Busse's *9. Armee* on 18 April, the three corps of the army were divided in three. At Schwedt the northern-most corps, the *101. Armee-Korps*, was able to maintain its positions for a time but, after the front had been torn open, it had to bend its southern flank back to the west and hold along the line of the Finow Canal. *General* Weidling's *LVI. Panzer-Korps* was sent to the threatened northern wing of the *XI. SS-Korps*, which had been forced back by the Soviet advance. The *11. SS-Freiwilligen-Panzergrenadier-Division "Nordland"* was sent to that threatened corps on 18 April. The *XI. SS-Korps* was able hold its own by and large, but then had to fall back to the west as a result of its open northern flank. It later ended up in the Halbe Pocket.

At that time, *Armeegruppe Steiner* was established north of the Finow Canal. It was composed of all sorts of different formations. On 21 April Hitler issued the following order to *General der Waffen-SS* Felix Steiner:

It is the essential mission of *Armee-Abteilung Steiner* to establish and maintain contact under all circumstances with the forces of the *LVI. Panzer-Korps* (Author's Note: The *11. SS-Freiwilligen-Panzer-Grenadier-Division "Nordland"*, the *18. Panzergrenadier-Division*, the *20. Panzergrenadier-Division*, *Panzer-Division "Müncheberg"* and elements of the *9. Fallschirmjäger-Division*) that are near and southeast of Werneuchen. It will do this by attacking from the north with the *4. SS-Polizei-Division* (Author's Note: Brought from Danzig/Hela) and elements of the *5. Jäger-Division* and the *25. Panzergrenadier-Division*. Those elements — which need to be as strong as possible — will be freed up by the *3. Marine-Division*.

It is expressly forbidden for any unit to fall back to the west. Officers who do not unconditionally follow this order are to be arrested and shot on the spot. I make you, yourself, responsible with your own head for carrying out this order.

The fate of the capital of the German Reich depends on the success of your mission.

signed: Adolf Hitler

It was an impossible order. It showed how far Hitler had become removed from reality. The order called for operations with divisions that no longer consisted of anything more than battered remnants. The designated line of defense had long-since been overrun.

***

In the morning of 22 April the positions of the *11. SS-Freiwilligen-Panzer-Grenadier-Division "Nordland"* on both sides of Mahlsdorf was already under heavy enemy pressure. They became untenable. In the northeast, Soviet formations were at Lake Weiß and had already achieved a penetration in the north, where the *Polizei* battalion was positioned. At about 1300 hours, the evacuation of Biesdorf was ordered. The situation had also quickly become hopeless there as well. The Soviets followed close behind. In the north they were at Pankow, in the south at Köpenick. From that point on, divisional-level cohesion was lost. Only *Kampfgruppen* were employed. The trains units moved to Pichelsberg and, a little later, to the Zoo in Berlin. *SS-Sturmbannführer* Ternedde raced to the division command post at Berlin, where he remained in the officer reserve. The trains units were combed out. Many men were ordered into action. The *II./SS-Panzer-Grenadier-Regiment 24 "Danmark"* never linked up with the regiment again. It was supposed to have linked up after having been transported back from Hohenlandin at the beginning of the battle for Berlin. Only the *8./SS-Panzer-Grenadier-Regiment 24 "Danmark"* made contact with the regiment.

The rifle companies of the *II./SS-Panzer-Grenadier-Regiment 24 "Danmark"* only made it to Werneuchen. The route south from there to the regiment had already been blocked by the Soviets. The *5., 6.,* and *7./SS-Panzer-Grenadier-Regiment 24 "Danmark"* defended at the airport, but then had to fall back to the west and linked up with *Armee-Gruppe Steiner.*

In the afternoon of 22 April in Biesdorf there was strafing by airplanes and sudden concentrations of artillery. Soon reconnaissance trips by liaison officers determined that the Soviets were in Lichtenberg and already threatened the north flank and rear of the *11. SS-Freiwilligen-Panzer-Grenadier-Division "Nordland"*. The order arrived: "Back to Karlshorst!" By midnight the enemy had penetrated to the racetrack. The *16./SS-Panzer-Grenadier-Regiment 24 "Danmark"* and the regiment's assault platoon, commanded by *SS-Untersturmführer* Christensen, threw the Soviets back.

The remnants of *SS-Panzer-Grenadier-Regiment 23 "Norge"*, *SS-Panzer-Grenadier-Regiment 24 "Danmark"*, *SS-Panzer-Aufklärungs-Abteilung 11*, *SS-Flak-Abteilung 11* and *SS-Pionier-Bataillon 11* fought bitterly at Karlshorst. Weapons, ammunition and, most of all, fighting men were in short supply. The remnants of *SS-Flak-Abteilung 11* were committed at Adlershof to ward off an enemy attack from Eichwalde.

After two fruitless attempts, the Soviets came with armored support right across the Karlshorst racetrack as morning approached. Karlshorst was evacuated on 23 April at about 0800 hours. The formations were pulled back to Baumschulenweg. One element of the remaining armored cars of *SS-Panzer-Aufklärungs-Abteilung 11* fell back to the northwest and made it via Friedrichshain to Neukölln. At that point, the command post of the *11. SS-*

Freiwilligen-Panzer-Grenadier-Division "Nordland" was located there. *General* Weidling, the commanding general of the *LVI. Panzer-Korps*, had issued the following order on the previous day: The *11. SS-Freiwilligen-Panzergrenadier-Division "Nordland"* is corps rearguard and covers the Spree bridges from Treptower Park to Adlershof.

The *LVI. Panzer-Korps* was to move to the south to *Armee Busse*, although that order was soon countermanded. The *LVI. Panzer-Korps* remained in Berlin.

SS-Sturmbannführer Lohmann and *SS-Untersturmführer* Schluifelder (battlefield commission). Schluifelder was the acting commander of the *1./SS-Panzergrenadier-Regiment 49 "De Ruyter"*. He was killed in action on the Ozoli Heights south of Preekuln on 24 January 1945.

Per Sörensen as a Danish officer. He was killed in action as the regimental commander of *SS-Panzergrenadier-Regiment 24 "Danmark"* on 24 April 1945 in Berlin.

SS-Sturmbannführer Krügel. He was killed in action as the regimental commander of *SS-Panzeregrenadier-Regiment 24* on 16 March 1945 during an immediate counterattack on the Altdamm Rail Station.

The Battle for Berlin

On 20 April 1945 there was a bustle of activity in the cellar bunkers of the German Chancellery. On the occasion of Hitler's 56th birthday, Keitel, von Ribbentrop, Bormann, Goebbels and others congratulated him. There was no other trace of the once "glorious *Führer* birthdays".

The military situation had rapidly worsened for the Germans. The breakthroughs at Wriezen, Seelow, Frankfurt/Oder and Forst/Cottbus could no longer be stopped, let alone closed. A counterattack from the Eberswalde bridgehead to the south to establish contact with the *LVI. Panzer-Korps*, which was fighting near Strausberg, never got past the beginning stage. *General* Weidling's corps had open flanks and was pushed back farther and farther to the west along the route of *Reichstraße 1*. A Russian assault wedge was aimed at Fürstenwalde from Görlsdorf (west of Seelow). In order to intercept it, the *32. SS-Freiwilligen-Grenadier-Division "30. Januar"* was brought up from its position south of Frankfurt/Oder and moved to the Fürstenwalde area. With an additional assault wedge south of Frankfurt/Oder, a possible encirclement of the southern group of the *9. Armee* (*XI. SS-Panzer-Korps, Festung Frankfurt/Oder, V. SS-Gebirgs-Korps*) was clearly impending. At the same time, the *V. Armee-Korps*, which had been split off from *Heeresgruppe Mitte* at Forst, sought contact with the *9. Armee*.

In the meantime, *General* Wenck had organized the new *12. Armee* in the Wittenberg — Dessau area. It occupied a front facing the Americans. It consisted of the last German reserves from troop schools and draftees born in 1927/28. The seven divisions so formed bore ceremonial names from German history, but the personnel and equipment were, in the truest sense of the words, thrown together from the very last reserves of manpower and the final sweepings of the arsenals.

When, on 21 April, the northern Russian pincers reached Oranienburg, the *Generalkommando III. (germanisches) SS-Panzer-Korps* was elevated from a corps headquarters to *Armeegruppe Steiner*. It was tasked with covering the southern flank of the *3. Panzer-Armee* (von Manteuffel), which was still on the lower Oder. Steiner's line of defense ran along the Oder—Spree Canal connection.

General Weidling intended to bring the *LVI. Panzer-Korps*, which was fighting with open flanks, to the southern group of the *9. Armee*. It would then move back to the west with the *9. Armee*, passing south of Berlin. In the daily report of *Heeresgruppe Weichsel* to the *OKH* for 21 April it states: "The *LVI. Panzer-Korps* has fought its way back to the outer line of the Berlin fortifications with its right wing at the east edge of Lake Müggel and its left wing west of Dahlwitz-Hoppegarten." In its first daily report for the "Berlin Defensive Area," the following could be read:

In the eastern part of Berlin, Erkner...was captured by the enemy. Enemy spearheads were east of Lake Müggel. North of the Müncheberg — Berlin road, the enemy attacked with strong armored support from jump-off points at Alt-Landsberg, Blumberg and south of Bernau. Weak remnants of the *Volkssturm* battalions, which had been thrown into the outer blocking lines, passed through the lines of the security forces in the main line of resistance. Enemy attacks on sectors A and B ensued in the late afternoon. (Author's Note: Berlin was divided into defensive sectors. Sectors A and B faced east.) Harassing fire from heavy artillery and attacks by ground-attack aircraft impeded German movement and rearward movement of the civilian population. The enemy advanced into the northern blocking zone with armored forces, crossing *Reichsstraße 109* (Prenzlau — Berlin). (Author's Note: That area was defended by the *Wachregiment* (Lehndorff) and elements of the *9. Fallschirmjäger-Division*)...Command post in Sector C moved from Köpenick to Niederschönweide; for Sector G from Wittenau to Reinickendorf.

On 22 April the Battle for Berlin flared up in the eastern outskirts. On that day, *General* Weidling summoned all the commanders of the *LVI. Panzer-Korps* to his command post in the retirement home in Biesdorf and made known to them his decision to lead his corps to the *9. Armee* so as to fall back to the west with it, passing south of Berlin. Those present felt that defending the heap of ruins that was Berlin would be insane. Everything concerning the southwest movement of the corps was distributed. The *11. SS-Freiwilligen-Panzer-Grenadier-Division "Nordland"* was to defend the Spree bridges at Ober-Schöneweide to secure the crossing by the other divisions. The command post of the *LVI. Panzer-Korps* was moved to Rudow in the southern outskirts of Berlin.

Hitler, who had learned of the southwest movement of the *LVI. Panzer-Korps*, was in a rage. Weidling reported to Hitler, as ordered, with two officers of his staff on 23 April at 1800 hours in the *Reich* Chancellery. Among other things, he reported he had been ordered by Busse to establish contact with Busse's *9. Armee* south of Berlin. Hitler disapproved of that plan. He ordered the *LVI. Panzer-Korps* to move into Berlin and made Weidling the new Berlin local-area-commander. Hitler informed those present of his plan for the relief of Berlin from the north and the south by Wenck's and Steiner's forces.

The order to turn around struck the soldiers of the *LVI. Panzer-Korps* like a bombshell. Berlin was a mousetrap! Nevertheless, the orders were followed for the most part.

On 23 April, *SS-Panzer-Grenadier-Regiment 24 "Danmark"* held a bridgehead in Oberschöneweide/Rummelberg. The Russians made two successive concentric attacks and were repulsed. Then mortars, antitank guns and tank main guns hammered away and shot to pieces the few nests of resistance. T

34's rolled forward. "Back over the bridges!" — That was the only salvation. Three bridges were blown up in that sector. The Nordic volunteers reestablished themselves firmly on the west bank.

Other *Kampfgruppen* of the *LVI. Panzer-Korps* were in Britz, Mariendorf and Lankwitz. Elements of *SS-Artillerie-Regiment 11* went into position in Britz and fired off their last remaining ammunition.

SS-Sturmbannführer Sörensen, who had occupied the Niederschönweide sector of the Spree with a hastily assembled group of soldiers, sought contact on his flanks. There was none. Farther to the north were the remnants of *SS-Panzer-Grenadier-Regiment 23 "Norge"*, similarly devoid of contact in the Spree defense.

SS-Pionier-Bataillon 11 was intended to close the gaps existing between the regiments of the *11. SS-Freiwillignen-Panzergrenadier-Division "Nordland"* in Treptower Park. However, before it could do that, the Soviets had already crossed the Spree in assault boats and occupied it. Farther to the north were Soviet observation balloons, which were used to direct artillery fire.

The men of the *11. SS-Freiwilligen-Panzer-Grenadier-Division "Nordland"* remained on the banks of the Spree. They passed around the latest rumor: "The division was going to be pulled out for rapid refitting in the Rathenow area. Then it would help the encircled remnants of Busse's *9. Armee* fight their way free." The men did not know that Soviet spearheads were already outside of Rathenow.

During the night of 23/24 April, *SS-Sturmbannführer* Sörensen went to see *Generalmajor der Waffen-SS* Ziegler at Neukölln. The situation was thoroughly discussed. Nobody knew exact details of anything. Ziegler promised to commit the combat engineer battalion at Treptower Park to force back the Soviets who had penetrated the Spree defenses and close the gaps between the regiments. "As for the rest, use your own best judgement!" said Ziegler.

SS-Sturmbannführer Sörensen went back to Niederschönweide. His command post was in a brewery. He was able to grab no more than a few hours sleep. In the morning of 24 April, *SS-Pionier-Bataillon 11* was not yet there. *SS-Unterstrumführer* Gordon, a regimental liaison officer, went back again to Ziegler. The division command post had moved from the Neukölln unemployment officer to a large office building farther into the city. Heavy fighting in Neukölln had engaged the combat engineers. Gordon raced back. His vehicle was fired on in Treptower Park. The devil was also on the loose in Niederschöneweide.

The remnants of *SS-Panzer-Grenadier-Regiment 24 "Danmark"* fell back to a tributary canal of the Spree. The abundance of small bridges detracted from the value of that line of defense. It had to be abandoned within an hour. A new main line of resistance was established in a half-circle around the

Köllnische-Heide railroad station. The situation intensified from one hour to the next. There were strong enemy movements from Treptower Park towards Neukölln. The Soviets worked their way farther forward at the Grünau station of the urban rail line.

The *11. SS-Freiwilligen-Panzer-Grenadier-Division "Nordland"* prepared an immediate counterattack against Treptower Park. The last tanks of *SS-Panzer-Regiment 11 "Hermann von Salza"* and the remnants of *SS-Panzer-Aufklärungs-Abteilung 11* prepared for it. But the counterattack never took place.

To the south, Konjew's divisions had reached Mariendorf and Britz. Elements of the division were also engaged in heavy fighting there. Britz was still full of trains units and artillery. Armored cars and the last of the *Tigers* launched an immediate counterattack and brought Konjew's armored spearheads to a halt.

While that was taking place, the *Kampfgruppe "Danmark"* sector became less fluid. Soviet attacks did not take place, but enemy sharpshooters positioned themselves along the urban rail line and at the Schöneweide railroad station.

SS-Sturmbannführer Sörensen stood by a lamp post and observed the movements on the railroad embankment. One shot — Sörensen fell backward. Two men dragged him into a doorway. Nothing was visible, but the glazed eyes showed that he was dead. With shaking hands they unbuttoned his shirt. It seemed too much to believe — *SS-Sturmbannführer* Sörensen was dead!

A *Schwimmwagen* belonging to the *13./SS-Panzer-Grenadier-Regiment 24 "Danmark"* brought the dead commander to the division command post at Neukölln. *SS-Unterscharführer* Scholles, a companion of Sörensen for many years, went with him. The commander of the *14./SS-Panzer-Grenadier-Regiment 24 "Danmark"*, *SS-Obersturmführer* Petersen, assumed command of *Kampfgruppe "Danmark"*.

Only then did Scholles discover how dangerous the Soviet penetration through Treptower Park to Neukölln was. Divisional tanks and *Flak* controlled the streets at the Neukölln unemployment office. Scholles was sent on with the dead commander to the division headquarters. In Pichelsdorf, the remains were handed over and prepared for the burial.

The *16./SS-Panzer-Grenadier-Regiment 24 "Danmark"* and the regiment's assault platoon were relieved by naval forces. Those units were sent to the trains and later pulled security at the Jungfernheide.

On 24 April the *III./SS-Artillerie-Regiment 11* had no more ammunition. The battalion, which was in firing positions at Britz, limbered up and moved by way of Neukölln, Kreuzberg and the Schöneberg railroad station to near the Tempelhof airfield where it then found quarters in a group of summer homes.

"Only the drivers stay with the vehicles and guns! Form up by batteries at the main entrance to Tempelhof airfield!" A portentous arrangement. And so it continued. No ammunition, no more fuel. Soon there was nothing left but infantry.

The men of the batteries of the *III./SS-Artillerie-Regiment 11* assembled at the main entrance. The commander, *SS-Sturmbannführer* Potschka, addressed them. The men were then assigned to squads and platoons and issued weapons. Then they moved out toward Neukölln. The battalion went into position at the canal along the Sonnenallee.

The commander of *SS-Panzer-Grenadier-Regiment 23 "Norge"*, *SS-Obersturmbannführer* Körbel, was wounded. *SS-Sturmbannführer* Ternedde was ordered by the division commander to assume command of the combined remnants of the division's regiments. The adjutant of *SS-Panzer-Grenadier-Regiment 24 "Danmark"* was severely wounded. He chose to end his own life in the hospital at the radio tower when the collapse came.

On 25 April, the defenses along the Spree and the Teltow Canal finally collapsed. Step by step, the German forces were forced back into the center of the city. *Generalmajor* Ziegler was relieved and placed under house arrest in the *Reich* Chancellery because he could not hold the Teltow Canal — Spree line. As of noon, 25 April, the remnants of the division were commanded by *Generalmajor* Krukenberg. He had come to Berlin at the last moment with a *Kampfgruppe* from the *33. Waffen-Grenadier-Division der SS "Charlemagne"*. Ziegler's relief was a senseless decision. Ziegler could no longer hold the positions with decimated formations. Everything was lacking. Tanks, guns and trucks were blown up because ammunition had run out.

During the night of 24/25 April, the remnants of the *16./SS-Panzer-Grenadier-Regiment 24 "Danmark"* and the regimental assault platoon provided security at the Jungfernheide. They oriented to the northwest, since the enemy was also expected from that direction.

SS-Untersturmführer Christensen and *SS-Oberscharführer* Illum, who were holding together the remnants of the above-named units, had taken quarters in a little summer inn. In addition to several vehicles, the small fighting force still had a radio. On 24 April the radio operator had vainly attempted to contact the division, but at that time the division no longer had a radio set.

SS-Untersturmführer Dirksen arrived in the morning of 25 April with new orders: "*Gruppe* Christensen/Illum will be relieved during the day by *Volkssturm* and employed with the *III./SS-Panzer-Grenadier-Regiment 24 "Danmark"* at Neukölln.

Shortly thereafter the conversation turned to the commander who had been killed on the preceding day, Per Sörensen. The men decided that Dirksen should go to the division to see whether a few men of the old

Freikorps should be permitted to attend to the burial. They remembered that, in the confusion at Strausberg, *SS-Obersturmbannführer* Klotz had been left lying unburied in a chapel. That should not happen to Per Sörensen.

Dirksen drove back. The division made no objections and assembled an honor guard. Three combat engineers made a coffin. The proprietor of the inn suggested the cemetery at Lake Plötzen as the final resting place.

After a lot of back and forth with the director of the cemetery, a burial plot was finally assigned and the grave dug. The truck arrived with the deceased. Eight radio operators and the old *SS-Sturmscharführer* Hermann served as honor guard. The coffin was placed on the planks and the little ceremony began.

The two Danish officers fought for composure and gave *SS-Sturmscharführer* Hermann the sign. He stepped to the open grave:

We stand here at a grave and take leave of a courageous Danish comrade who was an exemplary officer and the leader of *SS-Panzer-Grenadier-Regiment 24 "Danmark"* — Per Sörensen!

At this time I must also offer thanks from my countrymen to whom you and many of your Danish comrades have remained loyal to the end. May you find peace here in the heart of this bleeding city!

While Hermann spoke, tears ran down the cheeks of all those present. Then Hermann gave the sign to lower the casket. Three salvos rang out over the open grave. A woman threw flowers into the grave. Each of the men threw in a handful of earth. *Ich hatte einen Kameraden* closed the burial ceremony.

The final phase of the Battle of Berlin began on 25 April. In Neukölln, the defenders on the tributary canal of the Spree had to fall back. Soviet tanks rolled across the Tempelhof airfield. The Russians were at Spandau and at the Avus. Berlin was encircled! The time of the small assault troops had arrived. There were no more battalions. There were signs of sinking combat morale as the rush of events threw together officers and soldiers, *Panzergrenadiere*, artillerists, tank crews, *Volkssturm* men, aviators, Hitler Youth, men of the *Waffen-SS* and of the navy. The fronts became increasingly enmeshed. Blocks of houses, piles of debris and house facades were the scenes of the fighting.

Armored spearheads of the 1st Ukrainian Front, coming from the southeast, already engaged the movements of the *LVI. Panzer-Korps* on the morning of 24 April. The 8th Guards Army of the 1st Belorussian Front, some of whose units had crossed the Dahme at Grünau and Schmöckwitz, exerted pressure from the east. The spearheads of both fronts joined hands that same day at the Schönefeld airfield. With that action, the southern group of the *9. Armee* was surrounded. According to statements by Weidling, all of his formations that came into Berlin had a total strength of 15,000 men. Added to that were the *Volkssturm* units that were then locally attached.

On 24 April, when the Battle of Berlin developed fully, many supply units still got out of Berlin on *Reichstraße 5* before that was closed off by the Russians at Nauen. On that same day, as described above, the Danish commander of *SS-Panzer-Grenadier-Regiment 24 "Danmark"*, Per Sörensen, was killed while holding open the Spree crossings in Ober-Schöneweide. That day the *33. Waffen-Grenadier-Division der SS "Charlemagne" (französische Nr. 1)*, which had been badly battered in Lower Pomerania and which was being refitted in the Neustrelitz area, received orders to organize a *Kampfgruppe* to relieve Berlin.

The *Kampfgruppe* consisted of combat-ready units of the division that were combined into a battalion commanded by *SS-Hauptsturmführer* Fenet and of the division *Begleit-Kompanie* (headquarters escort company) commanded by *SS-Obersturmführer* Weber. The *Kampfgruppe* was brought into Berlin, shortly before the outer ring around Berlin was closed on 25 April at Ketzin, by the division commander, *Generalmajor der Waffen-SS Dr. jur.* Krukenberg. Krukenberg spoke perfect French and possessed intimate local knowledge of Berlin. At about the same time Russian and American spearheads joined hands at Torgau on the Elbe. The French volunteers were brought forward to Neukölln and attached to the *11. SS-Freiwilligen-Panzer-Grenadier-Division "Nordland"*. Dr. Krukenberg was given acting command of the division after the former commander, *Generalmajor der Waffen-SS* Ziegler, was placed under house arrest.

***

At this point, let us see what was happening to the other formations of the *III. (germanisches) SS-Panzer-Korps*.

The *LVI. Panzer-Korps* was swept away by a massed commitment of infantry and armored divisions west of Küstrin. The northern wing of the *9. Armee* — the *101. Armee-Korps* — was forced to the north behind the Hohenzollern Canal. The southern wing, the *XI. SS-Korps*, held temporarily at Frankfurt/Oder, but then had to be pulled back under the weight of the Soviet attacks and threats to its flanks. It ended up in the Halbe Pocket that formed between Zhukov's (central) and Konjew's (southern) advancing formations.

General Weidling's *LVI. Panzer-Korps* was split up. In its sector, Zhukov's armor rolled forward to Berlin on *Reichsstraße 1* and *Reichsstraße 158*. Like giant serpents, his armies rolled through Strausberg, Werneuchen and Eberswalde. Zhukov's northern group rolled through Birkenwerder past Oranienburg and toward Nauen.

Marshal Konjew's 1st Ukrainian Front rapidly gained ground to the west from the Forst area and swept away the German *4. Panzer-Armee*. An assault group soon reached the Elbe at Torgau and joined hands with the US 1st Army. Konjew's main forces, however, turned to the north and threatened Berlin from the south.

Somewhat later, Marshal Rokossowski's 2nd Belorussian Front attacked near Stettin and threw back the *3. Panzer-Armee.*

In detail: On 18 April, the *23. SS-Freiwilligen-Panzergrenadier-Division "Nederland"* with *SS-Freiwilligen-Panzer-Grenadier-Regiment 48 "General Seyffard"* and the *II./* and *III./SS-Artillerie-Regiment 54* was sent to the *XI. SS-Korps.* It occupied new positions southwest of Müncheberg. After bloody fighting, and after it had became evident that encirclement threatened in the area southeast of Berlin, *Kampfgruppe "Nederland"* and other units of the *9. Armee* fought their way back. A shortage of ammunition and fuel led to the loss of all heavy equipment. *SS-Obersturmbannführer* Scheibe, the commander of *SS-Freiwilligen-Panzer-Grenadier-Regiment 48 "General Seyffard"*, and many other members of the division were killed. Every step westward had to be fought for. The remnants were able to fight their way through toward Wittenberg to *Armee Wenck.* The *12. Armee* was formed in the Wittenberg area under General Wenck. All available men who could carry arms from the Saale/Elbe area were sent to the *12. Armee.*

In the north, *Armee-Abteilung Steiner* was formed from the staff of the *11. Panzer-Armee.* It consisted of all available men who could carry weapons between the Oder and Schleswig-Holstein: Seamen, aviators, replacement units and remnants of shattered divisions were sent to it. In the end, *Armee-Abteilung Steiner* comprised seven battalions and the *4. SS-Polizei-Division,* which had been brought up from Hela.

And what about the *Generalkommando III. (germanisches) SS-Panzer-Korps?* After the *11. SS-Freiwilligen-Panzer-Grenadier-Division "Nordland"* and the *23. SS-Freiwilligen-Panzergrenadier-Division "Nederland"* had been attached to other army corps, this corps headquarters had the *27. SS-Freiwilligen-Grenadier-Division "Langemarck"* and the *28. SS-Freiwilligen-Panzergrenadier-Division "Wallonien"* at its disposal. In addition, it also had *SS-Freiwilligen-Panzer-Grenadier-Regiment 49 "de Ruyter"* and the *I./SS-Artillerie-Regiment 54,* both of which were staged south of Gartz.

On 18 April 1945 the forward observer of the *2./SS-Artillerie-Regiment 54* noted in his personal diary:

No radio contact. During the morning the combat engineers were actively working in the Nipperwiese and the Oder marshes. Heavy weapons went into position. The enemy searched for mines. He occupied assembly areas in the Oder marshes, east of the river. Everything was visible. The best of targets and no order to "Fire at will!"

Because of shortage of ammunition, the German guns did not fire. The Soviets were able to carry out preparations for their attack in the Schwedt — Stettin sector without interference.

On 20 April the positions of a police regiment at the demolished *Autobahn* bridge south of Stettin were under Soviet fire. The enemy assault that followed forced the police regiment onto the high ground southeast of

Hohenzahden. By 1500 hours the Soviets captured the hills. The Soviet bridgehead had been formed.

One battalion of the *28. SS-Freiwilligen-Panzergrenadier-Division "Wallonien"* was employed for an immediate counterattack. An artillery preparation was needed to support the counterattack but did not take place due to lack of ammunition.

The Walloon volunteers stormed the high ground without support, recaptured Niederzahden and thus regained command of the river crossing. However, the Soviets threw new troops over the river during the night. The river crossing was, for all practical purposes, no longer contested. Artillery without ammunition and a *Luftwaffe* without fuel! The infantry weapons of the Walloon volunteers were powerless.

Nevertheless, the Walloon volunteers did their best to hurl the enemy back into the river on 21 April. The attempt failed with high casualties. In similar fashion, there was seesaw fighting at two additional bridgeheads upstream. The Oder defense fell apart on 23 April between Schwedt and Stettin. The battered German formations fell back on defensive positions farther to the west.

There was a similar development at Greifenhagen. *Kampfgruppe Schellong*, as the remnants of the *27. SS-Grenadier-Division "Langemarck"* were also called, blocked the bridges across the East and West Oder, but soon had to give up even the West Oder line. Three battalions, and the artillery regiment that was still in training, took another firm stand in the Schöningen — Pargow — Staffelde — Mescherin line.

But that line also could not be held with weak forces against a superior enemy. On the railroad line between Kolbitzow and Tantow a new main line of resistance was formed. That could be held initially. During the night of 23/24 April, the Soviets forced their way through to Tantow with infantry and armor. *Kampfgruppe "Langemarck"* fell back to the west. Units of *"Langemarck"* and *"Wallonien"* held the Brüssow line until 25 April.

Farther south, with its command post in Kasekow, was *SS-Freiwilligen-Panzer-Grenadier-Regiment 49 "de Ruyter"*. That regiment also had to fall back, occupying a new defensive position in Ratzebruch (east of Gramzow).

"Hitlerjugend"-Bataillon 27 was able to link up with *Kampfgruppe "Langemarck"*. Under *SS-Hauptsturmführer* Stange it fought bravely in the Prenzlau area. However, on 25 April the Soviets captured Prenzlau.

In the meantime, Berlin had become encircled. On 24 April Konjew's and Zhukov's forces joined hands at Potsdam. On that same day, Hitler named *General* Weidling as the Berlin local-area commander.

General Steiner received orders to attack from the north with his army group — which was not an army group at all — and relieve the beleaguered capital. In the south, *Armee Wenck* was supposed to advance against Beelitz, Ferch and Potsdam and break the stranglehold.

Armeegruppe Steiner managed no more than a shallow thrust over the Finow Canal before its strength was exhausted. In the south, Wenck made only slow forward progress.

General Steiner, concerned for his volunteers who had been drawn into Berlin, ordered the commander of the *4. SS-Polizei-Grenadier-Division*, *SS-Standartenführer* Harzer, to hold open the Spandau bridge on the *Heerstraße* with his right wing. The message was sent by radio to the fighting troops: "The *Heerstraße* is being held open to the west. Come out!"

But that did not take place. Harzer's companies could not hold for long and, by then, most of the German troops fighting in Berlin no longer had telephone or radio communications. On 25 April there was heavy fighting in and around Spandau. On Weidling's map of the city, additional thick red arrows were aimed at Reinickendorf, Weißensee, Treptow, Neukölln, Tempelhof, Grunewald and Dahlem.

Wenck's attack groups reached the area of Ferch on 27 April. The encircled garrison of Potsdam and 3,000 wounded broke out and were received by Wenck's forces. Ten thousand men were saved. With that, however, the offensive strength of the *12. Armee* was broken. Nevertheless, Wenck was able to hold on long enough for the remnants of the *9. Armee*, including the remnants of the *11. SS-Freiwilligen-Panzer-Grenadier-Division "Nordland"*, to reach his lines from the Halbe Pocket. An additional 40,000 men crossed the Elbe with the *12. Armee* and made it into American captivity.

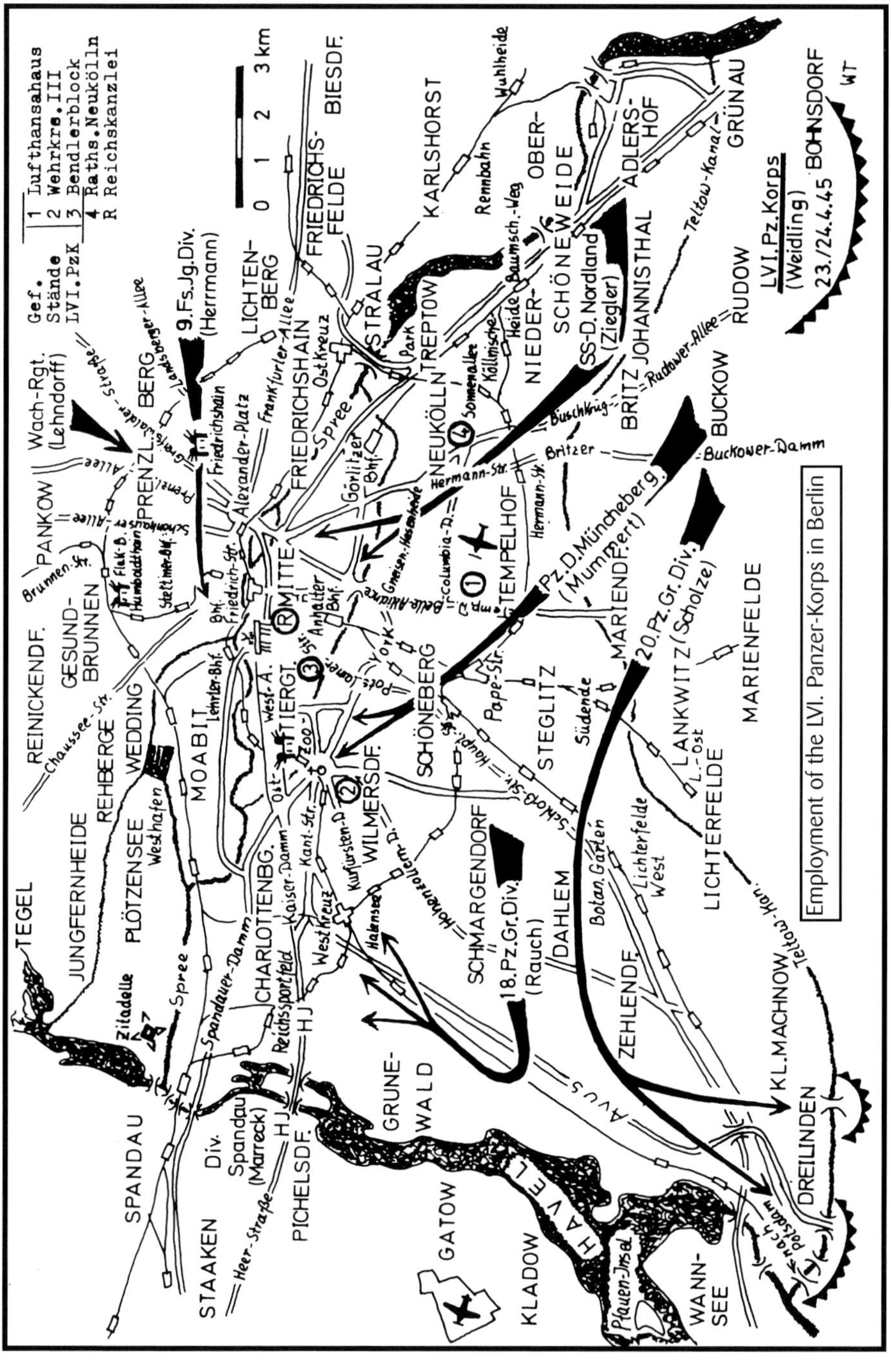
Gef.
Stände
LVI.PzK
1 Lufthansahaus
2 Wehrkrs.III
3 Bendlerblock
4 Raths.Neukölln
R Reichskanzlei
0 1 2 3 km
LVI.Pz.Korps
(Weidling)
23./24.4.45
WT
9.Fs.Jg.Div.
(Herrmann)
Wach-Rgt.
(Lehndorff)
SS-D.Nordland
(Ziegler)
Pz.D.Müncheberg
(Mummert)
20.Pz.Gr.Div.
(Scholze)
18.Pz.Gr.Div.
(Rauch)
Div.
Spandau
(Marreck)
HJ
TEGEL
JUNGFERNHEIDE
PLÖTZENSEE
REINICKENDF.
REHBERGE
WEDDING
GESUNDBRUNNEN
PANKOW
PRENZL. BERG
LICHTENBERG
FRIEDRICHSHAIN
FRIEDRICHSFELDE
BIESDF.
KARLSHORST
STRALAU
TREPTOW
NEUKÖLLN
NIEDERSCHÖNEWEIDE
OBERSCHÖNEWEIDE
ADLERSHOF
GRÜNAU
BOHNSDORF
JOHANNISTHAL
BRITZ
BUCKOW
RUDOW
TEMPELHOF
MARIENDF.
MARIENFELDE
LANKWITZ
LICHTERFELDE
STEGLITZ
SCHÖNEBERG
MITTE
TIERGT.
MOABIT
CHARLOTTENBG.
WILMERSDF.
SCHMARGENDORF
DAHLEM
ZEHLENDF.
KL.MACHNOW
DREILINDEN
WANNSEE
GRUNEWALD
GATOW
KLADOW
HAVEL
PICHELSDF.
STAAKEN
SPANDAU
Zitadelle
Spree
Westhafen
Reichssportfeld
Spandauer-Damm
Heer-Straße
Kaiser-Damm
Kant-Str.
Kurfürsten-D.
Hohenzollern-D.
Westkreuz
Halensee
Zoo
West-A.
Ost
Lehrter-Bhf.
Bhf. Friedrich-Str.
Stettiner-Bhf.
Flak-B. Humboldthain
Brunnen-Str.
Chaussee-Str.
Schönhauser-Allee
Prenzl.-Allee
Greifswalder-Straße
Landsberger-Allee
Alexander-Platz
Friedrichshain
Frankfurter-Allee
Ostkreuz
Görlitzer Bhf.
Anhalter Bhf.
York
Pots-damer
Belle-Alliance
Gneisen-Hasenheide
Columbia-D.
Hermann-Str.
Sonnenallee
Köllnische Heide
Baumsch.-Weg
Rennbahn
Wuhlheide
Teltow-Kanal
Rudower-Allee
Buschkrug
Britzer
Buckower-Damm
Pape-Str.
Südende
Schloß-Str.
Haupt-Str.
Botan. Garten
Lichterfelde West
L.-Ost
Teltow-Kan.
Potsdam
AVUS
Plauen-Insel
Park

Employment of the LVI. Panzer-Korps in Berlin

25 April: The Russian Assault On The Center Of Berlin

On 25 April, the formations of the *LVI. Panzer-Korps* occupied their new defensive sectors as Weidling ordered:

A and **B** (East Berlin): Immobile units, *Volkssturm* and *Hitlerjugend*, all under the command of *Generalmajor* Bärenfänger

C (Neukölln): *11. SS-Freiwilligen-Panzer-Grenadier-Division "Nordland"* (*Dr.* Krukenberg)

D (Tempelhof and Steglitz): *Panzer-Division "Müncheberg"* (Mummert)

E (southwest Berlin and the Grune Woods): *20. Panzergrenadier-Division* (Scholze)

F (Spandau and Charlottenburg): *Hitlerjugend, Volkssturm* and mixed formations led by *Oberstleutnant* Eder

G and **H** (north Berlin): Mixed formations and remnants of the *9. Fallschirmjäger-Division* (*Oberst* Herrmann)

Z (city center): *Kampfgruppe* (*Generalmajor der Waffen-SS*) *Mohnke* and *Luftwaffe* forces from the German Air Ministry (*Oberstleutnant* Seifert).

Reserve: The remainder of the *18. Panzergrenadier-Division* in the Grune Woods. While the German formations were listed with their original designations, they were only a shell of what they had been.

While the new organization of the defensive sectors was still in progress, the Russians started their major assault on the center of Berlin. Tschuikow wrote in his memoirs of immense artillery fire and two bombing attacks with 1,486 aircraft. There was no more German fighter defense.

In the Neukölln sector, a Russian attack on Treptower Park proved threatening to the *11. SS-Freiwilligen-Panzer-Grenadier-Division "Nordland"*. For a time, the remnants of *SS-Panzer-Grenadier-Regiment 23 "Norge"*, *SS-Artillerie-Kampfgruppe Potschla* (employed as infantry) and the *SS-Panzer-Aufklärungs-Abteilung 11* held their positions along the ring road at Sonnenallee and at the Landwehr Canal, as did the remnants of *SS-Panzer-Grenadier-Regiment 24 "Danmark"* at the urban rail line at Neukölln and Hermannstraße. However, due to enemy pressure and the great gaps in the lines, the German units had to fall back farther and farther into the core of the city. Similar developments took place in the other defensive sectors of

Berlin.

In the meantime, the French *SS-Bataillon Fenet* and *Kompanie Weber* (*33. Waffen-SS-Grenadier-Division "Charlemagne"*) had arrived at the Gneisenau army post at the Tempelhof airfield. *Dr.* Krukenberg employed them immediately as tank hunter/killer teams in dangerous gaps in the front at the Hermannsplatz. In the evening and during the following night the French knocked out 14 Russian tanks.

During the situation conference in the bunker at the *Reich* Chancellery during the night of 25/26 April, *General* Weidling gave a pessimistic report on the defense of Berlin. *General* Krebs, the chief of staff of the *OKH*, gave a far more optimistic sketch of the overall situation and looked to the relief attacks that Steiner and Wenck had been ordered to mount for Berlin's salvation. Dönitz also wanted to contribute to that and expressed the wish that his best people, the cadre of the *U-Boot* schools, be flown into Berlin.

On the basis of *General* Krebs' optimistic report, *General* Weidling ordered the *11. SS-Freiwilligen-Panzer-Grenadier-Division "Nordland"* and *Panzer-Division "Müncheberg"* to launch a counterattack to clean up the dangerous penetrations at Tempelhof Airfield and in Neukölln.

During the morning hours of 26 April, elements of *Panzer-Division "Müncheberg"* attacked southward from the northwest end of the Tempelhof Airfield with its last ten tanks, but the attack soon came to a halt in the Russian defensive fire.

SS-Bataillon Fenet assembled before daybreak at the Hermannsplatz and at the Hasenheide and set out with the last tanks of the *11. SS-Freiwilligen-Panzer-Grenadier-Division "Nordland"* along the Hermannstraße and the present-day Karl-Marx-Straße to recapture the ring-road position on both sides of the Neukölln railroad station.

When *SS-Hauptsturmführer* Fenet's battalion set out at 0600 hours, the Russian assault on the center of Berlin had begun. Nevertheless, the French soldiers moved forward in the streets to the south and southeast with pluck and bravado. A few tanks and assault guns of the *11. SS-Freiwilligen-Panzer-Grenadier-Division "Nordland"* provided support. The attack gained ground in bitter house-to-house and street fighting and over walls and ruins. At the Neukölln city hall, the battalion's reserve platoon was caught in a sudden concentration of artillery fire as it was closing up. Fifteen French soldiers were killed and almost all of the other members of the platoon were wounded.

Farther forward, their comrades fought it out with the Russians and forced their way ever closer to the ring road, which was to be the new main line of resistance. At about 0700 hours the battalion was ordered to halt the attack and go back to its starting position. The French volunteers did not understand what was going on at all. Go back now, when they were so close to the objective of their attack? They were called back, however, because the attack of their neighbor on the right, *Panzer-Division "Müncheberg"*, had been unsuccessful and also because the defense had collapsed at other locations. Weidling therefore resolved to pull the front back to the canal system of the inner city.

SS-Hauptsturmführer Fenet, wounded in the foot and supported by his messengers, still led his battalion. He checked with his company commanders. They agreed to hold fast in the Neukölln city hall until new orders arrived. The city hall and its immediate surroundings became a center of defense that the French held with iron determination. The constantly repeated Russian attacks were repulsed and hurled back with bloody losses. Approximately 30 Russian tanks and antitank guns were knocked out by the French soldiers and the few tanks of the *11. SS-Freiwilligen-Panzer-Grenadier-Division "Nordland"* in the attack and then in the defense. Messengers raced through the ruins under extremely heavy fire and maintained contact with the companies. Twenty-year old Millet was conspicuous for his exemplary bravery. He was killed in the afternoon at the Neukölln city hall.

The Russians exerted every effort to capture the city hall. The situation became critical when Russian forces worked their way around that defensive bastion. They then approached from the rear to within 100 meters. At that point, another attack was launched with armored support. At that crucial juncture, a tank from the *11. SS-Freiwilligen-Panzer-Grenadier-Division "Nordland"* approached from a side street and knocked out the foremost Russian T 34, giving the defenders a little breathing space. The defenders knocked out two more Russian tanks with *Panzerfäuste*. As a result, that attack also collapsed.

In the afternoon of April 26 the situation of the French defenders at the Neukölln city hall became increasingly critical. There was no longer any contact to the flanks. Nevertheless, the position was still held due to the unshakable fighting spirit of the volunteers. The 19-year-old Roger particularly excelled in hand-to-hand combat. He was called "the black devil" by his comrades. And Cap, the diminutive Flemish soldier, held an entire street in check with his machine gun and stopped the Russian advance. When several assault guns rolled back to resupply with ammunition, the situation again became extremely critical.

At 1900 hours it was reported to Fenet that the Russians were close to the Hermannsplatz. Based on that bad news, the battalion commander decided to fall back to the only street that was still clear of the enemy. In leapfrog fashion, the battalion and the three *Sturmgeschütze* fell back and firmly established themselves on the Hermannsplatz.

On 25 and 26 April, *SS-Bataillon Mrugalla*, assembled from Berlin offices and replacement units, held the Silesian railroad station. *Kampfgruppe Bärenfänger* held at Friedrichshain and Prenzlauer-Berg. The *11. SS-Freiwilligen-Panzer-Grenadier-Division "Nordland"* was located between the

Görlitz railroad station and Neukölln. *Panzer-Division "Müncheberg"* was at Tempelhof, and the *18. Panzergrenadier-Division*, under *Generalmajor* Rauch, was in Schmargendorf and Schöneberg.

In the evening of 26 April, based on his personally conducted inspection of the front, *General* Weidling reported the visible signs of disintegration among his units to the chief of staff of the *OKH*, *General* Krebs. He also reported the deep Russian penetrations at Spandau, in the west harbor area, in the Grune Woods and Zehlendorf, in Tempelhof, Neukölln, Friedrichshain and in the Jungfernheide. Krebs again calmed Weidling with the assurance that the attack by *Armee Wenck* would get through on the next day at the latest and reestablish contact with Berlin. In actual fact, Wenck's attack made only slow forward progress and had set as its primary objective the relief of the *9. Armee*, which had been encircled at Halbe after being held too long by Hitler in positions on the Oder and in the city of Frankfurt. A further assault by both armies to Berlin, as ordered by Hitler, was pure Utopia.

During the night of 27 April, the defenders of Berlin fell back to the innermost ring of defense. The *11. SS-Freiwilligen-Panzer-Grenadier-Division "Nordland"* assembled the remnants of *SS-Panzer-Grenadier-Regiment 23 "Norge"* and *SS-Panzer-Grenadier-Regiment 24 "Danmark"* and employed them at the Anhalter railroad station — Cottbuser Platz — Gendarmen Markt. According to statements by *Dr.* Krukenberg, the regiments were filled out with *Hitlerjugend*, *Volkssturm* and men who had become separated from units of all branches of the *Wehrmacht*. As a result, they had attained a strength of about 600 men. Sections and *Kampfgruppen* were formed that were designated with the name of the officer or noncommissioned officer leading them. For example, the group of *SS-Unterscharführer* Burgkart, with the division staff until 25 April, had a strength of 30 men. It consisted of members of all units of the *Wehrmacht, Hitlerjungen* and two *Bund deutscher Mädel* girls (League of German Girls), who were employed as messengers.

A 100-man *Kampfgruppe* commanded by *SS-Untersturmführer* Bachmann was formed from the trains elements of *SS-Panzer-Grenadier-Regiment 24 "Danmark"* and the lightly wounded there who were staged at the Berlin Zoo. *Kampfgruppe Bachmann* was employed in a semicircle at the Hallesches Tor with the task of blocking off the Hallescher Platz to the south. Initially, there was no contact with *SS-Panzer-Grenadier-Regiment 23 "Norge"* on the left.

In the evening of 26 April, the French soldiers of *SS-Bataillon Fenet* continued to hold off the Russians at the Hermannsplatz. Supported by several *Sturmgeschütze*, they repulsed all attacks and knocked out several Russian tanks. As midnight approached, the French soldiers went back as ordered and assembled in the Thomaskeller near the Anhalter railroad station. The battalion was then inserted between *SS-Panzer-Grenadier-Regiment 23 "Norge"* and *SS-Panzer-Grenadier-Regiment 24 "Danmark"*. The commander of the *1./SS-*

Bataillon Fenet, SS-Untersturmführer Labourdette, was killed during those operations. The command post of the *11. SS-Freiwilligen-Panzer-Grenadier-Division "Nordland"* was set up in the opera house on the Unter-den-Linden. A *Kampfgruppe* commanded by *Luftwaffe Oberst* Seifert went into position on the right. *Kampfgruppe Seifert* had its command post in the *Reich* Air Ministry.

The defensive sector of the *11. SS-Freiwilligen-Panzer-Grenadier-Division "Nordland"* then began at the Jannowitz Bridge on the Spree and ran approximately along Neander- and Prinzenstraße as far as the Landwehr Canal. It then ran along the canal Belle-Alliance-Platz. A *Kampfgruppe* defended the Anhalter railroad station. The neighbor on the right was *Kampfgruppe Seifert*.

The last heavy weapons of *11. SS-Freiwilligen-Panzer-Grenadier-Division "Nordland"* —infantry guns and light field-howitzers — were positioned in the zoo, where the trains units were also staged. The last combat-ready assault guns and tanks, including some *Königstiger*, were positioned on the streets that led into the center of the city. Everything that was still available was brought in for the defense of the inner ring, but there was little available. The final stages of the Battle of Berlin began under a bad sign.

The Final Phase of the Battle for Berlin

In addition to *Bataillon Fenet* of the *33. Waffen-Grenadier-Division der SS "Charlemagne" (französische Nr. 1)*, a battalion came by road to Berlin before the city was completely encircled on 24 April. It was from the *15. Waffen-Grenadier-Division der SS (lettische Nr. 1)*, which had been badly battered in Lower Pomerania and had been staged in the Neuruppin area.

One day later, *Flugkapitän* Hanna Reitsch flew the new Commander –in-Chief of the *Luftwaffe*, von Greim, into Berlin in a *Fieseler Storch*. Göring was in southern Germany and was laying claim as Hitler's successor. As a result, he had been removed by Hitler as Commander-in-Chief of the *Luftwaffe*. The small plane crash-landed on the *Ost-West-Achse* (East-West Axis), which had been converted into a landing strip.

On 28 April, a daredevil pilot flew out both of the injured to Rechlin. During the night of 26/27 April a weak naval battalion (von Schulen) was flown in to Gatow and led on to the inner city of Berlin where it was attached to *11. SS-Freiwilligen-Panzer-Grenadier-Division "Nordland"*. That was the last use of the Gatow airfield. On 27 April it was captured by the Soviets.

By the evening of 26 April, the defenders in the northern part of the city of Berlin were forced back to the urban railroad ring. The Humboldthain *Flak* tower was the backbone of the defense there. In the eastern part of the city, the front took the following shape: Prenzlauer-Allee — Friedrichshain *Flak* tower — dropping back to the Alexanderplatz — Schloß — Spittelmarkt — Belle-Alliance-Platz and then, cutting through Schmargendorf and the Grune Woods to the Havel, including the Pichelsdorf bridges. All signs pointed to the Soviets starting their major attack on the inner city on the next day.

Under the shadow of the impending attack, the defenses of the center of Berlin were divided into east and west sectors. *Oberstleutnant* Seifert commanded the west sector with his command post in the *Reich* Air Ministry. *Generalmajor der Waffen-SS* Dr. Krukenberg commanded the east sector with his command post in the State Opera House. The Wilhelmstraße was the dividing line.

Initially, the western sector was only weakly held, since *Panzerdivision* "Müncheberg" was still defending in Wilmersdorf and Schöneberg. The eastern sector, in which the remnants of *SS-Panzer-Grenadier-Regiment 23 "Norge"*, *SS-Panzer-Grenadier-Regiment 24 "Danmark"*, *SS-Panzer-Aufklärungs-Abteilung 11* and *SS-Bataillon Fenet* had organized the defense, was already being probed by weak Soviet attacks. Weidling wrote the following in his report on the final fighting:

At 0500 hours on 27 April, the Russians began their major attack on both sides of the Hohenzollerndamm after a heavy artillery preparation and very strong support from the air. My command post at the end of the Hohenzollerndamm in the buildings of *Wehrkreis III* was under heavy fire...Heavy artillery fire covered the Potsdamer Platz and Leipziger Straße. Brick and stone dust hung in the air like thick fog. The motor vehicle in which I was going to *Generalmajor* Bärenfänger (sector A) made only slow progress. Shells were bursting everywhere...We left the vehicle near the Schloß and proceeded...on foot to the Alexanderplatz...We had to move forward by dashes across the Alexanderplatz to the subway station...From platform E we had to go through the subway tunnel to the Schillingstraße station, where Bärenfänger had his command post...Bärenfänger reported heavy attacks on the Frankfurter Straße...He requested additional forces and ammunition be brought up. I could not promise him anything...On the way back I visited a totally overfilled hospital. The doctors had virtually no capability to care for the wounded. Light and water were totally lacking.

Marshal Konjew's 1st Ukrainian Front advanced farther into Berlin from the south with the 3rd and 4th Guards Tank Armies. In the other sectors, it was Marshal Zhukov's 1st Belorussian Front. Tschuikow's 8th Guards Army

311

was in the southeast and Bersarin's 5th Shock Army and Katukow's 1st Guards Tank Army were in the east. The 3rd Shock Army and the 2nd Guards Tank Army came from the north with a broad envelopment of the inner city to the west.

Armor supported the Red Army soldiers in the streets. The racket of the weapons and the hiss of the flamethrowers were everywhere. The German lines broke in many places. Only a few units held their positions. Remnants of the *9. Fallschirmjäger-Division* (*Oberst* Hermann) and *Wach-Regiment Lehndorff* from *Panzer-Korps Großdeutschland* were in north Berlin. In the east, *Generalmajor* Bärenfänger commanded a hastily assembled formation of *Hitlerjugend*, *Volkssturm* and *Waffen-SS* (*Bataillon Mrugalla*). In the southeast were remnants of *11. SS-Freiwilligen-Panzer-Grenadier-Division "Nordland"* (*Dr.* Krukenberg). Remnants of *Panzerdivision "Müncheberg"* (Mummert) were in Wilmersdorf and the *18. Panzergrenadier-Division* (Rauch) was in the Grune Woods. *Hitlerjugend* commanded by *Obergebietsführer Dr.* Schlünder defended the Havel bridges at Pichelsdorf. The *20. Panzergrenadier-Division* (Scholze) was in the southern Grune Woods and held the bridges over the Teltow Canal open for Wenck's *12. Armee*, which had been given the mission of relieving Berlin from the south. In sector Z (for *Zentrum/Zitadelle* around the *Reich* Chancellery) were hastily assembled forces that had been thrown together under command of *Generalmajor der Waffen-SS* Mohnke.

A counterattack by the *18. Panzergrenadier-Division* along the Avus quickly collapsed and the attackers were forced back to the Kurfürsten-Damm. A *Tiger* of *schwere SS-Panzer-Abteilung 503* at the Halensee railroad station and another *Tiger* at the Heerstraße station stood up to the attacking Russians and solidly supported the German infantry.

The Belle-Alliance-Platz was the key to Wilhelmstraße and Friedrichstraße. Those streets led directly to the *Reich* Chancellery. It was therefore understandable that the Russians made particular efforts at that square and along those streets since they hoped to capture Hitler alive.

When the bridges at the Hallesches Tor were prepared for demolition, the defenders fell back to the Hallescher Platz. The bridges went up in the air as the Russians were just in front of them. Nevertheless, the attackers attempted to continue advancing again and again. *SS-Unterstumführer* Bachmann of *SS-Panzer-Grenadier-Regiment 24 "Danmark"* held the position with his *Kampfgruppe,* which included Germans, Danes and ethnic Germans from Transylvania and the Banat. Again and again, artillery, mortar, antitank and tank rounds hailed down on the defenders. The situation became critical when the Russians then attempted to cross the Landwehr Canal at numerous places and succeeded in several. The only reserve, the platoon of Danish *SS-Unterstumführer* Dirksen, came to the assistance of the defenders at that hour of extreme need and the position held for that day.

The remnants of *SS-Panzer-Aufklärungs-Abteilung 11*, consisting of

Germans, ethnic Germans, Danes and Swedes, fought at the Anhalter railroad station. In the evening, the battalion fell back to the north into Seifert's sector.

On 27 April, the battle began in the inner city. The French volunteers of *Bataillon Fenet of* the *33. Waffen-SS-Grenadier-Division "Charlemagne" (1. französische)* fought their way back from Neukölln and assembled at the city-center railroad station. *SS-Hauptsturmführer* Fenet was supported by loyal messengers and did not leave his people in spite of his wounds. *Dr. Krukenberg,* who succeeded Joachim Ziegler as the commander of *11. SS-Freiwilligen-Panzer-Grenadier-Division "Nordland",* knew how his French soldiers had performed in Neukölln and decorated the brave with the Iron Cross.

***

A *Kampfgruppe* of about 100 men was put together from the trains elements of *SS-Panzer-Grenadier-Regiment 24 "Danmark".* It also included many men who had become separated from their units and men who had been lightly wounded. The commander of the *Kampfgruppe* was *SS-Untersturmführer* Bachmann, the leader of the communications section of the *II./SS-Panzer-Grenadier-Regiment 24 "Danmark".* While the fighting raged all around, *Kampfgruppe Bachmann* occupied positions on 26 April at the Hallesches Tor . In a half-circle, the position barred the Hallescher Platz toward the south and had contact with the units of *11. SS-Freiwilligen-Panzer-Grenadier-Division "Nordland"* that had pulled back to the Kottbuser Tor.

On 27 April, the Soviets launched concentric attacks. In many places there was no longer any holding them back. *Volkssturm,* staffs of the units stationed in Berlin and soldiers without combat experience streamed back into the inner city. Everywhere yawned gaps that could no longer be closed. Only a few combat-experienced units still stood against the Soviets. *Generalmajor* Bärenfänger commanded the defense in the Prenzlauer/Frankfurter Allee from his command post in the Schillingstraße subway station. To the south, the last remnants of *11. SS-Freiwilligen-Panzer-Grenadier-Division "Nordland", 33. Waffen-SS-Grenadier-Division "Charlemagne" (1. französische)* and the Latvian *Füsilier-Bataillon Nr. 15* fought against the Soviets. To the west, the remnants of the *18.* and *20. Panzer-Grenadier-Divisionen, Wach-Bataillon Großdeutschland* and *Panzerdivision "Müncheberg"* were decisively engaged. There were even remnants of a Spanish company and a group of Swiss volunteers in action.

In the meantime, Hitler sat in the bunker at the *Reich* Chancellery and waited for the great turnaround that Steiner and Wenck would bring to pass. However, the relief forces had long since been brought to a standstill. All the radio messages starting with, "I order...." were to no avail. On 27 April, the final collapse began.

On that day the situation also became critical for *Kampfgruppe Bachmann*. Heavy artillery fire took the first casualties. The fragmentation effect was tremendous on the cobblestone streets. The Hallesches Tor and Belle-Alliance-Platz were keys to Wilhelmstraße and Friedrichstraße. As noon approached, the Soviets pressed against the German centers of resistance in the Charlottenstraße. The bridge east of the Hallesches Tor was blown up. When the demolition party prepared the bridge at the Hallesches Tor for demolition, *Kampfgruppe Bachmann* was pulled back to the Belle-Alliance-Platz. Although the bridge was blown, it was only damaged and remained passable for armor. In the meantime, *SS-Untersturmführer* Dirksen had brought up all available remnants of *SS-Panzer-Grenadier-Regiment 24 "Danmark"* and had taken over that sector of the defense. There were no longer heavy weapons. Even the *13./SS-Panzer-Grenadier-Regiment 24 "Danmark"* was employed as an infantry company; its guns were back with the trains elements.

The remnants of *SS-Panzer-Aufklärungs-Abteilung 11* defended the Anhalter railroad station. Two infantry guns of the *8.SS-Panzer-Grenadier-Regiment 24 "Danmark"* supported Saalbach's men.

The defenders of the Belle-Alliance-Platz came under fire from Soviet tanks. At 1430 hours a Soviet tank was positioned on the damaged bridge and provided support for an infantry attack along the canal. *SS-Untersturmführer* Dirksen and his men launched an immediate counterattack, which gained them a short breather. One enemy tank was knocked out. Soviet infantry were able to gain a firm foothold in several blocks of houses. *Kampfgruppe Dirksen* was dispersed and forced back to the subway station under the Friedrichstraße, to Charlottenburg and to the north. The stretch of subway beneath the Friedrichstraße had been opened up by several bomb craters. As darkness fell, a machine-pistol and hand-grenade duel developed there with the Germans below and the Russians above. Units of *Kampfgruppe Dirksen* were forced back about 200 meters south of Kochstraße. *SS-Obersturmführer* Christensen was given command of the Friedrichstraße sector. His command post was in the Kochstraße subway station. At that time, the command post of *11. SS-Freiwilligen-Panzer-Grenadier-Division "Nordland"* was in the city-center subway station.

In the meantime, the front became increasingly convoluted in the heart of Berlin. Nobody knew who lurked around the next corner. Every street, every house, every story in every house was bitterly contested. The Russians' primary objective was the *Reich* Chancellery. They wanted to capture Hitler alive. On 28 April the last soldiers of the *33. Waffen-SS-Grenadier-Division "Charlemagne" (1. französische)* were committed at Belle-Alliance-Platz. Six Soviet tanks were knocked out. *SS-Hauptsturmführer* Fenet rallied his men to attack. *SS-Unterscharführer* Vaulot's squad reached the canal one more time, but concentric fire from the ruins and an artillery barrage forced the French soldiers back again.

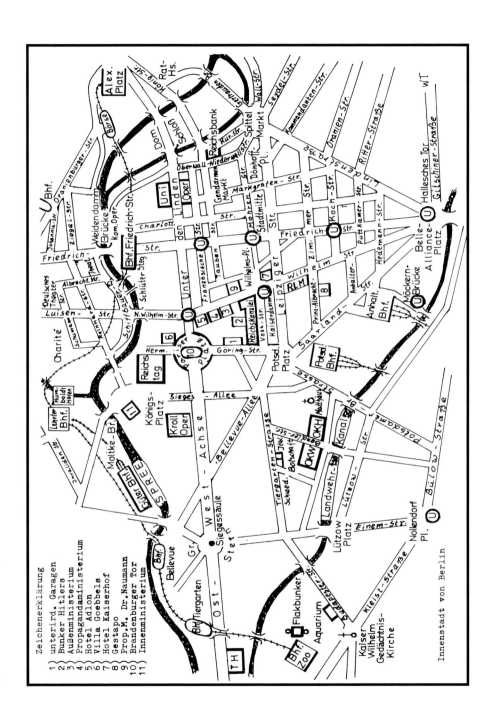

Innenstadt von Berlin

Zeichenerklärung

1) unterird. Garagen
2) Bunker Hitlers
3) Außenministerium
4) Propagandaministerium
5) Hotel Adlon
6) Villa Goebbels
7) Hotel Kaiserhof
8) Gestapo
9) Prop.M. Dr.Naumann
10) Brandenburger Tor
11) Innenministerium

315

On 29 April, the French fighters were able to repulse an armored attack on the Wilhelmstraße. Several volunteers knocked out their fourth and fifth tanks with *Panzerfäuste*. *SS-Unterscharführer* Vaulot was the first French soldier to receive the Knight's Cross. *SS-Oberscharführer* Apollot knocked out six Soviet tanks and, with his squad, brought a Russian attack to a standstill. *SS-Hauptsturmführer* Weber, formerly commander of the French division's combat-training center, kept control of his sector and knocked out his thirteenth tank. Apollot and Weber also received the Knight's Cross, along with *SS-Hauptsturmführer* Fenet, additional brave men of *11. SS-Freiwilligen-Panzer-Grenadier-Division "Nordland"* and *schwere SS-Panzer-Abteilung 503* on 29 April.

Numerous bomb craters had rendered Friedrichstraße impassable for tanks. The men of *Kampfgruppe "Danmark"* had that to thank for the fact that no heavy fighting developed there. They fended off all Soviet infantry advances from their position in the Kochstraße subway station.

That morning, *Kampfgruppe Bachmann* was relieved by men of the *13./SS-Panzer-Grenadier-Regiment 24 "Danmark"*. *Kampfgruppe Bachmann* launched an attack south from the Kochstraße subway station. With losses, Bachmann's men made it to the corner of Friedrichstraße and Puttkamerstraße and were able to establish themselves in the Herold Insurance building. *SS-Untersturmführer* Bachmann was wounded. Two of his men got Bachmann to a provisional hospital in the Hotel Adlon. *SS-Unterscharführer* Scholle's group then established itself firmly in the Herold building.

Kampfgruppe "Charlemagne" adjoined on the right. A *Spieß* from *SS-Panzer-Grenadier-Regiment 24 "Danmark"* and his men had fortified themselves on the left side of the Friedrichstraße. Farther on, in contact with that group, were the remnants of *SS-Panzer-Grenadier-Regiment 23 "Norge" and SS-Panzer-Grenadier-Regiment 24 "Danmark"*, both commanded by *SS-Sturmbannführer* Ternedde. His command post was in the old *Reich* bank. In the evening of 28 April, a 4-kilometer-square sector of the inner city was still held.

During the morning hours of 29 April, a battalion of the 79th Rifle Corps succeeded in crossing the ruined Moltke Bridge over the Spree. The Red Army soldiers occupied a large building and, as ordered, prepared for the assault on the *Reichstag*.

The bitter fighting continued on 29 April. Remnants of *SS-Panzer-Grenadier-Regiment 23 "Norge"* and *SS-Panzer-Grenadier-Regiment 24 "Danmark"* fought at the Spittelmarkt. Here is a report from a small *Kampfgruppe* of *SS-Panzer-Grenadier-Regiment 23 "Norge"*:

The Russians came through the subway and then tried to get into the mountain of ruins through Seydelstraße. But they did not succeed. They responded to their failure with a furious barrage of artillery and mortar fire. It crashed and roared in the ruins. Walls collapsed, timbers and beams flew into the air. Then the fire let up.

The sound of scraping and screeching announced the tanks. The men of *SS-Panzer-Grenadier-Regiment 23 "Norge"* positioned themselves with *Panzerfäuste* in the first story of the Weinitschke House at the corner of Wallstraße.

The tanks fired in all directions. The *Panzerfäuste* answered them. Two Soviet tanks were hit in the Wallstraße. They then blocked the way to the Spittelmarkt. The tanks that were behind them backed up and made it around the corner where the post office was on the square. Three tanks hesitantly felt their way forward and fired for all they were worth. Then they ran out of ammunition and turned around. As they turned, another *Panzerfaust* found its target. The crew of the tank bailed out and disappeared around the Weinitschke corner.

Half an hour went by. The "Norwegians" assembled in a house that was close to the Gertraude bridge and kept a sharp eye on the square. Then there was movement at the subway steps.

A head cautiously rose and looked around. The commander of the *Kampfgruppe* ordered: "Quiet — let them approach! Open fire only on my command!"

Eight Russians then came bent over across the Spittelmarkt. Then the German weapons spoke. Only one of the Russians made it back to the subway. Again a hail of steel came down on the Germans.

Daylight gave way to dull red light from fires. The ruins and remnants of walls gave a spectral effect in the light of the fires. A squad of "Norwegians" disappeared into a cellar. They had barely established themselves there when a stream of napalm hissed into the cellar vaults. They fled the cellar and made it into an adjoining room.

There the *Spieß* of the headquarters company of *SS-Panzer-Grenadier-Regiment 23 "Norge"*, *SS-Hauptscharführer* Danner, found his men. He had dashed into the ruined residence from the Niederwallstraße with food containers and sacks of rations.

As midnight drew near — just as the *Spieß* left again — a hellish spectacle occurred. All of a sudden the mess gear went flying and half-smoked cigarettes fell to the floor. The Soviets had come across the street and were making their way down the steelwork of the burnt-out stairs. It was impossible to keep anything straight in the bitter hand-to-hand combat with hand grenades and machine pistols. The "Norwegians" leaped back and disappeared into the small Kurstraße. Soon afterward, an immediate counterattack hurled the Soviets back.

Again the defenders and attackers faced each other. Barely ten meters away, the Soviets burrowed their way among the stone columns, their faces clearly recognizable in the light of the fires. Then the order came: "*Kampfgruppe 'Norge'* fall back to Kurstraße!" The men carefully withdrew and made it to the new line over the mountain of rubble. One part found refuge in a cellar.

"I leaned against the wall of a collapsed cellar, since it was as if the heavens were getting even darker. A giant fellow, a Russian, leaped across the narrow gap and landed right between us. One of us raised his machine pistol and cut down the Russian, who fell between us and lay dead. A wild man! We searched his pockets and found one watch after another. His rank insignia showed he was a First Lieutenant."

That was *SS-Oberscharführer* Zühlke's account. The Soviets got no further there.

On 29 April the fighting also continued in the Friedrichstraße and Wilhelmstraße. The Soviets did not get a step farther there. The soldiers of *Kampfgruppe "Charlemagne"* repeatedly knocked out attacking Soviet tanks.

Sharpshooters lurked. Each tried to outwit the other. A swastika flag was waved from a entryway beside the Herold building. The Soviets replied with furious fire. But they gave away their positions. German sharpshooters had waited for that and opened intensive fire on the nests of Soviet sharpshooters.

Several times a T 34 turned into the Puttkamerstraße from the Wilhelmstraße. It remained about 300 meters distant from the pockets of German resistance and fired for all it was worth. The southern sector of Wilhelmstraße, Friedrichstraße and the Spittelmarkt also repulsed all enemy attacks on 30 April.

SS-Flak-Abteilung 11, which had knocked out its last tanks at Strausberg, in Neukölln and at Tempelhof airfield with its cannon, had been forced to destroy its heavy equipment and guns because of shortage of ammunition and fuel. From then on it was employed as infantry. The last 63 men fought as infantry under *SS-Hauptsturmführer* Holzboog.

Two of the six *Tigers* of *schwere SS-Panzer-Abteilung 503* that had gone into Berlin were staged at the old *Reich* bank. They attacked when the Russians attempted to cross the Schloß Bridge. Tank commanders Turk and Diers knocked out several Russian tanks on the far side of the Spree. They had been providing the infantry with cover. Turk's tank had to remain at the *Reich* bank with steering problems. Diers was moved to the zoo with his tank to act as a reserve. The remaining *Tigers* of the battalion supported the southern sector of the *18. Panzergrenadier-Division* and *Panzer-Division "Müncheberg"* at the Westkreuz and Halensee trains stations and on the Kurfürsten-Damm.

As the situation continued to deteriorate on 29 April and only isolated pockets of resistance were holding out, Turk's *Tiger* was able to move to Potsdamer Platz thanks to the driving skill of his driver. It was there that it fought its last fight.

Dier's *Tiger* at the time was in position at the Kroll Opera House. It took the Russian tanks supporting the attacking infantry on the far side of the Spree under fire.

On the evening of 29 April, *General* Weidling submitted his plan for a breakout to the west, a plan which his staff had painstakingly worked out. Concentrating the last 40 tanks, the breakout would take place in three assault wedges along the Heerstraße over the Stößensee and Havel bridges at Pichelsberg, which were still held by *Hitlerjugend* units. Hitler rejected the plan. He still set his hopes on Steiner and Wenck.

The *Wehrmachtsbericht* for 29 April reported Soviet attacks against the relief armies of Steiner and Wenck. That indicated the German counterattack was threatened with failure. Other reports, which made the rounds among the defenders, stated that Wenck's spearheads were approaching Tempelhof. Rumors abounded and last hopes were pinned to them. Soon, however, even the last hopes vanished, hopes that were not restricted to the common man, but were also shared by the command. Hopes are the only explanation for the resistance to the last. First: Hopes that were illusory, even as they were created, that the western Allies would join with the Germans at the last moment to fight against the Russians. Second: Hopes that Berlin would be relieved and thus make it possible to be captured by the Americans.

***

It is unclear who defended the *Reichstag*. Presumably it was a hastily assembled force composed of army, navy, *Luftwaffe* and *Waffen-SS*.

At the midday situation conference on 29 April, Hitler asked *Generalmajor der Waffen-SS* Mohnke:

"Where are the Russians?"

"In the north, just in front of the Weidendammer Bridge. In the east, at the Lustgarten. In the south at the Potsdamer Platz and at the *Reich* Air Ministry. In the west in the zoo, 300-400 meters from the *Reich* Chancellery."

"How long can you hold them?"

"Twenty-four hours at the most."

That was the bitter reply.

The last situation conference with Hitler in the bunker at the *Reich* Chancellery was at 2200 hours. In response to questions radioed to the *OKW*, which was then located at Fürstenberg, came the shattering news that Wenck's and Steiner's relief attacks were not moving and that the *9. Armee* was surrounded at Halbe. The *Wehrmachtsbericht* announced: "The heroic struggle in the center of the capital of the *Reich* continues with undiminished intensity..."

After the Russian failure to storm the *Reichstag* on 29 April, Stalin sent strict orders that it must be accomplished on 30 April so that on May Day the world could be informed that Berlin had fallen. That demand was passed on with emphatic orders from the staffs of the highest commands down to the regiments.

The Thirtieth of April was a Monday. After Hitler had rejected his original proposal to break out of Berlin, *General* Weidling called his sector commanders together at his command post in the Bendlerblock to discuss the situation and possible measures to be taken with them. The outcome: Break out of Berlin in small groups! Hitler endorsed that decision at 1345 hours. In the written message that was brought by a courier it read:

319

To the commander of the Berlin defensive area, *General der Artillerie* Helmut Weidling:

As a result of the shortage of ammunition and rations for the defenders of the capital of the Reich, I give my permission for a breakout...

Too late! Events were moving too fast. On 30 April the fighting flared up around the *Reichstag* and continued throughout the day. According to statements by Colonel Sintschenko, the commander of the 756th Rifle Regiment, his soldiers, Kantarija and Jegorow, hoisted the Red Flag on the dome of the *Reichstag* at 2030 hours. "After I had reported to General Schatilow," said Sintschenko, "I went out to look at the Red Flag. For me that was a proud sight. That was the final victory over fascism."

The picture of the Red Flag that the world saw was clearly staged (compare the times: day vs. night). According to the most recent research by a German publishing company in Russia, it was a woman who raised the first Red Flag on the *Reichstag*. It was made from bed ticking.

That day, 30 April 1945, Hitler shot himself in the bunker of the *Reich* Chancellery. But only a few people discovered that at first. After Hitler's death, Goebbels, Bormann, Krebs and Burgdorf discussed what should happen next. Their thoughts about the military and the political situation, a cease-fire and a new regime were pure fantasy. Only *Großadmiral* Dönitz, who was in Flensburg, was informed that Hitler had appointed him to head the new regime. Weidling, who had already given his troops instructions for the breakout, was called back again to the *Reich* Chancellery, where *General* Krebs ordered him to establish contact with the Russians. During the night of 30 April/1 May a soldier with a white flag, Krebs, *Oberst* von Dufving and the Latvian *SS-Obersturmbannführer* Neilands as translator went to the Russians to negotiate with them for a cease-fire. They met at the Potsdamer Bridge near the Anhalter rail station.

The German delegation of negotiators was passed on from the command post of the 35th Guards Rifle Division to the command post of the 8th Guards Army in an apartment house at the Schulenburgring at Tempelhof. The Germans appeared before Colonel General Tschuikow, the Commander-in-Chief of the army. *General* Krebs presented proposals. Tschuikow telephoned the Commander-in-Chief of his Front, Marshal Zhukov. In turn, Zhukov contacted Moscow. Stalin directed: "...There is nothing to discuss with Krebs or any other *Nazis* except unconditional surrender."

Krebs had to remain. *Oberst* von Dufving, Weiding's chief of staff, went back to the *Reich* Chancellery to inform Goebbels, Bormann and the other senior officials what the Russians were demanding. Around 0500 hours, Zhukov's deputy, General Sokolowski, who was involved in the negotiations, reported to Zhukov:

The Germans are playing games. Krebs said he was not empowered to offer an unconditional surrender. Further, he stated, only the new German government could decide that. Krebs wants to initiate a cease-fire in order to assemble the Dönitz government in Berlin. I think we should blow them straight to hell if they don't agree to an unconditional surrender immediately!

And that was how it remained. Cease fire, to gain as much time as possible? No! Capitulation!

On 1 May, at 1400 hours, the German negotiators were back in the *Reich* Chancellery. More discussions. One last attempt to stand up against the inevitable. At 1515 hours the last radio message was sent from Berlin to *Großadmiral* Dönitz at Flensburg-Mürwik: "The *Führer* died yesterday at 1530 hours. His last will and testament of 29 April passed on the office of *Reich* president to you..."

General Weidling and his chief of staff von Dufving waited at the *Reich* Chancellery for the entire afternoon, but there were no final orders or instructions from Krebs, the chief of staff of the *OKH,* nor from Goebbels. The mood of the final collapse prevailed all around them.

At 1900 hours, Weidling and von Dufving left the *Reich* Chancellery and returned to their command post in the Bendlerblock. In the meantime, *General* Krebs and *General* Burgdorf shot themselves at the *Reich* Chancellery. Goebbels, his wife, Magda and their six children died from poison.

On 1 May the battle for the inner city of Berlin raged on undiminished. Very few learned anything of the negotiations with the Russians or of the death of Hitler.

In the evening of 1 May, *General* Weidling again assembled all commanders and leaders of units that could be contacted at his command post. He informed them of the situation and his decision that he would sign the unconditional surrender on 2 May, as demanded by the Russians. The units were free to break out of the encircled city.

During the night of 1/2 May, the combatants in their positions in the ruins learned from the leaders of their units that Hitler was dead and of the decision to break out. Squads, platoons and *Kampfgruppen* prepared to break out, each going in a different direction. It had been coordinated with *General* Weidling that he would not sign the surrender until the morning of 2 May.

After making contact with the Russians by radio, von Dufving stood for the third time in front of Tschuikow: "Unconditional surrender, yes or no?"

Oberst von Dufving replied to Tschuikow: "Yes!"

Agreements and arrangements were made over radio and telephone. Then, on 2 May at 0430 hours, one German and two Russian emissaries stood before the Bendlerblock to bring *General* Weidling to the 8th Guards Army at Tempelhof.

At 0500 hours the victor and vanquished stood facing each other, saluted and took their places. Colonel General Tschuikow spoke. An interpreter translated. *General* Weidling listened, looking tired and worn out. The chief of staff of the 8th Guards Army, General Beljawski, then placed one document in German and one in Russian in front of Weidling. Weidling glanced over them, reached for a pen with a trembling hand and signed the surrender for the Berlin area of command. The word "unconditional" pressed down like a hundred-pound weight.

Weidling was then required to issue a final order to his troops, demanding the cessation of the fighting. At noon on 2 May, Russian loudspeaker trucks drove through the streets making the order known to the defenders and inhabitants.

Late in the afternoon, Weidling and other German generals and high officers were driven through Berlin to give them another look at the extent of the destruction. On 6 May *General* Weidling was brought back again to Berlin from the officers' prisoner-of-war camp at Strausberg to sign the surrender a second time. That time it was before whirring motion-picture cameras and clicking still cameras for Russian newsreels for the Russian people. On 9 May a Russian airplane took off from Strausberg, Zhukov's headquarters, taking Weidling and other high officers to Moscow. That was the beginning of a long journey through prison camps and prisons, a journey that many did not survive.

In the evening of 2 May, Stalin issued an order of the day to the Red Army in which he praised the performance of the troops and commanders of the 1st Belorussian and 1st Ukrainian Front:

…By 2100 hours, our troops in Berlin had captured more than 70,000 German soldiers and officers…Today, on 2 May at 2330 hours, the capital of our homeland, Moscow, salutes…the heroic troops…in honor of this historical event, the conquest of Berlin…with 24 salvos of artillery from 324 guns…"

Weidling had freed the commanders of their formations to either surrender and go into captivity with him or to attempt to break out of the encircled city on their own. At about midnight of 1/2 May that was discussed among the defenders. Many troop commanders assembled their last loyal men to break out. Many soldiers, however, had already decided on their own or in small groups to disappear or to attempt to break out, for the Red Army soldiers were already in a victory frenzy.

***

Heavy fighting had marked 30 April in other locations in Berlin. In Wilhelmstraße, the French soldiers of *Kampfgruppe "Charlemagne"* were forced back. The Soviets made extensive use of flamethrowers.

Heavy fighting developed around the Herold building. Explosions thundered through the cellar. The Russians penetrated along the Charlottenstraße to Kochstraße, reaching it at 1300 hours. The Russians strengthened their

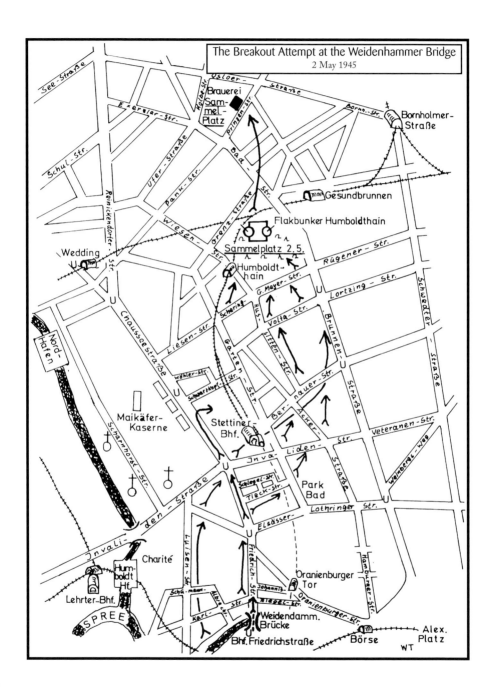

The Breakout Attempt at the Weidenhammer Bridge
2 May 1945

drive from there and along the Leipziger-Straße toward Friedrichstraße. By 1600 hours the Soviets were able to gain possession of a gateway near the Herold building through the cellars on the Puttkamerstraße.

That day was filled with continued bitter fighting. Small *Kampfgruppen* stood and fought entirely on their own. Nobody knew anything significant about the others. Each fought as best he could. Now let us turn to the words of *SS-Unterscharführer* Scholles, the leader of a group in the Herold building. His group included men from *SS-Panzer-Grenadier-Regiment 24 "Danmark"*, the *Kriegsmarine*, the *Volkssturm* and one *Reichs-Arbeit-Dienst* man. They were Germans, Danes and Latvians.

If we were to avoid going to the dogs, we had to immediately regain possession of the entryway. An immediate counterattack that followed a heavy hand grenade preparation failed due to defensive fire from the house in back. A second immediate counterattack was prepared. It was to take place when darkness fell. For that we created a hole in the wall. The counterattack was to go through the right-hand rooms of the Herold building and through the back court.

In the meantime it had become dark. The Russians attempted to broaden their penetration and break into the Herold building. The fighting reached its high point and disintegrated into repeated new individual engagements. At about midnight, the Russians attempted to bring a machine gun into position in a room adjoining the entryway. We forced them out with gunfire. That was the moment for the immediate counterattack.

At the head of the assault group, I ran through the breach in the wall into the long adjoining room. My assault rifle chattered. The Russians scattered. We pursued them. While all that was going on, the naval people in the covering squad threw hand grenades into the entry. They stopped throwing grenades when we got close. I dashed into the entryway, convinced that no more Russians were in it. The men behind me hung back a bit.

I was already at the entrance to Puttkamerstraße and wanted to check out the street. I threw another hand grenade — all this happened in seconds — when there was gunfire behind me, no more than three meters away. Ricochets zipped through the gateway. My left leg was suddenly heavy as lead. Blood trickled down. Again I ran right past the Russians and into the adjoining room. After thirty meters I collapsed. Three of my men were instantly beside me and dragged me back through the cellar room. How could that have happened? Although I had spent many long hours in the entryway, I had never noticed the little doorman's room.

Four men of the *II./SS-Panzer-Grenadier-Regiment 24 "Danmark"* dragged me over the rubble in the darkness to the Kochstraße subway station. The platform was overflowing with soldiers and civilians. What was happening? Everyone talked of withdrawing. Only where? Christensen came. I told him what happened at Puttkamerstraße. Hitler was said to be dead. *SS-Obersturmführer* Christensen awarded me the Iron Cross, First Class I and entered it in my *Soldbuch*. Then he left to bring back the *Kampfgruppe*.

In the meantime a medic attended to me. Four naval soldiers picked up my stretcher and carried me to the city-center subway station. Everything was in a state of confusion. At the station I hoped to find the command post of *11. SS-Freiwilligen-Panzer-Grenadier-Division "Nordland"* and the dressing station. They were not there. (Author's Note: The command post and aid station were actually one level farther down in the subway station.) Soldiers and civilians were close packed at that subway station as well. The naval soldiers set me down. A nurse gave me a pain pill and a bottle of red wine, which I greedily drained. Then I fell asleep.

At that same hour, *SS-Obersturmführer* Birkedahl-Hansen, the commander of the *8./SS-Panzer-Grenadier-Regiment 24 "Danmark"*, was also looking for the divisional command post at the subway station. He was seriously ill with jaundice. He was sent from one place to another. Finally, he returned to the trains elements in the zoo. A *Major* informed Birkedahl-Hansen about a planned breakout. He pointed out the breakout route of the defenders in the southwest sector on a map. Birkedahl-Hansen gathered all the men of the trains and joined with the *Major*. Carrying only the bare necessities, they set off toward Charlottenburg, but found that the Russians were already at the Zoo Bunker. After brief fighting they continued, but several lost contact. The darkness swallowed others. Vehicles were being blown up everywhere.

Scholles and Birkedahl-Hansen had been unable to find the division command post at the city-center subway station. On 1 May 1945 at 2000 hours, the acting commander of *SS-Panzer-Grenadier-Regiment 24 "Danmark"*, *SS-Sturmbannführer* Ternedde, was ordered to the division command post. At that time it was still in the city-center subway station. The division commander, *Generalmajor* Krukenberg, gave Ternedde the following orders:

Berlin is encircled by the enemy. Hitler is dead. The remnants of *SS-Panzer-Grenadier-Regiment 23 "Norge"* and *SS-Panzer-Grenadier-Regiment 24 "Danmark"* are to withdraw from their former positions at 2300 hours and assemble, ready for a breakout, at the Weidendammer bridge. The breakout will be supported by the remnants of *schwere SS-Panzer-Abteilung 503* and combat vehicles of *SS-Panzer-Aufklärungs-Abteilung 11*. The objective of the breakout is to the north and link-up with Armee-Abteilung Steiner at the Finow Canal.

And what were the prospects for carrying out those orders at that point? That night a messenger crawled through the wasteland of rubble at the Spittelmarkt and disappeared into a great cellar in which many soldiers and civilians were staged. Names were read out and those called were requested to come along. They were all men from *SS-Panzer-Grenadier-Regiment 23 "Norge"*. The word was that the Russians had achieved a penetration somewhere. It was said that the men who had been called were to mount an immediate counterattack. They left the cellar and the night swallowed them up.

They assembled in the vaults of the *Reich* Bank. There were also civilians and soldiers there as well. They listlessly eyed the newcomers. With scorched eyebrows, the eyes looked out of their sockets like ghostly apparitions. The men greedily sucked at cigarettes as they filled magazines and stuffed their pockets with hand grenades. Then they went through the Hausvogteiplatz across "Unter den Linden" to the Friedrichstraße railroad station — over ashes and rubble, past burnt-out vehicles and dead soldiers and civilians. Everywhere crooked steel beams stuck up in the air. Household furniture and machines were scattered in the street. Numerous fires blazed everywhere.

Shouts, instructions. The men moved off in another direction. The immediate counterattack at the *Reich* Chancellery was cancelled and replaced by one at the state opera house on "Unter den Linden".

The men entered the great lobby. There they heard: "Hitler is dead!" The place was also crawling with soldiers from all arms of the service. But some sort of command structure still seemed to function in that anthill. They then moved on across Friedrichstraße to the Weidendammer bridge.

There the men discovered that they were to attempt a breakout. With support from the last available friendly tanks and assault guns, the breakout was to proceed along Friedrichstraße toward the Stettiner railroad station. It was midnight. The breakout force was staging close to the Friedrichstraße railroad station and at the Weidendammer bridge.

Generalmajor der Waffen-SS Joachim Ziegler, who had been held at the *Reich* Chancellery until Hitler's death, raced back to his *11. SS-Freiwilligen-Panzer-Grenadier-Division "Nordland"*. Without any assigned responsibility, he wanted to be there for the breakout. *Generalmajor der Waffen-SS* Wilhelm Mohnke, the local area commander for the defense of the *Reich* Chancellery, had recommended the breakout to the divisional leadership.

The breakout group at the Weidendammer bridge got moving. The lead element — *Tigers* and *Sturmgeschütze* — rolled across the bridge and shoved the tank barricade aside.

The German armored spearhead fired to all sides, but the Russians were also awake. Their barrier of antitank guns barked at the breakout element. Tanks showed up and joined in. The Russian defense pounded the Germans from houses and street corners. The Soviets fired into the dense, tightly packed group. Once again all Hell broke loose. They would never make it through there!

Groups broke loose and tried other directions. The units lost cohesion. One batch of 50 men and a *Sturmgeschütz* rolled along the Schiffbauerdamm toward the Lehrter railroad station. It was shot up on Albrechtstraße. The solution seemed to be: Disappear into cover and make it through in small groups. Among those killed during that breakout attempt were *Generalmajor der Waffen-SS* Ziegler, *SS-Sturmbannführer* Rudolf Saalbach, the commander of *SS-Panzer-Aufklärungs-Abteilung 11,* and many other officers and men.

***

The battle for the city center increasingly became a battle of intertwined

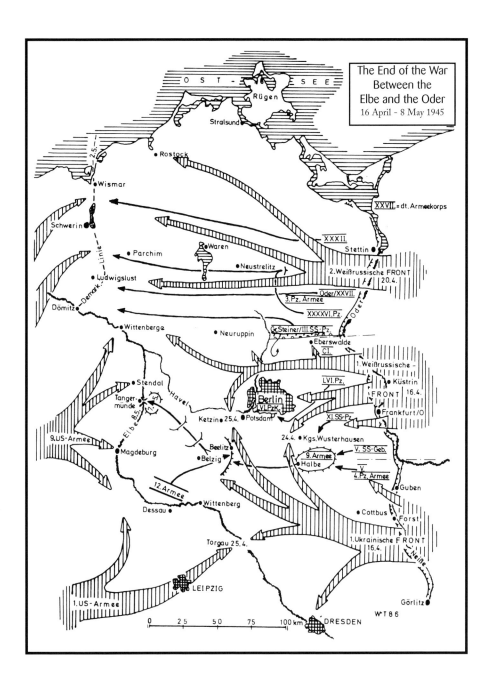

The End of the War
Between the
Elbe and the Oder
16 April - 8 May 1945

OST - SEE

Rügen

Stralsund

Rostock

Wismar

Schwerin

Parchim

Waren

Neustrelitz

Ludwigslust

Dömitz

Wittenberge

Neuruppin

XXXII.

Stettin

2.Weißrussische FRONT
20.4.

Oder/XXVII.
3.Pz. Armee

XXXXVI.Pz.

Gr.Steiner/III.SS-Pz.

Eberswalde
C.I.

1. Weißrussische –

Küstrin

LVI.Pz.

Berlin
V LV.Pz.K

FRONT 16.4.

Frankfurt/O

Stendal

Tanger-
münde

Havel

Ketzin 25.4. Potsdam

XI.SS-Pz.

24.4. Kgs.Wusterhausen

9.US-Armee

Magdeburg

Beelitz

Belzig

9.Armee
Halbe

V. SS-Geb.

V.
4.Pz. Armee

Guben

12.Armee

Wittenberg

Dessau

Cottbus

Forst

1.Ukrainische FRONT
16.4.

Torgau 25.4.

LEIPZIG

1.US-Armee

Görlitz

0   25   50   75   100 km

DRESDEN

W-T 86

XXVII. = dt. Armeekorps

2.5.

Demark-Linie

Oder

Elbe 8.5.

Neiße

individual actions. The *Kampfgruppen* — twenty to thirty men strong and named after their leaders — held islands of defense and ruins on the streets that led to the center of the city. They were made up of Europeans who had volunteered for the "crusade against Bolshevism" in the German army: Norwegians, Swedes, Danes, French, Latvians, Luxemburgers, Spaniards and ethnic Germans from southeast Europe.

They were often men whose countries were under the yoke of the Soviet Union or regimes dependent on the Soviet Union. Or they came from lands that had to bow to the Soviet Union, such as the small country of Finland. In Finland's case, there had already been volunteers from Sweden, Norway and Denmark, who had courageously fought the Soviet aggressor in the Finnish-Russian Winter War of 1939.

Then there were nationally minded French soldiers who saw the people's-front governments in their country as preparing the way for Bolshevism. They wanted to prevent Stalin's world dominance. They imagined a united Europe similar to what they had already experienced in the *Waffen-SS* volunteer formations. For them, a "United Europe" was no empty piece of rhetoric. They had already taken it to heart: A European Union, similar to what is being sought with such great effort now.

But why were they still fighting, with defeat before their eyes? Because they still hoped to be relieved by Wenck's *12. Armee* and Steiner's *Armeegruppe*. If relieved, it would bring an acceptable end to their fighting. And they fought because there were still comrades fighting at their side whom they did not want to leave in the lurch. Their loyalty to their German comrades and to Europe thus became a tragedy of great proportions.

***

SS-Obersturmbannführer Neilands and 80 Latvians had repulsed every attack on 1 May on "Unter den Linden". After the failure of the initial cease-fire negotiations, he and the remnants of his *15. lettisches Füsilier-Bataillon* barricaded themselves in the Civilian Air Ministry building. They were determined to fight to the bitter end, for they knew what awaited them. They had long since lost their homeland.

On 2 May in the morning there was a dead silence. Not a single Russian or German soldier was to be seen. Then they learned of the powerful break-out attempts during the night. The Latvians had been forgotten.

The Latvians then made their way through the ruins of the city to Pankow and reached a square where thousands of German soldiers awaited captivity. The remnants of the Latvian unit disbanded there and each one tried to escape captivity on his own.

The French had a similar experience. On 1 May the battle raged in their sector with undiminished fury. When the Soviets employed flamethrowers, the French had to fall back. On 2 May, the remnants of *Kampfgruppe*

"Charlemagne" were near the Civilian Air Ministry when German and Russian soldiers showed up with white flags. That was the end. In Bendlerstraße, the occupants of the Bendlerblock assembled for one last time. They marched past their commander, *General* Weidling, on their way to captivity.

White flags were raised at the Zoo Bunker, the final bulwark on the Ost-West-Achse. The *Flak* guns fell silent. They had been the terror of the Soviet tanks to the very end. Soldiers waited with resignation for their captivity.

***

We can read about the final hours before the end in the notes of the wounded *SS-Unterscharführer* Scholles, who had sunk into the deep sleep of exhaustion after emergency medical care in the city-center subway station.

I do not know how long it was, but when I awoke, the frightening word "Withdraw!" rang in my ears. And nobody knew what was going on. Everyone did his best to withdraw, even though withdrawal was no longer possible. In front and behind, to the right and left, possibly even overhead in the street were the Russians! But everyone flowed back toward the north. I lay helpless on my stretcher and prayed and called for someone to take me with them.

Then two motorcycle messengers from *SS-Panzer-Grenadier-Regiment 24 "Danmark"* came along. They assured me that they would not leave me in the lurch. They brought over two more comrades and carried me with them. Along the way they found a cart onto which they loaded me and which they then moved along the subway tracks. At the Französische Straße station they set me down. Everything again came to a standstill. I no longer felt any pain and fell asleep again. When I woke up it was the same old picture. A close-packed crowd where nobody knew what they were waiting for. It became light. The 2nd of May dawned. Suddenly a loud voice demanded attention: "Men! In front of us, above us and behind us are Russians! A Russian Commissar demands our surrender! Comrades, do you want to surrender?"

Cries of yes and no! Heated debates. Agreement. Refusal. One officer asked all officers to come forward for negotiations with the Russian Commissar. Then came the decision. "Comrades! Berlin is already in the enemy rear area. The city commander has signed the capitulation. Even the last centers of resistance have surrendered. Russian tanks are on all the streets. Any attempt to break out is doomed to failure. All of the soldiers of the *Wehrmacht*, the *Waffen-SS* and the *Volkssturm* are to lay down their weapons and be treated as prisoners of war. Women, children and civilians can go home. The wounded will go into hospitals. Don't anybody be stupid!"

I accepted that order with calm indifference. Everyone slowly shoved their way to a subway shaft at the Französische Straße. My cart was pushed along with the crowd. Beside me lay a severely wounded man. A few took their own lives. Pistol shots cracked repeatedly. Everyone clambered upwards. Nobody paid any more attention to the wounded. Our cart had finally been let go in the crush. All the others had left. After a while the Russians came along, shining flashlights all around. A Russian pushed our cart along. Occasionally he checked out the corpses. Gradually he amassed a mountain of pistols, watches, rings and all sorts of things on our wagon. The Russian was talkative. "Woina kaputt, Chitler kaputt! You hospital and then home!" He said that over and over again. When he got to the ladder he left our cart, gathered his assembled booty and left us to our fate.

I had a clean shot through the lower leg. I climbed down from the wagon, crept on all fours to the ladder and, with unspeakable agony, dragged myself up. The soldiers were already marching to the north. Up above, it was swarming with Russians. I made it a few meters from the "Unter den Linden" station to the surface.

Cold, wet weather greeted me. I was cold. Exhausted, I leaned against the remains of a wall. On Friedrichstraße and "Unter den Linden" there was busy traffic. Nowhere were there any more sounds of fighting. Finally, two slightly wounded men from *Kampfgruppe "Charlemagne"* came along. They dragged me along with them to the Hotel Adlon, where a Red-Cross flag was flying.

Breakout or Captivity

General Weidling, the local-area commander for Berlin, had given his troops free choice between going with him into captivity or breaking out. Many soldiers rallied around their officers to attempt to break out with them. Others wanted to try to get out of encircled Berlin in small groups or individually. During the night of 1/2 May 1945, there was great activity among the defenders. Two directions appeared to be the main choices for breaking out. One led over the Weidendammer bridge to the north, toward Oranienburg and to *Armeegruppe* Steiner. The other led through Spandau-Staaken to the west and southwest to Wenck's *12. Armee*, which was still believed to be at the Havel River in the Ketzin — Brandenburg area.

During the night of 1/2 May, the defenders withdrew from the last positions and bastions of defense and assembled at the announced departure points.

The soldiers of the *11. SS-Freiwilligen-Panzer-Grenadier-Division "Nordland"* quietly left their positions at the Gendarmenmarkt, Leipziger-Straße and Potsdamer-Platz and assembled at the urban railroad overpass and railroad station at Friedrichstraße to break out to the north. At the same time, *General* Ziegler, staff officers of the *OKH* and party notables left the *Reich* Chancellery in groups, intending to break out to the north. The Friedrichstraße railroad station teemed with men and vehicles. The last *Königstiger*, commanded by *SS-Unterscharführer* Diers, was to force the breach.

SS-Unterscharführer Diers had been at the Kroll Opera House with his *Tiger*. His final position was at the "Unter den Linden" subway station. The order reached him there to assemble at the Friedrichstraße railroad station. The heavy tank clattered to the assembly point. Three or four tanks and *Sturmgeschütze* and eight *SPW* from the division were already there or closing up. It took some time before the armored vehicles made their way through the mass of men.

The *Königstiger* took the lead over the Weidendammer bridge. It stopped at the road barricade just beyond it. The mass of people followed close behind the armored vehicles. *SS-Sturmbannführer* Ternedde, who led the assembled remnants of *SS-Panzer-Grenadier-Regiment 23 "Norge"* and *SS-Panzer-Grenadier-Regiment 24 "Danmark"*, and the divisional adjutant, *SS-Sturmbannführer* Bergfeld, had their hands full with organizing the teeming mass of people for the breakout.

Right after midnight the breakout got moving. The *Königstiger* shoved the antitank barricade to the side and rolled on to the Humboldthain *Flak* tower, which had been held as an island of defense by *General* Bärenfänger and his people. Dier's tank came through and roused the Russians, who had advanced through the Alexanderplatz as far as Ziegelstraße. The alerted Russians then opened fire on the breakout group with every weapon they had. Behind Diers, a *Sturmgeschütz* was hit and set afire. It blocked the road, which had been narrowed by the rubble of collapsed buildings. Russian mortars and artillery laid down heavy fire on the area. An *SPW* with the severely wounded commander of *SS-Panzer-Regiment 11*, *SS-Obersturmbannführer* Kausch, was buried under the collapsing wall of a house. Chaos spread among the breakout party. Again and again, groups attempted to break through. Many made it as far as the northern outskirts. Several had already been shot to pieces on Friedrichstraße or Chaussee-Straße.

SS-Unterscharführer Beresniak, of the *3./SS-Panzer-Aufklärungs-Abteilung 11*, had been attached to Mohnke's staff with his *SPW* since 28 April. (His company was the so-called "Swedish Company", since most of the Swedish volunteers had been assigned to it. Its commander was the Swede, Pehrsson, who was able to "disappear" in the Swedish embassy on Tiergarten-Straße with several of his people.) *SS-Unterscharführer* Beresniak had crossed the Weidendammer bridge with his *SPW* just as a *Sturmgeschütz* in front of him was hit by an antitank gun and went up in flames. Beresniak's *SPW* crew joined in the ensuing firefight, sweeping the windows where muzzle-flashes were evident with fire from their 4.7cm *Pak/Flak*.

Sometime between 0200 hours and 0300 hours (2 May) the *Sturmgeschütz* finally burned out. At that point, there was only isolated fire. Beresniak had dozed off from exhaustion. His driver, Szeckerich, woke him up. Beresniak, who quickly grasped the situation, asked his driver: "Hans, what do you think? Should we move out?" The answer: "With you, I'd go to hell and back!"

Those sentences expressed the boundless mutual trust, that each would stick by the other in the most hopeless situations. That was comradeship in the truest sense of the word. Beresniak, the cautious, somewhat phlegmatic Rumanian German —as was his entire crew — said only: "Well then, let's go, Hans!" A new breakthrough followed behind him.

Beresniak's *SPW* was knocked out by Russian gunfire somewhere near the Stettin railroad station. Beresniak, severely wounded, survived that and the ensuing imprisonment in Russia that lasted more than ten years before he could return to his homeland, the Banat.

There were many breakout groups that headed north past the Stettin railroad station, through the ruins of Chaussee-Straße and Garten-Straße, and reached the Humboldthain *Flak* bunker through Husitten-Straße and Brunnen-Straße. That was also where Dier's *Königstiger* ended its journey with track problems. The groups disintegrated at Humboldthain. The order: "Continue in small groups or individually." Many came together for the last time in the brewery north of Humboldthain on Prinzenstraße. They talked things over — and came to no conclusions. Some individuals continued onward, many shot themselves and the others surrendered when Russian troops reached the brewery.

*****

It was no different at the zoo and the *Flak* bunker there. The trains elements were at the zoo as well as the remaining heavy weapons of the *11. SS-Freiwilligen-Panzer-Grenadier-Division "Nordland"*. *Generalmajor* Mummert, commander of *Panzer-Division "Müncheberg"*, was determined to break out to the west through Spandau with the remnants of his division. The Havel bridges in Pichelsdorf and Spandau were still held by *Hitlerjugend Kampfgruppen*. Elements of the *11. SS-Freiwilligen-Panzer-Grenadier-Division "Nordland"* at the zoo joined up with Mummert. During the night of 1/2 May, at the same time that the breakout was in progress at the Weidendammer bridge, Mummert's breakout got moving.

Remnants of the *18. Panzergrenadier-Division* crossed the Havel bridge in Spandau on 1 May, but the Russians then strengthened that weak point in their encirclement. In the morning of 2 May the situation was as follows: The Heerstraße bridge at Pichelsdorf was blown up; the Schulenburg bridge in Spandau-Wilhelmstadt and the railroad and road bridges at the Spandau main railroad station were covered by fire from Russian heavy weapons, especially the road bridge.

The traffic jam of vehicles lengthened in front of the Schulenburg Bridge. During the breaks in the fire, soldiers, motor vehicles and tanks raced over the bridge again and again. Many men and vehicles were hit, and remained on or at the bridge. Finally, *SS-Untersturmführer* Schäfer's *Königstiger* made it. It had blown apart the Russian barriers at Spandau with its 8.8 cm main gun. But that tank then met its own end at Staaken.

During the course of 2 May, many breakout groups closed up to the spearhead in Staaken. Discussions followed. *General* Mummert and officers who were determined to fight worked to organize the soldiers and set up the lead elements.

At 0600 hours on 3 May, things got going again. A light field howitzer of the *18. Panzergrenadier-Division* shot the Russian barricade to pieces. Then several armored vehicles, staff cars and trucks moved over the fields. Masses of men stormed behind them — soldiers and civilians by the thousands — in large and small groups.

The armored spearhead and several groups broke through the Russian blockade. Many dead and wounded were left lying on the fields at Staaken. Many did not attempt the breakout and waited in Staaken to be taken prisoner.

The Russians pursued the breakout groups with particular attention because they suspected that those groups included extremely high level military and political figures. Ground-attack aircraft attacked them unceasingly.

Some high ground on the Döberitz Training Area proved to be an insurmountable obstacle. When the armored spearhead drew near, the Russians opened up on it with a murderous fire. The last armored vehicles, ambulances with wounded, staff cars and trucks were shot to pieces. There were heavy losses, also among the civilians who had joined the soldiers. Any remaining cohesion fell apart.

Small groups still tried to continue. Many surrendered and were taken prisoner. Others continued to the southwest and reassembled in the patches of woods in the southern part of the training area. On the morning of 4 May, they tried to break through via Ketzin to Wenck's *12. Armee*, which they assumed was still on the other side of the Havel. The Russians in the Ketzin area were surprised. they were already celebrating the news of the fall of Berlin, Soon, however, they regained the initiative and smashed those last breakthrough attempts.

All trace of *Generalmajor* Mummert, *SS-Sturmbannführer* Herzig (the commander of *schwere SS-Panzer-Abteilung 503*), and of battalion surgeon *Dr.* Cappell was lost in the Ketzin area. Selnes, a Norwegian, and Kipp, Witschas and Lehner, all Germans, were captured in that area. From that group, only *SS-Hauptscharführer* Schramm from *SS-Panzer-Regiment 11* and a single comrade made it across the Havel. On 6 May, however, they were captured by the Russians near the Elbe.

A small group led by the Dane, Birkedahl-Hansen, reached the Nauen State Forest. Travelling only by night, that group reached Warnemünde and then crossed the Baltic Sea to Denmark in a small cutter.

It is impossible to indicate numbers regarding the breakout groups at Spandau, Staaken and Döberitz. Various reports indicate ten thousand or more.

***

While the combat elements of the *11. SS-Freiwilligen-Panzer-Grenadier-Division "Nordland"* fought in Berlin, the field trains were moved to the Friesack area. After the Soviets succeeded in forming a bridgehead at Ketzin, the field trains assembled an alarm company that was employed there. The alarm company was decimated. Remnants came back to Friesack and were forwarded to the division rallying point at Kyritz. On 9 May 1945 elements of those supply units and of the division staff entered American captivity at Ludwigslust/Elbe.

The Remnants of the 9. Armee Break Out of the Halbe Pocket

On 25 April Berlin was enclosed in a large Pocket. On the same day, Russian and American troops joined hands at Torgau on the Elbe. It was not until the northern wing of the *9. Armee* was forced back to Berlin by the Russians that Hitler gave permission to pull back the southern wing, which was still holding its positions at Frankfurt/Oder. Too late! The forces of the *XI. SS-Panzer-Korps*, the *V. SS-Gebirgs-Korps* and the *V. Armeekorps* (split off from *Heeresgruppe Mitte*) that were fighting their way back were surrounded in a forested region between Löpten — Hermsdorf — Märkisch Buchholz and Halbe.

At the same time, the *12. Armee* (Wenck), set out from the Wittenberg — Dessau area to relieve Berlin and reached Belzig. One day later it reached the Lehnin — Beelitz area. Hitler's expectation that the *9. Armee* and the *12. Armee* would give the decisive turnaround in the battle of Berlin after they joined was pure fantasy. Busse's *9. Armee* was shattered and the *12. Armee*, after breaking contact with the Americans and being "turned around", was too weak for that mission. From the very beginning, *General* Wenck had in mind no more than the rescue of the remnants of the *9. Armee*.

At 1400 hours on 28 April 1945, all of the formation commanders in the surrounded forces who could be contacted reported as ordered in the head forester's office at Hammer for a situation conference. *General* Busse outlined the situation of the *9. Armee*. After thorough discussion, the decision was

334

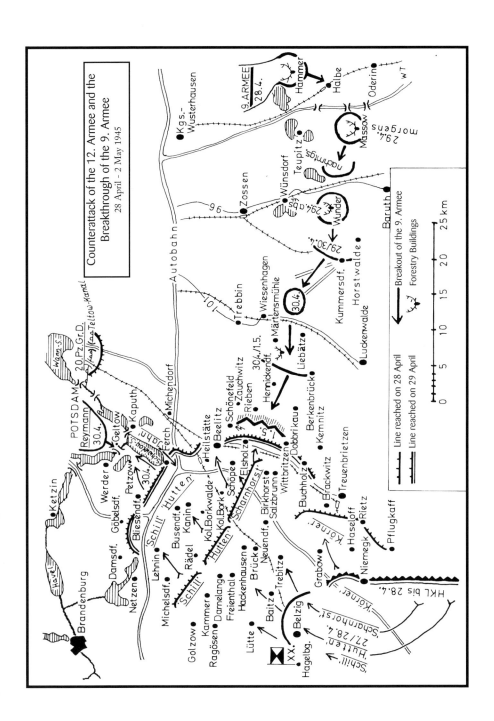

Counterattack of the 12. Armee and the
Breakthrough of the 9. Armee
28 April - 2 May 1945

reached to break through to the west at 1800 hours. The *9. Armee* would proceed through Halbe to the *12. Armee*, which was in the Beelitz area.

All available ammunition for the remaining heavy weapons was fired off. The last *Königstiger* of *schwere SS-Panzer-Abteilung 502* (Hartrampf) rolled off to Halbe. The little village in the middle of the fir-forests of Mark Brandenburg had changed hands several times. It was, at that time, held by strong Russian forces, which met the breakout force with a murderous fire. The heavy tanks received extremely heavy fire from antitank guns. In addition, their movement was restricted in the narrow village streets and they had to pull back. The Cottbus-Berlin *Autobahn* was finally crossed beyond Halbe to the west, and the breakout group assembled at the forester's house at Wunder. I have described in detail the breakout at Halbe during the night of 28/29 April in my book, "Das Ende zwischen Oder und Elbe, Der Kampf um Berlin, 1945". Terrible things took place during the breakout attempt.

During the night of 29/30 April, the breakout forces passed through the Kummersdorf firing range and reached the Märtensmühle — Liebätz area. On 1 May they passed through the lines of the *12. Armee* at Beelitz — Wittbrietzen. The death march of the *9. Armee* came to an end. The route of the breakout was soaked with the sweat and blood of innumerable soldiers and civilians. Many of them found their final resting place as unknown soldiers in the forest cemetery at Halbe. A great many of their comrades and fellow travelers lie buried in the woods between Halbe and Beelitz or remained, unburied, along the way. Many of their resting places will never be found again. The sandy soil of Mark Brandenburg has erased the traces of the murderous events.

The unfortunate survivors of the *9. Armee* made it over the Elbe to the Americans at Tangermünde. They were protected by the *12. Armee* as it fell back to the west. Among them were the Dutch volunteers of *SS-Freiwilligen-Panzer-Grenadier-Regiment 48 "General Seyffard"* of the *23. SS-Freiwilligen-Panzergrenadier-Division "Nederland"*. Its sister regiment, *SS-Freiwilligen-Panzer-Grenadier-Regiment 49 "de Ruyter"*, had been attached to the *547. Volks-Grenadier-Division* at Schwedt . It made its way back north of Berlin with the *3. Panzer-Armee*, where it reached the demarcation line on both sides of Schwerin. There it was taken prisoner by US forces.

The End of Heeresgruppe Weichsel in Northern Germany

When Zhukov's 1st Belorussian Front launched its offensive on Berlin against Busse's *9. Armee* on 16 April, von Manteuffel's *3. Panzer-Armee* on the lower Oder was granted a brief respite before it, too, was drawn into the final battle for Germany. Its opponent, Rokossowski's 2nd Belorussian Front, had smashed the *2. Armee* in East Prussia and was still on the move to the lower Oder. The mission of the 2nd Belorussian Front: Smash the *3. Panzer-Armee*, cover the northern flank of "Operation Berlin" and reach the Anklam — Wittenberge line within 10-12 days.

On 20 April, Rokossowski initiated operations with his first units. Although his 49th and 70th Armies were unable to gain bridgeheads on the west side of the Oder, his 65th Army (Batow) formed a bridgehead at the *Autobahn* bridge south of Stettin. That bridgehead was heatedly contested in the days that followed. As a result of the rapid westward progress of "Operation Berlin," the *3. Panzer-Armee* also had to evacuate its forward-echeloned positions and fall back incrementally to the west.

The next line of resistance was the Randow-Bruch position on both sides of Schmölln. It was held on 25 and 26 April. Fighting there were elements of the *27. SS-Freiwilligen-Grenadier-Division "Langemarck"*, the *28. SS-Freiwilligen-Panzergrenadier-Division "Wallonien"* and *SS-Freiwilligen-Panzer-Grenadier-Regiment 49 "de Ruyter"* of the *23. SS-Freiwilligen-Panzergrenadier-Division "Nederland"* (which was attached to the *547. Volks-Grenadier-Division*).

One day later, the *Jugend-Bataillon* of the *27. SS-Freiwilligen-Grenadier-Division "Langemarck"* under *SS-Hauptsturmführer* Stange fought with bravado at Prenzlau. However, the *3. Panzer-Armee* then had to retreat quite rapidly as a result of the fall of Berlin. On 28 April it reached the Ueckermünde — Strasburg — Joachimsthal line. On 29 April it was on both sides of Neustrelitz. The *33. Waffen-Grenadier-Division der Waffen-SS "Charlemagne" (französische Nr. 1)*, joined the retreat there. It had been in the process of being reconstituted. (One of its battalions had been sent to Berlin — *SS-Bataillon Fenet* — and met its end there.) *Armeegruppe Steiner*, with the *4. SS-Polizei-Division*, the *4. Marine-Division* and *Luftwaffen-Kampfgruppe Schirmer*, joined the retreat to the west in the Oranienburg area. At that point, all the formations were concerned with reaching the Western Allies, who had advanced to the area on both sides of Schwerin.

Along with small, still-intact army formations, *Kampfgruppe "1001 Nacht"* (*Major* Blancbois) with *SS-Panzer-Jagd-Abteilung 560 z.b.V.* (*SS-Hauptsturmführer* Markowz) and its *"Hetzer"* served as rear guard. They held the pursuing Russians at a distance and made it possible for their army comrades of the *XXVII. Armee-Korps* to march west.

On 1/2 May the main body of the *3. Panzer-Armee* reached the Rostow — Güstrow — Plauer-See — Kyritz line. The Mecklenburg isthmuses were defended by the rearguards. The march continued and the fighting retreat went on.

On 2 May 1945, the first units of the *3. Panzer-Armee* crossed the demarcation line on both sides of Schwerin and went into British or American captivity.

On 3 May *SS-Freiwilligen-Panzer-Grenadier-Regiment 49 "de Ruyter"* reached the Parchim area. The Russians pursued closely along the Plau — Lübs road. Since many German march groups of the *XXVII. Armee-Korps* were still on the way to the west, Lohmann's regiment was ordered to once again form a bulwark and hold on until all the units had passed the demarcation line. The commander of the *II./SS-Freiwilligen-Panzer-Grenadier-Regiment 49 "de Ruyter"*, *SS-Sturmbannführer* Petersen, reported:

> Once more, my battalion and the remnants of *SS-Freiwilligen-Panzer-Grenadier-Regiment 49 "de Ruyter"* had to defend at a time when the higher headquarters had already had made it across the demarcation line to the Western Allies. One last time our men dug foxholes — this time just east of Parchim. Two of the *Sturmgeschütze* that were attached to the regiment came forward and, according to standard operating procedures, went into position at the line of riflemen. Farther back, the three last heavy infantry guns of the regiment prepared to fire. Everything was coordinated to the "nth" degree in order to give the Russians a warm welcome.

> Then they came, confident of complete victory. Eight, nine, twelve Russian tanks rolled down from right to left into a ravine-like valley. The defenders were feverish at the weapons. But all maintained perfect fire discipline, as ordered. The lead tank came to a halt at the destroyed bridge over the stream. Suspecting nothing, the other eleven moved up, one after another. Then the German command rang out:

> "Left gun take the lead tank, right gun the rear tank. Open fire!"

> All Hell broke loose at once. The *Sturmgeschütze* knocked out all of the tanks, one after another. The steep terrain blocked the Russian tanks in their attempt to turn around and move up the slope. The chaos was complete.

> In the meantime, two armored cars with white stars on them approached from Parchim. They were waved forward from the firing position of the heavy infantry guns to the observation position at the front. The men in the foxholes whispered to each other that the *Amis* were coming. They would help us in the fight against the Russians.

> The armored cars stopped at the observation point on the road. The hatches opened. Two American officers of the US 7th Armored Division observed the con-

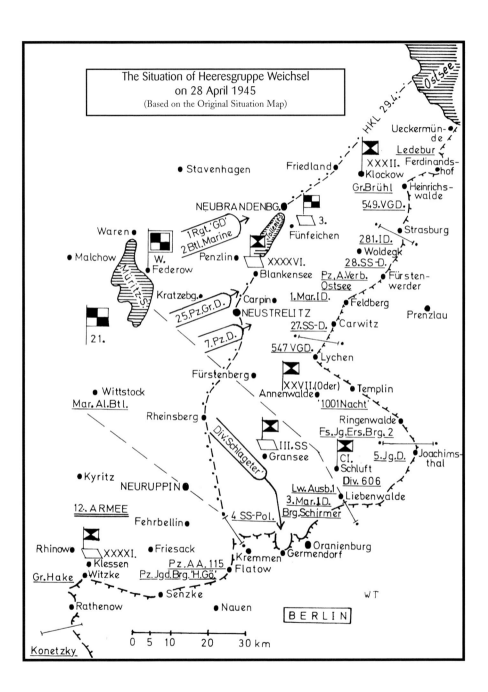

The Situation of Heeresgruppe Weichsel
on 28 April 1945
(Based on the Original Situation Map)

Ostsee

HKL 29.4.

Ueckermün-
de
Ledebur
XXXII. Ferdinands-
Klockow   hof
Gr.Brühl • Heinrichs-
549.VGD.   walde

• Stavenhagen   Friedland•

NEUBRANDENBG.•

Waren •   3.
                    Fünfeichen   • Strasburg
                              281.ID.
• Malchow   W.   Penzlin•   • Woldegk
          •Federow   XXXXVI.   28.SS-D.
                    •Blankensee   Pz.A.Verb. •Fürsten-
          Kratzebg.•   Ostsee   werder
                    Carpin•   1.Mar.ID.
          25.Pz.Gr.D. NEUSTRELITZ   •Feldberg
                              • Prenzlau
          7.Pz.D.   27.SS-D. •Carwitz
          21.   547 VGD.
                              •Lychen
          Fürstenberg•
                    XXVII.(Oder) • Templin
• Wittstock   Annenwalde•   '1001Nacht'
Mar.Al.Btl.   Ringenwalde•
          Rheinsberg•   Fs.Jg.Ers.Brg.2
                    III.SS   5.Jg.D. •Joachims-
                    •Gransee   CI.   thal
                              •Schluft
•Kyritz   Lw.Ausb.I Div.606
     NEURUPPIN•   3.Mar.ID. •Liebenwalde
12.ARMEE   Brg.Schirmer
          Fehrbellin•
                    4 SS-Pol.
Rhinow•   •Oranienburg
     XXXXI.   •Friesack •Kremmen •Germendorf
  •Klessen   Pz.A.A.115 •Flatow
Gr.Hake •Witzke   Pz.Jgd.Brg.'H.Gö.'
              •Senzke   W T
•Rathenow   •Nauen   BERLIN

          0 5 10   20   30 km

Konetzky

tinuing fight with the Russian tanks through their field glasses.

It continued for a while. A tense time. Then the field glasses dropped to their chests and two hands flew up to their caps in a military salute — to us, and the salute was returned by many.

The *Sturmgeschütz* commanders didn't see any of that and kept on firing as if it were their final obligation. I do not know any of their names.

Farther to the rear, the two olive-green armored cars with the white stars shifted into reverse and rolled back to Parchim. The leader of the combat patrol could report to the US 7th Armored Division in Schwerin how far the Russians were from the demarcation line.

In the evening of 3 May, *General* Hörnlein thanked *SS-Obersturmbannführer* Lohmann for the performance of *SS-Freiwilligen-Panzer-Grenadier-Regiment 49 "de Ruyter"* in its final fighting as the rearguard for the *XXVII. Armee-Korps*. The next morning the regiment went into American captivity. Since the direct route had already been blocked by the Russians, the regiment had to take a route across the moor. Petersen wrote:

It was a sunny morning as we walked across the moor. No more tanks followed us. To be sure, the men still had all their weapons and equipment with them, the tools of war, but there was a completely different feel about that day's walk on the spongy moor — no direct anxiety. It was a balance between times, between war and peace, a peace that, after all the years of war, was still beyond our grasp and not yet comprehensible, even for the last men of *SS-Freiwilligen-Panzer-Grenadier-Regiment 49 "de Ruyter"* who had fought just the day before.

Farther north, the remnants of the *27. SS-Freiwilligen-Grenadier-Division "Langemarck"*, the *28. SS-Freiwilligen-Grenadier-Division "Wallonien"* and the *33. Waffen-SS-Grenadier-Division "Charlemagne"* crossed the demarcation line into British captivity between Bad Kleinen and Wismar.

Farther southeast at the Elbe between Lenzen and Tangermünde, *Armeegruppe Steiner* and the *12. Armee* approached their end. Remnants of the *12. Armee* and *9. Armee* crossed the Elbe bridge at Tangermünde, which had been repaired in makeshift fashion, into American captivity.

On 6 May 1945, there was intense activity at the crossing sites at Tangermünde and Schönhausen. The question was repeatedly raised whether all the soldiers of the *Wehrmacht* could cross over in the period of time that had been agreed on between the Americans and the *12. Armee* at the surrender. The Russians drew ever nearer and pressed on the narrowing German bridgehead.

Among the many formations that crossed the river on 6 May were the remnants of *SS-Panzer-Aufklärungs-Abteilung 10* (which had been forced away from the *10. SS-Panzer-Division "Frundsberg"* at Cottbus) and the *23. SS-Freiwilligen-Panzer-Grenadier-Division "Nederland"* and its *SS-Freiwilligen-Panzer-Grenadier-Regiment 48 "General Seyffard"*. (*SS-Freiwilligen-Panzer-Grenadier-Regiment 49 "de Ruyter"* had been attached to the *547. Volks-Grenadier-Division*, as previously described.) Other units to

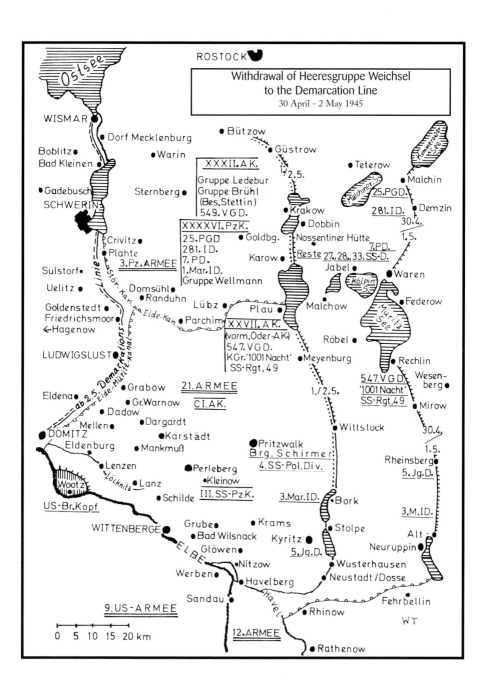

ROSTOCK

**Withdrawal of Heeresgruppe Weichsel
to the Demarcation Line**
30 April - 2 May 1945

Ostsee

WISMAR
Dorf Mecklenburg
Boblitz
Warin
Bad Kleinen
Gadebusch
Sternberg
SCHWERIN
Crivitz
Plahte
3.Pz.ARMEE
Sülstorf
Uelitz
Domsühl
Randuhn
Goldenstedt
Friedrichsmoor
←Hagenow
Parchim
LUDWIGSLUST
Grabow
21.ARMEE
Eldena
Gr.Warnow
CI.AK.
Dadow
Mellen
Dargardt
DÖMITZ
Karstädt
Eldenburg
Mankmuß
Lenzen
Perleberg
Wootz
Lanz
Kleinow
Schilde
III.SS-PzK.
US-Br.Kopf
WITTENBERGE
Grube
Krams
Bad Wilsnack
Glöwen
Kyritz
Nitzow
Werben
Havelberg
Sandau

XXXII.AK.
Gruppe Ledebur
Gruppe Brühl
(Bes.Stettin)
549.VGD.
XXXVI.PzK.
25.PGD
281.ID.
7.PD.
1.Mar.ID.
Gruppe Wellmann

Bützow
Güstrow
1/2.5.
Teterow
Malchin
Krakow
25.PGD.
281.ID.
Demzin
Dobbin
30.4.
Goldbg.
Nossentiner Hütte
7.PD.
1.5.
Karow
Reste 27, 28, 33.SS-D.
Jabel
Waren
Kölpin-S.
Lübz
Plau
Malchow
Federow
XXVII.AK.
(vorm.Oder-AK)
547.VGD.
KGr.'1001 Nacht'
SS-Rgt.49
Röbel
Meyenburg
1./2.5.
Rechlin
547.VGD.
'1001 Nacht'
SS-Rgt.49
Wesenberg
Mirow
30.4.
Wittstock
1.5.
Pritzwalk
Brg.Schirmer
4.SS-Pol.Div.
Rheinsberg
5.Jg.D.
3.Mar.ID.
Bork
3.M.ID.
Stolpe
5.Jg.D.
Alt-
Neuruppin
Wusterhausen
Neustadt/Dosse
Fehrbellin
Rhinow
WT

9.US-ARMEE

0 5 10 15 20 km

12.ARMEE

Rathenow

cross were the *schwere SS-Panzer-Abteilung 502* and the *32. SS-Freiwilligen-Grenadier-Division "30. Januar"*. Most of them crossed over the emergency footbridge at Tangermünde to the other side of the river. *SS-Standartenführer* Kempin, commander of the *32. SS-Freiwilligen-Grenadier-Division "30. Januar"*, discharged approximately 148 men of his division. It was all he had been able to assemble.

At 2200 hours, Kempin and his small staff were the last to cross the Elbe. On the other side, the German soldiers were led by soldiers of the US 102nd Infantry Division to the collecting points at Tangermünde and Stendal.

The weapons fell silent. Behind the European volunteers of the *Waffen-SS* lay months, years of fighting. They had been filled with sacrifice and deprivation. They had voluntarily accepted that in order to take part in the "crusade against Bolshevism" and block Stalin's world domination. They made the vision of a United Europe under German leadership a part of themselves and put their lives at stake for that ideal. Behind them lay the graves of comrades who had grown dear. They tortured their brains with thoughts and more thoughts. They bore no guilt, but they suspected that they would suffer from hate and persecution in their homelands. They received the first confirmation that their commitment had not been in vain when, a few years later, the "Iron Curtain" came down on that line at which, in May of 1945, their struggle for a United Europe had come to an end. They had fought for a Europe of the Fatherlands, whose outlines — blurred indeed — had begun to emerge in their imagination. The final confirmation came with the collapse of the Soviet Union in 1989.

Now that the Russian archives also stand open to the historians of the West, German historian Werner Maser has proved in his book *"Der Wortbruch — Hitler, Stalin und der zweite Weltkrieg"* (Breach of Promise — Hitler, Stalin and the Second World War):

…how Hitler and Stalin simultaneously bargained with the Western Allies and why Stalin resolved on a pact with Hitler and how, from then on, both dictators conceived and prepared measures that changed more than just Europe under the screen of their unholy alliance.

The research into and presentation of the Soviet plans for an attack on Germany is especially explosive. Maser's conclusion:

Hitler's "Operation Barbarossa" forestalled Stalin's strategic concentration in 1941 for the planned attack on Germany by only a few hours.

And the question emerges as to what would have become of Europe if Germany had not anticipated and thwarted the drive for world domination of the Soviet Union with a preventive strike? The Red Army would have overrun all of Europe clear to the English Channel in a single sweep! Seen in that light, the struggle of the European volunteers for a free and united Europe makes sense and is justified. They were the protagonists of that Europe that is so painstakingly being constructed today.

Appendices

Appendix 1: Precursor Formations

After the occupation of Denmark and Norway by the *Wehrmacht* (April 1940), many young Norwegians and Danes volunteered to serve in *SS-Regiment "Nordland"*, which was then being formed as the third regiment in the newly forming *SS-Division "Wiking"*. After war broke out with the Soviet Union (June 1941), recruitment strengthened in lands occupied by Germany to volunteer for service with Germany against the Soviet Union. The motivation: A crusade against communism. In the course of that, *"Legion Niederlande"* was formed in Holland, the *"Freikorps Danmark"* in Denmark, the *"Legion Norwegen" (Viken-Bataillon)* in Norway and the *"Finnisches Freiwilligen-Bataillon" (III. (finnisches)/SS-Regiment "Nordland")*. The latter was sent back to Finland in the summer of 1943. The three other battalions went into the nucleus of what would later become the *11. SS-Freiwilligen-Panzer-Grenadier-Division "Nordland"* and *23. SS-Freiwilligen-Panzergrenadier-Division "Nederland"*.

SS-Regiment "Nordland"

During the first half of April 1940, the *Wehrmacht* occupied Denmark and Norway in *Unternehmen Weserübung*.

The order for the formation of *SS-Standarte "Nordland"* had already been issued by 20 April 1940. The regiment was to consist of a combination of Danish and Norwegian volunteers. Recruiting began in those countries, with response from many young ethnic Germans from mainland Denmark as well as Danes and Norwegians. The first North-Schleswig volunteers illegally crossed the border and were assembled at the Hamburg-Langenhorn *SS*-barracks.

After suitable arrangements had been made with the Danish government and the newly installed administration in Norway, recruiting began openly and the volunteers were sent to Germany. By early summer 1940 the *I./SS-Regiment "Nordland"* had already been formed at Klagenfurt-Lendorf. The other battalions and the regimental units were organized shortly thereafter at Wien-Schönbrunn. After the organization was completed, *SS-Regiment "Nordland"* had the following structure:

I, II. and *III./SS-Regiment "Nordland"*: Each with three rifle companies and one machine-gun company.

Regimental units:

Regimental staff
13./SS-Regiment "Nordland": Infantry guns
14./SS-Regiment "Nordland": Antitank guns
15./SS-Regiment "Nordland": Motorcycle company
16./SS-Regiment "Nordland": Combat engineers
17./SS-Regiment "Nordland": Motorcycle reconnaissance
One regimental supply section

When, in September 1940, it was ordered that the *SS-Division (mot.)* with the name *"Wiking"* was to be organized from "...men coming from racially-related lands (Norway, Denmark and Holland)...", *SS-Regiment "Nordland"* had nearly reached its full authorized establishment. The commander of the regiment was *SS-Obersturmbannführer* Fritz von Scholz, a highly decorated officer from the Austro-Hungarian Army of the First World War. Within a short time he won the hearts of his subordinates, who soon named him "Old Fritz".

The commander of the *I./SS-Regiment "Nordland"* was *SS-Sturmbannführer* Polewacz. The *II./SS-Regiment "Nordland"* was first commanded by *SS-Sturmbannführer* Fortenbacher, then by *SS-Sturmbannführer* Stoffers. The commander of the *III./SS-Regiment "Nordland"* was *SS-Sturmbannführer* Plöw.

After completion of basic training and the first company-and battalion-level exercises, *SS-Regiment "Nordland"* transferred to become part of *SS-Division "Wiking"* in February/March 1941 at the Heuberg Training Area. The final contingents of volunteers, including Finns, joined the regiment at that location. Exercises involving larger formations were carried out at Heuberg.

In June 1941, as part of the redesignated *SS-Infanterie-Division (mot.) "Wiking"*, *SS-Regiment "Nordland"* moved by rail to the Guhrau area of Silesia and, shortly thereafter, in a road march to the assembly area for the Russian campaign (*Unternehmen "Barbarossa"*) near Lublin. The division and the *9. Panzerdivision* were attached to the *XIV. Armee-Korps (mot.)* (later redesignated a *Panzer-Korps*) of *Panzergruppe 1* (later *1. Panzer-Armee*) of *Generaloberst* von Kleist.

The campaign against Russia began on 22 June 1941. After German forces overcame the Russian border positions and Lemberg was captured on 30 June 1941 by formations of the *XXXXIX. Gebirgskorps (1. Gebirgsdivision)*, the motorized formations began a fast-moving advance. *SS-Division "Wiking"* rotated its regiments through the advance-guard position. *SS-Regiment "Nordland"* saw its first action at Tarnopol. A pursuit ensued. The offensive was then delayed by stubborn resistance at Satanow on the Stalin Line.

In mid-July, the *III. Armee-Korps (mot.)* (von Mackensen) had reached the

Fastow area outside of Kiev. It was far ahead of its flank formations. *SS-Regiment "Nordland"* was directly attached to the corps to protect its long, open northern flank. The regiment occupied a widely extended defensive position north of *Rollbahn Nord* (the road from Shitomir to Kiev), while other elements of *SS-Division "Wiking"* concentrated for the battle of the Uman Pocket.

SS-Regiment "Nordland" prevented the Russian formations that had been shoved aside by the formations of the *6. Armee* from reaching the road to Kiev. When other German units had closed up, *SS-Regiment "Nordland"* followed its division, which was already farther south and west of the Dnjepr. Security duty on the Dnjepr and the capture of Dnjeprodhershinsk followed. When the *III. Armee-Korps (mot.)* formed a bridgehead at Dnjepropetrowsk, units of *SS-Regiment "Nordland"* were brought into the bridgehead on ferries on 31 August.

On 1 September, the *198. Infanterie-Division*, commanded by *Generalleutnant* Roettig, took over the eastern portion of the Dnjepropetrowsk bridgehead. *SS-Regiment "Nordland"* was attached to the division. Both formations relieved the *13. Panzer-Division*, which had taken the first small bridgehead in a *coup de main*. The *60. Infanterie-Division (mot.)* was to the left of the *198. Infanterie-Division*.

On 2 September 1941, the bridgehead was enlarged by two to three kilometers on all sides by offensive operations. *SS-Regiment "Nordland"*, on both sides of the stone-paved road to Podgorodnoje, was in the center of the two army divisions. The Dnjepropetrowsk bridgehead was held in spite of daily infantry attacks and heavy pounding by Russian artillery and air. *SS-Regiment "Nordland"* paid a high price in blood. According to the *198. Infanterie-Division* war diary, the regiment had a combat strength of 58 officers and 1,928 noncommissioned officers and men on 30 August 1941. On 7 September 1941, it had 49 officers and 1,493 noncommissioned officers and men.

During the night of 7/8 September 1941, *SS-Regimenter "Germania"* and *"Westland"* moved into the bridgehead and broadened it with attacks through the village of Kamenka on 8 and 9 September. The Dnjepropetrowsk bridgehead fulfilled an important task in relation to the battle of the Kiev Pocket. It pinned Russian formations and also served as a starting point for the further advance to the east by *Panzergruppe von Kleist*.

On 29 October 1941, the onset of frost made the roads passable again. At long last, supplies came forward. During the advance of *Panzergruppe von Kleist* on Rostow and Schachty, *SS-Regiment "Nordland"* crossed the Nagalnoje sector in the Diakowo-Bobrikowo area.

In the meantime, the *III. Armee-Korps (mot.)* had captured Rostow on 21 November 1941. However, the Russian southern front soon launched a counteroffensive and forced the corps to evacuate Rostow on 28 November and withdraw.

SS-Division "Wiking", advancing toward Schachty on the northern wing of the *XIV. Armee-Korps (mot.)* (von Wietersheim), soon lost contact with its left neighbor, the *1. Gebirgsdivision*. As a mountain-infantry formation and as a result of strong enemy resistance in front of the heights at Darjewka, the *1. Gebirgsdivision* had fallen far behind. Since *SS-Regiment "Germania"* was pinned south of Astachowo and *SS-Regiment "Westland"* had to be employed to deal with a crisis between the *III.* and *XIV. Armee-Korps (mot.)*, *SS-Regiment "Nordland"* ended up with the task of again covering the long, open northern flank of *Panzergruppe von Kleist*. And that was exactly where the Russians set out to encircle the entire southern wing of the German Eastern Front, pushing it back against the Sea of Azov and destroying it.

On 17 November 1941, the Soviets began their attempt to break through the greatly overextended front of *SS-Regiment "Nordland"*. The Russian assault intensified from one day to the next. Astachowo became a hot spot. It was held for a long time by the *II./SS-Regiment "Nordland"*. When the *Panzergruppe* began a general retreat, *SS-Regiment "Nordland"* became a part of it. The positions had to be held during the day. It was only with the onset of darkness that the battalion could fall back to the next locality. The motorcycle troops remained as the last elements. They covered the withdrawal of the rifle companies which had to march on foot since the motor vehicles had been withdrawn far to the rear to avoid the danger of encirclement.

During the retreat in November 1941, the actual strength of *SS-Regiment "Nordland"* was significantly reduced. Nevertheless, it made it possible for *Panzergruppe von Kleist* to pull back through Tusloff to the Mius. Germans, Danes, Norwegians and Finns of *SS-Regiment "Nordland"* had withstood the assault of five fresh Soviet divisions and a tank brigade during the period from 17-23 November and made possible the formation of a new front. For that, the commander of the regiment, *SS-Oberführer* Fritz von Scholz, was awarded the Knight's Cross.

Severely decimated and completely exhausted, the men of *SS-Regiment "Nordland"* were granted a few days of rest in Amwrosjewka. Instead of the desired return to Germany for reconstitution, the regiment was reorganized. The *III./SS-Regiment "Nordland"* (*SS-Sturmbannführer* Plöw) and the *15., 16.* and *17./SS-Regiment "Nordland"* were disbanded and their men taken into the *I.* and *II./SS-Regiment "Nordland"*.

SS-Regiment "Nordland" then consisted of only two battalions. It was employed during the winter of 1941/42 in the Mius sector between Malopetrowsk and Demidowka. In the course of the winter, *SS-Division "Wiking"* exchanged regiments and battalions several times within its sector, giving a number of units a chance for some rest in Amwrojewka and Uspenskaja. After Russian attacks at the start of the new year had been repulsed, things remained calm on the Mius Front.

During the summer of 1941, the *"Finnisches Freiwilligen-Bataillon der Waffen-SS"* —formerly *"SS-Freiwilligen-Bataillon Nordost"* — was organized and brought to combat readiness under *SS-Sturmbannführer* Hans Collani, first at Wien-Schönbrunn, then at Stralsund and at the Groß-Born Training Area. The first contingent of Finnish volunteers —soldiers who had been trained in the Finnish Army — had already proven themselves in the *III./SS-regiment "Nordland"* (*SS-Sturmbannführer* Plöw). Starting on 3 December 1941, the *"Finnisches Freiwilligen-Bataillon der Waffen-SS"* rolled by rail from Groß-Born to the Eastern Front. It traveled in increments through Winniza — Dnjepropetrowsk — Rutschenkowo, arriving on 18 January 1942 at Amwrosjewka, where it was attached to *SS-Division "Wiking"*. The battalion was employed in the Skeljansk sector on 21 January.

After reciprocal reliefs and associated refitting, *SS-Regiment "Nordland"* was on the southern wing of the division in the spring of 1942. It was committed as a regiment in the Alexejewka — Alexandrowka — Demidowka sector. The *"Finnisches Freiwilligen-Bataillon der Waffen-SS"* became the *III. (finnisches)/SS-Regiment "Nordland"* on 23 May 1942.

In the course of the reorganization, *SS-Division "Wiking"* received a *Panzer-Abteilung*, thus becoming a *Panzergrenadier-Division*. At the same time the *Armeekorps (mot.)* was renamed *Panzerkorps*, the *Panzergruppen* became *Panzer-Armeen* and the regiments of *"Wiking"* became *Panzergrenadier-Regimenter*. During the reorganization, the machine-gun companies were disbanded and their platoons incorporated into the rifle companies as the fourth platoon of the rifle company. The last company of the battalion became the heavy company with a combat-engineer platoon, *Pak* platoon, infantry-gun platoon and signals platoon. Of the regimental companies, only the *13./SS-Panzergrenadier-Regiment "Nordland"* was left with its heavy infantry guns. As the offensive of *Heeresgruppe-Süd* started toward Stalingrad and the Caucasus, the *III. (finnisches)/SS-Panzergrenadier-Regiment "Nordland"* as well as other battalions of the division still lacked motor vehicles. The battalion therefore remained at Mokryj-Jelantschik until the vehicles arrived.

The *I.* and *II./SS-Panzergrenadier-Regiment "Nordland"* started the new offensive on 21 July 1942 as part of *SS-Panzergrenadier-Division "Wiking"*. On 24 July Rostow was captured. Next came the crossing of the Don and an eventful advance by the *1. Panzer-Armee* and the *17. Armee* (henceforth *Heeresgruppe A*) toward the Caucasus.

During the advance through the Kuban region, *SS-Panzergrenadier-Regiment "Nordland"*, together with *SS-Panzer-Abteilung "Wiking"*, under *SS-Sturmbannführer* Mühlenkamp, and other formations of the division, captured Bjelaja-Glina on the Tichorezk — Salsk railroad line on 1 August. On 3 August, *Kampfgruppe von Scholz* (*I.* and *II./SS-Panzergrenadier-Regiment "Nordland"* and elements of *SS-Panzer-Abteilung" Wiking"*) was given the mission of capturing Krapotkin and securing the bridge across the Kuban intact. The *coup de main* failed. The Russians blew up the bridge that was important for the continuation of the offensive before the first tanks and *Panzergrenadiere* could get to it.

In the meantime, *SS-Panzergrenadier-Regiment "Germania"* formed a bridgehead over the Kuban a bit farther south at Grigoripolenskaja. On 7 August, *SS-Panzergrenadier-Regiment "Nordland"* and *SS-Panzer-Abteilung "Wiking"* moved out of bridgehead. While engaging Russian rearguards, the *Kampfgruppe* reached the next river barrier, the Laba River, on the same day. During the night of 7/8 August, the *I./SS-Panzergrenadier-Regiment "Nordland"* formed a small bridgehead at Termigogenskaja. The *II./SS-Panzergrenadier-Regiment "Nordland"* and *SS-Panzer-Abteilung "Wiking"* reached the river at Tenginskaja. However, both bridgeheads were abandoned when *SS-Panzergrenadier-Regiment "Germania"* gained a bridgehead at Petropaulowskaja that was better for the continued advance.

On 10 August 1942, the *I./SS-Panzergrenadier-Regiment "Nordland"* and *SS-Panzer-Abteilung "Wiking"* established a bridgehead over the next river, the Bjelaba. On the following day the advance continued from there to Beloretschenskaja, which was under simultaneous frontal attack by other elements of the division. That established the starting point for the advance into the wooded Caucasus.

Within the framework of *SS-Panzergrenadier-Division "Wiking"*, *SS-Panzergrenadier-Regiment "Nordland"* advanced about 30 kilometers as the crow flies into the wooded Caucasus. It then captured several oilfields and, due to the mountains and forests, remained at Asfaltewaja to provide security until the *Jägerdivisionen* of the *XXXXIV. Jägerkorps* (de Angelis) had closed up. The light-infantry formations were better equipped and trained for such terrain. The *III. (finnisches)/SS-Panzergrenadier-Regiment "Nordland"* pushed through to the regiment with new motor vehicles and, on 16 August, captured the village of Lineinaja.

In the meantime, *SS-Panzergrenadier-Division "Wiking"* was transferred from the West Caucasus to the Terek and was attached to the *LII. Armee-Korps* (Ott), which had formed a bridgehead over the Terek at Mosdok. On 26 September 1942, *SS-Panzergrenadier-Regiment "Nordland"* attacked Malgobek from that bridgehead while *SS-Panzer-Abteilung "Wiking"* and *SS-Panzergrenadier-Regiment "Westland"* advanced along the valley from Nishni Kurp to Ssagopschin. After initial success, the first attack suffered heavy losses and bogged down. Additional attacks did not lead to significant success. The battalions of *SS-Panzergrenadier-Division "Wiking"* were swapped out several times and employed at the critical points, with the result that the overall combat strength of the division shrank at a frightening rate.

SS-Panzergrenadier-Regiment "Germania" finally arrived from the West Caucasus on 4 October. On 5 October it captured the oil city of Malgobek. The fighting for the Malgobek ridge lasted for days. On 16 October the *III.*

(finnisches)/SS-Panzergrenadier-Regiment "Nordland" captured the high ground (target reference point 701), however, the offensive against Grossny then had to be broken off due to exhaustion and lack of combat power.

In the meantime, the *III. Panzer-Korps* conducted an offensive along the high mountains toward Ordshonikidse. The *13. Panzer-Division* reached the outskirts and was encircled. To free that division, *SS-Panzergrenadier-Division "Wiking"* was relieved at Malgobek-Ssagopschin by the *50. Infanterie-Division*, which had been brought from the Crimea. It was then sent in a road march to the Ordshonikidse sector. The *II./SS-Panzergrenadier-Regiment "Nordland"* arrived first and drove an attack wedge through to the *13. Panzer-Division* on 10 November. On 10 and 11 November, the *13. Panzer-Division* was then able to make its way back through the blocking position that had been formed in the meantime at Fiagdon. *SS-Panzergrenadier-Regiment "Nordland"* occupied a portion of that new position.

In the course of the events at Stalingrad, the sack at Ordshonikidse was evacuated during the second half of December 1942. The freed-up *23. Panzer-Division* and *SS-Panzergrenadier-Division "Wiking"* were then sent to the *4. Panzer-Armee* (Hoth), which was fighting in the Kalmuck Steppe. Only the *III. (finnisches)/SS-Panzergrenadier-Regiment "Nordland"* remained behind and was temporarily attached to the *III. Panzer-Korps*. That battalion secured the mountain flank in several positions until the end of 1942.

At Christmas 1942, the *I./* and *II./SS-Panzergrenadier-Regiment "Nordland"* entrained at Prochladny. At the end of the year they arrived in the Remontnaja area. In the meantime, the *4. Panzer-Armee* attack to relieve Stalingrad had failed. The *4. Panzer-Armee*, consisting of the German *LVII. Panzer-Korps* and two Rumanian corps, fell back to the west in a fighting retreat before heavy enemy pressure.

As 1942 ended and 1943 began, the *I./* and *II./SS-Panzergrenadier-Regiment "Nordland"* defended Remontnaja, Simnowniki, Orlowskaja and Krasnoje Snamja. The *III. (finnisches)/SS-Panzergrenadier-Regiment "Nordland"* rejoined the regiment there.

There were changes in command: *SS-Brigadeführer* Fritz von Scholz assumed command of a Latvian brigade. *SS-Obersturmbannführer* Joerchel became the new commander of *SS-Panzergrenadier-Regiment "Nordland"*.

SS-Panzergrenadier-Division "Wiking" defended the Proletarskaja bridgehead from 17 to 19 January. From 18 to 21 January, the *III. (finnisches)/SS-Panzergrenadier-Regiment "Nordland"* defended Jekaterinowka, which was on the line of retreat of the division. *SS-Panzergrenadier-Regiment "Nordland"* held a series of defensive positions for specified times at Gigant (22 January), Zelina (23 January), Jergorlyskaja (24 and 25 January), Metschetinskaja (25 to 30 January), Kagalnizkaja (31 January) and Gawrilow (2 to 4 February 1943). Contact was then established with the *1. Panzer-Armee* which had to come from Terek and pass through the Rostow bottleneck.

In continuing the offensive that had started at Stalingrad, Russian armies had advanced far to the west and, by the end of January 1943, had crossed the Donez at several places. Their objective was to cut off and destroy the entire southern portion of the German Eastern Front. One of the Russian assault groups, Armored-Group Popoff, had already reached Krasnor-Ameiskoje. *SS-Panzergrenadier-Division "Wiking"*, which had been freed up at Bataisk, was committed against Popoff's group on 4 February 1943. *SS-Panzergrenadier-Regiment "Nordland"* took part in the destruction of Popoff's armored group from 11 to 19 February 1943 as part of the divisional offensive, which attacked Krasnor-Ameiskoje from the south.

A further advance to the north took place from 22 February to 3 March 1943. *SS-Panzergrenadier-Regiment "Nordland"* was employed on the left flank of the division. The Donez was reached on 3 March and a new front established. That ended the crises that had erupted as a part of the military catastrophe at Stalingrad.

In mid-April 1943, *SS-Panzergrenadier-Regiment "Nordland"* occupied a sector in the Ssrednij-Sawodskoje area along the Donez southwest of Isjum.

The regiment was then withdrawn from the front and assembled in the Losowaja area. There it turned over weapons, equipment and motor vehicles to other units of *SS-Panzergrenadier-Division "Wiking"*.

At the end of April 1943, *SS-Panzergrenadier-Regiment "Nordland"* entrained and was transported by rail to the Grafenwöhr Training Area, where it was built up to become the *11. SS-Freiwilligen-Panzergrenadier-Division "Nordland"*.

Winter 1940/41: Range firing of the *I./SS-Regiment "Nordland"* at Gleinach. From right to left: *SS-Standartenführer* von Scholz, *SS-Untersturmführer* Salge, *SS-Sturmbannführer* Polewacz, *SS-Untersturmführer* Bergfeld, *SS-Hauptsturmführer* Lang and *SS-Untersturmführer* ?

The range is closed down at Gleinach.

Above: Company day room in Klagenfurt-Lendorf.

Below: Summer 1941: The *I./SS-Regiment "Nordland"* during a halt on a road march. The vehicles have been placed under cover for operational security purposes. In the middle is the battalion commander, *SS-Sturmbannführer* Polewacz

Below right: At the range in Klagenfurt-Kreuzberg.

Summer 1941: Main Supply Route "North" at Shitomir.

Summer 1942: Crossing the Don at Rostow.

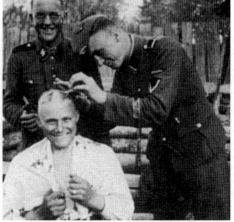

Left: Winter 1941/42 in the Mius Position outside of Kutscherowo: Covered in muck and lice and half-starved to death! From left to right: Langhein, Tieke, Raßmussen, Ratschkowski and Johannsen. **Right**: Phsical hygiene in the field: Not too short, please!

Christmas Eve 1942 on the train from the Caucasus to the Kalmücken Steppes. A Christmas tree has been decorated with paper and lights.

Left: Winter 1942/43: *SS-Untersturmführer* Handtke and *SS-Unterscharführer* Schütz. **Right:** A pig for the field kitchen.

Appendix 2: Organization and Disbanding of the Finnish Volunteer Battalion

(Karl-Heinz Ertel)

After the Soviet Russian — Finnish Winter War in March 1940 was ended by the Peace Treaty of Moscow, there were several months of peace in the relations between the two states. However, during the summer the Soviet Union increased its pressure on Finland. In January 1941 the Soviet Union recalled its ambassador from Finland and concentrated troops on Finland's southeast border. It appeared that Finland would suffer the same fate as the Baltic States, which had been declared Soviet Republics on 20 July 1940.

"During the Winter War, Germany had taken the position of a declared neutral, indeed, it had maintained a restrained viewpoint"[1]. After the conquest of Norway, German interest in the Scandinavian lands increased. Transit arrangements with Sweden and Finland safeguarded railroad and motor-vehicle transport for supplying the German troops stationed in Norway.

After the *Waffen-SS* started recruiting Norwegian volunteers at the end of 1940 for *SS-Regiment "Nordland"*, confidential inquiries regarding recruiting were also initiated in Finland at the beginning of 1941. On 1 March 1941, the Director of the *SS* Main Office, *SS-Gruppenführer und Generalleutnant der Waffen-SS* Gottlob Berger, officially asked the Finnish ambassador in Berlin for permission to recruit Finnish volunteers. On 9 March 1941 the German Foreign Office then placed that request before the Finnish government. Opinions in the Finnish government were decidedly conflicting. Finally, however, the experience of isolation during the February crisis gave the impetus. According to Professor Mauno Jokipili, who has engaged in intensive research into German-Finnish relations during the Second World War[2], Finland grasped that straw and gave permission for the recruitment of volunteers in Finland.

The Finnish government, particularly Marshal Mannerheim, would have preferred to have had a Finnish unit formed in the German Army in the tradition of the *27. königlich preußichen Jägerbattailon*[3] of the First World War. In the end, however, the plan of the *Waffen-SS* was endorsed. It was: "to bind the *Reich* morally to Finland in the event of an attack by the USSR and to train volunteers in Germany in a unit with modern equipment and training that would be available for employment in a struggle with the Soviet Union."[4]

On 15 June 1941, the *SS-Freiwilligen-Bataillon "Nordost"* was finally organized at Wien-Schönbrunn. On 14 September 1941, it was renamed the *Finnisches Freiwilligen-Bataillon der Waffen-SS*. After basic training, primarily at the Groß-Born Training Area, the battalion joined *SS-Division "Wiking"* in the southern sector of the Eastern Front in January 1942. The battalion fought in the ranks of *SS-Division "Wiking"* until April 1942, receiving recognition from senior commanders for its outstanding performance.

When the two-year obligation of the volunteers came to an end, the Germans sought an extension. In the meantime, however, the internal political situation in Finland had changed greatly.[5] The Finnish parliament had passed a law preventing Finns from serving in a foreign military when Finland was at war. Although no obstacle was placed in the path of leaving the battalion, any new obligation was to be limited to six months. The *OKW* made known to Marshal Mannerheim that Germany did not wish to cause a conflict of conscience for the Finnish volunteers and therefore waived the return of the battalion to German service. "With that, an episode that had provided an especially honorable chapter in the history of Finnish-German military fellowship drew to a close."[6]

[1] J. K. Paasikivi: "Meine Moskauer Mission 1939-1941." Hamburg, 1966

[2] Jokipii, Mauno: "Ein Strohhalm für Finnland. Die Hintergründe, die zur Aufstellung des finnischen SS-Bataillons im Winter 1941 führten" in Wilhelm Tieke: "Das Finnische Freiwilligen-Bataillon der Waffen-SS", Osnabrück 1979.

[3] George H. Stein/Peter Krosby: "Das Finnische Freiwilligen-Bataillon der Waffen-SS, eine Studie zur SS-Diplomatie und zur ausländischen Freiwilligen-Bewegung." in: Vierteljahrehefte für Zeitgeschichte 1966, 4. Heft.

[4] Berger to Himmler, 12 April 1941.

[5] Waldemar Erfurth: "Der Finnische Krieg, 1941-1944", Munich 1978.

[6] Ibid.

Summer 1943: Ruhpolding. The *III. (finnisches)/SS-Regiment "Nordland"* marches to its last massed formation in front of *General der Waffen-SS Steiner* on the occassion of its being released from German service.

Appendix 3: The Music-Platoon of the Finnish Battalion

Karl-Heinz Ertel

As recruitment began for volunteers, people in Finland were already thinking of organizing a music platoon. Reserve Lieutenant Tauno Pajunen was selected as the bandmaster.

Pajunen had already started learning music in the Finnish Navy as a 12-year-old. In 1926 he received a teaching position at the Finnish military music school. After that he spent four years at the conservatory in Helsinki. Today it is known as the "Sibelius Academy". After additional civilian studies, he passed his audition as Music Officer in the Finnish Defense Corps at Helsinki on 20 April 1937. After that, he led several music platoons in the Defense Corps until he transferred as a reserve lieutenant to the staff of the Defense Corps at Etelä-Pohjamma and, at the same time, took over directing the city orchestra and the chorus of the singing fellowship of Seinajoki.

At Etelä-Pohjamma he learned of the recruiting for the *Wehrmacht*. When he announced his interest, he received an invitation to the office of the *Ingenieurbüro Rata* in Helsinki. Recruiting for the battalion was conducted under that cover address. There he met Major Riekki, who conducted the entire operation. The major informed him that a Finnish volunteer battalion was to be formed in Germany and the formation of a music platoon was also planned. Pajunen arrived at Stralsund on 7 June 1941 with the last transport from Finland. He traveled from there to Vienna where, on 15 June 1941, the battalion was formed.

After basic training had started at Vienna, the battalion was transferred to Stralsund on 9 July 1941. About the middle of July, the battalion commander, *SS-Hauptsturmführer* Hans Collani, called Pajunen to his office and informed him that a music platoon would be formed for the battalion and that Pajunen was to lead it.

An order of the day was immediately issued to the companies stating that all men who played wind instruments were to report. After they had reported, Pajunen called the men to him individually to determine whether they met the prerequisites for membership in the music platoon. Most of them had already taken part in music platoons in the Defense Corps in Finland or in local wind-instrument orchestras. It was especially gratifying that there were several noncommissioned officers among the candidates.

Pajunan chose the Finnish Sergeant First Class Erkko Antonen and offered to make him the *SS-Stabsscharführer (Spieß)* of the music platoon. When Pajunen reported the results of his action to the commander, he was told that he had to travel to Berlin to secure instruments, music and other necessities. When Pajunen raised the question of payment for the instruments, he was told that he need not be concerned about that. The *SS-Führungshauptamt* would attend to payment. His concern was exclusively to make sure that he got everything that was needed. (Pajunen never did discover how much the final bill was.) The commander sent the German *SS-Untersturmführer* Wentz to assist Pajunen on the trip to Berlin.

On 11 August 1941, the Finnish military attaché in Berlin, Light Infantry Colonel Walter Horn, visited the battalion at Stralsund. Pajunen had to report to Colonel Horn on 12 August and then went with him and Wentz to Berlin.[7] A few days after they had completed their task in Berlin, the instruments, music and other material arrived at Stralsund.

Pajunen had the instruments brought to the intended rehearsal room and issued them to the music platoon. He had the following instruments:

2 piccolos
1 oboe
6 clarinets
1 bassoon
4 horns
2 cornets
3 trumpets
1 tenor horn
2 trombones
1 euphonium
2 bass tubas
1 set of drums
    27 instruments in all

Practice began immediately. The first days of practice were extremely difficult, since the men first had to become familiar with their instruments and with one another. The band leader also had to get to know his men and the men had to get to know their director. The practice time was strictly limited. The morning was available for practice, a highly welcome break from close-order drill and other barracks duties. On the other hand, the men also had to take part in the strenuous combat training.

The music platoon gave its first concert to the battalion in the evening of 14 August. When, on 25 August 1941, the battalion was sent to the Groß-Born Training Area, the music platoon played at the head of the column as it marched to the railroad station. Pajunen said that the music platoon also played the marching song, *"Wir fahren gegen Engelland"* ("We are Marching Against England") which was not actually supposed to be played on marches. He did not know that at the time. After arriving at the training area, the music platoon carried on with its training while the men took part in combat training in the afternoon. The music platoon gave a series of open-air concerts on the square between the company quarters, on the terrace of the officers' club, in front of the military hospital and in front of the commander's quarters.

The battalion had a day of major celebration on 15 October 1941 when it was sworn in. A large delegation from Finland appeared and Colonel Horn presented the battalion with a banner that had been sewn by wives of former light infantrymen of the *27. königlich preußichen Jägerbattailon*. The musical side of the festivities was provided by the music corps of the *SS-Führungshauptamt*, while the men of the music platoon took part in the swearing in with their unit.

On 3 and 4 December the long-awaited transfer to the Eastern Front began. Railroad transports arrived in Winniza on 8 December 1941. After the motor vehicles had arrived, a road march then continued to the east. The onset of winter surprised the battalion in Kirowograd, where several days were allotted for rest. Initially the commander wanted a concert there, but in the end it was cancelled.

In the middle of January the battalion joined *SS-Division "Wiking"* in the Mius position. The carefully packed instruments were stored at the division's base at Amwrossieka. After the withdrawal from the Caucasus, the battalion again passed through that place and Pajunen was able to make sure that the instruments were still there. It is no longer possible to determine whether the instruments were brought along on the retreat from the Mius position.

Many of the men of the music platoon were killed during the battalion's combat actions or later in the Finnish army. The *Spieß* of the music platoon, Erkki Antonen, lost his left arm as a Light Infantry Lieutenant in the fighting at Portinhoikka. A company commander in the Finnish battalion, Tauno Pohynjanlehto, took part in that engagement as commander of a tank company. He later ran into Antonen and asked him why he had brought his severed arm to the dressing station. Antonen replied: "My wristwatch was still on it."[9]

[7] Tauno Pajunen: "Suomalaisen vapaehtoisen SS-pataljoonan soittokunta", unpublished manuscript.

[8] Diary entry of Colonel Horn: "Vänr. Pajunen oli Berliinissa hakitoja suoritamassa, 12 -14 August 1941.

[9] Letter, Tauno Pohjanlehto to the author, 29 September 1983.

Appendix 4: The Battalion Marching Song

On 9 February 1942 Pajunen, the Finnish war correspondent, Jukka Tyrkkö, and *SS-Obersturmführer* Hortling (who was later killed in action) were lying on their bunks at Bachmutski (Mius position), when Soviet harassing fire came down on the village. German artillery positioned behind the village replied with a sudden concentration of its own. That inspired Pajunen to compose a march. Tyrkkö wrote lyrics, and the first verse of the marching song of the *Finnisches Freiwilligen-Bataillon* was soon completed. The marching song was completed the next day. On 8 March the two presented their work to the commander at the command post. The commander was greatly pleased and plied the two with cognac and cigarettes. The battalion adjutant, *SS-Untersturmführer* Hirt, was given the task of translating Tyrkkö's words into German that fitted the melody.

The march is not well known, although it was later printed in Finland. A Finnish singer once sang the song on the German radio. Tyrkkö, in any case, was later regularly greeted in his favorite watering hole with the melody of the march.

Appendix 5: Banat Swabians in the Waffen-SS

Many Germans from areas of Europe beyond the boundaries of the *Reich* served in the *Waffen-SS* during the war. The Fellowship of the Banat Swabians has created a memorial to the sacrifices made by the Banat Germans in producing a record of their ordeals in a large-format, 680-page book. The Banat Germans were ethnic Germans who had been settled in an area bounded by present-day Hungary, Rumania and the former Yugoslavia by Empress Maria Theresa in 1718.

It is a moving documentation of what happened to those Germans, many of whose men voluntarily served during the war with the *Waffen-SS*. They were outstanding soldiers and earned great honor. We feel it a distinct duty to speak out for those who stood firmly with the Germans and with their own people in the hour of greatest need in German history. They never disavowed their German heritage. They were the successor generation of the multitude of German settlers, who came from almost all the lands of the former Austrian Empire and from many parts of the *Reich*, who had come to the Banat to cultivate an unkempt land. They came as town citizens, as miners and as peasants. Threatened by epidemics and Turkish raids, they created a land rich in grain and blossoming with industry. Just before the First World War there were about 500,000 Germans in the Banat and north of the Marosch River.

Those who are unfamiliar with the development and relationships in southeast Europe often ask how it came about that a portion of the ethnic Germans subject to compulsory military service came to serve in the Rumanian army while others served in the German Army and whether they served voluntarily or were drafted.

The answers are not simple, since the situation was complicated and not easily simplified. The description that follows of the service in the German Army by ethnic Germans from Rumania — 90% of whom served in formations of the *Waffen-SS* — is a factual examination. There is no attempt to justify things. The intent is merely to note how and why those Germans in Rumania chose to serve in the German Army as opposed to the Rumanian one.

In several situations that were often determined by specific, local events, most of them moved freely and without direct or indirect pressure from one army to the other. They attempted to choose the lesser of two evils. Granted, the superior leadership and better quality of armament and supplies, as well as the social help given to family members at home, aided in their choice. The catastrophe at Stalingrad resulted in Germans from the dispersed Rumanian formations joining up on their own with German units. They had no choice in their assignment to the *Waffen-SS*. They were never asked. The majority could just as well have been mustered into the army formations or the *Luftwaffe*. The fact that the units of the *Waffen-SS* represented only about

10% of the German fighting forces did much to justify the hope that they would find more of their fellow countrymen in the *Waffen-SS* formations. As a rule, that was also the case.

In the 18th and 19th centuries and up until the end of the First World War, ethnic Germans throughout the entire Austro-Hungarian Empire discharged their military obligations in the Imperial Austro-Hungarian Army. At that time, that caused no problems in terms of the various nationalities living together. The garrisons were either within the large areas of German settlement or in old Hungary, lower Austria and the Steiermark. Rarely was a Banat Swabian or a Transylvanian Saxon assigned to inner Bohemia or Moravia or in the southern Slavic area. The Banat Germans served primarily in Temeschburg, Segedin, Großwardein, Ofenpest, Preßburg, Ödenburg, Vienna and Graz.

With the exception of the revolutionary years of 1848/49, for as long as the Austro-Hungarian Monarchy existed, the Germans of those lands never presented a problem of loyalty to the state, since they were never required to fight for the state against their own nationality. They were also never placed in a situation where they were faced with a decision for their own nationality against the state.

In contrast, the Germans in Bessarabia, Dobrudscha and Russia were faced with that conflict during the First World War. The same conflict faced southeast Germans in 1941, primarily those in Yugoslavia. In spite of the rapid capitulation of the Yugoslavian army in April 1941, a number of ethnic Germans were killed in the fighting against the German troops that advanced into Yugoslavia.

A similar problem faced the Rumanian Germans when, on 23 August 1944, Rumania, changed sides. Until that point, it had been fighting as an ally of Germany against a common enemy. The majority of the Germans in Rumania who were capable of military service — men between 17 and 45 years of age — along with tens of thousands of women capable of labor — 18 to 35 years of age— were sent to Russia for compulsory labor. However, numerous ethnic Germans were also serving with Rumanian military units and thus came into combat against brothers and cousins on the German side.

The legal side of service in the German Army resulted from an agreement between the German and Rumanian governments. The majority of the young Germans from the Banat came into German service in three large batches. Only after the flight of ethnic Germans in the fall of 1944 were older age groups also brought in as *Volkssturm* and for various services.

1. The So-Called 1,000-Man Action (1940)

An exhaustive presentation cannot be given here due to space limitations. A closer examination of the details and a citation of all the relevant sources can be found in the documents relating to the fate of Germans in Rumania that were published by the *Bundesminister für Vertriebene, Flüchtlinge und Kriegsgeschädigte* (German Federal Minister for Expelled Persons, refugees and Those Who Have Suffered in War).

The aforementioned action took place in January 1940 and, in agreement with the Rumanian government, brought about 1,000 volunteers to Germany in June of that year. The transport took place on ships of the Danube Steamship Company. Those mustered in Bessarabia and the Buchenland embarked at Galatz, those from the Dobrudscha at Cernavoda and the Germans from the Banat and Transylvania embarked in Orschova. At the muster in Vienna, the majority went to the *Waffen-SS and* about 200 to the army *Regiment "Brandenburg"*. An additional 100 went to the *Organisation Todt*, schools, or were employed in the economy.

No recruitment was needed for that action. Quite the contrary. Overall, it was conducted in secret to avoid large-scale pressure on the reception stations from men subject to compulsory military service. Wild suppositions ran rampant regarding the final purpose of this action. It appeared that neither the people in higher places nor the leadership of the ethnic Germans nor, for that matter, the German or Rumanian governments had any clear idea of what was actually intended.

For a long time, it appeared that those 1,000 men were to receive military or business training in Germany and then return to Rumania as instructors, primarily for the renewal and modernization of the Rumanian Army. The number who actually returned as instructors and for liaison to the Rumanian Army at the end of 1940 probably did not exceed 200.

How vague the thinking was at the time is clear from the fact that, at first, a time span of 6 months was being discussed. That was hardly sufficient for military training, and even less so for training in business pursuits. It is certain, however, that at the time the German government had no military intentions for those men. Germany had completed its campaign against Poland with only limited losses and had no shortage of soldiers. The proposal for these measures had been made by the Rumanian foreign minister, Gafencu, at the end of April 1940. They may have rested on the already discernible threat from its neighbor to the east, who was already reaching his hand out for Bessarabia and the Bukovina. Rumania thus wanted closer ties with Germany, which was strong at the time, and to reform its armies with German help.

Indeed, the execution of the 1,000 man action coincided with the Soviet occupation of Bessarabia and the Bukovina on 27 June 1940. Germany, at the time, was concerned with a shortage of workers and, in 1939, about 1,600-1,700 Dobrudscha Germans were brought back to Germany, primarily for the *Reichsarbeitsdienst*.

2. The So-Called 3,000-Man Action and the Yugoslavian Campaign

German military instructors had been in Rumania since September 1940. During the first three months of 1941, an increasing level of concern was particularly evident in the call up of the next age group for the draft — men born in 1920/21. There was talk of a so-called 3,000-man action. Indeed, something like that was already in the works, but was meeting opposition. Although their reasons differed, both the German Ambassador in Bucharest, von Killinger, and the new head of the Rumanian government, Ion Antonescu (since September 1940), were opposed to further recruiting action. The leaders of the ethnic Germans also resisted the thinning out of the population of ethnic Germans. The leader of the ethnic Germans, Andreas Schmidt said in February 1941: "Every man who can bear weapons is to serve in the Rumanian armed forces by order of the *Führer*."

Soon afterward, an event took place that threw all previous thinking onto the rubbish heap and made it possible for many young men of the Banat who were liable for military service to join German units. During the German campaign against Yugoslavia in April 1941, several German units passed through the Banat on their way to Belgrade. When those formations — *Luftwaffe*, army *Infanterie-Regiment (mot.)* "*Großdeutschland* and *SS-Division* "*Das Reich*" — left the Banat at the end of April, a large number of ethnic Germans, primarily from the Banat, went with them.

Since June of 1941 about 45,000 ethnic Germans from Rumania were stationed on the Eastern Front in units of the Rumanian armed forces. They were highly thought of and, indeed, proved competent and reliable. Nevertheless, they were denied almost all access to promotion. There were very few German reserve officers and those came almost exclusively from the former Imperial Austro-Hungarian Army. When the opportunity arose for those soldiers to transfer to the German Army in June and July of 1943, most of them availed themselves of the opportunity. The text of the agreement between the two governments is reproduced in the next section.

3. Agreement between the Governments of Germany and Rumania

The German Government and the Rumanian Government agree that Rumanian citizens of German ethnicity may serve in the *Wehrmacht* and the *SS* if the following conditions are met:

I. Enlistment

1. Rumanian citizens of German ethnicity who have turned 18 by 1 April 1943 may volunteer to enlist in the *Wehrmacht/SS*. Those who enlist in the *Wehrmacht/SS* under this agreement retain their Rumanian citizenship with all its rights and privileges. The same rights are also accorded those volunteers who, when mustered, turned out to be unsuitable for service or who were sent back to Rumania for other reasons.

2. Enlistment is not permitted for Rumanian citizens of German ethnicity under the following circumstances:

a) Active officers and noncommissioned officers. Reserve officers and reserve noncommissioned officers may enlist in the *Wehrmacht/SS* only by permission of the Rumanian General Staff.

b) Active and reserve officers, noncommissioned officers, naval ratings and soldiers of commands, units and administrative units on the Taman, the Crimea and on the Black Sea coast as far as the Dnjestr.

Also ineligible are men in Rumania who are in march units already selected for large formations on the Taman or Cuban.

c) Active corporals and sergeants of units within Rumania who are members of the 1942 and 1943 call-ups, excepting students at the reserve officer school and reserve noncommissioned officer school.

d) Specialists of all current call-ups from the years 1942, 1943 and 1944. Specifically: Telephone repairmen; radio telegraphers; range finders; surveyors; meteorologists; flamethrower troops; gunners of field guns, howitzers, infantry guns, mortars, and antitank weapons; armorers; members of the tank arm; and, all members of the navy and the air force.

e) Specialists of all ranks and age groups who are needed by the army and the economy. Specifically: Opticians; chemists; automotive mechanics; electricians; radio repairmen; vulcanizers; and, machinists.

f) Veterinarians and engineers. Only 60 medical doctors of all specialties may be approved for enlistment in the *Wehrmacht/SS* by the Rumanian General Staff. Their service may follow individually or as a group. Their departure and return to Rumania is not limited to a fixed period of time. Those 60 physicians may only be employed in the *Wehrmacht/SS*.

g) Those declared indispensable (exempt from the draft), that is, those who belong to undertakings which affect armament for the military and the national economy and who are identified in plans for industrial mobilization. Also included are those who are exempt from the draft as members of the metallurgic industry.

The ethnic German group in Rumania may apply for annulment of the exempt status and freeing for enlistment in the German *Wehrmacht/SS* for people specified above whose employment in the above-named industries is not absolutely necessary upon application to the Rumanian General Staff and, if required, provision of a replacement.

3. Rumanian citizens of German ethnicity who desire to enlist in the *Wehrmacht/SS* must report by 30 May 1943 to the enlistment commission of the ethnic German group in Rumania, where they must give a written declaration, witnessed by the representative of the enlistment-zone command. In the declaration, it must explicitly state that the applicant "voluntarily" reports for service in the German *Wehrmacht/SS* . The Rumanian government guarantees that it will not permit sanctions of any sort by anyone against those

who do not want to enlist. The list of volunteers compiled by the mustering commission shall be given to the enlistment-zone command at its headquarters, where the list will be examined with respect to the exceptions provided for in the present agreement. Those Rumanian citizens of German ethnicity who are, at the time, already in the Rumanian Army are to give their declaration to the unit concerned. The enlistment-zone command will send the personnel files of those men who do not belong to its area of responsibility to the responsible enlistment-zone commands so that they can make the necessary entries.

II. Transport Out Of Rumania

Those volunteers who are released to the ethnic-German group in Rumania are to be assembled by the agency of the ethnic-German group in transport units and are to have left Rumania by 31 July 1943. Those volunteers are to take with them no more than:

The clothing and underwear that they have on their bodies and one change of underwear.

Rations for the period of transportation and an additional two days rations for use after their arrival in Germany.

The amount of money specified in the existing economic agreement.

It is forbidden to take gold and jewelry, with the exception of a wedding band and watch.

The same restrictions apply for those returning to Germany from leave and on official journeys. Inspection and permits to arrive in/leave Rumania are the exclusive responsibility of the Rumanian authorities.

III. Relationships with Rumania

1. All those men who enter the *Wehrmacht/SS* as a result of this agreement are forbidden to wear German uniforms when in Rumania (on leaves, on official journeys, etc.) except during the time in transit to or from the country.

These restrictions also apply to areas administered by the Rumanian government.

Those who violate these provisions fall under the punishment provisions of Rumanian law.

2. No Rumanian citizen of German ethnicity can be employed in Rumania or in territory administered by Rumania in German political or economic administrative or military formations.

3. The Rumanian state is in no way responsible for support of or compensation to the families of the volunteers during the time of their service in the *Wehrmacht/SS*.

The Rumanian State is not in any way responsible for pension or compensation to those who become incapable of employment or to survivors of those who may be killed. Those obligations belong to the German *Reich*.

4. All Rumanian citizens of German ethnicity who are in the service of the German *Reich* are subject to Rumanian laws during the time that they are in Rumanian territory or in areas administered by the Rumanian state. Those who are guilty of an offense in Rumania or in areas administered by Rumania will be tried in an accelerated process and, in the event of conviction, the penalty will be postponed and the person turned over to the German military. At the end of the war they can return to Rumania and fulfill the terms of their sentence.

All Rumanian citizens of German ethnicity who are legally sentenced and who are in military or civil imprisonment or are with military units will be turned over to the German *Wehrmacht/SS*. Serving of their sentence will be postponed until the end of the war.

Those who are currently involved in proceedings before a military court will receive judgement in an accelerated proceeding. They will also receive the same treatment.

5. No Rumanian citizen of German ethnicity who is in the service of the German *Reich* may spend more than 30 days leave in one year in Rumania.

IV. Special Provisions

1. All Rumanian citizens of German ethnicity who are presently in the service of the German *Reich* with permission of the Rumanian state fall under the provisions of this agreement.

2. All Rumanian citizens of German ethnicity who have illegally left Rumania also fall under the provisions of this agreement if they are employed in German military *SS* units or in the military economy or in military economic organizations.

Bucharest, 12 May 1943

The Authorized Representative of the German Government

Manfred *Freiherr* von Killinger

Special Emissary and Authorized Minister of the *Reich*

The Authorized Representative of the Rumanian Government

General I. Steflea

Chief of the Royal Rumanian General Staff

From a photo-copy of Document NO-2236, Military Tribunal Case XI (Wilhelmstraße Proceeding): Files of the personal staff, *Reichsführer-SS*, Folder 8.

Enlistments took place, mostly between May and August 1943, in the home villages of the Germans according to the guidelines of the *Wehrmacht* rather than the eligibility criteria of the *Waffen-SS*. A total of about 50,000 Rumanian Germans served in the German Army, starting in the summer of 1943. (About 55% of them were from the Banat. After the award of northern Transylvania and Sathmar to Hungary in 1940, that approximated the amount of ethnic German representation.) The majority of them were again assigned to the *Waffen-SS*. Many of them served in the *7. SS-Freiwilligen-Gebirgs-Division "Prinz Eugen"*, the *4. SS-Polizei-Division*, the *5. SS-Division "Wiking"*, the *11. SS-Freiwilligen-Panzergrenadier-Division "Nordland"*, the *23. SS-Freiwilligen-Panzergrenadier-Division "Nederland"* and in many other *SS*-units. Some, however, served in the *Wehrmacht*, the *Luftwaffe*, the *Organization Todt* or in industry. Thus, in large measure, the question regarding the voluntary nature of their service is answered. As was already the case with the first two groups of inductees, the overwhelming majority of those who enlisted or who transferred to the German military in 1943 did so voluntarily. It was wartime and few were ever asked whether they wished to enter the *Wehrmacht*, *Waffen-SS*, *Luftwaffe* or the *Kriegsmarine*. The induction criteria mentioned above demonstrate that.

For most of those inducted into the *Waffen-SS*, that assignment resulted in serious consequences after the war. Many died in captivity. Those ethnic Germans who served in the Rumanian army suffered an above-average casualty rate. The number of those killed is estimated at about 7,000. Those who served in the German Army also made an extraordinarily high sacrifice. The preliminary estimate in the Bonn documents by the Religious Search Service amounted to between 8,000 and 9,000 killed, approximately 15% of the total inducted from Rumania.

After the war there were isolated voices raised by those who wished to justify measures taken against the Germans in Rumania by referring to their service in the *Waffen-SS*. That specious argument must be decisively refuted in the interest of historical truth. The absurdity of that claim is clearly proven by the simple and incontrovertible fact that numerous ethnic Germans who, for whatever reasons, served during the war in the Rumanian Army, were handed over to the Russians as prisoners at the end of 1944, while still wearing Rumanian uniform. Many, however, were discharged in Rumania for a short period and then, in February 1945, deported to Russia as forced laborers. Very few of the wives and family members of those soldiers were spared from compulsory labor in Russia or the later internal exile (1951) to the Baragan Steppes.

It should again be made emphatically clear that the transfer from the Rumanian to the German Army in the summer of 1943 was made with full agreement, not only of the Rumanian government (see the agreement above), but also from the military and the local authorities. Rumania entered the war on the German side because Russia had occupied two Rumanian provinces (Bessarabia and the northern Bukovina) in 1940, during a time of peace between the two countries. Rumania thus naturally had a major interest in a victory for Germany and its allies. When, after Stalingrad, at the beginning of 1943, the inadequacies of the Rumanian army became increasingly obvious, the Rumanians were inclined to depend more and more upon its larger ally as the guarantor of victory. The Rumanians were convinced that the provision of two to three divisions of ethnic Germans would make a significant contribution to that end, the more so since it entailed no obligations from Rumania and kept Rumania's sacrifices and efforts within bearable limits.

Thus it can be stated with certainty that those responsible in Rumania were not yet thinking of that action functioning as an alibi. Fifteen months later it was falsely transformed and put to that service.

The high value that was placed on that service by the Rumanians can be seen, for example, in the numerous and spirited speeches made by official representatives of the Rumanian state, including members of the general staff, at the departure of individual transports of volunteers.

What were the primary reasons for the transfer of most of the Rumanian Germans from the Rumanian to the German Army? Proper understanding of the motive requires a short look back to historical developments.

More so than the Transylvanian Saxons with their 800-year tradition of settlement in a foreign land, the Banat Swabians had several unfortunate experiences during the course of more than 200 years spent under varying state authorities. The experiences never shook their loyalty, but did restrain their patriotism to within measured bounds.

Toward the end of the reign of Maria Theresa in 1779, the crown-lands of the Banat passed to Hungary. The German settlers were, in all actuality, sold with their estates to predominately Magyar magnates under flagrant breach of the conditions of settlement. At that point in time, the colonists had not yet grown to form an ethnic group with sufficient clout to defend itself. Driven by bitter necessity and ubiquitous deadly fever and plague, they had been forced to wrest the ground required to grow their food from fever-breeding swamps and the uncultivated steppe. Drawn together from all regions of the *Reich* of that period, it required a considerable period of time for them to develop a real feeling of community as a racial group. Thus, in 1779, they had hardly noticed their change in status from free imperial citizens to becoming vassals of the Magyars. Upright and modest, they were accustomed to obediently conform to the dictates of their superiors as if they were coming from a superior level of wisdom. When they realized, with the passage of years, that they were tied to the soil and had been betrayed, the realization came too late. Understandably for them the revolution of 1848/49 was neither a question of high politics nor of the predominance of Austria or Hungary, but simply of regaining fundamental civic liberties and relief from the crushing property levies.

After both of those had been attained, they demanded a certain level of self government under a Swabian count of their own in the so-called "Bogarosch Swabian Petition". But their demand was in vain. Instead, they received some rights in the newly formed crown-land of *"Serbische Wojwodschaft und Temescher Banat"* for the short time span of 11 years. However, surrounded as they were by the outbreak of nationalistic passions among the Magyars and the Slavs, they found that, without the protection of a strong German or Habsburg government, they were subject to foreign despotism. After the "Austro-Hungarian Accord" of 1867, the weakening of the Habsburg power that came as a result of the unfortunate German dualism brought difficult conditions in all areas of their lives. Their governing class generally fell victim to the ongoing Magyarization, while the mass of the village population were forcibly reduced to a minimal cultural level. Thus they were and remained the objects of the state's arbitrary might without self-determination.

When the opportunity arose in 1918/19 to join with the Transylvanian Saxons and escape the massive pressure of Magyarization, the Banat Swabians set all of their hopes on the formation of the new state. However, thanks to the narrow-mindedness of the victorious powers at Trianon, the ethnic Germans became 2/3 members of that new state. The Banat, a natural and geographical unity, was arbitrarily split, although a Banat delegation in Paris submitted a memorandum with the request to attach the entire Banat to Rumania.

The soldiers who returned home from the First World War were awakened to the systematic intellectual repression. After spending years in the trenches with members of many German ethnic groups, including actual Swabians from Germany, they no longer believed in the asserted superiority of the Magyar nation, nor were they ready to accept their previous position as the "dumb Swabians". The Danube Swabians became aware of their own self-worth after being in the midst of an oppressive nationalism for more than half a century. The national consciousness rapidly grew to completion, especially among the Swabians in that portion of the Banat that belonged to Rumania.

After the economic and political rebirth of Germany's strength in the 1930's, the ethnic Germans abroad quite naturally turned to their parent country and sought protection and help there in regaining the rights that had been recognized by charter but that were generally denied. Basically, it had nothing to do with National Socialism. Similar support would have been desired whether the regime had been a democracy — either a monarchy or a republic.

The development of widespread autonomy — for example, in the area of the German educational system in Rumania — was favored and accelerated by the circumstance that, along with other southeast European states, Rumania became closely aligned with the German *Reich*. It needed Germany in order to keep its threatened eastern provinces or, when they were lost, to regain them.

All of that explains the thoroughly understandable enthusiasm for Germany and the readiness to cast one's lot with it. We were Germans and pledged allegiance to our nationality. It was a relationship that was considered obvious and natural for all the other peoples of the earth and was only held against the Germans because of a fundamental dislike of them.

What made it easier for ethnic Germans with a military obligation to personally exercise the option to choose the German over the Rumanian Army was the more than unsatisfactory situations and relationships in the Rumanian Army. It would have been hard to top the corruption that had been present in peacetime. The Germans were seen by their superiors as an inexhaustible source of personal enrichment. Whoever was able to bribe the entire hierarchy of superiors, from corporal to captain — and often much farther up the line — received abundant leave and favors. Anyone who opposed that practice hardly ever saw his family, was harassed by his superiors and became all too familiar with corporal punishment.

Naturally, there were exceptions and there was generally good comradeship among the troops at the front. However, apart from that, no matter how skillful and brave he might be, there was hardly any chance for a German to rise above the lowest enlisted rank, practically no army pay and no organized care for the families of soldiers. Organization, supply and rations were generally miserable. Corruption behind the front also played a significant role. Command and control of units was generally exercised from a point much farther to the rear than in the German Army. In the event of the slightest difficulty, that led all too often to chaotic situations. The frontline soldier on the Eastern Front constantly observed the difference between the two armies. Thus, it required little time for thought in deciding to switch to the German Army, particularly since the German Army was fighting for the same cause.

The ethnic Germans neither wanted nor started the war, nor could they end it. And they did not in any way betray their Rumanian fatherland.

H.F.

Appendix 6: German Cross in Gold Recommendation for SS-Obersturmführer Eugen Deck

SS-Freiwilligen-Panzer-Grenadier-Regiment 49 "de Ruyter"

Regimental command post
10 February 1944

Recommendation for the Award of the German Cross in Gold
to *SS-Obersturmführer* Eugen Deck
(born 10 February 1914 in Mörsch)

(Author's Note: This recommendation is truncated to reflect only Deck's operations with *SS-Freiwilligen-Panzer-Grenadier-Regiment 49 "de Ruyter"*. The preceding five reasons are based on Deck's service with *SS-Panzer-Aufklärungs-Abteilung "Wiking"* and then with the *Finnisches Freiwilligen Bataillon der Waffen-SS*.)

6. During the fighting retreat in February 1944, the *II./SS-Panzergrenadier-Regiment 49 "De Ruyter"* blocked the Luga River crossings at Ssala and Pulkowo-Keikino. During the night of 31 January/1 February 1944, the enemy was able to cross the Luga with one battalion and penetrate Pulkowo, which was defended by the *6./SS-Freiwilligen-Panzer-Grenadier-Regiment 49 "de Ruyter"*. When the inexperienced and exhausted troops were involved in difficult night fighting, the full weight of responsibility rested on the company commander, *SS-Obersturmführer* Deck. He reassembled the scattered elements of the company, stubbornly held on to the houses with them and intercepted the Soviet penetration into the village. After the arrival of the regiment's motorcycle platoon, he launched an immediate counterattack with them and the remnants of his company. At the front of his men, he ejected the enemy in five hours of tough house-to-house fighting. Although he was wounded in the fighting, he remained with his company. After withdrawal was ordered, he covered the withdrawal of the company with a machine gun.

SS-Obersturmführer Deck displayed extraordinary courage in this operation and through his personal example he inspired the badly battered remnants of his company to new resistance and carried them along with him in an immediate counterattack. It was due to his courageous behavior that the *6./SS-Freiwilligen-Panzer-Grenadier-Regiment 49 "de Ruyter"* was able to disengage without enemy pursuit.

This recommendation is enthusiastically endorsed by the division.

Division Command Post, 14 February 1944

Signed: Wagner
SS-Oberführer and Division Commander

Corps Headquarters
Corps Command Post, 23 February 1944
III. (germanisches) SS-Panzer-Korps
Adjutant

A highly regarded *SS* officer of many years whose courage is almost legendary and whose innumerable acts of bravery appear to justify fully the award of the German Cross in Gold.

Commanding General
Signed: Steiner
SS-Obergruppenführer und General der Waffen-SS

The German Cross in Gold was awarded to *SS-Obersturmführer* Eugen Deck on 12 March 1944.

Appendix 7: Knight's Cross Recommendation for SS-Oberscharführer Philipp Wild

Recommendation for the Award of the Knight's Cross to
SS-Oberscharführer Philipp Wild
Tank Commander in the
1./SS-Panzer-Abteilung 11 "Hermann von Salza"

4. SS-Panzer-Grenadier-Brigade "Nederland"

Brigade command post
17 March 1944

Strong enemy air units bombarded the bridgehead and city of Narwa during the nights of 6/7 and 7/8 March in unremitting attacks, each of which lasted for ten to eleven hours. On 8 March 1944 at 0700 hours, two and a half hours of intense artillery barrage began, which supported an attack that followed by the 63rd Guards Rifle Division. That attack was supported by 14 tanks and conducted on a narrow front against the northeast pillar of the bridgehead.

Twelve tanks broke through the main line of resistance and advanced as far as the positions of the heavy infantry weapons of *SS-Freiwilligen-Panzer-Grenadier-Regiment 48 "General Seyffard"*.

At that critical moment, *SS-Oberscharführer* Wild, *1./SS-Panzer-Abteilung 11*, joined the fight with his *Panther* and, in an extremely short time, destroyed all of the T 34's that had broken through.

As a result of his decisive intervention, he substantially thwarted the enemy's plans to roll up the Narwa bridgehead.

The destruction of those tanks was additionally decisive. Because of their loss, the ongoing infantry attacks, which were supported by isolated tanks, could be repulsed.

Signed: Wagner
SS-Oberführer and Brigade Commander

Corps Headquarters,
III. (germanisches) SS-Panzer-Korps

The engagement of *SS-Oberscharführer* Wild was decisive in the continued holding of the Narwa bridgehead.

Commanding General
Signed: Kleinheisterkamp
SS-Gruppenführer und Generalleutnant der Waffen-SS

Recommend approval.

Signed: Frießner
General der Infanterie and
Commander in Chief, *Armee-Gruppe Narwa*

Recommend approval.

Signed: Model
Generaloberst
Acting Commander of *Heeresgruppe Nord*

Also endorsed by *Reichsführer SS* Himmler.

SS-Oberscharführer Wild was awarded the Knight's Cross on 21 March 1944.

Appendix 8: Recommendation for the Oakleaves to the Knight's Cross for SS-Brigadeführer und Generalmajor der Waffen-SS Fritz von Scholz

Corp Headquarters
Corps command post
February 1944
III. (germanisches) SS-Panzer-Korps

Recommendation for the Award of the Oakleaves to the Knight's Cross to
SS-Brigadeführer und Generalmajor der Waffen-SS
Fritz von Scholz

(Born 9 December 1896 in Pilsen. Highly decorated officer in Austro-Hungarian Army in First World War. Knight's Cross as the commander of *SS-Regiment "Nordland"* in December 1941.)

Justification for the recommendation:

SS-Brigadeführer Fritz von Scholz has continued to prove he is outstanding as a division commander and as an example to his troops in active operations during the fighting in the northern sector of the Eastern Front from 16 January 1944 to the present time.

His division was given the mission of blocking superior enemy forces advancing along the Kipen — Narwa main supply route and stopping the enemy's advance on Narwa.

In the course of the heavy fighting, crises continually arose which were repeatedly mastered due to the personal intervention and example of the division commander.

On 28 January 1944, the enemy succeeded in breaking through between the remnants of the *10. Luftwaffen-Feld-Division* and the *61. Infanterie-Division* which were positioned south of the Kipen — Narwa main supply route on both sides of Osertizy. By advancing to the northwest, the enemy blocked the route at Gurlewo. There was danger at Osertizy that *Kampfgruppe Lohmann* of the *11. SS-Freiwilligen-Panzergrenadier-Division "Nordland"* and elements of the *10. Luftwaffen-Feld-Division* adjoining it to the south (with its division staff) would be encircled by the enemy. An immediate counterattack at nighttime from Ljalizy through Gurlewo by division commander *SS-Brigadeführer* Fritz von Scholz opened the route, threw back the enemy and opened the way to Ljalizy for the units that were stationed to the east and the division staff of the *10. Luftwaffen-Feld-Division*.

On 1 February 1944, the *11. SS-Freiwilligen-Panzergrenadier-Division "Nordland"* was pulled back from Jamburg to Dubrowka. The enemy outflanked the division both to the north and to the south with strong forces and attacked the units of the division that were fighting there along the main supply route. *SS-Brigadeführer* von Scholz was the soul of the resistance. He knew the remnants of the *61. and 227. Infanterie-Divisionen* and the *10.*

Luftwaffen-Feld-Division falling back to the west through Narwa required time for that movement. In spite of heavy enemy attacks with armor, the units of the division warded off an enemy thrust and repeatedly smashed the incessant enemy attacks in up to regimental strength.

The stubborn defense on both sides of Jamburg, on both sides of Dubrowka and on both sides of Komarowka, as well as the ongoing defense against superior enemy forces amounting to several divisions, established the prerequisites for the orderly occupation of the Narwa bridgehead and for the assembly of forces to occupy the northern Narwa position.

Additionally, the steadfastness of the units and the firm leadership of the *11. SS-Freiwilligen-Panzergrenadier-Division "Nordland"* provided time for bringing up *Panzergrenadier-Division "Feldherrnhalle"* and additional reinforcements. It also allowed the remnants of the *61.* and *170. Infanterie-Divisionen* and the *10. Luftwaffen-Feld-Division* to be brought back, where those formations could be organized west of Narwa.

The performance of the units and the leadership of *SS-Brigadeführer* Fritz von Scholz thereby established the prerequisites for the continued conduct of the fighting at the Narwa front and, as a result, should be considered decisive factors at this critically important front.

The personal commitment and the example provided by *SS-Brigadeführer* Fritz von Scholz, as well as his moral fiber, made it possible for the soldiers to give it their all. His example served the still inexperienced division well in establishing an obstinate defense.

Commanding General
Signed: Steiner
SS-Obergruppenführer und General der Waffen-SS

SS-Brigadeführer von Scholz was awarded the Oakleaves to the Knight's Cross on 12 March 1944 as the 423rd recipient. After his death in action at the Tannenberg Position, Fritz von Scholz was posthumously promoted to *SS-Gruppenführer und Generalleutnant der Waffen-SS* and, on 8 August 1944, was the 85th soldier to be awarded the Swords to the Oakleaves to the Knight's Cross.

Appendix 9: Recommendation for the Swords to the Oakleaves to the Knight's Cross for SS-Obergruppenführer Steiner

Armee-Abteilung Narwa
Headquarters, 4 August 1944

I recommend the Commanding General of the *III. (germanisches) SS-Panzer-Korps, SS-Obergruppenführer* Steiner, for the award of the Swords to the Oakleaves to the Knight's Cross.

SS-Obergruppenführer Steiner, who was awarded the Oakleaves to the Knight's Cross on 24 December 1942, has repeatedly excelled with unremitting personal involvement and leadership up front at the critical points in the fighting. Thanks to his effective, decisive leadership, he has had an extraordinary share in the present successes of the *Armee-Abteilung*.

Specifically:

1.) In especially difficult conditions, he organized the *11. SS-Freiwilligen-Panzer-Grenadier-Division "Nordland"* and the *4. SS-Panzer-Grenadier-Brigade "Nederland"*. In a partisan-infested area of Croatia, he not only trained the units and formations, but also participated actively in the fighting.

2.) It is thanks to his initiative and self-sacrificing decisiveness that all the enemy attacks at the Oranienbaum Pocket were repulsed by units that were still new and without combat experience.

3.) The Russian breakthrough of the Leningrad and Oranienbaum Fronts in January 1944 placed renewed, extremely heavy demands on the commands of the almost immobile formations. It was thanks to his toughness that the formations of his corps remained firmly under control and successfully fought their way to Narwa in a battle of maneuver.

4.) When it became clearly evident in July 1944 that the attack by the 2nd Shock Army was impending, he immediately oversaw the defensive planning of the Tannenberg Position by personal instruction to all the officers. Although the enemy repeated his attacks daily against the *III. (germanisches) SS-Panzer-Korps* with numerically greatly superior forces and with extremely massive expenditure of materiel, it is thanks to him that the intended breakthrough was totally unsuccessful up to this point. The success of that defense is especially attributable to the actions of *SS-Obergruppenführer* Steiner.

Signed: Grasser
General der Infanterie
Acting Commander of *Armee-Abteilung Narwa*

SS-Obergruppenführer Steiner, with his *III. (germanisches) SS-Panzer-Korps,* achieved a defensive success that was decisive for the entire Eastern Front. With his two weak divisions and one brigade, he held the Narwa Front unshakably firm against the Soviet 2nd Shock Army and 8th Army that attacked with 11 divisions and 6 armored formations. More than 1,020 tanks were knocked out. The enemy suffered extremely heavy losses. Decisive to that outcome was Steiner's great personal decisiveness and his equally brave and flexible conduct of battle.

The recommendation is enthusiastically endorsed.

Headquarters, 5 August 1944
Signed: Schörner
Generaloberst and Commander-in-Chief of *Heeresgruppe Nord*

SS-Obergruppenführer Steiner was awarded the Swords to the Oakleaves to the Knight's cross on 10 August 1944

Appendix 10: Recommendation for the German Cross in Gold for SS-Hauptsturmführer August-Georg Loderhose

11. SS-Freiwilligen-Panzergrenadier-Division "Nordland"
Division Command Post, 16 December 1944

Recommendation for the Award of the German Cross in Gold
to *SS-Hauptsturmführer* August-Georg Loderhose
Regimental Surgeon, *SS-Panzer-Artillerie-Regiment 11*
(Born 30 July 1908 in Frankenberg.)

(Author's Note: In the original justification for the recommendation, three actions in combat by Loderhose as a medical officer of *SS-Artillerie-Regiment 5 "Wiking"* were cited (Dnjepropetrowsk, Lutimaya and Astachowo). Additional justifications then followed)

4.) When the enemy achieved a penetration at Vasa on 12 February 1944, the medical clearing station of the *4. SS-Panzer-Grenadier-Brigade "Nederland"* was located at the Olgino Estate, 5 kilometers west of Narwa. During the period from 10 to 14 February 1944, it was under extremely heavy fire from enemy artillery and mortars.

Although the main lines had to be moved back to the vicinity of the clearing station after the penetration, *SS-Hauptsturmführer* Loderhose, on his own initiative, remained at his clearing station with elements of his company. He cared for all those who were wounded in the fighting under extremely difficult conditions. Thanks to the calm and firm leadership of the company commander, all difficulties were overcome. That was in spite of the fact that contact with the enemy had to be reckoned with at any time after the main lines had been penetrated and the clearing station was under constant mortar fire. All the more remarkable was the fact that *SS-Hauptsturmführer* Loderhose's medical company was in its first operation and the number of motor vehicles issued was absolutely inadequate.

Although the clearing station was hit several times by mortar fire, all of those who were wounded were speedily cared for and evacuated. That was thanks to the tremendous esprit of all the officers and men of the company who were involved. The clearing station was not moved until the penetration had been sealed off and the fighting around Vasa — Riigi had been concluded.

5.) During the Russian attempt to break through from the south and from Kriwasoo to the Waiwara — Narwa main supply route, the medical clearing station of the *4. SS-Panzer-Grenadier-Brigade "Nederland"* was located in Namika between the two penetrations of the enemy at the Waiwara railroad station and the Auwere railroad station.

When a penetration succeeded at the Waiwara railroad station in the early morning hours of 16 February, a Russian combat group that had infiltrated was only separated from the clearing station of the *4. SS-Panzer-Grenadier-Brigade "Nederland"* by a narrow stretch of woods. It presented an immediate threat to the clearing station. Loderhose promptly intervened personally with the assistance of two *Sturmgeschütze* that were at the clearing station. They pinned and captured the 30 enemy.

In spite of continuous concentrated enemy attacks, *SS-Hauptsturmführer* Loderhose and his clearing station remained — on his own initiative — in the immediate area of action. It was the only medical unit in the entire area of the formations involved, and it cared for a large number of wounded with exemplary devotion to duty.

On 18 March 1944, after a month under constant extremely heavy fire from artillery, mortars and Stalin organs, his clearing station reported its 5,000th patient. Particularly during the first days of that heavy defensive fighting, it was only due to the personal commitment of Loderhose, who ruthlessly secured every vehicle that could be freed up, that all of the wounded were transported to the nearest medical facilities, which lay more than 30 kilometers farther to the rear.

It was only because of Loderhose's personal decision to remain in the immediate area of the fighting, his devotion to duty and decisiveness under the most difficult working conditions that all of the troop units fighting in the Narwa — Waiwara railroad station area were cared for, thus assuring the preservation of the combat power of the troops. His performance of duty was emphasized in the corps operations officer's report to *Armee-Abteilung Narwa*.

6.) During the withdrawal movement from Narwa to the Tannenberg Position at the end of July 1944, *SS-Hauptsturmführer* Loderhose remained right behind the new main line of resistance with a forward dressing station after the actual medical clearing station of the company had been moved back to Woka. On 28 July 1944, the forward dressing station was fired on by a Stalin tank that had broken through. This followed days of extremely heavy fire from artillery and mortars. The building was hit repeatedly. It was entirely thanks to the overall courageous and decisive behavior of *SS-Hauptsturmführer* Loderhose that no panic occurred among the numerous wounded whose care was never interrupted. In spite of several direct hits to the building that housed the medical clearing station, work was resumed immediately after the operating room had been moved.

During six days more than 1,600 wounded were accepted. All urgent cases received immediate care on the spot and then were forwarded to the company's actual medical clearing station in Woka. Because of the thoughtful and resolute behavior of the medical company commander and his tireless activity with the small number of men who were available — particularly after two of the company's surgeons were wounded and losses had also occurred among the medical officers of other units — all tasks were fully accomplished.

SS-Hauptsturmführer Loderhose was the last to leave the forward dressing station during the night of 29/30 July. He did not leave until the building housing the forward dressing station had been destroyed by fire from artillery, mortars and tanks and ongoing low-level aerial attack and after the main line of resistance had stabilized and the heavy defensive fighting had come to an end. Loderhose's remarkable service was complicated by the manifold difficulties related to the low level of readiness of his company, which resulted from a shortfall of 80 men and the totally inadequate issuance of motor vehicles. It was only thanks to the initiative of Loderhose that those difficulties could be overcome.

SS-Hauptsturmführer Loderhose received the Iron Cross, Second Class for the fighting at Boguslaw from 21 to 25 July 1941 and the Iron Cross, First Class for the fighting at Smela from 2 to 3 August 1941. He is recommended for this high decoration because his performance has always been worthy of such an award.

———

Corps Headquarters
III.(germanisches) SS-Panzer-Korps
Corps Command Post, 21 February 1944
Adjutant

RECOMMEND APPROVAL!

Signed: Steiner
SS-Obergruppenführer und General der Waffen-SS

———

SS-Hauptsturmführer Loderhose was awarded the German Cross in Gold on 20 January 1945.

23. SS-Freiwilligen-Panzergrenadier-Division "Nederland"
Division Command Post, 26 January 1945

Ia Diary No. /45 Secret

(Author's Note: Copy from War Diary No. 4, Enclosure 132)

Evaluation of Formations

1.) *SS-Freiwilligen–Panzer–Grenadier–Regiment 49 "de Ruyter"*: The regiment does not have any combat power after its withdrawal from the front. The infantry strength of the battalions ranges from 10-20 men each. The heavy weapons of the regiment have almost all been lost and the crews are almost totally unavailable since they have been employed entirely as infantry after the loss of the weapons. The trains units personnel are still essentially intact, so the administrative framework exists for reconstituting the formation.

2.) *SS-Artillerie-Regiment 54:* The regiment's personnel strength continues to decrease. It has suffered substantial losses through employment as infantry in alarm units. Although replenishment with personnel is required for full combat readiness, it can be considered ready for action.

3.) *SS-Pionier-Bataillon 54:* The battalion possesses no combat power. Other than the adjutant and one company commander, it no longer has any combat-engineer officers or noncommissioned officers. Its combat strength consists of about 10-15 men. The rear-area units of the battalion are still essentially intact.

For the Commander:
(signature illegible)
SS-Untersturmführer

Note: From this evaluation, it is clear that the *23. SS-Freiwilligen-Panzergrenadier-Division "Nederland"* had ceased to exist, for all practical purposes. The same was true for the *11. SS-Freiwilligen-Panzer-Grenadier-Division "Nordland"*. In spite of that, they were still counted on in Lower Pomerania and miracles were expected from them. The formations were hurriedly refitted after arriving in Stettin, in part by impressing soldiers seized from raids on movie theaters. Within two or three days the divisions were thrown back into the fighting.

Appendix 12: Recommendation for the Award of the Oakleaves to the Knight's Cross to SS-Obersturmbannführer Albrecht Krügel

11. SS-Freiwilligen-Panzer-Grenadier-Division "Nordland"
Division Command Post, 31 October 1944

Recommendation for the Award of the Oakleaves to the
Knight's Cross of the Iron Cross to
SS-Obersturmbannführer and Regimental Commander
Albrecht Krügel

(born 22 April 1913 in Nordhorn. Active-duty officer. Presently commander of *SS-Panzer-Grenadier-Regiment 24 "Danmark"*)

Endorsement and justification through corps headquarters of the *III. (germanisches) SS-Panzer-Korps*:

During the fighting in Kurland, the *11. SS-Freiwilligen-Panzer-Grenadier-Division "Nordland"* was in the center of constant attritional blows from the Soviets after it had withdrawn from the extremely heavy fighting at the Narwa and Düna.

SS-Obersturmbannführer Krügel was conspicuous for the heroic example he repeatedly displayed during that fighting. It is in large part due to his superior command of his regiment that a decisive critical situation was mastered.

SS-Obersturmbanführer Krügel significantly reduced the burden on the division command by his sense of responsibility and demonstration of initiative. He proved his fighting spirit and tactical understanding in a combat situation that was complicated by the breadth of the area and the unique requirements of maneuver warfare.

Corps Command Post, 29 November 1944

Recommend approval!

Signed: Steiner
SS-Obergruppenführer und General der Waffen-SS

---

11. SS-Freiwilligen-Panzer-Grenadier-Division "Nordland"
Division Command Post, 25 November 1944
Commander

Efficiency Report Narrative
for
SS-Obersturmbannführer Albrecht Krügel

He continues as a highly experienced commander in offensive and defensive operations. On 16 November 1944 he was awarded the Oakleaves to the Knight's Cross. His equally masterful ability at both leading and judging men leads to the expectation that, within a very short time, he will be an outstanding division commander.

His clear mental capability and great skills make him outstandingly suited to command a school for officer candidates. He possesses the unlimited loyalty of both officers and men.

Signed: Ziegler
SS-Brigadeführer und Generalmajor der Waffen-SS

SS-Obersturmbannführer Albrecht Krügel was awarded the Oakleaves to the Knight's Cross of the Iron Cross on 16 November 1944 as the 651st recipient of the award.

Appendix 13: Recommendation for the Award of the German Cross in Gold to SS-Obersturmführer Johannes Hellmers

(Author's note: From the personnel file of *SS-Obersturmführer* Johannes Hellmers, born 23 October 1918 in Denmark. At the time of the recommendation for the German Cross in Gold, he was the company commander of the *6./SS-Freiwilligen-Panzer-Grenadier-Regiment 49 "de Ruyter".*)

Justification for the award of the <u>German Cross in Gold</u> on 2 November 1944. Endorsed by *the 4. SS-Panzer-Grenadier-Brigade "Nederland"* and the *III. (germanisches) SS-Panzer-Korps.*

During the withdrawal movement of *the 4. SS-Panzer-Grenadier-Brigade "Nederland"* from the Narwa Front to Latvia, *SS-Obersturmführer* Hellmers and elements of his company were cut off from his unit by strong Soviet armored forces south of Pernau. The attempt to reach German lines failed since the enemy had already secured all of the roads, villages and wooded areas.

SS-Obersturmführer Hellmers skillfully and courageously fought his way through the Soviet security in nighttime movements. In some places, the Soviets hunted the weak German group with dogs. It was only after ten days that *SS-Obersturmführer* Hellmers, along with *SS-Oberscharführer* Tyssen and *SS-Rottenführer* Kais, reached German lines in a state of complete exhaustion and debilitation.

SS-Obersturmführer Hellmers is an ethnic German volunteer from Denmark. Since joining the *III. (germanisches) SS-Panzer-Korps* he has repeatedly demonstrated outstanding zeal and imaginative leadership. During the current fighting southeast of Libau he has continued to particularly distinguished himself in combat.

The two *SS* men who fought their way through together with Hellmers have already been awarded the Iron cross, First Class for their courageous conduct.

SS-Obersturmführer Hellmers was awarded the German Cross in Gold on 18 December 1944.

Recommendation for the award of the Knight's Cross to the Iron Cross to *SS-Obersturmführer* Johannes Hellmers on 30 January 1945.

During the fighting in the Kaleti area, the company occupied the line of the former command posts 400 meters east of Kaleti as the main line of resistance. The company had been assembled from the remnants of a battalion. *SS-Obersturmführer* Hellmers commanded that company.

On the morning of 25 January, the Russians attacked with tanks and 200 men from the woods in front of the position. The Russian attack penetrated into the section of trenches and rolled up half of it. In that apparently hopeless situation, *SS-Obersturmführer* Hellmers decided to launch an immediate counterattack with a few men. At the front of his soldiers with his machine pistol, he stormed forward and ejected the enemy from the trench with bloody losses.

Although twice wounded during the action, he remained in the main line of resistance and, with his men, repulsed with infantry weapons fire all further attempts by the enemy to capture the main line of resistance.

It was thanks to his initiative and outstanding personal courage that the main line of resistance in the Kaleti area was held on 25 January to its full extent, and the enemy was prevented from breaking through at Kaleti. His resistance was decisively significant for the entire sector between Purmsati and Skuodas.

SS-Obersturmführer Hellmers was awarded the Knight's Cross on 5 March 1945.

Appendix 14: Breakthrough of Korps Tettau to the Oder Front

(Editor's Note: The following material is provided to augment the account Tieke has provided in the main text of this book concerning the confused situation existing around the Oder Front at the beginning of 1945 and leading to the final Battle of Berlin. Although this text repeats some material found in the main body, it also offers additional insights into that period.)

Because of the numerous gaps in the records (reports, orders, war diaries), it is not possible to reliably reconstruct the fighting in Lower Pomerania at the beginning of 1945. It primarily involved troop units that were born from necessity and formed from replacement and alarm units or formations that were in the process of organization. Nevertheless, the attempt will be made to trace at least the paths of the *15. Waffen-Grenadier-Division der SS (lettische Nr. 1)* and the *33. Waffen-Grenadier-Division der SS "Charlemagne" (französische Nr. 1)* that were in the process of formation, as well as *SS-Freiwilligen-Panzergrenadier-Regiment 48 "General Seyffard"* and the officer and noncommissioned officer training units of *SS-Sturmbannführer* Scheibe and *SS-Hauptsturmführer* Hämel that were at the Hammerstein Training Area.

Hammerstein was the collection point for all of the newly organized or refitted formations of the *III. (germanisches) SS-Panzer-Korps*, which was still employed at that time in Kurland. The basis for this report are the books: *"Die Eroberung Pommerns durch die Rote Armee"* ("The Conquest of Pomerania by the Red Army") by Erich Murawski; *"Tragedy of the Faithful"*; "In the Firestorm of the Last Years of the War" by Wilhelm Tieke; and, various written and verbal contributions to the author by those who took part in the fighting.

At the start of February 1945, the 1st Belorussian Front (Zhukov) reached the Oder at several places and formed bridgeheads. Its deep flanks in Lower Pomerania and Silesia were such great "unknowns" that Marshal Zhukov first requested the elimination of the threats to them before he was willing to begin the final battle, Operation Berlin.

On 15 February, Zhukov's fears were confirmed. The *11. SS-Panzer-Armee* (Steiner) launched Operation *"Sonnenwende"* against the deep flank of the 1st Belorussian Front and relieved the beleaguered city of Arnswalde. The German forces were too weak for additional operations so *"Sonnenwende"* had to be broken off on 25 February 1945.

In the meantime, the Soviets regrouped. After *"Sonnenwende"* had fizzled out, the 1st and 2nd Belorussian Fronts attacked to the north on their interior fronts from the area north of Schneidemühl in order to reach the Baltic Sea. With that, the widely stretched German front in Lower Pomerania and West Prussia would be split apart and rolled up on both sides.

Additional operations would then encircle and destroy east of the lower Oder the *2. Armee* (*Generaloberst* Weiß) and the *3. Panzer-Armee*

(*Generaloberst* Raus) — which had replaced the staff of the *11. SS-Panzer-Armee*.

On 24 February 1945, after a forty-minute artillery preparation, the newly inserted Soviet 19th Army (2nd Belorussian Front) started to break through the German front at the boundary between the *3. Panzer-Armee* and the *2. Armee*. The initial phase of the attack hit the *XVIII. Gebirgs-Korps (2. Armee)*, which defended along the Konitz — Hammerstein railroad line with the Pomeranian *32. Infanterie-Division* on the left and *Gruppe Ax* — remnants of the *15. Waffen-Grenadier-Division der SS (lettische Nr. 1)*, remnants of *SS-Freiwilligen-Panzer-Grenadier-Regiment 48 "General Seyffard"* and training units from the Hammerstein Training Area. The *33. Waffen-Grenadier-Division der SS "Charlemagne" (französische Nr.1)*, which had been brought from the *"West Prussia"* Training Area at Konitz, was in reserve behind the front.

The French volunteers soon had to be employed at critical points, a battalion at a time. As a result, the division was never employed as a complete formation. The units were scattered to all four winds. The *XVIII. Gebirgs-Korps* had to pull its formations back to Lake Groß Ziethen — Stegers — Kudde.

On 25 February, the 2nd Belorussian Front employed the III Guards Tank Corps to force the final breakthrough in the German front. With numerous tanks carrying infantry, the tank corps broke through the defenses of the *XVIII. Gebirgs-Korps*, with *Schwerpunkte* along the Hammerstein — Kudde — Baldenburg and Schlochau — Stegers — Baldenburg roads. By evening the spearheads had reached Schönau and Eickfier.

On 26 February, the III Guards Tank Corps captured the small city of Baldenburg and fanned out to the south to Stepen, to the west to Porst and Bublitz and to the northwest to Drawehn. The fall of Baldenburg started the penetration of the Pomeranian Position. The northern portion of the Pomeranian Position was occupied by replacement, training and alarm units that could offer little resistance to Soviet armor. The *15. Waffen-Grenadier-Division der SS (lettische Nr.1)*, the *33. Waffen-Grenadier-Division der SS "Charlemagne" (französische Nr. 1)* and *SS-Freiwilligen-Panzer-Grenadier-Regiment 48 "General Seyffard"* were severely decimated. Following that, those units of the French *SS* division that could be contacted were assembled in Köslin where they were encircled by Russian forces the next day. The main column was smashed during a breakout in groups that was led by Division Commander Puaud. One group, under *SS-Brigadeführer Dr. jur.* Krukenberg, joined *Korpsgruppe von Tettau*. Two smaller groups were forced aside to Kolberg and Danzig and made it by sea to Stettin and thence to the new assembly area at Neustrelitz.

After the breakthrough at Baldenburg, the *2. Armee* in Danzig and West Prussia was in danger of being cut off. The army withdrew the

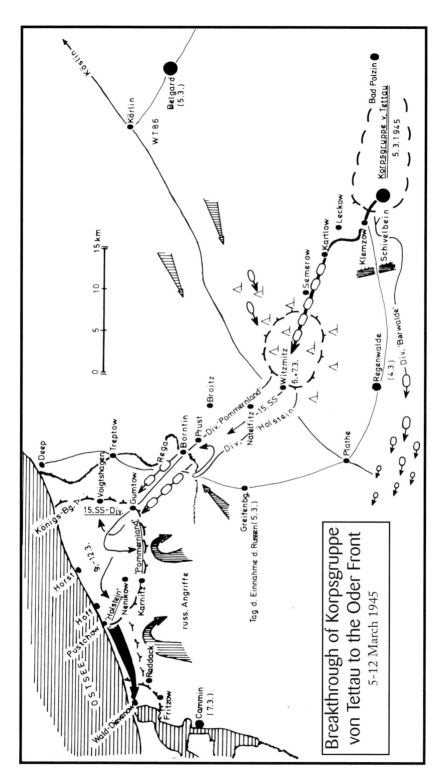

Breakthrough of Korpsgruppe
von Tettau to the Oder Front
5-12 March 1945

Generalkommando VII. Panzer-Korps from its southern front and attached the *7. Panzer-Division* (*Dr.* Maus) and the *4. SS-Polizei-Division* (Harzer) to it. The latter division was en route by rail from Stargard. Both divisions were concentrated in the Rummelsberg area for a counterattack that was intended to close the gap in the front between the *3. Panzer-Armee* and the *2. Armee.*

The *3. Panzer-Armee* also took countermeasures. *Panzerdivision "Holstein"* was brought up from Stargard and combined with provisional divisions *"Pommernland"* and *"Bärwalde"* to form *Korpsgruppe von Tettau*, which was assigned the mission of advancing from the area northwest of Baldenburg against the III Guards Tank Corps, which had broken through, and establishing contact with the *VII. Panzer-Korps (2. Armee)* which was to attack from the east.

On the other side, the Soviet 19th Army was hesitant in following the III Guards Tank Corps and Rokossowski had to halt the Guards' armor so that the Soviet 19th Army could close up and secure the flanks for the time being.

The Russians were faster in bringing up troops. On 27 February they captured Neustettin, an important pillar of the Pomeranian Position. The counterattack by the *VII. Panzer-Korps* and *Korpsgruppe von Tettau* never got off to a start. Heavy fighting developed during which the *VII. Panzer-Korps* was forced back to the Rummelsberg area and *Panzer-Division "Holstein"* to the Bublitz area. In the meantime, two additional Soviet armies advanced on to the north and, on 1 March, reached the Baltic Sea northeast of Köslin.

The 1st Belorussian Front launched an attack to the north from the Stargard — Reetz area on 1 March to destroy the *3. Panzer-Armee* which was already threatened on its eastern flank. The focus of the attack was on the *III. (germanisches) SS-Panzer-Korps* (Unrein) in the area east of Stargard and on the *X. SS-Armee-Korps* (Krappe) farther to the east.

That fighting was described elsewhere in this book and "In the Firestorm of the Last Years of the War". After the breakthrough to the Baltic Sea was completed, the *2. Armee* was continually compressed and finally eliminated in the Danzig — Gdingen area. Several formations were evacuated over the Baltic Sea to Stettin.

While that was taking place, the *X. SS-Armee-Korps* with the *5. Jägerdivision*, the *Division z.b.V. 402* and the *163. Infanterie-Division* was encircled and destroyed in the Falkenburg area. Elements of that corps fought their way through to the west and rejoined German forces at the Oder.

Korpsgruppe von Tettau was, in the meantime, involved in heavy fighting west of the lost Pomeranian Position and still held on in the area south and east of Bad Polzin. After more days filled with fighting, it was surrounded by Russian forces in the Bad Polzin — Schivelbein area. *General* von Tettau, who still commanded more than 10,000 men of various divisions, including remnants of the *15. Waffen-Grenadier-Division der SS (lettische Nr.1)*, the *33.*

Waffen-Grenadier-Division der SS "Charlemagne" (französische Nr. 1) and *SS-Freiwilligen-Panzer-Grenadier-Regiment 48 "General Seyffard"* ordered the corps to break out to the west in order to regain contact with German forces.

When *General* von Tettau decided to break out, he had not an inkling of the actual situation. Communications had broken down. However, he hoped for a relief effort by the *3. Panzer-Armee* to establish contact with his own and the *X. SS-Armee-Korps*. In the meantime, the *X. SS-Armee-Korps* had been destroyed and Marshal Zhukov had then given his 3rd Shock Armee the mission of destroying *Gruppe von Tettau*.

On 4 March, at about 2200 hours, *General* von Tettau issued the order to break out to the west. Only the most necessary ammunition, ration and medical vehicles were to be brought along. Everything else was to be destroyed. The units were ordered to avoid becoming decisively engaged. Instead, they were to bypass heavy enemy resistance and carry on the march in the general direction.

In the morning of 5 March 1945 *Korpsgruppe von Tettau* set out in heavy snowsqualls just north of Schivelbein along the road to Regenwalde. *Panzer-Division "Holstein"* proceeded on the right, *Division "Pommernland"* in the center and *Division "Bärwalde"* on the left. The *15. Waffen-Grenadier-Division der SS (lettische Nr. 1)*, including *SS-Freiwilligen-Panzer-Grenadier-Regiment 48 "General Seyffard"* and *Gruppe Hämel*, followed as rearguard.

After the first enemy outposts had been pushed aside, it turned out that the road to Regenwalde was blocked by strong Russian forces. In accord with von Tettau's basic order to bypass strong enemy defenses, *Division "Pommernland"*, *Panzer-Division "Holstein"* and the *15. Waffen-Grenadier-Division der SS (lettische Nr. 1)* moved through the villages of Leckow — Kartlow — Semerow in the forest area southeast of Witzmitz.

Division "Bärwalde" was forced off to the south. The division commander ordered the division to fight its way through in small groups and assemble in the Plathe area. The division was wiped out as events took charge and situations rapidly changed. Several groups reached the Langenberg bridgehead opposite Pölitz by 24 March and were brought over to the western shore of the Stettiner Haff by the navy.

On 5 March, at the same time that *Korpsgruppe von Tettau* had reached the Witzmitz forest area, the small city of Greifenberg, barely 15 kilometers farther west, was given up under heavy enemy pressure by a breakthrough-group of the *33. Waffen-Grenadier-Division der SS "Charlemagne" (französische Nr. 1)* led by *SS-Oberführer* von Veil. *Gruppe von Veil* drew back to the west to Cammin.

While elements of *Panzer-Division "Holstein"* formed a bridgehead over the Körlin — Plathe road, the main body of *Korpsgruppe von Tettau* formed a hedgehog position on 6 March in the forest southeast of Witzmitz. That day von Tettau finally regained radio contact with the *3. Panzer-Armee*. He learned from the army that the Wollin bridgehead, which was the breakout objective, had been crushed by the Russians and he would have to fight his way through to Dievenow instead.

General von Tettau decided to push through to the north so as to assemble his forces at Horst on the Baltic Sea. Then, protected by the forested dunes and the steep coast, he would break through to the Dievenow bridgehead. In the course of getting to Horst, *Panzer-Division "Holstein"* had to form a bridgehead across the Rega north of Greifenberg. However, because of heavy enemy pressure, that bridgehead could not be held. At that point, *Division "Pommernland"* formed a bridgehead at Borntin that was successfully held. While the main body of *Korpsgruppe von Tettau* gradually closed up on 8 March through the Borntin bridgehead, the spearheads of *Division "Pommernland"* had already reached the Gumtow area and by evening were at Horst on the Baltic Sea.

While all that was taking place, the *15. Waffen-Grenadier-Division der SS (lettische Nr. 1)*, including *Gruppen Scheibe* and *Hämel*, secured the "wandering pocket" as rearguard south of Witzmitz. That was where remnants of the *X. SS-Armee-Korps* and units of the *33. Waffen-Grenadier-Division der SS "Charlemagne" (französische Nr. 1)* that had fought their way through from the Belgard area joined up with *Gruppe von Tettau*.

During the nights from 7 to 11 March, 16 *Ju-52* aircraft dropped containers with ammunition and motor fuel in the locations where *Gruppe von Tettau* was at that time.

During the night of 8/9 March, *Korpsgruppe von Tettau* occupied the planned bridgehead position at Horst just in time to repulse strong Russian attacks in the western portion of the bridgehead.

The bridgehead position extended from Pustchow through Dresow — Karnitz (*Panzer-Division "Holstein"*) — along the railroad line to Gumtow (*Division "Pommernland"*) — Zedliner Berg — Voigtshagen to Königsberg in the forested dunes at the Baltic Sea (*15. Waffen-Grenadier-Division der SS (lettische Nr. 1)*). The Soviets strengthened their efforts to destroy *Korpsgruppe von Tettau*. They erected strong defensive barriers, especially in the breakout direction to the west.

On 10 March Russian formations attacked all along the front, particularly in the south, which was held by *Division "Pommernland"*. The division held only with extreme effort and by giving up some ground. It was high time for the breakthrough to the Wald-Dievenow bridgehead that was being held with great difficulty by two naval battalions. The breakthrough was set for 10 March at 2200 hours.

Panzer-Division "Holstein" formed the spearhead of the attack with one *Fusilier* battalion and the attached *Artillerie-Fahnenjunker-Regiment* from

Groß Born, led by *Oberstleutnant* Buchenau. The breach was struck in hard, seesaw night fighting, often man-to-man with cold steel. On 11 March, at about 0930 hours, the first elements of the breakout reached the Wald-Dievenow bridgehead. As ordered, *Panzer-Division "Holstein"*, which no longer had any tanks, formed a combat-outpost line along the south flank of the narrow breakthrough corridor. That line was held in seesaw fighting until the breakout by *Korpsgruppe von Tettau* was complete. On 11 and 12 March an endless procession of misery made up of refugees and soldiers flowed along the Baltic Sea to the west under fire from Russian heavy weapons.

On the German side, the cruiser *Admiral Scheer* and the torpedo boat *T 33*, as well as the naval artillery on the Isle of Wollin, took part in the fighting. The route of retreat was repeatedly blocked by Russian forces and had to be cleared again.

The rearguard of *Division "Pommernland"* and the *15. Waffen-Grenadier-Division der SS (lettische Nr. 1)* was supposed to hold the area at Hoff until 0600 hours in the morning of 12 March, but strong enemy pressure from Ninikow forced the commander of the rearguard to order withdrawal at 0500 hours. Since the flank security of *Division "Holstein"* did not hold, the rearguard had to repeatedly fight its way clear. Throughout 12 March 1945, the last groups of *Korpsgruppe von Tettau* made their way to the safety of the Wald-Dievenow bridgehead, which was then evacuated.

At noon on 12 March 1945, the *Wehrmachtsbericht* reported: "...On the Baltic Sea coast, a strong German force fought its way back to the Dievenow bridgehead against stubborn Bolshevik resistance..."

In addition to the army formations which made it out of the bridgehead at Dievenow, the following *SS* units and formations were eventually able to return to their parent units or organizations west of the Oder: The *15. Waffen-Grenadier-Division der SS (lettische Nr. 1)* and the *33. Waffen-Grenadier-Division der SS "Charlemagne" (französische Nr. 1)*, as well as remnants of *SS-Freiwilligen-Panzer-Grenadier-Regiment 48 "General Seyffard"* and of training and replacement units of the *III. (germanisches) SS-Panzer-Korps* (Scheibe and Hämel) that had been at the Hammerstein Training Area.

During the night of 19/20 March 1945, the Oder bridgehead held by the *III. (germanisches) SS-Panzerkorps* at Stettin-Altdamm was also evacuated. The Oder River was then the new front line.

Appendix 15: The "New" I./SS-Panzer-Grenadier-Regiment 23 "Norge" and I./SS-Panzer-Grenadier-Regiment 24 "Danmark"

In the fighting during the retreat from the Oranienbaum Pocket to Narwa in January 1944 the *I./SS-Panzer-Grenadier-Regiment 23 "Norge"* and the *I./SS-Panzer-Grenadier-Regiment 24 "Danmark"* suffered heavy losses. Both battalions were disbanded and their soldiers assigned to the other battalions of the regiments. A small cadre from both battalions went to Germany to reconstitute the battalions. As a result of great crises, both new battalions were sent to the *5. SS-Panzer-Division "Wiking"* north of Warsaw in November 1944. The two battalions remained with that division for the remainder of the war. (Wilhelm Tieke)

Reconstitution of the *I./SS-Panzer-Grenadier-Regiment 23 "Norge"* and its Employment with the *5. SS-Panzer-Division "Wiking"*

Herbert Mallis

The *11. SS-Freiwilligen-Panzergrenadier-Division "Nordland"* was formed during the summer of 1943 at the Grafenwöhr Training Area. At the same time, the *4. SS-Freiwilligen-Panzergrenadier-Brigade "Nederland"* was formed in Thüringen. Both formations were combined to form the *III. (germanisches) SS-Panzer-Korps*.

During the organization of the division, *SS-Panzer-Grenadier-Regiment 23 "Norge"* was formed from the old *SS-Regiment "Nordland"* and additional contributions from the *5. SS-Panzergrenadier-Division "Wiking"*, as well as from the *SS-Freiwilligen-Legion "Norwegen"*.

The *I./SS-Panzer-Grenadier-Regiment 23 "Norge"* was built upon a foundation of 600 volunteers from the *SS-Freiwilligen-Legion "Norwegen"*, which had been formed at Fallingbostel in the summer of 1941 and had last fought as part of the *2. SS-Infanterie-Brigade (mot.)* at the Leningrad Front. In March 1943, the *SS-Freiwilligen-Legion "Norwegen"* was brought back to Grafenwöhr and used to form the *I./SS-Panzer-Grenadier-Regiment 23 "Norge"*.

The commander of the battalion became *SS-Hauptsturmführer* Fritz Vogt, a front-line officer who had proven outstanding as a member of *SS-Division "Verfügungs"* during the campaign in France and had received the Knight's Cross to the Iron Cross.

The battalion was transferred to Croatia as part of the *11. SS-Freiwilligen-Panzergrenadier-Division "Nordland"* and, at the end of 1943, transferred to and employed at the Oranienbaum Pocket in the northern sector of the Eastern Front. When the German front collapsed in January 1944 under the immense Soviet offensive, the courageous *I./SS-Panzer-Grenadier-Regiment 23 "Norge"* was employed as a "fire brigade" and bled white at various hot spots. The remnants of the battalion were split up among the two

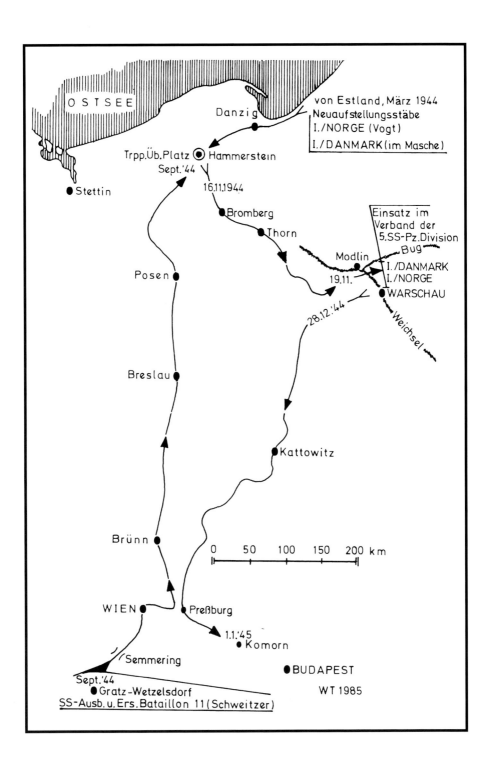

OSTSEE

Danzig

von Estland, März 1944
Neuaufstellungsstäbe
I./NORGE (Vogt)
I./DANMARK (im Masche)

Trpp.Üb.Platz ⊙ Hammerstein
Sept.'44

16.11.1944

● Stettin

● Bromberg

● Thorn

Einsatz im
Verband der
5.SS-Pz.Division

Modlin

Bug

I./DANMARK
I./NORGE

19.11.

WARSCHAU

● Posen

28.12.'44

Weichsel

● Breslau

● Kattowitz

● Brünn

0   50   100   150   200 km

WIEN ●   ● Preßburg

1.1.'45
● Komorn

Semmering

Sept.'44
● Gratz-Wetzelsdorf

● BUDAPEST

WT 1985

SS-Ausb. u. Ers. Bataillon 11 (Schweitzer)

other battalions of the regiment. Only a small organizational staff led by *SS-Hauptsturmführer* Fritz Vogt traveled to the Hammerstein Training Area to organize a new *I./SS-Panzer-Grenadier-Regiment 23 "Norge"*.

SS-Freiwilligen-Panzergrenadier-Ausbildungs- und Ersatz-Bataillon Graz-Wetzelsdorf

The *11. SS-Freiwilligen-Panzergrenadier-Division "Nordland"* had its replacement battalion in Graz-Wetzelsdorf. The complex was planned by an architectural bureau from Berlin and the construction was carried out during 1939-1940. The style of architecture was appropriate to the Alps. As a result of the war, the officers club, banquet room and swimming pool were not completed. Today the post is used by the Austrian Army and named the *"Belgierkaserne"* (Belgian Barracks) in commemoration of the Styrian *Infanterie-Regiment 27 "Leopold, König der Belgier"*. (Belgium belonged to Austria until 1797).

Starting in July 1944, recruits of age groups 1926 and 1927 and convalescent soldiers from the hospitals arrived daily at the facilities at Graz-Wetzelsdorf. Training began for the young recruits, many only sixteen and a half years old. *SS-Hauptsturmführer* Willi Schweitzer was commander of the divisional *Ausbildungs- und Ersatz-Bataillon*. He rode at the head of the battalion as it marched to exercises on his charger. Basic training ended in mid-September. Except for a training cadre, the battalion moved to the Hammerstein Training Area for formation training.

Since the battalion took no heavy weapons or vehicles along, entraining went smoothly and quickly. The rail transport proceeded over the Semmering Pass to Vienna. There was a long stop in Vienna, during which the Viennese soldiers were able to briefly visit their families. The journey continued over the Danube to Preßburg. There, during a stop for messing, a member of the battalion was struck and killed by an express train — the first member of the battalion to be killed. The next stops were Brünn, Breslau and Posen. On 18 September 1944, the transport finally arrived at its destination at Hammerstein.

The young soldiers from Graz-Wetzelsdorf were received at the Hammerstein freight station by officers and noncommissioned officers of the training staffs of the *I./SS-Panzer-Grenadier-Regiment 23 "Norge"* and the *I./SS-Panzer-Grenadier-Regiment 24 "Danmark"* (which was also being reformed). Their decorations showed they were front-line soldiers. With them and the transportation officers, the march to Hammerstein continued with a new song on their lips.

New Assignments and Formation Training at Hammerstein

Barracks were assigned by companies at the Hammerstein Training Area. Each man filled his straw sack and stowed his equipment and personal items in his locker.

Approximately 1,000 men lined up the following morning on the parade ground at Hammerstein, all from SS-Freiwilligen-Panzergrenadier-Ausbildungs- und Ersatz-Bataillon Graz-Wetzelsdorf. They became the new I./SS-Panzer-Grenadier-Regiment 23 "Norge" and I./SS-Panzer-Grenadier-Regiment 24 "Danmark". Thus, each battalion started with 500 men, with daily additions from convalescents returning from hospitals and men returning from home leave to the organizational staff. The duty positions were filled as follows:

I./SS-Panzer-Grenadier-Regiment 23 "Norge"

Battalion Commander: *SS-Hauptsturmführer* Fritz Vogt.

Battalion Adjutant: *SS-Obersturmführer* Radke.

Battalion Surgeon: *SS-Obersturmführer Dr.* Storm (Norwegian)

Messenger section: One *SS-Oberscharführer*, two *SS-Unterscharführer* and 10 *SS-Panzergrenadiere.*

1./SS-Panzer-Grenadier-Regiment 23 "Norge": *SS-Obersturmführer* Rendemann

2./SS-Panzer-Grenadier-Regiment 23 "Norge": SS-Obersturmführer Fechner

3./SS-Panzer-Grenadier-Regiment 23 "Norge": SS-Obersturmführer Stüwe

4. (schwere)/SS-Panzer-Grenadier-Regiment 23 "Norge": SS-Obersturmführer Kiefer (4 heavy machine guns, 4 mortars, 2 light machine guns, 2 7.5cm *Pak*)

Weapons, vehicles and equipment were gradually brought up to levels authorized for the German Army. Total strength: Approximately 600 men.

I./SS-Panzer-Grenadier-Regiment 24 "Danmark"

This battalion was also organized under *SS-Sturmbannführer* Hermann at Hammerstein. Organization, armament and equipment were similar to those of the *I./SS-Panzer-Grenadier-Regiment 23 "Norge".* Details are not available.

The heavy losses of the *I./SS-Panzer-Grenadier-Regiment 23 "Norge"* in the northern sector of the Eastern Front and at Narwa could not be made up with Norwegian volunteers, so there were only about 40 Norwegian officers, noncommissioned officers and men in the new battalion.

SS-Hauptsturmführer Fritz Vogt placed the emphasis in the training at Hammerstein on combat-related training, based on his long years of war experience. The emphasis was on camouflage, close-quarters combat, combat patrolling and combating armor. Along with that was formation training at the squad, platoon, company and battalion level. The training was hard and complemented by night exercises. Every fourteen days there was a 35-kilometer march with assault pack and, in between, attack maneuvers. Vogt's motto: "Sweat saves blood". The young soldiers were highly motivated and the battalion was soon ready for combat. In the meantime, the battalion was also sworn in. Camp and motorpool guard was performed by the individual companies of the battalion at that point.

One man of the *1./SS-Panzer-Grenadier-Regiment 23 "Norge"* deserted and was condemned to death by court martial. On 4 November 1944 he was shot before the assembled battalion on a firing range at the training area.

In November 1944, the *11. SS-Freiwilligen-Panzergrenadier-Division "Nordland"* was decisively engaged in Kurland. Kurland had already been separated from the other German fronts. The Kurland army was in a hopeless situation. Supply was only possible by sea. No more troops were sent. As a result, it was a complete unknown as to whether the newly organized battalions of the division would be able to get to their regiments.

Employment at the Front with the *5. SS-Panzer-Division "Wiking"*

In the meantime, the situation had also intensified at Warsaw. On 16 November 1944, the *I./SS-Panzer-Grenadier-Regiment 23 "Norge"* and the *I./SS-Panzer-Grenadier-Regiment 24 "Danmark"* received orders to join the *5. SS-Panzer-Division "Wiking"*, which was employed in the so-called "wet triangle" at Modlin-Warsaw. That division had suffered heavy losses in personnel in the Kowel Pocket.

On 16 November 1944, the battalions entrained at the Hammerstein freight station and left that same day. Only a few knew the destination of the journey.

The rail transport ran through Bromberg and Thorn to the east. In the gray dawn of 17 November, constant flashes and the thunder of the guns indicated the location of the front to the east. Detraining took place before full daylight at the Modlin railroad station followed by a road march to the old fortress of Modlin, where the platoons and companies were quartered for the rest of the day in the casemates. At about midnight of 17/18 November, the battalions moved to the front, dismounting at Olschew and Olschewenika. The vehicles moved back. The companies advanced about a kilometer to the main line of resistance, relieving an army battalion there, probably from the *542. Infanterie-Division*.

The positions were well constructed, with machine gun and billeting dugouts that, in part, extended to the outskirts of the village and included the potato cellars. In that sector north of Warsaw, the young soldiers of the *I./SS-Panzer-Grenadier-Regiment 23 "Norge"* and the *I./SS-Panzer-Grenadier-Regiment 24 "Danmark"* were confronted with the war.

It started with nerve-wracking positional warfare. The Russian positions were 50 to 100 meters away. In between there were mines and wire obstacles. It was always necessary to be on guard, day and night. Russian sharpshooters were always lurking. Artillery and mortar fire came down on the positions. Both of the young battalions suffered losses in dead and wounded.

A combat patrol was scheduled for 6 December with the objective of bringing in Soviet prisoners for interrogation regarding enemy intentions. The 3rd platoon of the *2./SS-Panzer-Grenadier-Regiment 23 "Norge"* conducted the patrol and brought in one prisoner. The combat patrol suffered one killed and four wounded.

The shooting and skulking went on day and night. Both sides fired at anything that moved. On 22 December the Norwegians, Sydeng and Herstad, were killed. It appeared that Christmas would be quiet. There was mail and personal items were available from the *Spieß*. The cook had pulled out all the stops to provide the men with a Christmas dinner.

At 0300 hours on 25 December, the Russian artillery suddenly laid down an intense artillery barrage on the German positions. The Christmas quiet was rudely interrupted. When the artillery barrage let up, the Russians broke into the trenches of the *I./SS-Panzer-Grenadier-Regiment 23 "Norge"*. *SS-Untersturmführer* Östrin from Oslo was killed. The Russians were ejected in an immediate counterattack. Dead and wounded remained hanging in the barbed wire and were riddled by murderous infantry fire without anyone being able to help them. One Russian was knocked unconscious in a bunker by a German who hit him with a hard sausage that he had received as a Christmas gift. The Russian was then taken to the battalion command post for interrogation. It turned out that the Russians had come to take the Christmas gifts from the Germans. That was how tight their supply situation was.

On 26 December 1944, the *5. SS-Panzerdivision "Wiking"*, including the *I./SS-Panzer-Grenadier-Regiment 23 "Norge"* and the *I./SS-Panzer-Grenadier-Regiment 24 "Danmark"*, was relieved in the "wet triangle" by army units. The *Schwerpunkt* had shifted to the Budapest area. Soon the Hungarian capital was encircled by the Red Army.

Employment in Hungary

Entraining of the *5. SS-Panzer-Division "Wiking"* for employment in Hungary took place in the darkness at various railroad stations at Modlin. In the interest of secrecy, the transport trains left by night.

The *I./SS-Panzer-Grenadier-Regiment 23 "Norge"* spent New Year's Eve on a train. There was an abundance of rations and personal goods so the New Year could be properly celebrated. In the course of the celebrations, a noncommissioned officer was killed and three additional soldiers wounded due to carelessness with a hand grenade. Battalion commander Vogt was furious and had the railroad car doors locked from the outside. They were not opened until the arrival in Komorn (Komarom) the following morning.

After unloading at Komorn, the battalion assembled at the outskirts of the city, as a means of camouflaging against aerial observation. The Russians had broken through the German front at several places and were close to

Komorn. The *5. SS-Panzer-Division "Wiking"* was employed in the Tata area in a counterattack that was intended to continue to relieve Budapest.

At about 1800 hours on 1 January 1945, the employment order arrived for the *I./SS-Panzer-Grenadier-Regiment 23 "Norge"*. It was assigned a flank guard mission for the attack formation of the division along the Komorn — Tata road.

After five kilometers, the battalion reached the small village of Döglöd Puszta without enemy contact. At about midnight, it was at the completely destroyed village of Boldogas. The numerous dead Soviet soldiers evidenced the severity of the fighting that had raged there. At the time the *I./SS-Panzer-Grenadier-Regiment 23 "Norge"* entered Boldogas, the spearhead of the division was already fighting at Tata. When the fighting ended there, the battalion was brought forward to Tata.

On 2 January, the *I./SS-Panzer-Grenadier-Regiment 23 "Norge"* advanced through Banhida to Fölsögalla, which was captured on 3 January after heavy fighting.

On 4 January, Bicske was attacked. In the early morning hours of 5 January, the battalion joined up with *SS-Panzer-Regiment "Wiking"* (Darges) shortly outside of Bicske. Two kilometers outside of Bicske the attack came to a halt and went no farther. The Soviets counterattacked from strongly defended Bicske and put the divisional spearhead in a threatening situation. *SS-Panzer-Regiment "Wiking"* and the *I./SS-Panzer-Grenadier-Regiment 23 "Norge"* formed a hedgehog position in the Hegeyks Estate. The estate was surrounded by a high wall, giving it good potential for defense.

Hegeyks was defended for seven long days by units of *SS-Panzer-Regiment "Wiking"* and the *I./SS-Panzer-Grenadier-Regiment 23 "Norge"* against the repeated surges of Russian attacks. Losses were high. Rations and ammunition were short. The "Fort of the Unyielding", as it was named in the newspapers, held as ordered, but the Soviets gradually increased their strength in the area so much that the relief attack on Budapest had to be broken off from there. The next attempt would be an advance toward Budapest from the south. With that, there was no longer any reason to hold the Hegeyks Estate. A breakout was ordered.

On 12 January, the defenders of Hegeyks broke out to the west and passed through the lines of the newly formed German defensive front. The *I./SS-Panzer-Grenadier-Regiment 23 "Norge"* assembled at Tarjan and, in the course of 12 January, moved by road march to Veszprem at the northwest point of Lake Balaton. After four days of rest and refurbishing weapons and equipment, the battalion was committed in a new attempt to relieve Budapest.

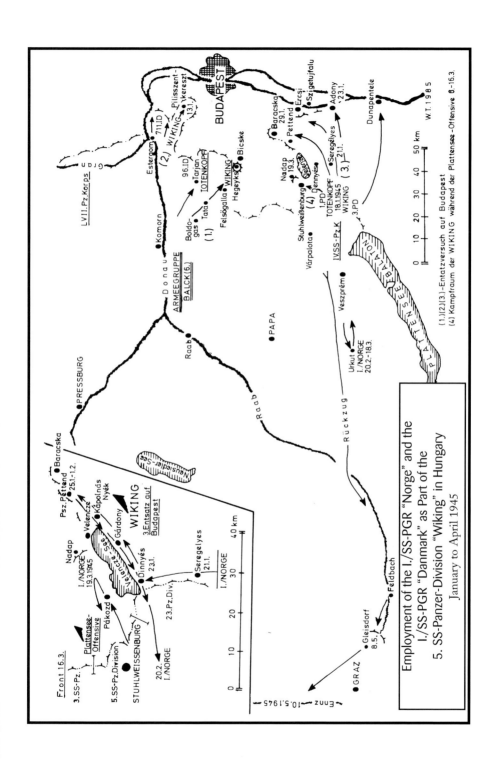

Employment of the I./SS-PGR "Norge" and the
I./SS-PGR "Danmark" as Part of the
5. SS-Panzer-Division "Wiking" in Hungary
January to April 1945

(1.)(2)(3)-Entsatzversuch auf Budapest
(4) Kampfraum der WIKING während der Plattensee-Offensive 8.-16.3.

W.T. 1985

Relief Attack from the South

After the failure of two attacks to relieve Budapest from the area east of Komorn, the new relief attack would come from the south. The *IV. SS-Panzer-Korps* (Gille) was in command. From north to south between Lake Velencze and Lake Balaton were staged the following formations: the *1. Panzerdivision,* the *3. SS-Panzerdivision "Totenkopf",* the *5. SS-Panzerdivision "Wiking"* (including the *I./SS-Panzer-Grenadier-Regiment 23 "Norge"* and the *I./SS-Panzer-Grenadier-Regiment 24 "Danmark"*) and the *3. Panzerdivision.*

On 16 January the *I./SS-Panzer-Grenadier-Regiment 23 "Norge"* moved from Veszprem to Berhida-Papkeszi area (at the northwest point of Lake Balaton) and assembled there for the attack. After a sudden concentration of fire by German artillery on 18 January at 0430 hours, the attack of the *IV. SS-Panzer-Korps* began. Because of the strong Russian defense, the formations only advanced slowly. On the morning of 21 January, the *5. SS-Panzer-Division "Wiking"* finally crossed the north-south Sarviz Canal west of Dinnyes and Seregelyes. As noon drew near, the *I.SS-Panzer-Grenadier-Regiment 23 "Norge"* captured Seregelyes. An armored attack with mounted infantry seriously threatened the battalion, which was then forced back to the western outskirts of Seregelyes. During that fighting, the battalion's wounded, the battalion surgeon, *Dr.* Storm, and two medics fell into Russian hands and were killed. It was a black day for the battalion.

On 23 January, the battalion advanced through Dinnyes and then along Lake Velencze as flank security for the division.

On 24 January, the battalion attacked strongly defended Pettend. The fighting raged all night long. Then, in the morning hours of 25 January, the place was finally captured. The battalion formed a hedgehog position in the extensive palace holdings.

In the meantime, the Russians reformed and mounted a counterattack. They attacked the left flank of *SS-Panzer-Division "Wiking"* with a strong armored formation. The division had its spearhead at Baracska and its right wing at the Danube. The counterattack, which was conducted with 180 tanks, struck the *I.SS-Panzer-Grenadier-Regiment 23 "Norge"* at Pettend Puszta with its full weight. The battalion knocked out 36 tanks, six of which were knocked out personally by battalion commander Fritz Vogt. The authors of various books have written that it was only the heroic fighting of the *I./SS-Panzer-Grenadier-Regiment 23 "Norge"* that prevented the Russians from destroying the *5. SS-Panzer-Division "Wiking".* Fighting raged around Pettend for three days.

The strong Russian counterattack forced the *IV. SS-Panzer-Korps* to break off the relief attack on Budapest. The force ratios were too unequal. At the beginning of February, *SS-Panzer-Division "Wiking"* fell back by bounds under heavy Russian pressure between Lake Velencze and the Danube to the *Margarethe* Position at the Sarviz Canal on both sides of Seregelyes.

In that withdrawal, the *I./SS-Panzer-Grenadier-Regiment 23 "Norge"* fell back along Lake Velencze. That retreat and the subsequent fighting in the *Margarethe* Position between Dinnyes and Seregelyes exacted more great sacrifices from the battalion. On 3 February, the commander of the *2./SS-Panzer-Grenadier-Regiment 23 "Norge"*, *SS-Obersturmführer* Fechner, was killed. On 5 February, the commander of the *4./SS-Panzer-Grenadier-Regiment 23 "Norge"*, *SS-Obersturmführer* Kiefer, was killed, as was *Oberscharführer* Gräz on 8 February. The fighting to regain and hold the *Margarethe* Position lasted until mid-February. The Russians had already penetrated it in several places. When the *I./SS-Panzer-Grenadier-Regiment 23 "Norge"* was withdrawn from the front on 19 February, it still had one *SS-Hauptsturmführer*, one *SS-Obersturmführer*, two *SS-Unterscharführer* and 32 men.

10 February 1945 (from the war diary of *Heeresgruppe Süd*): An additional reduction in the combat power of the *5. SS-Panzer-Division "Wiking"* as a result of the release of the *I./SS-Panzer-Grenadier-Regiment 23 "Norge"* and the *I./SS-Panzer-Grenadier-Regiment 24 "Danmark"* to their parent units — as ordered by the *SS-Führungshauptamt* — was prevented by the *OKH* in response to a request by *Armeegruppe Balck*. The units will continue to remain with the *5. SS-Panzer-Division "Wiking"*.

On 15 February 1945, the *I.SS-Panzer-Grenadier-Regiment 24 "Danmark"* and the barely 100-man strong *I./SS-Panzer-Grenadier-Regiment 23 "Norge"* held a trench position at Dinnyes. The sector was about 1,800 meters long. The *I./SS-Panzer-Grenadier-Regiment 23 "Norge"* was responsible for defending about 500 meters of the position.

Late in the afternoon, the Russians attacked the sector held by the *I./SS-Panzer-Grenadier-Regiment 24 "Danmark"*. Soviet tanks moved up to about 100 meters from the main line of resistance and shot the trenches to bits. No friendly tanks or armor-piercing weapons were available. The men of the *I./SS-Panzer-Grenadier-Regiment 23 "Norge"* gave their Danish comrades the best fire support they could under the circumstances, but they could only watch as the *I./SS-Panzer-Grenadier-Regiment 24 "Danmark"* was wiped out. The commander, *SS-Sturmbannführer* im Masche, has been missing ever since.

The same thing happened to the *I./SS-Panzer-Grenadier-Regiment 23 "Norge"* as evening approached. Vogt issued the order to fall back to the edge of the woods about 200 meters to the rear. The woods were covered by artillery fire of all calibers and many of the battalion's men were killed or wounded.

Refitting At Urkut

The remnants of the *I./SS-Panzer-Grenadier-Regiment 23 "Norge"* reached the small village of Urkut (west of Veszprem) by evening of 20 February 1945. The men found shelter in the empty houses on the outskirts of the village. The relationship with the Hungarian populace was good. A few days of rest and delousing, bathing and fresh underwear worked wonders. Weapons and equipment were cleaned and supplemented.

A few days later replacements arrived for the battalion: Soldiers from the *Luftwaffe* and the *Kriegsmarine*, as well as members of the battalion returning from hospitals. The battalion soon numbered 250 men again. Training began, but, in spite of the fact that every opportunity was exhausted, the battalion remained a motley bunch in *Luftwaffe* and *Kriegsmarine* blue as well as field-gray uniforms. It was never able to regain the old combat spirit and level of performance.

On the morning of 1 March 1945 the battalion said farewell to its former commander. Fritz Vogt had been promoted to *SS-Sturmbannführer* in the meantime and assumed command of *Panzer-Aufklärungs-Abteilung 5* of the division (at Kapolsk at the time). Vogt thanked his soldiers for their accomplishments in action and awarded the Iron Cross, Second Class and the Close-Combat Clasp in bronze (17 recorded days of close-quarters combat) to all who had been with the battalion since its first employment at Modlin. Several received the Iron Cross, First Class. At a later date, the men received the Infantry Assault Badge (the battalion had 13 recorded offensive operations). Vogt turned the battalion over to *SS-Sturmbannführer* Barth.

The training continued, but the lack of officers and noncommissioned officers had a markedly negative effect. The losses of weapons and equipment could only be replaced with difficulty or not at all. A new operations order arrived in the midst of the refitting.

From Lake Velencze to the End of the War

While the *I./SS-Panzer-Grenadier-Regiment 23 "Norge"* was being refitted in Urkut, the Lake Balaton offensive of the newly arrived *6. SS-Panzer-Armee* (Dietrich) was launched between Lakes Balaton and Velencze. The objective: Regaining the Danube in the direction of Budapest. The offensive began on 6 March. On 16 March, the offensive had to be broken off as the result of strong opposition and the start of strong counterattacks. Russian breakthroughs farther to the north in the Bakony Forest forced *Heeresgruppe Süd* into comprehensive regrouping. The *6. SS-Panzer-Armee* (Dietrich) and the *6. Armee* (Balck) were finally forced into the defensive. The *5. SS-Panzer-Division "Wiking"* was ordered to hold Stuhlweißenburg under all circumstances.

The non-combat-ready *I./SS-Panzer-Grenadier-Regiment 23 "Norge"* had to be employed in those circumstances. At that time, the company commanders were:

1./SS-Panzer-Grenadier-Regiment 23 "Norge": SS-*Obersturmführer* Radke
2./SS-Panzer-Grenadier-Regiment 23 "Norge": SS-*Obersturmführer* Strömsnes (Norwegian)

3./SS-Panzer-Grenadier-Regiment 23 "Norge": *SS-Obersturmführer* Huber.

On 18 May, the battalion received new orders to occupy and hold Hill 351 southwest of Nadap. The companies advanced widely dispersed, under attack by Russian ground-attack aircraft. At about 1500 hours, the first casualties occurred on the forward slope of Hill 351 due to the low-flying aircraft. Among them was the commander of the *2./SS-Panzer-Grenadier-Regiment 23 "Norge"*, *SS-Obersturmführer* Strömsnes. Due to heavy enemy fire coming from Nadap, it was not possible to recover his body during the day. Later, the press of rapidly changing events prevented its recovery.

At about 1800 hours, murderous artillery fire opened up on the battalion. It had gone into position in the meantime. Hill 351 was plowed up by shells. The battalion suffered heavy losses. The author was also wounded in that action and his assistant machine gunner was killed. An infantry attack carried out from Nadap at dusk forced the remnants of the battalion back to the west.

Heavy fighting developed during the retreat. The Russians broke through at several places and encircled the *5. SS-Panzer-Division "Wiking"* in Stuhlweißenburg. On 22 March the breakout to the southwest took place. The dispersed elements of the division passed through the lines of the *10. SS-Panzer-Division "Hohenstaufen"* in the Berhida-Papkesi area directly north of Lake Balaton. The latter division had formed a blocking line there. *Panzer-Aufklärungs-Abteilung 5 "Wiking"*, commanded by *SS-Sturmbannführer* Fritz Vogt, was employed covering the retreat to the Hungarian-Austrian border. On 3 April Fritz Vogt was killed at Fürstenfeld at the border. On 30 March 1945 he had been awarded the Oakleaves to the Knight's Cross.

The retreat was conducted in stages. On 30 March 1945 the remnants of the *I./SS-Panzer-Grenadier-Regiment 23 "Norge"* blocked the Körmend road at Heiligenkreuz in the Raab Valley. At that point, the battalion was led by *SS-Obersturmführer* Radke after *SS-Sturmbannführer* Barth had been wounded. It then fell back in the Raab Valley to Breitenfeld. The Russian advance was brought to a temporary halt. The battalion had suffered further heavy losses, including almost all the Norwegians. It was once again filled out with all possible replacements. At that point, the soldiers were sworn in to *Großadmiral* Dönitz, who had taken over the leadership of the *Reich* after Hitler's suicide.

There, east of Graz, in the valley of the Raab, the fighting of the *5. SS-Panzer-Division "Wiking"* of *Heeresgruppe Süd* came to an end. *General* Rendulic, an Austrian, had assumed command of *Heeresgruppe Süd*, but he could do no more than arrange the capitulation. *Heeresgruppe Süd* was about to lay down its arms. The intention of the army group was to lead its troops into American captivity across the Ennz, which had been set as the demarcation line between the Russians and the Western Allies.

In order to ensure an orderly rearward movement of the units of the *5. SS-Panzer-Division "Wiking"*, the battalion was employed yet again in the morning of 8 May 1945 south of Gleisdorf on the mountain slopes of the Raab Valley to delay the advance of the Russians. The battalion then conducted a fighting withdrawal, providing cover for the division in the Mur Valley through Graz, Bruck on the Mur, Murau, Tamsweg, Mauterndorf and then to the north over the Tauer Pass to Radstadt. On 12 and 13 May the units of the division arrived in Radstadt, where they were disarmed by the Americans and then sent through Wagrain into the Kleinarlbach Valley. The men of the division were held prisoner in the steep mountain valley until 31 May 1945. It was only accessible from the north. The division was then sent in a road march to the Eberfing prisoner-of-war camp at Bad Tölz. Very few of the early members of the *I./SS-Panzer-Grenadier-Regiment 23 "Norge"* were still around for the trip to the camp.

SS-Untersturmführer Fritz Kauerauf a platoon leader in the *1./schwere SS-Panzer-Abteilung 503*. He was also a master gunner for the *Panther* and *Tiger* tanks. He wrote the section starting on the next page concerning the final operations of the battalion.

Appendix 16: schwere SS-Panzer-Abteilung 503

Fritz Kauerauf

(Note from Wilhelm Tieke: These documents relating to the employment of *schwere SS-Panzer-Abteilung 503* in the final fighting from the end of January to May 1945 at Küstrin, in Pomerania, around Arnswalde, at Danzig, Stettin and Berlin prove that these men were warriors.)

There was hardly a single tank which escaped the fate of being knocked out at least once. It was, in itself, far too large a target. It moved and halted in the center of events, naturally drawing all the enemy fire. It frequently lacked any infantry escort. The crew knew no more than what the commander shared with them — whether it was the direction of movement given to the driver or the target area for the gunner and radio operator with the main gun and two on-board machine guns, one of which was rigidly coupled to the main gun. The loader, who was responsible for the ammunition, without which no tank could effectively fight, saw nothing at all!

Those circumstances demanded men who could react with lightning speed, grasp the situation and take appropriate action. They were men who possessed the highest standards of soldierly virtue such as enthusiasm, steadfastness and a spirit of sacrifice and who evidenced all of those qualities in a constant, reciprocal interdependence in dealing with constantly changing situations. That was the only way that a tank crew could function. The crew had to constantly search for success, remain mobile and skillfully apply its massive firepower. Otherwise, it would not fulfil its mission. *Schwere SS-Panzer-Abteilung 503*, with its 43 *Königstiger*, was such a unit. After a year of conscientious training, its remarkable endeavors helped a large share of the threatened populace to escape to western Germany from a terrible fate in the east. Consequently, the battalion also served the future of Germany.

At the end of February 1945, I made contact with the unit by letter. That was after I had recovered to the point where my life was no longer in danger from the head injuries, the (thank God!) not-too-serious burns and the amputation of my left lower leg that resulted when my tank had been knocked out on 9 February at Klein Silber in Pomerania. As a result, the unit mailed the effects that had been assembled for shipment to my parents to me at the reserve-hospital at Uetersen (Holstein). On 17 July 1945, after the war had ended, the English showed up at our hospital with two armored cars (!) and an ambulance and took me prisoner from my bed — I had required a subsequent amputation. Strange to say, they were quite friendly and brought me my possessions. They had fallen into their hands in Hamburg and contained such things as my *Soldbuch*, wristwatch, fountain pen and papers. They showed a certain friendliness and respect for me because they not only saw what had happened to me, but because they also had a letter to me from *SS-Obersturmführer* Max Lippert. It had also fallen into their hands in the same mailbag. They knew its content. They also turned that letter over to me. They let me know that we were ideologically closer to them then the "allies" against whom we had fought. It would not have been possible for them to have treated me any more fairly!

What Max Lippert wrote was actually a war diary of the *1./SS-Panzer-Abteilung* 503. It read:

Location classified, 12 April 1945

Dear Comrade Kauerauf!

Yesterday, when I returned from hospital, I found your letter of 5 March. It read it was necessary to amputate your left foot. Now that you have survived the worst part — thanks to your youth — you will make it through the rest. My best wishes for a speedy recovery!

Now for what has been happening: Menke is NOT dead. You are wrong there. He has been in action again for a long time now. The company has lost the following (killed around Arnswalde): Schaal, Jäger, Schlachta, Ludwigs, Knorr, Belda, Thies, Krenn (?), Martin Peter and Franz R. The maintenance team had to be employed as infantry twice. Killed around Danzig in March: Heinrich, Nolte, Dietzen, Jeserer, Klünder, Kremann, Müller G., Melzer and Fürbacher. Missing: Kofler and Grupe. Not returning from Küstrin: Allmer, Fell, Fischer, Möller, Nottrot and Sturm. That is a list that will probably increase. Officers killed: Kaes, König and Grimmiger. Wounded: Meinl, Schäfer, Johannigmayer, Bellé and myself. The battalion has been split in two. One element is in Danzig and the other at the Oder. Very soon, however, they should be reunited! Brommann has knocked out 66 and was named yesterday in the Army Report. He has, however, lost an eye.

Our effectiveness was quite pleasing, and it could have been much better if the tactical employment had been different. However, the split employment with which our commitment had begun pursued us as our fate and did not seem to want to come to an end. It is superfluous to state that none of our vehicles made it out of Danzig. Instead of my wonderful *1./schwere SS-Panzer-Abteilung 503*, I now have a mixed bag. Only my own and Bender's men are still with me. It is so sad that I really cannot think about it.

At the moment things are quiet. We are keeping watch here until they come up behind us. Haake has married. He got out of Küstrin but has not yet showed up here. He could at least let us hear something from him. I send you my best wishes for a speedy recovery!

Heil Hitler!
Your comrade, M. Lippert

That letter was a report of the situation of the unit at the time it was written. It was all the more important since it included the lists of killed, wounded and missing that were no longer being compiled in the usual bureaucratic fashion. *SS-Obersturmführer* Max Lippert died on the field of battle a few weeks later in Berlin.

After my release from the hospital in August 1946 and following several transfers while in British custody, I passed on all the information I had gained about members of our battalion to the German Red Cross, where the information was passed on to the search service. The German Red Cross deserves thanks that it considered the *Waffen-SS* as a part of the army and never allowed the fact that we were soldiers to be questioned. It did so in spite of extreme pressure — sometimes internationally — and sometimes to its own disadvantage. An intensive correspondence with members and men returning who had belonged to our unit followed. I have preserved all that.

The second report that follows comes from *SS-Sturmmann* Lothar Tiby. At the time, he was a young tank driver. Today, after his return from captivity in Russia, he is the director of a factory of a well-known industrial enterprise with a bachelor's degree in engineering. He kept these notes with him through the long years of Russian captivity. Lothar Tiby recorded accurate details which, naturally, reveal much about life in a tank of the *1./schwere SS-Panzer-Abteilung 503.*

25 January 1945: We were issued 36 *"Königstiger"* at Camp Senne (Padeborn) and entrained, heading "East". (6 training tanks were already on hand.)

28 January 1945: Detrained some units of the battalion in Pomerania in the Wedell area. Other units of the battalion were sent on toward Küstrin and Gotenhafen. As a result, the battalion was not committed as a complete formation.

31 January 1945: Our company (company commander *SS-Obersturmführer* Lippert) attacked with four tanks and *Fallschirmjäger.*

Our crew: Commander, *SS-Unterscharführer* Löchner; gunner, *SS-Unterscharführer* Klöckner; driver, *SS-Sturmmann* Tiby; radio operator, *SS-Sturmmann* Horak; loader, *SS-Sturmmann* Unkel.

Objective for the day: Regentin. About 15 kilometers were covered without contact with Russian armor.

Russian losses: 80 antitank guns and heavy losses of infantry.

Friendly losses: One tank commander killed by a round to the head. No tanks lost. The *Fallschirmjäger* lost about 30% killed and wounded.

1 February 1945: Attack with contact with Russian armor. Our tank took the lead; it ran over a mine and received damage to the tracks. The company commander's tank went up front to provide cover while we changed the track. Heavy Russian mortar fire on both tanks during the repair.

Friendly losses: Löchner, back injury; Horak, thigh injury; Unkel, leg injury; the driver of the command tank, Öchsle, head injury (blind). All four were transported to hospital. Klöckner and Tiby, minor injuries — remained on duty.

New Crew: Commander, Grünhofer; gunner, Klöckner; driver, Tiby; radio operator, Breitenstein; loader, Badke.

Attack with objective for the day. Additional 10 kilometers attained.

2 February 1945: Another 5 kilometers advance, then withdrawal to avoid encirclement.

3 February 1945: At maintenance facility in Neu Wedell for minor repairs. Strong Russian combat patrol destroyed at the outskirts of the city. New front sector: Arnswalde.

4 February 1945: Attack with four tanks of our company from Arnswalde to a place 5 kilometers outside of Arnswalde, where German infantry was encircled. Strong resistance from Russian tanks and antitank guns. Three friendly tanks were disabled. Lippert took over as commander in our vehicle, which was still in action. Two enemy tanks knocked out. We took direct hits that did not penetrate. Our vehicle was immobilized. There was a second attack with four additional tanks from our battalion. The encircled infantry were relieved and our tank was recovered.

6-20 February 1945: Our vehicle was with the maintenance company at Stargard. The battalion was encircled in Arnswalde. Relieved from outside on 18 February.

21 February-14 March 1945: Our vehicle is now in Berlin-Tempelhof for repairs. The repairs are expected to take several months. In Berlin we took over a vehicle with minor repairs.

15 March 1945: Back to the battalion in the central sector of the Oder. The battalion now has only 10 tanks.

20 March 1945: Our wounded radio operator, Horak, was back again, on duty in our new vehicle. New commander: Bender.

1-15 April 1945: Staged at Frauenhagen.

6 April 1945: Ordered to march via Angermünde to Strausberg.

8 April 1945: In position on the road from Bukow in expectation of Russian armored spearhead advancing on Berlin. We knocked out 12 Russian tanks with our vehicle. The 10 tanks in our battalion knocked out a total of 64 Russian tanks.

Friendly losses: One tank and several more with minor damage. Our own tank suffered damage to the track-tension adjuster and the power-turret traverse.

19 April 1945: The Russians broke through to and encircled our maintenance company. The two tanks there were immediately repaired. One tank was knocked out during the first breakout attempt. During the second breakout attempt with our vehicle, two Russian tanks were knocked out by us. Forced our way to Berlin with the maintenance company. Outside of Berlin, we knocked out two more Russian tanks.

22 April 1945: While our vehicle was being towed to the maintenance company, our radio operator, Horak, was severely wounded for the second time and transported to hospital.

24 April 1945: The ring around Berlin was closed by the Russians. The remaining tanks of our battalion were distributed in Berlin. In our first employment in Berlin on the Mecklenburgstraße we knocked out four Russian tanks.

25 April 1945: Employed at the Heerstraße railroad station.

26 April 1945: Employed at the Halensee railroad station.

28 April 1945: Our battalion commander, *SS-Obersturmbannführer* Herzig, and four additional commanders from our battalion were awarded the Knight's Cross by

Hitler at the *Reich Chancellery*.

29 April 1945: Out tank commander, *SS-Unterscharführer* Bender, received a stomach wound while outside the vehicle. Semik is our new commander.

30 April 1945: One Russian tank was knocked out at the Halensee railroad station. Commander Semik was severely wounded by a mortar round while outside the vehicle. *SS-Hauptscharführer* Scholte is our new commander.

1 May 1945: Five more Russian tanks knocked out at the Halensee railroad station. That was our last contact with enemy armor. We have knocked out a total of 28 Russian tanks with our tank.

2 May 1945: Breakout attempt to the west with our battalion's last two tanks. Our vehicle with tank commander Lippert; the second vehicle with Knight's Cross recipient Schäfer from the *3./schwere SS-Panzer-Abteilung 503*. The hard fighting lasted all day against a greatly superior enemy. Heavy losses in vehicles, infantry and civilians on our side and very high losses in personnel carriers and infantry for the Russians as a result of our two tanks. In a renewed breakthrough attempt, Schäfer's tank took a direct hit that killed two of the crew and severely injured the others. Additional breakout attempts were impossible. We destroyed our vehicle, the last of our battalion's tanks.

3 May 1945: *SS-Obersturmführer* Lippert was shot in the head and killed during an attempt to get out to the west as an infantryman. The experience of our own tank crew illustrates the high casualty rate of our battalion during the three months of continuous action. We had six different tank commanders, three radio operators and two loaders. Only Klöckner and Tiby were in action from start to finish.

Reports similar to the above could have come from all of the tanks of the battalion, even if they had not been in service for the entire period. It remains to be said that *schwere SS-Panzer-Abteilung 503* was condemned to death by its being employed in the final struggles for Berlin. Wherever those largest and strongest of the German tanks appeared, they, were the last hope and a certain backstop for all the soldiers, troop officers, refugees and populace in the effort to stem the flood of the overwhelming Russian onslaught. For the men of the *Königstiger* that meant: "Fight to the last tank! Provide an example to the end!" Knowing that, Max Lippert wrote: "It is so sad that one cannot even think about it."

We close with a letter from the mother of our fallen *Ordonnanzoffizier*, Adolf Grimmiger. This letter, an answer to my letter informing her of her son's death, applies to all our soldiers who offered their lives in loyal performance of their duty!

Schwäbisch Gmünd, 23 January 1947

Dear Herr Kauerauf,

We received your letter of 30 December and thank you deeply for it. We had already learned the sad news of the death of our beloved Adolf from two of his comrades. It is very sad to us that our dear son had to be killed right at the end after he had served with such inspired devotion in the heaviest fighting. We have received nothing officially, since his death came during the sad time of the desperate collapse. We have had to make a great sacrifice. Of our four children, we have lost three.

Our son, Walter, was killed on 23 September 1944 in action as a battery commander with his *Sturmgeschütz Abteilung* during the heavy fighting at Arnhem. He is buried in Bocholt on the German-Dutch border.

Our only daughter died giving birth to her fourth child in April 1945. She, too, was a victim of this unfortunate war. As a result, I had a heart attack. It was too much for my nerves. With God's help I have had a good recovery, but the loss and the longing for my dear children prevents me from feeling happy at any time.

God gives us a burden, but he also helps us carry it. That I have learned in rich measure! I often feel bitter sorrow that our soldiers, who have done so much and given their all with upright hearts, are now condemned. They were heroes in the truest sense, both those who have fallen and those who yet live. They gave their best for their fatherland and their fellow men. I often think how my sons would have suffered over the sad and dismal end.

Dear *Herr* Kauerauf, I thank you from my heart for your sympathy. I wish you all the best in your path through life.

Heartfelt best wishes from the mother of Adolf,

Frau Eugenie Grimminger

I bow in respect to my comrades of *SS-Königstiger-Abteilung 503* and their families.

SS-Untersturmführer and Knight's Cross recipient Karl Brommann and his crew.

From left to right: *SS-Untersturmführer* Adolf Grimminger (killed in action at Danzig), *Dr.* Karl-Heinz Cappell (killed in a breakout attempt at Berlin) and *SS-Sturmbannführer* Fritz Herzig (battalion commander of the *schwere SS-Panzer-Abteilung 503*).

Five tank commanders in front of a training tank. From left to right: An unknown comrade from the army; Heinrich (killed in action at Danzig); Kauerauf (wounded in Pomerania); Semik (wounded and missing in action in Berlin); and, Löchner (wounded and missing in action in Pomerania).

Appendix 17: Swedish Volunteers in Formations of the Waffen-SS

Organization, Wartime Service and End of the "Swedish Company" of SS-Panzer-Aufklärungs-Abteilung 11 "Nordland" in the Fighting for Estonia, Kurland, Pomerania and Berlin, 1944-1945.

Preliminary Remarks

A total of about 175 Swedish soldiers served in the ranks of the *Waffen-SS* between 1940 and 1945. Approximately 30-40 Swedish soldiers were killed during the fighting in the Soviet Union, the Baltic lands, Hungary , Pomerania and Berlin. Until 1943, the Swedish soldiers were scattered throughout the units of the *Waffen-SS*. An intentional gathering of them took place in mid-1943 in the formation of the newly organized *III. (germanisches) SS-Panzer-Korps*.

SS-Panzer-Aufklärungs-Abteilung 11 was formed within the 11. SS-Freiwilligen-Panzer-Grenadier-Division "Nordland". Its commander was SS-Hauptsturmführer Rudolf Saalbach, who had been a company commander in the 5. SS-Panzer-Division "Wiking". It was organized in two reconnaissance companies (armored cars with 2 cm guns), two SPW companies (Panzergrenadiere in armored personnel carriers) and one heavy company (including, among other elements, an antitank platoon armed with the short-barreled 7.5-cm cannon). The company commanders in 1943 were SS-Obersturmführer Lorenz, Heckmüller, Kaiser, Viehmann and Schmidt. The total strength of the battalion was about 800 men.

The "Swedish Company" of *SS-Panzer-Aufklärungs-Abteilung 11 "Nordland"*

The *3./SS-Panzer-Aufklärungs-Abteilung 11* was composed of three light *SPW* platoons with ethnic German *Panzergrenadiere* from Rumania and the 4th (heavy) Platoon, which was armed with mortars and heavy machine guns on *SPW*. That platoon was made up of Swedish volunteers and included about 40 soldiers. As a rule, it included 1-2 officers, 5 noncommissioned officers and 30-35 men. Because there were also many Estonian Swedes — a Swedish speaking group that had resided in Estonia since about 1400 — in the company, the whole unit was called the "Swedish Company". In addition there were other Scandinavian volunteers and several Swiss in the battalion. The burden of the later fighting was born by the ethnic German recruits from Rumania, who were numerically predominant.

The company commanders of the *3./SS-Panzer-Aufklärungs-Abteilung 11* from 1943 to 1945 were: *SS-Obersturmführer* Walter Kaiser (killed in 1944), *SS-Obersturmführer* Hermann Ahrens (killed in 1944) and *SS-Obersturmführer* Hans-Gösta Pehrsson (Swedish; since deceased). Acting commanders for short periods of time were: *SS-Obersturmführer* Walter Buchholz (deceased), *SS-Untersturmführer* Rune Ahlgren (Swedish; killed in 1944), *SS-Untersturmführer* H. M. (Swedish), *SS-Untersturmführer* G. E. (Swedish) and *SS-Untersturmführer* Höök (killed in 1944).

Thanks to its outfit of vehicles, *SS-Panzer-Aufklärungs-Abteilung 11* was a highly mobile unit that was weak in personnel but strong in firepower. Its later employment in Estonia, Kurland and Pomerania was in decidedly mobile combat — flank security, immediate counterattacks and fighting retreat — so the advantages of the unit could be utilized. As one of the best formations of the division, it was considered as a "fire brigade" and was only infrequently employed as an entire battalion. It was frequently employed as separate companies and with other units, even outside the *III. (germanisches) SS-Panzer-Korps.* A brief description in the form of excerpts with eyewitness reports follows, which relate the fighting up to its total destruction in the Battle of Berlin in 1945. Although the number of Swedish soldiers was only minimal, their fate is presumably representative of that of most of the Scandinavian volunteers in the *III. (germanisches) SS-Panzer-Korps.*

The Oranienbaum Pocket and the Narwa Bridgehead, 1944

After formation and training in 1943 at Grafenwöhr and in Croatia, the *III. (germanisches) SS-Panzer-Korps* was transferred to the Leningrad Front (Oranienbaum) at the end of November 1943 with the *11. SS-Freiwilligen-Panzer-Grenadier-Division "Nordland"* (*SS-Brigadeführer* von Scholz) and the *4. SS-Freiwilligen-Panzergrenadier-Brigade "Nederland".* All signs pointed to an imminent Soviet offensive to relieve Leningrad. On 14 January 1944, the Soviet assault broke loose with support from heavy naval guns (Kronstadt).

With tenfold superiority, the Soviets broke through the positions of the Luftwaffen-Feld-Divisionen and threatened the positions of the division. SS-Panzer-Aufklärungs-Abteilung 11 was employed everywhere as fire brigade, wherever things got too hot. We attacked at Kostalitzi. It was our first baptism of fire. For many it was also their last. But we succeeded in stopping the Russians. Thanks to that, our comrades from SS-Panzer-Grenadier-Regiment 23 "Norge" and the 4. SS-Panzer-Grenadier-Brigade "Nederland" could withdraw. We suffered great losses and almost every one of the survivors was slightly or severely wounded. We were only able to break our way through at night. (Franz Bereznyak, former *SS-Unterscharführer* of the "Swedish Company" to the author, 18 January 1978.)

The *III. (germanisches) SS-Panzer-Korps* organized its defense in the approaches to Narwa. Alongside it, in addition to army formations, was the newly organized *20. Waffen-Grenadier-Division der SS (estnisches Nr. 1),* whose regiments played a large role in the later defensive fighting. The Narwa combat area offered many historical associations. Founded by Danes, the city was an outpost of the German Order of the Knights Templar. During Estonia's "Swedish Period" (1561-1721), Charles XII conquered a superior Russian army at Narwa.

The new main line of resistance ran from the coast (Hungerburg) along the Narwa River around the German Narwa bridgehead. In the south, marshland stretched to Lake Peipus. The Narwa Front was already under Russian attack in the first days of February. However, the front held. Nobody expected that the defense of the city would last from February until July 1944.

The attempt by Soviet naval battalions to capture the coastal village of Meereküla by a *coup de main* was smashed by units of *SS-Panzer-Aufklärungs-Abteilung 11* and Estonian police units that were there. The later Russian attempt to attack at Auwere southwest of Narwa in order to encircle the *III. (germanisches) SS-Panzer-Korps* also failed. The "Swedish Company" was one of the units that took part in the fighting at Auwere. On 19 April 1944, the man who had commanded the company until that time, *SS-Obersturmführer* Kaiser, was killed at Sooküla. Because of his human qualities, Kaiser was much loved by the Swedish volunteers.

SS-Obersturmführer Hans-Gösta Pehrsson

After Kaiser's death, the Swedish *SS-Obersturmführer* Hans-Gösta Pehrsson finally assumed command of the *3./SS-Panzer-Aufklärungs-Abteilung 11* in July 1944 and led it during the battles of Estonia, Kurland, Pomerania and Berlin. Pehrsson was the highest ranking and most highly decorated Swedish soldier in the *Waffen-SS*. He was decorated with the Honor Roll Clasp of the German Army, the Iron Cross, Second Class, the Iron Cross, First Class, The Close Combat Clasp in Silver, the Tank Assault Badge, the Infantry Assault Badge and the Wound Badge in Silver.

Born at Karlskrona (Sweden) in 1910, he was a chemist in civilian life. He volunteered for the war and had been fighting since July 1941 in *"Freikorps Danmark"*. At Lake Ilmen, he was a *SS* noncommissioned officer and leader of a machine-gun platoon. He completed the officer-candidate course at *Junkerschule Tölz* in 1943. Before assuming command of the *3./SS-Panzer-Aufklärungs-Abteilung 11*, he was a platoon leader in the battalion. At the end of 1944 he was the acting commander of the battalion for a short period of time. He was decorated with the Honor Roll Clasp of the German Army on 25 December 1944 for particular bravery in the fighting around Trekni at Preekuln (Kurland) in October 1944. His final service was as intelligence officer of the *11. SS-Freiwilligen-Panzergrenadier-Division "Nordland"* under *SS-Brigadeführer* Ziegler. That duty assignment commenced on 15 April 1945 with simultaneous promotion to *SS-Hauptsturmführer*. After further wounds and capture by the Russians during the final Battle of Berlin, he fled to Sweden in June 1945. He died in Stockholm in 1974 after serious illness.

Gösta Pehrsson was a good comrade. Loyal, honorable and courageous, he possessed an abundance of military knowledge and ability. He helped those in need, even when it endangered his life to do so. The life of a comrade meant even more to him than his own, because he bore the responsibility for his men and his company. It was a responsibility he enjoyed. He was an agreeable, good, kind-hearted man. I saw my comrade, Gösta, for the last time at Preekuln in 1944. (Sepp Schirmer, former *SS-Obersturmführer* and company commander, *4./SS-Panzer-Aufklärungs-Abteilung 11* to the author, 14 April 1976.)

SS-Obersturmführer Pehrsson was a man of iron nerves. Pehrsson was proud of the blue-gold Swedish cross on his left shoulder. As a leader, he was a great guy. As a soccer player, however, he was hopeless. We played daily in the rest area at Mummassare and I always dribbled around him. But that's life! He was greatly respected and honored by everyone, but he was rather a "loner" who had little contact with others. His clear thinking always resulted in positive decisions and the young soldiers had no worries about going through Hell for him. (*Dr. med.* Jonel Orelt, former medic in *SS-Panzer-Aufklärungs-Abteilung 11* to the author, 5 May 1976).

Pehrsson was a man with many human qualities and showed no signs at all of political fanaticism. In mid-1944, he understood that the war was long-since lost for Germany. Morale had noticeably suffered after the extraordinarily bloody fighting around Narwa and the shocking experiences. While the *3./SS-Panzer-Aufklärungs-Abteilung 11* was in the rest area at Sillamäe during May/June 1944, Pehrsson, on his own initiative, assisted exhausted, disillusioned and extremely young soldiers and Estonian-Swedes of his company to flee to Sweden instead of forcing them into the hopeless fighting.

The Evacuation of Estonia and the Fighting in Kurland 1944

At the end of July 1944, the Narwa bridgehead was evacuated by the *III. (germanisches) SS-Panzer-Korps*. A Russian breakthrough south of Lake Peipus at Dorpat endangered the south flank of the Narwa front. On 27 July, the Soviet formations reached Dünaburg. *SS-Panzer-Aufklärungs-Abteilung 11* fought as part of *Panzergruppe Strachwitz* on the Düna to stop the Soviet breakthrough to Riga. The hard-hitting and mobile companies of the battalion played a significant role in the fact that the front held in front of Riga. The collapse of *Heeresgruppe Mitte* rendered the German northern front untenable. The formations of the *III. (germanisches) SS-Panzer-Korps* evacuated all of Estonia at the beginning of September and organized for the defense of Riga and Kurland. In the several months of Kurland battles that followed, the battalion was continuously employed. The losses up to that time had been murderous. A Swedish *SS-Untersturmführer* in *SS-Aufklärungs-Abteilung 11*, Rune Ahlgren, who had broken off his officer's training course at the Stockholm Military School to join the *Waffen-SS*, was killed in the fighting on the Düna on 30 October 1944.

The days spent in the Preekuln area were black days for the *3./SS-Panzer-Aufklärungs-Abteilung 11*. Trekni was the name of the place. Pehrsson received orders for the company directly from *SS-Brigadeführer* Ziegler: "This is a strategic point on which the fate of Mitau and Libau depend. Attack, occupy and hold under all circumstances to the last man".

After the attack, when we had occupied the Russian hill with the bunkers, Pehrsson's company had only a few men left. It was horrible, man-to-man butchery. The Russians knew how important it was and put everything they had into recapturing the hill. We repulsed their superior forces for four days, beating back every attack. On the fifth day we had to fall back. Pehrsson's command post was about 100 meters behind the bunker line. I will never forget the moment when he saw us falling back. "Cowards, back to your positions!" he yelled, although he knew that we could have done nothing else. And then he stormed forward ahead of us. With twelve men we surprised the Russians. They were so confident of victory that they did not expect an attack. We captured more than 100 prisoners. After the fight we emptied Pehrsson's alcohol-filled canteens. Thereupon he gave the following radio report to *SS-Sturmbannführer Saalbach*: "Position recaptured. If a case of schnapps is not here soon, we will abandon the position." Saalbach personally came with a case of schnapps. He knew that Pehrsson kept his word. (Franz Bereznyak).

After participating in four Kurland battles, the remnants of the *III. (germanisches) SS-Panzer-Korps* were pulled out of the Kurland Pocket and shipped to Stettin for reorganization and refitting. In the Pomeranian area, the burned-out companies of *SS-Panzer-Aufklärungs-Abteilung 11* were equipped with new *SPW* fitted with cannon, antiaircraft guns and mortars. They also received new personnel carriers.

The Battle for Pomerania 1945

On 12 January 1945, the German Weichsel Front collapsed. The Soviet armies advanced to Lower Silesia and Küstrin on the Oder. In order to strengthen the front south of East Pomerania, the *III. (germanisches) SS-Panzer-Korps* — then commanded by *Generalleutnant* Unrein in place of *SS-Obergruppenführer* Steiner, who had been named Commander-in-Chief of *Panzer-Armee-Oberkommando 11* — was among those formations employed at Arnswalde, Stargard and in the Altdamm bridgehead.

We then proceeded from Freiheide to Stargard, where we repeatedly had to attack to relieve some bunch that had gotten in trouble. At Hornsburg we had the mission of defending the sound detectors. Pehrsson's bunker took a direct hit. His driver, Wintergerst, and his messenger, Franz Kaul, were killed. Pehrsson and his radio operator, Köstner, were slightly wounded. We were surrounded. I brought Pehrsson back through swamps and woods in my SPW...

South of Stettin, in the Oder Marshes, we bivouacked in the woods. After several quiet days, during which promotions and decorations were awarded, it was back to Küstrin. (Franz Bereznyak).

The *11. SS-Freiwilligen-Panzergrenadier-Division "Nordland"* was seriously battered at the Stettin-Altdamm bridgehead. The division commander, *SS-Brigadeführer* Ziegler, therefore ordered the evacuation of the Altdamm bridgehead, contrary to a direct order from Adolf Hitler, in order to save the formations from final destruction.

It was a badly battered *SS-Panzer-Aufklärungs-Abteilung 11* that then rattled through Stettin a second time, a month and a half later, this time toward the west. In the bombed-out city, Soviet artillery had already started to finish what the bomber formations had begun...We only noted all that mechanically. Only then did we fully realize how infinitely weary and exhausted we were. It was impossible to follow a chain of thought to the end. The exhaustion took the form of pure apathy. The crews of the vehicles hung limply at their positions. (Notes of a Swedish platoon leader in the *3./SS-Panzer-Aufklärungs-Abteilung 11* — E. W. — in 1947).

The Swedish *SS-Untersturmführer* H. M. was severely wounded for the second time at Vossberg (Pomerania). On 10 March 1945, the Swede, Arne Johansson, was killed at Großwächtlin and his countryman, Ragnar

Gustaffson, was killed on 5 March at Massow. Danish volunteers buried him at the Lüttkenhagen Estate.

During counterattacks in Pomerania, the Swedish volunteers of the *3./SS-Panzer-Aufklärungs-Abteilung 11* also observed Soviet transgressions against the civilian population. In part, that resulted from the undisciplined condition that losses had brought about in the Red Army, from the incitements by Ilja Ehrenburg and the refusal of higher German party officials to allow timely evacuation of civilians from the combat zone.

During the Russian assault on Seelow in mid-April 1945, the "Swedish Company" was particularly heavily hit by the massive, intense Russian artillery barrage. The remaining *SPW* raced to the west. The remnants of the *3.* and *4./SS-Panzer-Aufklärungs-Abteilung 11* went into position along the Seelow — Müncheberg road. The retreating *Fallschirmjäger* of the *9. Fallschirmjäger-Division* passed through their lines and then joined them in launching an immediate counterattack, but the companies then had to fall back to the west again. The final Battle for Berlin and, with it, the complete destruction of *SS-Panzer-Aufklärungs-Abteilung 11 "Nordland"* was on the horizon.

The Final Act: The Struggle for Berlin

Hitler ordered the *LVI. Panzer-Korps* (*General der Artillerie* Weidling), to which the *11. SS-Freiwilligen-Panzergrenadier-Division "Nordland"* had been attached since 17 April 1945, to move in from the southeast toward Berlin. That instruction set the final seal on the fate of that corps and the division. On 25 April, the Russians reached Potsdam and Döberitz. Berlin was surrounded. By order of Goebbels and Hitler, the civilian population was not evacuated in good time — as had likewise happened in Pomerania — and suffered heavily in the ensuing fighting. In the final hours, irresponsible higher commands sent a *Kampfgruppe* of the *33. Waffen-Grenadier-Division der SS "Charlemagne" (französische Nr. 1)*, a battalion of the *15. Waffen-Grenadier-Division der SS (lettische Nr. 1)* and even naval units without infantry experience to Berlin. Thus, willy-nilly, the city was defended by French, Danish, Norwegian, Swedish, Swiss and Latvian as well as German soldiers.

The *11. SS-Freiwilligen-Panzer-Grenadier-Division "Nordland"* fell back, step by step, into the inner city of Berlin through Strausberg — Mahlsdorf — Biesdorf — Karlshorst. *SS-Panzer-Aufklärungs-Abteilung 11* covered the flanks at Friedrichsfelde and crossed the Spree at Stralau. The way then led through Oberschöneweide, Köpernick and Treptow. The battalion launched counterattacks at Rudow and Britz, among other places, and fell back to Neukölln.

We established ourselves firmly outside the city at Karlshorst, by the big racetrack. Heavy fighting developed there around the track and the immediate area. Our mortars were positioned on the green turf in the center of the racetrack. The other companies were employed as infantry. Whistling and howling, the Russian rounds tore into the stables and grandstands. Wooden benches and walls splintered and spun through the air. Concrete structures crumbled. We were surrounded again, but again we were able to break out. (Swedish *SS-Oberscharführer* E.W.).

During the Battle of Berlin, the commander of the *11. SS-Freiwilligen-Panzer-Grenadier-Division "Nordland"*, *SS-Brigadeführer* Joachim Ziegler, demonstrated remarkable personal courage in speaking out against the directives of Hitler and *General* Weidling regarding the defense of Berlin. Ziegler was not only an outstanding soldier but also a man of the highest character with heartfelt feelings for his soldiers. He evaluated the situation without illusions. Because Ziegler refused to force the foreign volunteers who had been entrusted to him into the hopeless battle and instead, attempted to save the division from commitment in the city, he was relieved of command of the division on 25 April 1945 and replaced by *SS-Brigadeführer Dr.* Krukenberg. Ziegler was then placed under house arrest at the *Reich* Chancellery. He was killed on 2 May 1945 in an attempt to break out of Berlin.

The burnt-out formations of the *11. SS-Freiwilligen-Panzer-Grenadier-Division "Nordland"* finally occupied the defensive sector Unter den Linden — Spittelmarkt — Lindenstraße — Hallesches Tor — Landwehrkanal and defended the government quarter alongside *Kampfgruppe Mohnke* (replacement units of the *1. SS-Panzer-Division "Leibstandarte SS Adolf Hitler"*). What was left of *SS-Sturmbannführer* Saalbach's *SS-Panzer-Aufklärungs-Abteilung 11* and *Bataillon Fenet* of the *33. Waffen-Grenadier Division der SS "Charlemagne" (französische Nr. 1)* were employed at the Anhalter railroad station. *SS-Hauptsturmführer* Pehrsson was the last *Ic* (intelligence officer) of the division. Following Ziegler's relief, Pehrsson returned to his old *3./SS-Panzer-Aufklärungs-Abteilung 11*. According to statements made by Pehrsson after the war, the fighting troops in Berlin were then plagued by the *Gestapo* and by "flying courts-martial" and thus robbed of their last illusions.

Our mission consisted of reconnaissance and conducting immediate counterattacks. On 27 April we mounted the last attack in a street in the eastern part of the city. The enemy had cut off six SPW there. We were able to get four of them. Two had to be abandoned. (Franz Bereznyak).

SS-Haupsturmführer Pehrsson and *SS-Unterscharführer* Bereznyak and three *SPW* of the *3./SS-Panzer-Aufklärungs-Abteilung 11* were attached to the *Reich* Chancellery and the staff of *SS-Brigadeführer* Mohnke on 27 April. They were employed as liaison elements and maintained contact with the various units. On 1 May *SS-Panzer-Aufklärungs-Abteilung 11* was informed that a breakthrough was planned at the Weidendammer Bridge. Pehrsson said farewell to the remaining men with a handshake and the words: "Men, the war is over. It's time to save yourself if you can." Most of them went to the Weidendammer Bridge, the last hope to get out of the witch's cauldron. Pehrsson's command vehicle took a direct hit shortly thereafter in the Friedrichstraße. It killed his driver, Johansson. Pehrsson, wounded, was captured by the Russians. He escaped in June 1945 and finally made it to Sweden as one of the few survivors of the "Swedish Company" of *SS-Panzer-Aufklärungs-Abteilung 11*.

SS-Obersturmführer Siegfried Lorenz, commander of the *1./SS-Panzer-Aufklärungs-Abteilung 11*, reported on the hopeless breakout attempt during the night of 2 May 1945:

In the meantime, I had learned that Steiner's relief attack from the direction of Oranienburg had failed and Hitler had committed suicide. During the night of 1/2 May a breakout was organized over the Schiffsbauerdamm Bridge to the north. It was horrible to see the many burned, dead soldiers under the commuter railroad bridge at the zoo.

What was still capable of moving was ready. In the front was my *SPW* with a machine gun and cannon. Behind me was an *SPW* from the *3./SS-Panzer-Aufklärungs-Abteilung 11*. The remaining *SPW* followed. I crossed the bridge. In front of us was a roadblock. Everything stopped. The Russian artillery fire got stronger and stronger. Tanks started firing, too.

There was the sound of an impact and my driver was silent. A sharpshooter had fired an explosive bullet through the vision slit. My hand found no more face there. I pulled my dead comrade off of his seat. Then I shifted the *Pak-SPW*. I did the aiming myself at the corner window across from me and hit. The sharpshooter did not bother us. We drove like the devil. I lost all concept of time. I read a sign saying Danziger Platz and, in the distance, I already saw Russian infantry and white flags everywhere. I said, "Comrades, that's the end of this war." We rolled the last *SPW* into the nearby deep cesspool. The men disappeared. The *Spieß* of the *2./SS-Panzer-Aufklärungs-Abteilung 11* and his wife committed suicide. Except for two of my people, I have not seen any of the others to this day. (Written communication to the author, 15 October 1983.)

SS-Unterscharführer Bereznyak was able to break out with his *Flak-SPW* over the Weidendammer Bridge and get to the Stettin railroad station in north Berlin. His report also provides a "closing chord" for the "Swedish Company" and the units of the *11. SS-Freiwilligen-Panzer-Grenadier-Division "Nordland"* in the final Battle of Berlin. Killed for a long-lost cause.

After a few minutes we heard the noise of tank tracks from the same direction from which we had just come. A *SPW* drew up and stopped in a cloud of steam. It was Bruno Sprintz from the Swedish platoon. He had a mortar vehicle with a hit in the radiator. The vehicle was boiling over. I wanted to take him and his crew — they were Swedes — with me in my vehicle. But he begged me to give him a tow. The Swedish crew remained in the towed vehicle. We shoved off in the belief that the worst was now behind us. Soon we discovered that we had only had a brief chance to catch our breath.

I wanted to break out to the northwest. The towed vehicle broke loose at an intersection. In one street I saw Russian tanks. A woman screamed out an open window. I just said, "Hans, move out!" But it was too late. Crash! A jet of flame and I saw how the crew was enveloped in flame. The driver had collapsed and the vehicle moved on like a torch in the wind…

Swedish volunteers. Pehrsson is standing third from the left. By the end of the war, he had been promoted to *SS-Hauptsturmführer* and served as the Intelligence Officer for the *11. SS-Freiwilligen-Panzergrenadier-Division "Nordland"*.

Chier, the Swedish war correspondent, and his driver.

Appendix 18: SS-Brigadeführer und Generalmajor der Waffen-SS Joachim Ziegler: A Remarkable Military Career

Lennart Westberg

Joachim Ziegler was born in 1904 in Hanau (Main) to an old Huguenot family. His father was killed in 1914 before Verdun as a cavalry officer. Ziegler spent his youth and school years with his mother and siblings in Darmstadt, where he passed his examination on completing secondary school in 1923. His interest in nature led him to work toward a career in forestry. He was interested in the humanities, musically gifted and talented in sports. For financial reasons, he joined *Reiter-Regiment 16* in 1923. His talents in leading troops and planning were soon recognized. Even as a young officer, Joachim Ziegler was conspicuous for his independent thinking and objectivity.

As a *Leutnant* with *Reiter-Regiment 4* at Potsdam, Ziegler experienced the conversion of the cavalry to tanks and was company commander in *Panzer-Regiment 6* of the *3. Panzer-Brigade* (*Hauptmann* in 1933). During the Spanish Civil War, he was one of the specialists who was assigned to the German *Panzer-Abteilung* that was in Spain (Spanish Cross in Gold in 1939). After returning to Germany, Ziegler was adjutant of the *3. Panzer-Brigade* (Berlin). During the Polish campaign he received the Iron Cross, Second Class as a company commander.

He served in the French campaign as a General Staff *Major*. He was employed as the *Ic* (intelligence) of the *7. Panzer-Division* under *Generalmajor* Rommel. He received the Iron Cross, First Class on 28 June 1940 and was then made a permanent general-staff officer.

Joachim Ziegler saw further employment as a general-staff officer in motorized and armored formations during the Russian campaign. He was promoted to General-Staff *Oberst* in 1943. He was chief of staff of the *XXXIX. Panzer-Korps*, where he received the German Cross in Gold in 1944. Since 1937, Ziegler had a "picture-book career". He was a general-staff officer with more than three years of experience on all parts of the Eastern Front. All of his personal evaluations spoke of him as a commanding personality who was far above the average.

As a result of high losses and the great expansion of the field formations of the *Waffen-SS* starting in 1943, there was a chronic shortage of officers, not only among the troops, but also in the higher staffs. Although itself short of personnel, the *OKH* transferred 25 general-staff officers from the army to the *Waffen-SS* in mid-1943. Some of those who were transferred at that time later were accepted of their own volition as active *SS*-officers. Effective 15 June 1943, *Oberst im Generalstab* Joachim Ziegler was detailed to the *Waffen-SS* and assigned to the newly forming *III. (germanisches) SS-Panzer-Korps* as its chief of staff. That resulted from a direct request of the commanding general,

General Steiner, who had met Ziegler in the Caucasus in 1942 and valued his professional qualifications.

As chief of staff of the *III. (germanisches) SS-Panzer-Korps*, Ziegler had experienced the Soviet offensives on the northeast front (Oranienbaum Pocket) and the fighting in the Narwa bridgehead (February-July 1944). The previous commander of the *11. SS-Freiwilligen-Panzergrenadier-Division "Nordland"*, *SS-Brigadeführer* von Scholz, was killed on 27 July 1944. *SS-Oberführer* Ziegler was named as his successor, simultaneously assuming the active rank in the *Waffen-SS* of *Generalmajor der Waffen-SS*. From that time on, Ziegler commanded the division during the extremely hard and turbulent fighting in Estonia (Knight's Cross on 5 September 1944), Latvia, Kurland and Pomerania up to the final end of the division in the Brandenburg — Berlin area in April 1945.

Ziegler was noted not only for his outstanding professional capabilities, but also as a humane and understanding commander who led the division with circumspection and a calm disposition. He was obviously a man who followed the dictates of his own conscience and was no rigid follower of orders. The well being of his soldiers was his first priority. In particular, he resisted to the last a senseless "squandering" of his division, because it consisted to such a great extent of foreign military volunteers. That is illustrated primarily by his uncompromising attitude toward the senseless Battle of Berlin.

The last phase of the final battle began at the Oder with the attack by the Red Army on 16 April 1945 from its bridgeheads at Küstrin and Wriezen. It soon became the final battle for the capital city itself. When the foreign volunteers of the *11. SS-Freiwilligen-Panzer-Grenadier-Division "Nordland"* and the *23. SS-Freiwilligen-Panzergrenadier-Division "Nederland"* were scattered to the winds during the fighting on the Oder and attached to other corps headquarters, *SS-Obergruppenführer* Steiner emphatically advised Ziegler to avoid being drawn into the city of Berlin under any circumstances. That would mean the end of the division. As later events proved, Ziegler constantly kept Steiner's advice in mind. After the *11. SS-Freiwilligen-Panzer-Grenadier-Division "Nordland"* was transferred from the area of the *III. (germanisches) SS-Panzer-Korps*, Steiner and Ziegler remained in contact through a radio relay of the *XXXXVI. Panzer-Korps*. Both pinned their final hopes on the advance of the Western Allies and held to the opinion that the foreign volunteers should be spared the final battle.

The *11. SS-Freiwilligen-Panzergrenadier-Division "Nordland"* was attached to the *LVI. Panzer-Korps* (*General der Artillerie* Weidling) effective 17 April 1945. On 23 April 1945, Hitler gave Weidling orders that the *LVI. Panzer-Korps* was to move to Berlin to take part in the defense of the capital. As it turned out, the order was a death sentence for those formations.

The Russians closed their circle around the city on 25 April at Potsdam. Under all circumstances, Ziegler wanted to prevent his division from being sacrificed in that insane operation. He first argued with Weidling's operations order and increasingly did his best to obstruct its execution. After 23 April, Ziegler apparently transferred important elements of his division — among others, essential units of the signals battalion — to the western section of Berlin. His intention was, in part, to raise questions about the combat power of the division; in part to have his division positioned for a breakout from Berlin. While Ziegler moved into a conflict situation, Weidling was under heavy pressure from the *Reich* Chancellery to employ the *LVI. Panzer-Korps* as ordered.

When Ziegler refused Weidling's questionable order to attack on 25 April with the *11. SS-Freiwilligen-Panzer-Grenadier-Division "Nordland"* to reach the eastern outskirts of Berlin and, instead, ordered the division radio net to go to radio silence, *General* Weidling removed Ziegler from command of the division.

SS-Brigadeführer Dr. Krukenberg was named as Ziegler's successor. Krukenberg had been ordered to Berlin with a *Kampfgruppe* of the *33. Waffen-Grenadier-Division der SS "Charlemagne (französische Nr. 1).* After his relief, Ziegler was held at the *Reich* Chancellery under house arrest until 2 May 1945.

During the night of 2 May 1945, the remnants of the *11. SS-Freiwilligen-Panzer-Grenadier-Division "Nordland"* and *Kampfgruppe Mohnke* (replacement units of the *1. SS-Panzer-Division "Leibstandarte SS Adolf Hitler")* assembled for an attempt to break out of Berlin. However, most of the attempts to break through at the Weidendammer Bridge and in north Berlin ended catastrophically due to the massed Russian opposition. Many men of the *11. SS-Freiwilligen-Panzer-Grenadier-Division "Nordland"* were killed in those attempts. Among them was *Generalmajor* Joachim Ziegler, who was killed early on 2 May 1945. The reports on his death are, in part, contradictory. It has been determined that he was killed in the area of Humboldthain (Brunnenstraße).

Appendix 19: Recommendation for the Oakleaves to the Knight's Cross of the Iron Cross for SS-Brigadeführer und Generalmajor der Waffen-SS Joachim Ziegler

Corps Headquarters
Corps Command Post, 17 April 1945
III. (germanisches) SS-Panzer-Korps

Recommendation for the award of the Oakleaves to the Knight's Cross of the Iron Cross to *SS-Brigadeführer und Generalmajor der Waffen-SS* Joachim Ziegler

(Born 18 October 1904 in Hanau. Active officer. Until 1 July 1943, active in various official positions in the 100,000-man-army and the *Wehrmacht*. As of 1 July 1943, detailed from the army to the *Waffen-SS*. Until 31 July 1944, Chief of Staff of the *III. (germanisches) SS-Panzer-Korps*. From 1 August 1944 to the present day, division commander of the *11. SS-Freiwilligen-Panzergrenadier-Division "Nordland".*)

Justification for the recommendation:

On 23 January 1945, after an intense, heavy artillery preparation, the Russians started the expected offensive toward Libau from the Preekuln area with units of 3 armies and the main body of the 3rd Guards Mechanized Corps (Confirmed: 8 divisions and 3 armored regiments).

After the Russians had smashed most of the units occupying the main line of resistance, the Russians achieved a deep penetration, in spite of bitter resistance from isolated pockets of resistance. *SS-Brigadeführer* Ziegler, recognizing the looming breakthrough, immediately intervened personally. He ruthlessly shut down supply operations so that the alarm units thus freed up could be led forward into blocking positions. He then personally led the small division reserves that were available in a counterattack.

It was only thanks to the personal, untiring, courageous commitment of his own person on the battlefield, especially on 24 and 25 January 1945...that *SS-Brigadeführer* Ziegler prevented the breakthrough to Libau.

On 15 February 1945, in spite of shortages of fuel and ammunition, the *11. SS-Freiwilligen-Panzergrenadier-Division "Nordland"* started the ordered relief attack on Arnswalde. Knowing that *Panzergrenadier-Regimenter* that had been given no more than a brief refitting could only achieve success through his own intervention and surprise of the enemy, *SS-Brigadeführer* Ziegler not only joined the regimental commanders in personally scouting in every detail for the attack from the main line of resistance but, from the very beginning of the attack, placed himself at the front of the foremost battalion.

After breaking the first enemy resistance, Ziegler started his armored group on a ruthless advance to Arnswalde. By 1400 hours, the armored group had reestablished contact with Arnswalde.

By pursuing with the *Panzergrenadier-Regimenter* and making full use of all the reserves, the enemy — most of the 7th Guards Cavalry Corps — was defeated...

As a result of this unique feat of leadership by *SS-Brigadeführer* Ziegler, not only was the enemy smashed with only extremely limited German casualties — seven dead and one wounded in one regiment — but also, for the first time and in a very short time, an encircled fortress was freed (1,000 wounded, 1,100 combatants and 7,000 civilians). The enemy was forced to give up planned attack operations in order to replace his shattered formations by regrouping.

During the heavy defensive fighting in Pomerania, beginning with the enemy breakthrough that was intended to split the front, the *11. SS-Freiwilligen-Panzergrenadier-Division "Nordland"* was constantly in the *Schwerpunkt* of the defense beginning 3 March 1945.

The division was under attack by the 2nd Guards Tank Army, elements of the 61st and 47th Armies and elements of the 3rd Shock Army.

In spite of Russian superiority in both numbers and weapons, the breakthrough to Stettin was stopped every time and the Altdamm bridgehead was formed within the framework of the orderly accomplishment of the withdrawal movements that had been ordered.

On 17 March 1945, after an extremely heavy fire preparation and after bringing up fresh forces, the enemy again attempted to advance through Altdamm to Stettin so as to split the bridgehead and capture the Oder crossings.

Ziegler's own and attached battalions had combat strengths of less than 100 men. Ammunition had been in sort supply since 10 March 1945.

In full knowledge of the enemy intentions, *SS-Brigadeführer* Ziegler remained at his forward command post (about 2 kilometers behind the main line of resistance) under continuous fire. With his staff, he temporarily defended his command post against enemy who had broken through. In spite of the total exhaustion of the men and the high casualty rate among officers, which led to a lack of leadership, he repeatedly organized the resistance. Because the radio equipment had been destroyed, it was no longer possible for observed fire. The shortage of ammunition prevented effective use of pre-planned fire. A large number of the infantry weapons had been put out of action or lost their crews. Radio and wire connections were continually broken and friendly armor was no longer mission capable.

It was only through his own outstanding, courageous, personal intervention in critical situations and his willingness to make sacrifices that *SS-Brigadeführer* Ziegler held the bridgehead for the time period that had been ordered.

SS-Brigadeführer Ziegler was the soul of the resistance. During the time period from 3 to 18 March 1945, the *11. SS-Freiwilligen-Panzergrenadier-Division "Nordland"* knocked out 194 tanks.

In recognition of his personally outstanding courageous action in Kurland and Pomerania in both attack and defense, *SS-Brigadeführer* Ziegler is recommended for the award of the Oakleaves to the Knight's Cross of the Iron Cross.

Signed: Steiner
SS-Obergruppenführer und General der Waffen-SS

SS-Brigadeführer Ziegler was awarded the Oakleaves to the Knight's Cross of the Iron Cross on 28 April 1945

Appendix 20: Court-Martial Practice in the III.(germanisches) SS-Panzer-Korps from 1943-1945

Lennart Westberg (Sweden)

To date, there has been practically no documentary evidence to support the accusation frequently raised that the judicial system of the *Waffen-SS* was especially harsh or, in comparison to *Wehrmacht* procedures, even "cruel". On the contrary, there are many indications that this claim is a postwar legend. There are practically no contemporary files available relating to the administration of justice by *Waffen-SS* courts-martial. Many of the files of the troop-unit staffs relating to punishments and those files that were preserved by the judicial section of the *SS* Main Office relating to courts-martial of the *Waffen-SS* were destroyed in 1945.

According to corroborating statements given in interviews, however, there are credible indications that, at least as far as the formations of the *III.(germanisches) SS-Panzer-Korps* are concerned, the accusation of particular harshness does not apply. Briefly, and without scholarly aspirations, the court-martial practice of that corps, which consisted in part of Scandinavian volunteers, will be described.

By Himmler's orders, the Scandinavian volunteers of the *Waffen-SS* were to be punished less severely. The minimum legally specified punishments were allowed to be less for "Germanic" volunteers. In addition, there was a widespread practice by division commanders of passing on the sentences to the commanding general, *SS-Obergruppenführer* Steiner, so that judgements that appeared inappropriately harsh could be reduced to the correct level at a higher command level. Finally, the *III. (germanisches) SS-Panzer-Korps* was staffed with judicial personnel of obvious discernment and full judicial qualifications. That included, among others, *SS-Obersturmbannführer* Ulrich Dümichen as corps judge and *Dr.* Karl Hachmeister as field judge of the *11. SS-Freiwilligen-Panzergrenadier-Division "Nordland"*.

On 3 June 1944, Steiner evaluated his corps judge as follows: "A military judge of the best type, the sort that troops can only wish for. A skilled psychologist who understands the troops precisely and therefore receives their complete trust..." (Berlin Document Center / Personnel file: Ulrich Dümichen). Dümichen had shared responsibility since 1936 for the creation of new *SS* and police judicial procedures. Later on he was active as the head of the *SS- und Polizeigericht III* (*SS* and Police Court) in Berlin and as a field judge for the *Waffen-SS*. If that were not known, however, the suspicion might exist that the rapid expansion of the *Waffen-SS* in wartime may have had the possible result that insufficiently trained judicial personnel were available for the responsibility-laden judicial staffing of the new *SS* divisions.

The *III. (germanisches) SS-Panzer-Korps* had punishment and assault platoons in *SS-Panzer-Pionier-Bataillon 11* and the *Korps-Panzer-Pionier-*

Bataillon. Those were units in which offenders and those arrested could rehabilitate themselves and were primarily used in construction of positions under enemy fire. Instructions to place Scandinavian convicts in the *Waffen-SS* prison camp at Danzig-Matzkau were apparently never issued. It is necessary to distinguish between the corps' own "in-house" punishment platoons and *SS-Sturmkompanie 103*, which consisted of former inmates of the *SS* prison camp at Danzig-Matzkau. In mid-1944 it was attached to the *III. (germanisches) SS-Panzer-Korps*. After the heavy fighting in the Narwa bridgehead (Estonia), the surviving riflemen of that unit were considered rehabilitated and incorporated into *SS-Panzer-Grenadier-Regiment 24 "Danmark"*. A second penal unit made up of noncommissioned officers, who had been stripped of their rank, was attached to the *III. (germanisches) SS-Panzer-Korps* in April 1945 north of Oranienburg. That unit disappeared in the Havelberg area.

When the *III. (germanisches) SS-Panzer-Korps* was transferred to Croatia during its training period in 1943 and was in danger of sinking into partisan warfare with all its negative associations, it was thanks to responsible troop commanders and judges that that did not lead to excesses. According to information provided by the Ludwigsburg Center to Investigate Nazi Crimes, there have been no accusations from Yugoslavia or elsewhere against the behavior of the *11. SS-Freiwilligen-Panzergrenadier-Division "Nordland"* or the *4. SS-Freiwilligen-Panzergrenadier-Brigade "Nederland"* in Croatia. (*Oberstaatsanwalt Dr.* Rückerl to the author, 10 November 1981.)

SS-Obersturmbannführer Ulrich Dümichen:

If we had to punish, we sought to make the sentence a means of education and deterrence for the troops. *SS-Obergruppenführer* Steiner, with whom I had a trusting, cooperative working relationship, guaranteed a sympathetic and more than fitting judgement. In the area of his command, chivalry ruled, even where it concerned an inhuman opponent. The civilian population benefited particularly from his protection...Crime in the *III. (germanisches) SS-Panzer-Korps* was a mirror of the history of this unit.

In addition to the offenses that are unavoidable in any human community, certain offenses accumulated in special situations. Those had to be met with understanding, but also with harsh measures. During the time the corps was being organized in the summer of 1943 in the Franconian region of Germany, there were a series of desertions among the Dutch recruits, who were still half children. In situations that were similar but entirely independent of each other, young soldiers simply ran away from the unit in the direction they presumed led to their homeland. Since those flights took place without any preparations and on the spur of the moment, most ended within hours and the offenders were returned to the unit.

Questioning constantly revealed the same picture. The subject had imagined that the life of a soldier would be quite different. He just wanted to go home because he had had enough of the Waffen-SS. The minimum punishment for desertion was a year in military prison. Since that was an unacceptable outcome, a certain amount of judicial manipulation was required to transform the act to absence without leave and change the punishment from penal confinement to probation until the end of the war.

In addition, the unit leaders were instructed to take educational measures to put a speedy end to such teething problems. All in all, the situation with regard to criminality among the troops continued quite favorably right to the end. The troops were, indeed, disillusioned, but their morale was unshaken...The war did have one good side to it that was quite different than in a peacetime situation: It offered the opportunity to atone for past misdeeds. Thus, the guilty party could erase the black spot on his record by special service. In that situation, one could dispense with the defamatory sentences of peacetime that, as a rule, do more harm than good...

For me, the time spent as an *SS* judge offered me the opportunity as a relatively young man to bear responsibility for the fate of human beings. It was a situation that came about because of the war. Punishment was not foremost in mind. Instead, I attempted to exert an educational effect on the fate of the individual and also within the community of soldiers. I had the good fortune to encounter understanding in almost all the military legal authorities with whom I interacted. That was particularly true in my relationship with General Steiner...(Ulrich Dümichen to the author, 15 September 1980)

Appendix 21: Duty Positions Held in the III. (germanisches) SS-Panzer-Korps (listed sequentially)

Corps Headquarters

Commanding Generals: *General der Waffen-SS* Steiner; *General der Waffen-SS* Kleinheisterkamp (acting commander); *General der Waffen-SS* Steiner; *General der Waffen-SS* Keppler; *General* Unrein; and, *General der Waffen-SS* Steiner

Chiefs of Staff: *SS-Obersturmbannführer* Sporn; Ziegler; and, *SS-Obersturmbannführer* von Bockelberg

Corps Quartermaster: Sporn

Corps Surgeons: Unbehauen and *SS-Hauptsturmführer* Dittmar

Corps Artillery Commanders: *SS-Standartenführer* Kryssing and *Oberst* Kresin

Corps Signal Officers: *SS-Obersturmbannführer* Rüger and *SS-Obersturmbannführer* Weitzdörfer

Corps Engineer: *SS-Obersturmbannführer* Schäfer

Corps Medical Battalion Commander: ?

Corps Logistics Officer: *SS-Obersturmbannführer* Scheingraber

Corps Provost Marshal: *SS-Obersturmbannführer* Grossner

Officer reserve: *SS-Obersturmbannführer* Stoffers, Vollmer and Dahm

11. SS-Freiwilligen-Panzer-Grenadier-Division "Nordland"

Divisional Commanders: *SS-Brigadeführer* von Scholz; *SS-Brigadeführer* Ziegler; and, *SS-Brigadeführer* Krukenberg

Operations Officers: *SS-Sturmbannführer* Ziemssen; *SS-Obersturmbannführer* von Bockelberg; *SS-Obersturmbannführer* von Bock und Pollach; and *SS-Sturmbannführer* Winczek

SS-Panzer-Abteilung 11 "Hermann von Salza"

Commander: *SS-Obersturmbannführer* Kausch

The battalion consisted of a headquarters company and four tank companies. Effective February 1945, it was redesignated a regiment. The commander of the *I./SS-Panzer-Regiment 11 "Hermann von Salza"* was *SS-Hauptsturmführer* Grathwol.

SS-Panzer-Aufklärungs-Abteilung 11

Commander: *SS-Sturmbannführer* Saalbach

The battalion consisted of a headquarters, two armored-car companies, two companies with cross-country vehicles and a heavy company.

SS-Pionier-Bataillon 11

Commanders: *SS-Sturmbannführer* Bunse and *SS-Sturmbannführer* Voß

The battalion consisted of three combat-engineer companies and a supply section.

SS-Nachrichten-Abteilung 11

Commanders: *SS-Sturmbannführer* Weitzdörfer; *SS-Obersturmbannführer* Schlotter; and, *SS-Hauptsturmführer* Schnick

The battalion consisted of one radio and one wire company.

SS-Flak-Abteilung 11

Commanders: *SS-Obersturmbannführer* Plöw and *SS-Sturmbannführer* Kurz

The battalion consisted of thee heavy and one light battery.

SS-Panzerjäger-Abteilung 11 (Sturmgeschütz)

Commanders: *SS-Hauptsturmführer* Roensch and *SS-Sturmbannführer* Schulz-Streek

The battalion consisted of a headquarters and supply company and three antitank companies

SS-Wirtschafts-Bataillon 11

Commander: *SS-Sturmbannführer* Conrad

The battalion consisted of a headquarters and four companies (rations, clothing, repair)

Divisional Field Hospital

Military Police Section

SS-Nachschub-Bataillon 11

Commander: *SS-Sturmbannführer* Gläsker

The battalion consisted of a headquarters and eleven companies and supply sections

SS-Instandsetzungs-Abteilung 11

Commander: *SS-Hauptsturmführer* Buck

The battalion consisted of two maintenance companies and an armament platoon

SS-Feld-Ersatz-Bataillon 11

Commander: *SS-Obersturmbannführer* Lang

The battalion consisted of a headquarters and four companies

SS-Artillerie-Regiment 11

Commander: Karl

I./SS-Artillerie-Regiment 11: *SS-Hauptsturmführer* Müller and *SS-Hauptsturmführer* Wischmann (three batteries of light field guns)

II./SS-Artillerie-Regiment 11: *SS-Sturmbannführer* Fischer (three batteries of light field guns)

III./SS-Artillerie-Regiment 11: *SS-Sturmbannführer* Potschka (three batteries of heavy field guns)

SS-Panzer-Grenadier-Regiment 23 "Norge"

Commanders: *SS-Obersturmbannführer* Jörchel; *SS-Sturmbannführer* Stoffers; *SS-Obersturmbannführer* Knöchlein; and *SS-Obersturmbannführer* Körbel

I./SS-Panzer-Grenadier-Regiment 23 "Norge": *SS-Sturmbannführer* Finson and *SS-Hauptsturmführer* Vogt

II./SS-Panzer-Grenadier-Regiment 23 "Norge": *SS-Sturmbannführer* Krügel; *SS-Sturmbannführer* Scheibe; *SS-Hauptsturmführer* Wichmann; and, *SS-Hauptsturmführer* Spörle

III./SS-Panzer-Grenadier-Regiment 23 "Norge": *SS-Sturmbannführer* Lohmann; *SS-Hauptsturmführer* Gürz; and *SS-Hauptsturmführer* Hoffmann

SS-Panzer-Grenadier-Regiment 24 "Danmark"

Commanders: *SS-Obersturmbannführer Graf* von Westphalen; *SS-Obersturmbannführer* Krügel; *SS-Obersturmbannführer* Klotz; *SS-Sturmbannführer* Sörensen; and, *SS-Sturmbannführer* Ternedde

I./SS-Panzer-Grenadier-Regiment 24 "Danmark": *SS-Sturmbannführer* Martinsen; *SS-Sturmbannführer* Fischer; *SS-Hauptsturmführer* Wichmann; and, *SS-Hauptsturmführer* Sörensen

II./SS-Panzer-Grenadier-Regiment 24 "Danmark": *SS-Hauptsturmführer* Walther; *SS-Hauptsturmführer* Hämel; *SS-Hauptsturmführer* Bergfeld; and, *SS-Sturmbannführer* Sörensen

III./SS-Panzer-Grenadier-Regiment 24 "Danmark": *SS-Sturmbannführer* Neegard-Jakobsen; *SS-Sturmbannführer* Kappus; and, *SS-Hauptsturmführer* Ternedde

4. SS-Panzer-Grenadier-Brigade "Nederland"

Brigade Commander: *SS-Brigadeführer* Wagner

Operations officer: *SS-Sturmbannführer* Ziemssen and *SS-Sturmbannführer* von Bock

Reconnaissance Company: *SS-Obersturmführer* Kuhne

Signals Company: ?

Supply Elements: ?

Maintenance Company: ?

Medical Company: ?

SS-Pionier-Bataillon 54

Commander: *SS-Hauptsturmführer* Wanhöfer

The battalion consisted of a headquarters, three combat-engineer companies and a supply section.

SS-Panzerjäger-Abteilung 54 (Sturmgeschütz)

Commanders: *SS-Sturmbannführer* Schock; *SS-Hauptsturmführer* Grotwohl; and, *SS-Hauptsturmführer* Aigner

SS-Artillerie-Regiment 54

Commanders: *SS-Sturmbannführer und Oberstleutnant der Schutzpolizei* Schlüter

The regiment had a *Flak* platoon within its headquarters.

I./SS-Artillerie-Regiment 54: *SS-Sturmbannführer* Schlüter; *SS-Sturmbannführer* und *Major der Schutzpolizei* Hofer; and, *SS-Hauptsturmführer* Rüschoff

II./SS-Artillerie-Regiment 54 (effective spring of 1944): *SS-Hauptsturmführer* Topeters; *SS-Hauptsturmführer* De Veer; *SS-Hauptsturmführer* Aigner; and, *SS-Hauptsturmführer* De Veer

III./SS-Artillerie-Regiment 54 (effective December 1944): *SS-Sturmbannführer und Major der Schutzpolizei* Hofe (a mixed battalion with some 8.8 cm *Flak*)

SS-Freiwilligen-Panzer-Grenadier-Regiment 48 "General Seyffard"

Commanders: *SS-Obersturmbannführer* Vitzhum; *SS-Obersturmbannführer* Jorchel; *SS-Obersturmbannführer* Benner; *SS-Obersturmbannführer* Scheibe (when reformed in the spring of 1945)

I./SS-Freiwilligen-Panzer-Grenadier-Regiment 48 "General Seyffard": *SS-Sturmbannführer* Geiger; *SS-Hauptsturmführer* Tröger; and, *SS-Sturmbannführer* Betzwieser.

II./SS-Freiwilligen-Panzer-Grenadier-Regiment 48 "General Seyffard": *SS-Sturmbannführer* Breymann

SS-Freiwilligen-Panzer-Grenadier-Regiment 49 "de Ruyter"

Commanders: *SS-Obersturmbannführer* Collani; *SS-Sturmbannführer* Bunse; *SS-Sturmbannführer* Lohmann; *SS-Obersturmbannführer* Klotz; and, *SS-Sturmbannführer* Lohmann

I./SS-Freiwilligen-Panzer-Grenadier-Regiment 49 "de Ruyter": *SS-Hauptsturmführer* Meyer; *SS-Sturmbannführer* Walther; and, *SS-Sturmbannführer* Unger

II./SS-Freiwilligen-Panzer-Grenadier-Regiment 49 "de Ruyter": *SS-Hauptsturmführer* Diener; *SS-Hauptsturmführer* Frühauf; *SS-Hauptsturmführer* Ertel; *SS-Obersturmführer* Scholz; *SS-Sturmbannführer und Major der Schutzpolizei* Petersen.

Appendix 22: SS-Flak-Abteilung 11 "Nordland"

The battalion was activated on 1 December 1943 at the North Arys Training Area in East Prussia.

Organization:

>Headquarters Company
>
>3 Batteries with 8.8 cm *Flak*. Within each battery was also a 2-cm *Flak* platoon. (The latter were later replaced by quad *Flak* guns.)
>
>1 battery with 3.7 *Flak*. (Later replaced with twin-barreled pieces.)

Vehicles: Armored and unarmored heavy and medium prime movers. The trains and ammunition vehicles were predominately *Opel-Blitz* trucks.

Duty Positions

Battalion commanders: *SS-Sturmbannführer* (later *SS-Obersturmbannführer*) Walter Plöw and *SS-Hauptsturmführer* (later *SS-Sturmbannführer*) Kurz

Adjutants: *SS-Untersturmführer* Adam Dieterich and *SS-Untersturmführer* Georg Anweiler

Signals officer: *SS-Hauptscharführer* Schneidemeier

Administrative officer: *SS-Obersturmführer* Heinz Schneider (also commanded the headquarters battery)

Liaison officer: *SS-Untersturmführer* (later *SS-Obersturmführer*) Besch

Ordnance officer: *SS-Untersturmführer* (later *SS-Obersturmfüher*) Fred Prescher

Battery commanders:

1./SS-Flak-Abteilung 11: *SS-Obersturmführer* (later *SS-Hauptsturmführer*) Leube (later Wirth)

2./SS-Flak-Abteilung 11: *SS-Obersturmführer* (later *SS-Hauptsturmführer*) Delfs

3./SS-Flak-Abteilung 11: *SS-Obersturmführer* (later *SS-Hauptsturmführer*) Mende

4./SS-Flak-Abteilung 11: *SS-Obersturmführer* (later *SS-Hauptsturmführer*) Holzboog

Ethnic composition of the formation: Primarily ethnic Germans from Transylvania and the Swabian Banat; Dutch; Dutch-speaking Belgians; and, volunteers from Scandinavian countries.

Appendix 23: The Reconstitution of
SS-Panzer-Grenadier-Regiment 24 "Danmark" (mid-April 1945)

The regiment was brought almost completely to authorized strength by the addition of elements from naval replacement battalions and about 200 personnel from *SS-Panzer-Abteilung 11 "Hermann von Salza"*. The *I./SS-Panzer-Grenadier-Regiment 24 "Danmark"* was committed in Hungary with the *5. SS-Panzer-Division "Wiking"* after it had been formed. The rest of the regiment was committed 10 kilometers west of Schwedt (Oder). The regimental command post was in Hohenlandin.

Regimental commander: *SS-Obersturmbannführer* Klotz

Regimental adjutant: *SS-Hauptsturmfüher* Lührs

The regimental headquarters company had an assault platoon consisting of 2 light machine guns and ten assault rifles. The commander of the headquarters company was *SS-Untersturmführer* Starke

II./SS-Panzer-Grenadier-Regiment 24 "Danmark" (teil-mot.)

Battalion commander: *SS-Sturmbannführer* Sörensen

Adjutant: *SS-Untersturmführer* Raßmussen

Assault platoon leader: *SS-Unterscharführer* Steindor

5./SS-Panzer-Grenadier-Regiment 24 "Danmark": *SS-Hauptsturmführer* Seyb

6./SS-Panzer-Grenadier-Regiment 24 "Danmark": *SS-Oberscharführer* Pösch (submitted for a battlefield commission)

7./SS-Panzer-Grenadier-Regiment 24 "Danmark": *SS-Untersturmführer* Stippernitz

8./SS-Panzer-Grenadier-Regiment 24 "Danmark": *SS-Obersturmführer* Birkedahl-Hansen. (The company had 4 heavy machine guns, 88 mm mortars, 2 light infantry guns and 2 75 mm *Pak*)

III./SS-Panzer-Grenadier-Regiment 24 "Danmark" (mot.)

Battalion commander: *SS-Sturmbannführer* Ternedde

Adjutant: *SS-Untersturmführer* Krieger

Assault platoon leader: ?

9./SS-Panzer-Grenadier-Regiment 24 "Danmark": *SS-Hauptscharführer* Pärschke

10./SS-Panzer-Grenadier-Regiment 24 "Danmark": *SS-Untersturmführer* Scheel

11./SS-Panzer-Grenadier-Regiment 24 "Danmark": *SS-Untersturmführer* Dirksen

12./SS-Panzer-Grenadier-Regiment 24 "Danmark": *SS-Hauptsturmführer* Meier

The companies had an average strength of 80 personnel with 10 light machine guns and 30 assault rifles.

Regimental Companies

13./SS-Panzer-Grenadier-Regiment 24 "Danmark": *SS-Hauptsturmführer* Laerum (heavy infantry guns and mortars)

14./SS-Panzer-Grenadier-Regiment 24 "Danmark": *SS-Obersturmführer* Petersen (*Flak*)

15./SS-Panzer-Grenadier-Regiment 24 "Danmark": ? (Horse-drawn section)

16./SS-Panzer-Grenadier-Regiment 24 "Danmark": *SS-Untersturmführer* Christensen (combat engineers)

The regiment also possessed a field-replacement company.

Appendix 24: Personnel Strengths

Authorized Strengths

General-Kommando III. (germanisches) SS-Panzer-Korps: 204 officers / 943 noncommissioned officers / 3,319 enlisted personnel and 334 *HiWis*: 4,416 total personnel

11. SS-Freiwilligen-Panzer-Grenadier-Division "Nordland": 558 officers / 3,391 noncommissioned officers / 12,612 enlisted personnel and 931 *HiWis*: 16,561 total personnel

4. SS-Panzer-Grenadier-Brigade "Nederland": 325 officers / 1,895 noncommissioned officers / 6,740 enlisted personnel and 434 *HiWis*: 8,960 total personnel

Total corps personnel: 29,937

Note: Above aggregate figures do not include *HiWis*, since they were considered auxiliaries and not intended to be employed in combat.

Actual Strengths

30 June 1944

General-Kommando III. (germanisches) SS-Panzer-Korps: 96 officers / 484 noncommissioned officers / 2,086 enlisted personnel: 2,666 total personnel

11. SS-Freiwilligen-Panzer-Grenadier-Division "Nordland": 355 officers / 1,857 noncommissioned officers / 8,788 enlisted personnel: 11,000 total personnel

4. SS-Panzer-Grenadier-Brigade "Nederland": 220 officers / 1,319 noncommissioned officers / 5,175 enlisted personnel: 6,713 total personnel

SS-Panzer-Grenadier-Regiment 23 "Norge" (reconstituted): 9 officers / 33 noncommissioned officers / 327 enlisted personnel: 369 total personnel

SS-Panzer-Grenadier-Regiment 24 "Danmark" (reconstituted): 6 officers / 50 noncommissioned officers / 324 enlisted personnel: 380 total personnel

Total corps personnel: 20,928

25 May 1944

SS-Panzer-Grenadier-Regiment 23 "Norge": 1,379 (of which 810 belonged to combat units)

SS-Panzer-Grenadier-Regiment 24 "Danmark": 1,503 (of which 1,175 belonged to combat units)

In comparison, each regiment had 3,200 soldiers in September 1943

20 September 1944

General-Kommando III. (germanisches) SS-Panzer-Korps: 100 officers / 487 noncommissioned officers / 1,957 enlisted personnel: 2,544 total personnel (with an additional 19 *HiWis*)

11. SS-Freiwilligen-Panzer-Grenadier-Division "Nordland": 328 officers / 1,818 noncommissioned officers / 8,334 enlisted personnel: 10,889 total personnel (with an additional 284 *HiWis*)

4. SS-Panzer-Grenadier-Brigade "Nederland": 178 officers / 1,170 noncommissioned officers / 5,182 enlisted personnel: 6,530 total personnel (with an additional 113 *HiWis)*

Total corps personnel: 19,963

Appendix 25: Foreign Composition of the
11. SS-Freiwilligen-Panzer-Grenadier-Division "Nordland"

15 September 1943

Danes: 33 officers / 162 noncommissioned officers / 1,191 enlisted personnel: 1,386 total

Norwegians: 20 officers / 50 noncommissioned officers / 464 enlisted personnel: 534 total

Swedes: 0 officers / 3 noncommissioned officers / 39 enlisted personnel: 42 total

25 May 1944

Danes: 37 officers / 220 noncommissioned officers / 852 enlisted personnel: 1,109 total

Norwegians: 21 officers / 48 noncommissioned officers / 269 enlisted personnel: 338 total

Swedes: 2 officers / 8 noncommissioned officers / 19 enlisted personnel: 23 total

In addition, there were a few Swiss and Finns. Additional Danes, Norwegians, Swiss and Finns came to the division when the *I./SS-Panzer-Grenadier-Regiment 23 "Norge"* and the *I./SS-Panzer-Grenadier-Regiment 24 "Danmark"* were reconstituted and returned to the division.

Appendix 26: Foreign Composition of the
4. SS-Panzer-Grenadier-Brigade "Nederland"

25 May 1944

Dutch: 39 officers / 291 noncommissioned officers / 2,406 enlisted personnel: 2,736 total

Belgians: 2 officers / 8 noncommissioned officers / 10 enlisted personnel: 20 total

Ethnic Germans from Rumania constituted about 33% of the total strength.

Appendix 27: Knight's Cross Recipients of the III. (germanisches) SS-Panzer-Korps

Corps and Corp Troops

SS-Obergruppenführer und General der Waffen-SS Felix Steiner (Knight's Cross as the commander of *SS-Regiment "Deutschland"*; Oakleaves as commander of the 5. *SS-Panzer-Division "Wiking"*; and, Swords as commanding general of the *III. (germanisches) SS-Panzer-Korps*)

SS-Standartenführer Max Schäfer (Knight's Cross as the commander of *SS-Pionier-Bataillon 5 "Wiking"*; Oakleaves as the corps engineer and the leader of a *Kampfgruppe*)

SS-Sturmbannführer Fritz Hertzig (Battalion commander of the *schwere SS-Panzer-Abteilung 503*)

11. SS-Freiwilligen-Panzer-Grenadier-Division "Nordland"

SS-Gruppenführer und Generalleutnant der Waffen-SS Fritz von Scholz (Knight's Cross as the commander of *SS-Regiment "Nordland"*; Oakleaves as the commander of the *11. SS-Freiwilligen-Panzer-Grenadier-Division "Nordland"*; and Swords as the commander of the *11. SS-Freiwilligen-Panzer-Grenadier-Division "Nordland"*)

SS-Sturmbannführer Fritz Bunse (Battalion commander of *SS-Pionier-Bataillon 11*)

SS-Sturmbannführer Rudolf Saalbach (Battalion commander of *SS-Panzer-Aufklärungs-Abteilung 11*)

SS-Obersturmführer Georg Langendorf (Acting commander of the *5./SS-Panzer-Aufklärungs-Abteilung 11*)

SS-Sturmbannführer Hanns-Heinrich Lohmann (Battalion commander of the *III./SS-Panzer-Grenadier-Regiment 23 "Norge"*). Oakleaves as *Obersturmbannführer* and commander of *SS-Panzer-Grenadier-Regiment* 49 "De Ruyter"

SS-Hauptsturmführer Heinz Hämel (Company commander of the *7./SS-Panzer-Grenadier-Regiment 24 "Danmark"*)

SS-Hauptsturmführer Walter Seebach (Company commander of the *5./SS-Panzer-Grenadier-Regiment 24 "Danmark"*)

SS-Obersturmbannführer Arnold Stoffers (Regimental commander of *SS-Panzer-Grenadier-Regiment 23 "Norge"*)

SS-Obersturmbannführer Albrecht Krügel (Knight's Cross as battalion commander of the *II./SS-Panzer-Grenadier-Regiment 23 "Norge"* and Oakleaves as the regimental commander of *SS-Panzer-Grenadier-Regiment 24 "Danmark"*)

SS-Oberscharführer Philipp Wild (Tank commander in *SS-Panzer-Abteilung 11 "Hermann von Salza"*)

SS-Unterscharführer Casper Spork (Gun commander of a cannon vehicle of the *5./SS-Panzer-Aufklärungs-Abteilung 11*)

SS-Unterscharführer Egon Christoffersen (Squad leader of the *7./SS-Panzer-Grenadier-Regiment 24 "Danmark"*)

SS-Hauptsturmführer Josef Bachmeier (Battalion commander of the *II./SS-Panzer-Grenadier-Regiment 23 "Norge"*)

SS-Obersturmbannführer Paul Albert Kausch (Knight's Cross as the battalion commander of *SS-Panzer-Abteilung 11 "Hermann von Salza"* and Oakleaves as regimental commander of *SS-Panzer-Regiment 11 "Hermann von Salza"*)

SS-Brigadeführer und Generalmajor der Waffen-SS Joachim Ziegler (divisional commander of the *11. SS-Freiwilligen-Panzer-Grenadier-Division "Nordland"*, and Oakleaves as divisional commander).

SS-Hauptsturmführer Martin Gürz (Battalion commander of the *III./SS-Panzer-Grenadier-Regiment 23 "Norge"*)

SS-Oberscharführer Albert Hektor (Platoon leader in *SS-Panzer-Grenadier-Regiment 24 "Danmark"*)

SS-Obersturmbannführer Friedrich Wilhelm Karl (Regimental commander of *SS-Artillerie-Regiment* 11)

SS-Sturmbannführer Hermann Potschka (Battalion commander of the *III./SS-Artillerie-Regiment 11*)

SS-Hauptsturmführer Richard Spörle (Battalion commander of the *II./SS-Panzer-Grenadier-Regiment 23 "Norge"*)

SS-Hauptscharführer Siegfried Lüngen (Acting commander of the *5./SS-Panzer-Grenadier-Regiment 23 "Norge"*)

SS-Obersturmbannführer Fritz Knöchlein (Regimental commander of *SS-Panzer-Grenadier-Regiment 23 "Norge"*)

SS-Sturmbannführer Karlheinz Schulz-Streek (Battalion commander of *SS-Sturmgeschütz-Abteilung 11*)

SS-Obersturmführer Willi Hund (Acting commander of the *7./SS-Panzer-Grenadier-Regiment 23 "Norge"*)

SS-Untersturmführer Karlheinz Gieseler (Assault group leader in *Kampfgruppe Nordland* in Berlin)

Received earlier: *SS-Hauptsturmführer* Fritz Vogt (Knight's Cross as a platoon leader in the *2./SS-Panzer-Aufklärungs-Abteilung "Verfügungs division"* and Oakleaves as the battalion commander of the *I./SS-Panzer-Grenadier-Regiment 23 "Norge"* (while attached to the *5. SS-Panzer-Division "Wiking"* in Hungary)

4. SS-Panzer-Grenadier-Brigade "Nederland"

SS-Brigadeführer und Generalmajor der Waffen-SS Jürgen Wagner (Knight's Cross as the regimental commander of *SS-regiment "Germania"* and Oakleaves as the divisional commander of the *23. SS-Freiwilligen-Panzergrenadier-Division "Nederland"*)

SS-Hauptsturmführer Hans Joachim Rühle von Lilienstern (Battalion commander of the *I./SS-Freiwilligen-Panzer-Grenadier-Regiment 48 "General Seyffard"*)

SS-Hauptsturmführer Günter Wanhöfer (Battalion commander of *SS-Pionier-Bataillon 54*)

SS-Rottenführer Derek Elsko Bruins (Gun commander of a *Sturmgeschütz* in *4. SS-Panzer-Grenadier-Brigade "Nederland"*)

SS-Obersturmbannführer Wolfgang Jörchel (Regimental commander of *SS-Freiwilligen-Panzer-Grenadier-Regiment 48 "General Seyffard"*)

SS-Obersturmführer Helmut Scholz (Knight's Cross as acting commander of the *7./SS-Freiwilligen-Panzer-Grenadier-Regiment 49 "de Ruyter"* and Oakleaves as acting commander of the *II./SS-Freiwilligen-Panzer-Grenadier-Regiment 49 "de Ruyter"*)

SS-Hauptsturmführer Carl-Heinz Frühauf (Battalion commander of the *II./SS-Freiwilligen-Panzer-Grenadier-Regiment 49 "de Ruyter"*)

SS-Obersturmbannführer Hans Collani (Regimental commander of *SS-Freiwilligen-Panzer-Grenadier-Regiment 49 "de Ruyter"*)

SS-Hauptsturmführer Hans Meyer (Battalion commander of the *I./SS-Freiwilligen-Panzer-Grenadier-Regiment 49 "de Ruyter"*)

SS-Hauptsturmführer Karl Heinz Ertel (Regimental adjutant of SS-Freiwilligen-Panzer-Grenadier-Regiment 49 "de Ruyter")

SS-Sturmbannführer und Major der Schutzpolizei Wilhelm Schlüter (Regimental commander of *SS-Artillerie-Regiment 54*)

SS-Rottenführer Stefan Strapatin (Signals section leader in *SS-Freiwilligen-Panzer-Grenadier-Regiment 49 "de Ruyter"*)

SS-Untersturmführer Albert Rieth (Acting battery commander of the *2./SS-Artillerie-Regiment 54*)

SS-Hauptscharführer Georg Schluifelder (Acting company commander of the *1./SS-Freiwilligen-Panzer-Grenadier-Regiment 49 "de Ruyter"*)

SS-Sturmbannführer und Major der Schutzpolizei Otto Petersen (Battalion commander of the *II./SS-Freiwilligen-Panzer-Grenadier-Regiment 49 "de Ruyter"*)

SS-Obersturmführer Clemens Behler (Battery commander of the *3./SS-Artillerie-Regiment 54*)

SS-Kanonier Walter Jenschke (*Flak* section leader in the *II./SS-Artillerie-Regiment 54*)

SS-Obersturmführer Johannes Hellmers (Acting company commander in *SS-Freiwilligen-Panzer-Grenadier-Regiment 49 "de Ruyter"*)

SS-Sturmbannführer und Major der Schutzpolizei Lothar Hofer (Battalion commander of the *II./SS-Artillerie-Regiment 54*)

SS-Sturmbannführer Siegfried Scheibe (Regimental commander of *SS-Freiwilligen-Panzer-Grenadier-Regiment 49 "de Ruyter"*)

Received earlier: *SS-Sturmmann* Gerardes Mooymann (Gun commander in the *SS-Panzerjäger-Kompanie* of *SS-Legion "Nederland"*

Appendix 28: Honor Roll of the German Army

III. (germanisches) SS-Panzer-Korps

25 November 1944: *SS-Obersturmbannführer* Max Schäfer (Corps engineer and leader of a *Kampfgruppe*)

11. SS-Freiwilligen-Panzer-Grenadier-Division "Nordland"

5 November 1944: *SS-Obersturmführer* Fritz Sidon (Acting commander of the *9./SS-Panzer-Grenadier-Regiment 24 "Danmark"*)

25 November 1944: *SS-Obersturmführer* Fritz Gärdtner (Acting commander of the *2./SS-Panzer-Grenadier-Regiment 24 "Danmark"*)

17 December 1944: *SS-Obersturmführer* Willi Hund (Acting commander of the *7./SS-Panzer-Grenadier-Regiment 23 "Norge"*); *SS-Hauptsturmführer* Rudolf Ternedde (Battalion commander of the *III./SS-Panzer-Grenadier-Regiment 24 "Danmark"*); and, *SS-Hauptsturmführer* Per Sörensen (Leader of a *Kampfgruppe* in *SS-Panzer-Grenadier-Regiment 24 "Danmark"*)

25 December 1944: *SS-Unterscharführer* Alfred Jonstrop (Section leader of the Headquarters Company of *SS-Panzer-Grenadier-Regiment 24 "Danmark"*); *SS-Obersturmführer* Franz Lang (Battalion commander of the *Feld-Ersatz-Bataillon* of *11. SS-Freiwilligen-Panzer-Grenadier-Division "Nordland"*); and, *SS-Sturmbannführer* Fischer (Battalion commander of the *II./SS-Artillerie-Regiment 54*)

7 January 1945: *SS-Hauptscharführer* Kalr Ewald (Headquarters section leader of the *2./SS-Feld-Ersatz-Bataillon 11*) and *SS-Hauptsturmführer* Franz Thomalla (Acting commander of the *1./SS-Feld-Ersat-Bataillon 11*)

4. SS-Panzer-Grenadier-Brigade "Nederland"

17 December 1944: *SS-Oberscharführer* Johann Täubl (Forward observer of the *5./SS-Artillerie-Regiment 54*)

Appendix 29: Images from the Estate of Joop Cuypers

These images were graciously provided by Max Cuypers, a relative of those mentioned in the photo captions (Max Cuypers was his grandfather). Members of the Cuypers family fought with various formations of the *III. (germanisches) SS-Panzer-Korps*. Friends and acquaintances served with other "Germanic" formations of the *Waffen-SS* as well. It is believed all of these pictures are previously unpublished.

Left: *SS-Schütze* Joop Cuypers in Hamburg in April 1941. At the time he was a member of *SS-Standarte Nordwest*. His *Erkennungsmarke* (dog tag) reads: *893 — 3. SS-Freiwilligen-Stab Nord-West*.

Above right: *SS-Schütze* Max Cuypers in Hamburg in April 1941. At the time he was a member of *SS-Standarte Nordwest*.

Right: *SS-Schütze* Heinz Martens in 1941. At the time, he was a member of *SS-Regiment "Westland"*. His *Erkennungsmarke* reads: *26 – 1/E – SS-WESTLAND*.

Above left: *SS-Sturmmann* Joop Cuypers in 1942. At the time, he was a member of *SS-Freiwilligen-Legion "Niederlande"*.

Above: *SS-Sturmmann* Joop Cuypers in 1942. At the time, he was a member of *SS-Freiwilligen-Legion "Niederlande"*.

Left: *SS-Sturmmann* Karel Weber in 1942. At the time, he was a member of *SS-Freiwilligen-Legion "Niederlande"*. His *Erkennungsmarke* reads: -3 SS-Freiwilligen-Stab Nord-West.

Above left: *SS-Sturmmann* Frans van Dyck in 1942. He was assigned to the *5. SS-Panzer-Division "Wiking"*. He was a recipient of the Wound Badge in Black.

Above right: *SS-Unterscharführer* Max Cuypers in 1943. At the time, he was a member of *4. SS-Panzer-Grenadier-Brigade "Nederland"*.

Right: *SS-Unterscharführer* Max Cuypers at Kroana (Pomerania) in 1943.

Opposite page, bottom: *SS-Unterscharführer* Joop Cuypers in 1943. At the time, he was a member of the *10. SS-Panzer-Division "Frundsberg"*. His *Erkennungsmarke* read: -1-3. / SS-Stu.Gesch.Abt 10.

Opposite page, top: *SS-Rottenführer* Frans van Dyck on 2 June 1943 while on leave at Mechelen (Belgium). At the time, he was a member of the *III. (germanisches) SS-Panzer-Korps.*

This page: Sisak (Croatia) in September 1943. Recruits are being sworn in as members of SS-*Sturmgeschütz-Abteilung 11.* The camp had to be on alert all the time for the possibility of partisan attacks.

455

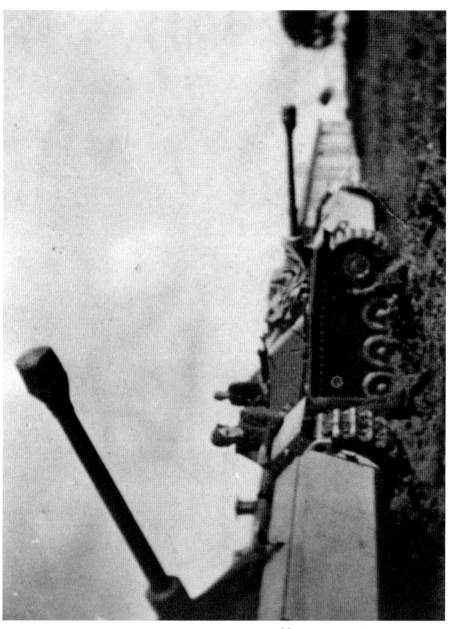

Opposite page: Washing vehicles in the Kupa River. From left to right: ?, ? (driver), *SS–Unterscharführer* Willi Kupka, *SS–Rottenführer* Heinz Martens and *SS–Unterscharführer* Müller (gun commander). River bathing was allowed under protection of the guards.

This page: Assault guns in Sisak (Croatia) in September 1943. In front: *SS–Unterscharführer* Müller. In back: *SS–Rottenführer* Heinz Martens.

457

This page:
Another view of
SS-Rottenführer
Heinz Martens
with his assault
gun.

Opposite page: A
Sturmgeschütz III,
Ausführung G is
prepared for anti-
partisan duty.
Joop Cuypers is
to the right on
top of the vehi-
cle.

459

Top: Personnel of the *SS-Sturmgeschütz-Abteilung 11* in Croatia in September 1943. Front left: *SS-Untersturmführer* von Renteln. Second from the left: *SS-Unterscharführer* Willi Kupka (driver). Front right: *SS-SS-Untersturmführer* Schalinski. Behind him on the top row: *SS-Unterscharführer* Vetter.

Left: *SS-Untersturmführer* Sioek, a platoon leader in *SS-Sturmgeschütz-Abteilung 11*.

Top: *SS-Unterscharführer* Max and Joop Cuypers in October 1944. At the time, both were members of the *4. SS-Panzer-Grenadier-Brigade "Nederland"*.

Right: *SS-Rottenführer* Heinz Martens in 1944. At the time, he was a member of *SS-Sturmgeschütz-Abteilung 11*. He was a recipient of the Eastern front Medal, the *Flak* Combat Badge, the Wound Badge in Black and the General Assault Badge.

This page: *SS-Instandsetzungs-Abteilung 11* in the Oranienbaum Pocket at Wolosowo on 19 January 1944. To the right: *SS-Rottenführer* Heinz Martens. In the middle: *SS-Unterscharführer* Hermes. On the left: A toolmaker from Wolosowo.

Opposite page: The same three hard at work replacing a torsion bar.

Above: A disabled *Panther* during the withdrawal from Oranienbaum to Luga. The tank commander was ordered to defend his vehicle to the last round before destroying it.

Opposite page: Assault gun in the Oranienbaum Pocket in January 1944. To the right is *SS–Unterscharführer* Steiner. He was killed shortly after his promotion to *SS–Oberscharführer* that same month.

Right: An antitank position at the Bohr Estate northeast of Narwa in February 1944. The gun belonged to *SS–Panzerjäger–Abteilung 11.*

Opposite page: Infantry positions at the Bohr Estate.

Above: The Narwa Bridgehead on 11 March 1944. This assault gun from *SS-Panzerjäger-Abteilung 54* is in a firing position at "Schotfeld Lilienbach" on the road from Narwa to Jamburg.

Opposite page: Another view of the infantry positions seen on the previous two pages.

Top: Narwa after aerial bombardment and artillery fire in March 1944. **Opposite page**: The main street of Narwa in March 1944. The assault gun in the background was commanded by the platoon leader, *SS–Untersturmführer* Stübner, who was killed on 10 March 1944 when his *Sturmgeschütz* took a direct hit. **Bottom**: The railway bridge over the Narwa. It suffered a direct hit during the bombing of 6/7 March 1944.

Above: The factory near the Narwa River falls was severely damaged during the bombardment. Opposite page, top: Narwa shortly after the bombardment. Left: *SS-Rottenführer* Heinz Martens. Right: *SS-Sturmmann* Schalinski. This bomb crater was about 20 feet from the shelter where Heinz and two others had taken cover. Opposite page, bottom: The Narwa bridgehead in March 1944. Below: The Narwa bridgehead in the spring of 1944. Standing to the front right: *SS-Untersturmführer* von Renteln. From left to right on top: *SS-Sturmmann* Schalinski (driver); *SS-Oberscharführer* Papmeier (gun layer); *SS-Rottenführer* Heinz Martens; *SS-Sturmmann* Holleman; ? (driver); and, *SS-Sturmmann* ? (driver).

473

The billeting area, which was blasted to ruins during the night of 6/7 March 1944.

A view of Narwa from the Russian side of the river. Both fortresses — the "Ivangorod" and the "Hermania" — can be seen in the background. Right: *SS-Unterscharführer* Joop Cuypers.

The Fortress "Ivangorod" from a bridge over the Narwa.

The Fortress "Hermania" on the Estonian side of the Narwa River.

Another view of Narwa in June 1944.

The Narwa Bridgehead —in June 1944. Here: The Dutch cemetery.

"Strongpoint West" in the Narwa bridgehead. Here: A *Sturmgeschütz III*, *Ausführung F* in July 1944. Standing on the right in front with the overseas cap: *SS-Unterscharführer* Joop Cuypers. Top right: *SS-Rottenführer* Walter Borchert. Second from the right on top: *SS-Hauptscharführer* Reinhart.

"Strongpoint North" at the Narwa Bridgehead. From left to right: *SS-Rottenführer* Rinus Kuiper, *SS-Unterscharführer* Joop Cuypers, *SS-Unterscharführer* Rudolf Witte, *SS-Rottenführer* Walter Borchert, ? and ? The house in the background was hit at night when these men from *SS-Panzerjäger-Abteilung 54* were asleep in it.

SS-Unterscharführer Richard Koch, a motorcycle messenger. He was a friend of Frans van Dyck and was killed in Estonia in 1944.

SS-Rottenführer Frans van Dyck (right) with *SS-Rottenführer* Reimann, who was killed in Estonia in 1944.

Moving from Lake Peipus to Dorpat, where Derk Elsko Bruins is about to receive his Knight's Cross. From left to right: *SS-Unterscharführer* Rudolf Witte, *SS-Untersturmführer* Römmelt, *SS-Rottenführer* Derk Elsko Bruins, ? (loader) and ? (driver).

Maintenance halt while moving to the Estonian harbor of Pernau in September 1944. From there, *SS-Panzerjäger-Abteilung 54* would be shipped to East Prussia.

The Königsberg harbor on 27 September 1944 after the safe arrival of the battalion.

Left: *SS-Grenadier* Max Cuypers Sr. in November 1944. He was assigned to the *34. SS-Freiwilligen-Grenadier-Division der Waffen-SS "Landstorm Nederland"*. His *Erkennungsmarke* read: *Fr.Brig.Lst.Ned. – 319 -*. **Right**: Unknown *SS-Rottenführer* (believed to be Vogel, who was a friend of the family). He is in training to become a *SS-Unteroffizier*. He was the recipient of the Eastern-Front Medal, the Iron Cross, Second Class and the Infantry Assault Badge.

An unknown *SS-Grenadier*, who is believed to have been a cook in the *34. SS-Freiwilligen-Grenadier-Division der Waffen-SS "Landstorm Nederland"*. This picture is believed to have been taken in November 1944.

Neuhammer am Queiss in Lower Silesia in November 1944. A road march with map and compass.

A group of noncommissioned officers at the Neuhammer am Queiss Training Area in November 1944. Left to right: *SS-Unterscharführer* Hofmann, ?, ?, *SS-Rottenführer* Heinz Martens, ?, *SS-Unterscharführer* Rudolf Witte and ?

A group of noncommissioned officers at the Neuhammer am Queiss Training Area in December 1944. Left to right: *SS-Unterscharführer* Rudolf Witte, *SS-Unterscharführer* Hofmann and *SS-Rottenführer* Heinz Martens. The rest are unknown.

Rank Comparisons

Enlisted

US Army	*German Army*	*Waffen-SS*
Private	*Schütze*	*SS-Schütze*
Private First Class	*Oberschütze*	*SS-Oberschütze*
Corporal	*Gefreiter*	*SS-Sturmmann*
(Senior Corporal)	*Obergefreiter*	*SS-Rottenführer*
(Staff Corporal)	*Stabsgefreiter*	(None)

Noncommissioned Officers

US Army	*German Army*	*Waffen-SS*
Sergeant	*Unteroffizier*	*SS-Unterscharführer*
Staff Sergeant	*Feldwebel*	*SS-Oberscharführer*
Sergeant First Class	*Oberfeldwebel*	*SS-Hauptscharführer*
Master Sergeant	*Hauptfeldwebel*	*SS-Sturmscharführer*
Sergeant Major	*Stabsfeldwebel*	*(None)*

Officers

US Army	*German Army*	*Waffen-SS*
Lieutenant	*Leutnant*	*SS-Untersturmführer*
First Lieutenant	*Oberleutnant*	*SS-Obersturmführer*
Captain	*Hauptmann*	*SS-Hauptsturmführer*
Major	*Major*	*SS-Sturmbannführer*
Lieutenant Colonel	*Oberstleutnant*	*SS-Obersturmbannführer*
Colonel	*Oberst*	*SS-Oberführer or SS-Standartenführer*
Brigadier General	*Generalmajor*	*SS-Brigadeführer*
Major General	*Generalleutnant*	*SS-Gruppenführer*
Lieutenant General	*General der Panzertruppen* etc.	*SS-Obergruppenführer*
General	*Generaloberst*	*SS-Oberstgruppenführer*
General of the Army	*Feldmarschall*	*Reichsführer-SS*